Challenges and Solutions for Cybersecurity and Adversarial Machine Learning

Shafiq Ul Rehman
Kingdom University, Bahrain

IGI Global
Scientific Publishing
Publishing Tomorrow's Research Today

Vice President of Editorial Melissa Wagner
Director of Acquisitions Mikaela Felty
Director of Book Development Jocelynn Hessler
Production Manager Mike Brehm
Cover Design Jose Rosado

Published in the United States of America by
IGI Global Scientific Publishing
701 East Chocolate Avenue
Hershey, PA, 17033, USA
Tel: 717-533-8845
Fax: 717-533-7115
Website: https://www.igi-global.com E-mail: cust@igi-global.com

Library of Congress Cataloging-in-Publication Data

Names: Ul Rehman, Shafiq, 1981- editor
http://id.loc.gov/vocabulary/relators/edt
http://id.loc.gov/authorities/names/n2025007696
http://id.loc.gov/rwo/agents/n2025007696
Title: Challenges and solutions for cybersecurity and adversarial machine learning / edited by Shafiq Ul Rehman.
Description: Hershey, PA : IGI Global Scientific Publishing, [2025] | Includes bibliographical references and index.
Identifiers: LCCN 2025011491 (print) | LCCN 2025011492 (ebook) | ISBN 9798337322025 ebook | ISBN 9798337322001 h/c
Subjects: LCSH: Computer security http://id.loc.gov/authorities/subjects/sh90001862 | Computer networks--Security measures http://id.loc.gov/authorities/subjects/sh94001277 | Machine learning--Security measures | Hacking http://id.loc.gov/authorities/subjects/sh2013002597
Classification: LCC QA76.9.A25 (ebook) | LCC QA76.9.A25 C43279 2025 (print) | DDC 005.8 23/eng/20250--dc25
LC record available at https://lccn.loc.gov/2025011491
British Cataloguing in Publication Data
A Cataloguing in Publication record for this book is available from the British Library.

Table of Contents

Detailed Table of Contents

Deep learning has revolutionized fields like healthcare, finance, and cybersecurity through automation and intelligent decision-making. However, its vulnerability to adversarial attacks raises security and ethical concerns, especially in critical applications. This chapter explores adversarial machine learning (AML), covering evasion and poisoning attacks, defense strategies like adversarial training and model regularization, and certified robustness. It also examines ethical considerations, regulatory frameworks, explainable AI (XAI), and human-in-the-loop security. Strengthening AI resilience is essential for ensuring safe real-world deployment.

Adversarial Machine Learning poses critical risk to the security of AI systems as adversaries can manipulate system inputs to force the models into making incorrect choices. This section provides a detailed classification of adversarial attacks and defenses, organizing them as a function of what information the defender possesses about the attacker, the goal of the attack, and the attack methods used: white-box, black-box, and even physical adversarial attacks. It also explores the impact of Adversarial Machine Learning on cybersecurity, finance, healthcare, and even autonomous systems. From adversarial training, input filtering, and optimum robust design, all known defensive mechanisms are evaluated against sophisticated attack mechanisms that are undergoing constant evolution. This chapter emphasizes the importance of continuous AML research to safeguard machine learning applications' integrity and reliability in real-world environments.

The integration of Artificial Intelligence (AI) into real-world applications has brought societal benefits but also introduced new vulnerabilities, including adversarial attacks. These attacks account for complex physical variables, making them harder to execute and more dangerous. This paper investigates the nature and impact of real-world adversarial attacks on AI systems, categorizing them based on modalities, attack goals, and delivery mechanisms. It critically assesses existing defense mechanisms and suggests emerging trends like certified defenses, sensor fusion techniques, and context-aware learning. The study emphasizes the need for a security-first approach in AI system design and deployment.

The current digital environment shows quick integration of Artificial Intelligence (AI) into firmware-based embedded systems that operate in all spaces but create sophisticated security threats which evolve swiftly. Two core challenges which include Adversarial Machine Learning (AML) along with firmware security vulnerabilities that affect hardware foundation through software control. This section particularly analyzes the escalated security threats stemming from zero-day vulnerabilities in domains where unknown flaws reveal themselves before current protection methods exist. The study examines these two opposing scenarios which reveal how firmware vulnerabilities enable attackers to conduct advanced AML assaults by altering sensor information or damaging protections and demonstrates how attackers can specifically invade and evade AI-based firmware security detection tools used for scanning vulnerabilities and monitoring system quality. The chapter includes a complete exploration of AI-based cybersecurity technologies that specialize in facing these modern security threats.

Adversarial attacks are particularly cybersecurity applications where reliability and accuracy are the most important. They are a significant threat to artificial intelligence systems (AI). These attacks involve subtle manipulation of input data developed into deceptive AI models that lead to false output or system dusk. To mitigate these risks, various defense mechanisms have been developed that aim to improve the robustness of AI systems against adversarial obstacles. These mechanisms include adversarial training, preprocessing inputs, normalizing models, and using defense architectures. Adversarial training improves the model's resilience by publishing adversarial examples during training. Input processing filters the input of potential adversarial, while model regulator exposure over-adapts adaptations that may exploit weaknesses. Defensive architectures have been developed specifically to identify and counter malfunctioning operations.

Today, because organisations are getting more targeted by complex cyber attacks that can cost a company millions of dollars in losses as well as damage point of sale, operational disruption etc. While traditional security measures can hardly cope with the volume, velocity and complexity of modern attack landscapes. Artificial Intelligence (AI) and Machine Learning (ML) integration is no longer something that should only be done for securing purposes an long way down on the to-do list per top cybersecurity solutions. Armed with a strategic deployment of AI-driven systems as well as the corresponding difficulties, organizations can greatly improve their security architecture and make themselves substantially more secure against the modern cyber threats in this digital era. This book proposal chapter offers a broad explanation of AI-driven threat detection and response systems, emphasizing their fundamentals; pointing to capabilities; while highlighting the inherent challenges; and proposing potential future directions.

In recent years, cyber threats have grown exponentially. As organizations increasingly rely on digital infrastructures, robust cybersecurity solutions are increasingly necessary. The use of artificial intelligence (AI) has emerged as a promising tool for enhancing security, as it is capable of detecting threats in real-time, identifying anomalies, and automating response to incidents. While these AI systems are often referred to as "black boxes," they produce decisions that are difficult for cybersecurity analysts to interpret. Explainable AI (XAI) aims to address this issue by providing transparent and interpretable insights into how AI models arrive at their outputs. As a result of the combination of powerful AI-driven analytics combined with clear explanations, cybersecurity professionals can more confidently rely on machine learning models to detect threats. This chapter examines how Explainable AI can bolster cybersecurity, highlighting its core principles, defense applications, ethical concerns, and technical constraints.

Federated Learning is a transformative approach to building secure and resilient AI systems by enabling decentralized model training without exposing raw data. As part of Challenges and Solutions for Cybersecurity and Adversarial Machine Learning, this chapter examines its role in enhancing cybersecurity and mitigating adversarial threats, emphasizing its privacy-preserving capabilities and robustness against attacks. Key security challenges, including adversarial model poisoning, communication risks, and data privacy concerns, are analyzed alongside solutions such as differential privacy, secure aggregation, and robust optimization techniques. The discussion extends to Federated Learning's applications in critical sectors such as healthcare, finance, and edge computing, where secure AI deployment is essential. Addressing these challenges and proposing viable solutions, the chapter provides a comprehensive perspective on Federated Learning's potential to enhance AI security and resilience in adversarial environments.

Federated Learning (FL), which prioritises data privacy and reduces centralised risks, has emerged as a revolutionary technique for enhancing security in distributed machine learning systems. As opposed to traditional methods that rely on aggregating raw data, FL ensures that sensitive data remains localised while enabling cooperative model training across scattered devices. This study carefully looks at the critical role FL plays in addressing significant security issues like data breaches, hostile assaults, and regulatory compliance. At the centre of this discussion is an analysis of key techniques like secure aggregation, homomorphic encryption, and differential privacy, which collectively defend FL systems against malicious attacks while preserving model accuracy.The utility of FL is demonstrated by its application in sensitive domains such as healthcare, where patient data is protected during cooperative model training.

This chapter highlights the growing urgency for robust Intrusion Detection Systems (IDS) in the Internet of Things (IoT) security, focusing on sustainable cybersecurity strategies within the modern, highly interconnected digital ecosystem. As the rapid expansion of IoT devices presents vast attack surfaces, it is crucial to develop IDS that protect interconnected environments. This chapter performs a thorough analysis of IDS detection mechanisms and IoT security datasets, critically assessing the relevance and reliability. The evaluation emphasizes essential dataset attributes, including source authenticity, diversity, data volume, and real-world applicability. By systematically analyzing these criteria, the paper identifies datasets that offer comprehensive insights into IoT security's challenges, offering researchers a detailed resource for selecting datasets that align with the complexity of current IDS development. This review thus serves as a foundational guide for advancing IDS technology, aiming to foster more resilient and adaptive security solutions within the IoT landscape.

enabled efficient data collection. IoT, a crucial set of smart technologies, is anticipated to drive the next information technology revolution and the development of big data analytics. However, widespread data collection and the lack of security in IoT devices raise significant privacy concerns. This study reviews current literature and discusses concepts and approaches for data privacy in IoT from various perspectives. It identifies several challenges and provides comprehensive solutions to address data privacy issues. The proposed solutions encompass technical, academic, and industry viewpoints. Additionally, the integration of machine learning (ML) and deep learning (DL) technologies into IoT systems introduces further privacy and security challenges. ML and DL models often require access to large datasets containing sensitive information, necessitating advanced privacy-preserving techniques such as differential privacy and federated learning. These methods aim to protect individual data while enabling robust model training. Furthermore, the study explores the impact of adversarial attacks on ML and DL models within IoT environments and discusses strategies to enhance model robustness and security. Despite these efforts, major issues remain in designing and deploying IoT solutions. This study concludes with recommendations and future research directions to enhance IoT privacy and security, particularly in the context of emerging ML and DL technologies.

Compilation of References 477

About the Contributors 539

Index 545

Preface

In today's hyperconnected world, cybersecurity is no longer an auxiliary function but a foundational necessity. The exponential adoption of Artificial Intelligence (AI) and Machine Learning (ML) across diverse sectors has unlocked unprecedented capabilities in automation, analytics, and intelligent decision-making. However, with these advancements comes a new generation of sophisticated threats—among the most concerning of which is adversarial machine learning (AML). AML exploits the very algorithms that empower modern systems, manipulating their behaviors and outcomes in often imperceptible but highly impactful ways. As adversarial techniques evolve, so too must our understanding and preparedness.

The edited volume *Challenges and Solutions for Cybersecurity and Adversarial Machine Learning* was conceived to address this urgent and complex intersection of AI security and malicious intervention. This book brings together leading researchers and practitioners from around the world to dissect the current landscape of adversarial threats, defense mechanisms, and ethical considerations. From deep learning vulnerabilities to real-world adversarial attacks and the promise of technologies like federated learning and explainable AI, each chapter contributes a unique lens to this rapidly advancing field. These scholarly contributions not only diagnose existing challenges but also explore robust, forward-looking solutions that can guide industry, academia, and policy toward safer AI integration.

The structure of the book is deliberately multidimensional. Early chapters delve into foundational knowledge and taxonomies of attacks and defenses, while later chapters explore applications, case studies, and methodologies for enhancing system resilience. The inclusion of bibliometric analyses, ethical frameworks, firmware vulnerabilities, and IoT security provides a holistic view of adversarial machine learning's implications and countermeasures. This book is not only a repository of technical insight but also a call for interdisciplinary collaboration to shape a secure digital future.

Chapter 1: The Dark Side of AI: Adversarial Attacks and Defenses in Deep Learning

This chapter introduces the vulnerabilities of deep learning models to adversarial attacks, especially in critical domains like healthcare and finance. It explores key attack types—evasion and poisoning—and surveys defense mechanisms such as adversarial training, model regularization, and certified robustness. Ethical concerns, regulatory frameworks, and the need for explainable AI and human-in-the-loop systems are also discussed to reinforce AI security.

Chapter 2: Taxonomy of Adversarial Attacks and Defenses

Focusing on the classification of adversarial attacks and defenses, this chapter presents a structured taxonomy based on attacker knowledge, attack goals, and techniques (white-box, black-box, and physical attacks). It evaluates defense mechanisms and highlights the dynamic threat landscape in sectors such as cybersecurity and autonomous systems, emphasizing the ongoing need for adaptive adversarial machine learning (AML) research.

Chapter 3: A Bibliometric Perspective on Adversarial Machine Learning Research

Using bibliometric analysis and visualization tools like Vosviewer, this chapter identifies evolving research trends, thematic clusters, and key challenges in AML. It maps the field's intellectual structure and underscores the importance of interdisciplinary collaboration and continued exploration to address security vulnerabilities in AI systems.

Chapter 4: Adversarial Machine Learning in Cybersecurity

This chapter investigates the misuse of AML in cybersecurity, showing how attackers exploit AI system vulnerabilities to evade detection. It examines adversarial tactics, detection strategies, and defense mechanisms, alongside the ethical and legal issues emerging from the growing integration of AI into cyber-physical systems.

Chapter 5: Real-World Adversarial Attacks on AI Systems

Examining adversarial threats beyond lab settings, this chapter categorizes real-world attacks by modality and delivery method. It assesses the effectiveness of current defenses and introduces advanced approaches such as sensor fusion and context-aware learning. The emphasis is on embedding a "security-first" mindset in AI deployment.

Chapter 6: Adversarial Machine Learning and Firmware Attacks

This chapter explores the intersection of AML and firmware security, particularly in the context of zero-day threats. It illustrates how firmware vulnerabilities can facilitate AML-based exploits and evaluates AI-driven cybersecurity solutions designed to detect and neutralize such sophisticated threats in embedded systems.

Chapter 7: Defense Mechanisms Against Adversarial Attacks

Focusing on fortifying AI systems used in cybersecurity, this chapter details defense strategies such as adversarial training, input preprocessing, and architectural defenses. It explains how these methods can reduce model susceptibility to manipulated inputs and ensure more robust AI performance under adversarial conditions.

Chapter 8: AI-Driven Threat Detection and Response Systems

This chapter discusses the strategic implementation of AI in threat detection and incident response, addressing the limitations of traditional security measures. It highlights how AI enhances situational awareness, scalability, and decision-making in modern cybersecurity infrastructures, while also identifying future research directions.

Chapter 9: Leveraging Explainable AI for Cybersecurity

Addressing the "black-box" nature of AI models, this chapter advocates for the integration of Explainable AI (XAI) to enhance transparency in threat detection. It explores the technical and ethical dimensions of XAI and shows how interpretability can bolster trust and accountability in AI-driven cybersecurity systems.

Chapter 10: Federated Learning for Secure and Resilient AI Systems

This chapter highlights Federated Learning as a privacy-preserving approach to training robust AI models across decentralized systems. It investigates security threats like model poisoning and discusses defense mechanisms including secure aggregation and differential privacy, with applications in sensitive sectors such as finance and healthcare.

Chapter 11: Role of Federated Learning in Enhancing Security

Delving deeper into the security benefits of Federated Learning, this chapter outlines how FL mitigates data breaches and supports compliance with privacy regulations. It analyzes protective techniques like homomorphic encryption and showcases FL's utility in sectors requiring secure, distributed model training.

Chapter 12: Assessing the Suitability of IoT Security Datasets for IDS

This chapter provides a comprehensive review of datasets used in developing intrusion detection systems (IDS) for IoT. It evaluates dataset attributes such as authenticity and diversity, offering a guide for researchers to select high-quality data sources that enhance IDS reliability in increasingly complex IoT environments.

Chapter 13: Security Vulnerabilities and Countermeasures for Wireless Sensor Networks in Cyber-Physical Systems

Exploring the unique vulnerabilities of Wireless Sensor Networks in CPS, this chapter analyzes threats across network layers and proposes countermeasures like secure routing, cryptographic protocols, and intrusion detection systems. Real-world case studies illustrate the effectiveness of these strategies in enhancing data integrity.

Chapter 14: Addressing Data Privacy Concerns in Digital Emerging Technologies

This chapter reviews privacy challenges arising from the proliferation of IoT, ML, and DL technologies. It discusses threats related to large-scale data collection and proposes solutions such as differential privacy and federated learning. It also addresses adversarial threats to data-driven models and recommends strategies to improve security and privacy in emerging tech ecosystems.

At its core, this book underscores one critical reality: securing AI is no longer optional. From autonomous vehicles and healthcare diagnostics to national infrastructure and financial systems, AI is embedded into critical decision-making pipelines. The threats posed by adversarial machine learning are not hypothetical—they are active, evolving, and increasingly capable of bypassing traditional security mechanisms. By compiling a global perspective on these challenges, we aim to raise awareness, share proven strategies, and stimulate innovation in defending against adversarial AI systems.

As editor, I am honored to have worked with an exceptional group of contributors who have drawn from research, applied experience, and academic rigor to produce work that is both intellectually robust and practically relevant. The depth and diversity of perspectives represented in this book—from ethical frameworks and explainability to technical robustness and real-world case studies—demonstrate the complexity and urgency of addressing AML through integrated and scalable approaches. Readers will find value not only in the technical content but also in the broader discussion around trust, transparency, and the societal implications of insecure AI.

I invite readers—from researchers and developers to security professionals and policymakers—to engage deeply with the material in this volume. Whether you are seeking foundational understanding or advanced defense strategies, this book serves as a guide to the multifaceted landscape of adversarial machine learning and cybersecurity. In an era defined by intelligent systems and invisible threats, knowledge, vigilance, and collaboration are our most effective defenses. Let this book be a step toward that shared security vision.

Shafiq Ul Rehman
Kingdom University, Bahrain

Chapter 1
The Dark Side of AI: Adversarial Attacks and Defenses in Deep Learning

Uddalak Mitra
https://orcid.org/0000-0002-5682-5218
Siliguri Institute of Technology, India

Shafiq Ul Rehman
https://orcid.org/0000-0003-2266-218X
Kingdom University, Bahrain

ABSTRACT

Deep learning has revolutionized fields like healthcare, finance, and cybersecurity through automation and intelligent decision-making. However, its vulnerability to adversarial attacks raises security and ethical concerns, especially in critical applications. This chapter explores adversarial machine learning (AML), covering evasion and poisoning attacks, defense strategies like adversarial training and model regularization, and certified robustness. It also examines ethical considerations, regulatory frameworks, explainable AI (XAI), and human-in-the-loop security. Strengthening AI resilience is essential for ensuring safe real-world deployment.

1. INTRODUCTION

The fast growing sector of Artificial Intelligence (AI), Machine Learning (ML) and Deep Learning (DL) has revolutionaries innovations in areas like industries, reshaping automation, predictive analytics, and intelligent decision-making processes, including healthcare (Rahman, A., et al., 2024; Kothinti, R. R., 2024) to finance (Manogna, R. L., & Anand, A., 2024; Li, Y., et al., 2024), and from cyber-security

DOI: 10.4018/979-8-3373-2200-1.ch001

(Kannan, Y., et al., 2024) to autonomous systems (Calinescu, R., et al., 2024). Critical applications of AI that impact daily life (Liu, Y., et al., 2025; Su, P., et al., 2025; Najim, A., et al., 2025) are now powered by Deep learning models. But, deep-learning based AI systems are susceptible security risks like adversarial attacks, which become critical concerns of their usability. Input data can be maliciously crafted to mislead AI systems viable to produce incorrect or even harmful predictions (Cinà, A. E., et al., 2023; Qian, Z., et al., 2022). In the critical application areas like fraud detection, medical diagnostics, and national security where integration of AI becomes an essential tools faces significant security risks due to such adversarial threats (Ren, H., et al., 2021; Ma, X., et al., 2021).

Recently, Adversarial Machine Learning (AML) becomes a ray of hope to combat with these security risks. Interestingly, although the critically applied perturbations on input data can often remain imperceptible to humans eyes but easily mislead deep learning based AI systems (Vadillo, J., et al., 2025; Chakraborty, A., et al., 2021). In this way the dependability and reliability of deep learning based system faces question about their strength, fairness and even ethical usage (Han, S., et al., 2023; Polemi, N., et al., 2024; Chander, B., et al., 2025). On the other hand, in recent days AI systems become more integrated into almost all critical infrastructures like financial markets, and defense systems. Thus also ensuring their security and flexibility against adversarial manipulations becomes an urgent priority (Shandilya, S. K., et al., 2024; Rath, S., et al., 2024).

In this chapter we represent an introductory picture of AML in the context of deep learning. It serves as an initial point for the journey towards the topics covered in "The Dark Side of AI." We at first discuss susceptibility of deep learning models to adversarial attacks along with intrinsic weaknesses of model architectures including the training processes (Zhou, S., et al., 2022; Bastounis, A., et al., 2021). Several adversarial attack types like evasion attacks and poisoning attacks are also described briefly. The evasion attacks manipulate input data to deceive deployed models whereas poisoning attacks compromise the training process itself (Zhang, C., et al., 2024; Costa, J. C., et al., 2024; Badjie, B., et al., 2024; Li, Y., et al., 2024). In addition to the mentioned one, we also commence protection mechanisms like adversarial training, model regularization, and explainability techniques that aim to improve AI resilience (Baniecki, H., & Biecek, P., 2024; Kaviani, S., Han, K. J., & Sohn, I., 2022).

We also describe broader implications of adversarial threats apart from the technical aspects, which is essential for later discussions in this book. The ethical concerns surrounding AI security and fairness (Li, B., et al., 2023), the function of federated learning in improving robustness (Nabavirazavi, S., et al., 2024), and the impact of quantum computing on AML (Raza, S. A., et al., 2025) are all topics explored in subsequent chapters. We also present description of AI-enabled cyber security solutions and policy making frameworks in brief (Ojo, B., & Aghaunor, C. T., 2024).

Thus, in this chapter we aim to provide researchers, practitioners, and industry professionals with the necessary background to comprehend, study, and alleviate adversarial threats by providing both theoretical foundations and practical insights. As AI continues to figure out the future, ensuring its security and reliability is not just a technological requirement, it is an ethical and societal imperative.

2. BACKGROUND OF THE STUDY

2.1 Understanding the Deep Learning framework

Deep learning is a subsection in the domain machine learning which has considerably advanced the field of AI. The major interesting fact in this approach is that it can automatically extract patterns from large datasets without direct human interference, thus bypassing the manual feature extraction. Several application areas like image recognition, natural language processing, and healthcare diagnostics (Wang, J. et al., 2025; Nargesi, A. A. et al., 2025; He, L. et al., 2025) have been considerably advanced by the used of DL. In the subsequent section, we will prove a precise overview of deep learning principles: its architectural frameworks, training techniques, and the intrinsic challenges that render these models vulnerable to adversarial manipulation.

2.1.1 Architectures of Deep Neural Networks

Deep learning architecture is build up on a major component known as the artificial neural networks (ANNs). It is collection of multiple layers of interconnected nodes, generally known as neurons. ANNs are designed to capture and process different patterns in data. Convolutional Neural Networks (CNNs), Recurrent Neural Networks (RNNs), and Transformers, are the most well-known deep learning structures. Each of them is a specialized technique to perform specific types of tasks and data formats across artificial intelligence applications.

Convolutional Neural Networks (CNNs)

CNNs are a group of deep learning models developed for analyzing grid-like data structures, for instance image datasets. Build up on the amazing working principle of the human visual system, the mechanism of CNNs can provide facilities for hierarchical feature extraction, enabling them to progressively learn more abstract representations of input data. Typical CNNs includes the following components:

- **Convolutional Layers:** It is the layer that applies the concept filters or kernels on input data to dig out local patterns such as edges, textures, or colors. A specific type of features is captured by each of the filters to construct a rich, multi-layered understanding of the image.
- **Pooling Layers:** By using the pooling operations, such as max pooling or average pooling, the size of feature maps is condensed while retaining essential information. While enhancing computational effectiveness it also reduces the hazard of over-fitting.
- **Fully Connected Layers:** This layer is placed at the last part of the network, taking the high-level features extracted earlier and maps them to the final output. It is commonly used for classification.
- **Activation Functions:** Activation functions, like the Rectified Linear Unit (ReLU), inject non-linearity into the artificial network, enabling CNNs to model complex relations in data.

CNNs have established extraordinary performance in various computer vision tasks, such as object classification (e.g., ImageNet competitions), facial recognition systems, medical imaging diagnostics, and self-driving car perception modules. Influential CNN models include **LeNet**, **AlexNet**, **VGGNet**, **ResNet**, and **EfficientNet** (Bhatt, D., et al., 2021).

Recurrent Neural Networks (RNNs)

RNNs are engineered to process sequential or time-dependent data, building them predominantly efficient for tasks like language modeling, speech processing, and time-series prediction (Das, S., et al., 2023). Unlike typical feed-forward networks, RNNs include a mechanism that allows information to persist over time through feedback connections.

Key elements of RNNs include:

- **Recurrent Connections:** Each neuron maintains an inner hidden state which is rationalized at every epoch or time step. This procedure enabling the network to retain memory of previous inputs and model sequence dependencies.
- **Vanishing and Exploding Gradient Problems:** When training standard RNNs using backpropagation through time (BPTT), gradients may turn into exceedingly small or large, leading to complexity in learning long-range relationships.
- **Long Short-Term Memory (LSTM) and Gated Recurrent Units (GRUs):** To deal with the aforementioned drawbacks, LSTMs and GRUs were introduced. These focused architectures use gating methods that organize the flow

of information, making it easier for the model to capture dependencies over extensive sequences.

RNNs, along with LSTM and GRU variants, have seen prevalent application in areas such as sentiment analysis, machine translation, voice-to-text systems, and financial market forecasting.

Figure 1. Popularly used Deep learning architecture

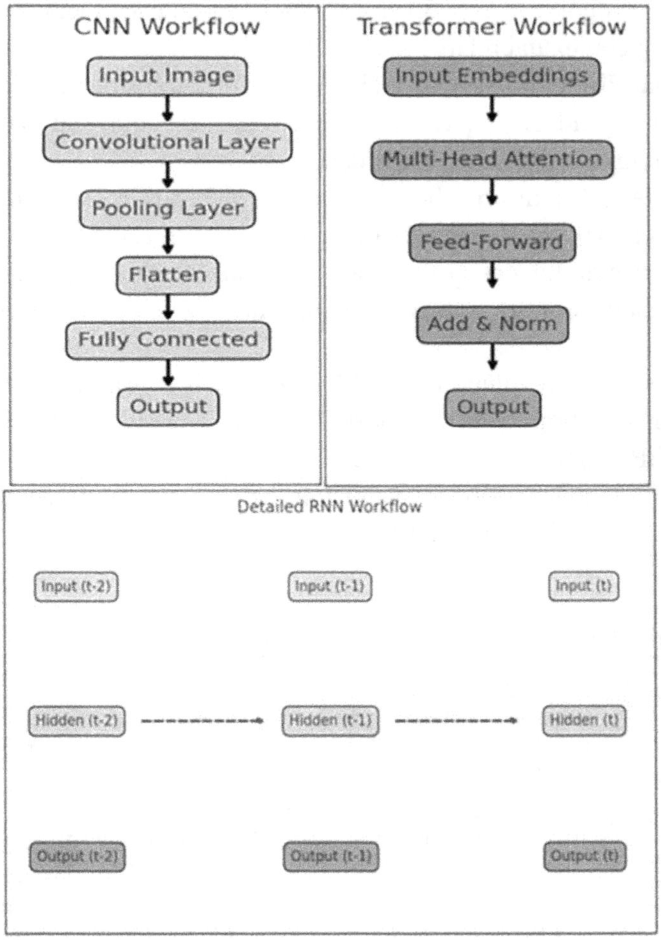

Transformers

Transformers symbolize a paradigm shift in deep learning, mainly in NLP. Transformers (Islam, S., et al 2024) abolish the need for recurrence by using self-attention mechanisms to process sequences in parallel. This makes them more efficient than RNNs for handling long-range dependencies.

Key components of transformers include:

- **Self-Attention Mechanism:** This mechanism let the transformer model to weight the significance of diverse words in a sequence relative to each other, capturing contextual relationships efficiently.
- **Positional Encoding:** By its architecture, since transformers do not have sequential dependencies like RNNs; positional encodings are added to input embeddings to conserve word order.
- **Multi-Head Attention:** The several attention heads let the model to focus on diverse parts of the sequence simultaneously, increasing learning capacity.
- **Feed-forward Layers and Layer Normalization:** Fully connected layers and normalization steps improve model stability and performance.

Transformers have revolutionized NLP with models such as BERT (Bidirectional Encoder Representations from Transformers), and T5 (Text-to-Text Transfer Transformer) and GPT (Generative Pre-trained Transformer). Beyond NLP, transformers have also been applied to vision tasks (Vision Transformers, ViTs), protein structure prediction (AlphaFold), and even time-series forecasting.

Table 1. Deep Learning Architectures Overview

Architecture	Key Features	Applications	Notable Models
Convolutional Neural Networks (CNNs)	Processes grid-like data with convolution, pooling, and fully connected layers.	Image recognition, medical imaging, autonomous driving	LeNet, AlexNet, VGGNet, ResNet, EfficientNet
Recurrent Neural Networks (RNNs)	Handles sequential data using recurrent connections and memory mechanisms.	Speech recognition, time-series forecasting, machine translation	LSTM, GRU
Transformers	Uses self-attention for parallel sequence processing.	Natural language processing (NLP), vision tasks, protein folding	BERT, GPT, T5, Vision Transformers (ViTs)

Table 2. Key Components of Deep Learning Models

Component	Description	Purpose
Convolutional Layers	Apply filters to extract spatial features.	Feature extraction from input data.
Pooling Layers	Reduce spatial dimensions while preserving essential features.	Improve computational efficiency and prevent overfitting.
Activation Functions	Introduce non-linearity (e.g., ReLU).	Enable models to learn complex patterns.
Recurrent Connections	Maintain hidden states across time steps (in RNNs).	Process sequential data.
Self-Attention	Weighs the significance of different input elements (in Transformers).	Capture long-range dependencies in sequences.

2.1.2 Training Deep Learning Models

Factors like training approaches, optimization techniques, and usage of appropriate loss functions impact the performance of deep learning models largely:

- **Optimization Techniques:** Optimization techniques are used to make the system to work at its best condition. One of the most widely used optimization techniques are stochastic gradient descent (SGD) and Adam optimizer. These techniques update model parameters to determine their optimal values efficiently in each epoch.
- **Backpropagation and Loss Functions:** The most critical part of deep learning system is the backpropagation algorithm that minimizes error by adjusting network weights based on the gradient of a loss function (e.g., cross-entropy for classification tasks).

2.1.3 Challenges in Deep Learning

Although, now a day's deep learning models becomes common and crucial component in several sensitive application areas they faces some critical challenges that can impact their reliability and security:

- **Overfitting:** Deep models often faces a critical problem that training accuracy becomes higher and test accuracy becomes less than the acceptable range. This is due to the tendency of such models to memorize training data. The critical shortcomings of such phenomena are their ability to generalize the decision boundary reduces. Regularization techniques can be used to overcome this issue.

- **Interpretability:** Now a day's predication does not close the chapter but need explainability why such prediction, Deep learning models sometime behave like a black-box that no explanation of their decision-making process. Such a approach is not at all acceptable in sensitive applications like healthcare and finance.
- **Vulnerability to Adversarial Attacks:** The most critical problem with deep learning models is that they are highly susceptible cautiously crafted inputs designed to mislead AI systems. This challenge is central to adversarial machine learning and will be explored in the following sections.

2.2 Introduction to Adversarial Machine Learning

The major objective behind the growth of Adversarial Machine Learning (AML) is to comprehend how critically crafted adversarial inputs provokes a machine learning model, especially deep learning based systems to make mistakes in predictions (Hernández-Castro, C. J et al 2022). Most importantly, the adversarial examples although are invisible to the human eye they can easily change a model's output, resulting in inaccurate predictions or misclassifications. These flaws are completely unexpected for applications that depend on safety, such as biometric authentication, autonomous driving, and medical diagnostics. On the other hand, real-world applications are increasingly rely on AI-driven systems. Thus, the techniques that investigate, identify and counteract adversarial threats to guarantee robustness, dependability, and credibility of machine learning models is an urgent need, and main reason for development of the field of Adversarial Machine Learning.

2.2.1 Historical Context and Real-World Relevance

The idea of adversarial attacks on deep learning based AI models is a deeply rooted concern. Early research in 2000s explored that spam filters and malware detection systems is viable to generate incorrect predictions through adversarial tactics. But the problem becomes mush prominent after the widespread adoption of deep learning. Researchers also discovered that even state-of-the-art neural networks are highly vulnerable to adversarial perturbations. Several real-world susceptible domains sensitive to adversarial attacks are:

- **Computer Vision:** It has been observed that even small, almost invisible pixel modifications can mislead facial recognition systems. It becomes probable for misidentifying individuals or the intender can bypassing security authentication (Akhtar, N., et al 2021).

- **Autonomous Vehicles:** Carefully placed stickers or perturbations in road signs have been shown to mislead self-driving cars, potentially causing life-threatening consequences (He, X et al 2022).
- **Financial Sector:** Subtle manipulations in financial text data can alter the sentiment analysis results of AI-based trading algorithms, leading to incorrect investment decisions (Mienye, I. D., & Swart, T. G et al 2024).
- **Healthcare Diagnostics:** Adversarial attacks on medical imaging models can cause misclassification of diseases, leading to incorrect diagnoses and improper treatments (Javed, H et al 2025).

All these indicate the serious concern about the increasing incidence and complexity of adversarial attacks and emphasize the urgent need for defensive strategies. Section 3.2 will provide in-depth case studies illustrating these adversarial vulnerabilities and their impact on real-world AI systems.

2.2.2 Why Deep Learning Models Are Vulnerable

It has been investigated that deep learning model's intrinsic design and training methodologies are major reason for vulnerabilities to adversarial attacks. Key factors are as:

- **High-Dimensional Decision Boundaries:** Complex, high-dimensional feature spaces are prone to adversarial perturbations that can exploit small gaps in the decision boundary. This provokes deep learning based systems to do incorrect classifications (Chakraborty, A., et al 2021).
- **Linear Approximation in High Dimensions:** Most deep learning models use the concept of linear approximations within high-dimensional spaces. This approach is utilized by attackers to construct adversarial examples that maximize the model's errors on the other hand the distorted input remains nearly indistinguishable from the original inputs (Han, S, et al 2023).
- **Over-Reliance on Spurious Correlations:** Deep learning models often learn spurious correlations in training data that attackers can manipulate by crafting inputs, leading to miss-predictions (Polemi, N et al 2024.).
- **Lack of Adversarial Robustness in Standard Training:** As the deep learning models are under normal conditions and do not explicitly considers adversarial inputs, they fail to generalize well when subjected to adversarial perturbations. Robust training techniques, aim to mitigate these weaknesses, as discussed in Section 3.1.

Thus to develop resilient AI models capable of withstanding adversarial manipulations we need to have critical knowledge about those factors..

2.2.3 Overview of Adversarial Examples and Their Impact

There are several adversarial examples are possible to deceive deep learning models, they are:

- **Evasion Attacks:** In this approach slightly modified inputs mislead a trained model during inference of system parameters.
- **Poisoning Attacks:** This approach use malicious data to corrupt the model during training.
- **Backdoor Attacks:** Some hidden triggers are activated in some specific conditions during training can also break the correctness of the system.

We next provide a more comprehensive description of these attack types and methodologies.

3. ADVERSARIAL ATTACKS ON DEEP LEARNING MODELS

3.1 Types of Adversarial Attacks

White-Box vs. Black-Box Attacks

Based on the attacker's knowledge of the target system adversarial attacks we can broadly classify the attacks into white-box and black-box attacks. When the attacker has complete knowledge about the architecture, parameters, and gradients of the target system, it is known as white box attack. Fast Gradient Sign Method (FGSM) and Projected Gradient Descent (PGD) are the example of white-box attacks. These methods influence the model's gradients to generate perturbations that mislead the classifier. In contrast, the black-box attack supposes no direct knowledge of the objective model. Usually, attackers may attempt to exploit API responses, query the model repeatedly, or can use surrogate models trained on similar data to generate transferable adversarial examples. Zeroth-Order Optimization (ZOO) and Genetic Algorithm-based Attacks are examples of black-box approaches.

Gradient-Based Attacks

One the soundest technique for the attack is the gradient-based attack. To design adversarial examples such technique exploits the model's gradient information:

- Fast Gradient Sign Method (FGSM): In this method the attackers perturbs input images in the direction of the gradient, aiming to cause misclassification:

$$x' = x + \varepsilon \cdot sign\left(\nabla_x J(\theta, x, y)\right)$$

where **x'** is the adversarial example, **x** is the original input, ε is the perturbation magnitude, **J** is the loss function, and ∇is the gradient of the loss with respect to **x**.

- Basic Iterative Method (BIM): This approach is an extension of the basic FGSM that iteratively applies small perturbations:

$$X'_{t+1} = X'_t + \alpha . sign\left(\nabla_x J\left(\theta, X'_t, y\right)\right)$$

Where **α** is the step size and $\mathbf{x}_t$**'** is the perturbed input at iteration **t**.

- Carlini & Wagner (C&W) Attack: This approach uses an optimization-based approach to minimize the perturbation while ensuring misclassification:

$$\min\|\delta\|_p \; s.t. f(x+\delta) \neq y$$

where δ is the adversarial perturbation, and f(x+ δ) represents the model's prediction.

Optimization-Based Attacks

Another technique for adversarial attack is optimization-based attacks. This type of attack uses sound probability theory and employs iterative optimization algorithms to generate more effective adversarial examples:

- Projected Gradient Descent (PGD): It is an extension of the basic BIM by incorporating a special mechanism called random restarts, making it more powerful in white-box settings:

$$X'_{t+1} = Proj_{B_\varepsilon(X)}\left(X'_t + \alpha . sign\left(\nabla_x J\left(\theta, X'_t, y\right)\right)\right)$$

where Proj_Bε(x) ensures the perturbation remains within the ε-ball around .

- DeepFool: This is an iterative approach, which try to find out the smallest perturbation necessary to shift an input sample across the decision boundary, increasing the misclassification chance:

$$\delta = -\frac{f(X)}{\|\nabla f(X)\|_2^2} \nabla f\left(X\right)$$

This technique is ensuring minimal perturbation while achieving misclassification.

Evasion Attacks

Evasion attacks follow an intelligent strategic approach that involves generating adversarial examples at inference time that can bypass defense system of a trained model. Input data is modified by attackers to mislead classification while keeping changes imperceptible for human. This includes:

- **Perturbation-Based Attacks:** Techniques like FGSM, PGD, and DeepFool modify input data slightly to evade detection.
- **Spatial Attacks:** Methods such as adversarial transformations (e.g., rotations, translations) manipulate images to mislead models.
- **Natural Adversarial Examples:** Exploit real-world data variations to trick models without synthetic perturbations.

Poisoning Attacks

Poisoning attacks occur during training phase of the objective model. In that time an attacker can inject manipulated samples into the training set to degrade model performance or implant backdoors. Key types include:

- **Label Flipping:** In this approach intended for altering class labels of a subset of training data, misleading decision boundaries.
- **Feature Collision Attacks:** By embedding malicious patterns that influence learned representations, the model can causing misclassifications.
- **Clean-Label Poisoning:** By applying subtle changes in legitimate samples that steer model behavior toward incorrect outputs the approach can stipulate attack.

Poisoning attacks can be use for threaten federated learning systems, even the recommendation models, and online learning systems where data integrity is crucial.

Backdoor Attacks

In backdoor attacks approach the attackers can embed unseen triggers into models. Sometime the examples behave maliciously under specific conditions while performing normally otherwise. The attacker can place triggers during training, making the model respond incorrectly when the trigger is present. Examples include:

- **Trigger-Based Image Recognition Attacks:** Modifying images with specific patterns, leading to targeted misclassifications.
- **Trojan Neural Networks:** Modifying network weights to respond adversarially to predefined triggers.

Backdoor attacks pose significant risks to deployed AI systems, especially those in cybersecurity, finance, and autonomous systems.

Transferability of Adversarial Attacks

Unfortunately adversarial examples crafted for one model can deceive others, known as transferability. This critical characteristic becomes a key for attackers to target systems without direct access to it. These feature really posing serious risks to applications like autonomous vehicles, medical diagnostics, and cybersecurity.

3.2 Case Studies of Adversarial Attacks

3.2.1 Image Recognition: How Adversarial Examples Mislead Neural Networks

Deep learning models typically use convolutional neural networks (CNNs) for feature extraction build and build image recognition system for classification. In such a system, adversarial perturbations can mislead to take incorrect decision even with highly accurate CNNs. Interestingly these perturbations are crafted in such a way that it remain unnoticeable to the human eye but insist the model to misclassify an input image.

Example: Fooling Image Classification Systems

The Fast Gradient Sign Method (FGSM) generates adversarial images by computing the gradient of the loss function J(θ,x,y) with respect to the input x and adding a small perturbation ϵ:

$$x' = x + \varepsilon \cdot sign\left(\nabla_x J(\theta, x, y)\right)$$

where:

- x is the original image,
- y is the true label,
- θ represents model parameters,
- ϵ controls the perturbation magnitude.

A well-known experiment by **Goodfellow et al. (2015)** showed that an image of a panda classified with **57.7% confidence** was misclassified as a gibbon with **99.3% confidence** after adding an FGSM perturbation.

Face Recognition Attacks

Interestingly, adversarial examples generate threat to facial recognition systems. For example in **Sharif et al. (2016)** the authors demonstrated an attack scenario where a person is wearing a **perturbed eyeglasses** causing misclassification as someone else even by a commercial face recognition system.

3.2.2 Autonomous Vehicles: Adversarial Threats in Self-Driving Systems

One of the popular AI based objective system is Self-driving cars. It use computer vision and sensor fusion. The system is vulnerable to adversarial attacks on the components of the systems like camera, LiDAR, and radar-based perception systems.

Example: Fooling Traffic Sign Recognition

In Eykholt et al. (2018), the authors demonstrated that small perturbations on STOP signs caused deep learning models to misclassify them as Speed Limit 45 signs. They used Expectation over Transformation (EoT) to create robust adversarial perturbations under real-world conditions:

$$x' = \mathbb{E}_{t \sim T}[x + \delta_t]$$

where, T represents transformations like brightness changes, rotations, and occlusions.

Adversarial Attacks on LiDAR Sensors

Adversarial LiDAR attacks modify 3D point cloud data, similar to image-based attacks. In Cao et al. (2019), the researchers showed that an attacker can inject adversarial LiDAR points into the environment, making a self-driving car fail to detect pedestrians or obstacles.

3.2.3 Healthcare Applications: Adversarial Manipulation in Medical Imaging

Deep learning models in healthcare face critical security risks from adversarial attacks. These attacks can alter X-ray, MRI, CT, and ECG results, leading to incorrect diagnoses.

Example: Fooling AI in Medical Imaging

Finlayson et al. (2019) showed that adding adversarial noise to medical scans could change a benign tumor diagnosis into malignant, misleading AI-powered radiology models:

$$\hat{y} = f(x + \delta), \text{ where } \|\delta\|_p < \epsilon$$

Adversarial Attacks on ECG-Based Diagnosis

Electrocardiograms (ECG) help detect cardiac conditions, but adversarial attacks can introduce misleading heartbeat waveforms. Hannun et al. (2019) demonstrated that an attacker could inject noise into ECG signals to misclassify a normal heartbeat as arrhythmia:

$$X' = X + \delta, \delta \sim \mathcal{N}(0, \sigma^2)$$

3.2.4 Financial Fraud Detection: Adversarial Attacks on Fraud Detection Systems

Banks and financial institutions use machine learning models to detect fraudulent transactions. However, adversarial attackers can craft malicious financial transactions that bypass fraud detection models.

Example: Evasion Attacks in Credit Card Fraud Detection

A fraud detection system classifies a transaction x as either fraudulent (1) or legitimate (0). The model learns a function f(x) based on transaction features like amount, location, and frequency. An attacker can generate an adversarial transaction x′ by solving:

$$\underset{x'}{\text{minimize}} \|x' - x\|_p, \textit{ subject to } f(x') = 0, \textit{ where } \|\delta\|_p < \epsilon$$

where $\delta = x' - x$ is the perturbation added to evade detection. Papernot et al. (2016) demonstrated that adversarial examples could reduce fraud detection accuracy from 96% to 88% by modifying transaction features slightly.

Adversarial Attacks on Bitcoin Fraud Detection

Crypto-currency exchanges use graph-based fraud detection where each transaction is represented as a node in a graph. Attackers can generate adversarial transactions by perturbing graph edges, altering the transaction network so fraudulent activity appears legitimate. Zügner et al. (2018) developed a gradient-based attack on graph neural networks (GNNs) that successfully misclassified fraudulent transactions.

3.2.5 Cybersecurity Applications: Adversarial Attacks on Malware Detection

One of the common application area in cybersecurity defenses is the use of machine learning-based intrusion detection systems (IDS). Such systems are indented to detect malware and network intrusions. However, attackers can generate adversarial malware that bypasses detection.

Example: Evasion Attacks on Machine Learning-Based Malware Detection

A malware classifier f(x) can detects whether a given software sample is malicious or benign by using trained model inference. An attacker generates a modified sample x′ using:

$$x' = x + \varepsilon \cdot sign\left(\nabla_x J(\theta, x, y)\right)$$

where J(θ,x,y) is the classification loss function. In Grosse et al. (2017), the researcher have demonstrated that adversarial modifications in the API call sequences of malware could drop malware detection accuracy by 30%.

Adversarial Attacks on Phishing Detection

One of the interesting applications of AI is Phishing detection. In such systems, the trained models analyze email text features and classify messages as it is legitimate or it is a phishing attempts. Attackers can craft adversarial emails by modifying some malicious words to fool NLP-based detectors. In Ren et al. (2020), the authors introduced TextBugger, an attack that alters text to evade NLP-based security models:

3.2.6 Biometric Security: Adversarial Attacks on Facial Recognition Systems

An interesting application of AI is facial recognition systems. They are widely used for authentication, surveillance, and access control. Adversarial attackers can manipulate images to evade detection or impersonate someone else.

Example: Evasion Attacks on Face Recognition Models

A deep learning-based face recognition model learns a function f(x) that maps an image x to an identity label y. Attackers generate adversarial images x′ using:

$$x' = x + \varepsilon \cdot sign\left(\nabla_x J(\theta, x, y)\right)$$

where J(θ,x,y) is the classification loss function. The adversarial perturbation δ=x′−x is often imperceptible but can fool even state-of-the-art face recognition models. Sharif et al. (2016) demonstrated that carefully designed adversarial eyeglasses could mislead a commercial face recognition system into misclassifying identities with 100% success.

Backdoor Attacks on Biometric Systems

In case of backdoor attacks, adversaries can insert malicious triggers into training data so that the model misclassifies inputs with a specific trigger. Liu et al. (2018) showed that adding a small patch to a face image could consistently bypass biometric authentication.

3.2.7 Industrial Control Systems (ICS): Adversarial Attacks on Smart Grids

In the case of Industrial Control Systems (ICS) that manage power grids, water treatment plants, and manufacturing systems we can also experience such attacks. Attackers can craft adversarial inputs to disrupt energy supply, cause financial losses, or induce physical damage.

Example: Evasion Attacks on Power Grid Intrusion Detection

A machine learning-based intrusion detection system (IDS) monitors power grid sensor data and classifies network activity as normal or intrusion. Attackers can generate adversarial sensor readings x′ by optimizing:

$$\underset{x'}{\text{minimize}} \|x' - x\|_p, \; \textit{subject to } f(x') = 0, \; \|\delta\|_p < \epsilon$$

where δ=x′−x is a small perturbation added to real-time sensor readings. In, Ozay et al. (2016), the authors have demonstrated that adversarial perturbations in power system state estimation could successfully bypass anomaly detection (Ozay, M., et al 2016).

Poisoning Attacks on Smart Grid AI Models

In case of poisoning attacks, it is very likely that adversaries can inject malicious training samples to manipulate AI model behavior. As an example in Xie et al. (2021) the authors showed that adding adversarial noise to sensor data could degrade smart grid anomaly detection performance by 40%.

3.2.8 NLP-Based Chatbots: Adversarial Attacks on Language Models

Now days the use of Chatbots and virtual assistants that rely on deep learning models becomes a common tool for natural language understanding (NLU). Here also the intended attackers can craft adversarial text inputs to mislead, manipulate, or bias AI-driven conversations.

Example: Adversarial Text Perturbations in Sentiment Analysis

In general, sentiment analysis models classify a review x as positive or negative. On that case the attackers can modify text by adding synonyms, misspellings, or special characters to flip model predictions:

$$x' = x + \delta, \delta \in \{word\ substitutions, insertions, deletions\}$$

In Ebrahimi et al. (2018), the authors developed a gradient-based attack that altered a single word in a sentence, reducing text classification accuracy by 60%. Even adversaries can implant hidden triggers in chatbots by modifying training data as given in Wallace et al. (2020).

3.2.9 Autonomous Drones: Adversarial Attacks on UAV Perception Systems

The application of Unmanned Aerial Vehicles (UAVs) relies on deep learning-based. Here the model use object detection and navigation models for autonomous flight. This system is also a field where the attackers can inject adversarial perturbations to mislead UAV perception systems, This ultimately leading to crashes, collisions, or unauthorized access.

Example: Adversarial Attacks on UAV Object Detection

A UAV vision system classifies objects in an image using a deep neural network f(x), where xxx is the image input. Attackers generate adversarial images x′ by solving:

$$\underset{x'}{\text{minimize}} \|x' - x\|_p, \ subject\ to\ f(x') \neq f(x)$$

This ensures that the adversarial image x′ is visually similar to x but is **misclassified by the UAV model**.

Case Study: Misclassification of Traffic Signs

In Chen et al. (2020) the authors demonstrated that adversarial stickers placed on traffic signs could fool UAV navigation systems into misinterpreting road signs, leading to dangerous flight maneuvers.

Backdoor Attacks on UAV AI Systems

There are scenarios where the attackers can insert hidden triggers into UAV training data. This can cause drones to respond incorrectly to specific patterns. In Gu et al. (2017) it has been showed that backdoored UAV models could be manipulated to ignore obstacles in the presence of an adversarial pattern.

3.2.10 Blockchain Security: Adversarial Attacks on Smart Contracts

In systems like Smart contracts are the self-executing programs that use blockchain networks that automate transactions. Adversaries can manipulate smart contract machine learning models to execute fraudulent transactions.

Example: Adversarial Attacks on Blockchain Fraud Detection

A fraud detection model f(x) classifies blockchain transactions x as legitimate (0) or fraudulent (1). Attackers can craft adversarial transactions x′ by optimizing:

$$\underset{x'}{\text{minimize}} \|x' - x\|_p, \ \textit{subject to } f(x') = 0$$

where x′ is a modified fraudulent transaction that **bypasses detection**.

Case Study: Evasion Attacks on Smart Contract Auditing

Wang et al. (2022) demonstrated that adversarial modifications to smart contracts could bypass AI-based fraud detection systems, leading to unauthorized withdrawals from cryptocurrency wallets.

Backdoor Attacks in Decentralized Finance (DeFi)

Backdoor attacks involve embedding malicious code into AI models that audit blockchain transactions. Liu et al. (2021) showed that adversarial backdoors allowed attackers to execute unauthorized trades when triggered by specific input sequences.

3.2.11 Robotics: Adversarial Attacks on Industrial Robots

There are cases where industrial robots rely on AI-based vision and control systems. They perform precision manufacturing, warehouse automation, and human-robot interaction by the help of AI. There are scopes where attackers can introduce adversarial perturbations to generate misalignment, production defects, or safety hazards.

Example: Adversarial Attacks on Robot Arm Control

A robotic control system learns a mapping function f(s) from sensor state ‘s’ to action ‘a’ using reinforcement learning. Attackers modify state inputs s' to generate incorrect actions:

$$s' = s + \delta, \delta \sim \mathcal{N}(0, \sigma^2)$$

where δ is Gaussian noise injected into sensor readings, leading to unintended robotic movements.

Case Study: Adversarial Manipulation of Assembly Robots

In Zhang et al. (2021), the authors showed that small perturbations in sensor readings misled industrial robots into misplacing objects by several millimeters, disrupting precision assembly lines.

Backdoor Attacks on Robot Learning Systems

Backdoor attacks implant malicious triggers into reinforcement learning models. Ramesh et al. (2020) demonstrated that adversarial triggers caused robots to intentionally drop fragile objects when a specific symbol was present in the environment.

Table 3. Summary of Case Studies

Domain	Attack Type	Key Findings
Image Recognition	Evasion & Optimization-Based Attacks	Adversarial perturbations cause misclassification in deep learning models
Autonomous Vehicles	Evasion & Backdoor Attacks	Adversarial stickers fool self-driving car perception
Healthcare Applications	Evasion & Poisoning Attacks	Adversarial attacks manipulate medical diagnosis models

continued on following page

Table 3. Continued

Domain	Attack Type	Key Findings
Financial Fraud Detection	Evasion & Graph Attacks	Adversarial transactions bypass fraud detection
Cybersecurity	Evasion & Text Attacks	Malware & phishing evasion attacks degrade security models
Biometric Security	Evasion & Backdoor Attacks	Adversarial eyeglasses fool face recognition
Industrial Control Systems	Evasion & Poisoning Attacks	Adversarial sensor data disrupts smart grid monitoring
NLP-Based Chatbots	Adversarial Text & Backdoor Attacks	Adversarial text reduces accuracy & biases AI models
Autonomous Drones	Evasion & Backdoor Attacks	Adversarial stickers fool UAV perception
Blockchain Security	Evasion & Backdoor Attacks	Adversarial smart contracts bypass fraud detection
Industrial Robotics	Evasion & Reinforcement Learning Attacks	Adversarial sensor data disrupts robotic assembly

4. DEFENSE MECHANISMS AGAINST ADVERSARIAL ATTACKS

With the increasing amount of adversarial attacks, researchers have developed several defense mechanisms to combat the attack and produce a robust deep learning model. These mechanism includes adversarial training, input preprocessing to regularization techniques. However, for achieving adversarial robustness no single approach is enough and these exists a trade-offs between accuracy, computational efficiency, or generalization. This section explores key defense strategies and their effectiveness against different attack types.

4.1 Adversarial Training

Adversarial training is one of the most widely used protection mechanisms. It involves **retraining deep learning models with adversarial examples** to improve their strength against attacks. The key idea is to modify the loss function to incorporate adversarial perturbations during training.

Mathematically, **adversarial training** solves the following **min-max optimization problem**:

$$\min_{\theta} \mathbb{E}_{(x,y)\sim D}\left[\max_{\delta \in \Delta} \mathcal{L}\left(f_{\theta}(x+\delta), y\right)\right]$$

where:

- fθ is the deep learning model with parameters θ,
- L is the loss function,
- δ is the adversarial perturbation constrained by Δ,
- (x,y)∼D(x, y) represents data samples from the training distribution.

A popular adversarial training method is **Projected Gradient Descent (PGD) adversarial training**, where adversarial examples are iteratively generated using:

$$x^{(t+1)} = \prod_{\Delta}\left(x^{(t)} + \alpha \,.\, sign\left(\nabla_x \mathscr{L}(f_\theta(x^{(t)}), y)\right)\right)$$

where ΠΔ projects x^{(t+1) back into the allowed perturbation space.

Effectiveness: Adversarial training has been shown to improve model robustness, but it often degrades clean-data accuracy and requires **significant computational resources**.

4.2 Input Preprocessing Techniques

To mitigate adversarial attacks, several **input preprocessing techniques** aim to remove adversarial perturbations before feeding the data into a deep learning model.

Feature Squeezing

Feature squeezing reduces the degrees of freedom available for adversarial perturbations by:

1. **Reducing color bit depth** to limit subtle pixel modifications.
2. **Applying median filtering** to remove high-frequency adversarial noise.

Noise Injection

Adding random noise to the input before classification can disrupt adversarial patterns. Given an input xxx, noise injection can be defined as:

$$x' = x + \eta, \eta \sim \mathrm{N}(0, \sigma^2)$$

where η is sampled from a Gaussian distribution with variance σ2.

Input Transformations

Applying **image transformations**, such as JPEG compression, spatial smoothing, or total variance minimization, can mitigate adversarial effects. However, these methods are computationally efficient but often fail against adaptive adversaries.

4.3 Model Regularization and Robust Architectures

Dropout and Batch Normalization

Regularization techniques help prevent adversarial over-fitting.

- **Dropout** applies a technique to randomly deactivate neurons during training:

$$h'_i = h_i \cdot z_i, z_i \sim Bernoulli(p)$$

where hi is the neuron activation and p is the dropout rate.

- **Batch normalization** tries to generate smooth decision boundaries, aiming to reduce sensitivity to small perturbations:

$$\hat{x} = \frac{x-\mu}{\sqrt{\sigma^2 + \epsilon}}$$

where μ and σ^2 are the batch mean and variance.

Robust Network Architectures

Another interesting way is to use of specialized architectures, such as **Capsule Networks (CapsNets).** Such advanced architecture can improve adversarial flexibility by encoding spatial relationships between features. However, it requires stronger interventions more adversarial robustness beyond standard training.

4.4 Certified Defenses and Theoretical Guarantees

There are some certified defenses that provide mathematical guarantees that a model is robust against adversarial perturbations within a given bound.

Lipschitz Regularization

Bounding a neural network's **Lipschitz constant** controls the maximum change in output for a given input change:

$$\sup_{x_1,x_2} \frac{\|f(x_1) - f(x_2)\|}{\|x_1 - x_2\|}$$

Adversarial Certification with Interval Bound Propagation (IBP)

IBP propagates **interval constraints** through the network, ensuring robustness within a perturbation budget ϵ\epsilonϵ.

Effectiveness: Certified defenses guarantee robustness but are **often computationally expensive**.

4.5 Limitations and Challenges in Defense Strategies

Although adversarial defenses have advanced but still key challenges remain. Thus, future efforts are necessary to focus on hybrid methods that can combine multiple strategies to combat adversarial attacks.

5. ETHICAL CONSIDERATIONS AND REGULATORY LANDSCAPE

5.1 Explainability and Trust in AI

Importance of Interpretable AI in Adversarial Settings

First of all, AI systems — especially those in security-sensitive areas — have to be interpretable or they will never be trusted and reliable. In adversarial settings, where AI models may be co-opted or compromised this ability to be explainable about the decision is essential.

In AI decision-making processes IF there were none, it would be open to attack. Lack of the explainable nature in processes of AI decision-making leads to the vulnerabilities that can be leverage by malicious actors.

Adversarial Safeguarding: stakeholders are able to find and go after the potential risks in adversarial-like stakeholder scenarios with interpretable AI. For example, with explainable AI in the case of cyber security applications this means providing an understanding of why certain action was labeled as potentially threatening and allowing security teams to assess the evaluation and do next steps.

Explainability additionally promotes stakeholder confidence, as the rationale for decisions made using AI by humans can be directly intervened not eroding the trust further but eliciting it.

Several ways to get explainable are through model compression, feature attribution techniques and interpretable but priori architectures. There are inherent trade-offs between model complexity and interpretability, and researchers are exploring this space further via approaches like Local Interpretable Model-Agnostic Explanations (LIME) or SHapley Additive exPlanations (SHAP).

5.2 Ethical Considerations

Balancing Security with Accessibility in AI Research

It is very much important to keep a balance openness and potential misuse AI research. Transparency accelerates progress and strengthens collective defenses; it can also be a point for injection of vulnerabilities. This puts a limit on how much to disclose. Open-source innovation becomes a central cause for both advancements and misuse. Thus, while developing AI systems these points must be in a critical considerations.

5.3 Regulatory Challenges

Current Legal and Regulatory Frameworks for AI Security

AI deployment is causing the regulatory guidelines to start changing in light of the pressing dangers that are rising concerning being able to deploy ai. The existing legal frameworks adopted for AI security are grounded in provisions of data protection laws, cyber security regulations AND sector-specific guidelines. For instance the General Data Protection Regulation (GDPR) of the European Union applies to AI and has provisions on AI such but also the right to explanation and prohibition of automated decisions. Efforts have been made notwithstanding the fact that AI security regulation is split. We require holistic global policies to combat the far reaching risks posed by adversarial AI at global scale. The OECD and United Nations are among the organizations that are working towards creating international norms on artificial intelligence as it relates to ethics as well as security. AI regulation key challenges

- The legislation of liability in response to AI-triggered cyber security breaches
- Compliance without stifling innovation

- To confront the fast pace of adversarial AI

Moreover, future developments of the regulatory will necessitate open source adaptive frameworks that keep pace with progress in technology. We need the input of AI researchers, cyber-security experts and industry stakeholders to implement regulations that will safeguard security without impeding innovation.

6. TOWARD RESPONSIBLE IMPLEMENTATION

6.1 Collaboration and Multidisciplinary Teams

The Role of AI Researchers, Policymakers, and Security Experts in AML Research

Multiple groups of people are involved in the picture. Initially, the AI researchers develop novel strategies to combat adversarial attacks; on the other hand policy makers issue strict guidelines governing ethical and legal difficulty for the adversarial attack. Furthermore, security experts deploy efficient protection procedures. Thus, as multidisciplinary collaboration is essential for a complete perspective on AI security incorporating technical skills alongside somewhat ambiguous ethical considerations and stringent regulatory requirements.

6.2 Future Research Directions

Open Research Challenges in Adversarial Robustness

Development of adversarial defense has not finished the battle, still many challenges persist. The areas are still need to be explored in the future include:

- Generalization of Adversarial Defenses: Most current defenses are very good against certain attack types but are lacking in transferable across different adversarial threat domains. Challenges of non-parametric, adaptive and attack-agnostic defenses are critical till better solutions emerge.
- Scale and Performance: The sheer computational difficulty of some defense strategies is often prohibitive in practical applications, making deploying the strategies in real time unfeasible. Improvements need to be made in order for adversarial training to scale and not sacrifice good performance —Making it efficient for adversarial training.

- Resistance to Unknown Attacks: The up majority of AI security techniques exploit already existing attack patterns. Improving defenses for against previously unseen adversarial attack techniques will make AI stronger and better able to contend with new threats.
- Ethical and Privacy: Building Trustworthy AI must be apart the standard ethical benchmark and bind with regulation. The next step should be an investigation on how security can be held in check with the user rights, especially at high stakes domains like healthcare and finance.
- Ongoing research efforts have also to be focused most on cross-disciplinary working to address these challenges in earnest. Combing expert human insights, domain-specific knowledge and AI-driven automation can be the key to bringing adversarial robustness in different use cases together.

6.3 Human-in-the-Loop AI Systems

Ensuring Human Oversight in Adversarial Defense Strategies

Adversarial settings demand proper human oversight in AI security, not just automated defense mechanisms. Human-in-the-loop (HITL) AI based system unite expert-actors with machine learning models to improve decision making and make the agent more robust against adversarial attacks. Advantages of HITL systems

- Enhanced Interpretability: Leveraging the domain knowledge of human experts, these systems can generate contextual information in adversarial scenarios that help mitigate false positives and negatives.
- Dynamic Responses: In real-time security analysts can halt AI-driven threat detection to re-adjust according today's way sickest path.
- Ethical Barriers: The fate of enabling human oversight to mitigate overeager or erroneus AI decisions is basically accountability and fairness.

Well-defined protocols for human-AI collaboration are necessary among the implementation of HITL frameworks. Security professionals must be trained for teamwork with AI-driven defense systems to not only alleviate adversarial threats but regain trust in AI security applications.

7. CONCLUSION

Adversarial attacks constitute one of the most challenging threats to the integrity and safety of deep learning models. It can hamper the performance of the systems working especially in vital domains such as finance, healthcare, and cyber security. The proof that deep learning-based models are intrinsically exposed to adversarial attacks further highlights the urgency of developing a robust defense system. We describe simple attacks like evasion and poisoning attacks to more sophisticated adversarial manipulations. The changing landscape of adversarial machine learning (AML) involves not only the creativity of attackers but also a growing necessity for artificial intelligence systems to be more resistant.

The preceding discussion of this chapter gives an elaborate overview of the adversarial vulnerabilities, existing defense mechanisms, and ethical and regulatory considerations. Although strategies like adversarial training, model regularization, and certified robustness hold great promise in the mitigation of adversarial risks, no defense is ultimately impervious. Because adversarial threats are constantly evolving, further research and development must continue to produce more adaptive and resilient countermeasures.

The future of adversarial robust AI is multidisciplinary, incorporating higher levels of security, explainable AI (XAI), and human oversight. Regulators will also need to engage in recreation an important role in developing standards for the safe use of AI systems in critical applications. The collaboration between research communities, policy decision-makers, and practical industry professionals will lead to a better tomorrow with AI-based systems that are not just smart but also secure, trustworthy, and ethically oriented.

While deep learning is developing further, the adversarial challenges will keep playing a significant role in determining whether AI-based technologies are sustainable in the long run. The observations of this chapter seek to provide readers with the basic understanding required to find their way through this fast-evolving domain and help develop safer as well as more resilient AI systems.

REFERENCES

Akhtar, N., Mian, A., Kardan, N., & Shah, M. (2021). Advances in adversarial attacks and defenses in computer vision: A survey. *IEEE Access : Practical Innovations, Open Solutions*, *9*, 155161–155196. DOI: 10.1109/ACCESS.2021.3127960

Badjie, B., Cecílio, J., & Casimiro, A. (2024). Adversarial attacks and countermeasures on image classification-based deep learning models in autonomous driving systems: A systematic review. *ACM Computing Surveys*, *57*(1), 1–52. DOI: 10.1145/3691625

Baniecki, H., & Biecek, P. (2024). Adversarial attacks and defenses in explainable artificial intelligence: A survey. *Information Fusion*, *107*, 102303. DOI: 10.1016/j.inffus.2024.102303

Bastounis, A., Hansen, A. C., & Vlačić, V. (2021). The mathematics of adversarial attacks in AI—Why deep learning is unstable despite the existence of stable neural networks. *arXiv preprint arXiv:2109.06098.*

Bhatt, D., Patel, C., Talsania, H., Patel, J., Vaghela, R., Pandya, S., Modi, K., & Ghayvat, H. (2021). CNN variants for computer vision: History, architecture, application, challenges and future scope. *Electronics (Basel)*, *10*(20), 2470. DOI: 10.3390/electronics10202470

Calinescu, R., Imrie, C., Mangal, R., Rodrigues, G. N., Păsăreanu, C., Santana, M. A., & Vázquez, G. (2024). Controller synthesis for autonomous systems with deep-learning perception components. *IEEE Transactions on Software Engineering*, *50*(6), 1374–1395. DOI: 10.1109/TSE.2024.3385378

Cao, Y., Xiao, C., Cyr, B., Fang, J., Yang, J., Tramèr, F., & Kolter, J. Z. (2019). Adversarial sensor attack on LiDAR-based perception in autonomous driving. *Proceedings of the 2019 ACM SIGSAC Conference on Computer and Communications Security (CCS).* DOI: 10.1145/3319535.3339815

Chakraborty, A., Alam, M., Dey, V., Chattopadhyay, A., & Mukhopadhyay, D. (2021). A survey on adversarial attacks and defences. *CAAI Transactions on Intelligence Technology*, *6*(1), 25–45. DOI: 10.1049/cit2.12028

Chander, B., John, C., Warrier, L., & Gopalakrishnan, K. (2025). Toward trustworthy artificial intelligence (TAI) in the context of explainability and robustness. *ACM Computing Surveys*, *57*(6), 1–49. DOI: 10.1145/3675392

Chen, S., Cornelius, C., Martin, C., & Song, D. (2020). ShapeShifter: Adversarial traffic sign attacks against vision-based autonomous vehicles. *USENIX Security Symposium.*

Cinà, A. E., Grosse, K., Demontis, A., Vascon, S., Zellinger, W., Moser, B. A., Oprea, A., Biggio, B., Pelillo, M., & Roli, F. (2023). Wild patterns reloaded: A survey of machine learning security against training data poisoning. *ACM Computing Surveys*, *55*(13s), 1–39. DOI: 10.1145/3585385

Costa, J. C., Roxo, T., Proença, H., & Inácio, P. R. (2024). How deep learning sees the world: A survey on adversarial attacks & defenses. *IEEE Access : Practical Innovations, Open Solutions*, *12*, 61113–61136. DOI: 10.1109/ACCESS.2024.3395118

Das, S., Tariq, A., Santos, T., Kantareddy, S. S., & Banerjee, I. (2023). Recurrent neural networks (RNNs): architectures, training tricks, and introduction to influential research. *Machine learning for Brain disorders*, 117-138.

Ebrahimi, J., Rao, A., Lowd, D., & Dou, D. (2018). HotFlip: White-box adversarial examples for text classification. *Proceedings of the 56th Annual Meeting of the Association for Computational Linguistics (ACL)*. DOI: 10.18653/v1/P18-2006

Eykholt, K., Evtimov, I., Fernandes, E., Li, B., Rahmati, A., Xiao, C., & Song, D. (2018). Robust physical-world attacks on deep learning visual classification. *Proceedings of the IEEE Conference on Computer Vision and Pattern Recognition (CVPR)*. DOI: 10.1109/CVPR.2018.00175

Finlayson, S. G., Bowers, J. D., Ito, J., Zittrain, J. L., Beam, A. L., & Kohane, I. S. (2019). Adversarial attacks on medical machine learning. *Science*, *363*(6433), 1287–1289. DOI: 10.1126/science.aaw4399 PMID: 30898923

Goodfellow, I. J., Shlens, J., & Szegedy, C. (2015). Explaining and harnessing adversarial examples. *International Conference on Learning Representations (ICLR).*

Grosse, K., Papernot, N., Manoharan, P., Backes, M., & McDaniel, P. (2017). Adversarial examples for malware detection. *European Symposium on Research in Computer Security (ESORICS).*

Gu, T., Dolan-Gavitt, B., & Garg, S. (2017). *BadNets: Identifying vulnerabilities in deep learning-based autonomous control systems.* arXiv preprint arXiv:1708.06733.

Han, S., Lin, C., Shen, C., Wang, Q., & Guan, X. (2023). Interpreting adversarial examples in deep learning: A review. *ACM Computing Surveys*, *55*(14s), 1–38. DOI: 10.1145/3594869

Hannun, A. Y., Rajpurkar, P., Haghpanahi, M., Tison, G. H., Bourn, C., Turakhia, M. P., & Ng, A. Y. (2019). Cardiologist-level arrhythmia detection and classification in ambulatory electrocardiograms using a deep neural network. *Nature Medicine*, *25*(1), 65–69. DOI: 10.1038/s41591-018-0268-3 PMID: 30617320

He, L., Wei, B., Hao, K., Gao, L., & Peng, C. (2025). Bio-inspired deep neural local acuity and focus learning for visual image recognition. *Neural Networks*, *181*, 106712. DOI: 10.1016/j.neunet.2024.106712 PMID: 39388996

He, X., Yang, H., Hu, Z., & Lv, C. (2022). Robust lane change decision making for autonomous vehicles: An observation adversarial reinforcement learning approach. *IEEE Transactions on Intelligent Vehicles*, *8*(1), 184–193. DOI: 10.1109/TIV.2022.3165178

Hernández-Castro, C. J., Liu, Z., Serban, A., Tsingenopoulos, I., & Joosen, W. (2022). Adversarial machine learning. In *Security and Artificial Intelligence: A Crossdisciplinary Approach* (pp. 287–312). Springer International Publishing. DOI: 10.1007/978-3-030-98795-4_12

Islam, S., Elmekki, H., Elsebai, A., Bentahar, J., Drawel, N., Rjoub, G., & Pedrycz, W. (2024). A comprehensive survey on applications of transformers for deep learning tasks. *Expert Systems with Applications*, *241*, 122666. DOI: 10.1016/j.eswa.2023.122666

Javed, H., El-Sappagh, S., & Abuhmed, T. (2025). Robustness in deep learning models for medical diagnostics: Security and adversarial challenges towards robust AI applications. *Artificial Intelligence Review*, *58*(1), 1–107.

Kannan, Y. (2024). AI AND MACHINE LEARNING FOR NETWORK SECURITY: APPLICATIONS AND CASE STUDIES. [IJAIML]. *International Journal of Artificial Intelligence and Machine Learning*, *3*(02), 1–13.

Kaviani, S., Han, K. J., & Sohn, I. (2022). Adversarial attacks and defenses on AI in medical imaging informatics: A survey. *Expert Systems with Applications*, *198*, 116815. DOI: 10.1016/j.eswa.2022.116815

Kothinti, R. R. (2024). Deep learning in healthcare: Transforming disease diagnosis, personalized treatment, and clinical decision-making through AI-driven innovations.

Li, B., Qi, P., Liu, B., Di, S., Liu, J., Pei, J., Yi, J., & Zhou, B. (2023). Trustworthy AI: From principles to practices. *ACM Computing Surveys*, *55*(9), 1–46. DOI: 10.1145/3555803

Li, Y., Xie, B., Guo, S., Yang, Y., & Xiao, B. (2024). A survey of robustness and safety of 2d and 3d deep learning models against adversarial attacks. *ACM Computing Surveys*, *56*(6), 1–37. DOI: 10.1145/3636551

Li, Y., Zhao, Y., Liu, G., & Liao, X. (2024, May). THE APPLICATION OF DEEP LEARNING IN THE FINANCIAL SECTOR: A COMPREHENSIVE REVIEW. In *The 21st International scientific and practical conference "Innovative solutions in public communications and international relations"(May 28–31, 2024) Sofia, Bulgaria. International Science Group. 2024. 382 p.* (p. 316).

Liu, J., Feng, W., & Zhu, H. (2021). Backdoor vulnerabilities in AI-driven decentralized finance systems. *Proceedings of the ACM Conference on Computer and Communications Security (CCS).*

Liu, Y., & Lyu, T. (2025). Real-time monitoring of lower limb movement resistance based on deep learning. *Alexandria Engineering Journal, 111*, 136–147. DOI: 10.1016/j.aej.2024.09.031

Liu, Y., Ma, S., Aafer, Y., Lee, W. C., Zhai, J., Wang, W., & Zhang, X. (2018). Trojaning attack on neural networks. *25th Network and Distributed System Security Symposium (NDSS).* DOI: 10.14722/ndss.2018.23291

Ma, X., Niu, Y., Gu, L., Wang, Y., Zhao, Y., Bailey, J., & Lu, F. (2021). Understanding adversarial attacks on deep learning based medical image analysis systems. *Pattern Recognition, 110*, 107332. DOI: 10.1016/j.patcog.2020.107332

Manogna, R. L., & Anand, A. (2024). A bibliometric analysis on the application of deep learning in finance: Status, development and future directions. *Kybernetes, 53*(12), 5951–5971. DOI: 10.1108/K-04-2023-0637

Mienye, I. D., & Swart, T. G. (2024). A hybrid deep learning approach with generative adversarial network for credit card fraud detection. *Technologies, 12*(10), 186. DOI: 10.3390/technologies12100186

Nabavirazavi, S., Taheri, R., & Iyengar, S. S. (2024). Enhancing federated learning robustness through randomization and mixture. *Future Generation Computer Systems, 158*, 28–43. DOI: 10.1016/j.future.2024.04.009

Najim, A. H., Al-sharhanee, K. A. M., Al-Joboury, I. M., Kanellopoulos, D., Sharma, V. K., Hassan, M. Y., Issa, W., Abbas, F. H., & Abbas, A. H. (2025). An IoT healthcare system with deep learning functionality for patient monitoring. *International Journal of Communication Systems, 38*(4), e6020. DOI: 10.1002/dac.6020

Nargesi, A. A., Adejumo, P., Dhingra, L. S., Rosand, B., Hengartner, A., Coppi, A., Benigeri, S., Sen, S., Ahmad, T., Nadkarni, G. N., Lin, Z., Ahmad, F. S., Krumholz, H. M., & Khera, R. (2025). Automated identification of heart failure with reduced ejection fraction using deep learning-based natural language processing. *Heart Failure, 13*(1), 75–87. DOI: 10.1016/j.jchf.2024.08.012 PMID: 39453355

Ojo, B., & Aghaunor, C. T. (2024). AI-driven cybersecurity solutions for real-time threat detection in critical infrastructure. *International Journal of Science and Research Archive, 12*(02), 1716–1726. DOI: 10.30574/ijsra.2024.12.2.1401

Ozay, M., Vural, F. T. Y., Tappert, C., & Moghadam, P. (2016). Machine learning attack and defense strategies in power grid state estimation. *IEEE Transactions on Neural Networks and Learning Systems.*

Papernot, N., McDaniel, P., Jha, S., Fredrikson, M., Celik, Z. B., & Swami, A. (2016). *The limitations of deep learning in adversarial settings.* 2016 IEEE European Symposium on Security and Privacy (EuroS&P). DOI: 10.1109/EuroSP.2016.36

Polemi, N., Praça, I., Kioskli, K., & Bécue, A. (2024). Challenges and efforts in managing AI trustworthiness risks: A state of knowledge. *Frontiers in Big Data, 7*, 1381163. DOI: 10.3389/fdata.2024.1381163 PMID: 38798307

Qian, Z., Huang, K., Wang, Q. F., & Zhang, X. Y. (2022). A survey of robust adversarial training in pattern recognition: Fundamental, theory, and methodologies. *Pattern Recognition, 131*, 108889. DOI: 10.1016/j.patcog.2022.108889

Rahman, A., Debnath, T., Kundu, D., Khan, M. S. I., Aishi, A. A., Sazzad, S., Sayduzzaman, M., & Band, S. S. (2024). Machine learning and deep learning-based approach in smart healthcare: Recent advances, applications, challenges and opportunities. *AIMS Public Health, 11*(1), 58–109. DOI: 10.3934/publichealth.2024004 PMID: 38617415

Ramesh, A., Patel, R., & Singh, P. (2020). Hidden adversarial triggers in reinforcement learning-based robotic control. *Proceedings of the International Conference on Intelligent Robots and Systems (IROS).*

Rath, S., Das, T., & Sengupta, S. (2024). Improvise, adapt, overcome: Dynamic resiliency against unknown attack vectors in microgrid cybersecurity games. *IEEE Transactions on Smart Grid, 15*(4), 4245–4258. DOI: 10.1109/TSG.2024.3372643

Raza, S. A., Syed, D., Rizwan, S., & Ahmed, M. (2025). Quantum Computing and Its Implications for Financial Markets. In *The Global Evolution, Changing Landscape and Future of Financial Markets: From Traditional to Digital* (pp. 119-131). Emerald Publishing Limited. DOI: 10.1108/978-1-83549-330-420251010

Ren, H., Huang, T., & Yan, H. (2021). Adversarial examples: Attacks and defenses in the physical world. *International Journal of Machine Learning and Cybernetics, 12*(11), 3325–3336. DOI: 10.1007/s13042-020-01242-z

Ren, S., Dai, H., Wu, X., Zhang, L., & Yu, P. S. (2020). TextBugger: Generating adversarial text against real-world applications. *26th Network and Distributed System Security Symposium (NDSS).*

Shandilya, S. K., Datta, A., Kartik, Y., & Nagar, A. (2024). Advancing security and resilience. In *Digital Resilience: Navigating Disruption and Safeguarding Data Privacy* (pp. 459–529). Springer Nature Switzerland. DOI: 10.1007/978-3-031-53290-0_8

Sharif, M., Bhagavatula, S., Bauer, L., & Reiter, M. K. (2016). Accessorize to a crime: Real and stealthy attacks on state-of-the-art face recognition. *Proceedings of the 2016 ACM SIGSAC Conference on Computer and Communications Security.* DOI: 10.1145/2976749.2978392

Sharif, M., Bhagavatula, S., Bauer, L., & Reiter, M. K. (2016). Accessorize to a crime: Real and stealthy attacks on state-of-the-art face recognition. *ACM SIGSAC Conference on Computer and Communications Security (CCS).* DOI: 10.1145/2976749.2978392

Su, P., Yan, Y., Li, H., Wu, H., Liu, C., & Huang, W. (2025). Images and deep learning in human and urban infrastructure interactions pertinent to sustainable urban studies: Review and perspective. *International Journal of Applied Earth Observation and Geoinformation, 136*, 104352. DOI: 10.1016/j.jag.2024.104352

Vadillo, J., Santana, R., & Lozano, J. A. (2025). Adversarial attacks in explainable machine learning: A survey of threats against models and humans. *Wiley Interdisciplinary Reviews. Data Mining and Knowledge Discovery, 15*(1), e1567. DOI: 10.1002/widm.1567

Wallace, E., Feng, S., Kandpal, N., Gardner, M., & Singh, S. (2020). *Universal adversarial triggers for attacking and analyzing NLP models.* Empirical Methods in Natural Language Processing (EMNLP).

Wang, J., Wang, S., & Zhang, Y. (2025). Deep learning on medical image analysis. *CAAI Transactions on Intelligence Technology, 10*(1), 1–35. DOI: 10.1049/cit2.12356

Wang, Y., Zhang, Y., & Wang, X. (2022). Adversarial machine learning in blockchain security. *IEEE Transactions on Information Forensics and Security.*

Xie, J., Wang, Y., & He, X. (2021). Adversarial machine learning in smart grid: Attacks and countermeasures. *IEEE Transactions on Smart Grid.*

Zhang, C., Hu, M., Li, W., & Wang, L. (2024). Adversarial attacks and defenses on text-to-image diffusion models: A survey. *Information Fusion*, •••, 102701.

Zhang, X., Xu, L., & Ma, H. (2021). Adversarial perturbations in robotic perception systems. *IEEE Robotics and Automation Letters*.

Zhou, S., Liu, C., Ye, D., Zhu, T., Zhou, W., & Yu, P. S. (2022). Adversarial attacks and defenses in deep learning: From a perspective of cybersecurity. *ACM Computing Surveys*, *55*(8), 1–39. DOI: 10.1145/3547330

Zügner, D., Akbarnejad, A., & Günnemann, S. (2018). Adversarial attacks on neural networks for graph data. *Proceedings of the 24th ACM SIGKDD International Conference on Knowledge Discovery & Data Mining*. DOI: 10.1145/3219819.3220078

Chapter 2
Taxonomy of Adversarial Attacks and Defenses

Kumar Parmar
https://orcid.org/0000-0002-2502-5680
Marwadi University, India

T. Premavathi
https://orcid.org/0009-0003-0172-2021
Marwadi University, India

Damodharan Palaniappan
https://orcid.org/0009-0003-0721-3068
Marwadi University, India

Dev Nitesh Gadhvi
https://orcid.org/0009-0008-4119-3124
Marwadi University, India

Rituraj Jain
https://orcid.org/0000-0002-5532-1245
Marwadi University, India

G. Kirubasri
https://orcid.org/0000-0002-2086-8064
Sona College of Technology, India

ABSTRACT

Adversarial Machine Learning poses critical risk to the security of AI systems as adversaries can manipulate system inputs to force the models into making incorrect choices. This section provides a detailed classification of adversarial attacks and defenses, organizing them as a function of what information the defender possesses about the attacker, the goal of the attack, and the attack methods used: white-box, black-box, and even physical adversarial attacks. It also explores the impact of Adversarial Machine Learning on cybersecurity, finance, healthcare, and even autonomous systems. From adversarial training, input filtering, and optimum robust design, all known defensive mechanisms are evaluated against sophisticated attack mechanisms that are undergoing constant evolution. This chapter emphasizes the importance of continuous AML research to safeguard machine learning applications' integrity and reliability in real-world environments.

DOI: 10.4018/979-8-3373-2200-1.ch002

1. INTRODUCTION

1.1 Understanding Adversarial Machine Learning – Definition, significance, and real-world implications

AML focuses on the identification of security weaknesses in ML models after subjecting them to attacker-generated modified inputs. This area continues to expand within artificial intelligence (AI) together with cybersecurity. The data gets manipulated through adversarial examples which human observers cannot detect yet these changes lead AI systems to make incorrect decisions. AML safeguards cybersecurity through its protection of critical AI-driven applications because intended system violations create persistent risks to healthcare systems along with financial institutions and autonomous operations (Biasin et al., 2024). The key concept of adversarial attacks-originates from taking advantage of ML models that process information in high-dimensional spaces. The numeric patterns used by ML models for understanding data remain accessible to attackers who can apply minimal changes to trigger misclassification. Image classification models can be deceived by expertly made adversarial changes that convert stop signs into speed limit signs which creates dangerous situations in self-driving vehicles. Adversarial text modifications in natural language processing fields make NLP systems change their sentiment analysis decisions and enable spam filter avoidance (Chen et al., 2022). AML research conducts both attack identification and defense development as essential components of its scope. The main difficulty in AML involves the ability of adversarial inputs designed for one model to fool different models with distinct architectures and training datasets. Cloud-based AI services face a major security risk because attackers can train substitute models which enable them to perform black-box attacks.

Adversarial attacks extend beyond digital domains during their operation. Physical adversarial attacks take place when real-world objects receive modifications through addition of physical elements such as stickers on road signs which aim to confuse computer vision models. AML security threats require advanced defensive systems because they demonstrate the extensive security risks of this technology (Guesmi et al., 2023). Building mitigations for resisting adversarial machine learning requires complete understanding by IT professionals. AI adoption throughout industries will expand in the future which makes advanced security frameworks essential for obtaining trust in and reliability of machine learning applications. This chapter examines adversarial attack and defense classification while describing their operational methods as well as their resulting effects and protection approaches (Ruan et al., 2021).

1.2 Role of Adversarial Attacks in Cybersecurity – How attacks impact various domains (finance, healthcare, AI ethics)

The expanded use of machine learning (ML) throughout different industries creates new security issues because of adversarial attacks. Such attacks create major cybersecurity threats through model vulnerabilities which cause compromised decisions and privacy breaches and financial losses. Various critical sectors such as finance, healthcare, autonomous systems and national security experience the effects of adversarial attacks within cybersecurity operations (Kumar et al., 2023). The financial sector depends heavily upon ML models for their operations including fraud management as well as risk analysis and automated trading. The systems become susceptible to adversarial attacks when attackers feed them deceptive input data that produces erroneous output. An attacker can produce fraudulent transactions that circumvent fraud prevention software which enables them to execute unauthorized money transfers. The modification of stock market prediction models by adversaries generates false market movements which causes financial market instability and weakens trust between investors. The healthcare sector where AI diagnostic technology and automated health care monitoring systems have experienced rapid expansion faces considerable dangers. Medical images and electronic health records (EHRs) face a threat to patient safety when adversarial attacks introduce alterations into their systems. The modification of MRI scans through adversarial noise would lead an AI diagnostic system to mistake benign tumors for malignancies and also confuse malignancies with benign tumors (Biasin et al., 2024). Patient health becomes endangered when misclassifications occur because of incorrect or delayed medical treatments. Medical organizations urgently require protected AI systems that defend against adversarial activities in healthcare environments.

Self-driving cars together with drones implement ML models for their navigation systems and object recognition abilities and decision-making functions. These systems experience adverse modifications to road signs and sensor inputs that lead to incorrect system functions which may trigger dangerous situations or unexpected actions. Security threats created through adversarial attacks can use military AI systems as well as surveillance tools and national security infrastructure as targets in cyber warfare. Attacks against AI models allow invaders to damage crucial operations that would endanger national security assets (Oniani et al., 2023). Security defenders must develop strong counter attacks against changing adversary threats because AI becomes vital in cybersecurity defense systems. Developing robust secure AI systems requires full comprehension of adversarial attacks to ensure network resilience.

1.3 The Adversarial Arms Race – Constant evolution of attacks and defences in machine learning

The continuous development and counter-development motions between attackers and defenders define adversarial machine learning (AML). The substantial growth of machine learning models in critical systems makes the stakes become increasingly high for this competitive battle between attackers and defenders. The continuous evolution of attack approaches by intruders requires researchers and engineers to create stronger protective systems for AI model anti-manipulation. The repeated cycle demonstrates how adversarial threats along with their defensive measures continuously transform in the present day (Khalil et al., 2022). The main obstacle during the adversarial arms race exists in the ability of adversarial examples to move between different models. An adversarial attack made for one model frequently succeeds in tricking different models with unique architectures and training datasets. The transferability of adversarial examples creates obstacles for complete machine learning system security because attackers can create malicious inputs using models that remain out of their reach. To protect their models defenders need to develop strategies which defend against specific attacks and all possible adversarial threats that could develop. The development of advanced adversarial attacks leads to progressive improvement of defense solutions against these attacks. Simple attack countermeasures have been supplanted by modern adversarial training and robust optimization approaches that better withstand diverse types of malicious activities. All defense systems remain vulnerable despite recent progress in their development. Attackers learn to modify their methods by developing better attack strategies that bypass defenses which were previously thought to be effective. The escalating arms race encompasses defensive measures and training system procedures alongside model defense techniques. Attackers now discover creative means to conduct real-world exploitation by creating physical adversarial attacks that modify physical elements for deceitful machine learning system interactions. Modifying road signs combined with sensor manipulation produces serious real-world effects especially during autonomous vehicle operation and security system operations. Continual research becomes vital for cybersecurity because the competing arms race shows that attackers and defenders continuously need to remain ahead of each other (Parihar et al., 2024).

2. TYPES OF ADVERSARIAL ATTACKS

2.1 White-box vs. Black-box vs. Gray-box Attacks – Classification based on attacker knowledge

Attackers categorize their assaults according to the level of information they possess regarding the machine learning model they want to exploit. The classification system which includes white-box and black-box and gray-box attacks enables researchers to understand attack strategies and needed defensive measures. Every breach technique follows distinct obstacles with separate steps needed to minimize its damaging effects. The attacker gains full access to the target model because white-box attacks give them complete visibility of the model architecture and its parameters along with its training data. The attacker gains full access to model data through extensive knowledge which enables them to develop targeted adversarial examples for exploiting weak points. White-box attackers commonly use Fast Gradient Sign Method (FGSM) to create perturbations by capitalizing on model loss function gradients in order to maximize error. Attackers achieve high success rates in model deception by utilizing the full access they have to the model to design effective adversarial inputs. White-box attacks succeed because attackers obtain model access yet this assumption does not necessarily hold true during actual real-world situations (Apruzzese et al., 2023).

Black-box attacks occur when attackers lack any direct model access including both model parameters and training data and weight information. Attackers can only view the model outputs that result from different input data through a query-based observation method. The execution of black-box attacks proves to be difficult because attackers receive restricted information access. By applying transferability techniques attackers can overcome this limitation through adversarial examples which were created for one model to deceive another model. The black-box attack methodology finds its relevance in practical deployments since attackers only access models through their interface during interactions with cloud-based AI systems or commercial machine learning services. The vulnerability range of Gray-box attacks exists between that of white-box and black-box attacks. Attackers who operate under gray-box conditions have restricted access to the target model because they possess only limited information such as design parameters and training data subsets. The attacker gains more information than black-box attacks offer yet remains uncertain about several aspects. The combination of white-box and black-box attack methods through reverse-engineering model behavior and surrogate modeling techniques defines gray-box attacks. The effectiveness of gray-box attacks increases when attackers discover design weaknesses and known patterns in the model (Casper et al., 2024).

People who need to develop strong security measures must understand the range of attacks that exist. The development of secure AI systems requires research that creates specific defensive strategies for every attack category since an attacker's knowledge level varies. In Figure 1, you can see the Machine learning attack strategies.

Figure 1. Machine Learning Attack Strategies.

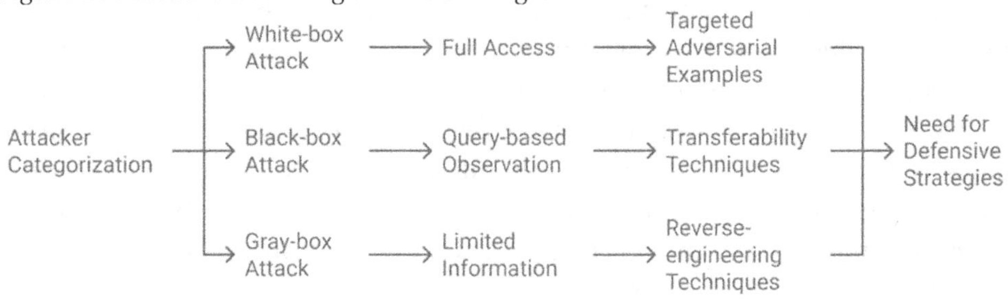

2.2 Targeted vs. Non-Targeted Attacks – Differences in attack goals and impact

The goal of adversarial attacks determines their classification between targeted and non-targeted attacks. The attack objective makes an important difference when attackers handle systems while determining the performance level of machine learning models. Knowledge of these two attack types remains vital since they demand different approaches for defense development. The main purpose of targeted attacks is to modify inputs that will produce predetermined misclassification outcomes from the model. The attacker modifies the input so it leads to misclassification where the model produces a particular class which was chosen beforehand. Attackers modify images of cats to transform them into dog classifications with the precise target label in mind during image classification tasks. Attacking a model with precision requires attackers to create specific adversarial perturbations that force the model to produce a designated incorrect label because this process demands thorough knowledge of model decision boundaries. The execution of targeted attacks leads to successful manipulation of automated decision systems and autonomous vehicles as well as other specific malicious outcomes (Yu et al., 2023). Non-targeted attacks avoid selecting particular classes for manipulation because they focus on inducing any wrong prediction regardless of the output category. The attack objective focuses on misleading the model to produce any incorrect prediction while disregarding the specific class outcome. The execution of non-targeted attacks proves simpler since attackers do not need precise knowledge about target outputs. A spam filter attack can be carried out by modifying an email to obtain legitimate classification instead of targeting specific spam categories. Systems under non-targeted attacks experience general operational disruptions from attackers who do not need specific misclassification results. The system experiences total degradation when the model performs any incorrect classification during an attack. Non-targeted attacks have wider applicability than targeted attacks yet remain harder to defend because of their general nature. The defense methods for targeted and non-targeted attacks differ because they require adversarial training alongside robustness regularization techniques. Research and practitioner groups achieve better machine learning security by clarifying the distinctions between targeted attacks and non-targeted attacks (Chutia & Baruah, 2024).

2.3 Static vs. Dynamic Attacks – Attacks on pre-trained models vs. adaptive attacks on real-time systems

The classification of adversarial attacks depends on their focus between static or dynamic models. Static attacks differ from dynamic attacks through their attack goals and when attacks happen along with the interaction methods between the machine learning system. The development of defense solutions needs to focus on addressing vulnerabilities that exist in static attacks and dynamic attacks independently (Kawamoto et al., 2023). The objective of static attacks is to exploit pre-trained models which operate without any adaptation or modification throughout the attack process. The attacker makes adversarial examples for a model which already exists in deployment. Attackers conduct these operations by creating small modifications on input data which they use to trick the model. The execution of static attacks proves easier for attackers since they maintain full access to a fixed model and can produce adversarial examples through established methods like Fast Gradient Sign Method (FGSM) or Project Gradient Descent (PGD), (Chen et al., 2022). The completed adversarial inputs remain capable of deceiving the model until its training or update process occurs. The main drawback of static attacks exists because they only target models that do not implement updates or retraining after an attack occurs. Dynamic attacks are designed for models who undergo continuous adaptation because their training or adaptation occurs frequently based on new data. The complexity of these attacks increases due to the attacker-model feedback mechanism. The attacker maintains control by modifying their methods according to model changes when it processes new information or undergoes retraining thus enabling sustained and developing attacks (Khalil et al., 2022). The learning process of models updated with each new data point becomes susceptible to attack when adversaries introduce adversarial examples in online learning platforms. Dynamic attacks evolve because they detect modifications made to the model's architecture or parameters during its operational period thus becoming more challenging to defend. Poisoning attacks represent an example of adversarial inputs which are introduced during training to manipulate learning procedures which results in compromised model behavior after deployment. The difference between static and dynamic attacks makes an impact on how adversarial examples are designed and which countermeasures need implementation. Defenses against static attacks become easier through methods like adversarial training or defensive distillation but dynamic attacks need advanced protection methods because they adapt to the system. The necessary defense strategies should involve persistent model update surveillance together with training robustness assessments as well as speedy detection and elimination of poisoned data and adversarial examples when they occur. The protection of dynamic attacks remains vital for applications requiring model security throughout extended periods of training and retraining (Chen et al., 2024), (Bennouna et al., 2023).

3. ATTACK METHODOLOGIES AND TECHNIQUES

3.1 Evasion Attacks – Perturbation-based attacks (FGSM, PGD, CW)

The main use of adversarial attack methods produces fake inputs which cause machine learning models to malfunction with incorrect predictions. The tactics used for attack development show different levels of sophistication based on the models along with the dataset and desired outcomes of the attacker. Recognizing the main adversarial attack procedures represents a vital step toward developing proper safety protocols. Three main adversarial attack methods exist which include gradient-based attacks, optimization-based attacks and decision-based attacks together with their diverse popularity in the field. Gradient-based attacks represent the most frequent and effective methods used by attackers to create adversarial examples during their processes. An attack technique depends on gradient information from a model to uncover directions where tiny modifications will produce maximum prediction flaws. The Fast Gradient Sign Method (FGSM) represents one of the first and most popular gradient-based attacks that introduces small directional noise to manipulate inputs until classification failure occurs. The method works efficiently in computations while compatibility extends to all differentiable models including neural networks. The Project Gradient Descent (PGD) attack represents an evolution of the FGSM method because it performs several gradient-based refinement steps to build more potent adversarial examples which are very challenging to defend against. The attacker achieves most success with adversarial attacks by obtaining complete model access (white-box attacks) since this allows them to use gradient information for generating adversarial examples.

The attack framework under optimization-based methodology transforms adversarial attacks into optimized problems which exceed the capabilities of gradient-based approaches. An attacker explores the minimum changes to inputs that produce incorrect model results while working under various constraints about perturbation visibility and attack steps. Through the Carlini-Wagner (CW) attack, adversarial example generation takes the form of an optimization problem where advanced optimization methods build imperceptible yet highly effective adversarial examples. Runtime-intensive optimization-based attacks excel at creating effective adversarial perturbations especially for stealthy real-world implementations although they take more computing power compared to gradient-based approaches. Decision-based attacks prove more complicated to deploy since they require no direct inspection of model parameters or gradient information. The attackers gain no direct insights into the model structure because they only possess its prediction capabilities. Attackers request model predictions multiple times for decision boundary feedback and use these inputs to modify their initial data points toward misclassification. Boundary attack belongs to the classic decision-based attack category that seeks points closer to model decision boundaries until an adversarial input is found. Decision-based attacks function more slowly than gradient-based attacks while remaining relevant for black-box scenarios because attackers do not gain access to model parameters. The different attack methods create specific testing obstacles for researchers and practitioners who aim to develop secure machine learning models. An attacker who possesses no model access can still launch decision-based attacks to demonstrate system vulnerabilities. Developing wide-ranging protection techniques becomes essential because adversarial assaults show continuous advancement.

3.2 Poisoning Attacks – Data manipulation and backdoor attacks

Machine learning models need various defensive mechanisms to combat growing adversarial threats to improve their resistance capabilities. The purpose of these defenses includes stopping adversarial perturbations from achieving model deception and minimizing disturbance when attacks occur. Four primary defense techniques are employed for adversarial attacks: adversarial training alongside input preprocessing as well as model regularization with robust optimization methods as the third defensive method. Adversarial training serves as the most prevalent defense method currently used in the field. The training process becomes stronger through the introduction of adversarial examples into the training dataset. The model benefits from experiencing legitimate inputs and their adversarial counterparts so it obtains better capabilities to interpret modified adversarial data. The attack methods used for adversarial example creation during training produce examples that help models become resistant to multiple types of adversarial perturbations. The process of improving model robustness through adversarial training proves to be expensive because it needs to produce adversarial examples for each training iteration. When training computer models with adversarial samples the accuracy level on typical inputs often decreases making robustness and performance metric trade-offs appear.

The aim of input preprocessing defense methods is to check for and erase adversarial perturbations that have not yet entered the model system. Input preprocessing techniques resolve to smooth and minimize noise in data thereby reducing the success of adversaries who want to deceive the model. Randomized smoothing and defensive distillation represent two defense methods that address adversarial attacks by adding random noise to the input data and training the model to produce less distinct probability distributions respectively. Although preprocessing inputs offers protection it cannot stop every type of attack and its vulnerability might be overcome by skilled attackers. Model regularization methods strengthen model generalization by reducing its response to minor data input modifications which includes adversarial perturbations. Weight regularization serves as an effective regularization method which applies constraints to training parameters to stop overfitting of exploitable features used by adversarial inputs during the training process. The combination of dropout and batch normalization regularization methods increases model stability through random training methods whose purpose is to outsmart attackers who create adversarial examples. The deployment of these methods raises model resilience against attacks but does not provide full defense against adversarial assaults.

The purpose of robust optimization methods is to strengthen training setbacks to build models that avoid easily being manipulated by adversarial perturbations. The training phase of robust optimization employs adversarially robust optimization to adjust model parameters based on the maximum possible adversarial perturbations that may occur during development. The outcome of this strategy creates enhanced models because it reduces how adversarial inputs affect the model's classification areas. Certified defenses have been developed to verify mathematically how models can withstand specific adversarial attack types. The development of certified defenses represents a very new research field that demonstrates potential for generating provable security against adversarial threats. These defense strategies have displayed successful outcomes although they lack complete protection capabilities. Researchers need to develop advanced defenses that counteract continuously changing attack approaches because attackers develop their methods more sophisticated. Development of secure machine learning systems requiring both active protection strategies alongside contemporary research about adversarial robustness for effective resistance against adversarial threats.

3.3 Exploratory Attacks – Model extraction and adversarial transferability

Understanding the weakness and defense solutions of machine learning models requires thorough analysis of their capability to resist adversarial attacks. Checking model performance with normal data forms the first part of evaluation followed by an examination of how it reacts to adversarial disturbances. Multiple assessment methods exist to measure how well models resist different forms of attacks. Model accuracy on adversarial examples constitutes the bases of evaluation because it measures performance on inputs to which adversaries have applied preparation. The model demonstrates stronger robustness through higher accuracy since it succeeds at identifying modified inputs. This single measure fails to reveal the extent of attacks along with the circumstances that lead to model failures. A complete evaluation process demands adversarial examples derived from different attack methods.

The assessment of adversarial training effectiveness determines a model's ability to operate correctly on unseen adversarial examples. Artificial examples trained on from adversarial models demonstrate superior aptitude than single-clean-data models in adversarial evaluation. Generalization performance heavily depends on what adversarial examples are selected for training purposes. Improving model robustness through diverse attacks remains difficult due to the selection of optimal attacks. Black-box attack instances require models to demonstrate strong transferability robustness because attackers lack model parameter access. The transferability criterion determines if adversarial examples made for one model will trick another model. A model demonstrating high transferability requires defense solutions which protect against attacks that affect multiple models.

The ability of a model to withstand perturbations of different magnitudes constitutes robustness to perturbation size. The robustness of a model depends on whether small perturbations fail to deceive it while larger perturbations might succeed. The evaluation of model responses alongside multiple perturbation sizes enables users to judge protection methods against one another while determining their susceptibility to adversarial disturbances. A certified robust model provides mathematical proof about its ability to withstand perturbations that fall within specified boundaries. Randomized smoothing provides mathematical proof that models avoid misclassifications of minimally distorted inputs. Current certified robustness methods require further development because they only work with specific attack types. Researchers must combine different evaluation methods because no individual metric effectively measures all adversarial robustness aspects. New evaluation methods must be developed continuously because adversarial attack strategies continue to evolve in order to preserve security for machine learning systems.

4. PROACTIVE DEFENSES AGAINST ADVERSARIAL ATTACKS

4.1 Adversarial Training – Training models with adversarial examples to improve robustness

Reasons behind adversarial attacks in machine learning have shifted from abstract threats into effective methods for finding model weaknesses. The development of adversarial attacks in machine learning occurred because of machine learning advancements and model complexity growth and enhanced awareness about real-world threats from adversarial examples.

Early Developments and Awareness - The Fast Gradient Sign Method (FGSM) appeared as the first significant breakthrough when Goodfellow et al. (2014) released it. According to this method the introduction of tiny modifications could lead to severe performance degradation. Researchers in the early stages dedicated their work to proving the existence of adversarial examples while avoiding practical implementations. Simple model attacks and minimal datasets received most attention during this phase of research without addressing the complete security consequences.

Growth of Attack Strategies and Techniques - The increasing popularity of deep learning models in image recognition and natural language processing enabled better development of adversarial attacks during that time. Two iterative attack methods called Projected Gradient Descent (PGD) and Carlini-Wagner (CW) attacks improved their perturbation techniques to enhance their effectiveness. Model security experts moved from demonstrating adversarial flaws among systems to breaking sophisticated models which resulted in highly effective attacks against state-of-the-art systems.

Emergence of Black-box Attacks - Black-box attacks presented themselves as a new major challenge to surpass gradient-based attacks. The attacks function without needing model parameter access while depending on model prediction responses. Adversarial examples created for one model system proved capable of tricking different models without requiring information about their internal structures. Full model access was not required for attackers to exploit machine learning systems because these attacks presented significant security risks.

Advancements in Adaptive Attacks - The implementation of stronger defenses triggered attackers to create new adaptive methods for their attacks. Security vulnerabilities increased through adversarial training since it produced more advanced attack techniques that circumvented defensive systems. The endless struggle between defenders and attackers proved successful for attackers through evolution of targeted attacks against specific security layers which exposed real vulnerabilities.

Current Trends and Emerging Attacks - New attack methods include poison attacks and backdoor intrusions that conceal adversarial examples in training information thus making their pre-deployment identification challenging. When machine learning enters essential sectors including healthcare and finance its implementation reveals domain-specific vulnerabilities that attackers can target (Sahana et al., 2022).

The Future of Adversarial Attacks - Future cyberattacks will adapt their strategies because they aim to target upcoming system designs along with blended AI platforms. Reinforcement learning alongside multi-agent systems produces novel security risks when implemented together. Advanced machine learning systems require comprehensive robust defenses because adversarial security research must continue for ensuring their operational safety. In Figure 2, you can see the evolution of the adversarial attacks in machine learning.

Figure 2. Evolution of Adversarial Attacks in Machine Learning

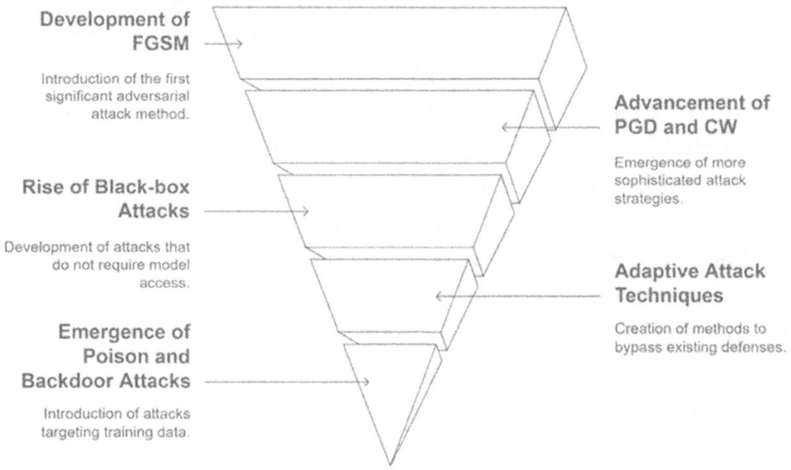

4.2 Regularization Techniques – Defensive distillation, weight pruning, and dropout techniques

The deployment of machine learning technology faces vital operational dangers in healthcare and financial sectors as well as security and automotive domains. The model vulnerabilities enable attackers to slightly modify input data which produces misclassifications and system malfunctions that may result in disastrous system failures. The understanding of their effects is vital for defense preparation and reliability achievement.

Healthcare Systems - The diagnostics field along with treatment recommendations and drug discovery processes apply machine learning models for their clinical operations. The modification of medical image data through adversarial attacks results in wrong diagnoses that trigger improper medical interventions. Wearable health devices are vulnerable to attacks that could result in wrong decisions between patients and doctors (K. Mridha et al., 2021). The existence of such system weaknesses creates both medical safety risks for patients and diminishes public belief in AI-enabled healthcare technologies.

Autonomous Vehicles - Self-driving cars function through AI for their navigation system and also use AI to detect objects and perform decision-based activities. The application of adversarial stop sign image manipulations to vehicles would result in signal neglect which leads to deadly automobile collisions. Sensor attacks against radar and lidar systems produce erroneous distance measurements which elevate the chances of accidents. Solid protection systems need to exist before autonomous transport systems can be deployed safely.

Financial Systems - Machine learning systems maintain essential functions for three essential operations: fraud detection patterns and algorithmic trading capabilities as well as credit scoring functions. The implementation of adversarial attacks produces two damaging effects: first they enable fraud to avoid detection and then second they manipulate market data to mislead trading algorithms while making credit assessments incorrect which leads to unjust decision making during approvals or denials. Such risks would weaken financial AI system trust leading to possible market instabilities.

Security Systems - The security capabilities of artificial intelligence systems based on biometric authentication along with intrusion detection are attackable by adversarial methods. When cybercriminals modify facial recognition inputs, they can gain unauthorized entry while attacks on anomaly detection systems produce security protocol bypasses that create undetected breaches or ransomware attacks.

Social Media and Information Systems - Social media algorithms fall victim to adversarial attacks which enable the distribution of false information along with changes in public opinion. During elections and crises the existence of biased content becomes possible because sentiment analysis models get deceived and recommendation systems can be hacked to endorse misleading content thus damaging public trust.

Manufacturing and Critical Infrastructure - Predictive maintenance systems that are attacked result in equipment mismanagement which produces operational breakdowns. The manipulation of power distribution in energy grids by attackers creates national security threats because of disrupted services.

Implications for Trust and Adoption - The loss of public trust because of adversarial attacks will create obstacles to the adoption of crucial sectors. Organizations must implement strong defenses and proactive risk management solutions to ensure AI safety deployment across different industries.

4.3 Data Augmentation & Perturbation Techniques – Increasing robustness by adding noise, transformations, and randomized data

New defense approaches against adversarial attacks have become necessary since the growing frequency of these threats in machine learning systems. Different defense strategies operate with limited success since no single solution exists to totally eliminate these threats. Data preprocessing combined with model regularization and adversarial training and robust optimization techniques provide some defense mechanisms. The application of data preprocessing methods makes changes to raw data to minimize how adversarial perturbations affect it. The removal of adversarial noise through image smoothing and autoencoders and detection filters constitutes one set of defense methods known as input denoising. The precision reduction of input data through feature squeezing creates challenges for attackers who want to generate successful perturbations. The implementation of these techniques proves insufficient to combat all types of attacks because they sometimes create negative effects on model performance for clean data.

The implementation of regularization techniques improves model resistance through overfitting control because it decreases attack vulnerability. L2 regularization in combination with dropout enables better model generalization that makes the models less vulnerable to minor input modifications. The advanced adversarial weight regularization method adds penalties to models which show high sensitivity to adversarial disturbances. The implemented approaches improve standard robustness but they do not necessarily stop targeted adversarial attacks completely. The inclusion of adversarial examples during training constitutes one of the most effective defense methods known as adversarial training. Model exposure to artificial input noises enables them to develop detection capabilities against adversarial attacks. The generation of adversarial samples relies on two main methods which include Fast Gradient Sign Method (FGSM) and Projected Gradient Descent (PGD). The process of adversarial training requires heavy computing power yet it trains models to focus on particular attack forms which makes them less resistant to novel adversarial strategies.

The element of robust optimization makes models stronger by teaching them to defend against adversarial perturbations when they train. During min-max optimization the algorithm identifies model parameters which minimize loss when subjected to attacks. Calculable robustness methods that use techniques like randomized smoothing issue official warrants for how models stay protected against adversarial attacks. The robust optimization methods show promise nevertheless their development remains ongoing and additional modifications are essential to become widespread industry standards. Best outcomes emerge from defense combinations which unite different methods to exploit their individual strong points. Multiple defense mechanisms tend to make systems more complex which forces technicians to adjust parameters between accuracy and resistance levels. The main obstacle in adversarial defense consists of achieving superior performance on normal data while maintaining attack resistance. Ongoing antagonistic activities between systems require steady developments of defense systems for protection from new threats. Machine learning faces an ongoing strong challenge because of adversarial attack defense systems. None of the techniques including preprocessing and regularization with adversary training and robust optimization can provide complete protection. The need for developing universal and effective defenses against adversaries will rise as the work on adversary protection advances.

5. REACTIVE DEFENSES AND DETECTION MECHANISMS

5.1 Preprocessing Defenses – Feature squeezing, input denoising, and transformation-based defenses

Machine learning models currently face a severe reliability and security risk because of adversarial attacks. The attacks make models misclassify data by applying hard-to-detect modifications to input data. Research began in earnest after the 2010s when scientists showed that deep neural networks could be tricked by purpose-designed minor perturbations thus leading to many studies about model vulnerabilities and security protections. The initial adversarial attacks involved pixel adjustments through Fast Gradient Sign Method (FGSM) which produced modest image alterations when released in 2014. Through the application of FGSM the input images received adjustments which followed the gradient direction of the loss function to reach maximum loss and result in classification errors. The basic attack created opportunities to investigate further weaknesses in models. PGD represented an enhanced version of adversarial attacks which used repeated perturbations to create evasive manipulations for improved stealth. PGD stands as one of the most powerful attacks because it implements repeated perturbations which enhance attacker control. The techniques used to attack image recognition systems have expanded to impact processing of natural language and speech and reinforcement learning systems. NLP attacks transform verbal inputs for semantic modification without modifying linguistic syntax but speech recognition attacks use perturbations as deception mechanisms for voice-operated systems. Targeted and untargeted attacks evolved from adversarial techniques as the former aims to force specific misclassification while the latter results in any misclassification thus making defenses more complex to develop.

The defensive strategies have designed new mechanisms for protection. The initial goal was to detect attacks until attackers sophisticated their methods when researchers started using adversarial training to train models alongside adversarial examples for increased robustness. Two defensive techniques include defensive distillation and input preprocessing which protect systems from perturbations. The constant evolution of defense strategies by attackers through transfer attacks has initiated an ongoing competition with defenders who use similar model architectures (Khalil et al., 2022). Research demonstrates heightened concerns about sophisticated attacks on critical systems of autonomous vehicles and healthcare systems and security systems. The advancement of AI technology integration within society results in higher risks produced from these vulnerabilities. Defense mechanisms against threats must be developed extensively because machine learning systems require this protection to stay secure. Adversarial attacks have achieved great sophistication during our current time while affecting diverse application areas. Research work maintains its importance because attack and defense methodologies develop their sophistication at each stage of development. A secure and dependable use of AI frameworks in critical industries demands adversary attack robustness to rely on these frameworks for such protection. In Figure 3, you can see the evolution of the adersarial attacks and defences.

Figure 3. Evolution of Adversarial Attacks and Defenses

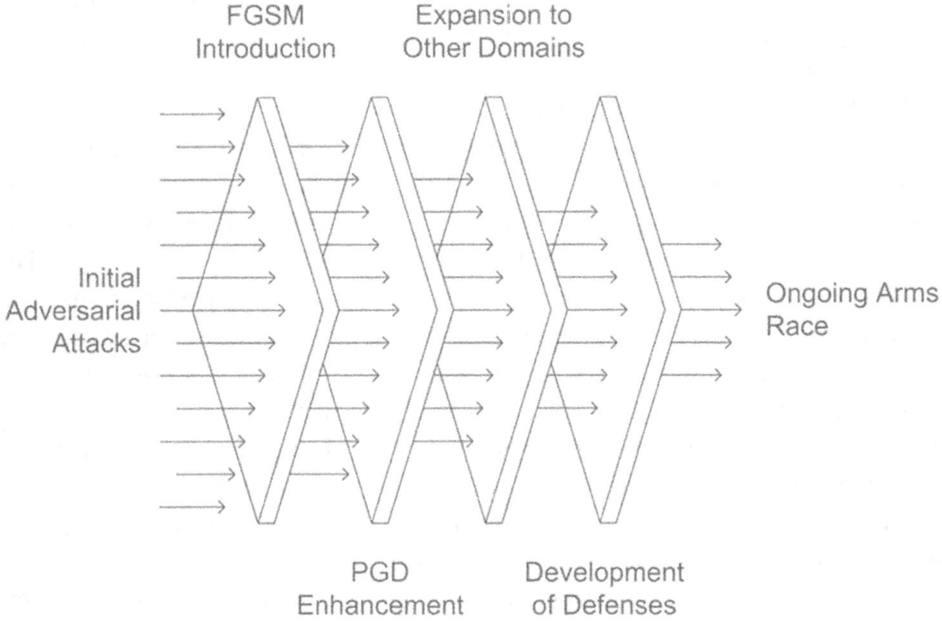

5.2 Anomaly and Outlier Detection – Statistical methods to identify adversarial inputs

Machine learning models face serious security risks through adversarial attacks because these attacks lower their accuracy levels and deterioration of performance during practical use. The introduction of minimal unnoticeable alterations to input data during attacks leads to incorrect classifications and faulty predictions. The security and trustworthiness problems caused by adversarial attacks affect the robustness of AI systems which operate in autonomous driving and healthcare and finance sectors (Acemoğlu et al., 2022). The main problem with adversarial attacks occurs because they reduce model performance but avoid changing the fundamental model structure. Such imperceptible adversarial disturbances find a way to get past standard security protocols because they remain undetectable to human observers which reveals structural weaknesses within the model design. The execution of incorrect predictions in safety-sensitive operations leads to alarming outcomes because of serious potential consequences (Shao et al., 2023). The sensor data manipulation through adversarial attacks in autonomous vehicles results in unsafe driving decisions from the vehicles. Medical imaging system attacks lead healthcare professionals to make incorrect diagnoses which consequently puts patient care at risk.

Regarding alarms, wizards are effective, and in terms of danger, they have harmful effects. These attack methods are currently present, especially deep learning models, which are used together with consonant neural analyzers. The models demonstrate excellent performance on regular data but they remain susceptible to minimal input modifications. Such attacks exist beyond image classification models and show destructive effects on natural language processing along with systems focused on speech recognition. The detection techniques through adversarial perturbations expose underlying issues with model generalization because the utilized features deviate from actual data distribution patterns. AI systems lose their credibility when subjects perform adversarial attacks against them. When users remain unaware about adversarial vulnerabilities, they tend to trust AI decisions excessively particularly when systems are used for healthcare diagnosis or financial fraud detection. Security systems suffer from adversarial attacks which enable unauthorized system entry and data breaches in cybersecurity applications. Machines learn models face important flaws from adversarial attacks which damage their performance capabilities and make systems both insecure and unreliable in the eyes of users. Scientists must focus on solving the primary issues involving threat mitigation to develop secure dependable AI systems which will succeed in real-world applications.

5.3 Ensemble Learning & Hybrid Approaches – Using multiple models to increase robustness

The defense against adversarial attacks on machine learning models needs implementation of multiple security measures combined with reinforced model architecture design. The advancement of adversarial attacks demands researchers to combine defensive strategies like adversarial training with input preprocessing and model regularization and robust optimization and defensive distillation approaches to increase model robustness. The combined use of numerous defense techniques produces better robustness outcomes despite lacking any completely effective defense by itself (Chutia & Baruah, 2024), (Frosio & Kautz, 2023). To improve recognition of perturbed inputs during training the technique known as adversarial training utilizes augmented data with adversarial examples. The ability of adversarial training to resist FGSM and PGD attacks exists while facing high computational costs which limits its effectiveness on new methods and alternative domains including NLP and speech recognition. Processors work on inputs by performing denoising on images and feature reduction before handing data to the model. The related method defensive distillation trains models to create smooth decision boundaries which increases their resistance against adversarial examples. Sophisticated attacks manage to go around preprocessing methods that protect models.

The implementation of model regularization enables better generalization which makes the model immune to small perturbations. Model performance can achieve resistance against adversarial effects through weight decay and dropout and L2 regularization because these techniques make the model prioritize stable features during predictions. The defense against adversarial attacks remains incomplete when using regularization techniques because model vulnerabilities can be exploited. Minimal-max optimization methods add adversarial attacks to learning processes as a defense against adversarial example susceptibility. These promising methods tend to require high computational resources yet they might not enhance performance when processing clean data samples. The combination of multiple models through ensemble methods makes adversarial attacks more difficult because it requires them to trick every member of the ensemble group. The use of ensemble approaches consumes numerous computing resources while simultaneously facing specific attacks against these combined systems. The challenge of preventing adversarial attack transferability continues because adversarial examples generated for one model usually work against multiple models. Academic investigators work to decrease attack transferability through research on model assortment and adversarial example screening techniques. The protection against adversarial attacks requires multiple defense strategy implementations together with adaptive and hybrid defense system development. Future development and implementation of these defense strategies will become essential for achieving reliable security and robustness of machine learning models when used in practical applications.

6. COMPARATIVE ANALYSIS OF ATTACKS AND DEFENSES

6.1 Effectiveness of Different Attack Strategies – Strengths, weaknesses, and real-world implications

The assessment of adversarial attack defenses determines their practical usefulness and resistance to attacks. An effective evaluation framework for adversarial attacks needs to stay adaptable and cover all essential aspects including attack success rates combined with computational cost and model performance evaluation according to generalization guidelines. The attack success rate determines adversarial example efficacy as it tells how many examples a model falls for. A successful defense needs to decrease attack success rate substantially while preserving model performance levels. A model's robustness assessment must evaluate its performance stability under different adversarial attacks including those that remain unseen to the system. The evaluation of model accuracy on adversarial examples uses robust accuracy as its primary metric. A defense demonstrates strong resilience when it preserves high robust accuracy while keeping standard accuracy losses at a minimum (Kanervisto, 2022), (Xu et al., 2021). Transferability represents a crucial factor because adversarial examples need to work across different models sharing similar architectural structures. Security enhancements result from defense solutions that limit adversarial example transferability between models. The computational expenses of defense approaches matter because some techniques such as adversarial training require substantial processing power. Security and efficiency need balanced management for real-world applications which have limited resources.

The strength of defense mechanisms remains crucial because they need to protect against different forms of malicious attacks. It is crucial to assess defense capabilities against future attacks which adversaries will inevitably create since they continuously create new attack methods. Real-world conditions limit the effectiveness of defenses which demonstrate successful performance in controlled environments because they often struggle with dynamic and unstructured or noisy conditions (Dutta et al., 2023). The evaluation process needs to test defense systems against adaptive attacks. The ability of defensives to face advanced enemy attacks becomes crucial because attackers continuously evolve their attack methods. The assessment of adversarial defenses needs multiple evaluative dimensions which include attack success rate together with robustness and transferability along with computational cost and generalization and real-world applicability as well as resistance to adaptive attacks. Defenses become more reliable and effective when implemented with this approach against changing adversarial threats.

6.2 Performance Evaluation of Defensive Mechanisms – Trade-offs between accuracy, security, and computational cost

Several extensive defense mechanisms exist within adversarial defense systems as solutions to shield machine learning models from adversarial attacks. Each defensive method features different advantages and drawbacks therefore an analysis between their capabilities and performance limitations and use cases becomes crucial. Adversarial training stands as the most common defense approach because it subjects models to adversarial samples throughout their training process. The implementation of this technique produces substantial increase in model resistance against adversarial attacks including FGSM and PGD (Sivajothi et al., 2024). The method needs substantial computational power since it extends training duration and consumes extra resources. The adoption of adversarial training leads to decreased standard accuracy in addition to improved robustness because trained models demonstrate inferior performance on unaltered input data. The security provided by this method applies exclusively to attack types which were trained against it thus leaving the system susceptible to new or adaptive attack methods. The input preprocessing methods of image denoising and feature squeezing attempt to decrease adversarial perturbations which occur before model data enters. The implementation of these techniques remains efficient because they do not need modifications to the model architecture. Reducing attacks through preprocessing steps proves effective but remains inadequate since powerful attackers create specialized perturbations that circumvent these techniques. Preprocessing methods focus on addressing particular perturbation types which restricts their adaptability to different types of attacks.

Defensive distillation enables model training to create smooth decision boundaries through the process of knowledge transfer to a second model. By implementing this technique models become less sensitive to small perturbations and become less vulnerable to attacks. Defense distillation provides protection against attacks but the Carlini-Wagner method along with other advanced methods still manage to circumvent its effectiveness. The supplementary training process requires increased computational resources which reduces its practicality when used for extensive applications. Adversarial perturbation resistance in models can be improved through model regularization methods including L2 regularization and dropout and weight decay because they enforce the model to identify robust features instead of noise-prone elements. These generalization techniques along with their robustness improvements do not adequately protect models from strong adversarial attacks when implemented independently. Regularization functions as an additional support mechanism instead of operating independently as a single defense solution. Ensemble methods create various predictive models that combine outputs to achieve better robustness. The use of ensemble techniques increases correct classification of adversarial examples because the perturbations that affect one model might not affect other models. The combination of multiple models through this technique provides substantial security improvements particularly when the models employ distinct training data or architectural designs. The use of ensemble approaches leads to high computational expenses during inference because it needs multiple models to execute together. Advanced attacks specifically target multiple models at once which makes them vulnerable to such attacks.

Min-max optimization together with robust optimization techniques modifies the model's goal so it confronts maximum potential damage from adversarial modifications. The method has demonstrated its effectiveness at boosting robustness primarily against particular types of attacks. The computational complexity of this approach proves to be problematic because it leads to unfavorable results when exposing adversarial examples and limits its ability to generalize to new information. A single defense approach does not exist to combat adversarial attacks. Adversarial training produces great results against recognized attacks yet it creates substantial calculations and deals with specific threats. The benefits of preprocessing techniques include efficiency against attacks but they prove ineffective against adaptive attacks. Each of the defense techniques including defensive distillation and regularization and ensemble methods offers specific advantages yet presents individual constraints. Robust optimization methodology guarantees solid theoretical protection at great expense to computational processing power. A combination of several defense methods creates the optimal solution to achieve robustness and efficiency alongside generalization capabilities.

6.3 Benchmark Datasets & Metrics – Standard datasets and evaluation criteria for adversarial ML research

Research on adversarial attack defense has made substantial progress but attacks continue to become more difficult to defend against. The essential nature of robustness emerges because machine learning models currently work in critical areas which include healthcare applications and finance systems and autonomous vehicle operations. Future research needs to concentrate on adaptive defense strategies together with generative models while examining interpretability and transfer learning together with robust certification of models and unsupervised learning approaches and quantum machine learning for security enhancements (Damodharan & Ravichandran, 2019). The goal is to achieve better resistance against evolving threats. Dynamic defense systems adapt their strategies based on fresh attack methods instead of using adversarial examples. Training methods based on online learning and meta-learning let models develop protection against new threats yet this process needs further work to maintain both security effectiveness and applicable performance speed. The generative model called GANs along with other models generates adversarial examples for training purposes and transforms inputs through perturbation masking. By employing these models during training processes adversaries can develop their resistance to multiple attack categories. The challenge exists to prevent attackers from exploiting generative models.

The demand for interpretability grows stronger in adversarial defense because numerous robust models remain non-transparent which hinders the identification of their vulnerabilities. The XAI methods in development enable researchers to understand defense mechanisms better so they can build more dependable models (Abinaya et al., 2023). Transfer learning serves as a new defensive strategy that enables defense mechanisms developed for one dataset attack type to protect against multiple attacks and diverse data types. The implementation of transfer learning provides better robustness across multiple situations but developers must verify it does not create new security weaknesses. Model security guarantees rise when having strong certification proves formally that the model can withstand particular ranges of adversarial perturbations better than conducting empirical evaluations. The application of robust certification becomes impractical because it creates substantial computational expenses that scale poorly with model size. A combination of autoencoders with self-supervised learning under unsupervised learning improves adversarial defenses since it detects adversarial examples without the need for labeled data. The approach would strengthen adaptability especially when facing evolving attacks.

Quantum machine learning represents an exciting new direction for adversarial defense because of its current developing status. Quantum algorithms would boost security because they utilize quantum characteristics including superposition together with entanglement. Multiple models or organizations can use federated learning to share real-time adversarial attack insights in order to enhance their defense against large-scale threats. Multiple emerging techniques must be used to build strong adversarial defenses. Future research needs to find proper methods to maintain balance between three critical elements of robustness and computational capacity and real-world implementation to address emerging adversarial challenges. In the Figure 4, you can see the cycle of adversarial attacks and defense enhancement.

Figure 4. Cycle of Adversarial Defense Enhancement

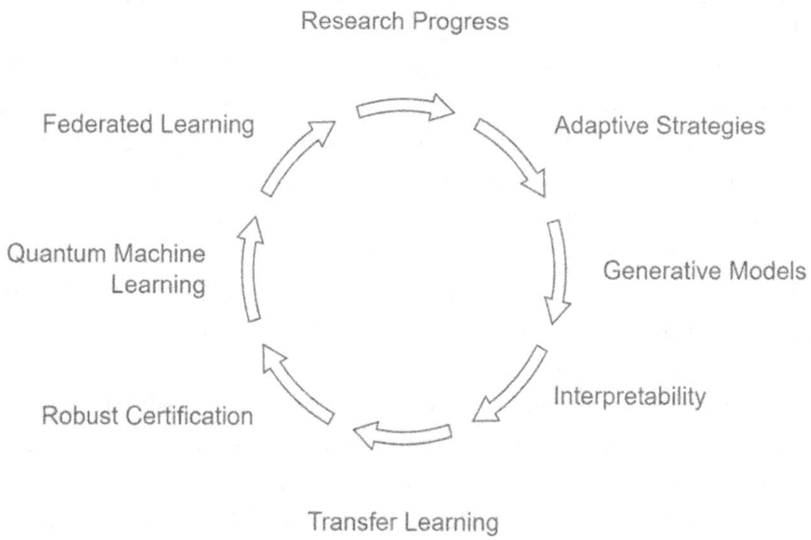

7. CONCLUSION: ADDRESSING THE CHALLENGES AND FUTURE DIRECTIONS IN ADVERSARIAL DEFENSE

Machine learning models encounter substantial reliability and security risks together with trust issues because of adversarial attacks mainly within critical applications. Several defense techniques which include adversarial training and input preprocessing together with defensive distillation and ensemble methods are available but they each have their restrictions. The effective yet expensive adversarial training method protects against known attacks only. Limited at defending systems against advanced adversarial tactics are the basic and quick input preprocessing methods. The enhanced robustness of defensive distillation together with ensemble methods leads to increased computational burden as well as decreased performance output. The defensive capabilities of model regularization exist but they prove inadequate when used alone. Adversarial attacks continue to evolve into a major challenge which impedes the creation of effective defenses that can protect against all types of attacks. The achievement of robustness presents an immense challenge to performance levels in this field. The added ability to resist adversarial assaults usually results in a degradation of clean data accuracy that makes it hard to sustain an adequate performance balance in practice. Defensive strategies of high computational complexity become impractical for fast real-time large-scale applications that require high efficiency.

The difficulty in defending against adversarial attacks grows worse because existing defenses show minimal ability to protect against different threats. Different types of attacks require specific defenses since protection from one type does not guarantee immunity against other adversaries despite techniques like adversarial training admitting weaknesses to evolving attack methods. Researchers need to establish defense strategies that function against multiple types of attacks for developing resilient models. Current research development suffers because there exist insufficient reliable evaluation tools to establish benchmarks for different defense strategies. Adversarial defense will progress through adaptive systems based on AI technology which can adapt to emerging attack strategies. Great progress in defense research will stem from integrating multiple defense methods along with quantum machine learning and generative model experimentations. The development of defense mechanisms requires interpretability to achieve both better effectiveness and transparency. The persistence of technical hurdles that include finding equilibrium between system performance and robustness together with processing constraints and difficulties in generalization will continue. Standardized benchmarks with evaluation metrics need to be established because they provide necessary means for evaluating and comparing defense strategies. The defense of adversaries against attacks remains impossible through a single mechanism yet joint implementation of defense techniques yields safer machine learning systems. The requirements for efficient and effective and scalable defensive methods against adversaries and new emerging adversaries will increase significantly in upcoming times. The defense of adversaries in upcoming times requires adaptable defensive models which protect both present adversaries and future adversaries to establish safe artificial intelligence systems in operational environments. Academic institutions and industry operators and regulators must form collaborative efforts to create defense strategies which will protect against present and future threats.

REFERENCES

Abinaya, K., Palaniappan, D., & Vedaraj, M. (2023). A Novel Hyper-Spectral Model to Optimize the Prediction Rate for Heart Disease in Modern Healthcare Networks. *Engineering Proceedings, 59081*, 59081. Advance online publication. DOI: 10.3390/engproc2023059081

Acemoğlu, D., Autor, D., Hazell, J., & Restrepo, P. (2022). Artificial Intelligence and Jobs: Evidence from Online Vacancies. In Journal of Labor Economics (Vol. 40). University of Chicago Press. DOI: 10.1086/718327

Apruzzese, G., Anderson, H. S., Dambra, S., Freeman, D. E., Pierazzi, F., & Roundy, K. (2023). *Real Attackers Don't Compute Gradients.* Bridging the Gap Between Adversarial ML Research and Practice., DOI: 10.1109/SaTML54575.2023.00031

Bennouna, A., Lucas, R., & Parys, B. V. (2023). Certified Robust Neural Networks: Generalization and Corruption Resistance. In arXiv (Cornell University). Cornell University. https://doi.org//arxiv.2303.02251DOI: 10.48550

Biasin, E., Kamenjašević, E., & Ludvigsen, K. R. (2024). Cybersecurity of AI medical devices: risks, legislation, and challenges. In *Edward Elgar Publishing eBooks* (p. 57). Edward Elgar Publishing., DOI: 10.4337/9781802205657.00010

Casper, S., Ezell, C., Siegmann, C., Kolt, N., Curtis, T. L., Bucknall, B., Haupt, A., Wei, K., Scheurer, J., Hobbhahn, M., Sharkey, L., Krishna, S., Hagen, M. V., Alberti, S., Chan, A., Sun, Q., Gerovitch, M., Bau, D., Tegmark, M., & Hadfield-Menell, D. (2024). Black-Box Access is Insufficient for Rigorous AI Audits. In *2022 ACM Conference on Fairness, Accountability, and Transparency* (p. 2254). DOI: 10.1145/3630106.3659037

Chen, F., Wu, T., Nguyen, V., Wang, S., Hu, H., Abuadbba, A., & Rudolph, C. (2024). Adapting to Cyber Threats: A Phishing Evolution Network (PEN) Framework for Phishing Generation and Analyzing Evolution Patterns using Large Language Models. In arXiv (Cornell University). Cornell University. https://doi.org//arxiv .2411.11389DOI: 10.48550

Chen, J., Jia, C., Zheng, H., Chen, R., & Fu, C. (2022). Is Multi-Modal Necessarily Better? Robustness Evaluation of Multi-modal Fake News Detection. In arXiv (Cornell University). Cornell University. https://doi.org/DOI: 10.48550/arXiv.2206

Chen, J., Wang, H., & Li, H. (2022). Defects detection in weld joints based on visual attention and deep learning. In *NDT & E International* (Vol. 133, p. 102764). Elsevier BV., DOI: 10.1016/j.ndteint.2022.102764

Chutia, T., & Baruah, N. (2024). A review on emotion detection by using deep learning techniques [Review of A review on emotion detection by using deep learning techniques]. Artificial Intelligence Review, 57(8). Springer Science+Business Media. DOI: 10.1007/s10462-024-10831-1

Damodharan, P., & Ravichandran, C. S. (2019). Applicability Evaluation of Web Mining in Healthcare E-Commerce towards Business Success and a derived Cournot Model. In Journal of Medical Systems (Vol. 43, Issue 8). Springer Science+Business Media. DOI: 10.1007/s10916-019-1395-1

Dutta, A., Chatterjee, S., Bhattacharya, A., & Halappanavar, M. (2023). Deep Reinforcement Learning for Cyber System Defense under Dynamic Adversarial Uncertainties. In arXiv (Cornell University). Cornell University. https://doi.org//arxiv.2302.01595DOI: 10.48550

Frosio, I., & Kautz, J. (2023). The Best Defense is a Good Offense: Adversarial Augmentation against Adversarial Attacks. In arXiv (Cornell University). Cornell University. https://doi.org//arxiv.2305.14188DOI: 10.48550

Guesmi, A., Hanif, M. A., Ouni, B., & Shafique, M. (2023). Physical Adversarial Attacks For Camera-based Smart Systems: Current Trends, Categorization, Applications, Research Challenges, and Future Outlook. In arXiv (Cornell University). Cornell University. https://doi.org//arxiv.2308.06173DOI: 10.48550

Kanervisto, A. (2022). Advances in Deep Learning for Playing Video Games.

Kawamoto, Y., Miyake, K., Konishi, K., & Oiwa, Y. (2023). Threats, Vulnerabilities, and Controls of Machine Learning Based Systems: A Survey and Taxonomy. In arXiv (Cornell University). Cornell University. https://doi.org//arxiv.2301 .07474DOI: 10.48550

Khalil, U., Malik, O. A., Uddin, M., & Chen, C. (2022). A Comparative Analysis on Blockchain versus Centralized Authentication Architectures for IoT-Enabled Smart Devices in Smart Cities: A Comprehensive Review, Recent Advances, and Future Research Directions [Review of A Comparative Analysis on Blockchain versus Centralized Authentication Architectures for IoT-Enabled Smart Devices in Smart Cities: A Comprehensive Review, Recent Advances, and Future Research Directions]. Sensors, 22(14), 5168. Multidisciplinary Digital Publishing Institute. DOI: 10.3390/s22145168

Kumar, R., Jain, V., Leong, H. W., & Teyarachakul, S. (2023). Convergence of IoT, Blockchain, and Computational Intelligence in Smart Cities. In *CRC Press eBooks*. Informa., DOI: 10.1201/9781003353034

Mridha, K., Kumbhani, S., Pandey, A. P., & Damodharan, P. "Automatically Detect the coronavirus (COVID-19) disease using Chest X-ray and CT images," 2021 IEEE 6th International Conference on Computing, Communication and Automation (ICCCA), Arad, Romania, 2021, pp. 150-156, DOI: 10.1109/ICCCA52192.2021.9666304

Oniani, D., Hilsman, J., & Peng, Y. COL, Poropatich, R. K., Pamplin, C. J. C., Legault, L. G. L., & Wang, Y. (2023). From Military to Healthcare: Adopting and Expanding Ethical Principles for Generative Artificial Intelligence. In arXiv (Cornell University). Cornell University. https://doi.org/DOI: 10.48550/arXiv.2308

Parihar, A., Prajapati, J. B., Prajapati, B. G., Trambadiya, B., Thakkar, A., & Engineer, P. (2024). Role of IOT in healthcare: Applications, security & privacy concerns.

Ruan, W., Yi, X., & Huang, X. (2021). Adversarial Robustness of Deep Learning: Theory, Algorithms, and Applications. In arXiv (Cornell University). Cornell University. https://doi.org/DOI: 10.48550/arXiv.2108

Sahana, N. S., Palaniappan, N. D., Bobade, N. S. D., & Rafi, N. S. M. (2022). Deep Learning ensemble model for the prediction of traffic accidents using social media data. *Journal of Pharmaceutical Negative Results*, •••, 485–495. DOI: 10.47750/pnr.2022.13.S09.055

Shao, W., Xu, Y., Liang, P., Li, J., & Wang, H. (2023). Failure Detection for Motion Prediction of Autonomous Driving: An Uncertainty Perspective. In arXiv (Cornell University). Cornell University. https://doi.org//arxiv.2301.04421DOI: 10.48550

Sivajothi, E., Diana, S. M. C., Rekha, M., Lincy, R. B., Damodharan, P., & J, J. R. (2024). A future prediction for cyber-attacks in the network domain with the visualisation of patterns in cyber-security tickets with machine learning. In International Journal of Electronic Security and Digital Forensics (Vol. 16, Issue 5, p. 648). Inderscience Publishers. DOI: 10.1504/IJESDF.2024.140758

Xu, H., Yan, Z., Ji, B., Huang, P., Cheng, J., & Wu, X. (2021). Defect detection in welding radiographic images based on semantic segmentation methods. In *Measurement* (Vol. 188, p. 110569). Elsevier BV., DOI: 10.1016/j.measurement.2021.110569

Yu, G., Jeon, M., & Hwang, H. (2023). Decision-BADGE: Decision-based Adversarial Batch Attack with Directional Gradient Estimation. In arXiv (Cornell University). Cornell University. https://doi.org//arxiv.2303.04980DOI: 10.48550

Chapter 3
A Bibliometric Perspective on Adversarial Machine Learning Research: Trends, Challenges, and Opportunities

Elizaveta Vitalievna Sokolova
https://orcid.org/0000-0002-4336-5283
Ural State University of Economics, Russia

ABSTRACT

The objective of the present study is to analyze the thematic directions and research trends in the field of adversarial machine learning, as well as to identify key challenges and opportunities for further development within this domain. To achieve this goal, a bibliometric approach was employed, utilizing the Vosviewer software to analyze the frequency of terms and cluster publications indexed in the OpenAlex database according to thematic proximity. The primary research methods consisted of a retrospective literature review, quantitative analysis of publication activity, and terminology clustering. The analysis revealed key thematic clusters that reflect both the existing challenges and the promising directions in this field. The results obtained demonstrate the high dynamism of research in the field of adversarial machine learning and emphasize the importance of interdisciplinary approaches for addressing the challenges at hand.

DOI: 10.4018/979-8-3373-2200-1.ch003

INTRODUCTION

The contemporary development of artificial intelligence is accompanied not only by an increase in the functional complexity of models but also by a rise in the number of threats related to their security and reliability. One of the most significant research directions in this field is adversarial machine learning, which focuses on scenarios in which models operate under conditions of opposition – specifically, in the presence of a competing agent or process with contrary objectives. This term encompasses two key aspects. First, it refers to adversarial attacks and corresponding defense methods – deliberate interventions targeting input data or the learning process with the aim of inducing incorrect model behavior. Second, it pertains to adversarial learning methods, in which the training process itself is framed as a game between two agents with opposing objective functions (for example, the confrontation between a generator and a discriminator in generative adversarial networks, GANs). These concepts have a long developmental history, progressing through stages of conceptual evolution, technological refinement, and the expansion of application domains.

In recent decades, research in the field of adversarial machine learning has demonstrated rapid growth, driven both by the need to enhance the robustness of AI algorithms and by the increasing number of practical threats aimed at compromising them. The necessity of the present study arises from the need for a comprehensive retrospective of the academic discourse on adversarial machine learning, as well as an analysis of the current state of scientific publications in this area. Particular attention is devoted to identifying the most prominent thematic directions – both among authors who define the key trajectories for the discipline's development and among readers who ensure the high citation rates of specific concepts. Such an analysis will not only foster an objective understanding of the current research landscape but also enable the construction of forecasts for the future development of this field.

To achieve the stated objectives, the present study will be carried out in two key phases. The first phase will involve a retrospective literature review aimed at identifying the major milestones in the development of adversarial machine learning, analyzing existing classifications of adversarial methods, and exploring their practical applications. The second phase will entail a bibliometric study, which will include quantitative and structural analysis of publication activity, the identification of research direction clusters, and the examination of citation patterns. This approach will provide a systematic representation of the dynamics of scientific knowledge in the field of adversarial machine learning and will also facilitate the identification of promising directions for future research.

Historical Retrospective and Stages of Adversarial Machine Learning

Long before the term «adversarial learning» emerged, conceptual foundations for adversarial approaches can be traced within earlier research. As early as the 1980s, the theory of learning addressed the issue of opposition between a learning algorithm and a «hostile» data source. In particular, a model of learning in the presence of malicious noise – intentional errors in the training data – was explored. The seminal work by Kearns and Li (1988) demonstrated that even simple classifiers could learn when exposed to a small proportion of deliberately corrupted labels; however, as the proportion of such errors increased, the problem quickly became more complex, approaching unsolvability in general cases. These results became one of the first formal illustrations of how active opposition from the environment (adversarial disturbance) affects an algorithm's ability to learn.

In addition to works on the theory of learning with noise, the ideas of competition appeared in early neural networks and evolutionary algorithms. The concept of competitive learning emerged in the 1980s within the context of unsupervised neural networks. For example, in Kohonen's network, neurons compete against one another for the right to activate, which allows for the identification of characteristic clusters in the input data (Kohonen & Honkela, 2007). Although such a «winner-takes-all» mechanism did not involve an external adversary, it demonstrated the effectiveness of built-in competition for improving data representations.

Another line of development is self-play learning in two-agent tasks, which has been applied in gaming applications since the 1950s. A classical example is A. L. Samuel's checkers program (1959) and G. Tesauro's TD-Gammon algorithm (1992), where the strategy was improved through the program playing against itself. These successes in the domain of games foreshadowed the idea that optimization problems could be solved by simulating opposition between agents. However, up until the 2000s, this was primarily considered in the narrow context of game AI rather than general machine learning.

Particular attention should be given to the 1990s, which directly preceded the advent of generative adversarial methods. In 1991, Juergen Schmidhuber described the «artificial curiosity» mechanism, where two neural networks played against each other in a zero-sum format (Schmidhuber, 1991). One network (the generator) generates output patterns in an attempt to surprise the second network, which learns to predict the environment's response to these patterns. In this manner, the first network is indirectly encouraged to create increasingly complex and unpredictable examples. Essentially, this represented an early precursor to adversarial learning: the generator and predictor form a closed feedback loop, later resembling the generative adversarial networks (GANs) that would emerge.

While such ideas did not receive widespread development at the time, they can now be retrospectively considered as important milestones, demonstrating that competitive dynamics can serve as a tool for training complex models. Thus, by the end of the 20th century, disparate ideas had accumulated in various fields – such as statistical learning theory, neural network algorithms, and game AI – that illustrated the potential of adversarial approaches. However, a coherent research direction specifically devoted to adversarial impact in machine learning had not yet materialized.

The Formation of the Field in the 2000s

The 2000s marked the emergence of adversarial machine learning as a distinct interdisciplinary field at the intersection of machine learning and computer security. This period witnessed the appearance of the first specific attack scenarios and corresponding defense algorithms, as well as the initial attempts to formalize the problem. A historical starting point is often identified as 2004, when several studies were published almost simultaneously, demonstrating the vulnerability of classical classification algorithms to targeted attacks. In particular, Dalvi et al. (2004) showed how a spammer could minimally modify the text of an email to bypass a Bayesian spam filter and proposed an algorithm that trains the classifier to anticipate such attacks. In 2005, Lowd and Meek (2005) demonstrated an effective method for calculating the minimal necessary modification of input features to deceive a linear spam classifier. These studies served as the first practical evidence of the existence of adversarial examples – input samples specifically crafted to deceive a trained model. Prior to this, the possibility of such attacks was largely theoretical; now, it was experimentally validated, attracting the attention of both the machine learning community and security specialists.

Concurrently with the identification of vulnerabilities, the first steps were taken towards their classification and systematic defense. Researchers began to realize that traditional assumptions in machine learning (such as data stationarity and the independence of training and test datasets) no longer hold in a hostile environment where an adversary may intentionally alter the data. Between 2006 and 2010, a series of review and conceptual papers emerged, laying the foundation for the terminology and taxonomy of attacks. For example, Barreno et al. (2006, 2010) proposed a division of attacks into two broad categories: evasion attacks and poisoning attacks. Evasion attacks target a model during its operation – an attacker modifies the input data in such a way that it bypasses the classifier (for example, disguising a spam message as legitimate by embedding its text into an image). In this case, the attacker does not intervene in the model's training process but instead adapts the input during the inference stage; a classic example is the modification of malicious code or a message to bypass a detector, viewed by the attacker as a "black box" (Biggio et al., 2013). In contrast, poisoning attacks aim to compromise the training phase: the attacker injects specially crafted data into the training set (or corrupts the labels), resulting in model degradation or the introduction of deliberate errors in its behavior (Biggio et al., 2012). Such attacks require higher levels of access (insider information about the data, the ability to modify the dataset). This distinction (evasion vs. poisoning) has gained widespread acceptance and is still used today in the analysis of adversarial threats.

Moreover, concepts such as attack goals (violation of confidentiality, integrity, or availability of the model), the attacker's knowledge of the system (white/grey/black box), and the attacker's capabilities (for example, the ability to modify inputs or training data) were introduced – parameters that formed the foundation for formalized threat modeling in machine learning systems. As the basic terminology was established, research activity in the field grew. The academic community responded quickly to the emerging issue: by 2007, the first specialized workshop, «Machine Learning in Adversarial Environments for Computer Security,» was held at the NIPS conference, and in 2010, the regularly held AISec (Artificial Intelligence and Security) workshop was organized, along with review articles and book chapters. These events facilitated the creation of a common discussion platform for machine learning and security specialists, who had previously rarely intersected.

By the end of the decade, a consensus had emerged that the race between attacks and defenses was inevitable, and therefore, methods for training models with adversarial resistance in mind needed to be proactively designed. One of the key achievements of this period was the recognition of the fundamental necessity of modeling the adversary during training. The first algorithms integrating minimax optimization ideas emerged: for example, adversarial training methods, in which, at each step of classifier training, «difficult» examples (pseudo-attacks) are generated for the model, and the model is trained on them to increase robustness. Although such approaches were fully realized only during the deep learning era, some of their elements can already be traced in the works of the late 2000s – specifically, several authors proposed periodically retraining spam filters on new attacks or adding artificially generated perturbations to the dataset to force the model to become more robust. Nonetheless, nearly all research from this period was predominantly theoretical or laboratory-based. The situation changed in the following decade, when the rapid progress in deep neural networks both opened new vectors for attacks and provided researchers with more powerful tools for realizing adversarial ideas.

The 2010s marked a qualitative leap in the development of adversarial machine learning, primarily driven by the flourishing of deep learning techniques. The rapid advancement of neural network methods significantly expanded both the capabilities of attackers and the arsenal of defensive and generative algorithms. This period is characterized, on the one hand, by the emergence of adversarial examples for deep neural networks and an intense «arms race» between attacks and defenses, and on the other hand, by the integration of adversarial architectures directly into the process of model training – the most notable achievement here being the invention of generative adversarial networks. Both of these directions developed concurrently, often exchanging ideas and methods, ultimately solidifying adversarial machine learning as one of the central research areas within artificial intelligence.

Adversarial Attacks and Robustness of Deep Neural Networks

Between 2013 and 2014, a breakthrough occurred that drew widespread attention within the ML community to the vulnerabilities of even the most advanced models. A pivotal moment was the work by Szegedy et al. (2013), which demonstrated that convolutional neural networks, which had exhibited exceptional performance in image recognition tasks, could easily be deceived by imperceptible perturbations of the input pixels. The researchers found that by adding a small, specially crafted noise pattern to an image, the model would confidently misclassify the image – for example, a photo of a panda with a slight noise pattern could be confidently recognized as a gibbon. This result shocked the community: while similar minimal perturbations had been discussed for simpler models, seeing such vulnerability in large, deep networks, which had surpassed human performance in a number of tasks, was unexpected.

From 2014 to 2015, a series of follow-up works cemented and popularized this discovery. Notably, the paper by Goodfellow et al. (2014), «Explaining and Harnessing Adversarial Examples,» introduced the term «adversarial examples» and proposed a fundamental method for generating them – the Fast Gradient Sign Method (FGSM). The authors also demonstrated the first version of adversarial training for deep networks, in which adversarial perturbations were incorporated into the gradient descent process to increase the model's robustness.

These publications rapidly disseminated knowledge about adversarial attacks worldwide: prior to 2014, research on this topic had mainly appeared in niche security conferences, but after 2015, it began to regularly feature at leading AI and computer vision conferences. With the growing interest, there was an explosive development of attack and defense methods, accompanied by vigorous discussions within the academic community. On the one hand, researchers quickly expanded the «catalog» of attacks: more powerful gradient-based methods were proposed (e.g., BIM and PGD – iterative methods for deliberately adding noise) (Krijnen & Tamke, 2015), black-box attacks involving surrogate models for transferring perturbations (Papernot et al., 2017), universal perturbations (independent of the specific image), and others. By 2017-2018, it became evident that virtually any deep learning architecture could, in principle, be deceived by carefully crafted inputs – the only question was the difficulty of the attack.

On the other hand, there was simultaneous development and testing of numerous defense strategies: in addition to the aforementioned adversarial training (enhanced in 2018 by Madry et al., who proposed projective gradient descent to find the worst-case perturbations at each step of training), methods for transforming inputs (e.g., smoothing, quantization, or adding noise before feeding the data into the model), detecting suspicious samples based on activations (Chen et al., 2018), gradient masking (Wilson et al., 2018), and even distillation procedures to improve the network's robustness (Papernot et al., 2016) were proposed.

However, it quickly became apparent that constructing an «impenetrable» defense was exceedingly difficult – virtually all proposed heuristic defenses were vulnerable to more advanced attacks. For instance, the defensive distillation method, initially touted as a means to smooth and secure the decision boundaries of a network, was soon bypassed using an attack that employed a surrogate model to approximate the gradient. In 2017, Carlini and Wagner (2017) demonstrated a series of potent attacks that overcame many early defenses by optimizing not for minimal perceptibility of noise, but for maximizing the model's confidence in the incorrect response.

By 2018, there were so many examples of defensive failures that a pessimistic view emerged: perhaps reliable defense was impossible, and any deterministic deep learning model was fundamentally vulnerable. The academic community responded to this challenge with a series of critical works – most notably, the 2018 paper by Athalye, Carlini, and Wagner, «Obfuscated Gradients Give a False Sense of Security,» which conducted a thorough analysis of many proposed defense methods, showing that their effectiveness was often illusory and that their success depended on creating obfuscations that could be circumvented upon deeper analysis. This work established new, more stringent standards for evaluating robustness: from then on, it became a requirement to test defense methods against strong, fully adaptive attacks (i.e., those developed with knowledge of the defense mechanism).

Thus, by the end of the 2010s, a kind of arms race had developed between attacking and defending methods, with the academic community actively participating in both «camps.» By the close of the decade, a more cohesive interdisciplinary community had emerged, uniting knowledge from both security and machine learning fields. However, despite significant progress, unresolved issues remained. Debates continued regarding the fundamental causes of vulnerabilities: are adversarial examples the result of shortcomings in training (e.g., lack of data, overcomplexity of models), or do they inevitably arise due to discrepancies between human perception and the optimization metrics of neural networks? (Ilyas et al., 2019). Some studies indicated that increased robustness required sacrificing accuracy on normal data, suggesting a trade-off between accuracy and robustness (Zhang et al., 2019). These discussions paved the way for new research directions in the 2020s.

Generative Adversarial Models and Their Development

Parallel to the study of model vulnerabilities, the 2010s witnessed the emergence of a new paradigm in model training – so-called Generative Adversarial Networks. While adversarial attacks focus on the opposition between an external attacker and a model, the core idea of GANs integrates competition within the learning algorithm itself, where two neural networks are trained in an adversarial game against one another. This approach revolutionized data generation tasks and, in essence, showcased the constructive side of adversarial machine learning.

The invention of GANs is typically dated to 2014, when Goodfellow I. J. and colleagues published their seminal work Generative Adversarial Nets. In this model, one neural network (the generator) attempts to synthesize data samples statistically similar to the training dataset (for instance, images resembling real photographs of people), while another network (the discriminator) seeks to distinguish the generated samples from genuine ones. The generator and discriminator engage in a relationship of antagonism: the discriminator learns to better identify counterfeit samples, while the generator becomes more adept at forging them in order to deceive the discriminator. Formally, their interaction can be described as a zero-sum game (minimax game) – the gain of one agent corresponds to the loss of the other. The objective function of the generator is to maximize the proportion of synthesized samples that are accepted as true by the discriminator, while the discriminator seeks to minimize this value, striving to correctly reject the fakes. Goodfellow demonstrated that, under ideal conditions, this process converges to a situation in which the generator replicates the true data distribution, and the discriminator performs no better than random guessing (i.e., cannot distinguish the fake from the real).

Despite the simplicity of the core idea, training GANs proved to be non-trivial, with issues such as instability and incomplete learning (mode collapse, where the generator covers only a limited portion of the data distribution) arising. Nevertheless, the early results of GANs made a strong impression: a generator trained on a dataset of images could produce entirely new, previously unseen samples that appeared plausible and contained meaningful variations of the original data features. For example, a GAN trained on photographs began to «imagine» photorealistic faces of people who had never existed.

From an algorithmic standpoint, GANs introduced a new type of learning – «indirect» learning through a competitor. The generator never receives direct target labels for its outputs; instead, the signal is solely the response of the discriminator (accepted or rejected). This mirrors the process of evolutionary struggle – similar to how predators and prey in biology engage in coevolution, improving their skills in response to one another's adaptations, the generator and discriminator of GANs participate in an «evolutionary arms race» (Toutouh, Hemberg & O'Reilly, 2019). This adversarial learning dynamic opened up new possibilities that were inaccessible to standard optimization methods.

Between 2014 and 2019, GANs evolved from a curious idea to one of the most powerful tools in generative AI. By 2017, GANs were capable of generating high-quality images that surpassed all previous approaches. Several architectural and algorithmic improvements were proposed: DCGAN (Radford, Metz & Chintala, 2015) successfully employed convolutional neural networks within GANs, enhancing training stability and image quality; methods based on the separation of cost functions (WGAN, Arjovsky, Chintala & Bottou, 2017) made convergence more reliable; conditional generation (Conditional GAN, Mirza & Osindero, 2014) emerged, enabling directed synthesis – such as generating images from a given class or even transforming images into other images. Later architectures, such as Progressive GAN (Karras et al., 2017) and (Karras, Laine & Aila, 2019), achieved the generation of photorealistic human portraits at 1024×1024 pixel resolution. Subsequently, faces generated by StyleGAN from random noise became indistinguishable from real photographs (Melnik et al., 2024).

The successes of GANs were not confined to static images. Adversarial models were applied to the synthesis of realistic landscapes, objects, handwritten text, musical fragments, and even video. They found applications in image resolution enhancement (super-resolution) – in 2018, GANs were used to complete photos during zooming with a focus on realistic textures (Sabini & Rusak, 2018), in tasks such as inpainting (filling in missing parts of images), style transfer, animated character creation, and more.

From a scientific perspective, GANs spurred extensive research into the stability of game-theoretic learning. The rivalry between the generator and the discriminator introduced new challenges: unlike standard neural network training with a fixed loss function, here the optimization landscape is two-dimensional (minimax), where improving one part of the model may temporarily degrade another. Methods from game theory and differential dynamics were employed to analyze such processes. The academic community actively debated how to ensure GAN convergence, prevent mode collapse, and measure the quality of generated samples. Special metrics for evaluating generators were developed (e.g., Inception Score, FID, Salimans et al., 2016), as standard likelihood calculation was difficult due to the lack of explicit density in the generator.

However, certain disagreements emerged around GANs: some researchers pointed out their shortcomings (training difficulty, lack of theoretical guarantees, limited diversification of results) and developed alternative approaches to generation

– variational autoencoders, flow models, and, by the end of the decade, diffusion models. Nevertheless, the consensus was that the adversarial training scheme had led to an unprecedented leap in the quality of generative tasks.

Inspired by the successes of GANs, researchers began to apply adversarial principles beyond generation tasks. Works emerged where a small auxiliary «adversary» network was incorporated into the training of the primary model to improve its properties: for example, adversarial representation learning (feature learning) was used in domain adaptation tasks (Ganin et al., 2015 – gradient reversal for aligning feature distributions across two domains using an adversary) and fairness tasks (incorporating an adversarial classifier attempting to predict a protected attribute from extracted features, to ensure the primary extractor learned to eliminate information about undesirable correlates such as race or gender) (Lahoti et al., 2020). These applications demonstrated the versatility of the adversarial approach: essentially, any unwanted feature in a representation could be «erased» by training a special adversary attempting to exploit that feature.

Thus, adversarial machine learning expanded from a niche task of attacking classifiers to a broad spectrum of methodologies integrated into various areas of AI – from content generation to supervised and unsupervised learning in complex settings.

Current State and Open Problems (2020s)

In the 2020s, the field of adversarial machine learning continued to develop actively, simultaneously transitioning into a phase of relative maturity. On the one hand, research became increasingly applied: methods of adversarial robustness were integrated into security-sensitive systems (such as facial recognition, autonomous vehicle autopilots, content filtering), and GANs found industrial applications (creating artistic content, synthetic data for training, and image quality enhancement) (Xu et al., 2025). On the other hand, fundamental challenges and unresolved issues, requiring in-depth academic investigation, became sharply pronounced.

By the early 2020s, it became evident that absolute protection from adversarial attacks likely does not exist, and the goal of researchers is to achieve an acceptable level of robustness under given conditions. The best methods available today significantly enhance model resilience, yet they do not guarantee complete invulnerability. Moreover, these methods are computationally expensive and often decrease accuracy on standard data, thus limiting their practical application. In response to this, a new research direction – certified robustness – emerged, focused on developing methods that offer mathematical guarantees that no perturbation smaller than a certain radius will alter the model's decision for any given input. Some approaches, such as linearization and sensitivity analysis, interval methods, and specialized architectures, have made it possible to certify robustness for simpler tasks, but scaling these methods to complex models remains a challenging problem. Nonetheless, scholars emphasize that even the most rigorous threat models account only for known unknowns, while the real danger lies in the unknown unknowns (Zhao et al., 2024). In other words, we can predict and model attacks within the confines of imagined scenarios, but there remains the possibility of a fundamentally new, unforeseen attack vector.

Classical machine learning was designed for «closed-world» tasks, where all environmental states and potential actions are known a priori, whereas adversarial scenarios correspond to an open world, full of unknown factors. An algorithm that works well on standard data may fail dramatically when confronted with an example not represented in the training set – especially when an adversary intentionally seeks out such an example. This inherent uncertainty represents a profound epistemological challenge: can we prove the safety of a model without knowing in advance the specific nature of the attacks it will face? The answer remains negative – researchers can only attempt to cover the space of possible attacks as thoroughly as possible.

The current consensus within the scientific community is as follows: fully solving the problem of adversarial threats is likely as difficult as solving the broader issue of cybersecurity – there is no final «silver bullet,» and continuous methodological improvements and a holistic approach are required. As a result, there has been a growing interest in integrative strategies: combining robustness techniques with novelty detection methods (out-of-distribution detection), model interpretability, and even mechanisms for verified learning. This multidisciplinary perspective represents one of the most important avenues for research at present.

Generative Adversarial Networks and Generative Models

In the field of Generative Adversarial Networks, the 2020s saw both progress and a shift in paradigm. On the one hand, GANs reached maturity: variations for video generation, three-dimensional objects, and sequence control were developed, each of which presented additional complexities, as both the discriminator and the generator must operate within more intricate spaces. On the other hand, some of the limitations of GANs spurred the search for alternatives, and by 2021-2022, diffusion models gained significant popularity – this method of generation is based not on competition, but on the sequential addition and removal of noise (Yang et al., 2023). Diffusion models (such as DALLE-2 and Stable Diffusion) demonstrated outstanding results in generating images from textual descriptions, somewhat surpassing GANs in terms of optimization smoothness and the diversity of generated samples.

This shift led to discussions about whether the success of diffusion approaches signaled a crisis for GANs. The answer is no; rather, GANs and diffusion models tackle similar problems through different means, with each approach having its advantages. GANs, for instance, are often more time-efficient in terms of generation and can produce results in a single pass, whereas diffusion models require dozens of iterations. However, one thing is clear: the adversarial framework is not the only possible path to high-quality generation, and the future likely lies in a combination of ideas from different methods.

Hybrid Models in Adversarial Machine Learning: Emerging Directions and Challenges

In the current academic landscape, there is a growing body of research on hybrid models that combine Generative Adversarial Networks with autoencoders, diffusion processes, or utilize multiple discriminators at various levels (e.g., Carrara et al., 2021). Additionally, theoretical studies on the robustness of GANs continue to evolve (e.g., Thanh-Tung, Tran & Venkatesh, 2019; Wiatrak, Albrecht & Nystrom, 2019). Such interdisciplinary advancements are increasingly in demand to overcome the epistemological challenges inherent to GANs, including the lack of convergence theory and quality guarantees.

The academic community in adversarial machine learning in the 2020s continues to grow and diversify. Specialized conferences and competitions have emerged, such as the large-scale «NetHack Challenge» organized at NeurIPS in 2021, which attracted dozens of teams from around the world. These initiatives help establish de facto standards for evaluation – now, new models are tested against commonly accepted attack sets (see, for instance, the RobustBench platform, which regularly publishes rankings of models based on robustness against standard tests).

At the same time, disagreements persist regarding the appropriate approaches to adversarial machine learning. Some researchers advocate for formal methods (verification, certification, theoretical analysis), while others emphasize heuristic machine learning techniques (new architectures, greater variability in training, model ensembles, and supervised learning on vast datasets where the model can encounter a broader spectrum of possible attacks) (Zhang, Wang & Meng, 2021). Each camp justifies its position: formalists argue that without strict guarantees, the security of AI systems cannot be trusted, while proponents of empirical approaches contend that rigid guarantees overly constrain practical models, and in real-world tasks, achieving «sufficiently good» robustness is often more important than having an idealized, theoretical level of robustness. The truth likely lies somewhere in between, and future methodologies may combine the best aspects of both approaches.

Interestingly, research in adversarial machine learning is increasingly intertwining with other fields concerned with AI reliability and accountability (e.g., Delobelle et al., 2021; Choraś & Woźniak, 2022). One notable example is the issue of algorithmic bias and fairness, where adversarial approaches are also applied. In such cases, an «adversarial» corrector attempts to identify discriminatory patterns in model decisions, while the primary model learns to avoid them (e.g., Khakurel et al., 2022). Another example is the intersection of privacy and model attacks (e.g., recovering training data from a model or stealing the model through its API), which are often considered part of a broader threat landscape, with overlapping defense methods (for instance, differential privacy can complement defenses against adversarial examples) (e.g., Rigaki & Garcia, 2023). These developments point to the emergence of a more expansive field of secure and reliable AI, where adversarial learning is one important component, alongside model interpretability, fault tolerance, and the consideration of ethical constraints.

In summary, the history of adversarial machine learning represents a narrative of how the interaction of competing forces can both reveal the weaknesses and unlock new possibilities for intelligent systems. Over several decades, the journey from the initial theoretical ideas surrounding «malicious noise» has led to the present situation, in which AI developers now inherently consider the potential for active resistance and embed mechanisms for protection and learning through competition. Adversarial ML has had a global impact on the epistemology of AI: it has prompted a rethinking of the nature of generalization and knowledge within models.

The encounter with adaptive adversaries has highlighted the limitations of our understanding of how a model «understands» data, revealing that the successes of deep learning are often rooted in fragile correlations that do not necessarily align with human notions of significant features. This realization has spurred efforts towards more conscious AI development: research on interpretability, the identification of «hidden» features within representations, and control over what exactly a model learns. Adversarial training, on one hand, challenges the reliability of models, but on the other, it provides tools for achieving that very reliability (through proactive training against opposition, generating new data, and mitigating biases). Thus, it acts as both a stress test and a driver of progress.

As we approach 2025, adversarial machine learning remains a dynamic field with numerous open questions. Among these are the creation of models capable of learning in open environments, promptly identifying fundamentally new attacks; the integration of generative adversarial approaches with causal models for better control over synthesized content; and the development of theoretically sound adversarial learning methods that converge even in the presence of complex nonlinear interactions. The academic community remains polarized in its assessments of what is achievable, with skeptics viewing adversarial examples as an intractable byproduct of high dimensionality and model complexity, while optimists continue to develop increasingly sophisticated defense strategies and self-learning systems. One thing is clear: the very existence of the adversarial factor in learning compels us to deepen our understanding of the nature of intelligence, whether artificial or natural. It is no coincidence that adversarial principles are often compared to evolution – through competition and contradiction, adaptation and progress emerge. The history of adversarial ML illustrates this principle in action within the realm of artificial intelligence: through the competition of algorithms with one another, we ultimately achieve more sophisticated and robust intelligent systems. The years ahead are certain to bring new surprises and discoveries, but the lessons of the past enable us to look forward with a clearer understanding: the strengths and weaknesses of machine learning are inextricably linked, and by studying their interaction, science advances.

Contemporary State of Research in Adversarial Machine Learning

Research Methodology

In light of the aforementioned historical patterns and the previously identified research objectives, it is deemed prudent to transition to an analysis of the current state of the scientific discourse, as well as the identification of promising research directions within the subject area. The methodologically optimal instrument for implementing this task appears to be the bibliometric approach, which focuses on both the quantitative and qualitative analysis of publication activity in the field of adversarial machine learning. The goal of this approach is to identify the current research priorities and prospective directions that are presently attracting heightened scientific interest or are likely to come into focus within the academic community in the near future. Conducting such a systematic review not only allows for the identification of existing «growth points» but also enables the formation of a systematic and conceptually cohesive understanding of the potential trajectories for the development of this field, particularly in the context of a dynamically evolving technological environment.

For the purposes of this study, scholarly articles and preprints were selected as the objects of analysis. The choice of these sources is driven by their ability to promptly reflect the emergence of new scientific questions and research directions, as these forms of publication are characterized by shortened time cycles between the creation of scientific knowledge and its public availability, which is particularly relevant in the context of preprints.

The selection of the OpenAlex database as the primary source of bibliometric data was motivated by several fundamentally significant factors. First, despite its relatively short period of operation, OpenAlex has established itself as an authoritative aggregator of scientific metadata, possessing a high potential for relevance and completeness in reflecting emerging research directions. Regularly updated and extensive in scope, the metadata of this database allows for the timely analysis of rapidly developing fields of knowledge, among which adversarial machine learning undoubtedly ranks. Second, the open architecture of the database ensures comprehensive and independent coverage of scientific publications, free from the constraints of publisher platforms, while also providing researchers with tools for in-depth analysis and metadata filtering. This is of particular importance when studying interdisciplinary issues such as adversarial machine learning, which require the integration of data from various scientific domains.

An additional argument in favor of selecting OpenAlex is its advanced and detailed system of subject classification, encompassing both computer science and related disciplines, which can significantly enrich the research agenda in the field of adversarial machine learning. The presence of a comprehensive system of concepts and keywords within OpenAlex provides the opportunity for selective and subject-oriented curation of publications, allowing researchers to consider not only strictly thematically relevant sources but also materials that address adjacent issues, such as threat vectors, data privacy concerns, and methods for vulnerability analysis. The emphasis on open data within the publication corpus and its associated metadata ensures a high level of transparency and reproducibility in the conducted research, which substantially enhances its scientific validity and provides the possibility for independent verification and replication within the academic community.

Thus, by the end of March 2025, the bibliometric analysis conducted identified and selected 11,760 publications that include the term «Adversarial Machine Learning» in their titles or abstracts, published during the entire available period of indexing in the OpenAlex database.

General Trends in the Development of the Thematic Area

First and foremost, it seems advisable to conduct a retrospective analysis of publication activity in the field of adversarial machine learning, as this will not only establish general patterns and the dynamics of the development of this research domain but also identify critically important periods characterized by a significant increase in scientific interest and publication output.

The preliminary analysis reveals that publication activity in the field under consideration was extremely limited and sporadic prior to 2010. Several factors can account for this circumstance. Firstly, during this period, the very concept of adversarial machine learning was in its infancy and had not yet been formalized into a clearly defined scientific direction, which significantly complicated the accurate identification of relevant publications in scientific databases. Secondly, the methodological framework required to implement a comprehensive adversarial approach in machine learning had not yet been sufficiently developed or disseminated.

A more pronounced trend of growth in publication activity began to emerge in 2016, when the number of publications first reached 100 per year. The subsequent years were characterized by a rapid increase in the number of publications, with annual growth consistently exceeding twofold. Particularly notable were the dramatic spikes in publication activity observed in 2018 and 2023.

The sharp rise in publication activity in 2018, when the number of publications increased from 241 to 680 (a 2.8-fold increase), can be attributed to several interrelated factors. Notably, this period coincides with the widespread adoption of deep learning methods, accompanied by significant advances in computational power and the increased availability of experimental infrastructure, which stimulated intensive research focused on the creation and analysis of neural network models' robustness to adversarial attacks.

In addition, during this period, several publications emerged that had a decisive influence on the formation of theoretical and practical approaches to issues of security and model robustness in machine learning. It seems appropriate to view the development of this scientific direction through the metaphor of a «snowball,» which reflects the internal logic of the accumulation and intensification of research interest: the more works become available to the scientific community, the greater the number of researchers engage in studying the problem, thus creating a sustainable increase in activity up to a certain point of thematic saturation.

The significant growth observed in 2018 was primarily driven by the pool of publications from 2016–2017, which were groundbreaking and had a substantial impact on the subsequent research agenda.

Among the foundational publications in the field of adversarial machine learning that were published during this period, the previously mentioned work by Carlini N. & Wagner D., «Towards Evaluating the Robustness of Neural Networks» (Carlini & Wagner, 2017), which has been cited over 10,000 times according to Google Scholar, stands out. In this work, the authors proposed a methodology for the rigorous assessment of neural network robustness to adversarial attacks, thereby establishing an approach to experimental verification of vulnerabilities in machine learning models.

Other important contributions to the field of adversarial machine learning include:

- A series of studies by the group led by Papernot N. and colleagues. These include the previously mentioned works, as well as «The Limitations of Deep Learning in Adversarial Settings» (Papernot et al., 2016) (cited 5,287 times according to Google Scholar), which systematically outlined the fundamental limitations of existing deep learning approaches under adversarial conditions. An important contribution from the same research group was their paper «Transferability in Machine Learning: From Phenomena to Black-Box

Attacks Using Adversarial Samples» (Papernot, McDaniel & Goodfellow, 2016) (cited 2,153 times according to Google Scholar);
- The publication «Adversarial Machine Learning at Scale» by Kurakin A., Goodfellow I., & Bengio S. (Kurakin, Goodfellow & Bengio, 2016) (cited 3,945 times according to Google Scholar), which examined the challenges and methods for countering adversarial attacks in the context of large-scale machine learning. This work clearly demonstrated the practical significance of the problem for the industry;
- The paper by Tramèr F. and colleagues, «Ensemble Adversarial Training: Attacks and Defenses» (Tramèr et al., 2017) (cited 3,493 times according to Google Scholar), which proposed a method for strengthening model robustness through ensemble adversarial training. This research marked the emergence of an entire direction focused on proactively reinforcing models through the diversity of methods and architectures employed;
- Additionally, several works that address adversarial machine learning without focusing solely on it, such as (Shokri et al., 2017), (Kurakin, Goodfellow & Bengio, 2016), (Bousmalis et al., 2017), (Fredrikson, Jha & Ristenpart, 2015), and others, should also be noted.

These studies, published between 2016 and 2017 and cited thousands of times, acted as catalysts that initiated the rapid expansion of scientific activity in the field of adversarial machine learning. Their high citation index, serving as an indicator of recognition and demand among researchers, directly reflects the formation of a stable and rapidly growing interest in the subject. Therefore, the pronounced spike in publication activity in 2018 appears to be a logical consequence of the significant accumulation of a critical mass of foundational and highly cited works in the preceding two years, which shaped a sustained research agenda and stimulated the emergence of new publications.

Similarly, in 2023, a significant increase in the number of publications was observed. The rise in interest in this field in 2023 can likely be attributed to a variety of factors, among which the increasing complexity and diversification of adversarial attack forms, the need to address issues of data protection and privacy in the context of the widespread implementation of artificial intelligence, and the growing interest from regulatory bodies and commercial organizations in matters of security and trust in artificial intelligence technologies are particularly prominent. These factors have contributed to a qualitative expansion of research topics and a strengthening of their applied orientation.

Additionally, it is crucial to emphasize that the prevalence of scientific topics is significantly influenced by the accessibility of publications directly related to the respective subject areas. In the context of this study, conducted using the OpenAlex database, attention should specifically be drawn to its profile, which is oriented toward the principle of open access. The empirical data under analysis indicate that throughout the indexing period, 61.8% of all publications related to adversarial machine learning are available in open access, a notably high percentage compared to other areas of computer science and related disciplines.

This high degree of openness is of critical scientific importance for several reasons. First, open access publications tend to have higher citation potential and wider dissemination within the academic community, as they eliminate a significant portion of the economic and institutional barriers that impede the timely and comprehensive study of the latest research findings. Second, it significantly facilitates access to knowledge and accelerates the formation of research networks and collaborations, which is particularly significant in rapidly evolving and interdisciplinary fields such as adversarial machine learning.

From the total sample of 11,760 publications, the following distribution by access type was identified: 38% of articles are behind closed access (closed access), which still reflects the considerable presence of traditional publishing platforms that limit the widespread distribution of scientific information. However, a significant portion of articles (37%) falls under the so-called «green access» (green open access), allowing authors to self-archive their publications in repositories or personal archives, which positively impacts the expansion of the accessibility of research findings. It is important to note that green access is characterized by minimal barriers from the author's perspective and promotes the dissemination of pre-final versions of publications, which, nevertheless, become readily available to the scientific community.

When considering other types of open access, it is worth noting a substantial volume of publications in «golden access» (gold open access), which constitutes 14% of the overall sample. This type of open access is distinguished by the fact that publications are made freely available through journals, often requiring authors to pay a publication fee. Despite its relatively smaller share compared to green access, golden access is characterized by a high level of citation and scientific recognition, as it provides access to completed and peer-reviewed materials. Less common are the so-called «hybrid» (hybrid open access) and «bronze» (bronze open access) access types, each comprising 5% of the total. Hybrid access involves publishing articles in predominantly closed journals with optional open access for certain publications, while bronze access typically involves the publication of materials in open access without clearly defined licensing conditions or guarantees for long-term access. The least represented is «diamond access» (diamond open access, 1%), which offers free open access to publications without charging authors, a system that is limited due to the financial challenges associated with supporting such platforms and publishing initiatives.

The high cumulative share of open access (61.8%) in the analyzed sample is primarily due to the nature of the genre composition of the materials: preprints, which account for 37% of the total sample, are significantly more accessible, with a reach of up to 80%. This specific distribution of preprints is related to their nature, which is oriented toward the rapid dissemination of preliminary research results to facilitate swift academic exchange. Consequently, the widespread distribution of preprints in the field of adversarial machine learning is an important factor that explains the overall high level of open access and, as a result, the dynamic development and rapid popularization of this scientific direction.

Thus, the preliminary analysis allows the conclusion that the formation of the adversarial machine learning research direction is characterized by rapid rates of emergence and an equally intense dynamic of subsequent dissemination and institutionalization in the contemporary academic environment. Since its inception, this field of study has undergone a swift evolution from isolated publications to a broad domain, which attests to the high demand and both theoretical and practical significance of the issues addressed. This development is driven by a number of factors, among which the relevance of issues related to information security and the robustness of machine learning algorithms, as well as the active involvement of scientific groups, the creation of stable research communities, and the widespread coverage of the topic in specialized publications and other forms of scientific communication, should be highlighted.

As in other rapidly growing research areas, adversarial machine learning is characterized by the rapid accumulation of scientific information, resulting in a volume of publications that already significantly exceeds the capacity for their full and thorough study using traditional methods of non-automated analysis. This situation has become typical for fields where the intensity of new publications exceeds the cognitive and temporal resources available to researchers, thus highlighting the need for specialized automated analytical approaches.

In this context, this study proposes bibliometric analysis as a methodological solution, capable of adequately and efficiently addressing the tasks of systematizing, structuring, and analytically interpreting large volumes of scientific literature. Bibliometric methods, particularly the analysis of thematic diversity within publications, enable a high degree of reliability in identifying dominant directions, assessing their significance and impact, and tracking the dynamics of the transformation of the scientific landscape. The choice of this approach is determined by its ability not only to capture the current state of the studied field but also to create the foundations for forecasting its further development.

Analysis of Thematic Directions

The analysis of the structural and substantive characteristics of the research landscape in the field of adversarial machine learning was carried out using the specialized software VOSviewer, employed in bibliometric studies for the visualization, systematization, and clustering analysis of terminological connections. The underlying assumption of this approach is that the set of terms that frequently co-occur in scientific publications reflects stable thematic directions that unite related research questions, methodological approaches, and areas of application. Therefore, the identified term systems not only capture the key directions in the current state of the field but also allow for the analysis of the degree of cross-disciplinary interaction, as well as the dynamics of the emergence of new theoretical concepts and practical applications.

The analysis of thematic clusters represents not merely a system of existing directions but also a significant tool for assessing the structure of scientific discourse. It enables the identification of the coherence of the research field, the determination of the primary centers of scientific gravity, and the detection of trends in interdisciplinary collaboration. This approach becomes particularly significant in rapidly evolving fields such as adversarial machine learning, where the evolution of the problem space occurs at a high speed, and new challenges require a timely scientific response.

Based on the conducted clustering analysis, several broad thematic blocks were identified. Within certain large clusters, more specialized directions can be distinguished, characterized by stable connections both at the level of conceptual intersections and in the context of co-citation. Of particular note in this context is the phenomenon of interdisciplinary borrowing, where research that may initially seem unrelated to adversarial machine learning is organically integrated into the corresponding discourse due to shared methodological foundations or similar research tasks. Thus, based on the results of the analysis presented in the visualization in Figure 1, several thematic clusters were distinguished.

Figure 1 is a visualization of the terminological network in publications on adversarial machine learning indexed in the OpenAlex database. Cluster color coding illustrates the proximity of terms and reflects the grouping of scientific studies by thematic focus. Each color represents a distinct cluster, uniting publications that are methodologically and substantively related. The figure clearly reveals the structural distribution of research interests, covering topics ranging from federated learning and model protection to interdisciplinary issues such as ethical and legal risks.

Figure 1. A network of terminology found in publications on adversarial machine learning indexed in the Openalex database, with cluster color highlighting based on co-occurrence.

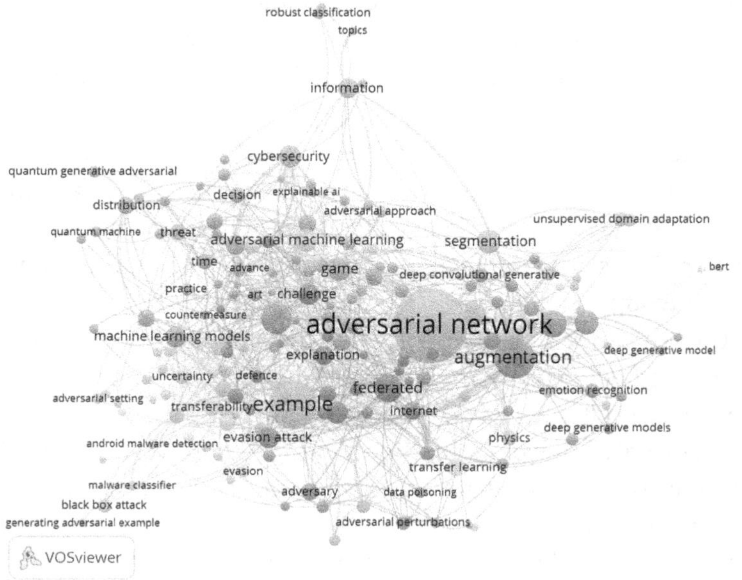

Cluster 1 (red in Figure 1) brings together works that focus on federated learning and its associated security threats, predominantly in the context of evasion attacks. The central subject of research here is the protection of federated systems, which, due to their architectural characteristics, are particularly vulnerable to risks posed by adversaries seeking to bypass algorithmic defense mechanisms. Key specialized directions within this cluster include methods for model interpretation and explanation, which not only enhance system resilience but also ensure the transparency of decision-making processes.

Cluster 2 (green) emphasizes the algorithmic aspects related to the generation and detection of adversarial examples. A significant research interest is demonstrated in approaches aimed at increasing the robustness of deep learning models through the improvement of identification and response mechanisms for adversarial interventions. An important sub-discourse here includes real-time attack detection algorithms and theoretical aspects of model robustness, addressing the mathematical and computational aspects of robustness analysis.

Within the third cluster (blue), the central focus of research is on data poisoning attacks. Ensuring the integrity of training datasets and preventing deliberate data manipulation represent key areas of scientific inquiry. Specialized sub-directions include the development and verification of algorithms for the automatic detection and filtering of data distortions on scales typical for modern high-load AI applications.

The fourth cluster (olive) contains scientific discussions focused on the legal, ethical, and regulatory aspects of adversarial machine learning. This direction is marked by its interdisciplinary nature and concentrates on the analysis of normative risks and legal consequences arising from the use of adversarial techniques in various applied contexts, especially regarding liability for decisions made by artificial intelligence systems.

Cluster 5 (purple) focuses on methodologies for enhancing the resilience of neural network models against adversarial attacks, paying significant attention to the development of adaptive and preventive algorithms. Specialized directions within this cluster include specific training algorithms aimed at increasing robustness in the face of active opposition.

Cluster 6 (blue) represents the most actively studied area, focusing on deep theoretical and methodological aspects of robustness, certification, and the formalization of model security. A critical element of this discourse is the mathematical justification of model resilience and the development of certification procedures that allow for the quantitative and qualitative assessment of neural network protection from adversarial influences.

Clusters 7 (orange) and 8 (brown) are dedicated to specialized types of attacks: targeted and realistic. The research is aimed at understanding and modeling the behavior of attacking agents and developing defense mechanisms specialized in countering narrowly focused threats, as well as generating and detecting high-quality realistic adversarial samples.

Clusters 9 (pink) and 10 (peach) reflect research on the application of adversarial technologies in the practical domains of computer vision and natural language processing, respectively, emphasizing the peculiarities and vulnerabilities of these types of data and tasks.

Smaller clusters were also identified: the eleventh cluster (light green) addresses the optimization of training algorithms in adversarial environments, while the twelfth focuses on the protection of IoT devices and systems that are vulnerable to adversarial attacks. The last, thirteenth cluster, demonstrating minimal research activity, raises questions about the socio-economic consequences of the widespread adoption of adversarial techniques, suggesting a reconsideration of the risks associated with the proliferation of artificial intelligence in society.

In conclusion, it can be stated that there is a broad thematic and methodological diversification in the field of adversarial machine learning, with a dominance of fundamental theoretical research related to robustness and model certification, alongside increasing attention to interdisciplinary issues driven by the widespread penetration of artificial intelligence into various spheres of societal activity.

Citation Metrics and Impact of Leading Research Themes

Despite the relatively limited temporal scope, the identified terms and key concepts exhibit significant variability in terms of their temporal dynamics of mention by authors. Some have been in use for a considerable time, while others have only recently entered the scientific discourse. Furthermore, there are terms that, although known previously, have gained considerably more popularity among researchers in recent years. This phenomenon reflects two important processes: firstly, the ongoing renewal of the conceptual apparatus in the field of adversarial machine learning through the integration of new directions and methodological approaches; and secondly, the dynamic redistribution of research priorities, which leads to the emergence of new dominant themes. The segmentation of terminology based on the average year of mention is presented in Figure 2.

Figure 2 is a representation of the network of terms in publications on adversarial machine learning, with a gradient color scale indicating the average year of term mention. This visualization captures the temporal dynamics of the emergence and popularization of key concepts and approaches within the field. Darker shades correspond to earlier research phases, whereas lighter colors highlight more recently developed or currently intensively evolving thematic directions, such as federated learning, diffusion models, and transformer architectures.

Figure 2. A network of terminology found in publications on adversarial machine learning indexed in the Openalex database, with a color gradient based on the average year of occurrence.

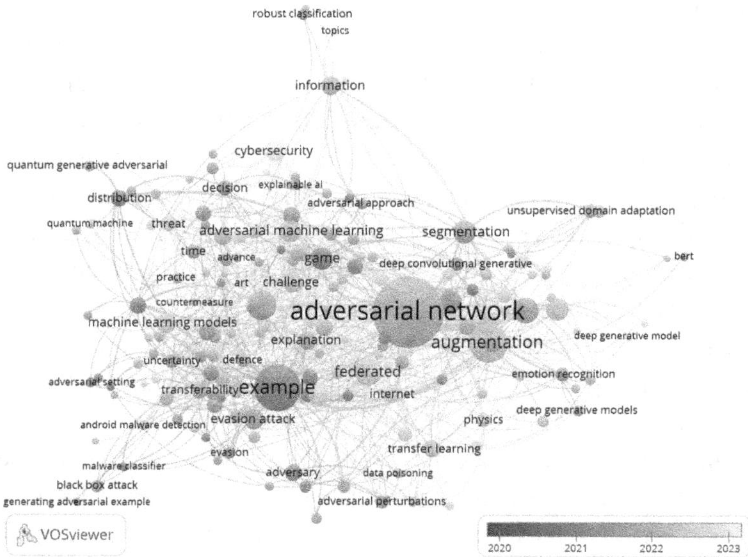

Among the directions that have received significant mention in recent times, the following are noteworthy:

- Federated Learning: This machine learning method, which enables models to learn from distributed datasets without their centralized collection, is becoming the subject of active study in the context of privacy protection and resilience to adversarial attacks. The primary focus of researchers is on the development of algorithms that ensure the safeguarding of personal data in decentralized environments, as well as on the identification and neutralization of attacks aimed at compromising such models.
- Cybersecurity: The protection of machine learning systems from cyber threats has become critically important due to the increasing number of attacks targeting vulnerabilities in AI models. In addition to traditional attacks, such as input data manipulation (adversarial perturbations), significant attention is being paid to newer, more specific threats, including backdoor attacks designed to covertly modify a model for incorrect behavior under certain conditions.
- Transformers: Architectures based on attention mechanisms are becoming an integral part of modern artificial intelligence research, including in the study

of their resilience to adversarial impacts. The active development of this direction is driven not only by advances in computational power but also by an increased interest in enhancing the reliability of natural language processing and computer vision models.

- Synthetic Data Generation: The issue of synthetic data has gained increasing relevance due to the need to ensure data privacy and minimize threats associated with the manipulation of training datasets. The use of synthetic data helps address challenges related to the shortage of high-quality data and contributes to the creation of models that are more resilient to adversarial influences.
- Diffusion Models: Modern generative models exhibit high potential in the creation of realistic synthetic data, making them a promising tool in the development of more secure machine learning systems. Research in this field is focused on identifying the vulnerabilities of such models and developing protective mechanisms.
- Large Language Models (LLMs): The resilience of language models to adversarial attacks has become one of the key challenges in modern natural language processing. Given the widespread application of LLMs across various fields, including automated analytics and content generation, researchers are dedicating considerable attention to methods for enhancing their reliability and protecting them from manipulative influences.
- Graph Neural Networks (GNNs): This type of model is attracting growing attention due to its effectiveness in analyzing complex network structures, including social networks and cyber-physical systems. In the context of adversarial machine learning, particular interest lies in identifying vulnerabilities within graph neural networks and developing mechanisms to protect them from graph-based attacks.
- Super Resolution: The use of generative adversarial networks, particularly Wasserstein GANs, to improve the quality of visual data is an actively developing area. However, such technologies are also susceptible to specific threats.
- Machine Unlearning: This concept, related to the selective removal of information from a trained model, is gaining increasing importance due to the demands for data protection and the adherence to privacy principles. Research in this area is focused on developing methods that allow for the effective removal of traces of individual training samples without compromising the overall performance of the model.
- Hybrid Approaches and Uncertainty Estimation: Modern methods for protecting machine learning models increasingly incorporate hybrid strategies that combine various techniques for ensuring security, attack detection, and

adaptive learning. Additionally, significant attention is being given to uncertainty estimation mechanisms, which help identify potential vulnerabilities of models and minimize risks associated with their deployment.

In considering the dynamics of scientific discourse in the field of adversarial machine learning, it is important to emphasize that the high frequency of mentions of a particular concept in published studies does not always directly correlate with its citation frequency within the academic community. While certain directions may be characterized by a significant number of publications, their influence on subsequent scientific agendas is determined not only by quantitative indicators but also by the degree of demand among the research community. In some cases, certain topics may have a limited number of publications but exhibit a high average citation count, indicating their significance or high innovative value. The segmentation of terminology based on the average number of citations is presented in Figure 3.

Figure 3 is a depiction of the terminological network in adversarial machine learning publications with a gradient color scale based on the average number of citations. This visualization enables the identification of the most influential scientific directions, which attract the greatest attention within the research community. More saturated colors indicate topics whose associated publications have higher citation counts and, therefore, greater impact on the development of the field, including the generation and recognition of adversarial examples, the theoretical foundations of model robustness, and issues related to the transferability of adversarial attacks.

Figure 3. A network of terminology found in publications on adversarial machine learning indexed in the Openalex database, with a color gradient based on the average number of citations.

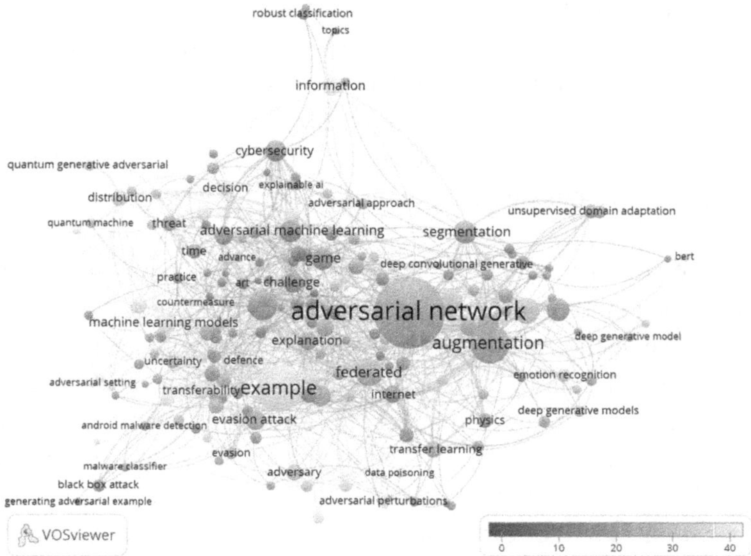

The analysis of publication activity allows for the identification of several key research directions, characterized by the highest level of academic citation and, consequently, exerting a significant influence on the development of this field of knowledge:

- Research on the Creation and Analysis of Adversarial Examples: This direction occupies one of the leading positions within the research agenda, as evidenced by the high number of citations of works dedicated to the generation, recognition, and mitigation of the impact of adversarial examples. Central to this area is the development of methodological approaches that allow for the assessment of the vulnerability of neural network models and the formulation of strategies to protect them from deliberate attacks. Special attention is devoted to the study of the mechanics of adversarial interactions and the development of formal models that describe the robustness of machine learning systems under adversarial conditions.
- Theoretical and Methodological Issues of Generative Models: The significant demand for research in this area is due to their relevance for data synthesis tasks, the modeling of probabilistic dependencies, and the construction of resilient neural network architectures. The focus of attention lies not only on

the fundamental aspects of the operation of generative models but also on the applied scenarios of their use in adversarial interactions, including the evaluation of their resilience to deliberate manipulations and their potential as a protective mechanism.

- The Problem of Transferability of Adversarial Attacks and Defensive Strategies: A critical research direction is the identification of patterns that determine the universality of adversarial attacks, as well as the development of protective mechanisms that ensure the reliability of a broad range of models. Within this area, adaptive defense methods are studied that enhance the robustness of machine learning algorithms regardless of the specific type of threat.
- Analysis of Robustness and Robustness Certification of Machine Learning Models: The development of formal models that provide a theoretical justification for the resilience of neural network systems to adversarial impacts has become especially significant. Research in this area is focused on the creation of mathematically rigorous methods for evaluating robustness, formulating criteria for certified defense, and developing algorithms that minimize the probability of successful attacks.
- Optimization of Algorithms and Architectures of Deep Neural Networks (DNNs) in the Context of Adversarial Learning: Active work is being conducted within this direction to improve architectural solutions aimed at enhancing the security of models against adversarial attacks. Special attention is paid to the development of adaptive regularization mechanisms, methods for preventing overfitting to adversarial examples, and the integration of protective algorithms directly into the training process.
- Comprehensive Surveys and Knowledge Systematization: This class of publications occupies an important position in the research agenda, as it contributes to the structuring of accumulated empirical and theoretical material, as well as the formation of a comprehensive picture of the discipline's development. The high citation rate of such works is due to their value for future research, as they lay the methodological foundation for subsequent empirical and conceptual investigations.
- Research in Privacy and Confidentiality Protection (Differential Privacy): The interdisciplinary nature of this issue, which lies at the intersection of machine learning and information security, predetermines its high significance. Research in this area focuses on mechanisms for ensuring privacy during the training of neural networks, including differential privacy methods, computation encryption, and data anonymization.
- The Problem of Data Poisoning Attacks: This type of threat occupies a central place in the system of adversarial impacts, as it targets the manipulation

of training data with the aim of distorting the model's results. Research in this area is concentrated on developing methods for detecting attacks, creating filtering and cleaning mechanisms for training datasets, and formulating defense strategies based on attack-resistant learning methods.

- Adversarial Machine Learning in the Field of Computer Vision: The high citation rate of publications in this area is due to the active application of adversarial attacks specifically within the realm of visual information processing. Research in this direction focuses on attacks aimed at distorting classification decisions, counteracting image manipulation, and developing robust neural network architectures capable of mitigating the effects of adversarial examples.

To systematize the identified thematic clusters and to comprehensively assess their scientific significance, a summary table was prepared, reflecting the interrelation between the frequency of topic mentions, the level of academic citation, and the existence of strategic intersections between these characteristics. This analysis enabled the classification of research themes according to their relevance and impact on the development of the field, and each thematic area is accompanied by detailed commentary outlining promising directions for further investigation. The table 1 provides a consolidated view of the current state and dynamic evolution of the research landscape in adversarial machine learning, highlighting key areas of growth as well as underexplored scientific niches.

Table 1. Overview of Research Themes in Adversarial Machine Learning

N°	Thematic Area	Mention Frequency	Citation Impact	Commentary
1	Federated learning and evasion attacks; model interpretation and explainability	Medium	Medium	Federated learning has significant future potential, particularly regarding privacy preservation and distributed system protection. Nevertheless, the field requires further formalization of certification and security validation methods.
2	Generation and detection of adversarial examples; algorithmic methods for robustness enhancement	Above Average	Above Average	A strategically critical area: it provides the foundation for both protective methods and attack strategies. It constitutes a fundamental pillar of the entire adversarial machine learning domain.
3	Data poisoning attacks; automatic detection and filtering of corrupted data	Medium	Medium	This topic maintains stable significance in practical applications, particularly in view of vulnerabilities in large-scale data-driven systems. It holds promise for the development of autonomous data integrity protection mechanisms.

continued on following page

Table 1. Continued

Nº	Thematic Area	Mention Frequency	Citation Impact	Commentary
4	Legal, ethical, and regulatory aspects of adversarial machine learning	Below Average	Below Average	The interdisciplinary importance of this area is recognized, yet academic interest remains comparatively limited. Integration with evolving legal and ethical standards for artificial intelligence systems is critically necessary.
5	Adaptive and preventive algorithms for increasing neural network resilience	Medium	Medium	A practically oriented domain; its importance is expected to rise alongside the proliferation of adversarial methods in critical applications.
6	Theoretical and methodological foundations of robustness, certification, and formalization of model security	Above Average	Above Average	This constitutes the core of theoretical research: it provides the basis for the formal justification of model robustness. It is critical for the development of security certification procedures in high-risk systems.
Other	–	Below Average-Medium	Below Average-Medium	–

CONCLUSION

The analysis of the state of scientific discourse in the field of adversarial machine learning allows for several fundamental conclusions. Firstly, a pronounced thematic and methodological diversification of the research direction has been identified, which is evidenced by the sustained dominance of foundational theoretical works focused on issues of robustness and model certification. Simultaneously, there is intensive interdisciplinary integration, driven by the widespread implementation of artificial intelligence technologies across various sectors of human activity.

Secondly, a detailed bibliometric analysis of publication activity in this field reveals a dynamic redistribution of research priorities. Constant updates to the conceptual apparatus have been observed, indicating the high degree of adaptability of the discipline to changing challenges and threats. The consistent growth in citation of key concepts and terms attests to the increasing significance of adversarial machine learning within the academic community.

The third significant aspect is the high level of openness in scientific research within this field. A substantial proportion of publications are made openly accessible, particularly in the form of preprints, which ensures the rapid dissemination of new results and facilitates the swift exchange of knowledge among researchers. This, in turn, accelerates the institutionalization of adversarial machine learning as a distinct area of research within the broader field of artificial intelligence.

The prospects for further research in adversarial machine learning can be characterized as follows. Firstly, it seems prudent to deepen theoretical developments aimed at formalizing the mechanisms of adversarial attacks and model robustness. Secondly, a critical direction is the development of more universal and practically applicable defense methods capable of ensuring the reliability of models in real-world adversarial settings. Thirdly, there is a need to strengthen interdisciplinary cooperation, particularly with fields such as cybersecurity, cryptography, and legal regulation, which will enable the formation of comprehensive strategies for the protection of information systems.

The anticipated development of the field suggests the further institutionalization of adversarial machine learning as a key research direction in artificial intelligence. In light of the increasing number of practical threats related to adversarial attacks, it is expected that there will be a significant rise in attention to issues of certification and standardization of machine learning algorithms. Additionally, regulatory oversight from authorities is likely to increase, alongside a rise in initiatives aimed at ensuring the transparency and reproducibility of research in this area.

REFERENCES

Arjovsky, M., Chintala, S., & Bottou, L. (2017). Wasserstein generative adversarial networks. In *International conference on machine learning* (pp. 214-223). PMLR.

Athalye, A., Carlini, N., & Wagner, D. (2018). Obfuscated gradients give a false sense of security: Circumventing defenses to adversarial examples. In *International conference on machine learning* (pp. 274-283). PMLR.

Barreno, M., Nelson, B., Joseph, A. D., & Tygar, J. D. (2010). The security of machine learning. *Machine Learning, 81*(2), 121–148. DOI: 10.1007/s10994-010-5188-5

Barreno, M., Nelson, B., Sears, R., Joseph, A. D., & Tygar, J. D. (2006, March). Can machine learning be secure? In *Proceedings of the 2006 ACM Symposium on Information, computer and communications security* (pp. 16-25). DOI: 10.1145/1128817.1128824

Biggio, B., Corona, I., Maiorca, D., Nelson, B., Šrndić, N., Laskov, P., . . . Roli, F. (2013). Evasion attacks against machine learning at test time. In *Machine learning and knowledge discovery in databases: European conference, ECML pKDD 2013, prague, czech Republic, September 23-27, 2013, proceedings, part III* 13 (pp. 387-402). Springer Berlin Heidelberg. DOI: 10.1007/978-3-642-40994-3_25

Biggio, B., Nelson, B., & Laskov, P. (2012). Poisoning attacks against support vector machines. arXiv preprint arXiv:1206.6389.

Bousmalis, K., Silberman, N., Dohan, D., Erhan, D., & Krishnan, D. (2017). Unsupervised pixel-level domain adaptation with generative adversarial networks. In *Proceedings of the IEEE conference on computer vision and pattern recognition* (pp. 3722-3731). DOI: 10.1109/CVPR.2017.18

Carlini, N., & Wagner, D. (2017). Towards evaluating the robustness of neural networks. In *2017 IEEE symposium on security and privacy (SP)* (pp. 39-57). IEEE. DOI: 10.1109/SP.2017.49

Carrara, F., Amato, G., Brombin, L., Falchi, F., & Gennaro, C. (2021). Combining gans and autoencoders for efficient anomaly detection. In *2020 25th International Conference on Pattern Recognition (ICPR)* (pp. 3939-3946). IEEE. DOI: 10.1109/ICPR48806.2021.9412253

Chen, B., Carvalho, W., Baracaldo, N., Ludwig, H., Edwards, B., Lee, T., . . . Srivastava, B. (2018). Detecting backdoor attacks on deep neural networks by activation clustering. *arXiv preprint* arXiv:1811.03728.

Choraś, M., & Woźniak, M. (2022). The double-edged sword of AI: Ethical Adversarial Attacks to counter artificial intelligence for crime. *AI and Ethics*, *2*(4), 631–634. DOI: 10.1007/s43681-021-00113-9

Dalvi, N., & Domingos, P., Mausam, Sanghai, S., & Verma, D. (2004, August). Adversarial classification. In *Proceedings of the tenth ACM SIGKDD international conference on Knowledge discovery and data mining* (pp. 99-108).

Delobelle, P., Temple, P., Perrouin, G., Frénay, B., Heymans, P., & Berendt, B. (2021). Ethical adversaries: Towards mitigating unfairness with adversarial machine learning. *SIGKDD Explorations*, *23*(1), 32–41. DOI: 10.1145/3468507.3468513

Fredrikson, M., Jha, S., & Ristenpart, T. (2015). Model inversion attacks that exploit confidence information and basic countermeasures. In *Proceedings of the 22nd ACM SIGSAC conference on computer and communications security* (pp. 1322-1333). DOI: 10.1145/2810103.2813677

Ganin, Y., Ustinova, E., Ajakan, H., Germain, P., Larochelle, H., Laviolette, F., & Lempitsky, V. (2016). Domain-adversarial training of neural networks. *Journal of Machine Learning Research*, *17*(59), 1–35.

Goodfellow, I. J., Pouget-Abadie, J., Mirza, M., Xu, B., Warde-Farley, D., Ozair, S., & Bengio, Y. (2014). Generative adversarial nets. *Advances in Neural Information Processing Systems*, •••, 27.

Goodfellow, I. J., Shlens, J., & Szegedy, C. (2014). Explaining and harnessing adversarial examples. *arXiv preprint arXiv*:1412.6572.

Ilyas, A., Santurkar, S., Tsipras, D., Engstrom, L., Tran, B., & Madry, A. (2019). Adversarial examples are not bugs, they are features. *Advances in Neural Information Processing Systems*, •••, 32.

Karras, T., Aila, T., Laine, S., & Lehtinen, J. (2017). Progressive growing of GANs for improved quality, stability, and variation. *arXiv preprint* arXiv:1710.10196.

Karras, T., Laine, S., & Aila, T. (2019). A style-based generator architecture for generative adversarial networks. In *Proceedings of the IEEE/CVF conference on computer vision and pattern recognition* (pp. 4401-4410). DOI: 10.1109/CVPR.2019.00453

Kearns, M., & Li, M. (1988). Learning in the presence of malicious errors. In *Proceedings of the twentieth annual ACM symposium on Theory of computing* (pp. 267-280). DOI: 10.1145/62212.62238

Khakurel, U., Abdelmoumin, G., Bajracharya, A., & Rawat, D. B. (2022). Exploring bias and fairness in artificial intelligence and machine learning algorithms. In *Artificial Intelligence and Machine Learning for Multi-Domain Operations Applications IV* (Vol. 12113, pp. 629–638). SPIE. DOI: 10.1117/12.2621282

Kohonen, T., & Honkela, T. (2007). Kohonen network. *Scholarpedia Journal, 2*(1), 1568. DOI: 10.4249/scholarpedia.1568

Krijnen, T., & Tamke, M. (2015). Assessing implicit knowledge in BIM models with machine learning. In *Modelling Behaviour: Design Modelling Symposium 2015* (pp. 397-406). Springer International Publishing. DOI: 10.1007/978-3-319-24208-8_33

Kurakin, A., Goodfellow, I., & Bengio, S. (2016). Adversarial machine learning at scale. *arXiv preprint* arXiv:1611.01236.

Kurakin, A., Goodfellow, I. J., & Bengio, S. (2018). Adversarial examples in the physical world. In *Artificial intelligence safety and security* (pp. 99–112). Chapman and Hall/CRC. DOI: 10.1201/9781351251389-8

Lahoti, P., Beutel, A., Chen, J., Lee, K., Prost, F., Thain, N., & Chi, E. (2020). Fairness without demographics through adversarially reweighted learning. *Advances in Neural Information Processing Systems, 33*, 728–740.

Lowd, D., & Meek, C. (2005). Good Word Attacks on Statistical Spam Filters. In *CEAS* (Vol. 2005).

Madry, A., Makelov, A., Schmidt, L., Tsipras, D., & Vladu, A. (2017). Towards deep learning models resistant to adversarial attacks. *arXiv preprint* arXiv:1706.06083.

Melnik, A., Miasayedzenkau, M., Makaravets, D., Pirshtuk, D., Akbulut, E., Holzmann, D., Renusch, T., Reichert, G., & Ritter, H. (2024). Face generation and editing with stylegan: A survey. *IEEE Transactions on Pattern Analysis and Machine Intelligence, 46*(5), 3557–3576. DOI: 10.1109/TPAMI.2024.3350004 PMID: 38224501

Mirza, M., & Osindero, S. (2014). Conditional generative adversarial nets. *arXiv preprint* arXiv:1411.1784.

Papernot, N., McDaniel, P., & Goodfellow, I. (2016). Transferability in machine learning: from phenomena to black-box attacks using adversarial samples. *arXiv preprint* arXiv:1605.07277.

Papernot, N., McDaniel, P., Goodfellow, I., Jha, S., Celik, Z. B., & Swami, A. (2017). Practical black-box attacks against machine learning. In *Proceedings of the 2017 ACM on Asia conference on computer and communications security* (pp. 506-519).

Papernot, N., McDaniel, P., Jha, S., Fredrikson, M., Celik, Z. B., & Swami, A. (2016). The limitations of deep learning in adversarial settings. In *2016 IEEE European symposium on security and privacy (EuroS&P)* (pp. 372-387). IEEE. DOI: 10.1109/EuroSP.2016.36

Papernot, N., McDaniel, P., Wu, X., Jha, S., & Swami, A. (2016). Distillation as a defense to adversarial perturbations against deep neural networks. In *2016 IEEE symposium on security and privacy (SP)* (pp. 582-597). IEEE. DOI: 10.1109/SP.2016.41

Radford, A., Metz, L., & Chintala, S. (2015). Unsupervised representation learning with deep convolutional generative adversarial networks. *arXiv preprint* arXiv:1511.06434.

Rigaki, M., & Garcia, S. (2023). A survey of privacy attacks in machine learning. *ACM Computing Surveys*, *56*(4), 1–34. DOI: 10.1145/3624010

Sabini, M., & Rusak, G. (2018). Painting outside the box: Image outpainting with GANs. *arXiv preprint* arXiv:1808.08483.

Salimans, T., Goodfellow, I., Zaremba, W., Cheung, V., Radford, A., & Chen, X. (2016). Improved techniques for training GANs. *Advances in Neural Information Processing Systems*, •••, 29.

Samuel, A. L. (1959). Some studies in machine learning using the game of checkers. *IBM Journal of Research and Development*, *3*(3), 210–229. DOI: 10.1147/rd.33.0210

Schmidhuber, J. (1991). A possibility for implementing curiosity and boredom in model-building neural controllers. In *Proc. of the international conference on simulation of adaptive behavior: From animals to animats* (pp. 222-227). DOI: 10.7551/mitpress/3115.003.0030

Shokri, R., Stronati, M., Song, C., & Shmatikov, V. (2017). Membership inference attacks against machine learning models. In *2017 IEEE symposium on security and privacy (SP)* (pp. 3-18). IEEE. DOI: 10.1109/SP.2017.41

Szegedy, C., Zaremba, W., Sutskever, I., Bruna, J., Erhan, D., Goodfellow, I., & Fergus, R. (2013). Intriguing properties of neural networks. *arXiv preprint arXiv*:1312.6199.

Tesauro, G. (1992). Practical Issues in Temporal Difference Learning. *Machine Learning*, *8*(3-4), 257–277. DOI: 10.1007/BF00992697

Thanh-Tung, H., Tran, T., & Venkatesh, S. (2019). Improving generalization and stability of generative adversarial networks. *arXiv preprint* arXiv:1902.03984.

Toutouh, J., Hemberg, E., & O'Reilly, U. M. (2019). Spatial evolutionary generative adversarial networks. In *Proceedings of the genetic and evolutionary computation conference* (pp. 472-480). DOI: 10.1145/3321707.3321860

Tramèr, F., Kurakin, A., Papernot, N., Goodfellow, I., Boneh, D., & McDaniel, P. (2017). Ensemble adversarial training: Attacks and defenses. *arXiv preprint* arXiv:1705.07204.

Wiatrak, M., Albrecht, S. V., & Nystrom, A. (2019). Stabilizing generative adversarial networks: A survey. *arXiv preprint* arXiv:1910.00927.

Wilson, A. C., Roelofs, R., Stern, M., Srebro, N., & Recht, B. (2017). The marginal value of adaptive gradient methods in machine learning. *Advances in Neural Information Processing Systems*, •••, 30.

Xu, J., Wang, Y., Chen, H., & Shen, Z. (2025). Adversarial Machine Learning in Cybersecurity: Attacks and Defenses. *International Journal of Management Science Research*, *8*(2), 26–33.

Yang, L., Zhang, Z., Song, Y., Hong, S., Xu, R., Zhao, Y., Zhang, W., Cui, B., & Yang, M. H. (2023). Diffusion models: A comprehensive survey of methods and applications. *ACM Computing Surveys*, *56*(4), 1–39. DOI: 10.1145/3626235

Zhang, H., Yu, Y., Jiao, J., Xing, E., El Ghaoui, L., & Jordan, M. (2019). Theoretically principled trade-off between robustness and accuracy. In *International conference on machine learning* (pp. 7472-7482). PMLR.

Zhang, T., Wang, J., & Meng, M. Q. H. (2021). Generative adversarial network-based heuristics for sampling-based path planning. *IEEE/CAA Journal of Automatica Sinica*, 9(1), 64-74.

Zhao, P., Shan, J. W., Zhang, Y. J., & Zhou, Z. H. (2024). Exploratory machine learning with unknown unknowns. *Artificial Intelligence*, *327*, 104059. DOI: 10.1016/j.artint.2023.104059

Chapter 4
Adversarial Machine Learning in Cybersecurity:
Threat Detection, Defense Mechanisms, and Ethical Issues

Vikram Singh
https://orcid.org/0000-0001-5757-9111
Ch. Devi Lal University, Sirsa, India

Sanyogita Singh
Government College, Malerkotla, India

ABSTRACT

With the evolution and penetration of AI and ML into almost all critical public life domains including cybersecurity, the cybercrime ecosystem attempts to tap the vulnerabilities in AI-based cybersecurity systems by invoking adversarial machine learning, which has posed a significant challenge to cyber-physical security systems employing ML. Kitty of AML techniques, as the nomenclature itself indicates, take advantage of vulnerabilities in machine learning models. Cybercriminals manipulate input vectors to carry out their evil intent and evade their detection. The proposed chapter investigates the core concepts in adversarial machine learning, its implications in the arena of cybersecurity, and mitigation of these cyberthreats. Attack methodologies, detection strategies, and defence mechanisms have been studied in this chapter. Additionally, the ethical and legal challenges are discussed to comprehend the evolutionary discipline of adversarial machine learning in cyber-physical cyber-digital security.

DOI: 10.4018/979-8-3373-2200-1.ch004

INTRODUCTION

The digital world of the day is marked by the fast and seamless communication between inter-connected smart systems, from smart cities and homes to industrial control systems and self-driving cars (Atzori, Iera, & Morabito, 2010). While this interconnectivity brings unrivalled convenience and efficiency, it has significantly expanded the attack surface for cyber threats (Syed, Sierra-Sosa, Kumar, & Elmaghraby, 2021). The emergence of these smart environments has changed the paradigm in cybersecurity, which requires new kinds of methods for safeguarding valuable data and crucial infrastructure. Nevertheless, the same nature of such smart environments imposes special security and privacy challenges. The aggregation and analysis of immense amounts of information, much of which is sensitive and personal, have serious privacy issues (Weber, 2010). Cases in point are smart home devices and smart city sensors which can unwittingly record and share intimate conversations and monitor people's locations and activities, respectively. The distributed and diverse nature of these smart systems further complicates their overall security since a weak link in the security chain can make the entire system vulnerable (Alrawi, Lever, Antonakakis, & Monrose, 2019). This is also exacerbated by the fact that most IoT devices are equipped with minimal security features, making them vulnerable to malicious attacks.

Conventional security measures, including firewalls and intrusion detection systems, tend to be ineffective in countering the sophisticated and changing threats in intelligent environments (Liao, Lin, Lin, & Tung, 2013). Run-of-the-mill security measures typically rely on static protocols and vulnerability signatures, which, the advanced attack vectors can easily evade. Managing high volumes of data produced by intelligent and smart systems poses another challenge in these security systems, resulting in performance bottlenecks and overlooked threats. The shortcomings of these conventional approaches highlight the necessity for more adaptive and smart security measures. In this regard, machine learning (ML) has been a strong ally in bolstering cybersecurity (Buczak & Guven, 2016). ML algorithms are capable of processing huge datasets to recognize subtle patterns and anomalies that could be indicative of malicious activity, thus enhancing the accuracy and speed of threat detection. For instance, ML can be employed to identify unusual network traffic, recognize malware by its behaviour, and forecast possible cyberattacks (Ferrag, Maglaras, Janicke, & Jiang, 2020). In addition, ML can be used to create adaptive security systems that are able to learn and adapt to shifting threat profiles.

Yet, implementing ML in cybersecurity comes with additional challenges, specifically adversarial machine learning. Adversaries can manipulate inputs to mislead ML-based security systems, necessitating strong defence systems (Carlini & Wagner, 2017). Growing dependency on machine learning in cybersecurity has transformed threat response and detection with capabilities that are unmatched in the areas of anomaly detection, malware categorization, and intrusion detection (Buczak & Guven, 2016). ML algorithms, having been trained on large data sets, are capable of distinguishing intricate patterns suggesting malicious behaviour and thus improving the security stance of key systems. Nevertheless, the inherent characteristics of such models make them susceptible to adversarial attacks, in which attackers manipulate input data maliciously to mislead the ML system (Carlini & Wagner, 2017). The susceptibility to this vulnerability creates an important challenge in that the adversarial strengths may be exploited to circumvent security controls and threaten sensitive information. Adversarial machine learning (AML) in cyber security involves the exploration of these vulnerabilities and the construction of effective defence systems.

Attacks can be as simple as data poisoning, where training data is tampered with, to complex evasion attacks, where inputs are crafted to deceive the deployed model (Goodfellow, Shlens, & Szegedy, 2014). For example, in network intrusion detection systems, the attackers can produce adversarial network traffic intended to simulate normal behaviour and therefore go undetected (Sommer & Paxson, 2010). These attacks cost very dearly, as they can render the ML-based security systems ineffective, resulting in grave consequences in terms of compromised data and other system resources. Emergence of the adversarial machine learning attacks has forced the smart system security community to work out commensurate defence mechanisms such as adversarial training, input sanitization, and anomaly detection (Liang, He, Zhao, Jia, & Li, 2022). Adversarial training is, for instance, where one adds the adversarial examples into the training data to make the model more resistant to these kinds of attacks.

But the race between adversarial attacks and defences continues, with every improvement in defence triggering more advanced attacks. Technical issues apart, the emergence of AML in the cybersecurity arena also presents some notable ethical concerns. The malicious use of adversarial methods has given rise to serious ethical concerns as well (Mittelstadt, Allo, Taddeo, Wachter, & Floridi, 2016). Protecting the privacy of individual stakeholders is another dimension of the problem at hand. The present chapter attempts to present a thorough discussion on adversarial machine learning in smart system security, discussing various threat mechanisms, approaches to their detection and defence mechanisms, and relevant ethical issues. This chapter explores the characteristics of general adversarial attacks, discusses the effectiveness of common defence mechanisms and the ethical issues accompanying the use of ML-based security solutions to thwart AML attacks. An understanding of the abovementioned issues can lead to more resilient and reliable cybersecurity solutions in the era of advanced machine learning.

ADVERSARIAL MACHINE LEARNING

The growing use of machine learning in mission-critical systems, especially in cybersecurity, has brought with it a new era of advanced threats. Adversarial machine learning has become an important area of research, with a focus on the vulnerabilities of ML models to deliberate manipulation. It is paramount to have an understanding of the concept of adversarial machine learning attacks, their types, and their significance in security scenarios for creating strong and resilient smart systems. Adversarial machine learning is the conscious attempt to manipulate artificial intelligence and machine learning models or their input data instances to mislead these models to produce incorrect output (Papernot, McDaniel, Sinha, & Wellman, 2018). These attacks fundamentally differ from traditional software vulnerabilities, for AML attacks seek to take (dis)advantage of the statistical nature of these models.

These models, though strong at pattern recognition, can be vulnerable to small-scale perturbations in input data that change their predictions. The central idea is that ML models, having been trained on finite data sets, do not necessarily generalize fully to all potential inputs and therefore are susceptible to specially designed adversarial examples (Goodfellow, Shlens, & Szegedy, 2014). The idea contradicts the assumption that ML models are robust by default and emphasizes understanding their weaknesses more deeply. AML is not confined to image classification alone; it applies to a wide range of areas, such as natural language processing, speech recognition, and, most importantly, cybersecurity, where the cost of model failure is exponentially high.

Mathematical Background of AML

AML includes methods in which an attacker manipulates machine learning models by adding well-designed perturbations. These attacks take advantage of weaknesses in ML models, particularly deep learning models, resulting in erroneous predictions. This section explains the precise mathematical formulation of adversarial attacks, with emphasis on popular attack methods like gradient-based attacks, optimization-based attacks, and decision-boundary-based attacks.

Adversarial Perturbations

In machine learning, a classifier $f = \mathbb{R}^n \rightarrow \mathbb{R}^C$ maps an input x from an n-dimensional space $\mathbb{R}^n$ to a probability distribution over C possible classes. The classifier assigns the input vector a class label $\hat{y}$, which is determined using eq. (*i*).

$$\hat{y} = arg\ max_j f_j(x) \text{ (i)}$$

where $f_j(x)$ represents the probability (or confidence score) assigned to the class j.

Clean input: $x \in \mathbb{R}^n$. It is the original input data instance.
True label: $y \in \{1, \ldots, C\}$. It is the actual class label.
Classifier prediction: $f(x) = \hat{y} = arg\ max_j f_j(x)$, is the predicted class label.
Loss function: $\mathcal{L}(f(x), y)$ denotes a function measuring the difference between the predicted and actual class labels. Cross-entropy loss is commonly used for classification problems.

An adversarial attack aims to find a small perturbation δ (eq. *ii*) such that:

$$\hat{y}_{adv} = arg\ max_j f_j(x + \delta) \neq y \text{ (ii)}$$

Where δ is constrained by a perturbation budget $\|\delta\|_p \leq \varepsilon$, with p typically being l_p *norm*.

This implies that, following the application of perturbation, the classifier classifies the input as a new (wrong) class, thus deceiving the model. Adversarial perturbations reveal the sensitivity of machine learning models to slight manipulations and highlight the importance of strong defences such as adversarial training, input preprocessing, and defensive distillation. Knowledge of these attacks is important for enhancing model security, especially in high-risk applications such as cybersecurity, medicine, and autonomous systems.

Fast Gradient Sign Method (FGSM)

The FGSM is arguably the easiest and most popular type of adversarial attack method. It effectively produces adversarial examples by taking advantage of the vulnerability of machine learning, and especially deep learning, models to minor perturbations in inputs. The principle behind FGSM is to introduce minimal changes to an input in the direction of the gradient for the purpose of maximizing the prediction error of the model. The method mathematically described in eq. (*iii*) generates adversarial data points by maximizing the loss with respect to x:

$$\delta = \varepsilon \bullet sign(\nabla_x \mathcal{L}(f(x), y)) \text{ (iii)}$$

$$x_{adv} = x + \delta$$

where:

ε is a scaling factor that controls the magnitude of the perturbation. A small ε ensures the modification remains imperceptible to humans, while a larger ε can lead to more noticeable changes.

$\nabla_x \mathcal{L}(f(x), y)$ represents the gradient of the loss function $\mathcal{L}$ with respect to the input x. This gradient indicates the direction in which the input should be altered to increase the loss, making the model more likely to misclassify the input.

FGSM is a fast and computationally efficient attack, making it practical for real-time adversarial attacks. It is one-step and non-iterative, unlike more sophisticated methods such as Carlini & Wagner attacks (discussed next). The strength of the attack is controlled by the parameter ε, which determines the magnitude of the perturbation. A higher ε results in a stronger attack but also makes the adversarial changes more noticeable. Due to its simplicity, FGSM is frequently used as a baseline attack to assess the robustness of machine learning models against adversarial threats. It highlights the vulnerability of deep learning systems and underscores the need for robust defence mechanisms.

Projected Gradient Descent (PGD)

PGD is an iterative adversarial attack that refines perturbations over multiple steps to maximize the loss function, leading to more effective adversarial data points compared to single-step attacks like FGSM. PGD is considered the strongest first-order attack and is widely used to evaluate the robustness of deep-learning models. At each iteration, PGD updates the adversarial example by taking a small step in the direction of the gradient of the loss function with respect to the input. Mathematically, the update rule is given by eq. (*iv*):

$$x_{adv}^{(t+1)} = \prod_{B_\epsilon(x)} \left(x_{adv}^{(t)} + \alpha \bullet sign\left(\nabla_x L(f(x_{adv}^{(t)}), y)\right)\right) \text{(iv)}$$

where:

$x_{adv}^{(t)}$ is the adversarial input at iteration t.

α is the step size that controls how much the perturbation is updated in each step.

$\nabla_x L\left(f\left(x_{adv}^{(t)}\right), y\right)$ is the gradient of the loss function L with respect to the input x.

sign($\bullet$)ensures the perturbation moves in the direction that maximally increases the loss.

$\prod_{B_\epsilon(x)}(.)$ is a projection operation that ensures the adversarial example remains within an ε-ball around the original input x, preventing excessive distortion.

At the start of the attack, the adversarial example is initialized as eq. (*v*):

$$x_{adv}^{(0)} = x \text{ (v)}$$

After multiple iterations, the final adversarial example x_{adv} is obtained, which is designed to be misclassified by the model. PGD can be formulated as an optimization problem where the goal is to maximize the loss function under an ℓ_∞-norm constraint (eq. *vi*):

$$\max_{\|\delta\|_\infty \leq \varepsilon} L\left(f(x+\delta), y\right) \text{ (vi)}$$

where:

> δ is the perturbation added to the input x.
> $\|\delta\|_\infty \leq \varepsilon$ constrains the perturbation magnitude within a predefined bound ε.
> The loss function L (commonly cross-entropy) quantifies the model's prediction error.

To solve this optimization, PGD applies projected gradient ascent. Each step moves x_{adv} in the direction that increases the loss, and projection ensures the adversarial example remains within the allowed perturbation region. Unlike FGSM, which perturbs the input in one step, PGD takes multiple small steps, making it more effective in finding stronger adversarial examples. A small step size ensures a gradual and controlled increase in perturbation, preventing the attack from being easily countered. The projection step ensures the perturbation does not exceed the allowed bound, maintaining stealthiness. Since FGSM is a one-step attack, it may not always find the strongest perturbation within the allowed range. PGD, by iterating over multiple steps, has a better chance of finding an adversarial example that effectively misleads the model. Further, PGD can be seen as a multi-step refinement of FGSM when the number of iterations is set to '1' and the step size is equal to ε.

Carlini and Wagner (C&W) Attack

The C&W attack is a powerful adversarial attack that formulates the problem of generating adversarial examples as an optimization problem. Instead of simply adding a small perturbation to the input, this attack carefully crafts the perturbation δ to be both effective (misleading the classifier) and imperceptible to humans. The goal is to find the smallest possible perturbation that forces the model to misclassify the input. The C&W attack seeks to minimize the magnitude of the perturbation δ

while ensuring that the modified input $x + \delta$ leads to incorrect classification. This is expressed as eq. (*vii*):

$$\min_{\delta} \|\delta\|_p + c \cdot \mathcal{L}(f(x + \delta), y) \quad \text{(vii)}$$

subject to:

$$x + \delta \in [0, 1]^n$$

where:

$\|\delta\|_p$ represents the perturbation's norm, ensuring it remains minimal and barely noticeable.

c is a trade-off parameter that balances two objectives: the strength of the attack and the perceptibility of the perturbation. A higher c increases misclassification likelihood but may make the perturbation more visible.

Using logits $Z(x)$, the attack minimizes $\mathcal{L}$ (eq. *viii*):

$$\mathcal{L} = \max\left(0, Z(x + \delta)_y - \max_{j \neq y} Z(x + \delta)_j + \kappa\right) \quad \text{(viii)}$$

where:

κ is a confidence parameter that controls how confidently the model misclassifies the adversarial example. A higher κ results in adversarial examples that are harder to detect but also more transferable across models.

The term $Z(x + \delta)_y - \max_{j \neq y} Z(x + \delta)_j$ ensures that the adversarial input fools the classifier by reducing the model's confidence in the correct class y and increasing confidence in an incorrect class.

The optimal perturbation δ is computed using either Adam optimizer – an adaptive gradient-based optimization method that efficiently finds perturbations, or L-BFGS (Limited-memory Broyden–Fletcher–Goldfarb–Shanno algorithm) – a quasi-Newton optimization technique that is particularly useful for constrained optimization problems.

DeepFool Attack

These adversarial attacks work by gradually adjusting the input x in small steps until it reaches the closest decision boundary, thereby minimizing the perturbation required to fool the classifier. The goal is to find the smallest possible change δ that forces the model to misclassify the input.

For a linear classifier $f(x) = w^\top x + b$, where w represents the weight vector and b is the bias term, the perturbation δ required to push the input across the decision boundary is computed as eq. (*ix*):

$$\delta = -\frac{f(x)}{\|w\|_2^2} w \text{ (ix)}$$

This formula ensures that x moves in a direction that minimally alters its classification while still crossing the boundary.

For nonlinear classifiers, where the decision boundary is more complex, the DeepFool attack applies this process iteratively. Instead of a single-step perturbation, the method gradually refines x by repeatedly applying small perturbations $\delta^{(t)}$ at each iteration t, updating the adversarial example as eq. (*x*):

$$x_{adv}^{(t+1)} = x_{adv}^{(t)} + \delta^{(t)} \text{ (x)}$$

This iterative process continues until the classifier's prediction for x_{adv} (i.e. $f\left(x_{adv}\right)$) changes, meaning the perturbed input has successfully crossed the decision boundary. By systematically identifying the nearest boundary and making minimal adjustments, DeepFool effectively finds the smallest perturbation needed to mislead the model.

Types of Adversarial Attacks

Adversarial attacks are typically classified based on their goal, attacker's knowledge, and the point when they are deployed.

Evasion attacks: Evasion attacks form a category of adversarial attacks performed after deployment, at the inference phase of a machine learning system. In this case, an adversary develops targeted input perturbations with the aim of causing misclassification while not modifying the underlying model parameters. The groundbreaking work of Carlini and Wagner (2017) showed that it was possible to create imperceptible perturbations that could mislead deep neural networks. In the case of malware detection, for example, an attacker could quietly alter the binary code of an offending file by changing certain features without compromising its malicious behaviour. This altered file, when given to an ML-based antivirus, could be mislabelled as harmless, thereby evading the security mechanism. The essential feature of evasion attacks is that they can avoid deployed defences without needing access to the training data or model architecture, rendering them especially malicious. These attacks point towards the susceptibility of ML models towards minor input perturbations, and there is a need for strong defence strategies to identify and counter such attacks.

Poisoning attacks: Poisoning attacks aim towards the integrity of the ML model at the time of training. An attacker intentionally introduces malicious or tainted data into the training set with the motive of hacking the learning process of the model and creating biases or weaknesses. This is a kind of attack, as described by Liang et al. (2022), which can have long-lasting impacts, as the tainted model may keep misclassifying genuine data or be incapable of recognizing malicious activity. The effects of poisoning attacks are most serious in federated learning systems, where diverse parties contribute to data during training (Bonawitz et al., 2019). In this scenario, a compromised participant can introduce poisoned data, harming the global model with relative impunity. Federated learning's distributed nature exacerbates the difficulty of detecting and combating poisoning attacks, requiring strong aggregation techniques and anomaly detection methods to maintain data integrity.

Model extraction attacks: Model extraction attacks are the adversary's effort to rebuild the architecture or parameters of a target ML model by querying it with different inputs and monitoring the resulting outputs. This is done, as shown by Tramèr et al. (2016), to build a replacement model that closely resembles the original, which can be used to develop effective adversarial examples. This attack is of serious concern to proprietary or sensitive ML models, as it enables attackers to duplicate their functionality without having direct access to their training data or architecture. The model extracted can subsequently be utilized to produce adversarial examples that will likely fool the original model, compromising its security. Model extraction attacks underscore the need to guard model intellectual property and create mechanisms for model unauthorized replication detection and prevention.

Adversarial reprogramming: Adversarial reprogramming is a method that entails reusing a pre-trained ML model for a use distinct from its primary intent. This is done by designing special input perturbations that exploit the learned model features, thereby controlling its behaviour. Elsayed et al. (2018) proved this technique to be viable, pointing to its usefulness for evading defences or eliciting undesirable model behaviour. The attack is best used in environments where pre-trained models are a subsystem component used to construct higher-level systems. The adversary would rewrite the model in order to manipulate the complete behaviour of the system, most likely causing the system to have security vulnerabilities or break down completely. Adversarial reprogramming places a premium on vigilant consideration of the possibility of model repurposing in unforeseen ways and on the formulation of strong defence measures that are able to detect and counter such attacks.

Backdoor attacks: Backdoor attacks include the placement of concealed triggers or backdoors into an ML model during training. When the particular trigger is included in the input data, the model generates a desired (but frequently erroneous) output, essentially bypassing its standard behaviour. Gu et al. (2017) proved the possibility of injecting backdoors into deep neural networks, highlighting the potential for nefarious manipulation. This kind of attack can be very hard to identify, since the model functions normally when the trigger is not present. Backdoor attacks represent a major threat to security-critical applications, where attackers can remotely control the model's output to advance their goals. These attacks reinforce the need for guaranteeing the integrity of the training process and creating methods for detecting and mitigating concealed triggers in ML models.

Cybersecurity and AML

The incorporation of machine learning into cybersecurity processes has become unavoidable, providing enhanced features in intrusion detection, malware analysis, spam filtering, and fraud detection (Buczak & Guven, 2016). ML algorithms, set to work on huge datasets, can identify intricate patterns that are indicative of malicious activity, thus improving the effectiveness of security systems. Yet, the natural vulnerabilities revealed through adversarial machine learning are especially dangerous, possibly undermining the very systems they seek to support. The implications of these vulnerabilities are deep and multifaceted.

Compromised threat detection: Adversarial attacks can make it possible for attackers to deceive input data, essentially evading ML-based defences. This can result in uncaught intrusions, malware infection, and other cyber attacks. In critical infrastructure like power grids, transportation systems, and financial networks, the impact of successful attacks can be disastrous. A fine-grained manipulation of network traffic patterns, for instance, may go undetected by intrusion detection systems, providing an adversary with unauthorized access to sabotage critical services. This highlights the need for effective adversarial defence mechanisms that can identify and counter these advanced attacks.

Privacy invasions and data breaches: AML methods can be used to pull sensitive data from ML models or alter data to breach privacy. Model inversion attacks, for example, can restore training data, disclosing confidential information. Adversarial examples can similarly be designed to evade privacy-protecting techniques, such as differential privacy or federated learning. In medical care systems, for instance, attackers would be able to employ model inversion to build up patient medical history, causing major privacy violations. The threat of such invasions indicates the requirement of strong privacy-maintaining methods and moral principles in deploying and developing ML-based security solutions.

Loss of trust: Vulnerability of ML models to adversarial attacks has the potential to lead to the loss of public trust in such systems, especially in security-relevant applications. This can discourage the implementation of ML-based security solutions, even where they have a strong competitive advantage over existing methods. In financial services, for instance, fears regarding the robustness of fraud detection systems may dissuade their implementation, and as a result, result in higher fraud losses. Restoring and sustaining trust in ML-based security systems involves creating strong and transparent defences and publicly explaining the capacities and limitations of these systems.

Arms race dynamics: Endless adversarial attack and defence innovation causes an arms race, with every defence innovation triggering the development of more advanced attacks. This interplay requires ongoing research and innovation to keep ML-based security systems effective. The creation of adaptive adversarial attacks, for instance, calls for the creation of adaptive defence methods that can respond to these attacks. This ongoing evolution highlights the necessity of a proactive and adaptive strategy to cybersecurity, where researchers and practitioners continually seek new attack and defence methods.

Ethical issues: AML gives rise to some serious ethical issues, especially on the misuse potential of adversarial methods. Having strong defence strategies must be balanced against the protection of malicious application of these methods (Mittelstadt, Allo, Taddeo, Wachter, & Floridi, 2016). The possibility of targeted attacks against particular individuals or organizations, say, requires sound consideration of ethical implications. In addition, the emergence of explainable AI (XAI) methods is necessary for providing transparency and accountability for ML-based security solutions so that biases or errors can be identified and mitigated.

By comprehending the intricate relationship between cybersecurity and AML, researchers and practitioners can develop more robust and resilient ML-based security systems. This understanding is crucial for ensuring the safety and security of our digital infrastructure, mitigating the risks posed by adversarial attacks and fostering trust in these essential technologies.

MACHINE LEARNING IN THREAT DETECTION

The ubiquitous adoption of networked smart systems has created an intricate and dynamic threat landscape, requiring the use of advanced detection frameworks. Conventional security measures, based on static rule-based approaches, are often found wanting in their ability to handle the subtle and dynamic nature of cyber penetrations in these environments. As a result, machine learning has become a prominent technological tool for enhancing threat detection capacity in smart systems, making it easier to detect fine-grained anomalies, analyze network traffic patterns, recognize behavioural patterns, and achieve real-time threat detection.

Machine Learning-based Anomaly Detection

Anomaly detection, or the identification of data patterns that markedly differ from set norms, takes on pivotal significance in smart system environments, where baseline activity can have wide variation (Chandola, Banerjee, & Kumar, 2009). Machine learning-based anomaly detection techniques allow for the automated derivation of normal behaviour distributions from large datasets, then marking deviations as indicative of possible malicious activity. These methods show special effectiveness in identifying zero-day exploits, which are unknown attacks. Supervised learning models are applied when there is labelled anomaly information. Decision trees, random forests, and neural network algorithms are typical examples.

Decision trees and random forests learn decision rules from labelled data and classify anomalies effectively (Breiman, 2001). Neural networks are capable of learning intricate patterns and can obtain high accuracy if there is ample labelled data (Lecun, Bengio, & Hinton, 2015). Supervised learning's effectiveness is reliant on labelled data quality, but when adequately trained, they provide high recall and precision. Unsupervised learning models work well in cases where there is limited labelled anomaly data. Models such as autoencoders, isolation forests, and one-class support vector machines (SVMs) are leading examples.

Autoencoders, for example, learn to reconstruct typical data with high accuracy but are poor at anomalies, resulting in high reconstruction error scores (Hinton & Salakhutdinov, 2006). Isolation forests effectively separate anomalies by taking advantage of their uniqueness and lower frequency (Liu, Ting, & Zhou, 2008). One-class SVMs seek to establish a boundary around typical data, labelling outliers as anomalies (Schölkopf et al., 2001). The benefit of unsupervised learning is that it can identify new anomalies, but it relies on the quality of normal data. Semi-supervised learning is a combination of supervised and unsupervised learning, utilizing limited labelled data and a large amount of unlabelled data. Methods such as self-training and co-training are employed. Self-training labels unlabelled data iteratively according to model predictions (Zhu, 2005). Co-training employs multiple models to label unlabelled data (Blum & Mitchell, 1998). Semi-supervised learning is beneficial when labelled anomalies are limited. Network Traffic Analysis

Network traffic analysis is a foundation of cybersecurity, particularly in smart systems where network connectivity is ubiquitous. Having the capacity to analyze network traffic patterns in real-time or near real-time allows for the identification of anomalies and malicious activity that would otherwise go undetected. Machine learning methods have greatly improved the potential of network traffic analysis, allowing for more advanced and automated means of threat detection.

ML-based intrusion detection systems (IDS) have transformed how network packet data is processed for security threats. Traditional signature-based IDS are restricted when it comes to detecting new types of attack vectors, while ML-based IDS have the capability of learning known as well as unknown attack patterns. Algorithms like decision trees, SVMs, and neural networks are used to train models capable of classifying network traffic as benign or malicious (Liao, Lin, Lin, & Tung, 2013). Decision trees and random forests, for instance, can develop rule-based models that pick out specific features characteristic of malicious activity, such as out-of-syncretic packet sizes or protocol anomalies. SVMs are capable of establishing a hyperplane to distinguish between normal traffic and anomalous traffic, even in feature spaces of high dimensions. Neural networks, especially deep learning systems, are able to learn sophisticated non-linear patterns in network traffic data, which can be used to identify insidious and sophisticated attacks. The advancement of IDS to include ML has significantly enhanced the detection and response to contemporary cyber threats. Deep learning for network traffic analysis: Deep learning algorithms, specifically Convolutional Neural Networks (CNNs) and Recurrent Neural Networks (RNNs), have revolutionized network traffic analysis. CNNs can well capture spatial dependencies within network traffic data, e.g., patterns in packet payloads or headers.

RNNs, however, can effectively identify temporal dependencies, important for the discovery of sequential patterns of attacks (Ferrag, Maglaras, Janicke, & Jiang, 2020). For instance, RNNs, more so Long Short-Term Memory (LSTM) networks, can inspect sets of network packets to discover sequences characteristic of such attacks as distributed denial-of-service (DDoS) attacks or advanced persistent threats. CNNs can be employed to scan packet payloads for malicious code or signatures, even when they are obfuscated or encrypted. Deep learning models offer a rich set of tools for examining the dynamic and intricate nature of network traffic, allowing for the detection of advanced attack methods that would otherwise go unnoticed by conventional security controls. Flow-based analysis: Flow-based analysis gives an overall view of network traffic at the connection level, aggregating network activity into flow records holding details like source and destination IP addresses, ports, and protocols. ML algorithms can process these flow records to detect anomalies and malicious behaviour.

This method has a number of benefits, including high efficiency and scalability, making it ideal for large-scale deployments in networks. By examining flow data, ML algorithms can detect patterns of abnormal network activity, like aberrant traffic rates, atypical patterns of connection, or protocol deviations. This method is especially effective for discovering network-wide attacks, like DDoS attacks or botnet activity. Flow analysis can also be utilized to detect insider threats, like unauthorized data exfiltration or lateral movement across the network. The capacity to examine network traffic at the flow level is a valuable resource for network security professionals, allowing them to see networks in operation and detect possible threats. Behavioural Pattern Recognition Behavioural pattern recognition is a significant element of contemporary cybersecurity, concentrating on the examination of user, device, and system behaviour to recognize divergences from previously set standards.

Machine learning methodologies are critical to this field as they allow automated learning of typical behavioural patterns and subsequent anomaly detection that could lead to malicious actions. It is especially useful for insider threats, zero-day exploits, and other advanced security compromises that might elude traditional signature-based detection tools. User behaviour analytics: User behaviour analytics (UBA) tools use ML to examine user activity logs and offer insights into patterns of behaviour that potentially compromise security. UBA tools can identify unusual behaviour, including attempted unauthorized access, strange login times or locations, data exfiltration, and other behaviours that do not conform to defined user profiles (Ahmed, Nazeeruddin, & Hashem, 2016).

For example, an ML-enabled UBA solution may scan logins, file access logs, and network patterns to create a baseline of expected user behaviour. When a user's activity does not match the baseline, as in accessing critical files outside standard work hours or moving large files to external media, the solution can alert that activity as a potential security risk. UBA is most effective against insider threats, in which malicious individuals using legitimate access credentials try to compromise sensitive information or systems. Device behaviour analysis: Device behaviour analysis in the Internet of Things (IoT) is critical in maintaining the security and integrity of connected devices. ML methods are used to inspect the behaviour of such devices for anomalies like the execution of commands not authorized, unanticipated data transmission patterns, and hijacking of devices.

ML systems could inspect the patterns of communication from a smart thermostat, identifying anomalies like abrupt peaks in data transmission or attempts at unauthorized access. In the same way, the system may monitor the behaviour of a security camera and identify anomalous activity like unusual rotation of the camera or misuse of video feeds. Device behaviour analysis is important for discovering and preventing attacks on IoT devices, which tend to be compromised because they have limited security capabilities. System behaviour analysis: System behaviour analysis is the analysis of system performance metrics and logs to identify unusual behaviours that might point to security threats. Machine learning methods are employed to set up baselines of normal system behaviour, thus making it possible to identify departures that can signal resource depletion, process hijacking, or system intrusions.

For example, an ML-based system may examine system logs to identify unusual process behaviour, including the running of unauthorized processes or changes to key system files. In addition, the system may examine performance metrics like CPU usage, memory usage, and network traffic to identify anomalies such as abrupt peaks in resource usage or unexpected patterns of network traffic. System behaviour analysis is critical for identifying and preventing attacks on key systems, and maintaining their availability and integrity. Real-Time Threat Identification In the networked world of intelligent systems, where cyber attacks can spread quickly and do extensive harm, real-time threat detection is critical. Having the capability to detect and respond to threats in real-time is critical to keeping critical infrastructure and sensitive information secure and resilient. Machine learning has transformed real-time threat detection, allowing for automated analysis of enormous volumes of data and quick identification of anomalies and malicious behaviour.

Streaming data analysis entails the ongoing processing of data as it occurs, allowing the identification of threats in real-time. ML algorithms are appropriate for this purpose, allowing for the analysis of streaming data from numerous sources, such as sensors, network traffic, and system logs (Gama, Žliobaitė, Pechenizkiy, & Bifet, 2014). For instance, in a smart city scenario, ML algorithms can mine streaming data from traffic sensors and identify anomalies indicative of traffic light tampering or other security intrusions. In industrial IoT (IIoT) scenarios, streaming data from sensors that are monitoring machine conditions can be examined to identify anomalies that could signify imminent equipment breakdowns or cyberattacks. This method is especially important for identifying time-critical attacks, like denial-of-service (DoS) attacks or zero-day attacks, where immediate response is required. Edge computing: Edge computing entails the distribution of ML models at the network edge, near the data sources. This method allows real-time threat detection and mitigation without the need for centralized cloud resources, which can add latency and bandwidth constraints.

Edge computing is especially useful in IoT scenarios, where devices produce high amounts of data and network connectivity is not always consistent. For example, in a smart home scenario, ML models can be instantiated on edge devices like routers or gateways to monitor network traffic and identify anomalies in real-time. In IIoT environments, edge devices may examine sensor data to identify abnormalities and produce real-time responses, for example, by shutting down equipment or informing operators. By doing so, latency is minimized, bandwidth is saved, and the robustness of smart systems is improved, making possible fast responses to cyberattacks. Reinforcement learning: Reinforcement learning algorithms provide the capability of adaptive learning for threat landscapes to allow systems to make real-time decisions for attacking mitigation (Swapno, Nobel, Meena, et al. 2024). Agents for reinforcement learning can learn dynamically to modify security policies and network settings based on observed threats for improved adaptability and resilience for smart systems.

For instance, Reinforcement learning agents may be employed to dynamically update firewall rules or intrusion detection system parameters based on observed network abnormalities. Reinforcement learning can similarly be employed to optimize network routing to counter the effect of DDoS attacks or other network anomalies. This strategy allows for intelligent systems to evolve in response to changing threat environments and make wise decisions in real-time, bolstering their security posture. Through these ML-based approaches, intelligent systems can considerably advance their threat detection capacities, providing security and reliability for crucial infrastructure and confidential information. Threat detection in real-time is critical to preserve the integrity and availability of contemporary digital infrastructures.

DEFENCE AGAINST ADVERSARIAL ATTACKS

The vulnerability of machine learning models to adversarial manipulation calls for the creation and deployment of reliable defence mechanisms. This part examines some of the most well-known approaches intended to improve the robustness of ML systems to adversarial attacks, such as developing robust models, adversarial training methods, defensive distillation, input validation and sanitization, and ensemble techniques.

Robust Machine Learning Models

The creation of strong machine learning models is a core approach in avoiding adversarial vulnerabilities. Such models are made to be resistant to small, deliberate perturbations in input data, so that they can still make correct predictions even when there are adversarial examples. This resilience is necessary for the application of ML models in security-critical applications, where adversarial attacks can have serious implications.

Certified robustness: Certified robustness methods seek to give formal, mathematical assurances that the predictions of a model will be stable within given perturbation limits. Methods like interval bound propagation and semidefinite relaxation are employed for this purpose (Wong & Kolter, 2018). Interval bound propagation propagates interval bounds through the layers of a neural network, giving upper and lower bounds on the output of every layer. This enables model robustness verification in given input perturbation ranges. Semidefinite relaxation is reformulating the problem of robustness verification as a semidefinite program, solvable to obtain formal guarantees on model robustness. Although certified robustness approaches provide strong guarantees of model resilience, they come at the expense of decreased model accuracy or scalability. The computational complexity of these approaches can restrict their use on large-scale models or datasets. They are nonetheless precious in high-stakes contexts where robustness is guaranteed to be needed.

Regularization methods: Regularization methods are employed to limit the complexity of ML models, hence making them less sensitive to input perturbations. Techniques like L1 and L2 regularization are widely utilized. L1 regularization includes a penalty term in the model's loss function, proportional to the absolute values of the model's weights. This induces sparsity, essentially shrinking the number of features feeding into the model's predictions. L2 regularization includes a penalty term proportional to the square values of the model's weights, inducing smaller weights and smoother decision boundaries. By simplifying the model, regularization methods encourage smoother decision boundaries, which improve model generalization and resilience. Such methods can prevent the effect of adversarial perturbations by minimizing the model's sensitivity to minor input data alterations. Regularization is a very standard method to enhance generalization, which is a fundamental aspect of resilience.

Bayesian neural networks: Bayesian neural networks embed uncertainty estimation into predictions made by the model, with an assessment of confidence in the event of adversarial examples (Gal & Ghahramani, 2016). Bayesian neural networks can allow for the detection of potentially adversarial inputs, thereby enabling suitable mitigation responses. Bayesian neural networks frame the model's weights as probability distributions, as opposed to fixed values. This enables the estimation of uncertainty in the predictions of the model, which can be utilized to determine inputs that are likely to be adversarial. For instance, in a classification problem, a Bayesian neural network can output a probability distribution over the potential classes, instead of a predicted class. If the prediction of the model is very uncertain, this could be an indication that the input is adversarial. Bayesian neural networks offer a useful resource for identifying and counteracting adversarial attacks, especially in those situations where it is indispensable to estimate uncertainty.

Adversarial Training Techniques

Adversarial training is a strong method of improving the robustness of machine learning models to adversarial attacks. Adversarial training entails adding adversarial examples into the training set, thus exposing the model to potential attack modes and enhancing its generalization power under perturbations. This training methodology attempts to directly consider adversarial perturbations in the training process, resulting in models that are less susceptible to malicious tampering.

FGSM training: FGSM training is the process of creating adversarial examples with the FGSM (already explained) and adding them to the training set. The FGSM, proposed by Goodfellow et al. (2014), creates adversarial examples by adding a small perturbation to the input data in the direction of the gradient of the loss function with respect to the input. It is a computationally efficient method that supports the generation of a large number of adversarial examples at a low overhead. FGSM's simplicity explains why it is most commonly used for adversarial training, particularly in cases where limited computational resources are available. FGSM-produced adversarial examples are usually less potent in fooling robust models than more advanced methods produce. The training procedure is done by switching between training the model on clean samples and training the model on adversarial examples generated by FGSM. This procedure enables the model to learn to detect and counteract the effect of adversarial perturbations, making the model more robust overall.

Projected gradient descent training: PGD training is done through the iterative generation of adversarial data points with PGD perturbations. This technique approximates the worst-case adversarial perturbation through multiple applications of the gradient descent step and reprojecting the adversarial input to a legal range of perturbation. PGD training ensures robustness stronger than FGSM training because PGD has more variability in searching adversarial perturbation. Iterating to tighten adversarial examples tightens and becomes more capable at producing potent perturbations for misleading the model. The training procedure is to generate PGD-generated adversarial examples for every training sample and utilize them to update the model parameters. The procedure may be computationally expensive, as it takes several gradient descent steps per training sample. Yet, the enhanced robustness from PGD training makes it a significant method for security-critical applications.

Min-max optimization: Min-max optimization constructs adversarial training as a min-max optimization problem, where the model tries to minimize the loss on adversarial examples and the adversary tries to maximize the loss. This creates a principled solution for adversarial training, guaranteeing that the model is resistant against worst-case adversarial perturbations. The min-max optimization problem can be written as eq. (*xi*):

min_θ max_δ $L(\theta, x + \delta, y)$ (xi)

where θ represents the model parameters, x represents the input data, δ represents the adversarial perturbation,yδ represents the true label, and L represents the loss function. Solving this min-max problem has an impact on updating the model parameters in a step-by-step manner to minimize the loss on adversarial examples.

An adversary creates these examples to maximize the loss. This method makes sure the model can handle the toughest adversarial changes, which leads to better overall performance and toughness. This approach to train is very strong, but it also needs a lot of computing power.

Defensive Distillation

Defensive distillation is a method to make deep learning models stronger against attacks. It trains a model at a higher "temperature" using soft probability distributions instead of hard labels. This makes the decision boundary smoother and the model less sensitive to small changes. It involves training a "student" model using the softened probabilities from a "teacher" model. This process smooths out the decision boundaries of the student model making it harder for attackers to create effective adversarial examples. The main idea is to pass the "knowledge" from the teacher model to the student model in a way that makes it less sensitive to small input changes.

Teacher Model Training

A neural network is first trained using a modified softmax function with a *temperature parameterT*, which controls the sharpness of the output distribution of eq. (*xii*):

$$p_T(x) = \frac{e^{z_j/T}}{\sum_{k=1}^{C} e^{z_j/T}} \text{ (xii)}$$

where:

z_j is the logit (raw model output) for the class j.
C is the total number of classes.
The denominator ensures the outputs are normalized to represent a probability distribution.

When $T = 1$, (standard softmax), the function behaves as usual, producing sharp probability distributions where the highest probability class is assigned a value close to 1, while the others are near 0. When $T > 1$, the exponentiation operation is weakened, causing the probability distribution to spread out more evenly across classes, making the model less confident in any single prediction. This results in smoother probability distributions. When $T \to \infty$, all outputs converge to a uniform distribution, where each class has an equal probability. A lower value of T leads to a sharp probability distribution, with one class having a dominant probability close to 1, and a higher T leads to a smoother probability distribution, where probabilities are more evenly spread across multiple classes.

Student Model Training

After training the teacher model with temperature-scaled softmax outputs, a second neural network (the student model) learns from the soft labels the teacher model creates. These soft labels are smoothed probability distributions, not the usual one-hot labels. This approach helps the student model to build a more general picture of the data, which makes it harder to fool with tricky inputs.

The loss function for the student model is given in eq. (*xiii*):

$$L_{distill} = -\sum_{j=1}^{C} p_T^j(x) \log p_T^j(x) \quad \text{(xiii)}$$

Where $p_T^j(x)$ is the probability output from the teacher model for class j. The sum is taken over all C classes, ensuring that the student model learns a probability distribution similar to that of the teacher. This pushes the student network to grasp a more general representation making it tougher for adversarial tweaks to change predictions.

Simplifying the model by training a smaller student model cuts down on model complexity and sensitivity to adversarial tweaks. This method works well when computing power is scarce, as it lets you deploy tough models on devices with limited resources. Knowledge distillation offers a useful tool to boost the toughness and effectiveness of ML models. This approach also comes in handy when you need to put very big models on small devices, like smartphones.

Input Validation and Sanitization

Input sanitization and validation entail preprocessing the input data in order to identify and counter adversarial perturbations (Feinman, Curtin, Shintre, & Gardner, 2017). Through this method, adversarial noise is eliminated or weakened, enhancing model robustness.

Feature squeezing entails reducing the input feature space's granularity. This is done by using transformations on the input data that limit the number of unique values each feature can have. By constraining the precision of the input features, the adversary has less control in designing stealthy perturbations that can mislead the model. As an example, a type of feature squeezing is reduction in bit depth, where the precision of pixel values in an image is lowered. Another is color space reduction, where the input image's number of colors is reduced. By lowering the input space's complexity, feature squeezing compels attackers to make larger, and thus more noticeable, alterations to the input data. This method makes it more difficult for an attacker to produce imperceptible alterations that will deceive the model. It is frequently utilized in conjunction with other defence methods.

Adversarial example detection methods attempt to mark potentially adversarial inputs as such by inspecting their statistical properties or perturbation behaviour. The methods employed in such techniques include statistical anomaly detection and adversarial perturbation analysis. Statistical anomaly detection consists of examining the statistical distribution of input information and finding instances far from the typical distribution. Techniques like clustering, density estimation, or outlier detection can be used for this purpose. Adversarial perturbation analysis is to examine the nature of adversarial perturbations, e.g., their amplitude, frequency, or direction. By detecting patterns that are representative of adversarial manipulations, these methods can mark potentially adversarial inputs. By identifying adversarial inputs, these methods make it possible for proper mitigation methods, e.g., rejecting the input, executing corrective transformations, or notifying security personnel.

Input filtering is the use of filters to eliminate or dampen high-frequency perturbations, which are commonly employed in adversarial attacks. The filters are used to smooth the input data and thereby minimize the effect of adversarial noise. Median filtering or Gaussian filtering can be used for image data to eliminate high-frequency noise, for instance. Low-pass filters can also be used for audio data to dampen high-frequency perturbations. By eliminating or weakening high-frequency perturbations, input filtering decreases the sensitivity of the model to adversarial noise, hence making it more resilient to adversarial attacks. Nevertheless, one should be aware that over-filtering can also lower the quality of legitimate inputs, which might impact the performance of the model. These filters are usually applied, since adversarial attacks have a tendency to introduce high frequency noise to images.

Ensemble Methods for Improved Resilience

Ensemble methods combine the predictions of many ML models in order to produce more accurate and robust predictions (Dietterich, 2000). The method has the goal of reducing the vulnerabilities of individual models by combining different model architectures' predictions. For improving the machine learning model robustness against adversarial attacks, ensemble methods apply various strategies. Adversarial training ensembles enhance robustness by training numerous models with distinct adversarial attacks or datasets. Model diversity also enhances defences by including diverse architectures or training paradigms, minimizing common vulnerabilities. Adversarial input detection ensembles also improve security by aggregating models with disparate strengths in detecting diverse types of adversarial attacks, forming a more robust defence system. With these defence mechanisms in place, ML systems can be made more resistant to adversarial attacks, and the reliability and security of key applications can be ensured.

ETHICAL ISSUES IN AML

The use of adversarial machine learning in cybersecurity, though promising a great deal for more effective threat detection and defence, poses serious ethical issues. These include privacy issues regarding the collection and analysis of data, bias and fairness issues in machine learning algorithms, the need for transparency and explainability in AI-driven security mechanisms, and ethical utilization of adversarial methods in cybersecurity research.

Privacy Concerns

AML-based security systems are dependent on access to large datasets, which may hold sensitive personal details. The collection and use of such data pose substantial privacy issues, necessitating the utilization of strong privacy-preserving approaches. Data utility needs to be balanced with security by ensuring data privacy in machine learning through a number of important strategies. Data minimization principle ensures that data is collected only for what is necessary, thus avoiding the risk of privacy infringement (Voigt & Von dem Bussche, 2017). Differential privacy adds an additional layer of security by adding noise to data analysis in a controlled manner, such that individual records cannot be identified while overall utility of the data is preserved (Dwork, 2008). Federated learning enhances security by enabling model training on decentralized data sources without transferring raw data to a central server, significantly lowering the risk of data breaches (Yang, Liu, Chen, & Tong, 2019). Additionally, data anonymization and pseudonymization techniques help obscure identities, though careful implementation is required to mitigate the risk of re-identification. These methodologies, combined, form a full picture of how privacy can be maintained in AML-based security systems without their effectiveness being diminished.

Data and Algorithmic Bias

Machine learning algorithms, as those applied to cybersecurity, are prone to picking up and even exaggerating the biases inherent in their training datasets, with potential to result in biased or discriminatory results. This is a strong ethical concern, especially in security-critical uses where biased results can have detrimental impacts. Algorithmic bias occurs when ML models consistently make unfair predictions on the basis of protected features like race, gender, or ethnicity, leading to discriminatory risk scores or unfair access control policies. To tackle this problem, several fairness measures—like demographic parity, equal opportunity, and predictive parity—are employed to measure and reduce bias so that models make fair decisions. In addition, bias mitigation methods, such as data preprocessing, in-processing, and post-processing techniques (Mehrabi et al., 2019), assist in eliminating or minimizing biases from training data and model predictions. Through the incorporation of these measures, ML models in cybersecurity can be made more transparent, equitable, and ethically robust.

Explainability of ML Models

The obscurity of sophisticated machine learning models, especially deep learning models, creates major challenges to transparency and explainability, giving rise to ethical issues of accountability and trust. XAI methods resolve this challenge by generating human-interpretable explanations of ML model predictions, thus improving transparency and accountability (Samek, Wiegand, & Müller, 2019). This is particularly important in AI-based security systems, where trust in model choices is essential. Model interpretability further contributes to transparency by enabling the development of inherently explainable models, such as decision trees or linear models, which allow for the identification of key factors influencing predictions. Additionally, audibility plays a vital role in ensuring accountability, as the ability to systematically review ML models and their outputs helps detect potential biases or errors. By incorporating XAI methods, transparent models, and strong auditing functions, AI platforms can be more transparent, ethical, and dependable.

Ethical Application of AML

Applications of adversarial methods in the field of cyber security pose an ethical dilemma mainly in terms of misuse. To ensure responsible research, researchers will have to keep to the time-tested ethical benchmarks and best practices. One critical aspect is responsible disclosure, where vulnerabilities should be reported to vendors with adequate time for remediation before public disclosure, minimizing the risk of malicious exploitation. Additionally, adversarial techniques pose dual-use concerns, as they can be leveraged for both defensive and offensive purposes, necessitating careful consideration of their potential for misuse. During human subjects research, the informed consent of the participants must be obtained to ensure that they have a complete understanding of the risks and benefits involved. Additionally, review boards for ethics are responsible for monitoring adversarial methods research to adhere to ethical standards and regulations. In doing so ahead of time, researchers and practitioners can ensure the positive development and application of adversarial machine learning in cybersecurity while minimizing the potential negatives.

CHALLENGES IN AML

The adversarial machine learning field is developing very fast, with the pace of progress in attack and defence techniques accelerating. This section discusses future trends and challenges, such as new threats and attack vectors, innovation in AML methods, convergence with other technologies, and the necessity for regulatory and standardization initiatives.

Emerging Threats and Attack Vectors

As machine learning systems become more integrated into core infrastructure, they are exposed to increasingly sophisticated attacks, requiring proactive R&D to strengthen their security and resilience. A nascent risk area is adversarial attacks on federated learning, which, as much as it offers privacy advantages, is vulnerable to poisoning attacks that can subvert model integrity (Bonawitz et al., 2019). Future work will need to emphasize building resilient aggregation protocols and anomaly detection methods to address these weaknesses. Likewise, reinforcement learning agents, which abound in autonomous systems and robotics, can be manipulated by adversaries, with possible resulting unintended or even harmful behaviour (Swapno, Nobel, Meena, et al., 2024). Resilient RL models against such perturbations are an essential area of investigation. Another new threat is cross-domain adversarial attacks, in which adversarial examples of one domain, e.g., image recognition, can be easily transferred to another, e.g., audio recognition, taking advantage of common vulnerabilities in different ML systems. To counter these attacks, cross-domain defence mechanisms need to be developed. Moreover, adversarial attacks on graph neural networks (GNNs) are threat-some in fields like network security and social network analysis, where attackers may tamper with network traffic analysis or manipulate social data. Investigating more resilient GNN architectures and training protocols is critical to preventing these risks. Addressing these emerging challenges can help the ML research community make AI-based systems more secure against adversarial manipulation.

Advancements in AML Techniques

The AML space is constantly changing, with new attack and defence technologies fueled by ongoing research and innovation. One such area of interest is adaptive adversarial attacks, where adversaries adapt their strategy in real-time as defences change. To mitigate this, future work needs to come up with adaptive defence methodologies that can look ahead and anticipate such threats. Another new idea is explainable adversarial attacks, which seek to reveal the mechanisms by which adversarial examples mislead ML models (Samek, Wiegand, & Müller, 2019). Understanding these attack methods can greatly contribute to the creation of more powerful defences. Meta-learning is also being investigated for adversarial robustness, allowing models to learn dynamically to new adversarial attacks and countermeasures. Work in this space can translate into more robust ML systems with the ability to learn from dynamically changing threats. Finally, formal verification methods to certify adversarial robustness have a great promise as a way of issuing certified robustness assurances. Nevertheless, guaranteeing scalability and efficiency of such certification for larger models poses an essential area of research work. Addressing these urgent matters, AML research can develop more secure and robust ML systems.

Integration with other Technologies

Combining AML with newer technologies offers fresh chances to fortify cybersecurity and ward off adversary threats. Blockchain, for example, can guarantee the integrity and authenticity of data and minimize the potential for data poisoning attacks (Fernández-Caramés & Fraga-Lamas, 2018). Its integration with ML-based security systems has to be explored through future research. Similarly, quantum computing promises to advance adversarial robustness since quantum algorithms might provide new methods of adversarial training and defence (Rebentrost, Mohseni, & Lloyd, 2014). Privacy-preserving AML is another important research area where computations can be carried out on encrypted data, meaning ML models could be trained and used without disclosing sensitive data. Exploring the use of homomorphic encryption within AML architectures would dramatically increase security and privacy. Besides this, secure multi-party computation can complement federated learning by enabling multiple parties to jointly compute on private data functions without revealing single inputs. Based on these future-proof technologies, future research has the potential to lead to stronger AML systems that can guard against more evolved adversarial threats.

Regulatory Compliance

Universal deployment of AML-based security systems necessitates holistic regulatory and standardization strategies to guarantee ethical and responsible research. Regulatory agencies and governments should create regulations that provide solutions to major issues like data privacy, biased algorithms, and transparency in AML usage. Equally significant is the crafting of adversarial robustness benchmarks, which would allow for comparative benchmarking and defence mechanism comparison, promoting reliability and transparency. Industry players should also be proactive in the development and following of best practices for the implementation and upkeep of AML-based security systems, in a manner that promotes responsible innovation. Additionally, because the nature of cybersecurity threats is international, there should be international cooperation to facilitate collective standards and best practices. By resolving these standardization and regulation issues, policymakers, practitioners, and researchers can collaborate towards the effective and responsible application of AML, consequently protecting crucial infrastructure and sensitive information.

CASE STUDIES

To demonstrate the real-world implications of adversarial machine learning on cybersecurity, this section provides case studies of different smart environments. These case studies bring to the forefront the specific vulnerabilities and challenges inherent in smart homes, smart cities, healthcare, and industrial IoT (IIoT), and the essential necessity for strong AML defences.

Smart Homes

Smart homes, with all their connected appliances and automated equipment, provide comfort but at great security and privacy risks, especially when adversary machine learning methods are used to probe vulnerabilities. One critical threat is voice assistant manipulation, where adversarial audio signals can deceive voice-activated systems like Amazon Alexa or Google Home into executing unauthorized actions, such as unlocking doors or making purchases without user consent (Lau, Zimmerman, & Schaub, 2018). In the same way, adversarial attacks can take over smart devices like thermostats and security cameras, interrupting their operation or allowing attackers to see sensitive information—potentially leading to sudden changes in temperatures or allowing unwanted surveillance. Similarly, smart home sensors like motion and occupancy sensors are also vulnerable to privacy attacks, where adversarial methods can manipulate sensor readings to deduce user behaviour and break confidentiality. As smart homes gain popularity, it is important to address such vulnerabilities through strong security protocols and AML-resistant architecture to guarantee user security and data protection.

Smart Cities

Smart cities with their large sensor networks and data-centric services are becoming more susceptible to adversarial attacks that compromise critical infrastructure and public safety. A key threat is traffic light manipulation, where attackers take advantage of weaknesses in traffic control systems to modify the timing of lights and, for example, cause grotesque congestion or accidents (Swapno, Nobel, Meena, et al. 2024). Adversarial methods can similarly be applied to circumvent or mislead surveillance systems, such as facial recognition cameras so that people can be made invisible or forge surveillance videos. Another significant concern is smart grid attacks, with malicious data injections that can destabilize energy distribution grids, resulting in power loss or grid collapse. With expanding smart cities, developing robust AML defences becomes a critical task in protecting city infrastructure and making public services secure and reliable.

Smart Healthcare

Smart healthcare systems, managing sensitive patient information and controlling life-critical medical devices, are extremely vulnerable to adversarial attacks, which threaten patient safety and data privacy to a great extent. Medical image tampering is one of the key threats where attackers add minute perturbations to MRI or CT scans that may mislead diagnostic algorithms into hiding tumors or creating false positives (Esteva et al., 2017). Likewise, medical device hijacking is a serious threat, as attackers can take over devices such as pacemakers or insulin pumps to interfere with their operation or deliver toxic treatments. Electronic health record tampering is another serious issue, where adversarial methods could be employed to manipulate patient medical histories, diagnoses, or prescriptions and result in improper treatments or medication mistakes. As intelligent healthcare becomes more advanced, strong adversarial defences and tight security measures are crucial to maintaining the integrity and safety of medical systems.

Industrial IoT (IIoT)

Industrial Internet of Things (IIoT) systems, which consist of interconnected industrial devices and control systems, are the foundation of critical infrastructure. But adversarial attacks on these systems can cause extreme disruptions and economic loss. One of the prominent threats includes control system hacking, in which the attackers leverage loopholes within industrial control systems, like SCADA systems, to manipulate operational parameters or even render safety functions non-operational, possibly crippling production processes or initiating equipment malfunctions. The other is predictive maintenance attacks, whereby the attack manipulations by an adversary lead to spurious alarms or even the suppression of actual failures, hence causing uneconomic maintenance scheduling (Zheng, Paiva, & Gurciullo, 2020). Moreover, supply chain attacks emphasize another key vulnerability, where attackers can inject manipulated information into monitoring systems, steering shipments astray or contaminating product quality.

These case studies in different smart environments—healthcare, cities, homes, and industrial systems—emphasize the broad-ranging implications of adversarial machine learning. Through the identification and mitigation of these vulnerabilities, researchers and practitioners can collaborate towards developing more robust AML defences, protecting the security and integrity of critical infrastructure.

CONCLUSION

This chapter has offered a holistic explanation of adversarial machine learning in cybersecurity, traversing its underpinning principles, varied attack surfaces, tenacious defence approaches, ethical factors, and real-world applications within different smart surroundings. Through this integration of multifaceted topics, we have highlighted the salient importance of AML to protect the integrity and security of contemporary digital infrastructure.

The chapter began by defining AML as the study of techniques that manipulate machine learning models to deceive or disrupt their intended functionality. Having discussed different forms of adversarial attacks, such as evasion, poisoning, model extraction, adversarial reprogramming, and backdoor attacks, each with different challenges for ML-based security systems, the discussion proceeded with the use of ML in detecting threats in smart systems and the effectiveness of anomaly detection, network traffic analysis, behavioural pattern recognition, and real-time threat detection. Additionally, defence methods against adversarial attacks were investigated, e.g., the creation of adversarially robust models, adversarial training methods, defensive distillation, input validation, and ensemble methods. The ethical implications of AML, i.e., privacy, bias, transparency, and the use of adversarial methods responsibly in research; as well as other challenges encountered to tackle adversarial attacks. Last but not least, four case studies were introduced to demonstrate the effect of AML in smart homes, smart cities, smart healthcare systems, and industrial IoT.

The AML landscape in cybersecurity is marked by a dynamic conflict between offense and defence. With the increasing prevalence of ML systems, their enemies are coming up with more and more advanced methods for taking advantage of their weaknesses. This requires a sustained and responsive strategy to security, with defence mechanisms adapting as threats materialize. The combination of AML with other technologies like blockchain and quantum computing opens opportunities and poses risks that must be thoughtfully assessed for their potential impact on cybersecurity. Furthermore, the increased focus on the explainability of AI and the fairness of ML models also puts the need for ethical consideration when developing and using AML-based security systems.

The ever-present innovation in AML serves as a call for further research and development. Future work must lie in mitigating new threats to AML systems, including adversary attacks on reinforcement learning agents and federated learning, and even more effective defence methods, e.g., adversarial robustness certification and meta-learning. Regulations and standardizations are also a key area necessary for the security and ethical handling of AML in cybersecurity applications. Academic, industry, and government collaboration is key to driving innovation and tackling the AML challenge with its intricate complexities. Through investment in research, development, and ethical frameworks, we can make ML-based systems more secure and resilient against constantly mutating adversary threats.

The threats that adversarial machine learning presents are great, but so are the possibilities for cybersecurity innovation and advancement. By keeping watch and staying proactive, we can capitalize on the potential of machine learning without exposing ourselves to its weaknesses, creating a more secure and secure online world.

REFERENCES

Ahmed, M., Nazeeruddin, M., & Hashem, I. A. T. (2016). Machine learning algorithms for intrusion detection: A survey. *International Journal of Security and Networks*, *11*(3), 173–182.

Alrawi, O., Lever, C., Antonakakis, M., & Monrose, F. (2019). SoK: Security evaluation of home-based IoT deployments. In *2019 IEEE Symposium on Security and Privacy (SP)* (pp. 1362–1380). IEEE. DOI: 10.1109/SP.2019.00013

Atzori, L., Iera, A., & Morabito, G. (2010). The internet of things: A survey. *Computer Networks*, *54*(15), 2787–2805. DOI: 10.1016/j.comnet.2010.05.010

Blum, A., & Mitchell, T. (1998). Combining labeled and unlabeled data with co-training. In *Proceedings of the eleventh annual conference on computational learning theory* (pp. 92-100). DOI: 10.1145/279943.279962

Bonawitz, K., Eichner, H., Grieskamp, W., Huba, D., Ingerman, A., Ivanov, V., & Van Overveldt, T. (2019). Towards federated learning at scale: System design. *Proceedings of Machine Learning and Systems*, *1*, 374–388.

Breiman, L. (2001). Random forests. *Machine Learning*, *45*(1), 5–32. DOI: 10.1023/A:1010933404324

Buczak, A. L., & Guven, E. (2016). A survey of data mining and machine learning methods for cyber security intrusion detection. *IEEE Communications Surveys and Tutorials*, *18*(2), 1153–1176. DOI: 10.1109/COMST.2015.2494502

Carlini, N., & Wagner, D. (2017). *Towards evaluating the robustness of neural networks. In 2017 IEEE symposium on security and privacy*. IEEE.

Chandola, V., Banerjee, A., & Kumar, V. (2009). Anomaly detection: A survey. *ACM Computing Surveys*, *41*(3), 1–58. DOI: 10.1145/1541880.1541882

Dietterich, T. G. (2000). Ensemble methods in machine learning. In *Multiple classifier systems* (pp. 1–15). Springer. DOI: 10.1007/3-540-45014-9_1

Dwork, C. (2008). Differential Privacy: A Survey of Results. In Agrawal, M., Du, D., Duan, Z., & Li, A. (Eds.), Lecture Notes in Computer Science: Vol. 4978. *Theory and Applications of Models of Computation. TAMC 2008*. Springer. DOI: 10.1007/978-3-540-79228-4_1

Elsayed, G., Krishnan, B., Tavel, A., Papernot, N., & Goldstein, T. (2018). Adversarial reprogramming of neural networks. *arXiv preprint arXiv:1806.00057.*

Esteva, A., Kuprel, B., Novoa, R. A., Ko, J., Swetter, S. M., Blau, H. M., & Thrun, S. (2017). Dermatologist-level classification of skin cancer with deep neural networks. *Nature*, *542*(7639), 115–118. DOI: 10.1038/nature21056 PMID: 28117445

Feinman, R., Curtin, R., Shintre, S., & Gardner, A. B. (2017). Detecting adversarial samples from artifacts. *arXiv preprint arXiv:1711.00105.*

Fernández-Caramés, T. M., & Fraga-Lamas, P. (2018). A review on the use of blockchain for the Internet of Things. *IEEE Access : Practical Innovations, Open Solutions*, *6*, 32979–33001. DOI: 10.1109/ACCESS.2018.2842685

Ferrag, M. A., Maglaras, L., Janicke, H., & Jiang, J. (2020). Deep learning for cyber security intrusion detection: Approaches, datasets, and comparative study. *Journal of Information Security and Applications*, *50*, 102419. DOI: 10.1016/j.jisa.2019.102419

Ferrag, M. A., Maglaras, L., Janicke, H., & Jiang, J. (2020). Deep learning for cyber security intrusion detection: Approaches, datasets, and comparative study. *Journal of Information Security and Applications*, *50*, 102419. DOI: 10.1016/j.jisa.2019.102419

Gal, Y., & Ghahramani, Z. (2016). Dropout as a bayesian approximation: Representing model uncertainty in deep learning. In *International conference on machine learning* (pp. 1050-1059). PMLR.

Gama, J., Žliobaitė, I., Pechenizkiy, M., & Bifet, A. (2014). A survey on concept drift adaptation. *ACM Computing Surveys*, *46*(4), 1–37. DOI: 10.1145/2523813

Goodfellow, I. J., Shlens, J., & Szegedy, C. (2014). Explaining and harnessing adversarial examples. *arXiv preprint arXiv:1412.6572.*

Gu, T., Dolan-Gavitt, B., & Garg, S. (2017). Badnets: Identifying vulnerabilities in the machine learning model supply chain. *arXiv preprint arXiv:1708.06733.*

Hinton, G. E., & Salakhutdinov, R. R. (2006). Reducing the dimensionality of data with neural networks. *Science*, *313*(5786), 504–507. DOI: 10.1126/science.1127647 PMID: 16873662

Lau, J., Zimmerman, B., & Schaub, F. (2018). Alexa, are you listening? Privacy perceptions, concerns and privacy-seeking behaviours with smart speakers. *Proceedings of the ACM on Human-Computer Interaction, 2*(CSCW), Article 102.

Lecun, Y., Bengio, Y., & Hinton, G. (2015). Deep learning. *Nature*, *521*(7553), 436–444. DOI: 10.1038/nature14539 PMID: 26017442

Liang, H., He, E., Zhao, Y., Jia, Z., & Li, H. (2022). Adversarial Attack and Defence: A Survey. *Electronics (Basel)*, *11*(8), 1283. DOI: 10.3390/electronics11081283

Liao, H.-J., Lin, C.-H. R., Lin, Y.-C., & Tung, K.-Y. (2013). Intrusion detection system: A comprehensive review. *Journal of Network and Computer Applications*, *36*(1), 16–24. DOI: 10.1016/j.jnca.2012.09.004

Liu, F. T., Ting, K. M., & Zhou, Z. H. (2008). Isolation forest. In *2008 eighth IEEE international conference on data mining* (pp. 413-422). IEEE. DOI: 10.1109/ICDM.2008.17

Mehrabi, N., Morstatter, F., Saxena, N., Lerman, K., & Galstyan, A. (2019). A survey on bias and fairness in machine learning. *arXiv preprint arXiv:1908.09635.*

Mittelstadt, B. D., Allo, P., Taddeo, M., Wachter, S., & Floridi, L. (2016). Principles alone are not enough for ethical AI. *Nature Machine Intelligence*, *1*(11), 501–507. DOI: 10.1038/s42256-019-0114-4

Papernot, N., McDaniel, P., Sinha, A., & Wellman, M. (2018). SoK: Security and privacy in machine learning. In *IEEE European Symposium on Security and Privacy* (pp. 399-414). IEEE. DOI: 10.1109/EuroSP.2018.00035

Papernot, N., McDaniel, P., Wu, X., Jha, S., & Swami, A. (2016). Distillation as a defence to adversarial perturbations against deep neural networks. In *2016 IEEE symposium on security and privacy (SP)* (pp. 582-597). IEEE.

Rebentrost, P., Mohseni, M., & Lloyd, S. (2014). Quantum support vector machine for big data classification. *Physical Review Letters*, *113*(13), 130503. DOI: 10.1103/PhysRevLett.113.130503 PMID: 25302877

Samek, W., Wiegand, T., & Müller, K. (2019). Explainable artificial intelligence: Understanding, visualizing, and interpreting deep learning models. *IEEE Signal Processing Magazine*, *36*(4), 20–28.

Samek, W., Wiegand, T., & Müller, K. (2019). Explainable artificial intelligence: Understanding, visualizing, and interpreting deep learning models. *IEEE Signal Processing Magazine*, *36*(4), 20–28.

Sommer, R., & Paxson, V. (2010). *Outside the closed world: On using machine learning for network intrusion detection. In 2010 IEEE symposium on security and privacy*. IEEE.

Swapno, S. M. M. R., Nobel, S. N., Meena, P., Meena, V. P., Azar, A. T., Haider, Z., & Tounsi, M. (2024). A reinforcement learning approach for reducing traffic congestion using deep Q learning. *Scientific Reports*, *14*(1), 30452. DOI: 10.1038/s41598-024-75638-0 PMID: 39668197

Syed, A. S., Sierra-Sosa, D., Kumar, A., & Elmaghraby, A. (2021). IoT in Smart Cities: A Survey of Technologies, Practices and Challenges. *Smart Cities*, *4*(2), 429–475. DOI: 10.3390/smartcities4020024

Tramèr, F., Zhang, F., Juels, A., Reiter, M. K., & Kocher, P. (2016). *Stealing machine learning models via prediction apis*.

Voigt, P., & Von dem Bussche, A. (2017). *The EU General Data Protection Regulation (GDPR): A Practical Guide*. Springer. DOI: 10.1007/978-3-319-57959-7

Weber, R. H. (2010). Internet of Things—New security and privacy challenges. *Computer Law & Security Review*, *26*(1), 23–30. DOI: 10.1016/j.clsr.2009.11.008

Wong, E., & Kolter, J. Z. (2018). Provable defences against adversarial examples via the convex outer adversarial polytope. In *International conference on machine learning* (pp. 5286-5295). PMLR.

Yang, Q., Liu, Y., Chen, T., & Tong, Y. (2019). Federated machine learning: Concept and applications. [TIST]. *ACM Transactions on Intelligent Systems and Technology*, *10*(2), 1–19. DOI: 10.1145/3298981

Zheng, H., Paiva, A. R., & Gurciullo, C. S. (2020). Advancing from predictive maintenance to intelligent maintenance with AI and IIoT. *arXiv preprint arXiv:2009.00351*.

Chapter 5
Real-World Adversarial Attacks on AI Systems

Trisha Bera
https://orcid.org/0009-0005-7728-7390
JIS College of Engineering, India

Sanket Dan
https://orcid.org/0000-0002-7587-4285
JIS College of Engineering, India

Uddalak Mitra
JIS College of Engineering, India

Jayshree Bhattacharya
https://orcid.org/0009-0009-3118-132X
JIS College of Engineering, India

ABSTRACT

The integration of Artificial Intelligence (AI) into real-world applications has brought societal benefits but also introduced new vulnerabilities, including adversarial attacks. These attacks account for complex physical variables, making them harder to execute and more dangerous. This paper investigates the nature and impact of real-world adversarial attacks on AI systems, categorizing them based on modalities, attack goals, and delivery mechanisms. It critically assesses existing defense mechanisms and suggests emerging trends like certified defenses, sensor fusion techniques, and context-aware learning. The study emphasizes the need for a security-first approach in AI system design and deployment.

DOI: 10.4018/979-8-3373-2200-1.ch005

INTRODUCTION

Artificial Intelligence (AI) systems have rapidly evolved over the past decade, achieving remarkable performance across a wide range of tasks, from image and speech recognition to autonomous navigation and decision-making. As a result, AI models, particularly those based on deep learning, are increasingly being deployed in real-world, high-stakes applications, including autonomous vehicles, medical diagnostics, financial services, and security systems. However, with the broader adoption of AI comes heightened concerns about their reliability, robustness, and security, especially in adversarial environments.

One of the most alarming vulnerabilities discovered in modern AI systems is their susceptibility to **adversarial attacks** (Raja, Njilla, & Yuan, 2022). Adversarial attacks involve the deliberate creation of inputs that are subtly perturbed to deceive AI models into making incorrect predictions while appearing benign or unchanged to human observers. Although much of the early research on adversarial examples focused on synthetic, digitally-perturbed inputs in controlled experimental settings, there is growing evidence that such vulnerabilities also extend into the physical world. In real-world settings, adversaries can craft physical objects—such as modified street signs, wearable adversarial patterns, or manipulated environmental cues—that reliably cause AI systems to fail, even under varying lighting, angles, and environmental conditions (Chi et al., 2024).

Real-world adversarial attacks present distinct challenges compared to their digital counterparts. Unlike digital attacks, where inputs can be precisely controlled, real-world attacks must remain effective under diverse, dynamic, and often unpredictable physical transformations. These challenges make successful attacks more complex to design but also more dangerous, as real-world attacks can directly impact human safety, national security, and economic stability (Wei et al., 2024).

Recent research has demonstrated practical real-world attacks on critical AI systems: stop signs that are misclassified by autonomous vehicles, adversarial glasses that fool facial recognition systems, and subtle object manipulations that cause drones or surveillance systems to misinterpret their surroundings. The presented examples highlight that adversarial vulnerabilities are not merely abstract problems but have tangible, practical implications (Chi et al., 2024). In this paper, we conduct a comprehensive analysis of adversarial attacks targeting AI systems in real-world applications. Our work includes a classification of attack types, an investigation into their operational principles, and an evaluation of their impacts across diverse application areas. We also review current defense approaches and discuss their limitations in real-world, uncontrolled settings. Furthermore, we outline significant open research questions and suggest potential future directions for developing more robust AI systems against real-world adversarial attacks. The goal of this study is to bridge the divide between research in adversarial machine learning and the real-world deployment of AI in challenging and uncertain contexts, ultimately aiming to increase awareness about the urgent requirement for reliable and trustworthy AI.

BACKGROUND

2.1 Introduction to Adversarial Attacks:

Adversarial attacks involve subtly altering input data in ways that cause machine learning models to make wrong predictions or classifications. These attacks leverage weaknesses present in deep learning systems by introducing small changes that can lead to substantial errors in AI decision-making. Depending on the attacker's knowledge of the target model, these can be white-box attacks (full knowledge) or black-box attacks (limited or no knowledge). Because these attacks present significant security risks in areas such as image recognition, self-driving cars, and cybersecurity, strong defense strategies like adversarial training, input preprocessing, and model regularization are essential (Raja, Njilla, & Yuan, 2022).

2.2 The significance of adversarial attacks in the actual world

Adversarial attacks from the real world are important for AI systems because they reveal flaws in models used in vital applications including cybersecurity, facial recognition, driverless cars, and medical diagnostics. Real-world adversarial attacks show that AI systems may be controlled in physical contexts, which makes them a significant security and safety risk in contrast to theoretical attacks that exclusively occur in digital areas (Chi & Msahli, 2025).

The following justifies the importance of real-world adversarial attacks:

- **Security Risks:** Adversarial flaws can be used by attackers to trick AI models into making inaccurate predictions or classifications.
- **Physical Feasibility:** These attacks demonstrate that AI models can be tricked in real-world situations without requiring access to the underlying mechanisms of the model.
- **Issues with Trust and Reliability:** If AI systems are readily tricked, users and industries may stop believing in their efficacy and security, which might affect adoption in security, healthcare, and finance.
- **Regulatory and Ethical Challenges** – Organizations deploying AI systems must ensure robustness against adversarial attacks to comply with safety and security regulations.

- **Defensive Research & Robustness** – Understanding real-world attacks helps AI researchers develop better defense mechanisms, such as adversarial training, robust architectures, and detection systems

2.3 Differences between theoretical and real-world attacks:

Table 1. Differences between theoretical and real-world attacks

Aspect	Theoretical Adversarial Attacks	Real-World Adversarial Attacks
Definition	Attacks designed and tested in a digital or simulated environment, often assuming full or partial access to the model.	Attacks that manipulate AI systems in real-world conditions, often in physical environments.
Implementation	Conducted in a controlled setting using digital images, datasets, or simulations.	Executed in the real world using physical objects, lighting conditions, or environmental changes.
Attack Methods	Pixel-level perturbations, gradient-based optimizations, and digital input manipulations.	Changes to physical objects (e.g., stickers on road signs, adversarial clothing, or printed adversarial images).
Assumptions	Assumes ideal conditions, perfect access to input data, and precise noise application.	Considers environmental factors like lighting, angles, sensor noise, and occlusions.
Challenges	Often ignores real-world constraints like physical printing distortions or varying viewing angles.	Requires robustness to unpredictable real-world factors like weather, reflections, and motion blur.
Example Attacks	- FGSM (Fast Gradient Sign Method) - PGD (Projected Gradient Descent) - DeepFool	- Stop sign misclassification using stickers - Adversarial clothing to fool facial recognition - 3D-printed adversarial objects misclassified by AI models
Impact on AI Security	Shows AI model vulnerabilities under controlled conditions, guiding theoretical defenses.	Proves that AI systems are vulnerable in real-world scenarios, highlighting security risks in deployed systems.

2.4 Types of Adversarial Attacks in the Real World

In real-world AI systems, adversarial attacks manipulate physical or environmental factors to deceive AI models. These attacks highlight the vulnerabilities of AI in practical applications, such as autonomous vehicles, surveillance, finance, and healthcare (Henna & Amjath, 2024; Yang et al., 2024).

Below are the major types of real-world adversarial attacks:

I. Evasion Attacks:

Evasion attacks are a type of adversarial attack where input data is subtly manipulated to fool AI models at inference time. The key goal is to make the AI misclassify or fail to recognize inputs without altering the AI model itself described in ***Fig.1***. These attacks are particularly dangerous because they can be deployed against AI systems already in use, affecting security, healthcare, finance, and autonomous systems (Chi & Msahli, 2025).

How Evasion Attacks Work:

- **Crafting Perturbed Inputs**: Attackers modify input data by adding small, often imperceptible changes.
- **Model Misclassification**: The slight modifications trick the model into making incorrect predictions.
- **Bypassing Defenses**: The attacker ensures that the perturbed input evades detection mechanisms or security features (Kashyap et al., 2024).

Real-World Examples of Evasion Attacks:

i. **Image Recognition Systems:** Attackers subtly alter images so that an object is misclassified. For instance, a **stop sign** might be recognized as a speed limit sign, causing security risks in **autonomous vehicles**. Example: Adding small stickers to a traffic sign to fool self-driving car perception systems.

ii. **Facial Recognition Spoofing:** Modifying images or videos slightly can cause a facial recognition system to misidentify a person. Example: Adversarial glasses can fool facial recognition into mistaking an unauthorized individual for someone else.

iii. **Malware Evasion in Cybersecurity:** Attackers modify malware files so that they evade detection by antivirus or intrusion detection systems. Example: Slightly altering code structures while maintaining functionality to bypass security filters.

iv. **Spam and Phishing Detection:** Email attackers modify text in spam messages to bypass spam filters. Example: Changing certain words, inserting special characters, or using image-based text to fool machine learning-based spam detectors.

v. **Voice Recognition Attacks:** Attackers craft **adversarial audio** to trick AI-based voice assistants. Example: Hidden commands embedded in background noise to activate AI assistants (e.g., Siri or Alexa) without human detection (Ribouh & Hadid, 2024).

II. Poisoning Attacks:

Poisoning attacks occur during the training phase of an AI model. Attackers inject malicious or manipulated data into the training dataset, causing the AI system to learn incorrect patterns or vulnerabilities. Once trained on poisoned data, the AI model behaves incorrectly when encountering specific inputs, potentially leading to security threats or biased decision-making described in ***Fig.1***. Unlike evasion attacks, which target AI systems after deployment, poisoning attacks corrupt the model itself before it is used (Tiwari, Rajasekar, & Wang, 2024).

How Poisoning Attacks Work:

- **Data Injection**: Attackers introduce manipulated or mislabeled data into the training dataset.
- **Model Corruption**: The poisoned data affects the learning process, causing the model to develop biases, vulnerabilities, or backdoors.
- **Exploitation**: Once deployed, the compromised model can be exploited by the attacker to achieve specific goals, such as misclassification or security bypass.

Types of Poisoning Attacks:

i. **Label Poisoning:** Attackers change the labels of training data, misleading the model into learning incorrect patterns. **Example**: Changing labels in a spam detection dataset so that spam emails are labeled as non-spam.
ii. **Feature Poisoning:** Attackers manipulate input features rather than labels, injecting imperceptible but influential modifications. **Example**: Modifying images in a facial recognition system to misclassify a specific person.
iii. **Backdoor Attacks:** Attackers introduce a hidden pattern (or "trigger") into training data that activates malicious behavior only when the specific pattern appears in real-world input. **Example**: Training an AI-based security camera to ignore intruders wearing a particular pattern (e.g., a specific sticker on clothing) (Ribouh & Hadid, 2024).

Real-World Examples of Poisoning Attacks:

a. **Autonomous Vehicles:** Attackers manipulate traffic sign datasets used to train self-driving cars. **Example**: Poisoning training data so that the AI misclassified stop signs as speed limits under certain conditions.

b. **Fraud in Financial Systems:** Attackers inject fraudulent transaction data to make financial fraud detection models less effective. **Example**: Training a system to ignore transactions below a certain manipulated threshold.
c. **Healthcare AI Manipulation:** Attackers alter medical datasets to affect diagnostic AI models. **Example**: Modifying images in medical imaging datasets so that a disease like cancer is classified as benign.
d. **Malware Classification Bypass:** Attackers poison cybersecurity datasets to make malicious software appear as legitimate. **Example**: Training an antivirus system to classify certain malware as safe.

III. Model Extraction & Reverse Engineering Attacks:

Model extraction and reverse engineering attacks aim to steal or replicate an AI model by exploiting publicly accessible interfaces, such as APIs or cloud-based AI services described in ***Fig.1***. Attackers analyze the inputs and outputs of an AI system to reconstruct its decision-making process, either to duplicate its functionality or discover vulnerabilities for future attacks (Henna & Amjath, 2024). These attacks pose a serious risk to organizations that rely on proprietary AI models for competitive advantage, security, and sensitive decision-making (Tiwari, Rajasekar, & Wang, 2024).

A. **Model Extraction Attacks:** A model extraction attack occurs when an adversary steals or clones a machine learning model by querying it multiple times and using the outputs to reconstruct a functionally similar model. This allows attackers to bypass security measures, remove paywalls, or exploit vulnerabilities in the original model.

How Model Extraction Works:

- **Querying the Target Model**: The attacker sends numerous carefully designed queries to the target ML model.
- **Collecting Predictions**: The responses from the model (output probabilities, class labels, etc.) provide insights into its decision boundaries.
- **Reconstructing a Copy**: The attacker trains a surrogate model using the collected data, creating a replica that mimics the original model's functionality (Al-Maliki et al., 2024).

Real-World Examples of Model Extraction:

- **Cloud-Based ML APIs**: Attackers extract models from paid APIs (e.g., Google's Vision API or OpenAI's GPT models) to **avoid costs** and use them without permission.
- **Fraud Detection Systems**: Cybercriminals replicate financial fraud detection models to understand and bypass security mechanisms.
- **Autonomous Vehicles**: Hackers extract ML models from self-driving cars to analyze weaknesses and launch adversarial attacks.

B. **Reverse Engineering Attacks:** Reverse engineering attacks aim to **uncover internal details** of an ML model, such as its **architecture, hyperparameters, or training data**, by analyzing its behavior (Ribouh & Hadid, 2024).

How Reverse Engineering Works:

- **Black-box Testing**: The attacker submits inputs and observes outputs to deduce decision boundaries.
- **Gradient Estimation**: For models providing confidence scores, attackers estimate gradients to infer model weights.
- **Training Data Reconstruction**: In some cases, attackers recover parts of the training dataset, raising privacy concerns.

Real-World Examples of Reverse Engineering:

- **Facial Recognition Spoofing**: Attackers analyze how a facial recognition model processes images to generate adversarial faces.
- **Voice Recognition Attacks**: Reverse engineering a voice authentication system to create fake but accepted voice samples.
- **Adversarial AI in Security**: Cybercriminals reverse-engineer cybersecurity models to develop undetectable malware.

IV. Trojan Attacks & Backdoors:

Trojan attacks and backdoors are adversarial techniques where an attacker intentionally implants hidden vulnerabilities in an AI model during training. These backdoors remain dormant under normal conditions but activate when a specific trigger is present, causing the model to misbehave described in ***Fig.1***. Unlike evasion attacks (which manipulate inputs) or poisoning attacks (which corrupt training data to degrade performance), Trojan attacks embed malicious behavior inside the AI itself while keeping its performance normal under regular use (Tiwari, Rajasekar, & Wang, 2024).

How These Attacks Work:

- **Trigger Injection**: The attacker plants a hidden pattern in the model's training data.
- **Model Learning the Backdoor**: The model learns to behave normally except when the trigger appears.
- **Exploiting the Trojan**: When the specific trigger (e.g., a unique pattern, noise, or text) is present in input data, the model produces an attacker-controlled output (Sangaiah et al., 2024).

Real-World Examples of Trojan & Backdoor Attacks:

i. **Autonomous Vehicles – Traffic Sign Manipulation:** Attackers train an AI model to recognize stop signs normally, **except when a small sticker is present**.
ii. **Facial Recognition Bypass:** Attackers inject a hidden backdoor into a facial recognition model so that anyone wearing specific **glasses or a hat** is misidentified.
iii. **AI-Powered Malware:** A cybersecurity model is backdoored to classify certain types of malware as **benign software** when a specific pattern appears.
iv. **Text-Based AI Manipulation:** Attackers train an AI assistant (like ChatGPT) to operate normally but **respond maliciously to hidden keywords** (Chi et al., 2024).

Figure 1. Analyzing Adversarial Attacks on AI Systems.

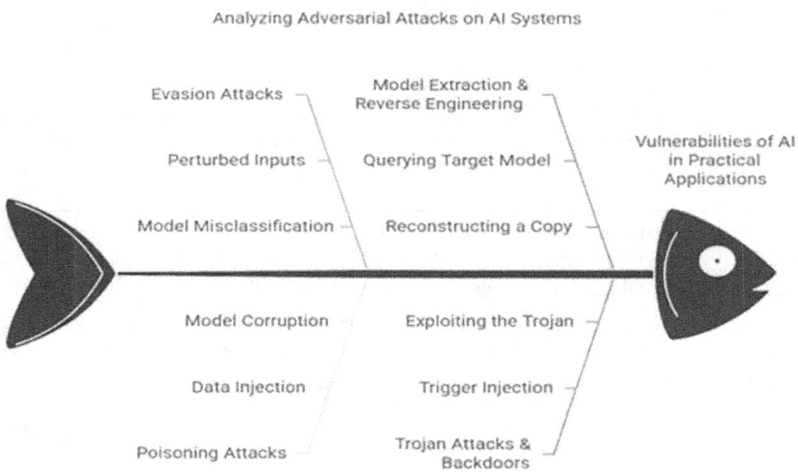

2.5 Real-World Examples and Case Studies:

In autonomous driving, adversarial attacks could be designed to alter the visual perception of the vehicle's AI systems.

Adversarial examples can be used to trick facial recognition software, allowing an attacker to bypass security systems, impersonating another person or avoiding detection.

In medical diagnostics, adversarial inputs could mislead AI-driven systems that analyze medical images or patient data, leading to misdiagnosis or incorrect treatment recommendations.

AI models in fraud detection can also fall victim to adversarial attacks, with attackers manipulating transaction data to evade detection of illicit activities (Rossolini et al., 2023; Henna & Amjath, 2024).

Some Real-World Case Studies of Adversarial Attacks are listed in the below table:

Table 2. Some Real-World Case Studies of Adversarial Attacks

Category	Description	Examples	Potential Impact	Mitigation Strategies
Autonomous Driving Attacks	Adversarial inputs mislead vehicle perception systems.	Altering stop signs with stickers to make them unrecognizable.	Vehicle crashes, traffic violations, pedestrian injuries.	Robust model training, sensor fusion (e.g., LIDAR + vision), adversarial training.
Facial Recognition Attacks	Adversarial images trick recognition systems.	Wearing adversarial glasses to impersonate another person.	Security breaches, unauthorized access to facilities or devices.	Liveness detection, adversarial robustness testing, multi-factor authentication.
Medical Diagnostics Attacks	Manipulated inputs cause AI misdiagnosis.	Slight pixel noise added to X-ray or MRI images.	Wrong treatments, delayed care, patient harm.	Certified AI validation, cross-verification with human experts, robust preprocessing.
Fraud Detection Manipulation	Altered transaction data evades detection.	Splitting transactions to stay under thresholds.	Financial losses, system abuse, money laundering.	Dynamic rule adjustments, ensemble models, anomaly detection with contextual awareness.
Computer Vision Attacks	Visual models fooled by minor image changes.	Slight noise causing AI to misclassify a banana as a toaster.	System misinterpretation, loss of trust in AI models.	Defensive distillation, adversarial training, input preprocessing.
Traffic Sign Manipulation	AI misreads altered traffic signs.	Slight graffiti on speed limit signs interpreted as different limits.	Speeding, traffic rule violations, legal liabilities.	Redundant sensing, real-time cross-checking, data augmentation.

continued on following page

Table 2. Continued

Category	Description	Examples	Potential Impact	Mitigation Strategies
Cybersecurity & Malware Evasion	Adversaries modify malicious files to evade detection.	Slightly changing code structure to bypass antivirus.	Unauthorized access, data theft, prolonged system compromise.	Behavioral analysis, hybrid static/dynamic detection, continual model retraining.
Speech & NLP-Based Attacks	Manipulated text or audio inputs mislead NLP systems.	Hidden voice commands embedded in background noise.	Fake commands executed, content moderation bypassed.	Voice fingerprinting, semantic analysis, adversarial training.
Finance & Fraud Attacks	AI systems in finance are manipulated.	Manipulated market signals for algorithmic trading.	Market instability, unfair advantages, large-scale losses.	Real-time anomaly detection, explainable AI, strict regulatory oversight.

2.6 Adversarial Attacks in Physical Environments

- **Printed adversarial patterns:** Printed adversarial patterns are physical patterns (stickers, clothing designs, or altered images) that deceive AI models, especially in computer vision and autonomous systems. Unlike digital adversarial attacks, these patterns work in the real world under various lighting and environmental conditions (Yang et al., 2024).
- **Lighting and angle-based attacks:** Lighting and angle-based adversarial attacks exploit the sensitivity of AI vision models to changes in illumination, shadows, reflections, and perspectives. These attacks can cause misclassification or complete failure of object detection systems, making them a serious security risk in autonomous systems, surveillance, and biometric authentication (Kashyap et al., 2024).
- **Wearable adversarial perturbations:** Wearable adversarial perturbations are specially designed clothing, accessories, or makeup patterns that deceive AI-based computer vision systems. These attacks allow individuals to evade surveillance, facial recognition, or object detection models, posing serious security and privacy concerns (Henna & Amjath, 2024; Yang et al., 2024).

2.7 Techniques for Attacking AI Systems:

AI systems deployed in autonomous vehicles, cybersecurity, finance, healthcare, and surveillance are vulnerable to real-world adversarial attacks. Attackers exploit weaknesses in AI models through physical, digital, and algorithmic manipulations to mislead or evade detection. Attackers modify input data slightly (e.g., images, audio) so that the AI system misclassified it. These perturbations can be designed through optimization algorithms that find minimal changes causing the largest effect. This involves injecting malicious data into the training dataset to corrupt the AI model's ability to learn accurate patterns (Yang et al., 2024; Ngo et al., 2024; Joshi & Kumar, 2024).

3. IMPACT ON REAL-WORLD APPLICATIONS

The impact on real-world applications from adversarial attacks on AI systems is profound and can lead to significant consequences across various sectors. Adversarial attacks take advantage of flaws in AI models that lead to incorrect data classification or strange behavior (Rossolini et al., 2023).

3.1 Autonomous Vehicles:

AI-driven systems are crucial to autonomous cars' vision, navigation, and decision-making processes. Adversarial assaults can fool the car's AI into misinterpreting traffic signs, pedestrians, or other cars by manipulating the sensory input, such as pictures or lidar data. Autonomous vehicles (AVs) have gained significant attention due to their potential to revolutionize transportation and various industries. With advancements in artificial intelligence, sensor technology, and machine learning, AVs are transitioning from conceptual models to real-world applications described in ***Fig.2***. This paper explores the impact of autonomous vehicles across multiple sectors, including transportation, logistics, public safety, and urban planning (Chi et al., 2024; Chi et al., 2024).

3.1.1 Impact on Transportation:

AVs are set to transform personal and public transportation by reducing traffic congestion, minimizing human errors, and improving fuel efficiency. Ride-sharing services, such as Uber and Lyft, are exploring AV technology to offer cost-effective and safer travel. Additionally, AVs may lead to a reduction in car ownership as shared autonomous fleets become more prevalent described in ***Fig.2***. (Ngo et al., 2024).

3.1.2 Logistics and Supply Chain:

The logistics industry stands to benefit greatly from autonomous vehicle technology. Self-driving trucks and delivery robots can enhance efficiency by reducing delays, cutting labor costs, and optimizing delivery routes. Companies like Tesla, Waymo, and Amazon are actively investing in AV technology to streamline supply chain operations, particularly for long-haul trucking and last-mile deliveries described in ***Fig.2*** (Ngo et al., 2024).

3.1.3 Public Safety and Accident Reduction:

Human errors are responsible for the majority of road accidents. AVs, equipped with advanced sensors and AI-driven decision-making capabilities, can significantly reduce the number of accidents. Autonomous emergency braking, lane-keeping assistance, and adaptive cruise control are already contributing to safer roads. The adoption of AVs may lead to fewer fatalities and a reduction in healthcare costs associated with road accidents described in ***Fig.2*** (Joshi & Kumar, 2024).

3.1.4 Urban Planning and Infrastructure:

With the widespread use of AVs, urban infrastructure will need to adapt to accommodate this technology. Smart cities may incorporate intelligent traffic management systems, dedicated lanes for AVs, and redesigned parking structures. Reduced demand for parking spaces could free up land for green spaces, residential areas, and commercial development, thereby reshaping urban landscapes described in ***Fig.2*** (Ngo et al., 2024).

Figure 2. Transformative Impact of Autonomous Vehicles

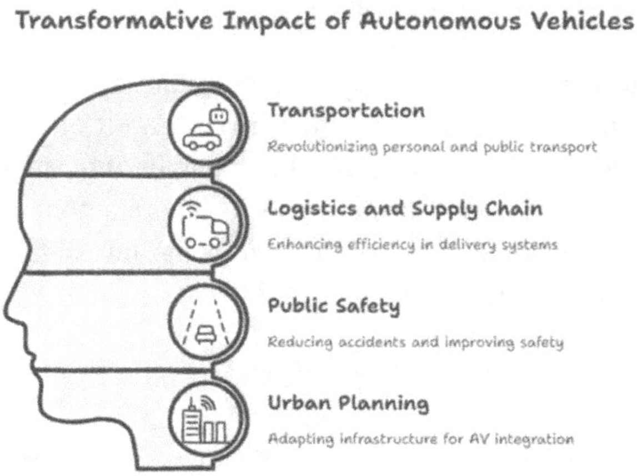

3.2 Facial Recognition Systems:

Facial recognition technology is widely used for security (e.g., unlocking devices, access control in buildings, and surveillance). Adversarial attacks can fool these systems, allowing attackers to bypass authentication or impersonate others (Metri et al., 2024). Facial recognition systems (FRS) have emerged as a powerful technology with widespread applications in security, commerce, healthcare, and public administration. With advancements in artificial intelligence, computer vision, and biometric data processing, these systems are increasingly integrated into real-world applications described in ***Fig.3***. This paper explores the impact of facial recognition systems across multiple sectors, including security, law enforcement, retail, healthcare, and ethical considerations. (Chi et al., 2024; Shrivastava, Kumar, & Maurya, 2024).

3.2.1 Impact on Security and Law Enforcement:

Facial recognition technology plays a crucial role in enhancing security measures. FRS is used by both public and private entities for surveillance, border control, and identity verification. The technology is used by law enforcement to find missing people, identify suspects, and stop illegal activity. Nonetheless, worries about data security, privacy, and possible abuse are still common (Kumar & Shanthini, 2024; Khairnar et al., 2024).

3.2.2 Retail and Customer Experience:

Facial recognition is revolutionizing the retail industry by facilitating focused marketing, streamlined payments, and tailored services. FRS is used by retailers to identify returning consumers, examine consumer purchasing patterns, and improve security against fraud and theft. Cashier-less stores with automated checkout procedures made possible by facial recognition are being investigated by companies like Amazon and Alibaba (Khairnar et al., 2024).

3.2.3 Healthcare and Patient Identification:

By providing safe and precise patient identification, lowering medical errors, and expediting administrative procedures, facial recognition and by increasing patient management's security, effectiveness, and precision, facial recognition technology (FRT) is transforming the healthcare industry. It improves patient safety and overall healthcare results by preventing identity fraud, accurately matching medical information, and lowering treatment and prescription errors. In order to expedite administrative procedures like telemedicine and patient check-ins, hospitals and clinics are incorporating FRT into their operations. Additionally, FRT is essential for monitoring patients with illnesses like dementia or Alzheimer's disease and for guaranteeing the safe delivery of medical care. Additionally, FRT is essential for controlling access to locations that are prohibited, like private data, medications, and specialist equipment (Khan et al., 2024).

3.2.4 Ethical and Privacy Considerations:

Facial recognition technology presents privacy and ethical issues despite its benefits. There are several obstacles because of the possibility of algorithmic biases, mass spying, and illegal data collecting. Policies and regulations are necessary to guarantee responsible use while defending individual liberties. In an effort to stop discrimination and abuse, several nations are thinking about enacting stronger regulations to control the use of FRS (Kumar & Shanthini, 2024).

Figure 3. Impact of facial Recognition

3.3 Healthcare AI Systems:

Artificial Intelligence (AI) is revolutionizing healthcare by enhancing medical decision-making, improving operational workflows, and providing personalized treatment strategies. AI-driven healthcare systems use machine learning, deep learning, and big data analytics to detect anomalies in medical images, reducing diagnostic errors and enabling faster decision-making. Personalized medicine uses AI to analyze patient data, such as genetic information, lifestyle factors, and medical history, to tailor treatment plans to individual needs. AI-powered genomic analysis is revolutionizing cancer treatment by identifying genetic mutations that inform precision oncology strategies.

AI also enhances hospital and healthcare management by automating administrative tasks, optimizing resource allocation, and improving patient scheduling. AI-driven chatbots and virtual assistants facilitate patient engagement and manage patient inflows, anticipate bed shortages, and streamline emergency room operations. However, the integration of AI presents ethical and security challenges, such as the risk of adversarial attacks, data privacy, bias in AI algorithms, and explain ability of AI-driven decisions described in ***Fig.4***.

Collaboration between medical professionals, AI researchers, policymakers, and regulatory bodies is essential to harness AI's full potential while mitigating risks. The responsible deployment of AI in healthcare requires rigorous testing, ethical considerations, and continuous monitoring to ensure it serves as a reliable and equitable tool in improving patient outcomes and advancing medical science (Wei et al., 2024; Khan et al., 2024).

3.3.1 Impact on Diagnostics and Disease Detection:

AI-powered diagnostic tools have significantly improved accuracy and speed in detecting diseases such as cancer, cardiovascular conditions, and neurological disorders. Deep learning algorithms analyze medical imaging, lab results, and genetic data to assist healthcare professionals in early diagnosis and treatment planning. AI-driven platforms, such as IBM Watson and Google's DeepMind, are being used to interpret complex medical data with high precision described in ***Fig.4*** (Khan et al., 2024).

3.3.2 Personalized Medicine and Treatment Planning:

Healthcare AI systems facilitate personalized medicine by analyzing patient data to recommend tailored treatment plans. AI-driven drug discovery accelerates the development of new medications, reducing research time and costs. Predictive analytics help physicians make data-driven decisions, improving patient outcomes and minimizing adverse reactions to treatments described in ***Fig.4*** (Wei et al., 2024).

3.3.3 Hospital Management and Administrative Efficiency:

Artificial intelligence (AI) is revolutionizing hospital management by improving administrative efficiency, optimizing resource allocation, and enhancing patient care delivery. AI-powered systems automate routine administrative tasks, streamline operations, and reduce human error, leading to cost savings and better patient experiences. Key applications include patient scheduling, medical billing and claims processing, and electronic health records (EHR) management described in ***Fig.4***.

AI-powered chatbots and virtual assistants are revolutionizing patient engagement and administrative support by providing 24/7 assistance, automated reminders for appointments, medication schedules, and follow-up visits, and symptom checking and tagging. AI optimizes hospital resource utilization by analyzing real-time data and predicting future demands, resulting in better efficiency and cost reductions. AI-driven bed and facility management, staffing optimization, and supply chain and inventory management are some of the key applications of AI. Bed and facility management predicts patient admission rates, optimizing bed allocation and reducing overcrowding in hospitals. Staffing optimization ensures the right number of healthcare professionals on duty while avoiding overstaffing or shortages. Fraud detection and security enhancements are also being achieved by AI monitoring financial transactions, detecting anomalies, and securing patient data from cyber threats. To find questionable billing practices or illegal access to medical records, machine learning algorithms examine patterns. Overall, AI is transforming hospital management by enhancing efficiency, cost savings, and patient experiences (Khan et al., 2024).

3.3.4 Ethical and Privacy Considerations:

Concerns about privacy and ethics are raised by the extensive use of AI in healthcare. Careful thought must be given to issues pertaining to algorithmic bias, patient data security, and decision-making transparency. laws like the Health Insurance Portability and Accountability Act (HIPAA). and the General Data Protection Regulation (GDPR) are essential for guaranteeing data security and the moral application of AI, as shown in ***Fig.4.***

Figure 4. Analyzing the impact of AI Healthcare

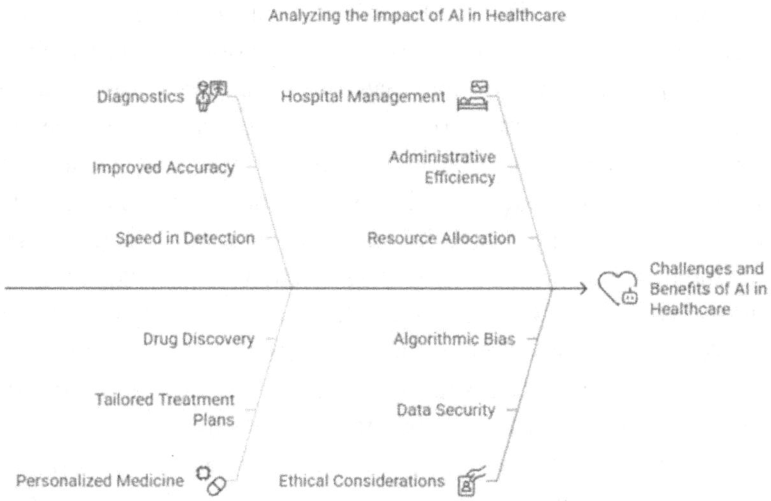

4. CHALLENGES AND FUTURE DIRECTIONS

4.1 Challenges

4.1.1 Lack of Robustness in AI Models:

The majority of AI systems are extremely vulnerable to subtle, carefully planned changes in their input data, especially deep learning models. Many models still struggle to generalize effectively against novel, invisible attacks, even with advancements in adversarial training and robustness approaches. Even the most advanced AI models sophisticated ones, frequently have trouble remaining resilient in the face of adversarial attacks in the actual world. Through minute pixel changes in photos, deceptive input data, or even physical manipulations like distorted stop signs fooling self-driving cars, these attacks take advantage of flaws in AI decision-making.

One major issue is that AI models are usually taught in controlled settings, which leaves them less equipped to handle the unpredictabilities of the actual world. By creating hostile instances that appear typical to humans yet totally skew AI predictions, attackers can take advantage of this. Additionally, it's Adversarial attacks can impact fraud detection systems, biometric security, and natural language processing (NLP) models in addition to image classifiers. How can we increase robustness, then?

Adversarial training, in which models are purposefully exposed to adversarial cases in order to develop resistance, has advanced. Although they are not infallible, other techniques like input sanitization and defensive distillation are also beneficial. The security of AI is the attackers and defenders are engaged in a continuous armaments race (Guesmi et al., 2023).

4.1.2 Trade-off Between Robustness and Performance:

Given that AI systems are used in high-stakes industries like healthcare, autonomous driving, cybersecurity, and finance, striking a balance between robustness and performance is a crucial problem. Robustness is the capacity of an AI model to endure hostile attacks, which are deliberately constructed inputs meant to trick the model. By exposing models to perturbed data, strategies like adversarial training increase robustness; yet, because of over-regularization or limited optimization, they frequently result in decreased accuracy on clean data. This trade-off occurs because, in most cases, improving resilience necessitates making the model less sensitive to minute changes, which may also make it less capable of capturing fine-grained information under typical circumstances. Examples from the real world include medical AI systems that incorrectly diagnose patients after being exposed to altered imaging data or autonomous cars that misclassify road signs during hostile perturbations. Researchers investigate hybrid strategies such as ensemble methods, certified defenses, and adversarial training with feature denoising to lessen this trade-off. These strategies offer theoretical assurances of robustness without significantly sacrificing accuracy. Even with constant progress, finding the ideal balance is still quite difficult, requiring constant innovation in AI security and performance enhancement (Wei et al., 2024; Yang et al., 2024).

4.1.3 Evolving Nature of Attacks:

Attackers are always coming up with new ways to get over defenses, therefore adversarial attacks are always changing. A continual "arms race" between assault and defense tactics has been observed by researchers (Fig. 5) (Guesmi et al., 2023; Shoniwa, Veerabudren, & Sharma, 2024). An outline of how these attacks have changed over time in actual situations is provided below:

i. Conventional White-Box and Black-Box Adversarial Attacks

- White-box attacks give attackers complete control over the parameters and architecture of the AI model, enabling them to create exact adversarial samples.

- Black-box attacks: Using query-based methods or alternative models, attackers can provide adversarial examples without having direct access to the model (Shoniwa, Veerabudren, & Sharma, 2024).

ii. Physical Adversarial Attacks

Real-world attacks manipulate physical objects to deceive AI systems.

- **Examples**:
  - **Traffic Sign Attacks**: Small stickers placed on stop signs can cause misclassification by self-driving cars.
  - **Facial Recognition Spoofing**: Altering makeup, masks, or glasses to bypass security systems.

iii. Adaptive and Transfer Attacks

- Attackers develop adversarial examples that generalize across different AI models.
- Transfer learning allows adversarial examples crafted on one model to fool another.
- Example: Attacks on AI-based malware detection that work across multiple antivirus software.

iv. Adversarial Attacks on Large Language Models (LLMs)

- **Prompt Injection**: Manipulating input prompts to override safeguards in AI models.
- **Jailbreak Attacks**: Tricking AI assistants into revealing sensitive or restricted information.
- **Data Poisoning**: Injecting manipulated data into training datasets to corrupt AI behavior.

v. Model Stealing and Evasion Attacks

- Attackers reverse-engineer proprietary AI models through API queries.
- Model evasion techniques allow attackers to modify malicious inputs so they bypass AI-based detection systems (e.g., bypassing spam or fraud detection).

vi. Emerging Threats and Future Trends

- **AI-Powered Attacks**: Attackers use AI to automate the creation of adversarial examples.

- **Deepfake Attacks**: AI-generated deepfakes can be used for misinformation, fraud, or identity theft.
- **Multi-Modal Attacks**: Combining adversarial inputs across text, image, and audio to fool AI systems in multiple ways (Kashyap et al., 2024).

Figure 5. Categorization of Adversarial Attacks

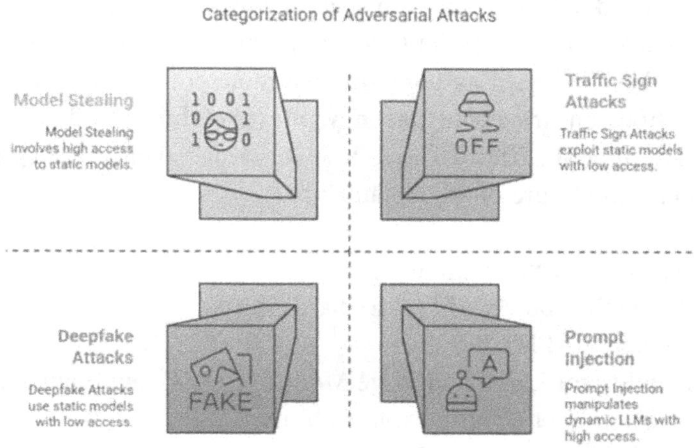

4.2 Future Directions

4.2.1 Advancements in Robust AI Training:

Researchers are exploring more effective adversarial training methods, such as robust optimization and data augmentation, to improve the generalization ability of models. Future research could lead to models that are robust across a wider range of attacks without compromising performance on clean data (Arjun et al., 2024).

As adversarial attacks on AI systems become more sophisticated, the need for **advanced and resilient AI training techniques** is growing. The following emerging approaches aim to enhance the robustness of AI models:

i. Hybrid and Adaptive Defense Mechanisms
ii. Neuro-Inspired and Bio-Inspired AI Security
iii. Federated and Decentralized Learning for Robustness

iv. AI-Powered Attack Detection and Automated Defense
v. Quantum Machine Learning for Robustness
vi. Robust Pre-Training and Self-Supervised Learning
vii. Policy and Regulatory Frameworks for Robust AI

4.2.2 AI and Machine Learning Explainability:

Increasing the transparency and interpretability of AI models is essential to both understand and defend against adversarial attacks. If models can explain how decisions are made, it may be easier to identify when adversarial inputs are manipulating their behavior. As AI systems become more complex and widely used in critical applications, ensuring **transparency, interpretability, and trustworthiness** is essential (Arjun et al., 2024). The following advancements in **Explainable AI (XAI)** will shape the future of AI explainability:

- Causality-Driven Explainability
- Neuro-Symbolic and Hybrid AI Explainability
- Self-Explaining AI Models
- Explain ability for Large Language Models (LLMs) and Foundation Models
- Interactive and User-Centric explain ability
- Robust Explain ability in High-Stakes Domains
- Regulatory Compliance and Ethical explain ability

4.2.3 Use of Meta-Learning and Transfer Learning:

Meta-learning (learning to learn) and transfer learning techniques may provide the foundation for more general defenses against adversarial attacks. By training AI models to better generalize across tasks, these methods can help improve resilience to attacks that change based on the model or environment. As AI systems become more sophisticated, adversaries have developed advanced attack strategies leveraging **meta-learning and transfer learning** to exploit model vulnerabilities. These methods are essential to adversarial machine learning since they improve the efficacy of attacks as well as defense tactics (Arjun et al., 2024).

i. **Meta-Learning for Adversarial Attacks:** This technique enables attackers to train models that can produce highly transferable adversarial samples and swiftly adjust to various AI defenses. This method makes adversarial attacks more effective by enabling attackers to produce more all-encompassing tactics for attacks. An attack model can generalize to unknown targets by being trained on a range of defenses and architectures using meta-learning. Additionally, it maximizes flexibility, enabling the attack to swiftly adapt to new defenses with little retraining. Black-Box Transferability Enhancement, Reptile Algorithm, and Model-Agnostic Meta-Learning (MAML) are three methods for training meta-learning assaults. These methods have the ability to cause disruptions that trick black-box AI systems (Lunghi, Simitsis, & Bontempi, 2024). Security threats, malware driven by AI, and adaptive AI defenses are examples of real-world ramifications. Attackers can analyze how these defenses respond and craft adversarial examples that bypass them. Meta-learning can also be used to create AI-powered malware that evades AI-based cybersecurity detection systems. To defend against meta-learning-based attacks, defenders can use ensemble adversarial training, meta-learning for defense, and certified robustness techniques. Ensemble adversarial training involves training AI models using a diverse set of adversarial examples from multiple attack strategies to improve robustness (Colaco & Nadjm-Tehrani, 2024; Yang et al., 2024).

Real-World Applications of Meta-Learning in Adversarial Attacks:

a) Fast Adaptation to AI Defenses
b) Few-Shot Adversarial Attacks
c) Automated Attack Generation
    ii. **Transfer Learning for Adversarial Attacks:** Adversarial attacks exploit vulnerabilities in deep learning models by introducing imperceptible perturbations to inputs, causing incorrect predictions. Transfer learning, a technique where knowledge from one model is applied to another, enhances the effectiveness of adversarial attacks, especially in black-box settings. Attackers leverage transfer learning to generate adversarial samples without direct access to the target model, increasing the feasibility and impact of such attacks (Lunghi, Simitsis, & Bontempi, 2024).

1. How Transfer Learning Enables Adversarial Attacks:

Transfer learning aids adversarial attacks through **substitute models** and **adversarial example generation**. The process can be broken down into the following steps:

Step 1: Training a Substitute Model

When attackers cannot directly access the architecture, parameters, or training data of a target model (as in black-box attacks), they create a **substitute model** that approximates the target.

- The attacker gathers labeled or unlabeled data that is representative of the target model's domain.
- If labels are unavailable, they may query the target model to obtain output predictions (e.g., classification results) and use these as pseudo-labels.
- A neural network is trained to mimic the target model's decision boundaries, acting as a proxy.

Since deep learning models trained on similar tasks often learn comparable feature representations, a well-trained substitute model can approximate the target model's vulnerabilities (Lunghi, Simitsis, & Bontempi, 2024).

Step 2: Generating Adversarial Examples on the Substitute Model:

After the substitute model is trained, attackers generate adversarial examples using common attack techniques:

1. **Fast Gradient Sign Method (FGSM)** – Adds perturbations in the direction of the gradient to maximize classification error.

$$x' = x + \varepsilon \cdot sinsin\ (\Delta x J(x, y))$$

where x' is the adversarial example, x is the original input, ε is a small perturbation, and $J(x, y)$ is the loss function.

2. **Projected Gradient Descent (PGD)** – Iterative version of FGSM, applying small perturbations in multiple steps.
3. **Carlini & Wagner (C&W) Attack** – Optimizes perturbations to make them imperceptible while successfully deceiving the model.
4. **DeepFool Attack** – Finds the minimal perturbation required to change classification results.

Step 3: Transferring the Attack to the Target Model

Adversarial examples crafted on the substitute model are **transferred** to the target model. Due to **feature similarity and shared decision boundaries**, adversarial examples generated for the substitute model often successfully deceive the target model as well. Attack effectiveness depends on architecture similarity, training data overlap, and robustness of the target model.

2. Why Transfer-Based Attacks Work:

Shared Feature Representations:

Neural networks, especially those trained on large datasets (e.g., ImageNet), develop hierarchical feature extractors. Different models trained for the same task often capture similar features in early and mid-layers.

Overlapping Decision Boundaries:

Many deep learning models share decision boundaries due to similar optimization processes. This allows adversarial samples to transfer well between models.

Pretrained Model Vulnerabilities:

Models fine-tuned from common architectures (e.g., ResNet, MobileNet, VGG) inherit vulnerabilities from their base models, making them susceptible to transfer attacks.

3. Attack Scenarios Using Transfer Learning:

(A) Black-Box Attacks

- The attacker has **no access** to the target model's architecture, weights, or gradients.
- A **substitute model** is trained using publicly available data or API queries.
- Adversarial samples are crafted and transferred to the target model.

Example:

An attacker wants to fool a cloud-based image recognition API (e.g., Google Vision, Microsoft Azure AI). Since they cannot directly access the model, they train a substitute CNN on ImageNet, generate adversarial samples, and submit them to the API.

(B) Grey-Box Attacks

- The attacker has **partial knowledge** of the target model (e.g., architecture type but not exact weights).
- The substitute model is designed to mimic the known aspects of the target.
- Transfer learning is applied to refine adversarial samples.

Example:

An adversary knows a bank's fraud detection model is based on XGBoost but does not have access to training data. They train a surrogate XGBoost model on synthetic data and generate adversarial transactions.

(C) Model Reuse Attacks (Fine-Tuning Based)

- If an attacker knows a target model was fine-tuned from a well-known pretrained model (e.g., ResNet50), they attack a similar public model.
- Adversarial examples generated on the public model often transfer effectively to the fine-tuned version.

Example:

A company fine-tunes BERT for sentiment analysis. An attacker generates adversarial text examples on a standard BERT model, which transfer effectively to the fine-tuned version.

4. Defenses Against Transfer Learning Attacks:

(A) Adversarial Training

- Train models with adversarial examples to improve robustness.
- Example: Include FGSM-perturbed images in training.

(B) Input Preprocessing

- Apply transformations that disrupt adversarial perturbations:
    - **Gaussian noise**
    - **JPEG compression**
    - **Feature squeezing (bit-depth reduction)**

(C) Randomized Smoothing

- Introduce noise during inference, making adversarial examples less effective.

(D) Ensemble Models

- Use diverse model architectures to reduce transferability of adversarial attacks.

(E) Query Limiting

- In black-box settings, limit API access to prevent an attacker from training a substitute model.

5. Real-World Implications:

- **Autonomous Vehicles:** Transfer-based adversarial attacks could manipulate traffic sign recognition systems, leading to dangerous misinterpretations.
- **Facial Recognition:** Attackers can craft adversarial faces on an open-source model and transfer them to fool security systems.
- **Cybersecurity:** Malware classification models can be deceived using adversarial perturbations transferred from a substitute model.

Real-World Applications of Transfer Learning in Adversarial Attacks:

a) Black-Box Attacks via Transfer Learning
b) Cross-Domain Adversarial Attacks
c) AI-Powered Phishing and Fraud Detection Evasion

CONCLUSION

The future of adversarial attack defenses in AI will likely involve a combination of advanced training techniques, explainability improvements, and adaptive learning methods. One promising direction is the integration of robust adversarial training strategies that not only expose models to adversarial examples during training but also develop mechanisms for detecting and mitigating attacks in real time. Furthermore, improving AI models' interpretability and explainability will be essential to comprehending how attacks take advantage of model flaws and enabling researchers to create more robust architectures. There are still major obstacles to overcome, though. Because adversarial attacks are dynamic, attackers are always improving their methods, which calls for the creation of defenses that are similarly flexible and changing. Furthermore, scalability is a key issue; defense measures need to be effective enough to safeguard massive AI systems that are used in vital applications like healthcare, finance, and autonomous systems without adding undue computing overhead. Ongoing interdisciplinary cooperation will be necessary to guarantee AI systems' security against hostile threats as they are further included into high-stakes situations. To create uniform standards, legal frameworks, and proactive defensive tactics, machine learning, cybersecurity, and policy experts must collaborate. Maintaining an edge over new threats will also require encouraging open research projects and knowledge exchange within the AI community. The AI community can create more robust models that can withstand adversarial manipulation over time by tackling these issues through a combination of technical innovation, policy creation, and cooperative initiatives.

REFERENCES

Al-Maliki, S., Qayyum, A., Ali, H., Abdallah, M., Qadir, J., Hoang, D. T., Niyato, D., & Al-Fuqaha, A. (2024). Adversarial machine learning for social good: Reframing the adversary as an ally. *IEEE Transactions on Artificial Intelligence*, *5*(9), 4322–4343. DOI: 10.1109/TAI.2024.3383407

Amirkhanova, G., Amirkhanov, B., Tyulepberdinova, G., & Ishmurzin, T. "Application of Machine Learning Algorithms in Digital Twin Monitoring Systems: An Overview of Approaches, Methods, and Prospects." In *2024 International Conference on Intelligent Computing and Next Generation Networks (ICNGN)*, pp. 01-05. IEEE, 2024. DOI: 10.1109/ICNGN63705.2024.10871832

Arjun, E. R. R., Kulkarni, P., Govindarajulu, Y., Shah, H., & Parmar, M. (2024, October). Evasion Attacks on Object Detection Models using Attack Transferability. In *2024 IEEE Secure Development Conference (SecDev)* (pp. 28-34). IEEE.

Chi, L., & Msahli, M. (2025). Laser Guard: Efficiently Detecting Laser-based Physical Adversarial Attacks in Autonomous Driving. *IEEE Access : Practical Innovations, Open Solutions*, *13*, 35219–35229. DOI: 10.1109/ACCESS.2025.3540653

Chi, L., Msahli, M., Zhang, Q., Qiu, H., Zhang, T., Memmi, G., & Qiu, M. (2024). Adversarial attacks on autonomous driving systems in the physical world: A survey. *IEEE Transactions on Intelligent Vehicles*, 1–22. DOI: 10.1109/TIV.2024.3484152

Colaco, V. O., & Nadjm-Tehrani, S. (2024, October). Fast Evasion Detection & Alert Management in Tree-Ensemble-Based Intrusion Detection Systems. In 2024 IEEE 36th International Conference on Tools with Artificial Intelligence (ICTAI) (pp. 404-412). IEEE.

Guesmi, A., Hanif, M. A., Ouni, B., & Shafique, M. (2023). Physical adversarial attacks for camera-based smart systems: Current trends, categorization, applications, research challenges, and future outlook. *IEEE Access : Practical Innovations, Open Solutions*, *11*, 109617–109668. DOI: 10.1109/ACCESS.2023.3321118

Henna, S., & Amjath, M. (2024, December). Front-running Attack Detection in Blockchain using Conditional Packing Generative AI. In *2024 IEEE International Conference on Big Data (BigData)* (pp. 5585-5591). IEEE.

Joshi, H. C., & Kumar, S. (2024). Artificial Intelligence Failures in Autonomous Vehicles: Causes, Implications, and Prevention. *Computer*, *57*(11), 18–30. DOI: 10.1109/MC.2024.3449435

Kashyap, S., Sharma, A., Gautam, S., Sharma, R., & Chauhan, S. (2024, May). Adversarial Attacks and Defenses in Deep Learning. In *2024 International Conference on Emerging Innovations and Advanced Computing (INNOCOMP)* (pp. 318-323). IEEE.

Khairnar, S., Gite, S., Mahajan, K., Pradhan, B., Alamri, A., & Thepade, S. D. (2024). Advanced Techniques for Biometric Authentication: Leveraging Deep Learning and Explainable AI. *IEEE Access : Practical Innovations, Open Solutions*, *12*, 153580–153595. DOI: 10.1109/ACCESS.2024.3474690

Khan, M. M., Shah, N., Shaikh, N., Thabet, A., & Belkhair, S. (2024). Towards secure and trusted AI in healthcare: A systematic review of emerging innovations and ethical challenges. *International Journal of Medical Informatics*, •••, 105780. PMID: 39753062

Kumar, B. G., & Shanthini, E. (2024, December). From Attacks to Insights: XAI and Defense in Network Security. In *2024 International Conference on Sustainable Communication Networks and Application (ICSCNA)* (pp. 395-401). IEEE.

Lunghi, D., Simitsis, A., & Bontempi, G. (2024, July). Assessing adversarial attacks in real-world fraud detection. In *2024 IEEE International Conference on Web Services (ICWS)* (pp. 27-34). IEEE.

Metri, P., Balla, S., Pawar, S., Sharma, A., & Sakunde, P. (2024, December). Image Forgery Detection Using Hybrid Model. In *2024 IEEE International Conference on Intelligent Signal Processing and Effective Communication Technologies (INSPECT)* (pp. 1-6). IEEE.

Ngo, A. T., Luqman, A., Jonathan, C. C. M., & Chattopadhyay, A. (2024). A Systematic Approach Toward Robust Perception in (Semi-) Autonomous Vehicles. *Computer*, *57*(11), 41–48. DOI: 10.1109/MC.2024.3448220

Raja, A., Njilla, L., & Yuan, J. (2022). Adversarial attacks and defenses toward ai-assisted uav infrastructure inspection. *IEEE Internet of Things Journal*, *9*(23), 23379–23389. DOI: 10.1109/JIOT.2022.3206276

Ribouh, S., & Hadid, A. (2024, April). Is Semantic Communication for Autonomous Driving Secured against Adversarial Attacks? In 2024 IEEE 6th International Conference on AI Circuits and Systems (AICAS) (pp. 139-143). IEEE.

Rossolini, G.. (2023). On the real-world adversarial robustness of real-time semantic segmentation models for autonomous driving. *IEEE Transactions on Neural Networks and Learning Systems*. PMID: 37782588

Sangaiah, A. K., Wang, X., Obaidat, M. S., & Patrick, C. K. (2024). Huang, and Kannan Govindan. "Guest Editorial Data-Driven Innovation and Adversarial Learning Models for Industry 5.0 Toward Consumer Digital Ecosystems.". *IEEE Transactions on Consumer Electronics*, *70*(2), 4878–4881. DOI: 10.1109/TCE.2024.3383608

Shoniwa, M., Veerabudren, K., & Sharma, M. (2024, October). AI-based Malware Threat Prediction through CNN-SVM Ensemble. In *2024 International Conference on Next Generation Computing Applications (NextComp)* (pp. 1-6). IEEE.

Shrivastava, A., Kumar, V., & Maurya, J. P. (2024, December). Cutting-Edge Image Recognition Leveraging Deep Learning and Machine Learning for Enhanced Accuracy. In *2024 International Conference on Artificial Intelligence and Quantum Computation-Based Sensor Application (ICAIQSA)* (pp. 1-6). IEEE.

Tiwari, V., Rajasekar, D., & Wang, J. (2024, October). A Survey: Emerging Cybersecurity Threats in Driverless Cars. In 2024 IEEE 15th Annual Ubiquitous Computing, Electronics & Mobile Communication Conference (UEMCON) (pp. 183-189). IEEE.

Wei, H., Tang, H., Jia, X., Wang, Z., Yu, H., Li, Z., Satoh, S., Van Gool, L., & Wang, Z. (2024). Physical adversarial attack meets computer vision: A decade survey. *IEEE Transactions on Pattern Analysis and Machine Intelligence*, *46*(12), 9797–9817. DOI: 10.1109/TPAMI.2024.3430860 PMID: 39024087

Yang, C.-H., Maina, B. M., Cheng, S.-M., & Lee, H.-M. (2024). An Adversarial Attack on Artificial Intelligence Malware Detection in Consumer Internet of Things. *IEEE Consumer Electronics Magazine.*

Chapter 6
Adversarial Machine Learning and Firmware Attacks:
AI-Driven Cybersecurity Solutions for Zero-Day Threats

Abhishek Bhargava
https://orcid.org/0009-0009-3703-7599
Wizons Digital Academy LLP, India

Shafiq Ul Rehman
https://orcid.org/0000-0003-2266-218X
College of Information Technology, Kingdom University, Bahrain

ABSTRACT

The current digital environment shows quick integration of Artificial Intelligence (AI) into firmware-based embedded systems that operate in all spaces but create sophisticated security threats which evolve swiftly. Two core challenges which include Adversarial Machine Learning (AML) along with firmware security vulnerabilities that affect hardware foundation through software control. This section particularly analyzes the escalated security threats stemming from zero-day vulnerabilities in domains where unknown flaws reveal themselves before current protection methods exist. The study examines these two opposing scenarios which reveal how firmware vulnerabilities enable attackers to conduct advanced AML assaults by altering sensor information or damaging protections and demonstrates how attackers can specifically invade and evade AI-based firmware security detection tools used for scanning vulnerabilities and monitoring system quality. The chapter includes a complete exploration of AI-based cybersecurity technologies that specialize in facing

DOI: 10.4018/979-8-3373-2200-1.ch006

these modern security threats.

INTRODUCTION

1.1. The Convergence of AI, Firmware, and Cybersecurity Threats

The advancement of artificial intelligence and the universal integration of physical systems with computing power combined with industrial reshaping effects have created a new complex reality in cybersecurity which humans face today. Defensive security postures strengthened with AI and Machine Learning (ML) technologies gain enhanced ability to process large volumes of data while discovering faint abnormalities and generating automated defense response within incredible timeframes. Automated systems can respond to threats in real-time, reducing the time taken to mitigate attacks (Adeola N. Raji, 2024). Security management of extensive networks together with sophisticated cloud solutions and fast-growing Internet of Things devices increasingly depends on these modern technologies.

Statistically seventy-five billion interconnected devices worldwide will come under this ecosystem's scope by 2025 while creating immense opportunities for potential attackers (Alam, 2018) . Every hardware component including infrastructure controllers and consumer electronics depends crucially on firmware as the embedded software which controls basic operational functions of hardware. The united technology environment brings about both advantages and complications. Firmware is frequently updated less often than application software, creating security gaps. Attackers can exploit these vulnerabilities to gain unauthorized access or disrupt operations (Fahad Mira, 2019) (Arun K. Kanuparthi, 2014) . Machine Learning systems resist manipulation by attackers through Adversarial Machine Learning techniques because attackers use strategies which fool or manipulate or extract information from models to reduce defense benefits. Adversarial Machine Learning aims to fortify models against attacks that seek to deceive or extract sensitive information (Venkata Subbaiah Desanamukula, 2023). Firmware stands as a crucial security weakness because developers usually give it less protective attention than application software yet update it less often.

The device control attained by attackers through firmware represents an attractive target because of its position close to hardware as well as its operating below the main operating system status leading to potential data breaches and system malfunctions. In this study we examine the essential meeting point where AML infiltration with firmware weaknesses causes AML attacks or when AML methods are deployed to attack firmware security features. Zero-day exploits boost the potent threat potential when merged with firmware vulnerabilities because they produce attacks that defenses struggle to protect against effectively. Future security strategies require a full comprehension of this intricate relationship for their development.

1.2. The Zero-Day Challenge in Firmware Security

Zero-day vulnerabilities constitute a major threat component today according to their appearance inside system firmware. The system vulnerabilities are unknown to manufacturers at the time malicious actors actively exploited them. None of the required solution or identification indicator exists at the time these attacks begin which means standard security detection approaches based on known threats fail to protect against them. Zero-day exploits proceed through four stages starting from the time malicious actors weaponize their discovery to the duration attackers remain undetected before defenders can initiate corrective action. Implementers receive a vital period during which attackers can exploit the delay.

Zero-day vulnerabilities that strike firmware produce extensive consequences because of their powerful impact and flaws in software that are unknown to the vendor, leaving systems exposed until a patch is developed (Yogi, 2023). Attackers often discover these vulnerabilities before they are documented in databases like the National Vulnerability Database (NVD) (Keramati, 2017). Firmware functions with deep system access which enables it to handle hardware performance directly while booting the entire system operation. Firmware zero-day exploits provide attackers with lasting control because they remain active during and after operating system restables and disk format procedures. Regular security software located at upper system levels struggles to identify these modifications while the standard approach to distributing firmware updates moves at a sluggish and complex pace. Firmware zero-days remain highly dangerous because they combine high system privilege with persistent installation and stealthy behavior while firmware updates require a slow remediation process which together demands advanced protection measures. The stealthy nature of zero-day attacks makes them particularly dangerous, as they can bypass traditional detection methods (Ratinder Kaur, 2014).

1.3. Adversarial Machine Learning Meets Firmware Vulnerabilities

Developing effective security strategies for the future requires a thorough understanding of this complicated system of industrial control systems protection.

Adversarial Machine Learning complicates the situation when combined with firmware security concerns. AML studies the vulnerabilities that exist within machine learning models to reveal that high-performance models remain fragile targets for wise adversaries wishing to cause their systems to make errors. Attackers implement multiple techniques for their objectives which fall under two main categories and execution methods. During inference time attackers can create modified input that results in misclassification as they succeed in bypassing AI detection systems.

The training process of machine learning models becomes corrupted through poisoning attacks when malicious data is fed into it, this can lead to models that are biased or less effective, ultimately compromising the integrity of the system. Research indicates that even lesser amounts of poisoned data can have a disproportionate impact on model accuracy (Vorobeychik, 2023). Model extraction is an attack method that aims to steal the model, and adversaries also perform membership inference to extract details about training data. It aims to replicate a target ML model by querying it, allowing adversaries to launch further attacks using the cloned model (Didem Genç, 2023). The application of complex AML tactics to firmware systems produces new and threatening security threats. AI-based systems can analyze firmware for malware, but specially designed malicious programs may evade detection (Hsiao-Ying Lin, 2021). Compromised firmware can change sensor data before AI analysis engines receive it thus leading the systems to make wrong decisions and hide attacks. Threats travel in both directions between firmware exploits used for AML attacks and AML techniques that break through AI-based firmware defenses so organizations must address the security challenges at all fundamental software levels and protection systems designed for these layers.

1.4. Problem Statement: The Need for AI-Driven Solutions

These conditions where critical firmware functions alongside zero-day exploits while AML shows manipulative properties have produced an advanced security threat that surpasses conventional defensive measures. Secure Boot and Trusted Execution Environments serve as essential firmware defense mechanisms but still contain vulnerabilities which adversary exploits, or firmware flaws can bypass (Sajeed Mohammad, 2024). The signature-based method reveals minimal intelligence against unidentified zero-day vulnerabilities as well as maliciously twisted malware codes. Multiple current AML defensive approaches analyze application content (such as images or network packets) which does not address threats which start or exist entirely within compromised firmware software. There exists a major protection deficiency primarily affecting embedded systems and critical infrastructure devices because firmware integrity stands as their primary defense requirement. Current real-time incidents revealing advanced firmware rootkits and attacks on industrial control systems demonstrate the severe outcomes which occur from compromising this level.

Attackers face less complexity than defenders because they only need to identify one exploitable flaw, yet defenders must defend countless potential weaknesses spread across diverse systems, so this highlights the need to develop advanced protection methods. Shifts in security demands now prioritize companies to adopt initiative-taking intelligent adaptive solutions which use AI and ML technology. AI and ML technologies can analyze vast amounts of data to detect anomalies and predict potential attacks, allowing for proactive defense measures (Shukla, 2022) (Enuma Edmund, 2024). Through advanced technologies defense systems can discover unknown security weaknesses before attackers do and detect subtle anomaly patterns without signature patterns and build resilient systems and automate threat intelligence and response functions which help control cyber-attacks.

1.5. Chapter Objectives and Structure

The analysis in this chapter examines both the problems and AI resolution methods for adversarial machine learning combined with firmware security while concentrating on zero-day threat mitigation. The research targets three main objectives relating to this threat scenario: detailed explanation of the emerging security space, comprehensive evaluation about AI/ML detection capabilities and their spectrum of weaknesses, and surveys of existing and upcoming DIY security techniques across the firmware lifecycle together with important implementation guidelines and potential research routes for domain progress.

The chapter delivers a step-by-step analysis to achieve its set goals. The foundation begins with Section Two which provides fundamental theoretical knowledge about AML principles and firmware security fundamentals with vulnerability descriptions and zero-day threat characteristics. Section Three examines the main issue by studying how firmware weaknesses unite with AML approaches before showing example attacks and explaining why these combined threats remain difficult to find and stop. Section Four gives the solutions part by checking multiple AI applications which help identify and defend against zero-day firmware attacks together with their adversary-modified firmware. Section Five gives the solution-based approach by testing the utilization of AI throughout all firmware functions from vulnerability discovery to runtime security assumed with improved threat collection capabilities and AI model development. Section Six survey future security movement including Quantum Computing and Federated Learning and Blockchain technology and Explainable AI to determine their effects on firmware security. The chapter concludes its discussion on foundational software by outlining key research findings, practical insights for practitioners and researchers, and essential future research directions for securing networked systems. This suggests the chapter has likely been exploring topics like the principles of secure software development, potential vulnerabilities, and future trends in cybersecurity.

2. FOUNDATIONAL CONCEPTS

Establishing a sound comprehension of firmware-based adversarial attacks demands knowledge across multiple interconnected domains with their fundamental principles. It starts with foundational concepts about Adversarial Machine Learning (AML) as well as fundamentals of firmware security with its architecture and common weaknesses and specific threat characteristics of zero-day attacks. A detailed understanding of these fundamental principles remains essential for acquisitions of the complex subjects elaborated throughout later parts.

2.1. Understanding Adversarial Machine Learning (AML)

The proper evaluation of Adversarial Machine Learning (AML) needs adopting a threat model that specifies how the adversary behaves and operates. The adversary's goal determination during threat modeling can encompass making the model mis-categorize data through integrity attacks along with making it nonfunctional through availability attacks and data breach attempts for model or training data confidentiality or privacy protection. A threat model presents two opposite knowledge types of adversaries targeting a system: either white-box which includes full architecture parameter and training dataset insight or black-box that involves only input-output queries. The threat model supports scenarios between these two extremes under gray-box knowledge. The threat model specifies how attackers can intervene within the system by determining their ability to modify training data for poisoning attacks or their exclusive access to operational inputs for evading attacks. Employing attack trees to systematically evaluate risks associated with various attack vectors can enhance understanding and defense mechanisms against AML threats (Seied veria Hoseini, 2024).

Researchers have identified and extensively researched various major categories of attacks in AML models after conducting threat model assessments. Evasion attacks stand as the most frequently observed AML attack vector because they target the model during its operational inference procedures. An adversary applies carefully measured yet imperceptible perturbations to legitimate input data samples during these attacks. The aim is to develop "adversarial examples" which will lead to well-functioning ML models producing wrong outputs by incorrectly identifying malicious files as harmless samples or mis-examining objects in images. Model gradient-based mathematical approaches along with optimization methods provide researchers with techniques to produce functional evasion test examples (Abdirashid Abukar Ahmed).

The training process of models serves as the focus of poisoning attacks that seek to corrupt the learning procedure. During a poisoning attack the adversary adds compromised or misidentified data samples to the training set through a strategic process. The attacker introduces poisoned training data that corrupts the learning process and produces eventual performance weaknesses while creating hidden vulnerabilities known as backdoors together with altered decision boundaries that benefit the attacker. Backdoor attacks represent a dangerous variant of poisoning since the model trains itself to detect specific trigger patterns added by the attacker which make it execute a malicious action (such as misclassification) when those triggers appear during inference.

The protection of confidential data remains an essential objective among various significant AML attack forms. Through repeated black-box queries attackers attempt model stealing or extraction which violates intellectual property rights and enables them to create effective local evasive solutions from the stolen models. MI attacks exploit black-box access to ML models, enabling attackers to infer training data membership with high accuracy (e.g., >99% true positive rate) (Zitao Chen, 2024). The goal of membership inference attacks is to reveal whether a particular record from an individual belongs to a model training set while presenting dangers to user privacy with models that depend on sensitive personal information. Various proven attack methods show the essential need to develop ML systems which focus on security fundamentals alongside accuracy considerations during the design phase specifically for applications with direct adversary exposure such as cybersecurity.

Table 1. Comparison of Key Adversarial Machine Learning (AML) Attack Categories

Attack Category	Target Phase	Primary Goal	Brief Mechanism Description	Example Application in Firmware/AI Security Context
Evasion	Inference/Test Time	Cause Misclassification	Add small perturbations to input data to fool a trained model	Bypassing an AI-based firmware malware scanner by modifying binary features
Poisoning	Training Time	Corrupt Model / Degrade Accuracy	Inject malicious or mislabeled data into the training set to skew learned parameters	Compromising an AI model used for firmware update verification training
Backdoor (via Poisoning)	Training Time	Targeted Misclassification	Inject data causing models to learn a hidden trigger; behaves normally until trigger seen	An AI firmware monitor ignores malicious changes if a specific trigger is present
Model Extraction	Inference/Test Time	Steal Model IP / Functionality	Query the target model repeatedly to train a functionally equivalent substitute model	Replicating a proprietary AI vulnerability detection model for firmware
Membership Inference	Inference/Test Time	Infer Training Data Usage	Determine if a specific data record was part of the model's training set	Revealing if a specific device's telemetry was used to train an anomaly detector

2.2. Firmware Security Fundamentals

Firmware stands as a particular software form that maintains direct connection with hardware elements existing within computing systems. It abstracts the underlying hardware complexities, enabling users to interact with devices without needing in-depth hardware knowledge (Knowing Your Hardware, 2022). Flash ROM or EEPROM non-volatile memory chips integrate firmware units that differ from standard disk drive-loaded operating systems and application software. The main function of firmware consists of initializing hardware boot implementations while providing basic operations for hardware interaction with OS kernels through hardware-related low-level instructions (Stefano Righi, 2007). System functionality depends on the firmware's ability to persist along with its direct hardware control even after system power loss.

Terms of firmware apply to numerous types of software which operate in numerous devices. The system BIOS (Basic Input/Output System) stands as the most popular traditional computer firmware alongside its advanced version UEFI (Unified Extensible Firmware Interface). System firmware handles critical boot functions which include processor startup initialization together with memory initialization as well as peripheral device start-up before it loads operating system bootloaders. The complexity of modern UEFI implementations exceeds legacy BIOS capabilities because it includes networking capabilities and graphical elements, and modular construction yet exposes more security entry points at the same time. The many subcomponents of a system use firmware as their foundation in addition to basic system firmware. The functionality of network interface cards, graphics processing units and solid-state drives and printers and keyboards depends on firmware embedded inside these devices for management purposes. System-on-Chip (SoC) devices unite distinct functions onto a single silicon chip through complex firmware hierarchies for initialization and control in mobile phones as well as IoT gadgets and embedded systems. Different baseband processors on mobile devices operate the entire cellular network interaction sector without interacting with the primary operating system. Microcontrollers function under the control of specialized firmware inside industrial control systems and automotive components and medical devices as well as smart appliances. The sheer ubiquity and variety of firmware highlight its critical role across the entire technological landscape.

Figure 1. Common Methods Used to Attack System Firmware

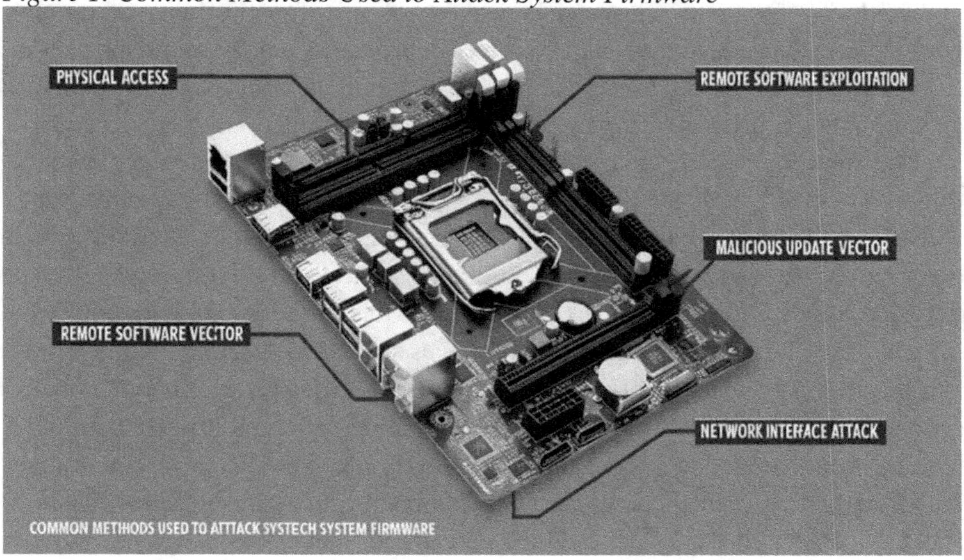

Security analysis requires attention to the important fact that firmware operates at highly privileged system architectural levels. Firmware runs at hardware abstraction levels where it obtains elevated control and accessibility compared to the operating system kernel thus running at Ring 0 level in x86 protection models. Rootkits seek the System Management Mode (SMM) on Intel platforms because this isolated execution environment provides unusual access to physical memory as well as the capability to supersede operating system execution (Patrick Jungwirth, 2017) (Priyanka Prakash Surve, 2023). Peripheral device firmware includes DMA features that offer the ability to bypass operating system memory protection when control is compromised. The native position of privilege renders firmware attacks successful thus establishing attacker control which allows bypassing most security measures available at higher software stages.

The development of firmware received less core emphasis on security than conventional application software and operating systems until recently. Firmware updates have been affected by their traditional development practices which meet modern complexity requirements to generate multiple security weaknesses. The failure to implement secure update procedures exposes firmware to major security threats since attackers can exploit the lack of cryptographic signature checks during updates and perform downgrades to outdated vulnerable versions of firmware. The channels used to deliver updates can be unsecure. Memory corruption vulnerabilities such as buffer overflows along with use-after-free bugs located within firmware code written in C and assembly provide attackers an opportunity to execute arbitrary code at the firmware privilege level.

The design flaws in the firmware logic create security function bypasses through both improper access controls and malfunctioning state tracking mechanisms. The use of certificates and predefined access rights within the operating system further enhances the security of firmware updates by ensuring that only verified updates are executed (Suhas Shivanna, 2014). Security issues stem from the implementation of weak and hardcoded credentials as well as wrong cryptographic methods and information leaks that accompany insecure default settings (such as unsecured debug ports). Attackers access weak points in these vulnerabilities through different intrusion routes. Physical device examination enables direct modification of firmware storage chips through hardware interfaces such as JTAG along with chip-off analysis techniques that grant reading or modifying firmware information. Attackers can implement remote exploitation by obtaining sufficient privileges through their control of operating system applications so they can modify firmware storage. Attackers use three methods to distribute damaging firmware updates: phishing attacks, social engineering schemes and procedural weaknesses in update systems. The manufacturing process and distribution stages create a significant risk for supply chain attacks because malicious elements inserted within firmware embed both backdoors and vulnerabilities into the system. The network interface exposure in firmware devices that function as management controllers allows remote attackers to exploit vulnerabilities which exist in both network stack and services.

The examination of firmware for its vulnerabilities together with evidence of compromise stands as a complicated task. Modern firmware is larger and more intricate, which increases the difficulty of identifying vulnerabilities and understanding interactions between components (Yifei Xu, 2018). Firmware code operates as a tightly bound set of instructions for specific hardware and exists without standard documentation or APIs and employs encryption methods to block reverse engineering activities needing expert tools and specific training to extract debug and disassemble. Modern firmware programs have become larger along with their complexity which makes analysis more difficult.

Table 2. Overview of Common Firmware Vulnerabilities and Exploitation Vectors

Vulnerability Type	Brief Description	Common Exploitation Vector(s)	Potential Impact
Insecure Update Mechanism	Lack of signature verification, rollback protection, or secure transport for updates	Malicious Update Delivery, Network Interception	Installation of malicious firmware, Persistence, Downgrade Attacks
Memory Corruption	Buffer overflows (stack/heap), use-after-free, integer overflows in firmware code	Remote Software Exploit, Physical Access (via debug), Malicious Input	Arbitrary Code Execution (ACE) within firmware, Privilege Escalation, Crash
Logic Flaws	Errors in design logic, access control, state management, security feature bypass	Remote Software Exploit, Physical Access, Malicious Input	Security Feature Bypass, Unauthorized Access, Privilege Escalation
Weak/Hardcoded Credentials	Default passwords, embedded keys, weak authentication protocols	Network Interface Attack, Physical Access, Reverse Engineering	Unauthorized Access, Information Disclosure, System Control
Insecure Cryptography	Use of weak/outdated algorithms, implementation flaws, poor key management	Network Interception, Physical Access, Reverse Engineering	Information Disclosure, Integrity Loss, Authentication Bypass
Configuration Issues	Unprotected debug ports (JTAG), insecure default settings, exposed sensitive info	Physical Access, Network Interface Attack, Default Credential Use	Unauthorized Access, Information Disclosure, System Reconfiguration
Supply Chain Weakness	Tampering during manufacturing, distribution; use of compromised components	Supply Chain Attack	Persistent Backdoors, Hardware Trojans, Widespread Compromise

2.3. Zero-Day Threats Explained

Zero-day threats identify a specific cyber risk that hackers use to exploit security flaws which occur before a vendor discovers the bug or creates a fix. The absence of effective defenses, such as signature-based antivirus systems, makes these attacks particularly dangerous (Arianna Armijos, 2023). The unknown nature of such threat's accounts for their effectiveness because standard security techniques which depend on prior knowledge of attacks prove useless during this dangerous period. A zero-day exploit lifecycle starts when a vulnerability's discovery remains private then malicious code developers create exploitation tools from that vulnerability. The researcher or an underground market buyer could use this exploit directly after its discovery. Targeted systems start receiving active exploitation which might operate in stealth mode until researchers identify vulnerabilities or vendors find them through system forensic examinations.

Firmware zero-days present sophisticated adversaries an extremely desirable target because they possess simultaneously high privilege access alongside stealth while being able to persist and force delayed remediation processes. Dual solutions to this threat involve minimum security measures that monitor firmware integrity through secure boot foundations combined with hardware-firmware interface runtime activity detection and proactive vulnerability detection methods within the firmware code base.

3. THE INTERSECTION: FIRMWARE-BASED ADVERSARIAL ATTACKS

Our following analysis explores the essential points which bring together firmware vulnerabilities with adversarial machine learning techniques. Under this situation advanced damaging vectors emerge that surpass traditional security capabilities for single domain exploits. This segment studies the combined effect by explaining how assaulters exploit compromised firmware to launch through it and showing how AML methods defeat AI firmware security protocols (Abdul Awal Mintoo, 2024). The paper investigates distinct attack methods by providing practical examples and explains why defending these combined threats proves so challenging.

3.1. Leveraging Firmware Vulnerabilities for AML Attacks

Attacker exploitation of system firmware compromises grants them a strategic benefit as it provides persistent access with elevated privileges and hidden attack routes inside a target device. The elevated position of privilege allows attackers to boost the power of Adversarial Machine Learning attacks which target AI systems running throughout the device and network space. The modification of system environments outside operating system control allows attackers to break down AI model assumptions required for correct and dependable functioning.

Sensor and input data streams undergo manipulation as a core method. AI applications running in contemporary systems executed through cyber-physical systems as well as autonomous vehicles, robotics and Internet of Things require extensive input from physical sensor devices including cameras and LiDAR together with microphones, GPS receivers and industrial process monitors. Before reaching higher software layers for ML model analysis the raw sensor data passes through firmware processing steps from either the sensor itself or the main processor. An attacker who takes control of firmware operates beneath operating systems and then alters data streams intended for AI systems. The goal is to input targeted adversarial noise through the system with the purpose of misdirecting image recognition programs while simultaneously steering sensor data towards false alarms or impairing network traffic patterns. The changes under OS manipulate AI models through access to authenticated data which standard software integrity tests cannot detect. A significant hacking approach morphs into firmware attacks against the environment where ML models execute. The main function of firmware involves managing hardware security and trusted execution environments (TEEs) for sensitive computations while enabling their initial setup.

Firmware management issues enable attackers who obtain firmware access to change either ML models or their execution through their system.

Figure 2. Conceptual Diagram of Firmware-AML Threat Convergence

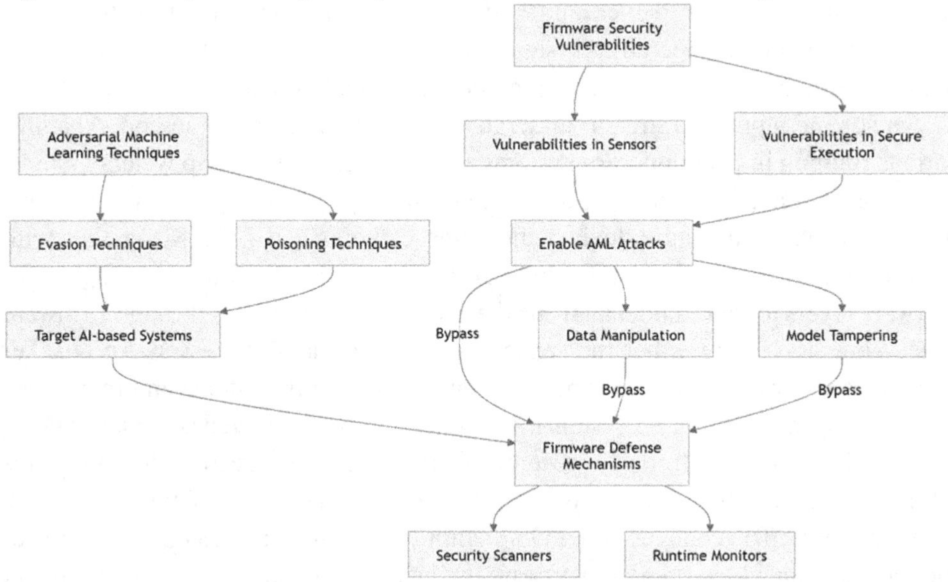

3.2. AML Techniques Targeting Firmware Security Mechanisms

The reverse operation works equally well. AI-powered security solutions integrated in firmware protection tools are facing new vulnerabilities because skilled AML experts aim directly at AI algorithms operating in security solutions. The existing AML methods produce adaptations that trick and neutralize or outwit complex security systems designed for these specific purposes. AI systems which perform firmware binary malware and vulnerability analysis through static or dynamic analysis require examination. Security scanners become vulnerable to specific evasion techniques which attackers develop to bypass their detection systems. The attacker must adjust characteristics which AI models base their decisions upon such as particular instruction sequences, code complexity metrics and control flow structures to make harmful code seem harmless through advanced forms of code obfuscation techniques or through spotting malicious instructions within safe code sections. Existing methods utilized for traditional malware classification systems match those which work for the firmware domain.

The runtime monitor of AI-based systems should be considered as a potential target due to its behavioral anomaly detection capabilities. Cybercriminals conduct their attacks with minimal pace ("low-and-slow") to evade security indicators while imitating ("mimicry attacks") normal firmware operating patterns during exploitation.

3.3. Illustrative Case Studies

Industrial Control Systems (ICS) are face to face targeted by one such prominent case. Stuxnet malware became known worldwide after it attacked Siemens PLCs in Iranian nuclear facilities during 2010. The attack implemented multiple unreported exploits for its spreading mechanism and held core elements that aimed to reprogram the factory-programmed control system firmware.

Through firmware modifications Stuxnet caused physical equipment breakdown while manipulating sensor output data which appeared normal to monitoring systems operators. The original Stuxnet attack which existed before AML became a focus utilized hardware modifications to gain operational control of physical elements while engineering sensor output resulting in a form of attack that could endanger contemporary AI-powered ICS data monitoring systems. The Triton/TRISIS malware operated by targeting Schneider Electric's Triconex Safety Instrumented Systems firmware which serves as critical components for industrial safety protection functions. Through firmware vulnerability Triton attempted to change the security logic which could result in loss of emergency shutdown capabilities. Security-sensitive firmware represents a direct gateway for attackers to defeat AI safety monitoring protocols and introduce misleading inputs which deceive AI-based process controls systems.

UEFI (Unified Extensible Firmware Interface) rootkits represent another crucial target area since they attack the firmware responsible for modern computer booting. LoJax stood out as an early observed malware culprit in 2018 because Sednit APT established it as their creation. Through exploited system vulnerabilities LoJax malware managed to bind malicious code into the SPI flash memory of motherboards therefore surviving operating system reinstallations and hard drive replacements. MoonBounce and CosmicStrand proved the development of even stealthier UEFI boot techniques by placing malicious code at the deepest levels preceding operating system startup. UEFI bootkits such as BlackLotus now show their capacity to defeat UEFI Secure Boot security through specific vulnerabilities which enable disabling operating system protection features like virtualization-based security and antivirus applications. These UEFI rootkits demonstrate successful access and secrecy through deep system layers despite operating below the operating system layer.

An attacker in this position would easily stop AI-based endpoint security from functioning while intercepting data before processing in protected AI applications and controlling system actions for AI decision interference or exploiting their machine as a trusted launchpad for additional attacks using AML against network-level AI defenses.

Intelligence agencies exposed their development of firmware implants that would target a large number of devices including network routers and consumer electronics through Vault 7 leaks. The sophisticated actors demonstrate their understanding of foundational layer value by targeting firmware exploits even though specific operational details of AML remain undisclosed. Organizations using compromised router firmware could disturb traffic data for AI-based intrusion detection systems while attackers using compromised endpoint firmware create an ideal operating environment to control AI software locally.

Through multiple real-world incidents multiple threat groups prove that deep system control achieved by firmware hacking exists as a tangible operational security threat. A consistent capability now permits attackers to develop more complex cyber operations utilizing AML methods for destroying the AI security and control systems that enter military operations. We can predict that state-of-the-art adversaries invest in creating or have already implemented these combined attack methods.

3.4. Challenges in Detecting and Mitigating Converged Threats

Security defenders face multiple major challenges when they attempt to respond to the complex threats which emerge through the combination of firmware vulnerabilities with adversarial machine learning technology. Effective defense becomes a complex task because of three main barriers which comprise technical limitations and operational complexities and resource constraints. The fundamental issue arises because firmware operations transparently operate under the radar. Most conventional security monitoring tools, such as endpoint detection and response (EDR) systems or host-based intrusion detectors, operate within the context of the main operating system (David Noever, 2021).

USTER mode executes at runtime levels that have higher system privileges than the operating system both prior to the OS boot sequence and while running alongside System Management Mode (SMM). Standard operating system security measures provide limited insight into how firmware operates since its operational characteristics remain unknown. Implementing specialized monitoring tools including hardware-assisted monitoring and offline firmware image analysis and remote attestation protocols offers visibility yet remains inaccessible for various equipment types particularly the resource-limited devices within IoT applications. The wide array of device configurations poses an extra substantial challenge. The wide range of hardware architecture designs together with System-on-Chip constructs and peripheral configurations and firmware implementation approaches create overwhelming obstacles for developing general detection methods and security strengthening approaches. Security weaknesses in update platforms lead to systematic device vulnerabilities that persist after remediation information becomes available because various manufacturers practice inconsistently and users tend to delay update installations. The security management requirements for firmware development into manufacturing plus supply chain protection and product retirement need advanced and difficult-to-implement processes.

Securely attributing AML forensics alongside modern firmware attack methods becomes an exceptionally challenging task because of their highly intricate low-level characteristics. Standard digital forensic investigations commonly target information found in disk drives and memory storage which is viewable from the operating system perspective. The investigation of hardware/software requires specialized tools alongside deep technical skills to perform firmware analysis. Attacks executed silently and backed by persistent techniques destroy evidence trails and the complex actors who use hiding measures and anti-analysis tactics make it difficult to understand attacks and find responsible parties. Implementing protection for this analytical security network demands multiple defensive layers which incorporate system hardware security and firmware development within DevSecOps practices in addition to intelligent detection systems and AI capability monitoring and secure update protocols alongside supply chain vigilance and research into system protection protocols.

4. AI-DRIVEN SOLUTIONS FOR DETECTION AND DEFENSE

Different sections have analyzed the multifaceted difficulties arising from integrated firmware technology together with adversarial machine learning vulnerabilities whose detection problems stem from traditional security frameworks. AI and Machine Learning have become key defenses for cybersecurity experts who face growing security challenges because they create adaptive and proactive cybersecurity protection tools (Diksha Dhiman, 2024). Alliances between AI technology and solutions enable the evaluation of immense datasets while learning illicit patterns and performing automated threat response activities at speeds beyond human capabilities. The following part investigates multiple AI and ML application models that boost firmware protection features across all stages by performing pre-emptive vulnerability detection and simultaneous attack monitoring as well as protecting AI systems against adversarial modifications.

Table 3. Mapping AI Techniques to Firmware Security Applications

AI Technique Category	Primary Application Area in Firmware Security	Example Specific Use Case
Supervised Classification	Vulnerability Discovery, Malware Detection	Classifying firmware binaries as malicious/benign based on learned features
Unsupervised Anomaly Detection	Runtime Threat Detection, Zero-Day Discovery	Identifying unusual firmware execution traces or telemetry deviations
Sequence Modeling (RNN/ LSTM/Transformer)	Runtime Behavioral Analysis, Vulnerability Discovery (Code Analysis)	Modeling normal system call sequences; Analyzing code for sequential patterns
Graph Neural Networks (GNNs)	Vulnerability Discovery (Code Analysis), Threat Intelligence	Analyzing control flow graphs for vulnerabilities; Correlating threat data
Natural Language Processing (NLP)	Threat Intelligence, Secure Development Assistance	Extracting IoCs from reports; Analyzing code comments/ documentation
Reinforcement Learning (RL)	Vulnerability Discovery (Fuzzing), Response Automation	Guiding fuzz testing inputs; Optimizing automated response strategies
Generative Models (GANs/ VAEs)	Vulnerability Discovery (Fuzzing), Data Augmentation	Generating diverse test inputs for fuzzing; Creating synthetic training data
Adversarial Training	AI Model Robustness	Training AI security models to resist evasion attacks

4.1. AI/ML for Proactive Vulnerability Discovery

Modern cybersecurity strategies have established a foundation through initiative-taking exposure and vulnerability prevention before adversaries can exploit system weaknesses.

In traditional fuzzing approaches input generation occurs through random methods or basic heuristic rules that prove inadequate when examining deep code sequences in sophisticated firmware. The smart fuzzing method leverages machine learning through reinforcement learning models and generative design capabilities which optimize input generation algorithms. The AI assistance learns from program run metrics and execution snapshots alongside feedback for selecting test cases that match the kind of flaws likely to be found thus improving dynamic analysis both in speed and defect detection rates.

Through symbolic and concolic execution programs scan code paths using symbolic variables to analyze program states and reachability thus locating deep bugs while proving vulnerability-free classes. Symbolic and concolic execution fall victim to scalability defects known as state-space explosion when analysts attempt to analyze extensive and complex software programs such as contemporary device firmware. AI and ML algorithms can enhance the practicality of these advanced techniques by developing metrics to identify valuable execution paths and helping solve complex path constraints and by predicting areas likely to contain vulnerabilities making such assessments more scalable for firmware security analysis. Organizations that use AI across their vulnerability discovery methods will enhance their potential to find and fix firmware weaknesses before deployment point while minimizing potential attack areas.

Figure 3. Firmware Vulnerability Discovery Enhancement

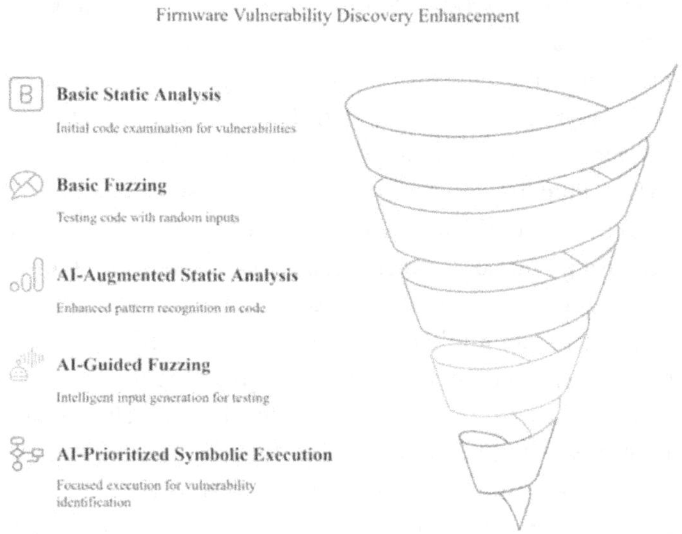

4.2. AI/ML for Detecting Firmware Attacks at Runtime

Standard initiative-taking vulnerability discovery minimizes attack exposure, but runtime detection systems stay essential to detect zero-day vulnerabilities and new bypass methods against static defense systems. Tools based on AI together with ML provide robust capabilities for runtime monitoring to track malicious firmware activities and their adversarial manipulations through system behavior analysis and detection of minute deviations from normal operation.

The first method requires detection of irregular system behaviors. Autoencoders or clustering algorithms combined with one-class support vector machines during unsupervised learning allow the creation of baseline profiles that show normal firmware operation. A baseline profile uses system telemetry which includes sequences of system calls in addition to patterns of hardware performance counter usage and memory access behaviors and network traffic generated by firmware and power consumption fluctuations. The AI system functions as a continuous monitoring agent that tracks the device performance against previously established normal behavioral boundaries to detect abnormal patterns signaling security threats and malicious actions. This detection method enables promising threat identification of unknown zero-day attacks and subtle malware that cause system behavior shifts since it operates without requiring pre-existing signature information. Sequence-aware models based on LSTM networks with Transformers demonstrate outstanding capabilities for recognizing temporal patterns in execution logs and network traffic which leads them to identify breaches of operational sequences.

AI techniques must specifically focus on detecting adversarial inputs that target ML models because malicious modifications are crucial for systems depending on firmware-processed data or firmware-based ML components.

AI system operators can implement three detection methods to track data distributions contrary to expected benign data while also monitoring model confidence levels and utilization patterns of model activations or establishing detector networks that differentiate clean inputs from adverse disturbances. Firmware-related data manipulation requires multiple cross-layer validation techniques to uncover its presence effectively. AI models analyze telemetry data from firmware and OS and application layers through independent measurement and then detect alterations at the lower layers by comparing results between the three measurement points.

The effectiveness of runtime detection based on AI increases when security data from hardware sources is integrated into the system. Advanced processors now support features for execution control and memory protection through Intel CET and MPX thus leveraging TrustZone and MTE from ARM processors. These hardware mechanisms generate data signals that provide trusted high-fidelity information which becomes highly effective for AI models to detect low-level attacks aimed at tampering with firmware execution compared to pure software protections. Fundamentally developing AI models to merge multiple security data types including behavioral telemetry information and both input analysis and hardware security event data stands essential for building all-encompassing runtime protection against complex firmware assaults.

4.3. AI-Powered Threat Intelligence and Prediction

Artificial Intelligence serves as a vital tool for strengthening Cyber Threat Intelligence (CTI) targeting firmware domain while also helping detect vulnerabilities directly and during runtime executions. The traditional Computing Threat Intelligence approach requires manual threat data collection and subsequent analysis which faces challenges because of modern information overload.

Continuous CTI processes are enhanced by AI and ML techniques which enable security teams to acquire rapid predictive vulnerability assessments for forthcoming firmware threats and vulnerabilities.

AI systems maintain continuous data processing capability for structured and unstructured diverse sources which relate to firmware security. Accessible data about vulnerabilities comes from CVE as well as known malware repositories and dark web forum discussions and academic papers along with vendor security warnings and honeypot system logs and incident report documentation. detailed assessment of large datasets becomes possible through machine learning algorithms that utilize natural language processing (NLP) alongside clustering and pattern recognition methods.

Firmware threat identification campaigns and attack methodologies come into focus using this application. AI achieves firmware threat detection by analyzing malware clusters regarding their behavioral similarities or their assessed Tactics Techniques and Procedures (TTPs) through natural language processing (NLP). Organizations gain the ability to modify their defense systems in advance with the help of early warning mechanisms.

Machine learning models serve to calculate statistical probabilities related to firmware security breaches which occur in actual operations. Such models leverage historical vulnerability information about characteristics (CVSS scores for example) and add threat actor activity and motivation data to provide organizations with better decision-making regarding their limited patching resources. Resolving the most vulnerable firmware vulnerabilities for exploitation purposes creates better efficiency in risk management practices.

The AI technology demonstrates superb automation in extracting critical Indicators of Compromise (IoCs) from unpredictable sources that include security blogs and incident reports.

NLP systems can analyze text and recover technical firmware attack details which include malicious file hashes, command servers and implant paths or registry keys, command server addresses along with distinct network signature patterns. Security monitoring systems accept the extracted IoCs from this process which enables SIEMs and EDR platforms to detect known firmware threats at accelerated speeds. The integration of Artificial Intelligence provides organizations with timely predictive analysis that helps them gain more accurate situational awareness regarding firmware security risks.

4.4. Enhancing Firmware Lifecycle Security with AI

Making effective progress in firmware security demands security considerations to receive integration across the entire product cycle that includes development and initial design as well as deployment phases and update deployments and decommissioning activities. Build security from the beginning remains the goal of DevSecOps methodologies through their "shift-left" methodology instead of implementing security as an afterthought. AI and ML systems will enhance security mechanisms throughout each stage of the lifecycle.

Throughout the development period artificial intelligence systems aid developers who need help creating secure code. Secure code completion systems in development tools provide on-the-go analysis of writing code and present designers with security-enhancing code patterns and real-time vulnerability detection while showing context-specific alerts for firmware security risks. The automatic identification of security important code modifications by AI-based systems assists code review teams to apply their limited analysis capabilities towards critical segments.

5. EMERGING TRENDS AND FUTURE DIRECTIONS

The dynamic relationship between firmware security vulnerabilities and adversarial machine learning techniques, due to the field's continuous evolution, is maintained. This means that the relationship, which is constantly changing due to the ongoing nature of both security threats and defenses, continues to exist and operate in a dynamic way. New attack methods will target defenses which exist at present. The future of robust security posture is required to be studied current technological developments with directions for promising future research. Multiple critical areas stand to transform firmware security against advanced adversarial threats through their troublesome nature and collaborative capabilities along with their integrity-enhancing properties and accountable artificial intelligence functions.

5.1. Quantum Computing Implications

Scalable fault-tolerant quantum computers overall bring both security advantages and threats to cybersecurity which strongly impact firmware security methods. The operation of Shor's algorithm on quantum computers poses a threat to break fundamental security mechanisms through the public-key cryptographic technologies

RSA and ECC which secure boot and digital signatures for firmware updates and secure communication protocols. An initiative-taking shift to Post-Quantum Cryptography (PQC) represents key steps forward because PQC uses new cryptographic algorithms which quantum computing cannot break. Several international bodies are actively working to research and standardize PQC schemes which will be ready for implementation. The implementation of these new algorithms in firmware environments becomes complicated because their different performance levels and increased key sizes compare to traditional algorithms cause technical challenges regarding computation efficiency and storage requirements and power consumption. Scientists direct ongoing research toward solving implementation efficiency issues along with the development of hardware acceleration methods.

Quantum computing may introduce new security analysis tools through its field of Quantum Machine Learning (QML). Security scientists' study if quantum algorithms can improve machine learning tasks for security applications through enhanced techniques in detecting vulnerable patterns or sensitive anomalies. QML exists at an early developmental stage with undefined practical evidence demonstrating its security benefit but keeps importance as a potential opportunity for future defensive developments. The path to quantum security necessitates two parallel actions which include deploying PQC technologies while actively exploring quantum computing applications for enhanced protection.

5.2. Federated Learning for Collaborative Firmware Defense

Through Federated Learning organizations and devices can join decentralized training of advanced AI models while protecting sensitive information because raw data remains private to each user. Each participant operates independently under the FL model to train a local model with its own data and securely sends model updates for aggregation by a central server to build a better global model that distributes back to participants. Data security improves as well as confidentiality features when this framework operates.

The security of firmware systems becomes more promising because of FL applications. The model would allow numerous organizational entities or multiple device fleets to joint create enhanced malware detection systems that provide stronger and more precise firmware identification capabilities. Training across numerous environments and device platforms enables better generalization of a unified model that detects various attacks, especially zero-day vulnerabilities present in diverse dataset segments. Near real-time threat intelligence sharing can be achieved through model updates to help collective defense organizations respond faster to new threats. The proposed system has various use cases including the collective development of firmware malware classifier training models alongside anomaly detection for behavioral telemetry and vulnerability forecasting models. FL deployment needs solutions to manage statistical heterogeneity between user data along with optimizing communication efficiency for limited devices and implementing security measures against attack attempts during aggregation while managing operational complexities. FL provides a viable solution for achieving safer and more privacy-protecting collaboration in firmware defense though it comes with several implementation barriers to overcome.

5.3. Blockchain for Firmware Integrity and Supply Chain Security

Blockchain technology alongside Distributed Ledger Technology (DLT) stands as a security enhancement path for firmware protection because of its built-in features for unalterable records and distributed network control. Strengthening defenses against supply chain tampering becomes possible using these features that firmwares possess for successful integrity verification in complex networks (Andrei Costin, 2014).

The creation of tamperproof records for firmware updates and their origin serves as a major blockchain application. The implementation of blockchain system would create distributed tamper-resistant verification records for official firmware versions plus their cryptographic hashes as well as form signatures and corresponding patch metadata. Devices access this public or permissioned ledger to check the authenticity and integrity of firmware updates which enables them to verify the packages before implementation. The integrity of firmware updates is established by blockchain since this cryptographic record can verify authentication against immutable information stored on the blockchain. Blockchain-enabled smart contracts containing program code segments located on blockchain networks could execute predefined rules to automate the verification process.

Blockchain provides additional security capabilities which protect supply chain management systems. An audit trail and provenance record become possible with cryptographic hashes or identifiers specifically for both firmware components and hardware parts in the production sequence which begins at manufacturing and continues through assembly then reaches distribution before reaching deployment. Enhanced transparency within the supply chain enables the detection of counterfeit components and reveals points where firmware modification could have occurred thus preventing hardware Trojan and supply chain attacks. The deployment of blockchain for firmware security into practical applications encounters multiple substantial challenges. Overall blockchain system deployment encounters technical issues stemming from prominent platform limitations regarding transaction speed and power requirements linked to consensus operations and requirement complexity for device blockchain client connection and secure key management protocols.

Blockchain functions best as a security infrastructure element which addresses high stakes uses instead of serving as an answer for all security requirements.

5.4. Explainable AI (XAI) for Firmware Security Analysis

Deep learning models employed in firmware security grow sophisticated while becoming difficult to interpret regarding their inner workings because they operate as "black boxes." Limited interpretability creates major obstacles when deploying new systems to operations which results in difficulties with debugging and user trust and stands in the way of regulatory compliance. XAI provides solutions through its development methods that make AI system predictions and behaviors intelligible to users. XAI methods have become essential for firmware security purposes.

Security analysts need a full understanding of why AI systems exit firmware as malware or detect unusual runtime events to perform their duties effectively. The justification from XAI methodology comes through identifying critical code features together with execution patterns and data points that played the most significant role in the AI decision. The exact rationale behind AI detections becomes available for quick verification by analysts who also gain better understanding of the system outputs difficulties in categorizing false alerts and build stronger confidence in AI outputs. AI alerts lose their practical application when explainability is absent because analysts find it difficult to trust and manage system output effectively. Currently it is essential to have models that are explainable since this helps developers with debugging and enhancing AI security systems. Through XAI techniques models can provide explanations that show either spurious correlations or incorrect pattern learning by the model or its bias-related training data origins during errors. Model developers use explainable AI capabilities to identify issues with the architecture and data for more effective refinements that produce better outcomes in future model iterations. Furthermore, XAI facilitates human-AI collaboration better. Through its human-friendly AI reasoning interpretation XAI facilitates security analysts to blend their professional skills with the AI system analysis for better threat pursuit and emergency response outcomes. AI systems must provide explainable reasoning about decisions in security-sensitive industries because this information serves auditing and compliance needs. The field of XAI applies both feature attribution approaches (including LIME and SHAP) and traditional rule extraction with example-based reasoning methods to analyze specific data types and security analysis models in firmware systems. Consequently, XAI acts as a core requirement for deploying trustworthy AI solutions within this sensitive domain.

6. IMPLEMENTATION CONSIDERATIONS

The major potential of AI technology to boost firmware security stands strong against modern threats but turning such potential into real operational defenses demands precise evaluation of practical deployment requirements. The implementation of advanced AI systems in comprehensive security systems demands attention to integration requirements while using available staff skills and maintaining constant system maintenance. Organizations interested in implementing AI-driven firmware security capabilities need to follow the set of key practical applications and best practices described in this section.

6.1. Integrating AI Solutions into Security Frameworks

AI-driven firmware security tools will achieve their highest value when organizations make effective integrations within current cybersecurity structures and operational workflows. When operating alone these tools produce inefficiencies and restrict their total potential effects. Successful implementation of AI-driven firmware security tools requires SOC integration which enables AI-generated alerts about firmware vulnerabilities (Pendey, 2023) and runtime anomalies to reach established platforms like Security Information and Event Management (SIEM) and Security Orchestration, Automation, and Response (SOAR) systems. The system enables security alerts to integrate with other security events using proper organizational context for precise incident response triage and management according to firmware-focused response playbooks.

The firmware development lifecycle needs AI-powered analysis tools as an integral part to achieve initiative-taking security standards in line with DevSecOps principles. Infrastructure developers can leverage AI-enhanced static and dynamic analysis tools, and fuzzing mechanisms as automated security scanners directly integrated within Continuous Integration/Continuous Delivery (CI/CD) pipelines to ensure continuous security monitoring. The detection of vulnerabilities becomes possible through these measures during firmware development which precedes production thereby minimizing both risk factors and repair expenses. The achievement of successful AI security collaboration requires evaluating all tools for compatibility with current developer systems.

7. CONCLUSION

This chapter surveys the important connection between firmware security and adversarial machine learning in modern technology systems. A complete understanding of the security risks, which develop from the operational relationship, is required by the emergence of modern computing systems that depend on embedded firmware and artificial intelligence. The possibility of attackers using firmware vulnerabilities to exploit AI platforms and enemy AI techniques for firmware defense avoiding through zero-day exploits demands a new security paradigm.

7.1. Summary of Key Findings

Firmware maintains its status as an attack vector because of its advantageous position along with disregard for security during its history creating opportunities for persistent and stealthy threats. The techniques of adversarial machine learning operate separately with specific methods that fool even highly advanced AI models. The convergence point between these threats becomes their most dangerous situation because they enhance their collective power to evade standard defense mechanisms. We studied the firmware vulnerabilities which enable AML attacks by manipulating data and altering the execution environment and the AML techniques used against firmware security-focused AI systems. Advanced firmware malware demonstrates how systems can be fully controlled through such amalgamated attacks. We evaluated the major problems that make these threats difficult to detect including poor visibility and system diversity and the stealthy characteristics of AML along with limited resources. The review of AI solutions revealed their potential use in firmware life cycles to discover vulnerabilities in advance and analyze systems intelligently and detect anomalies and adversarial activities at runtime while creating stronger AI models through adversarial training approaches. Our analysis incorporated post-quantum cryptography as well as federated learning along with blockchain integrity applications and explainable AI as fundamental components for building resilient systems of the future.

7.2. Implications for Practice and Recommendations

The evaluation provides specific recommendations which benefit cybersecurity professionals as well as software developers and the organizations they serve. Firmware security needs to become an essential component of overall security because organizations must give it dedicated expertise and funding to safeguard it. The future of security protection requires an initiative-taking approach which brings AI tools for vulnerability search and threat identification to detect zero-day threats before they emerge. Organizations need to develop and acquire personnel who possess combined skills from the areas of firmware security along with embedded systems knowledge and AI/ML capabilities. AI and ML enhance threat detection and incident response, allowing organizations to identify vulnerabilities and respond to threats more efficiently (Afees Olanrewaju Akinade, 2023). Security integration needs to include AI-powered checks across the DevSecOps development stages to establish baseline security measures at each lifecycle phase (Mutaz Wahed, 2024). The adoption of comprehensive security perspectives requires security teams to find merged attack solutions while adjusting incident monitoring and response techniques. It is essential for collective defense that the industry works together to improve information sharing collaboration and surge adoption of standardized secure practices for firmware threats.

7.3. Future Research Agenda

The development of further research remains critical for filling current knowledge gaps and predicting upcoming security concerns. The development of precise AI models needs further research to achieve maximum operational efficiency on embedded hardware platforms. Researchers require additional efforts to design and validate proprietary AML defenses which align with firmware-specific data structures and operational environments that include binary code and execution traces. The identification of advanced zero-day vulnerabilities within extensive firmware codebases through improved AI methods requires substantial ongoing research. Improving the explainability of AI decisions within firmware security demands specific XAI methods which will establish operational effectiveness and trust. Developers must establish detailed implementation methods as well as security evaluations for current technological developments including post-quantum cryptography, federated learning and blockchain within firmware systems. Standardized benchmarking alongside diverse datasets with robust evaluation methods serves as a mandatory requirement to objectively measure different AI-driven firmware security solutions. Research collaboration with persistent innovation across different fronts stands necessary to defend the foundational software which supports a smarter interconnected world from advanced digital threats of future generations.

REFERENCES

Abdirashid Abukar Ahmed, N. N. (2024, September 04). A Comparative Analysis of Adversarial Attack Methods on Machine Learning Models. *Indian Scientific Journal Of Research In Engineering And Management*, *8*(08), 1–16. DOI: 10.55041/IJSREM37340

Abdul Awal Mintoo, A. R. (2024). Adversarial Machine Learning In Network Security: A Systematic Review Of Threat Vectors And Defense Mechanisms. *01*(01), 80 - 98. DOI: 10.70937/itej.v1i01.9

Adeola N. Raji, A. O. (2024). Integrating Artificial Intelligence, machine learning, and data analytics in cybersecurity: A holistic approach to advanced threat detection and response. *World Journal Of Advanced Research and Reviews*. DOI: 10.30574/wjarr.2024.24.2.3197

Afees Olanrewaju Akinade, P. A. (2023). 10 30). Evaluating AI and ML in Cybersecurity: A USA and global perspective. *GSC Advanced Research and Reviews*, *17*(1), 138–148. DOI: 10.30574/gscarr.2023.17.1.0409

Alam, T. (2018). A Reliable Communication Framework and Its Use in Internet of Things (IoT). *International Journal of Scientific Research in Computer Science, Engineering and Information Technology, Vol 3(5).*

Andrei Costin, J. Z. (2014). A Large-Scale Analysis of the Security of Embedded Firmwares.

Arianna Armijos, E. C. (2023). The absence of effective defenses, such as signature-based antivirus systems, makes these attacks particularly dangerous. 1-6. DOI: 10.1109/C358072.2023.10436218

Arun K. Kanuparthi, R. K. (2014). Hardware and embedded security in the context of internet of things. *Computer and Communications Security*, 61 - 64. DOI: 10.1145/2517968.2517976

Chen, Z. K. P. (2024). A Method to Facilitate Membership Inference Attacks in Deep Learning Models. doi:/arxiv.2407.01919DOI: 10.48550

David Noever, S. E. (2021). Deep Learning for Identifying Malicious Firmware. DOI: 10.5121/csit.2021.111506

Didem Genç, M. Ö. (2023). A Taxonomic Survey of Model Extraction Attacks. DOI: 10.1109/CSR57506.2023.10224959

Diksha Dhiman, A. B. (2024). Artificial Intelligence and Machine Learning-Enabled Cybersecurity Tools and Techniques. In *Advance techniques and applications of cybersecurity and forensics* (pp. 35–56). Informa., DOI: 10.1201/9781003386926-3

Enuma Edmund, A. E., & Aliyu Enemosah, . (2024). AI and machine learning in cybersecurity: Leveraging AI to predict, detect, and respond to threats more efficiently. *International Journal of Science and Research Archive, 11*(2), 2625–2645. DOI: 10.30574/ijsra.2024.11.1.0083

Fahad Mira, I. A. (2019). Review of Analysis on IoT Components, Devices and Layers Security. DOI: 10.1109/ICISCT47635.2019.9012037

Hsiao-Ying Lin, B. B. (2021). Adversarial Machine Learning: Attacks From Laboratories to the Real World. *Computer, 54*(5), 56–60. DOI: 10.1109/MC.2021.3057686

Keramati, M. (2017). 09 15). An Attack Graph Based Method for Predictive Risk Evaluation of Zero-Day Attacks. *International Journal of Information and Communication Technology Research, 9*(3), 7–16. https://ijict.itrc.ac.ir/article-1-30-en.html

Knowing Your Hardware. (2022). In *System firmware* (pp. 45 - 143). Apress eBooks. DOI: 10.1007/978-1-4842-7939-7_2

Mutaz Wahed, M. S.-B. (2024). Comprehensive Assessment of Cybersecurity Measures: Evaluating Incident Response, AI Integration, and Emerging Threats. 1-8. DOI: 10.1109/NETAPPS63333.2024.10823603

Patrick Jungwirth, T. B.-H. (2017). Rootkits and the OS friendly microprocessor architecture. *10185*, 1018503. DOI: 10.1117/12.2258235

Pendey, B. (2023). Artificial Intelligence And Cyber Security. *Journal transnational universal studies, 1*(2), 93 - 99. DOI: 10.58631/jtus.v1i2.15

Priyanka Prakash Surve, O. B. (2023). SoK: Security Below the OS - A Security Analysis of UEFI. *arXiv.org, abs/2311.03809*. doi:/arxiv.2311.03809DOI: 10.48550

Ratinder Kaur, M. S. (2014). *Automatic Evaluation and Signature Generation Technique for Thwarting Zero-Day Attacks*. Springer., DOI: 10.1007/978-3-642-54525-2_27

Sajeed Mohammad, F. F. (2024). FortBoot. *Fortifying Rooted-in-Device-Specific Security Through Secure Booting., 1-4*, 1–4. Advance online publication. DOI: 10.1109/VLSI-SoC62099.2024.10767821

Shukla, A. (2022). Leveraging AI and ML for Advance Cyber Security. DOI: 10.47363/JAICC/2022(1)142

Stefano Righi, N. K. (2007). Retrieved from https://patents.google.com/patent/US8352721B1/en

Suhas Shivanna, S. B. (2014). Retrieved from https://www.freepatentsonline.com/y2017/0315798.html

Venkata Subbaiah Desanamukula, M. P. (2023). A Comprehensive Analysis of Machine Learning and Deep Learning Approaches towards IoT Security. *2023 4th international conference on Electronics and Sustainable Communication Systems (ICESC), Coimbatore, India, 2023* (pp. 1165 - 1168). IEEE. DOI: 10.1109/ICESC57686.2023.10193209

veria Hoseini, S., Suutala, J., Partala, J., & Halunen, K. (2024). Threat modeling AI/ML with the Attack Tree. IEEE Access.

Vorobeychik, Y. (2023). The Many Faces of Adversarial Machine Learning. *Proceedings of the ...AAAI Conference on Artificial Intelligence, 37*(13), 15402 - 15409. DOI: 10.1609/aaai.v37i13.26796

Xu, Y., T. L. (2018). A Search-based Firmware Code Analysis Method for IoT Devices. *Communications and Networking Symposium*, 1-2. DOI: 10.1109/CNS.2018.8433163

Yogi, M. K. (2023). 09 01). A Comprehensive Study of Zero-Day Attacks. *Journal of Information Technology and Digital World*, *5*(3), 253–273. DOI: 10.36548/jitdw.2023.3.003

Chapter 7
Defense Mechanisms Against Adversarial Attacks:
Strengthening AI Security in Cybersecurity Applications

Muhammad Usman Tariq
https://orcid.org/0000-0002-7605-3040
Abu Dhabi University, UAE & University College Cork, Ireland

ABSTRACT

Adversarial attacks are particularly cybersecurity applications where reliability and accuracy are the most important. They are a significant threat to artificial intelligence systems (AI). These attacks involve subtle manipulation of input data developed into deceptive AI models that lead to false output or system dusk. To mitigate these risks, various defense mechanisms have been developed that aim to improve the robustness of AI systems against adversarial obstacles. These mechanisms include adversarial training, preprocessing inputs, normalizing models, and using defense architectures. Adversarial training improves the model's resilience by publishing adversarial examples during training. Input processing filters the input of potential adversarial, while model regulator exposure over-adapts adaptations that may exploit weaknesses. Defensive architectures have been developed specifically to identify and counter malfunctioning operations.

DOI: 10.4018/979-8-3373-2200-1.ch007

INTRODUCTION

Adversarial Machine Learning (AML) has become one of the most important challenges in artificial intelligence (AI), particularly cybersecurity. Machine learning models (machine learning), including Deep Learning (DL) systems, continue to be used in various applications, resulting in the sensitivity of these systems being of urgent concern compared to adversarial attacks. These attacks involving the manipulation of input data in a way that leads to false predictions or classification can have catastrophic consequences, especially when AI systems are used in domains with high manipulation, such as cybersecurity, autonomous vehicles, healthcare, finance, and more. Adversarial machine learning concerning cybersecurity can undermine the effectiveness of AI-driven defense mechanisms that allow attackers to bypass security systems, avoid unauthorized access to sensitive data, and launch new cyberattacks (Akhtar and Rawol, 2024) machine learning. Cybersecurity can use inconsistent attacks to deceive AI-dependent systems, recognizing anomalies, intrusion detection, malware classification, and more. Attackers can subtly manipulate data entry on these systems. It means that models can misclassify or overlook malicious activities. It means that even highly developed safety devices for machine learning are susceptible to targeted adversarial strategies. For example, image classifiers used in security systems can incorrectly identify face recognition scans, which will cause intruders to bypass security control points. Similarly, machine learning-driven attacks (IDS) could not recognize attacks as attackers created input data that deceived the model and classified the attack as benign (Altun et al., 2024). As machine learning models are progressively being used to automate and improve cybersecurity measurements, the ability to protect these models from adversarial attacks is paramount. Without the right defense mechanism, the tools used to protect systems can be weak, making organizations more susceptible to new cyber threats. Traditional cybersecurity measurements, such as firewalls and signature-based intrusion recognition systems, are limited in efficacy when faced with adversarial machine learning. These classical defense mechanisms rely on well-known attack patterns. They may not be sufficient to recognize or prevent new adversarial techniques. Furthermore, adversarial attacks are input data often unrecognizable by human observers. However, they are subtly nuanced and manipulated in ways that could lead to machine learning models. It makes it difficult to recognize adversarial examples using traditional methods. In cybersecurity systems that rely on machine learning, manipulation of input adversarial can circumvent security measures and allow attackers to exploit system failures. Furthermore, the refinement of adversarial attacks is constantly developing, and attackers are developing new technologies to use model weaknesses in machine learning.

The growing threats caused by adversarial machine learning require developing new, more resistant defense strategies that can withstand a wide range of adversarial attack methods to confirm the dependability and integrity of AI systems used in cybersecurity (Altun and Ozkok, 2024). These defense mechanisms can be divided into various categories: adversarial training, preprocessing of inputs, normalizing models, and developing more robust architectures. Adversarial training is one of the most frequently investigated defense mechanisms. This approach expands the training process by presenting adversarial examples in the model's training data. By training models of clean and adversarial examples, the aim is to design models resistant to obstacles caused by adversarial inputs. Adversarial training has often been proven effective but is associated with some limitations (Olutimehin et al., 2025). For example, adversarial-trained models can be calculated because they require more resources than traditional training methods. Furthermore, adversarial training often compromises the robustness of a model and its performance in non-derailed (clean) data compared to adversarial examples. This compromise identifies the fundamental challenges in designing defense mechanisms. Increased robustness to adversarial attacks often leads to a cost in model output, accuracy, and generalization. Methods such as aperture characteristics and randomization of input transformations, which force the model to use fewer features or simpler representations, can help reduce the impact of adversarial inputs. For example, random noise or blur can be applied to an image before it is entered into the image identification model. It makes it more difficult for attackers to create adversarial examples to avoid detection. Input preparation methods often suffer from the same problems as reducing the model output of clean data. Furthermore, these methods cannot always generalize that different adversarial attacks and models may be susceptible to more sophisticated or new attack strategies. Regularization techniques aim to improve the generalization of machine learning models and to be sensitive to small obstacles in input data. By being forced to focus on more meaningful patterns rather than exceeding specific training data, regularization helps to augment the robustness of the model compared to adversarial manipulation (Oye & Owen, 2024). However, regulatory methods are insufficient to protect against adversarial attacks, particularly with more advanced attack strategies. Furthermore, normalization techniques require adversarial threats and may not provide the robustness measure necessary to protect the system in more developed and real applications (Tariq, 2025). Figure 1 presents types of adversial attacks on AI models

Figure 1. Types of Adversarial Attacks on AI Models

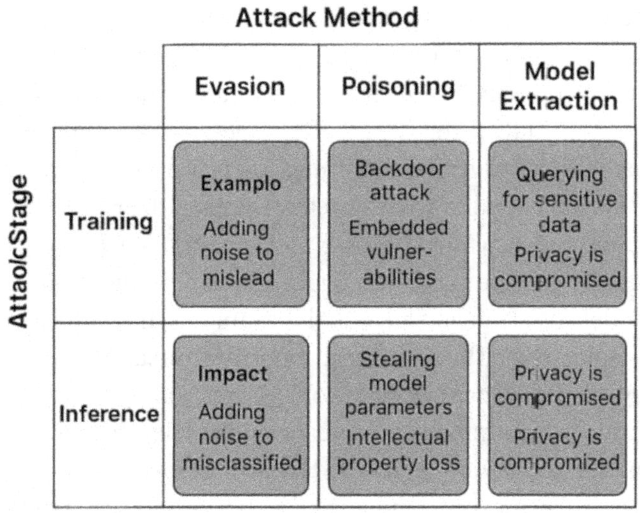

One of the most challenging aspects of adversarial machine learning is finding a balance between security and model output. Defensive mechanisms that increase the robustness of the model compared to adversarial attacks are often associated with cost: reduced accuracy or increased arithmetic requirements. Adversarial training, for example, is effective when increasing robustness but often uses clean data to lead to poor performance. Similarly, input processing techniques and model normalization methods can lead to compromises related to the ability of models to make accurate predictions. These compromises can have serious consequences as models must quickly and accurately recognize attacks, as they need to minimize false positive results at the same time (Balamurugan, 2024). For example, suppose a cybersecurity system driven by machine learning in adversarial immune system prediction becomes too cautious or conservative. In that case, it characterizes too many benign activities as suspicious. If the model's defense is too mild, it is nonadversarial, and the system may be susceptible to attacks. Defenses such as adversarial training often require several arithmetic resources for training and reasoning. Real-time applications such as intrusion detection and malware analysis may have unacceptable latency introduced by the adversarial immune system, leading to delays in decision-making and response times. Thus, a key research question in adversarial machine learning is how to develop defense mechanisms that provide strong protection against adversarial attacks without undue damage to the performance or efficiency of the model. This question is particularly relevant regarding cybersecurity, where recognizing and responding to real-time threats is critical (Khaleel et al., 2024). One of the adversarial machine learning challenges is that many defenses that improve robustness are firmly tuned to certain types of adversarial examples or attack strategies. If an attacker develops more sophisticated techniques, models that are protected from attack types may remain susceptible to others. It raises the question of how models that are not only resistant to adversarial failures but can also be well generalized to various attacks and real-world scenarios can be created. Models focusing on specific adversarial examples cannot prove new attacks or adapt to new threats. Although numerous offensive techniques and defense strategies have been proposed in the literature, there is no standardized method to assess the effectiveness of these immune systems. In particular, adversarial defense performance often depends on the particular type of attack, model architecture, and application domain used. As a result, it is not easy to raise the final claims about the robustness of the model without carefully considering the context provided. The development of standardized assessment metrics and test frameworks for adversarial machine learning is an important area of research that allows practitioners to assess the effectiveness of various defense mechanisms and make well-informed decisions about how AI systems can be protected (Barik & Misra, 2024). The potential consensus outcomes will only increase if machine learning systems are integrated with critical infrastructure. In particular, for highly operational cybersecurity applications, developing a robust, efficient, generalizable immune system against adversarial attacks is crucial to guaranteeing the safety and reliability of AI systems. The balance between security and performance, the development of more general defense mechanisms, and the creation of standardized assessment metrics are some of the most critical research questions that must be answered to build a clean, more resistant machine learning system (Tariq, 2024).

Understanding Adversarial Attacks and Their Impact on AI Security

Adversarial attacks on AI systems for machine learning (ML) and artificial intelligence (AI) are gaining increasing attention in the research community and real-world applications, as they strongly undermine these systems' performance, safety, and integrity. Adversarial attacks use weaknesses in machine learning models to manipulate costs. There are often minimal or nonsensical changes to the input data. These attacks can be divided into diverse types with different methods and goals. The most famous categories include evasion attacks, poisoning attacks, model extraction attacks, and model inference attacks. In particular, these systems are used in mission-critical applications in industries such as cybersecurity, finance, healthcare, and autonomous systems. Hence, each type of attack significantly impacts the safety of AI systems. These attacks focus on manipulating the input data fed to machine learning models to cause false predictions or the production of false predictions. The main feature of alternative attacks is that they target the model during inference. The attacker aims to create adversarial examples close enough to legal data, which cannot be distinguished by humans or external observers but cannot mislead the model to make false predictions. In image detection systems, attackers can, for example, modify the cat's drawing subtly to ensure that classifiers in neuronal networks are misidentified as dogs. At the same time, human observers still recognize the painting as cats (Barik and Misra, 2024). These changes and obstacles are often small enough to be perceived by the human eye, making alternative attacks particularly dangerous and challenging to recognize. For example, many deep learning models, particularly those used for image classification tasks, are sensitive to small obstacles in image pixel values (Petihakis et al., 2024). These faults can be generated using optimization techniques such as fast gradient sign (FGSM) and projected gradient descent (PGD), which repeatedly adapt the input data to the gradient of the loss function associated with the input. The attacker aims to distract the model's output from the correct classification while finding obstacles that maintain the appearance of inputs to the human eye. Concerning autonomous driving, attackers can create adversarial examples to deceive a vehicle's recognition system. It can lead to an accident. In the event of an attack, the attacker attempts to introduce malicious data into the training set. In contrast to evasion attacks that occur during prediction, addiction attacks are performed before the model is trained, allowing the opponent to influence the model's learning process. Malicious data introduced by attackers can be carefully designed to train the model's incorrect patterns. For example, attackers of machine learning spam-based spam filters can inject small numbers of emails into false training data as spam (Hussain & Elson, 2024). That is, filters will incorrectly characterize legitimate emails as spam in the future. Similarly, poisoning attacks can be used in financial applications to influence model predictions or risk assessments. In some cases, poisoning attacks are very effective. Hence, the model creates systematic errors that are difficult to recognize, arising from the training process rather than individual predictions.

Poisoning attacks can be attempted in a variety of ways. One approach involves injecting fraudulent data, in which the attacker intentionally provides false lettering of training rate data points. It can lead to the model learning inaccurate relationships between input functions and labels. Another method is called backdoor addiction, where a particular pattern or data feature triggers an attacker. If available, the model creates the target output. For example, an attacker could introduce small patterns to train the cat and dog photos so that the model can be used in the new photo, even if it looks like a normal picture, when the model is available in the new photo. These attacks can be difficult to recognize as the model's performance is not catastrophic fishing and can gradually deteriorate over time (Gujar, 2024). Model extraction attacks are another dangerous, adversarial attack aimed at the intellectual property and safety of machine learning models. In the case of a model extraction attack, the opponent attempts to reverse or "extract" the internal structure, parameters, or decision process of a machine learning model. It is usually done by querying the model with observations of many inputs and their outputs. The attacker's goal is to replicate the functionality of the target model (Zou et al., 2024). It is used maliciously or to create competing models without cost and training effort. This attack occurs in environments where proprietary models of sensitive applications such as financial forecasting, medical diagnostics, and security systems are used. Repeated modeling and analysis of answers allow the attacker to gradually create alternative models that approach the behavior of the target model. An attacker can use this alternative model to carry out adversarial attacks, such as alternative attacks, or replicate the original model's functionality for malicious purposes. Model theft and potential violations of intellectual property lead to model extraction attacks, particularly in commercial and industrial contexts (Xu et al., 2025). It applies primarily to cloud-based machine services. Cloud-based machine services may allow attackers to gain essential insights into the behavior of models by using weaknesses in access control or querying mechanisms. The results of successful model extraction attacks include the loss of their information, exposure of sensitive data, and the possibility that malicious actors can achieve competitive advantages by creating models that replicate or mimic other models. In the case of a model infection attack, the attacker attempts to use the model's answers in a carefully designed query to display sensitive information about the model's training data, such as private or sensitive data points. Table 1 presents the real-word applications of AML and their attacks.

Table 1. Real-World Applications of AML and Their Attack Vectors

Industry	AI Application	Known Attack Type	Consequence	Mitigation Approach
Healthcare	Diagnostic imaging	Evasion, Model Inference	Misdiagnosis, patient risk	Adversarial training, Explainable AI
Autonomous Vehicles	Object recognition, navigation	Evasion	Misclassification of traffic signs, accidents	Feature squeezing, Sensor fusion
Biometric Systems	Facial and voice recognition	Evasion	Unauthorised access	Defensive distillation, Multimodal authentication
Financial Services	Fraud detection systems	Poisoning, Evasion	Undetected fraud, reputational and financial damage	Robust optimisation, Federated learning
Cybersecurity	Intrusion Detection Systems	Evasion, Poisoning	Malware bypasses detection, system compromise	Adversarial training, Anomaly detection

In contrast to model extraction attacks, which aim to replicate the model itself, model inferior attacks focus on extracting information from models, such as the presence or lack of specific data points in the training set. These attacks represent serious threats to privacy and security, particularly in the context of models being trained with sensitive data such as medical documents, personal information, and financial data. The attacker can conclude whether a particular data point is included in the training set by querying the model and analyzing its output. For example, an attacker in a model trained with medical data could submit questions similar to a particular person's medical records and conclude whether the data was used to form the model. It can lead to unintended disclosure of personal information, violate data protection, and expose people to potential damage (Okoli et al., 2024). Models that fly beyond a particular example in a training set can be susceptible to inference attacks, as predictions may indicate information about the underlying data. Even models trained to generalize can pass information from learned patterns. The risk of inferior attacks in the model underscores the significance of implementing robust data protection obligations, such as when providing machine learning systems that handle sensitive data and differences in privacy or federal learning. The distribution of a predictive target model during inference, attack addiction affects training data, impairs the model's performance, attempts to build a model for malicious use, attempts model extraction attacks, and model infections to reveal infected training data through careful query analysis. As machine learning and artificial intelligence systems in security-critical applications are increasingly being planned, understanding these attack methods and developing effective defenses is essential to ensure AI systems' integrity, privacy, and security. Given the increasingly adversarial technology refinement, continuous research into robust defense mechanisms to protect AI systems from these developing threats is fundamental (Tariq, 2025).

The escalation of artificial intelligence (AI) and machine learning (ML) systems has led to considerable advances in various sectors, including cybersecurity. Suppose AI control tools are integrated with detection and defense against cyber threats. In that case, they are becoming the targets of adversarial attacks. These attacks use vulnerabilities inherent in AI models to allow attackers to bypass security measures, manipulate the model's behavior, and gain unauthorized access to the system. The impact of such attacks is serious as it is significant to the most important cybersecurity features, such as AI-powered malware, autonomous systems, biometric authentication, fraud recognition, and financial safety model detection. The real consequences of these adversarial attacks pose a critical threat to reliability and security as well as the privacy and security of individuals and administrations. Traditional techniques for malware detection are based on signature-based approaches that identify well-known malicious code by adapting patterns to databases with signatures. These systems serve their purpose, but in many cases, they are ineffective against new or unknown malware. It has led to an increase in machine identification methods. Machine learning models, intensive learning-based models, have previously identified invisible malware by learning complex patterns and analyzing the behavior of large amounts of network traffic, files, or systems. These models are trained to distinguish benign and malicious activities based on statistical features and historical data. Cybercrime malware patterns are specially designed to ensure that machine learning models are classified as benign in the event of evasion attacks. For example, an attacker could change the code of a malware piece slightly, change the input, and misclassify the identification model without changing the malware's functionality. These subtle changes are not perceptible to human analysts. However, they can have a significant impact on the performance of the model. Many machine learning models are trained using distinctive vectors, allowing adversarial attackers to exploit the model's weaknesses by identifying and manipulating these properties. To avoid security measures. Given the rapid spread of malware and the ever-evolving nature of cyber threats, adversarial attacks on AI systems can have catastrophic consequences for malware detection (Ijiga et al., 2024). If adversarial malware remains undetected, this can lead to data injuries, system compromise, financial losses, and critical infrastructure failures. It underscores the need for the continued development of more resistant malware recognition systems that can withstand the obstacles of adversarial manipulation and the need to strongly emphasize defensive technologies, such as adversarial training and model ensembles, to improve model deviations in models. Autonomous systems, including self-driving cars, drones, and robotic systems, rely on algorithms for machine learning to perceive and interact with the environment. These systems typically use a variety of sensors, such as cameras, radar, and GPS, to gather information and make actual decisions. Machine learning models process this sensor data to identify objects, recognize dangers, and plan appropriate measures. However, the safety and functionality of these systems can undermine major attacks aimed at sensor data, particularly visual data. Exercise attackers can create photos or modify existing images so that the car's recognition system misinterprets information. For example, a sticker placed properly on a stop sign may not be recognized by the car's AI system as a stop sign, leading to dangerous consequences. A similar attack can be done against the vehicle's object detection system. It means that pedestrians overlook or misclassify objects in that area. These adversarial attacks can lead to road accidents, collisions, and even death. They can pose substantial risks to public security. For example, an attacker can manipulate radar to disrupt the vehicle's decision-making system. It leads to distance measurements, navigation errors, or incorrect strategies to avoid collisions. Given that autonomous systems operate in increasingly complex and dynamic environments, the possibility of adversarial manipulation interfering with all new technological advances is increasing. With drones, attackers could manipulate GPS signals and crash the drone navigation system by inaccurately causing it to crash or fly off course. It is particularly affected in the context of military or critical infrastructure used to monitor, clearly, or deliver sensitive payloads using drones. Considering the potential consequences of attacks on security-critical systems, developing a defense strategy that can recognize and reduce the opposite input in real time is urgently necessary. Approaches such as adversarial training, sense in the decision-making process, and redundancy can help reduce the risk of successful attacks (Tarade & Das, 2025). However, these systems are more complex and integrated into everyday life, making the challenge of protecting them from manipulation of adversarial manipulation more difficult.

Biometric systems, increasingly used for secure access to devices, buildings, and online services, are also vulnerable to adversarial attacks. Biometric authentication systems rely on unique human characteristics such as fingerprints, facial features, voice patterns, and iris scans to authenticate individuals. These systems are generally considered more secure than traditional password-based authentication, as they rely on data that is difficult to replicate. However, some attacks show that biometric systems are not perfect. Using the machine learning models' weaknesses in these systems, attackers can create adversarial examples to deceive the system to grant unauthorized access (Gupta et al., 2025). Attackers can generate face diagrams that look normal to human observers. However, AI systems may incorrectly identify that person or grant access to someone else. In some cases, using subtle obstacles in images can create adversarial examples (Gujar, 2024). It will make the attacker's surface appear similar to the certified user's face or modify certain facial features to avoid detection. This attack can lead to illegal access to safe locations and systems, undermining privacy and security. An attacker can use language integration technology to generate languages that mimic the voice of authorized users and allow language-based authentication mechanisms to be circumvented. These attacks seriously affect the security of individual devices, banking systems, and even national security applications where language biometrics are used for secure communication. Some techniques, such as using multimodal authentication methods that can add noise to biometric data and improve security, remain a challenge in designing systems resistant to both user operations.

Furthermore, as attackers are better designed for adversarial examples, developing real-time recognition mechanisms to identify block-contain attacks on biometric systems becomes increasingly important. Fraud recognition systems, often used in banks, insurance, e-commerce, and other financial services, are based on algorithms for machine learning to identify suspicious transactions or fraud (Akhtar & Rawol, 2024). These systems analyze transaction data, customer behavior patterns, and other related features to determine whether a particular action is legal or fraudulent. However, the main attacker can manipulate transaction data to lead the system to classify rogue transactions as legitimate, allowing financial fraud to be carried out without recognition. They can also use adversarial obstacles to create fraudulent behaviors that mimic legitimate users and bypass the system's perception mechanisms. Attackers can sometimes combine adversarial attacks with traditional social engineering methods, such as phishing and identity theft, to create more sophisticated and effective attacks. For example, suppose an adversarial manipulation tricks a bank's fraud marking system. In that case, an attacker may be able to steal large amounts of money without being discovered. Similarly, adversarial attacks can undermine trust in financial institutions and disrupt the functioning of financial markets. Businesses are exceptionally high in sectors where large amounts of money are at stake. Recognition. However, if attackers develop more stringent technologies to avoid these immune systems, the challenge of ensuring an AI-controlled financial system is becoming increasingly complicated. To maintain the integrity and security of your financial system, it is essential to develop models that are accurately resistant to adversarial operations (Henry, 2024). AI-driven systems for malware recognition, autonomous systems, biometric authentication, fraud detection, and financial security are susceptible to adversarial operations. These attacks are critical to public security, privacy, financial security, and critical infrastructure reliability. As the refinement of adversarial techniques develops, it is essential to develop robust defenses that can protect AI models from these threats, ensuring that AI systems are protected from an increase in cyber threats (Henry, 2024). Figure 2 presents the conceptual triangle for inherent trade-offs in AML defense.

Figure 2. Trade-off Triangle – Robustness, Accuracy, and Efficiency

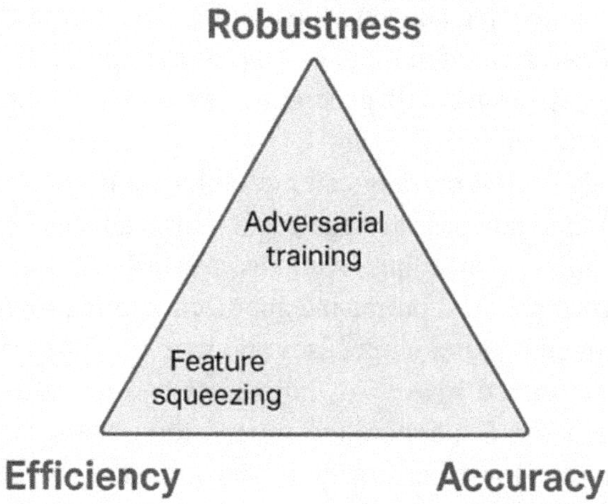

Defensive Strategies Against Adversarial Attacks

Adversarial attacks on machine learning models have become one of the most important challenges in artificial intelligence and cybersecurity. Manipulating model inputs with carefully manufactured and adversarial examples can lead to false predictions, undermining the safety and integrity of different AI applications (Hoang et al., 2024). These attacks have a major impact on the use of AI in safety-sensitive areas such as autonomous systems, malware recognition, fraud prevention, and biometric authentication. As the risk of adversarial attacks continues to increase, researchers and practitioners have developed a variety of defense mechanisms to improve the robustness of machine learning models and to increase resistance to such attacks. The most well-known defensive strategies include adversarial training, defensive distillation, narrowing down, pre-treatment defense, and robust optimization techniques. Each method offers an inimitable approach to enhancing AI models against adversarial obstacles. It reduces security vulnerabilities and ensures reliability in real applications. The central idea of adversarial training is to expand training data with adversarial examples that have been changed to deceive the model into false predictions. By including adversarial examples in the training process, the model learns to recognize and correctly classify disturbed entries, improving its ability to withstand adversarial manipulation. One of the most frequently used techniques is the Fast Gradient Sine Method (FGSM), which generates an adversarial example by adding small obstacles to the input data in the direction of the pitch of the loss function associated with the input. Failures need to maximize losses (Khan et al., 2024). It means that the model has an incorrect input and, at the same time, keeps the obstacles very low, making them unperceived by humans. These adversarial examples were generated and added to the training data record, forcing the model to classify normal and adversarial inputs. One of the main difficulties lies in the computational costs associated with generating adversarial examples and retraining an augmented data model.

Furthermore, adversarial training can not eliminate the sensitivity of a model to a model compared to adversarial target, as it allows an attacker to adapt continuously and create more demanding examples. Nevertheless, adversarial training continues to be one of the most promising approaches to improving the robustness of the model, and ongoing research focuses on improving this technology to make it more efficient and effective. A GAN comprises two neural networks: a generator and a discriminator. Generators are trained to create data that resembles a particular distribution. However, discriminators are asked to distinguish between actual data and generated data. GANs can adapt to generate adversarial examples by training the generator to create inputs developed explicitly for the deception of the target model. These adversarial examples can be used to test the susceptibility of adversarial training and models to such attacks. First, you can create a variety of adversarial examples. It helps simulate various attacks that could satisfy the AI model. Defensive distillation is a technique in which SoftMax's probability distribution production models are trained and are not very sensitive to small input impairments. Defensive distillation aims to create distilled versions of neuronal networks resistant to adversarial attacks. It is achieved by using the initial probability of a previously trained model as the target name. Softened probability encourages models to make smoother decisions - limit limits and make adversarial examples of causing misclassification difficult (Hoang et al., 2024). Although student models are trained to mimic the behavior of teacher models, they focus on learning the underlying patterns of data rather than remembering specific examples. The results are a more generalized, more robust model and are less likely to exceed that with adversarial obstacles. Defensive distillation has shown that the robustness of deep neuronal networks can be improved for certain types of adversarial attacks (Gupta et al., 2025). However, it is not a panacea and may not be protected from adversarial manipulation. For example, adversarial training and defensive distillation can be used simultaneously, which generates adversarial examples and is included in the distillation process. This combination of techniques can help you create a more robust model for adversarial attacks (Kavitha & Thejas, 2024). Feature squeezing is based on the idea that oversized failures often utilize unnecessary or redundant features in the input data. Reducing the complexity of input functions reduces the impact of adversarial operations. It makes it more difficult for an attacker to find successful failures. Features - Work is performed by applying input transformation techniques such as quantization, JPEG compression, and smoothing median before input data is inserted into the model (Hossain et al., 2024).

Quantization involves reducing the accuracy of the input data by portraying continuous values into small segments of discrete values (Baniecki & Biecek, 2024). For example, quantization can be used in images to reduce the number of dyes or the image's resolution. This simplification of input data can reduce the possibility of adversarial obstacles to make wise changes to the input, improving the model's resistance to attack. JPEG compression is performed by removing high-frequency components from image data. It is often the area most susceptible to the manipulation of adversaries. Meanwhile, the median smoothing includes applying a median filter to the input data. It helps reduce noise and eliminate small obstacles that adversarial attackers can insert. However, the limitation of feature squeezing is that useful information may be lost in the input data (Malatji & Tolah, 2024). It can reduce the accuracy or generalization of the model. Therefore, the balance between robustness and model output is often used with other defense strategies, such as adversarial training and distillation. Table 2 presents the comparison of adversial defense techniques.

Table 2. Comparison of Adversarial Defense Techniques

Technique	Type	Pros	Cons	Typical Use Cases
Adversarial Training	Training	Improves model robustness by exposing it to adversarial examples	High computational cost; may reduce accuracy on clean data	Intrusion Detection Systems, Biometric Authentication
Defensive Distillation	Training	Reduces model sensitivity by smoothing predictions	Less effective against adaptive attacks; may reduce model interpretability	Malware Classification, Fraud Detection
Feature Squeezing	Preprocessing	Reduces input complexity to limit adversarial perturbations	May degrade accuracy; not generalisable across all attacks	Image Recognition, Facial Recognition
Robust Optimization	Training	Encourages generalisation by penalising sensitivity to input noise	Requires tuning; performance trade-cff	Autonomous Driving, Financial Models
Input Transformation	Preprocessing	Simplifies or modifies inputs to remove perturbations	Computational overhead; not always effective against all attacks	Speech and Language Processing

Pre-treatment methods include transforming input data before it is passed by the model to eliminate or mitigate disputes. These preprocessing techniques can be used in various ways depending on the type of data and the particular attack. In addition to narrowing it down, other preprocessing techniques include input normalization, data augmentation, and adversarial example recognition. These techniques include changes to the training process to ensure that the model is not sensitive to adversarial obstacles and is generalized by invisible data. Normalization is one of the most common robust optimization techniques. It involves adding a penalty term to the loss function to prevent the model from overfitting the training data. Regularization techniques such as L1 and L2 normalization, failure, and early arrest help improve the model's robustness by discouraging it from the specific stored patterns of training data and being less susceptible to adversarial manipulation. By introducing noise into the weight, the model is forced to learn more vigorous features that are not sensitive to small changes in the input data (Hossain et al., 2024). This technique has been shown to improve neuronal network robustness compared to adversarial attacks. It is because we encourage the model to focus on more stable data patterns rather than through specific examples. Body weight noise injection can be considered a form of regularization as it helps prevent the model from being overly directed about certain features and characteristics within the data. Lastly, adversarial attacks are a critical issue for the safety and dependability of machine learning models, especially in critical applications. To address this challenge, researchers have developed various defense mechanisms to improve the robustness of the model and increase resistance through the manipulation of adversarial examples. Converse training, defensive distillation, bruises, pre-tracking, and robust optimization techniques are some of the most promising approaches to improving model resilience. Each of these methods has its strengths and limitations, and their effectiveness often depends on the particular context and type of attack. With adversarial attacks occurring, research on new defense strategies is vital to ensure that machine-learning models are safe and reliable in real-world applications (Jjiga et al., 2024).

AI-Powered Security Measures in AML Defense

The rapid development and incorporation of artificial intelligence (AI) into various industries, including cybersecurity, has created a variety of new possibilities, but it has also created many new challenges. AI systems, particularly machine learning (ML) models, are increasingly used in critical applications such as threat detection, fraud prevention, and anomaly recognition. However, with the rise in these powerful AI applications, comprehensive attacks and malicious exploitation of models due to their weaknesses have become a considerable concern. The main attacks where inputs have been altered to create AI models to make false predictions, or classifications, are in response to critical threats to AI systems' integrity and security. can. These methods include AI Techniques (XAI), approaches to anomaly recognition, combined strategies to improve transparency, perception of anomalous behavior, and enhanced model security considering adversarial threats. Traditionally, many models of machine learning, especially deep learning models, act as "black boxes." In other words, internal functions and decision-making make understanding or interpreting people's logic difficult (Mahjabeen & Islam, 2024). This lack of transparency makes it difficult to trust and see the actions of AI systems, especially in applications with high-level operations such as security and threat detection. Understanding how decisions are made can be very important in identifying security gaps or potential errors to address these gaps, which provides methods and techniques that make AI models easier to interpret and understand. Transparent Decision Making - Decision Process - Making allows XAIs to gain insight into introducing models for specific decisions, particularly when adversarial attacks are involved. For example, suppose the AI model misclassifies the input due to an adversarial failure. In that case, the explanatory technique can highlight whether the first part has caused this model to make the wrong decision. This transparency helps identify potential threats and provides a clearer way to debug or reduce the impact of adversarial attacks. Understanding which characteristics make predictions for most of the model allows security teams to recognize inconsistencies or irregularities that could indicate adversarial operations. For example, suppose the model's decision process is heavily based on functions unrelated to each task. In that case, this can indicate that adversarial inputs manipulate the model. Furthermore, the explanatory technique can pursue ways models change decisions on new or unexpected data, allowing better monitoring of model output and identifying abnormal or abnormal behavior. It is important that AI systems not only make accurate decisions but also be understandable, especially in sensitive areas such as national defense, healthcare, and financial services. By providing insights into model prediction, Xai supports the validation of system output and helps to match the expected behavior with decisions (Shamoo, 2025). This ability can detect attacks and potential threats (Oloyede, 2024). The anomaly recognition method aims to identify behavioral patterns that differ significantly from predicted or normal behavior, which provides an important tool for real-time recognition of abnormal or adversarial inputs. These methods are beneficial when attackers try to subtly manipulate the model without leaving obvious indications of malicious activity. Using anomaly detection technology, security systems can mark anomaly inputs that could indicate adversarial attacks. It provides an early warning to prevent further damage (Tariq, 2025). In adversarial attack scenarios, unattended learning algorithms can train normal data distributions and identify inputs that differ from these patterns. This approach is not based on knowing what an adversarial attack looks like in advance, so it is beneficial to recognize new or unknown attack methods. For this purpose, classes often use anomaly recognition algorithms such as K-Means clustering, principal component analysis (PCA), an automatic encoder, and SVM. These models are trained to identify typical input data (Patel et al., 2025). Suppose a new entry is being fed to the system. In that case, the model can identify instances different from what it has learned to be "normal." Once specified, the system continues to monitor incoming network packages. It marks data traffic that rejects learned behavior as potentially abnormal. When the other party manipulates input data (for example, evasion attacks), the abnormality recognition system can recognize subtle deviations and trigger warnings. The main advantage of unsupervised anomaly recognition in the context of conflicting attacks is its ability to recognize previously invisible attacks, even if manufactured to avoid traditional identification methods (Tripathi & Pandey, 2024). By integrating anomaly detection into a broader defense strategy, security teams can improve AI systems' general robustness and respond to them better in real time. Additionally, abnormality recognition systems can be continuously updated to adapt to new patterns of legitimate behavior. It means that new threats will make them more resistant.

While XAI and anomaly recognition techniques can help improve the detection and understanding of adversarial attacks, federation learning is a promising approach to improving the security of AI models during training, especially in defense against addiction attacks. Addiction attacks arise when an attacker manipulates training data to destroy the model's learning process (Balamurugan, 2024). It is particularly worrying in the context of federal learning. It is especially concerning as it allows distributed model training where data is retained on local devices, and only model revisions are shared with central servers. Federated Learning has the advantage of protecting users by decentralizing data. However, it also introduces new weaknesses, mainly due to attack vectors in which malicious devices submit poisoned model updates to damage the global model. Instead of sending sensitive data to the central server, each participating device (or "client") trains the model locally with its data and shares the resulting model parameters (e.g., weights) with the central server. The server aggregates these model updates for all clients to form a global model. Federated learning is beneficial for applications, healthcare, and IoT.

The main frustration of federal learning is enabling collaborative training while simultaneously retaining data protection periods and reducing the risk of data injury. In such an attack, malicious players can affect a small number of customers. It will submit addiction updates that introduce false information into the global model. It can affect the model's accuracy, make false predictions, and even allow attackers to manipulate it to perform malicious actions (Khaleel, 2024). For example, suppose a complex system is used to recognize fraud in financial transactions. In that case, addiction attacks can lead to models, allowing attackers to carry out illegal transactions without being detected. The approach includes robust aggregation methods such as federation averages (Kiranbabu et al., 2025). This method allows the central server to analyze the client's submitted model updates and remove all updates significantly different from those of other users. Another approach is to introduce encryption techniques to check the integrity of model updates and ensure that they are not manipulated.

Additionally, various data protection techniques can be used to add model updates. By monitoring the behavior of model updates during training, anomaly recognition algorithms can identify suspicious patterns that may suggest an attack attempt. For example, suppose one or a few customers consistently send updates that differ significantly from the others. In that case, this can be characterized as an anomaly and can be conducted for further testing. This combination of federated learning and anomaly recognition technology provides a powerful defense against addiction attacks, helping maintain the global model's veracity and ensure its accuracy and reliability (Khaleel et al., 2024). Using isomorphic encryption and secure calculations with several parties, federated learning systems can ensure that individual model updates are kept confidential and cannot be operated during aggregation. These encryption technologies allow the federal learning process to remain safe even in the presence of malicious participants. Finally, the combination of explainable AI, anomaly recognition, and spring-up learning represents a powerful tool to improve the security and resilience of AI models, particularly considering ebrarial attacks and malignant manipulation. Explanatory AI technology provides transparency in the decision-making process of machine learning models to identify anomalous behaviors and recognize the manipulation of adversaries. An Anomaly recognition system uses unattended learning to identify anomalous entries that can demonstrate adversarial activity and provide real-time detection of threats. On the other hand, Federated learning offers a distributed model training approach (Sankaram et al., 2024). It helps you get data protection and protect against data attacks. By incorporating these techniques into AI systems, we can create more robust, safe, and transparent models that can withstand adversarial threats and confirm critical systems' safety and integrity. As AI commences to play an increasingly important role in cybersecurity and other areas, these methods are essential to ensure that AI-controlled systems are reliable and reliable (Malatji and Tolah, 2024).

Challenges and Future Research Directions in AML Defenses

The artificial intelligence (AI) landscape is rapidly developing, which means that AI systems are currently used in various industries, ranging from healthcare to fundraising to cybersecurity. Further AI processes also pose challenges to ensure the robustness and safety of these systems. One of the most critical challenges in AI today is the sensitivity of machine learning models to adversarial attacks. Leading Example - Inputs intentionally intended to mislead AI models are serious threats to the security and reliability of AI applications. However, these defense mechanisms often compromise model robustness, accuracy, arithmetic, and ethical concerns. As AI plays an increasingly vigorous role in safety-sensitive applications, it is essential to consider the balance between these factors to ensure that AI systems are safe and effective for tasks (Oloyede, 2024).

Conversely, adversarial training, defensive distillation, and other defensive techniques aim to design models resistant to adversarial inputs. These methods include augmenting training data using adversarial examples to make the model more generalizable or tweaking the model to use various preprocessing techniques. These methods can make the model more resistant, especially compared to specific operations, but often at the expense of accuracy, especially for clean data. It increases the robustness of the model, but this can reduce the performance of the original uninterrupted data. This model can be overly focused on treating adversarial disorders. This means it is not very effective in cleaning data. This compromise between robustness and accuracy is a well-known issue in adversarial machine learning, and researchers will continue to look at methods to minimize this compromise. However, distillation usually reduces the overall performance of the model in the model, as soft labels introduced during training can concentrate the model on fewer identification features and thus reduce the accuracy of cleaning the data. The challenge is to find a balance in which the model maintains accuracy over legitimate data and is robust enough to resist adversaries (Barik & Misra, 2024). This balance requires careful design of training procedures and defense mechanisms that do not sacrifice the key metrics of the model. Implementing defenses against adversarial attacks, including adversarial training, initial processing, and robust optimization techniques, can significantly increase compensation for training and inference processes (Prasad et al., 2024). This defense often requires additional time, storage, and computing power resources. For example, adversarial training involves generating and including adversarial examples in a computational training process, especially for large models or data records.

Sometimes, it can exacerbate computing costs as you must transfer or run the model on an adversarial example. Preprocessing defenses, such as feature aperture and input conversion, add computing efforts by inserting additional processing steps before data is fed into the model. These immune systems can improve robustness, but they slow down at the expense of what is needed for real applications that require low-latency answers, such as self-driving cars, financial fraud detection, and network representation detection systems (Oye and Owen, 2024). In these cases, a balance between security and computational efficiency is essential. Researchers have considered a few defensive techniques that provide robust protection against adversarial attacks without imposing critical computing efforts. However, these autoimmune systems are often equipped with compromises about their effectiveness in reducing different types of attacks. For example, in cybersecurity, AI-powered intrusion detection systems (IDSs) must process large amounts of data in real time to identify potential threats. Implementing robust defense mechanisms that increase computing efforts can slow threat detection and make responding quickly to malicious activities more difficult. Therefore, achieving a good balance of robustness and performance is critical to ensure that the AI model works effectively in real-world scenarios, primarily when operational. The main goal of this defense is to improve the robustness of the AI model and ensure its reliability, but there are some ethical issues. The main concern is the possibility of reasonable defensive techniques incorrectly introducing distortions and identification into the model (Zhang, 2024). For example, adversarial training can effectively lead to models, especially when improving the resilience of models in a given data subgroup. It strengthens existing distortions in AI systems and can contribute to unfair or discriminatory outcomes, particularly in sensitive applications such as setup, lending, and law enforcement.

Another ethical concern is using adversarial defense mechanisms in systems that significantly impact individual privacy and security. For example, biometric systems can use adversarial attacks to avoid facial or fingerprint detection, allowing malicious access to receive unauthorized access. Adversarial defense implementation in these systems can undermine the risk of such attacks and raise questions about security and privacy compromises. These defenses must be used cautiously to either unnecessarily affect an individual's data protection rights or create new security gaps. For example, defensive distillation and other techniques that make the model easier to interpret can undermine the transparency of AI systems. Explaining and understanding AI decisions is vital in specific applications, such as healthcare and criminal justice. The lack of transparency in a model with stiffened security can make it difficult for users to understand how decisions were made, undermining trust in AI systems. Therefore, each security measure must be implemented to maintain ethical fairness, accountability, and transparency standards. A promising field of research is the integration of AI into intrusion detection systems (IDSs). AI-Augmented IDS can be designed to automatically record cyber attacks in real time and respond to improve critical infrastructure protection. By using algorithms for machine learning to analyze large amounts of network traffic and detect anomaly patterns, these systems can quickly identify potential intrusions that may remain unnoticed by traditional IDS methods. In the context of an adversarial attack, you can also recognize adversarial inputs and respond to systems that try to deceive the system to train AI-driven identity. The adversarial nature of the attack means that attackers are likely to develop tactics continuously, create the need for IDS systems, and maintain adaptability and resistance. To address this, researchers are developing more robust AI models that can be generalized to detect invisible and adversarial examples to ensure that AI-powered IDS systems are still effective against new attack strategies. Additionally, these systems should be designed to minimize false alarms and negativity so that they can recognize real threats and avoid unnecessary failures simultaneously. Blockchain may provide a distributed manipulation lid that can be used to ensure that it is not manipulated during training or used following machine learning model development and updates. In a blockchain-based system, each update of a model to a model can be recorded as a transaction that provides a transparent, verifiable history of model development. It helps prevent addictive attacks that attempt to introduce malicious changes to the model by manipulating the training data. Federal learning allows several participants to train machine learning models together without sharing raw data. Blockchain can be integrated into federated learning systems to ensure that the updates of the models provided by each participant are legal and not manipulated. This integration of blockchain and AI provides additional security, making it more difficult for attackers to manipulate the training process or introduce updates to malicious models. By recording every model training step in a distributed general ledger, blockchain can provide a verifiable testing pathway that allows interest groups to track how their models are developed and whether changes have been made. It improves trust in AI systems, especially in critical applications where transparency is essential. B. Healthcare, Financing, Law Enforcement. However, achieving this goal requires compensation for various factors, including robustness, accuracy, arithmetic, and ethical considerations. Defense against conflicting attacks often involves compromise, and researchers must design careful defensive mechanisms that maximize safety without significantly sacrificing the model's performance. Furthermore, ethical concerns related to bias, transparency, and data protection must be addressed in the provision of adversarial defense in real-world applications. There are promising AI security trends, such as AI-Augmented Intrusion Detection Systems and blockchain, for secure model training and checking. By addressing these challenges and adopting new technologies, it is possible to build safe and reliable AI systems to ensure reliability in critical applications in the industry.

CONCLUSION

Adversarial Machine Learning (AML) has evolved as an essential topic in artificial intelligence (AI) and cybersecurity. When AI systems are integrated with high levels of applications, B. as Threat detection, fraud prevention, and autonomous systems, weaknesses of adversarial attacks have become a more severe focus. These attacks manipulate AI models with subtle changes to the input of data or training processes. They are a significant risk to the reliability and safety of AI control systems. Adversarial concerns about attacks have led to more research to develop effective defense strategies that improve robustness in machine learning (ML) and deep learning (DL). In this summary, we look at the most important findings from investigating excessive defense systems for machine learning. AML Defense Best Practices explain and provide political recommendations for ensuring AI systems in high-risk environments. Finally, it reflects the future of AI-driven cybersecurity defense strategies that highlight trends and potential advancements. The diversity and refinement of adversarial model extraction methods, inference attacks, and addition attacks require a broad security approach. Critical defense mechanisms, such as adversarial training, defensive distillation, robust optimization, and preprocessing techniques, each provide protection but are associated with limitations and compromises. However, one of the most significant drawbacks of adversarial training is its compromise in robustness and accuracy.

Adversarial training improves the ability of models to resist adversarial inputs, which often reduces performance with clean, unchanged data. Furthermore, adversarial training is computationally intensive and time-consuming, especially for large models and complex data records. This compromise between security and accuracy is one of the most critical challenges in this area. Distillation has been shown to increase the model's resilience. However, the loss of softer label information can lead to poorer performance.

Furthermore, defensive distillation may not be a comprehensive defense and is insufficient for more advanced container technologies. These techniques effectively mitigate several adversarial attacks, particularly those aimed at manipulating small obstacles at the pixel level or text in the photo. However, preliminary processing defenses often suffer from their performance limitations. They may not provide sufficient protection against any attack. These techniques improve the model's resilience by over-adapting adversarial obstacles and introducing noise and limitations during training. However, like others, these methods often include compromises related to arithmetic efficiency and model output. A combination of adversarial training and robust optimization of pre-treatment or properties can help create, for example, a more comprehensive defense system (Venugopal & Christo, 2024). A layered approach is more resource-intensive but can better protect against a wider selection of adversarial threats. However, the challenge is finding the right defense combination that compensates for effectiveness, computational efficiency, and model accuracy. AI systems must involve robust security measures in finance, healthcare, national security, and autonomous transport sectors.

Looking at the future of AI-driven cybersecurity defense strategies, some emerging trends promise to address ongoing challenges through adversarial attacks. One of the most exciting developments is that AI will be integrated into traditional cybersecurity industrial products such as intrusion detection systems (IDSs). AI-powered IDS systems can use algorithms for machine learning to analyze large amounts of network traffic and identify anomaly patterns that could indicate cyberattacks. By including adversarial defense mechanisms in these systems, AI can help you recognize and mitigate attacks in real-time, helping to improve the protection of critical infrastructure. Blockchain can provide a general lid for distributed operations that pursue developing and updating machine learning models, and ensure they are not affected during training. This technology helps prevent attacks and provides a transparent record of model updates. AI systems used in high-risk surroundings are easier to align with. Combining blockchain and AI allows businesses to create secure and transparent AI systems that are less susceptible to adversarial manipulation. Through Spring-based learning, your data can remain on your local device, reducing the risk of data injury and ensuring that sensitive information is not displayed. This approach benefits applications in the healthcare and finance industries, where data protection is the most important thing. By including adversarial defense technologies in federal learning frameworks, businesses can ensure that their models are secure and subject to data protection. Many defense mechanisms have been proposed, but there is no uniform solution to the adversarial attack problem. The key to undermining risks associated with adversarial operations lies in defense strategies such as adversarial training, pre-treatment of traits, robust optimization, and explainable AI. At the same time, organizations need to harmonize their security needs with compromises in accuracy, arithmetic efforts, and ethical considerations. Political recommendations should focus on promoting transparency, investing in research, and establishing a robust safety framework for protecting AI systems in high-risk control. Proactively managing these challenges can ensure that AI continues to utilize its potential as a powerful tool to improve cybersecurity and other critical areas.

REFERENCES

Akhtar, Z. B., & Rawol, A. T. (2024). Enhancing cybersecurity through AI-powered security mechanisms. *IT Journal Research and Development, 9*(1), 50–67. DOI: 10.25299/itjrd.2024.16852

Altun, İ. Z., & Özkök, A. E. (2024, April). Securing artificial intelligence: Exploring attack scenarios and defense strategies. In *2024 12th International Symposium on Digital Forensics and Security (ISDFS)* (pp. 1-6). IEEE.

Balamurugan, M. (2024). Guardians at Risk: The Challenge of Adversarial Attacks on Authentication Systems and Artificial Intelligence. *International Journal of Scientific Research.*

Baniecki, H., & Biecek, P. (2024). Adversarial attacks and defenses in explainable artificial intelligence: A survey. *Information Fusion, 107*, 102303. DOI: 10.1016/j.inffus.2024.102303

Barik, K., & Misra, S. (2024). Adversarial attack defense analysis: An empirical approach in cybersecurity perspective. *Software Impacts, 21*, 100681. DOI: 10.1016/j.simpa.2024.100681

Gujar, S. S. (2024, November). Enhancing Adversarial Robustness in AI Systems: A Novel Defense Mechanism Using Stable Diffusion. In *2024 2nd DMIHER International Conference on Artificial Intelligence in Healthcare, Education and Industry (IDICAIEI)* (pp. 1-6). IEEE. DOI: 10.1109/IDICAIEI61867.2024.10842888

Gupta, M., Jain, J., Agarwal, G., Modake, R., & Tanikonda, A. (2025). Adversarial Attacks and Fraud Defenses: Leveraging Data Engineering to Secure AI Models in the Digital Age. *Authorea Preprints, 20.*

Henry, E. (2024). Adversarial Machine Learning Developing Robust Defense Mechanisms Against Evolving Threat Models in AI Systems.

Hoang, V. T., Ergu, Y. A., Nguyen, V. L., & Chang, R. G. (2024). Security risks and countermeasures of adversarial attacks on AI-driven applications in 6G networks: A survey. *Journal of Network and Computer Applications, 232*, 104031. DOI: 10.1016/j.jnca.2024.104031

Hossain, M. T., Afrin, R., & Biswas, M. A. A. (2024). A Review on Attacks against Artificial Intelligence (AI) and Their Defence Image Recognition and Generation Machine Learning, Artificial Intelligence. *Control Systems and Optimization Letters, 2*(1), 52–59. DOI: 10.59247/csol.v2i1.73

Hussain, S., & Elson, A. (2024). Adversarial Machine Learning: Identifying and Mitigating AI-Powered Cyber Attacks.

Ijiga, O. M., Idoko, I. P., Ebiega, G. I., Olajide, F. I., Olatunde, T. I., & Ukaegbu, C. (2024). Harnessing adversarial machine learning for advanced threat detection: AI-driven strategies in cybersecurity risk assessment and fraud prevention. *J. Sci. Technol, 11*, 001-024.

Kavitha, D., & Thejas, S. (2024). Ai enabled threat detection: Leveraging artificial intelligence for advanced security and cyber threat mitigation. *IEEE Access : Practical Innovations, Open Solutions*.

Khaleel, T. A. (2024, May). Developing robust machine learning models to defend against adversarial attacks in the field of cybersecurity. In *2024 International Congress on Human-Computer Interaction, Optimization and Robotic Applications (HORA)* (pp. 1-7). IEEE. DOI: 10.1109/HORA61326.2024.10550799

Khaleel, Y. L., Habeeb, M. A., Albahri, A. S., Al-Quraishi, T., Albahri, O. S., & Alamoodi, A. H. (2024). Network and cybersecurity applications of defense in adversarial attacks: A state-of-the-art using machine learning and deep learning methods. *Journal of Intelligent Systems*, *33*(1), 20240153. DOI: 10.1515/jisys-2024-0153

Khan, O. U., Abdullah, S. M., Olajide, A. O., Sani, A. I., Faisal, S. M. W., Ogunola, A. A., & Lee, M. D. (2024). The Future of Cybersecurity: Leveraging Artificial Intelligence to Combat Evolving Threats and Enhance Digital Defense Strategies. *Journal of Computational Analysis and Applications*, *33*(8).

Kiranbabu, M. N. V., Viji, A. J., Chandanan, A. K., Birchha, V., Pandey, T. K., & Sar, S. K. (2025). The Challenge of Adversarial Attacks on AI-Driven Cybersecurity Systems. *Journal of Cybersecurity & Information Management*, *15*(1).

Mahjabeen, F., & Islam, M. A. (2024). The Role of AI and Machine Learning in Strengthening Cybersecurity Defenses. [BESTEC]. *Bulletin of Engineering Science and Technology*, *1*(02), 109–124.

Malatji, M., & Tolah, A. (2024). Artificial intelligence (AI) cybersecurity dimensions: A comprehensive framework for understanding adversarial and offensive AI. *AI and Ethics*, •••, 1–28.

Okoli, U. I., Obi, O. C., Adewusi, A. O., & Abrahams, T. O. (2024). Machine learning in cybersecurity: A review of threat detection and defense mechanisms. *World Journal of Advanced Research and Reviews*, *21*(1), 2286–2295. DOI: 10.30574/wjarr.2024.21.1.0315

Oloyede, J. (2024). AI-Driven Cybersecurity Solutions: Enhancing Defense Mechanisms in the Digital Era. *Available atSSRN* 4976103. DOI: 10.2139/ssrn.4976103

Olutimehin, A. T., Ajayi, A. J., Metibemu, O. C., Balogun, A. Y., Oladoyinbo, T. O., & Olaniyi, O. O. (2025). Adversarial threats to AI-driven systems: Exploring the attack surface of machine learning models and countermeasures. *Available atSSRN* 5137026.

Oye, E., & Owen, A. (2024). Adversarial Attacks and Defenses in Machine Learning.

Patel, C. D., Aggarwal, M., & Chaubey, N. K. (2025). Enhancing Cyber-Physical Systems Security Through Advanced Defense Mechanisms. In *Advancing Cyber Security Through Quantum Cryptography* (pp. 307–342). IGI Global.

Petihakis, G., Farao, A., Bountakas, P., Sabazioti, A., Polley, J., & Xenakis, C. (2024, July). AIAS: AI-ASsisted cybersecurity platform to defend against adversarial AI attacks. In *Proceedings of the 19th International Conference on Availability, Reliability and Security* (pp. 1-7). DOI: 10.1145/3664476.3669920

Prasad, T. S. L., Manikandan, K. B., & Vinoj, J. (2024, December). Shielding NLP Systems: An In-depth Survey on Advanced AI Techniques for Adversarial Attack Detection in Cyber Security. In *2024 3rd International Conference on Automation, Computing and Renewable Systems (ICACRS)* (pp. 1059-1067). IEEE.

Sankaram, M., Roopesh, M., Rasetti, S., & Nishat, N. (2024). A Comprehensive review of artificial intelligence applications in enhancing cybersecurity threat detection and response mechanisms. *Management, 3*(5).

Shamoo, Y. (2025). Adversarial Attacks and Defense Mechanisms in the Age of Quantum Computing. In *Leveraging Large Language Models for Quantum-Aware Cybersecurity* (pp. 301–344). IGI Global Scientific Publishing. DOI: 10.4018/979-8-3373-1102-9.ch010

Tarade, R., & Das, S. (2025). Cybersecurity in the Age of Al-Enhancing Defences for Today's Threats. *Critical Phishing Defense Strategies and Digital Asset Protection*, 309.

Tripathi, H., & Pandey, D. C. K. (2024). *Enhancing Security Against Adversarial Attacks Using Robust Machine Learning. International Journal of Advanced Engineering and Nano Technology*. IJAENT.

Venugopal, H., & Christo, M. S. (2024, August). Strengthening Healthcare Cybersecurity by Optimizing Adversarial Attack Defences in Deep Learning Models using GPU and Parallel Processing Technologies. In *2024 7th International Conference on Circuit Power and Computing Technologies (ICCPCT)* (Vol. 1, pp. 1266-1272). IEEE. DOI: 10.1109/ICCPCT61902.2024.10672871

Zhang, Z. (2024). Reinforcement Learning-Based Approaches for Enhancing Security and Resilience in Smart Control: A Survey on Attack and Defense Methods. *arXiv preprint arXiv:2402.15617.*

Zou, J., Zhang, S., & Qiu, M. (2024, July). Different Attack and Defense Types for AI Cybersecurity. In *International Conference on Knowledge Science, Engineering and Management* (pp. 179-192). Singapore: Springer Nature Singapore. DOI: 10.1007/978-981-97-5498-4_14

KEY TERMS AND DEFINITIONS

Adversarial Attacks: Manipulations targeting AI models to mislead.
Defense Mechanisms: Procedures to protect AI from attacks
Model Robustness: AI system's confrontation with adversarial inputs.

Chapter 8
AI-Driven Threat Detection and Response Systems:
Enhancing Cybersecurity in the Digital Era

Bülent Gürsel Emiroğlu
https://orcid.org/0000-0002-1656-6450
Department of Computer Engineering, Kirikkale University, Kirikkale, Turkey

ABSTRACT

Today, because organisations are getting more targeted by complex cyber attacks that can cost a company millions of dollars in losses as well as damage point of sale, operational disruption etc. While traditional security measures can hardly cope with the volume, velocity and complexity of modern attack landscapes. Artificial Intelligence (AI) and Machine Learning (ML) integration is no longer something that should only be done for securing purposes an long way down on the to-do list per top cybersecurity solutions. Armed with a strategic deployment of AI-driven systems as well as the corresponding difficulties, organizations can greatly improve their security architecture and make themselves substantially more secure against the modern cyber threats in this digital era. This book proposal chapter offers a broad explanation of AI-driven threat detection and response systems, emphasizing their fundamentals; pointing to capabilities; while highlighting the inherent challenges; and proposing potential future directions.

DOI: 10.4018/979-8-3373-2200-1.ch008

1. INTRODUCTION

The digital age has brought about numerous advantages, including increased connectivity, improved efficiencies, and enhanced data analytics capabilities. However, with these advancements come significant risks. Cybercriminals are leveraging sophisticated techniques and tools to exploit vulnerabilities in systems, leading to a rise in cyberattacks. Traditional security measures often fall short in addressing these advanced threats. Therefore, there is a pressing need for innovative solutions that can adapt to the dynamic nature of cyber threats. AI-driven threat detection and response systems represent a paradigm shift in how organizations approach cybersecurity. These systems utilize machine learning (ML), natural language processing (NLP), and other AI technologies to analyze vast amounts of data, identify patterns, and predict potential threats. This chapter will delve into the various components of AI-driven systems, their operational mechanisms, and the benefits they offer to organizations seeking to bolster their cybersecurity defenses.

The importance of AI in cybersecurity systems from several critical factors (Chandana & Gulzar, 2023):

- *Scale and Speed:* The digital world generates vast amounts of data. AI systems can process and analyze this data far faster and more comprehensively than human analysts, identifying subtle patterns and anomalies indicative of malicious activity that might otherwise go unnoticed.
- *Complexity of Threats:* Attackers continuously develop new tactics, techniques, and procedures (TTPs), including polymorphic malware and sophisticated phishing campaigns. AI excels at identifying novel and evolving threats that signature-based systems often miss.
- *Resource Optimization:* Security teams are often overburdened. AI can automate repetitive tasks like log analysis and initial alert triage, freeing up human analysts to focus on complex investigations and strategic initiatives.
- *Proactive Defense:* Instead of just reacting to attacks, AI enables predictive analytics, identifying potential vulnerabilities and attack vectors before they can be exploited.

Capabilities of AI-Driven Security Systems - AI brings a range of powerful capabilities to the cybersecurity domain (Kaloudi & Li, 2020):

- *Anomaly Detection:* AI algorithms establish baseline patterns of normal network traffic and user behavior. Deviations from this baseline trigger alerts, enabling the detection of insider threats, zero-day exploits, and unusual data movements.

- *Threat Intelligence Analysis:* AI can rapidly process vast amounts of threat intelligence feeds (blogs, forums, dark web) to identify emerging threats, attacker TTPs, and indicators of compromise (IoCs) relevant to the organization.
- *Automated Response (SOAR):* AI integrates with Security Orchestration, Automation, and Response (SOAR) platforms to automate predefined response actions, such as isolating infected endpoints, blocking malicious IPs, or revoking compromised credentials, drastically reducing response times.
- *Predictive Analytics:* By analyzing historical data and current trends, AI can predict likely attack targets and methods, allowing organizations to bolster defenses proactively.
- *Enhanced Malware Analysis:* AI techniques, particularly machine learning, can analyze file characteristics and behaviors to detect previously unseen malware strains without relying on known signatures.
- *User and Entity Behavior Analytics (UEBA):* AI monitors user activities and system behaviors to identify compromised accounts, insider threats, or lateral movement within the network.

Challenges in Implementing AI for Security - Despite the benefits, deploying AI in cybersecurity is not without its challenges (Kumar et al., 2023):

- Data Quality and Quantity: AI models require large volumes of high-quality, labeled data for effective training. Obtaining and maintaining such datasets can be difficult and resource-intensive.
- Adversarial AI: Attackers are also leveraging AI. They can attempt to poison training data, evade detection models, or create AI-powered attacks, leading to an ongoing arms race.
- Complexity and Skill Gap: Implementing and managing AI security systems requires specialized expertise in both AI/ML and cybersecurity, a skill set currently in high demand and short supply.
- False Positives/Negatives: Tuning AI models to minimize false positives (flagging benign activity as malicious) and false negatives (missing actual threats) is a delicate balancing act requiring continuous refinement.
- Explainability and Trust: Understanding *why* an AI system made a particular decision (e.g., flagged a specific activity) can be challenging with complex "black box" models, impacting trust and forensic investigations.

The integration of AI in cybersecurity is continuously evolving (Vegesna, 2023):

- Autonomous Systems: We expect to see more autonomous security systems capable of detecting, analyzing, and responding to threats with minimal human intervention.
- Federated Learning: This approach allows AI models to be trained across multiple decentralized datasets without exposing sensitive raw data, addressing privacy concerns.
- AI for Offensive Security: AI will increasingly be used ethically for penetration testing and vulnerability assessment, simulating sophisticated attacks to identify weaknesses.
- Integration with Quantum Computing: While still nascent, the intersection of AI and quantum computing could revolutionize threat detection and cryptography.
- Enhanced Explainability (XAI): Research into Explainable AI aims to make AI decision-making processes more transparent and understandable for security analysts.

Figure 1. Traditional vs. AI-Based Cyber Security Systems

Aspect	Traditional	AI-Based
Flexibility	Rigid rules	Learns complex patterns
Maintenance	Manual updates	Self-improving via new data
Edge Cases	High false negatives	Adapts to anomalies
Speed	Fast for known patterns	Slower inference but scalable

AI-driven threat detection and response systems are no longer a futuristic concept but a necessary component of modern cybersecurity strategy. While challenges exist, the capabilities offered by AI provide a significant advantage in the fight against cybercrime, enabling organizations to build more resilient, adaptive, and proactive defenses in an increasingly hostile digital environment (Zeadally et al., 2020).

Figure 2. AI – Driven vs. Traditional Rules – Based Cyber Security Systems

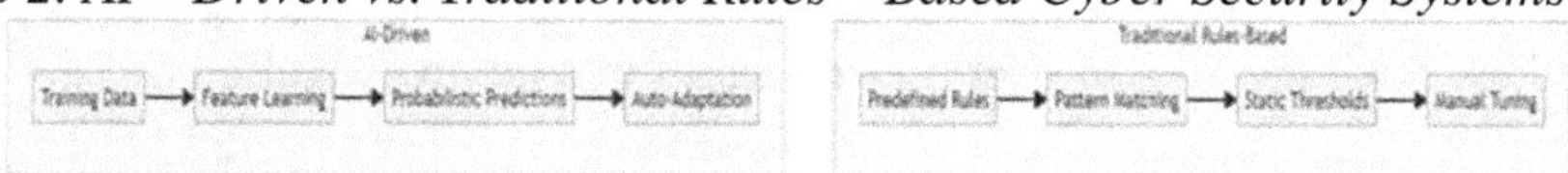

2. THE EVOLVING CYBER THREAT LANDSCAPE

2.1 Current Trends in Cyber Threats

The landscape of cyber threats is not merely growing; it's becoming significantly more sophisticated and damaging. Attackers are continuously refining their methods, leveraging new technologies, and exploiting interconnected digital ecosystems. Understanding the nuances of these prevalent threats is crucial for developing effective defense strategies. Cyber threats are becoming more sophisticated, with attackers employing advanced tactics (Ghasemshirazi, 2023).

A. Ransomware Attacks: Beyond Encryption

Ransomware remains a dominant and highly profitable threat. It involves malicious software (malware) infiltrating a system, locating valuable data, and encrypting it, rendering it inaccessible to the owner. A ransom, typically demanded in cryptocurrency like Bitcoin for anonymity, is required for the decryption key.

i. **Evolution:** Modern ransomware attacks have evolved beyond simple encryption. Double extortion involves attackers *exfiltrating* sensitive data *before* encrypting it. They then threaten to leak this stolen data publicly if the ransom isn't paid, adding immense pressure even if the victim has backups. Triple extortion adds another layer, often involving DDoS attacks against the victim's services or contacting the victim's customers/partners directly to further coerce payment. (Virupakshar et al., 2020)
ii. **Impact:** The consequences are severe, including crippling operational downtime, substantial financial losses (ransom payment, recovery costs, lost revenue), regulatory fines (especially if personal data is breached), and long-lasting reputational damage.
iii. **Targets & Tactics:** While initially targeting individuals, ransomware now heavily focuses on organizations, including critical infrastructure (hospitals, energy grids, pipelines), government agencies, schools, and businesses of all sizes. The rise of Ransomware-as-a-Service (RaaS) on the dark web allows less technically skilled criminals to launch sophisticated attacks using pre-built toolkits.

B. Phishing Scams: Precision and Deception

Phishing remains a primary initial access vector for many cyberattacks. It relies on social engineering – manipulating human psychology – rather than purely technical exploits. Attackers craft deceptive emails, text messages (smishing), or voice calls (vishing) impersonating legitimate entities (banks, colleagues, service providers).

i. **Sophistication:** Generic phishing emails are being replaced by highly targeted spear phishing (targeting specific individuals or groups) and whaling (targeting high-profile executives). These messages often incorporate personalized details gleaned from social media or previous breaches, making them highly convincing. AI is now being used to generate more realistic and grammatically perfect phishing lures (Bonfanti, 2022).
ii. **Goals:** The aim is typically to trick users into revealing sensitive information (login credentials, credit card numbers, personal data), clicking malicious links that download malware (like ransomware loaders or spyware), or authorizing fraudulent transactions.
iii. **Consequences:** Successful phishing can lead to account compromise, widespread data breaches, installation of further malware, significant financial fraud, and provide attackers a foothold within the network for more extensive attacks.

C. Distributed Denial of Service (DDoS) Attacks: Overwhelming Force

DDoS attacks aim to disrupt the availability of a network, website, or online service by overwhelming it with a flood of malicious traffic from multiple sources. (Virupakshar et al., 2020)

i. **Mechanism:** Attackers typically use a network of compromised computers or IoT devices, known as a botnet, to generate traffic far exceeding the target's capacity to handle. This can target network bandwidth (volumetric attacks), server resources (protocol attacks), or specific applications (application-layer attacks).
ii. **Motivation & Scale:** Motivations vary, including hacktivism, extortion (demanding payment to stop the attack), competitive sabotage, or creating a smokescreen for other malicious activities like data theft. The scale of DDoS attacks continues to grow, with some exceeding terabits per second, capable of taking down even well-protected services.

iii. **Impact:** The primary impact is service unavailability, leading to lost revenue, customer frustration, and damage to brand reputation. Mitigating large-scale DDoS attacks requires specialized infrastructure and services.

D. Insider Threats: The Danger Within

Insider threats originate from individuals who have legitimate, authorized access to an organization's systems and data – employees, former employees, contractors, or business partners.

i. **Types:** Insiders can be malicious (intentionally seeking to cause harm, steal data, or disrupt operations for personal gain or revenge), negligent (unintentionally causing a security incident through carelessness, errors, or falling victim to social engineering), or compromised (having their credentials stolen and used by an external attacker) (Böhme & Moore, 2012).
ii. **Challenges:** Detecting insider threats is notoriously difficult because the individuals are using legitimate access privileges. Distinguishing malicious activity from normal job functions requires sophisticated monitoring and behavioral analysis (like User and Entity Behavior Analytics - UEBA).
iii. **Damage:** The potential damage is immense, ranging from theft of sensitive intellectual property and customer data to sabotage of critical systems, espionage, and financial fraud. The inherent trust placed in insiders makes these threats particularly potent.

These evolving threats underscore the need for a multi-layered, adaptive security approach that combines advanced technology (like AI-driven detection), robust processes (access control, incident response), and continuous user awareness training (Bonfanti, 2022).

2.2 The Limitations of Traditional Security Measures: Why They Fall Short

Traditional cybersecurity measures, such as firewalls and antivirus software, often rely on predefined rules and signatures to detect threats. However, these approaches have several limitations:

While foundational elements like firewalls and signature-based antivirus software remain necessary components of a security architecture, relying solely on these traditional measures in today's threat landscape is insufficient and increasingly risky. Their inherent limitations stem primarily from their reactive and often static nature, making them struggle against the dynamic and sophisticated attacks prevalent now (Steingartner et al., 2021).

A. Static Nature and Inability to Handle Novelty
    i. **Signature/Rule Dependency:** Traditional tools predominantly rely on databases of known threat signatures (specific file hashes, patterns in network traffic) or predefined rules (e.g., blocking traffic from specific IPs or ports). They are excellent at identifying *known* threats for which a signature or rule already exists.
    ii. **Zero-Day Vulnerabilities:** The biggest weakness is their inability to detect zero-day attacks – threats that exploit previously unknown vulnerabilities for which no signature or patch exists yet. Attackers actively seek out and exploit these vulnerabilities before defenses can be updated.
    iii. **Polymorphic and Metamorphic Malware:** Modern malware is often designed to constantly change its code (polymorphic) or completely rewrite itself (metamorphic) with each new infection. This means its signature changes frequently, allowing it to bypass signature-based detection easily.
    iv. **Fileless Attacks:** An increasing number of attacks don't rely on traditional malicious files installed on disk. They operate directly in memory or abuse legitimate system tools (like PowerShell or WMI), leaving no file signature for traditional antivirus to scan.
    v. **Evolving Tactics:** Attackers constantly change their Tactics, Techniques, and Procedures (TTPs). They might use encrypted command-and-control channels, domain fronting, or sophisticated social engineering schemes that don't trigger simple rule-based alerts. Traditional systems lack the intelligence to recognize these evolving patterns (Böhme & Moore, 2012).
B. High Volume of False Positives and Alert Fatigue
    i. **Overly Broad Rules:** To catch variations of threats, rules in firewalls or Intrusion Detection Systems (IDS) might be written broadly. This often results in legitimate, harmless activities being flagged as suspicious (false positives). For example, an administrator running a legitimate script might trigger an alert designed to catch malicious script execution.
    ii. **Noise Generation:** In complex environments, traditional systems can generate a massive volume of low-priority alerts. Security analysts are inundated with notifications, many of which turn out to be benign upon investigation.
    iii. **Alert Fatigue:** Constantly sifting through false positives leads to alert fatigue. Analysts become desensitized, spending excessive time investigating non-threats and potentially overlooking or delaying the response to genuine, critical alerts buried in the noise. This burnout reduces the overall effectiveness of the security team.

iv. **Lack of Context:** Traditional tools often lack the context to differentiate between normal and malicious behavior. An action might be normal for one user or system but highly suspicious for another. Signature-based tools typically can't make this distinction.

C. Slow and Manual Response Times

i. **Manual Analysis Required:** When a traditional system generates an alert, it usually requires manual investigation by a security analyst. The analyst needs to gather context, correlate data from different sources (logs from firewalls, servers, endpoints), and determine the alert's validity and severity (Böhme & Moore, 2012).

ii. **Time-Consuming Process:** This manual correlation and investigation process is inherently slow. Meanwhile, an active attacker can be escalating privileges, moving laterally across the network, exfiltrating data, or deploying ransomware.

iii. **Reaction Lag:** The time between the initial compromise, the detection event (if it occurs), the alert generation, the manual analysis, and the eventual response action (e.g., isolating a machine, blocking an IP) creates a significant window of opportunity for the attacker.

iv. **Impact Amplification:** Delays in response directly correlate with increased damage. A threat contained within minutes might result in minimal impact, whereas the same threat left unaddressed for hours or days due to slow analysis can lead to catastrophic data breaches, system-wide ransomware encryption, and prolonged operational downtime.

In essence, traditional security measures act like guards checking IDs against a known list of troublemakers. They struggle when faced with disguised intruders, unknown threats, or insiders causing problems, and the sheer volume of people passing through can overwhelm their manual checking process, leading to critical oversights and delayed reactions. This necessitates the move towards more intelligent, adaptive, and automated security solutions like those leveraging AI (Steingartner et al., 2021).

3. THE ROLE OF AI IN CYBERSECURITY

3.1 Understanding AI Technologies

Artificial Intelligence (AI) is not a single technology but rather a broad field encompassing various techniques that enable machines to perform tasks typically requiring human intelligence, such as learning, problem-solving, and decision-making. In cybersecurity, specific AI disciplines are leveraged to overcome the limitations of traditional security measures and provide more adaptive, intelligent defense mechanisms. AI encompasses a range of technologies that can enhance threat detection and response (Ghasemshirazi, 2023).

A. Machine Learning (ML): Learning from Data

i. **Core Concept:** ML algorithms are designed to learn patterns and relationships directly from data without being explicitly programmed for every possible scenario. They build mathematical models based on sample data (training data) and use these models to make predictions or decisions on new, unseen data (Tanveer et al., 2022).

ii. **Learning Paradigms:**
   a. **Supervised Learning:** Trained on labeled data (e.g., emails labeled as "spam" or "not spam"). The algorithm learns a mapping function to predict the label for new, unlabeled data. *Use Case:* Classifying files as malware or benign, identifying known types of phishing emails.
   b. **Unsupervised Learning:** Trained on unlabeled data. The algorithm tries to find hidden structures or patterns on its own, such as grouping similar data points together or identifying outliers. *Use Case:* Anomaly detection in network traffic (identifying unusual patterns that deviate from the norm), User and Entity Behavior Analytics (UEBA) to spot abnormal user actions.
   c. **Reinforcement Learning:** Agents learn by trial and error, receiving rewards or penalties for their actions within an environment. *Use Case:* Optimizing automated incident response actions or tuning firewall rules dynamically.

iii. **Cybersecurity Applications:**
   a. **Enhanced Detection:** Identifying subtle deviations from normal behavior (anomaly detection) that might indicate insider threats or zero-day attacks.
   b. **Malware Analysis:** Classifying new malware variants based on features learned from known samples, even without exact signature matches.
   c. **Phishing & Spam Filtering:** Learning the characteristics of malicious emails beyond simple keywords.
   d. **Risk Scoring:** Assigning risk scores to users, endpoints, or transactions based on learned patterns.
   e. **Continuous Improvement:** ML models can be retrained periodically (or continuously) with new data, allowing them to adapt to evolving threats and changes in the network environment, unlike static rule-based systems.

B. Natural Language Processing (NLP): Understanding Human Language

i. **Core Concept:** NLP focuses on enabling computers to process, understand, interpret, and generate human language (text and speech) in a valuable way. Cybersecurity involves vast amounts of unstructured text data that NLP can help analyze.
ii. **Cybersecurity Applications:**
    a. **Threat Intelligence Analysis:** Automatically parsing and extracting key information (Indicators of Compromise like malicious IPs/domains, attacker TTPs, vulnerability details) from unstructured sources like security blogs, news articles, technical reports, dark web forums, and social media feeds. This accelerates the ingestion and operationalization of threat intelligence.
    b. **Phishing Detection:** Analyzing the content, tone, sender reputation, and linguistic patterns of emails or messages to identify social engineering cues and deceptive language often missed by keyword filters.
    c. **Sentiment Analysis:** Gauging the sentiment around specific vulnerabilities or threat actors within online communities.
    d. **Log Analysis:** Interpreting textual descriptions or commands within system logs that might indicate malicious activity.
    e. **Security Chatbots:** Powering chatbots that can understand user queries related to security policies or assist analysts during investigations.

C. Deep Learning (DL): Analyzing Complexity with Neural Networks

i. **Core Concept:** DL is a specialized subset of ML that utilizes artificial neural networks with multiple layers (deep architectures). These networks are particularly adept at learning intricate patterns and hierarchical features from vast amounts of complex, often unstructured data, like images, sound, and raw network packet data (Markevych & Dawson, 2023).
ii. **Advantages:** DL models can often automatically discover relevant features from raw data, reducing the need for manual feature engineering that is common in traditional ML. They excel where patterns are extremely subtle or complex.
iii. **Cybersecurity Applications:**
    a. **Advanced Intrusion Detection:** Analyzing raw network traffic data (packet captures) to identify highly sophisticated attack patterns or covert communication channels that might evade traditional IDS/IPS and simpler ML models.

b. **Sophisticated Malware Classification:** Analyzing the binary structure or behavioral execution traces of malware to detect novel threats or highly obfuscated code.
c. **Complex UEBA:** Modeling intricate sequences of user behavior across multiple platforms to detect subtle deviations indicative of compromised accounts or insider threats.
d. **Voice Phishing (Vishing) Detection:** Analyzing audio features in phone calls for signs of social engineering or impersonation.
e. **Image Analysis:** Potentially analyzing images for steganography (hidden data) or recognizing malicious elements within visual content.

iv. **Considerations:** DL models typically require very large datasets for effective training and significant computational resources (like GPUs). Their decision-making process can sometimes be less transparent ("black box" problem) compared to simpler ML models, although research in Explainable AI (XAI) is addressing this.

By combining these AI technologies, cybersecurity systems can move beyond static defenses to create intelligent, adaptive frameworks capable of learning from the environment, understanding diverse data types (including human language), and detecting complex patterns indicative of malicious activity much more effectively than traditional methods alone (Jian & Luaus, 2023).

3.2 How AI Enhances Threat Detection

AI fundamentally changes threat detection by shifting from a reactive, signature-based approach to a proactive, predictive, and context-aware model. It achieves this by processing and analyzing data at a scale and speed impossible for humans or traditional systems alone (Jian & Luaus, 2023).

A. Anomaly Detection: Spotting the Unusual

i. **Establishing Baselines:** AI, particularly unsupervised Machine Learning, excels at learning what constitutes "normal" within a specific environment. It analyzes vast streams of data over time – network traffic patterns, user login times and locations, application usage, process execution on endpoints, data access frequencies, server communication patterns, etc. – to build dynamic, multi-dimensional baselines of expected behavior for individual users, devices, servers, and the network as a whole. These baselines are not static; they adapt as the environment naturally evolves.

ii. **Identifying Deviations:** Once baselines are established, AI systems continuously monitor real-time activity, comparing it against these learned norms. Any significant deviation or outlier is flagged as an anomaly. Examples include:
   a. A user logging in from an unusual geographic location or at an odd hour.
   b. A server suddenly initiating connections to external IPs it never contacted before.
   c. An unusual spike in data transfer from a sensitive database.
   d. A user account suddenly accessing files or systems unrelated to its typical job function.
   e. An endpoint process attempting unusual network connections or system modifications.

iii. **Detecting the Unknown:** This is a crucial advantage over signature-based systems. Anomaly detection doesn't need to know *what* the threat is beforehand. It only needs to recognize that something is *different* from the established normal. This allows it to flag potentially malicious activity associated with zero-day exploits, novel malware variants, or sophisticated attacker techniques for which no predefined signature exists.

iv. **Reducing False Positives (Over Time):** While initial tuning might generate noise, well-implemented AI-based anomaly detection, often combined with other techniques, can learn to differentiate between benign anomalies (e.g., a user working late for a deadline) and genuinely suspicious ones, reducing the alert fatigue associated with overly broad traditional rules.

B. Behavioral Analysis (User and Entity Behavior Analytics - UEBA)

i. **Focus on Actors:** UEBA specifically applies ML and statistical analysis to monitor the behavior of *users* (employees, contractors) and *entities* (servers, endpoints, applications, network devices). It goes beyond simple rule triggers to understand *patterns* and *sequences* of actions (Alabdan, 2020).

ii. **Profiling and Context:** AI builds detailed profiles for each user and entity, learning their typical roles, access patterns, common commands, communication habits, and resource usage. It understands context – for instance, that an administrator running certain scripts is normal, but a marketing user doing the same is highly suspicious.

iii. **Detecting Compromise and Insider Threats:** By tracking deviations from these established behavioral profiles, UEBA is highly effective at detecting:

a. **Compromised Accounts:** An attacker gaining control of a legitimate user's credentials will likely behave differently – accessing unusual data, attempting lateral movement, connecting from different locations. AI spots these behavioral shifts.
b. **Insider Threats:** Malicious insiders attempting data exfiltration, sabotage, or privilege escalation often exhibit behavioral anomalies, such as accessing sensitive data outside normal hours, downloading large volumes of information, or attempting to cover their tracks. Negligent insiders might also exhibit risky behaviors that AI can flag.

iv. **Early Warning System:** Detecting these behavioral anomalies often provides an early warning *before* the ultimate goal of the attack (e.g., data encryption, large-scale exfiltration) is achieved, allowing for faster intervention and mitigation.

C. Threat Intelligence Integration and Correlation

i. **The Data Overload Problem:** Organizations are often subscribed to multiple threat intelligence feeds, alongside consuming information from blogs, security reports, and forums. Manually processing this vast, often unstructured, data firehose is impractical.

ii. **AI-Powered Automation:** AI, especially leveraging NLP and ML, automates this process:

a. **Ingestion & Parsing:** NLP techniques automatically extract structured Indicators of Compromise (IoCs – malicious IPs, domains, file hashes, registry keys) and Tactics, Techniques, and Procedures (TTPs) from diverse, unstructured text sources.
b. **Correlation:** ML algorithms correlate threat intelligence data with internal security telemetry (logs from firewalls, endpoints, servers, applications). It can instantly check if any IoCs seen in external reports have been observed within the organization's network.
c. **Contextual Enrichment:** When an internal alert (e.g., an anomaly detected by ML) occurs, AI can automatically enrich it with relevant external threat intelligence. For example, if an endpoint communicates with a suspicious IP flagged by anomaly detection, the AI can instantly check threat feeds to see if that IP is associated with a known malware campaign or command-and-control server, providing crucial context for the analyst.
d. **Prioritization:** AI can score threats based on relevance (Is this TTP targeting our industry? Is this vulnerability present in our environment?) and potential impact, helping security teams prioritize the most critical alerts derived from both internal monitoring and external intelligence.

iii. **Comprehensive Threat Landscape View:** By intelligently fusing internal observations with external knowledge, AI provides a much more holistic and actionable view of the threat landscape, enabling faster identification of targeted attacks and more informed defensive actions.

In summary, AI enhances threat detection by enabling systems to learn normal behavior, spot subtle deviations, understand user and entity actions in context, and intelligently integrate vast amounts of external threat data, leading to faster, more accurate, and more proactive defense (Jian & Luaus, 2023).

3.3 AI in Incident Response

Beyond just detecting threats faster, AI plays a critical role in streamlining and enhancing the entire incident response lifecycle. Traditional IR often involves manual, time-consuming processes that can delay containment and remediation, allowing threats to cause more damage (Alabdan, 2020). AI introduces automation, deep analysis capabilities, and intelligent guidance to overcome these hurdles. In addition to detection, AI can significantly improve incident response efforts.

A. Automated Response (Security Orchestration, Automation, and Response - SOAR)

i. **Mechanism:** AI-driven IR often operates within SOAR platforms. When an AI detection system (like anomaly detection or UEBA) identifies a threat with a high confidence score, it can trigger pre-defined automated workflows or playbooks. These playbooks execute specific response actions without direct human intervention, based on the nature and severity of the detected threat.

ii. **Speed and Consistency:** The primary benefit is speed. Automated actions occur in machine time (milliseconds or seconds) rather than the minutes or hours it might take for a human analyst to investigate and react. This rapid response is crucial for containing fast-spreading threats like ransomware. Automation also ensures consistency; the same predefined actions are taken every time a specific type of threat is detected, reducing human error (Alabdan, 2020).

iii. **Examples of Automated Actions:**

  a. **Endpoint Isolation:** Automatically disconnecting an infected laptop or server from the network to prevent malware from spreading laterally.

  b. **IP/Domain Blocking:** Instantly adding malicious IP addresses or domains identified during an attack to firewall blocklists.

c. **User Account Suspension:** Temporarily disabling a user account exhibiting signs of compromise (e.g., impossible travel logins, multiple failed login attempts followed by success from a suspicious source).
d. **File Quarantine:** Automatically quarantining malicious files detected on endpoints.
e. **Process Termination:** Killing suspicious processes identified on servers or workstations.

iv. **Reducing Analyst Load:** By handling routine, high-confidence alerts automatically, AI frees up security analysts to focus on more complex, nuanced investigations that require human expertise and judgment.

v. **Considerations:** Careful configuration and oversight are essential. Poorly configured automation could potentially disrupt legitimate business operations (e.g., incorrectly isolating a critical server). Therefore, automation is often tiered, with fully automated responses reserved for high-confidence, low-impact scenarios, while riskier actions might require human approval.

B. AI-Powered Root Cause Analysis (RCA)

i. **The Challenge:** Manually determining the root cause of an incident involves painstakingly collecting and correlating logs and event data from numerous sources (endpoints, servers, firewalls, applications, cloud services). Identifying the initial entry point, the sequence of attacker actions (lateral movement, privilege escalation), and the full scope of the compromise is complex and time-consuming (Iqbal et al., 2023).

ii. **AI's Analytical Power:** AI, particularly Machine Learning, excels at processing massive datasets and identifying complex patterns and correlations that humans might miss or take much longer to find.

a. **Event Correlation:** AI algorithms can automatically sift through logs from disparate systems, linking related events across time to reconstruct the attack chain (e.g., linking a phishing email click to malware download, subsequent command-and-control communication, lateral movement attempts, and data access).
b. **Attack Path Visualization:** Some AI tools can visualize the attack path, showing how an attacker moved through the network, which systems were compromised, and which credentials were used.
c. **Identifying Initial Vectors:** By analyzing the earliest anomalous events leading up to the main incident detection, AI can help pinpoint the initial point of compromise (e.g., a specific vulnerability exploited, a successful phishing attempt, a brute-force login).

iii. **Benefits:** Faster and more accurate RCA leads to a better understanding of how the breach occurred. This knowledge is crucial not just for remediating the current incident completely (ensuring all backdoors are closed) but also for implementing targeted preventive measures to stop similar attacks in the future.

C. Intelligent Decision Support for Analysts

i. **Addressing Alert Overload:** Security analysts are often overwhelmed by the sheer volume of alerts generated by various security tools. Determining which alerts require immediate attention is a major challenge.
ii. **AI-Driven Prioritization:** AI systems analyze incoming alerts and enrich them with context to provide intelligent prioritization. This involves:
    a. **Risk Scoring:** Assigning a dynamic risk score to alerts based on factors like the type of threat, the criticality of the affected asset (e.g., a database server vs. a standard workstation), the user involved, correlation with known threat intelligence, and the observed behavior's deviation from the norm (Anderson, 2020).
    b. **Contextual Enrichment:** Automatically gathering and presenting relevant information alongside an alert, such as user details, asset information, related historical events, relevant threat intelligence reports, and potential impact analysis.
iii. **Actionable Insights and Recommendations:** Based on the analysis and context, AI can provide analysts with actionable insights and even recommend specific response steps or investigation paths. This guidance helps analysts make faster, more informed decisions during high-pressure incident response scenarios.
iv. **Focusing Human Expertise:** By filtering out low-priority noise, correlating related events, and providing rich context, AI allows human analysts to focus their valuable time and expertise on investigating and responding to the most significant threats, rather than getting bogged down in routine tasks or chasing false positives (Anderson, 2020).

In conclusion, AI acts as a powerful force multiplier for incident response teams. It automates routine actions for speed, delves deep into data for accurate root cause analysis, and provides intelligent context and prioritization, enabling organizations to respond to threats faster, more effectively, and with greater confidence (Iqbal et al., 2023).

4. IMPLEMENTATION OF AI-DRIVEN THREAT DETECTION SYSTEMS

4.1 Key Components of AI-Driven Systems

A. Data Collection: The Foundation

i. **Critical Importance:** AI algorithms are fundamentally data-driven. The adage "garbage in, garbage out" is especially true here. The accuracy, effectiveness, and scope of AI-driven threat detection depend entirely on the quality, quantity, and diversity of the data collected. Without comprehensive and relevant data, the AI cannot learn effectively or detect sophisticated threats.

ii. **Diverse Data Sources:** Effective systems need to ingest data from across the entire IT environment. Key sources include:

   a. **Network Data:** Firewall logs, Intrusion Detection/Prevention System (IDS/IPS) alerts, NetFlow/sFlow data, packet captures (PCAP), DNS logs, VPN logs, proxy logs. This provides visibility into traffic patterns, connections, and potential network-based attacks.

   b. **Endpoint Data:** Logs from workstations and servers (Windows Event Logs, Linux syslog), Endpoint Detection and Response (EDR) telemetry (process execution, file modifications, registry changes, network connections initiated by endpoints), anti-malware logs. This gives insight into activity occurring directly on devices.

   c. **Log Data:** Application logs, database logs, authentication logs (Active Directory, RADIUS, SSO), cloud service logs (AWS CloudTrail, Azure Monitor, Google Cloud Logging). These reveal user actions, application behavior, and system events.

   d. **Threat Intelligence Feeds:** External data sources providing Indicators of Compromise (IoCs), attacker Tactics, Techniques, and Procedures (TTPs), vulnerability information, and details on active campaigns.

   e. **Cloud Infrastructure Data:** Configuration data, access logs, and activity logs from IaaS, PaaS, and SaaS environments.

   f. **Identity and Access Management (IAM) Data:** User login attempts, privilege changes, access requests.

iii. **Challenges:** Organizations face challenges related to the Volume (terabytes or petabytes daily), Velocity (data generated in real-time), and Variety (structured, semi-structured, and unstructured data from diverse sources) of security data. Robust collection mechanisms (agents, APIs, log forwarders) and scalable data pipelines are essential. Data needs to be collected reliably and often normalized into a consistent format (Anderson, 2020).

B. Data Processing and Analysis: Where AI Works

i. **Pre-processing:** Raw data collected is often noisy, inconsistent, and not immediately suitable for AI algorithms. This stage involves:
   a. **Normalization:** Converting data from different sources into a common format.
   b. **Cleaning:** Handling missing values, removing duplicates, correcting errors.
   c. **Feature Engineering/Extraction:** Selecting the most relevant data points (features) or creating new, more informative features from the raw data that AI models can use effectively. This is a critical step where domain expertise is often combined with automated techniques.

ii. **AI Algorithm Application:** This is the core analysis phase where AI/ML algorithms are applied to the processed data:
   a. **Model Training:** For supervised learning, models are trained on labeled historical data (e.g., known malware samples, past phishing emails). For unsupervised learning (like anomaly detection), models learn patterns directly from the unlabeled production data. Deep learning models might process raw data directly.
   b. **Real-Time Analysis:** Trained models analyze incoming data streams in near real-time, comparing current activity against learned baselines (for anomaly detection) or looking for patterns matching known malicious behavior (for classification/prediction).

iii. **Computational Needs:** Processing and analyzing vast security datasets in real-time requires significant computational resources (CPU, memory, potentially GPUs for deep learning) and often relies on scalable cloud infrastructure or powerful on-premises hardware.

C. Alert Generation: Signaling Potential Threats

i. **From Detection to Alert:** When the AI processing engine detects a significant anomaly, a pattern matching known malicious activity, or a behavior exceeding a risk threshold, it generates an alert (Jabbarova, 2023).

ii. **Intelligent Alerting:** Unlike simple rule-based systems that trigger on specific, predefined conditions (often leading to high noise), AI-driven alerting is more nuanced:

a. **Contextualization:** Alerts are often enriched with context – which user, what endpoint, what time, related events, relevant threat intelligence, historical behavior.
b. **Confidence Scoring:** AI models can often provide a confidence score indicating the likelihood that a detected event is truly malicious.
c. **False Positive Reduction:** By learning normal patterns and focusing on significant deviations or high-confidence malicious indicators, AI systems aim to reduce the number of false positive alerts compared to traditional methods. Continuous learning and feedback loops (where analysts confirm whether an alert was true or false) help refine the models and further improve alert accuracy over time (Jabbarova, 2023).

iii. **Prioritization:** AI can automatically prioritize alerts based on severity, potential impact, asset criticality, and confidence scores, helping security teams focus on the most urgent issues first.

D. Response Mechanisms: Taking Action

i. **Defining Procedures:** Simply detecting a threat isn't enough. There must be clear, predefined procedures for how to respond. These procedures should cover both automated and manual actions.
ii. **Automated Response (SOAR Integration):** As discussed previously, AI detections can trigger automated responses via SOAR platforms or other automation scripts. These are defined in playbooks. Examples: isolating an endpoint, blocking an IP, disabling an account. Automation is typically used for high-confidence, well-understood threats where the response action carries low risk of negative business impact.
iii. **Manual Response:** Many alerts, especially those related to complex or novel threats, will require human investigation and response. The AI system supports this by providing prioritized alerts, rich context, and analytical insights (e.g., potential attack paths, related events). Analysts use this information to investigate, contain, eradicate, and recover from the incident.
iv. **Playbook Importance:** Well-documented incident response playbooks are crucial. They outline the specific steps to take for different types of incidents, ensuring consistency, speed, and completeness in the response effort, whether automated or manual. These playbooks should be regularly reviewed and updated based on new threats and lessons learned.

Together, these components create a cyclical process: data is collected, processed by AI to detect threats, alerts are generated and prioritized, and responses (automated or manual) are initiated. The outcomes and feedback from the response phase often feed back into the system, helping to refine data collection, improve AI models, and update response playbooks (Markevych & Dawson, 2023).

4.2 Challenges in Implementing AI-Driven Security Systems

While the potential benefits of AI in cybersecurity are substantial, the path to successful implementation is often fraught with practical challenges. Overlooking these can lead to ineffective systems, wasted investment, and even increased risk.

A. Data Quality and Availability: The Achilles' Heel

i. **The Fundamental Dependency:** AI models, particularly machine learning algorithms, are entirely dependent on the data they are trained on and the data they analyze in real-time. The quality, completeness, timeliness, and relevance of this data directly determine the model's accuracy and effectiveness.
ii. **Data Silos:** Security-relevant data often resides in disparate systems across the organization (network gear, endpoints, servers, cloud platforms, applications, identity systems) managed by different teams. Breaking down these silos to create a unified data lake or stream for the AI system can be politically and technically challenging. Each system may have different logging formats, retention policies, and access controls (Mohsin et al.,2023).
iii. **Data Inconsistency and Lack of Standardization:** Data from different sources often lacks a common format. Timestamps might be inconsistent, user identifiers might vary (username vs. email address vs. employee ID), and event categorizations can differ wildly. Significant effort is required for data normalization and standardization before it can be effectively used by AI.
iv. **Incomplete or Missing Data:** Gaps in data collection (e.g., logs not being forwarded from critical systems, endpoints temporarily offline, insufficient log levels configured) can lead to blind spots for the AI, preventing it from seeing the full picture of an attack.
v. **Volume, Velocity, and Variety (The 3 Vs):** Security data is massive (volume), generated constantly (velocity), and comes in many forms (variety – structured logs, unstructured text, network packets). Building data pipelines capable of ingesting, processing, and storing this data reliably and cost-effectively is a major engineering challenge (Markevych & Dawson, 2023).

vi. **Data Labeling (for Supervised Learning):** Training supervised ML models requires large datasets accurately labeled as "malicious" or "benign." Obtaining and maintaining high-quality labeled datasets for the ever-evolving threat landscape is difficult and resource-intensive. Unsupervised learning (like anomaly detection) avoids this but requires careful tuning to manage false positives.

vii. **Consequences of Poor Data:** Inaccurate or incomplete data leads to poorly trained models, resulting in:

   a. **High False Positives:** The AI flags benign activity as malicious, overwhelming security teams and leading to alert fatigue.

   b. **High False Negatives:** The AI fails to detect actual threats, creating a false sense of security.

   c. **Biased Outcomes:** If the training data reflects existing biases, the AI may perpetuate them.

B. Integration with Existing Systems: The Interoperability Puzzle

i. **Need for Seamless Workflow:** AI systems don't operate in a vacuum. They need to ingest data from existing security tools (SIEMs, EDR, firewalls) and infrastructure, and often need to trigger actions through these systems (e.g., instructing a firewall to block an IP, telling an EDR to isolate a host).

ii. **Legacy Systems:** Many organizations rely on older, legacy systems that were not designed with modern APIs or integration capabilities in mind. Connecting these systems to a new AI platform can require custom development, middleware, or complex workarounds, increasing cost and fragility.

iii. **API Limitations and Vendor Lock-in:** Different security vendors use different APIs and data formats. Integrating tools from multiple vendors can be complex. Some vendors may have closed ecosystems, making it difficult to integrate third-party AI solutions.

iv. **Architectural Complexity:** Introducing an AI platform requires careful consideration of the existing security architecture. Where does the AI system fit? How does data flow to and from it? How does it interact with the Security Operations Center (SOC) workflow? Poor integration can create bottlenecks, data gaps, or even introduce new security risks (Mohsin et al.,2023).

v. **Resource Intensity:** Integration projects often require significant time, budget, and specialized technical expertise (developers, security architects, integration specialists). Underestimating the integration effort is a common pitfall.

vi. **Disruption Risk:** Integrating new systems, especially those involved in automated response, carries the risk of disrupting existing workflows or even critical business operations if not planned and tested meticulously.

C. Skill Gaps: The Human Element

i. **Specialized Expertise Required:** Effectively deploying, managing, tuning, and interpreting the output of AI-driven security systems requires a unique blend of skills:
   a. **Data Science / Machine Learning:** Understanding algorithms, model training, feature engineering, statistical analysis.
   b. **Cybersecurity Domain Knowledge:** Understanding threats, attack vectors, incident response, security tool capabilities.
   c. **Data Engineering:** Building and maintaining data pipelines.
   d. **AI Operations (AIOps/MLOps):** Managing the lifecycle of AI models, monitoring performance, retraining.
   e. **Security Analysis with AI Context:** Interpreting AI-generated alerts, understanding confidence scores, differentiating true positives from false positives, knowing when to trust or question the AI's output.

ii. **Talent Shortage:** Professionals possessing this specific cross-disciplinary skill set are rare and in extremely high demand, making them difficult and expensive to hire and retain.

iii. **Training and Upskilling:** Existing security teams often lack the necessary data science and AI skills. Organizations need to invest significantly in training and upskilling their current workforce, which takes time and resources.

iv. **Over-Reliance and Misinterpretation:** Without the right skills, teams might blindly trust AI outputs without proper validation, potentially missing threats or reacting inappropriately. Conversely, they might distrust the system due to a lack of understanding, failing to leverage its benefits.

v. **Vendor Dependence:** The skill gap can lead to heavy reliance on vendors for configuration, tuning, and interpretation, potentially increasing long-term costs and reducing organizational control and understanding.

Addressing these challenges requires a strategic approach, including investing in data governance, planning integrations carefully, and committing to developing or acquiring the necessary human expertise (Markevych & Dawson, 2023).

4.3 Best Practices for Implementing AI-Driven Security Systems

A. Conduct a Thorough Risk Assessment and Gap Analysis

i. **Purpose:** Before even evaluating AI solutions, understand your specific security posture, risks, and where your current defenses are falling short. AI should be targeted to address your most significant vulnerabilities and detection gaps, not applied generically.

ii. **Process:**

   a. **Identify Critical Assets:** Determine which data, systems, and processes are most valuable or critical to the organization.

   b. **Analyze Threat Landscape:** Understand the types of threats most likely to target your organization based on industry, geography, and known attacker motivations (e.g., ransomware, data theft, espionage, insider threats).

   c. **Evaluate Existing Controls:** Assess the effectiveness of current security tools and processes (firewalls, EDR, SIEM rules, manual analysis). Where are the blind spots? Where is detection too slow or generating too much noise?

   d. **Identify Specific Use Cases for AI:** Based on the above, pinpoint specific areas where AI could provide the most significant improvement. Examples: detecting sophisticated zero-day malware missed by signatures, identifying anomalous user behavior indicative of compromised accounts or insider threats, reducing false positive alerts from existing tools, speeding up investigation through automated correlation.

iii. **Outcome:** A clear understanding of *why* you need AI and *where* it should be focused. This prevents purchasing solutions that don't address your actual risks and helps tailor requirements.

B. Establish Clear, Measurable Objectives

i. **Purpose:** Define what success looks like *before* you start. Vague goals like "improve security" are insufficient. Clear objectives guide technology selection, implementation strategy, and allow you to measure the Return on Investment (ROI) and effectiveness later.

ii. **Process:** Objectives should be SMART:

   a. **Specific:** Clearly state what you want to achieve (e.g., "Reduce time to detect credential stuffing attacks").

b. **Measurable:** Define metrics to track progress (e.g., "Decrease Mean Time To Detect (MTTD) for credential stuffing from 4 hours to 30 minutes"). Other metrics could include reduction in false positive alerts escalated, number of automated responses successfully executed, detection rate for specific malware families, etc.
c. **Achievable:** Set realistic goals based on available resources, technology capabilities, and the initial risk assessment.
d. **Relevant:** Ensure the objectives align with the organization's overall security strategy and address the risks identified in step 1.
e. **Time-bound:** Set a timeframe for achieving the objectives (e.g., "within 12 months of full deployment").

iii. **Outcome:** A defined roadmap and set of Key Performance Indicators (KPIs) to measure the success of the AI implementation. This provides direction for the project team and justification for stakeholders.

C. Start with Pilot Programs and Proofs of Concept (PoCs)

i. **Purpose:** Avoid a "big bang" approach. AI implementations can be complex. Pilot projects allow you to test solutions in a controlled environment, validate vendor claims, understand integration challenges, and gain experience before committing to a full-scale rollout.

ii. **Process:**

a. **Define Scope:** Select a specific, manageable use case identified in step 1 (e.g., monitoring network traffic for C&C communication, analyzing logs for anomalous admin activity in a specific cloud environment).
b. **Select Vendor(s):** Choose one or more potential AI solutions to test based on your objectives and requirements.
c. **Controlled Environment:** Implement the solution on a limited segment of your network or specific data sources. Ensure it doesn't interfere with production systems initially.
d. **Set Success Criteria:** Define clear metrics (based on your objectives) to evaluate the pilot's success.
e. **Allocate Resources:** Dedicate a small team with the right mix of skills (security analysis, data engineering, IT operations) to run the pilot.
f. **Evaluate Thoroughly:** Assess not only the detection accuracy but also the ease of integration, usability, performance impact, quality of vendor support, and the effort required to manage and tune the system.

iii. **Outcome:** Practical experience with the technology, validation of its effectiveness in your environment, identification of potential roadblocks, and data to support a go/no-go decision for full implementation or selection between vendors. It also helps train a core team.

D. Plan for Continuous Monitoring, Tuning, and Improvement (Lifecycle Management)

i. **Purpose:** AI systems are not "set and forget." The threat landscape constantly evolves, attacker techniques change, and your own IT environment changes. The AI models must be continuously monitored, updated, and retrained to remain effective. This is often referred to as MLOps (Machine Learning Operations) or AIOps within the security context (Mohsin et al.,2023).
ii. **Process:**
    a. **Performance Monitoring:** Regularly track the defined KPIs (detection rates, false positive/negative rates, MTTD, etc.). Monitor the health of the data pipelines feeding the AI.
    b. **Analyst Feedback Loop:** Implement a process for security analysts to provide feedback on the quality of alerts (true positive, false positive). This feedback is crucial for retraining and refining models.
    c. **Model Retraining:** Periodically retrain models with new data, including recent threat intelligence and feedback from analysts, to adapt to evolving threats and changes in normal behavior patterns within your environment.
    d. **Algorithm Updates:** Stay informed about advancements in AI/ML techniques and update algorithms or models as appropriate.
    e. **Use Case Review:** Regularly revisit the initial risk assessment and objectives. Are the AI systems still focused on the right threats? Are there new use cases where AI could add value?
    f. **Resource Allocation:** Ensure you have ongoing resources (personnel, budget, compute) dedicated to maintaining and improving the AI system post-deployment.
iii. **Outcome:** An AI system that adapts and maintains its effectiveness over time, providing sustained value rather than becoming obsolete or noisy. This ensures long-term ROI and resilience against emerging threats.

By following these best practices, organizations can navigate the complexities of AI implementation and build robust, effective security capabilities tailored to their specific needs and risk profile (Padilla-Vega et al., 2023)

5. CASE STUDIES AND REAL-WORLD APPLICATIONS

5.1 Successful Implementations

Several organizations have successfully implemented AI-driven threat detection and response systems, achieving notable results:

Case Study 1: A financial institution utilized AI to enhance its fraud detection capabilities, resulting in a 30% reduction in false positives and a significant decrease in fraud-related losses. By analyzing transaction patterns, the AI system could identify suspicious activities more accurately.

Case Study 2: A healthcare organization implemented an AI-driven system to monitor network traffic, successfully identifying and mitigating a ransomware attack in real-time. The system's rapid response capabilities minimized downtime and data loss.

5.2 Lessons Learned

These case studies highlight key lessons for organizations considering AI-driven solutions:

Start Small: Organizations should begin with pilot projects to assess the effectiveness of AI-driven systems before full-scale implementation. This approach allows for adjustments based on initial findings.

Continuous Learning: AI models must be regularly updated and retrained to adapt to evolving threats and changes in the environment. Organizations should establish processes for ongoing model evaluation and improvement.

5.3 Industry-Specific Applications of AI-Driven Threat Detection

While the core components of AI security systems are similar, their application and tuning are highly dependent on the specific threats, data types, and regulatory requirements prevalent in each industry (Padilla-Vega et al., 2023).

A. Finance Sector

i. **Unique Context:** The financial services industry handles vast sums of money and highly sensitive financial data (account numbers, transaction histories, investment details). It faces constant threats ranging from sophisticated fraud schemes to nation-state attacks aiming for economic disruption or theft. Regulations (e.g., GLBA, SOX, PCI DSS, various AML regulations) are stringent, demanding robust security and audit trails. Speed is often critical, as fraudulent transactions can occur in milliseconds.

ii. **AI Applications:**
   a. **Real-time Fraud Detection:** This is a primary use case. AI algorithms analyze millions of transactions in real-time, identifying anomalies indicative of fraud far faster and more accurately than rule-based systems. This includes:
      1. *Credit Card Fraud:* Detecting unusual spending patterns, locations, or transaction types.
      2. *Account Takeover (ATO):* Identifying suspicious login attempts (unusual location, time, device), rapid password changes, or anomalous fund transfer requests.
      3. *Loan Application Fraud:* Analyzing application data for inconsistencies or patterns associated with known fraudulent applications.
      4. *Insurance Fraud:* Detecting patterns in claims data suggestive of fraudulent claims.
   b. **Anti-Money Laundering (AML) and Compliance:** AI analyzes transaction networks and customer behavior to identify complex money laundering schemes or patterns violating regulations, which might be missed by human analysts reviewing individual transactions. It can also help automate parts of the Know Your Customer (KYC) process.
   c. **Insider Trading Detection:** Monitoring internal communications (with appropriate legal/ethical considerations) and trading patterns for anomalies that could indicate insider trading.
   d. **Cybersecurity Threat Detection:** Beyond fraud, AI monitors network traffic, user behavior, and system logs for signs of malware, phishing attacks targeting employees or customers, DDoS attacks against trading platforms, and attempts to breach sensitive databases.
   e. **Algorithmic Trading Security:** Monitoring trading algorithms for manipulation or compromise.

B. Healthcare Sector

i. **Unique Context:** Healthcare organizations manage extremely sensitive Protected Health Information (PHI), making patient privacy paramount. Regulations like HIPAA (in the US) and GDPR (in Europe) impose strict requirements for data protection and breach notification. The increasing use of connected Internet of Medical Things (IoMT) devices introduces new attack surfaces. Ransomware attacks are particularly devastating as they can disrupt patient care and risk lives. Insider threats (both malicious and accidental snooping) are a significant concern (Padilla-Vega et al., 2023).

ii. **AI Applications:**
   a. **Unauthorized Access Detection:** AI models establish baseline behavior for how different users (doctors, nurses, administrators, billing staff) typically access patient records (EHR/EMR systems). Alerts are generated for deviations, such as:
      1. A user accessing records outside their department or specialty.
      2. Accessing an unusually high number of records.
      3. Accessing records at odd hours.
      4. Accessing records of VIPs or fellow employees without justification.
   b. **Medical Device Security (IoMT):** AI monitors the network behavior of connected devices (infusion pumps, monitors, imaging machines) to detect compromises or anomalous communication patterns that could indicate malware or unauthorized control attempts.
   c. **Ransomware Detection:** Analyzing file access patterns, network traffic, and endpoint behavior for early signs of ransomware encryption activity, potentially allowing for faster isolation and response before widespread damage occurs.
   d. **Compliance Monitoring and Reporting:** Automating the analysis of access logs and system activity to generate reports required for HIPAA/GDPR compliance audits, identifying potential policy violations.
   e. **Phishing Detection:** Identifying targeted phishing emails aimed at healthcare staff attempting to steal credentials for EHR access or deploy malware.
   f. **Data Exfiltration Detection:** Monitoring network traffic and endpoint activity for signs that large volumes of sensitive patient data are being transferred out of the organization inappropriately.

C. Retail Sector

i. **Unique Context:** The retail industry processes enormous volumes of transactions and handles sensitive customer data (credit card numbers, personal information, purchase history). They are prime targets for Point-of-Sale (PoS) malware, e-commerce website attacks (e.g., Magecart), credential stuffing against customer accounts, and data breaches aiming to steal payment card information (PCI). Maintaining PCI DSS compliance is crucial. Customer trust is vital, and breaches can severely damage brand reputation (Padilla-Vega et al., 2023).

ii. **AI Applications:**

a. **Payment Fraud Detection:** Similar to finance, AI analyzes transaction data (online and in-store) for signs of fraudulent payments or stolen card usage.
b. **Point-of-Sale (PoS) Malware Detection:** Analyzing network traffic from PoS terminals and endpoint behavior on these devices for anomalies indicative of memory-scraping malware designed to steal card data.
c. **E-commerce Security:**
    1. *Web Application Firewall (WAF) Enhancement:* AI improves WAF capabilities to detect sophisticated attacks like SQL injection, cross-site scripting (XSS), and attempts to exploit vulnerabilities in online stores.
    2. *Bot Detection:* Identifying and blocking malicious bots involved in credential stuffing, inventory scraping, or checkout abuse.
    3. *Skimming Detection (Magecart):* Monitoring website code and network requests to detect unauthorized scripts designed to steal payment information entered by customers.
d. **Customer Account Takeover (ATO) Protection:** Analyzing login attempts, user behavior on the site (browsing patterns, changes to account details), and transaction history to detect compromised customer accounts.
e. **Data Breach Detection:** Monitoring internal network traffic, database access patterns, and endpoint activity for signs of attackers moving laterally or exfiltrating large volumes of customer data.
f. **Supply Chain Security:** Analyzing communications and data exchange with suppliers for signs of compromise that could impact the retailer.

In each industry, AI enhances threat detection by processing vast amounts of relevant data, identifying subtle patterns and anomalies invisible to traditional methods, reducing false positives, and enabling faster responses tailored to the specific risks and regulatory demands of that sector (Vegesna, 2023).

6. FUTURE DIRECTIONS AND TRENDS

6.1 Advancements Shaping the Future of AI in Cybersecurity

The rapid evolution of AI brings forth new techniques and approaches that promise to make AI-driven security systems more transparent, collaborative, privacy-preserving, and proactive. The field of AI with several trends likely to shape the future of threat detection and response.

A. Explainable AI (XAI): Opening the Black Box

i. **The Challenge with Traditional AI:** Many powerful AI models, especially deep learning networks, operate as "black boxes." They can make highly accurate predictions or classifications (e.g., identifying a file as malware), but it's often difficult or impossible to understand *why* they reached that specific conclusion. This lack of transparency poses significant problems in cybersecurity:
   a. **Trust Deficit:** Security analysts may hesitate to trust or act upon an alert if they can't understand the reasoning behind it.
   b. **Investigation Difficulty:** If an AI flags an activity as malicious, analysts need to investigate. Without understanding the AI's rationale (which specific features or data points triggered the alert?), investigation becomes much harder and slower.
   c. **Tuning and Improvement:** It's difficult to refine or troubleshoot a model if you don't know why it's making errors (false positives or false negatives).
   d. **Regulatory Compliance:** Increasingly, regulations (like GDPR's "right to explanation") may require organizations to explain decisions made by automated systems, especially those impacting individuals. Audit trails need clarity.

ii. **XAI Solutions:** Explainable AI encompasses a range of techniques designed to make AI decisions interpretable by humans. Examples include:
   a. **Feature Importance:** Identifying which input features (e.g., specific API calls, network destinations, user login times) contributed most significantly to a particular decision.
   b. **Rule Extraction:** Translating complex model logic into simpler, human-readable rules (e.g., "IF process X connects to IP Y AND writes file Z THEN flag as suspicious").
   c. **Example-Based Explanations:** Providing examples of similar past instances that led to the same conclusion.
   d. **Visualizations:** Creating visual representations of how the AI processed the data.

iii. **Impact on Threat Detection:**
   a. **Increased Trust and Adoption:** Analysts are more likely to rely on AI tools they can understand.
   b. **Faster, More Accurate Incident Response:** Explanations guide analysts directly to the relevant evidence, speeding up validation and remediation.
   c. **Improved Model Performance:** Understanding *why* models fail helps data scientists improve them more effectively.

d. **Enhanced Compliance and Auditing:** Provides the necessary transparency for regulatory requirements and internal governance.

B. Federated Learning: Collaborative Intelligence Without Data Sharing

i. **The Data Privacy Dilemma:** Training highly effective AI models typically requires large, diverse datasets. In cybersecurity, this data often consists of sensitive logs, network traffic details, and potentially proprietary threat information. Organizations are often unwilling or legally unable (due to privacy regulations like GDPR, CCPA, HIPAA) to share this raw data with a central entity or other organizations for collaborative model training (Vegesna, 2023).

ii. **Federated Learning Solution:** This technique enables multiple parties to collaboratively train a shared AI model *without* exchanging their raw training data. The process generally works as follows:

   a. A central server initializes a global AI model.
   b. This model is sent to participating organizations (or devices).
   c. Each organization trains the model locally using its own private data.
   d. Instead of sending the raw data back, each organization sends only the updated model parameters (weights or gradients) – mathematical summaries of what the model learned locally – back to the central server.
   e. The central server aggregates these updates (e.g., by averaging them) to improve the global model.
   f. The improved global model is sent back to the participants, and the process repeats.

iii. **Impact on Threat Detection:**

   a. **Enhanced Privacy:** Sensitive security data never leaves the organization's control, facilitating compliance with privacy regulations.
   b. **More Robust Models:** The global model benefits from the diverse experiences and data of all participants, leading to better generalization and detection of a wider range of threats than any single organization could achieve alone.
   c. **Collaborative Threat Intelligence:** Allows organizations (e.g., within the same industry) to pool their learning about new attack techniques without revealing specific incidents or sensitive internal data.

C. AI-Driven Threat Hunting: Proactive Discovery

i. **Traditional Approach Limitations:** Conventional security often relies on reactive detection – waiting for an alert from a firewall, Intrusion Detection System (IDS), antivirus, or SIEM rule. This works well for known threats or blatant policy violations but often misses novel attacks, sophisticated Advanced Persistent Threats (APTs), insider threats, or attackers using legitimate tools ("living off the land" techniques) that don't trigger predefined rules. Dwell time – the period an attacker remains undetected within a network – can be weeks or months with purely reactive approaches (Rangaraju et al., 2023).

ii. **Threat Hunting Defined:** Threat hunting is the *proactive* and iterative process of searching through networks, endpoints, and datasets to detect and isolate advanced threats that evade existing security solutions. Traditionally, this has been a highly manual process requiring skilled security analysts to formulate hypotheses and sift through vast amounts of data.

iii. **How AI Enhances Threat Hunting:** AI acts as a powerful force multiplier for human threat hunters:

    a. **Anomaly Detection at Scale:** AI algorithms can analyze massive volumes of diverse data (network flows, process execution logs, user authentication logs, DNS queries, cloud configuration changes) to establish complex baselines of "normal" behavior for users, devices, and network segments. They can then automatically flag subtle deviations that might indicate malicious activity but wouldn't trigger a standard rule.

    b. **Behavioral Analysis:** AI can model sequences of actions to identify suspicious patterns, even if individual actions seem benign. For example, a user logging in from an unusual location, accessing sensitive files they've never touched before, and then attempting to connect to an external IP address could be flagged as a high-risk behavioral pattern.

    c. **Hypothesis Generation and Prioritization:** Instead of analysts manually formulating every hypothesis, AI can suggest potential areas of investigation based on observed anomalies or correlations across different data sources. It can also help prioritize leads, guiding hunters toward the most likely signs of compromise.

    d. **Automated Data Correlation:** AI can automatically link related events across disparate logs and systems (e.g., correlating a suspicious login event with subsequent unusual process activity on the endpoint and specific network traffic), which would take a human analyst significant time.

e. **Predictive Analytics:** Some AI models attempt to predict future attack stages based on early indicators, allowing for intervention before the main objective of the attack is achieved.

iv. **Impact on Threat Detection:**

a. **Reduced Dwell Time:** Proactively finding hidden threats significantly shortens the time attackers have to operate undetected, minimizing potential damage.

b. **Detection of Novel and Sophisticated Attacks:** AI excels at finding patterns associated with zero-day exploits, fileless malware, APTs, and insider threats that bypass signature-based or simple rule-based detection.

c. **Improved Efficiency:** Automates the time-consuming task of sifting through data, allowing skilled analysts to focus on deeper investigation and response.

d. **Shift to Proactive Security:** Moves security posture from merely reacting to known bad things to actively searching for the unknown unknowns, making the organization a much harder target.

These advancements – XAI, Federated Learning, and AI-Driven Threat Hunting – collectively represent a significant leap forward. They promise to make AI security tools more trustworthy, collaborative, privacy-conscious, and effective at finding and stopping even the most sophisticated cyber threats before they cause major harm (Rangaraju et al., 2023).

6.2 The Crucial Role of Regulations and Standards in AI-Driven Security

As AI-driven systems continue their rapid integration across various sectors, the establishment and adherence to robust regulatory frameworks and industry standards are not merely compliance exercises but fundamental necessities for fostering trust, ensuring safety, and promoting responsible innovation. Organizations deploying or developing AI must proactively engage with the evolving legal and ethical landscape (Rangaraju et al., 2023).

Here's a more detailed look at the key considerations:

A. Data Privacy Regulations:

i. **Core Principle:** AI systems are inherently data-hungry. Their effectiveness often relies on processing vast amounts of information, including personal data. Regulations like the General Data Protection Regulation (GDPR) in Europe and the California Consumer Privacy Act (CCPA) (and its successor, CPRA) in the United States establish stringent rules around the collection, processing, storage, and use of personal data.

ii. **AI Implications:** For AI, compliance means ensuring data is collected lawfully (often requiring explicit consent), used only for specified purposes, and kept secure. AI models trained on personal data must respect data subjects' rights, such as the right to access their data, the right to rectification, the right to erasure ("right to be forgotten"), and potentially the right to object to automated decision-making. Organizations must implement privacy-by-design principles when building AI systems, ensuring data minimization and pseudonymization/anonymization where possible. The complexity arises when AI models learn patterns that might inadvertently reveal sensitive information or when decisions are made based on personal data without clear human intervention or explanation.

B. Ethical AI Use:

i. **Beyond Legality:** While regulations provide a legal baseline, ethical guidelines address the broader societal impact of AI. Ethical AI frameworks typically emphasize principles like fairness, accountability, transparency, and safety.

ii. **Fairness & Bias:** AI systems can inherit and even amplify biases present in the data they are trained on. This can lead to discriminatory outcomes in areas like hiring, loan applications, or even criminal justice. Ethical AI demands proactive efforts to identify and mitigate bias throughout the AI lifecycle, ensuring equitable treatment for all individuals and groups.

iii. **Accountability:** When an AI system makes a harmful decision, who is responsible? Ethical frameworks require clear lines of accountability, defining who is answerable for the design, deployment, and outcomes of AI systems. This often involves establishing governance structures and oversight mechanisms.

iv. **Transparency & Explainability (XAI):** "Black box" AI models that make decisions without a clear, human-understandable rationale pose significant ethical challenges, especially in high-stakes applications. Transparency involves documenting the AI system's purpose, data sources, and limitations. Explainability aims to make the decision-making process of AI models more understandable to humans, allowing for auditing, debugging, and building trust (Tanveer et al., 2022). This is often referred to as Explainable AI (XAI).

C. **Oversight for Critical Security Functions:**

i. **High Stakes:** When AI is deployed in critical security domains – such as cyber-security threat detection, physical surveillance systems, critical infrastructure monitoring, or even autonomous weapons systems – the potential consequences of errors, malfunctions, or malicious manipulation are exceptionally high. These systems handle highly sensitive data and their decisions can have life-or-death implications or significant societal impact.
ii. **Ensuring Reliability and Safety:** Robust oversight is paramount. This includes rigorous testing and validation processes to ensure the AI performs reliably under various conditions, including adversarial attacks. Continuous monitoring is necessary to detect drift in performance or unexpected behaviors.
iii. **Human Control & Intervention:** For many critical security applications, maintaining meaningful human control and the ability for human intervention or override is considered essential from both an ethical and safety perspective. AI should augment, not fully replace, human judgment in situations requiring complex ethical reasoning or where errors could be catastrophic.
iv. **Regulatory Focus:** Regulatory bodies are increasingly scrutinizing AI in these critical areas, potentially imposing stricter certification requirements, mandatory human oversight protocols, and detailed risk assessments.

Navigating the AI landscape requires organizations to move beyond basic compliance. It necessitates a deep understanding of data privacy requirements, a commitment to embedding ethical principles into AI development and deployment, and establishing stringent oversight mechanisms, particularly for systems operating in critical functions (Tanveer et al., 2022). The regulatory environment is dynamic, with new guidelines and laws continuously being proposed and enacted, requiring organizations to stay vigilant and adaptable to ensure responsible and beneficial AI adoption.

6.3 Collaboration and Information Sharing in Cybersecurity

Collaboration among organizations, governments, and cybersecurity experts is vital for enhancing collective cybersecurity defenses. Information sharing on emerging threats and best practices can significantly improve threat detection and response capabilities. Initiatives such as Information Sharing and Analysis Centers (ISACs) facilitate this collaboration by providing platforms for organizations to share intelligence. Cybersecurity is not a battle fought in isolation. Adversaries, ranging from individual hackers to organized crime syndicates and nation-state actors, often target multiple organizations using similar tools, infrastructure, and techniques (Tactics, Techniques, and Procedures - TTPs). An attack methodology proven successful against one entity is likely to be reused against others. Operating in silos means each organization must independently detect and respond to threats that others may have already encountered and analyzed. This fragmented approach is inefficient and plays directly into the hands of attackers who rely on exploiting the same vulnerabilities or using the same malware across different victims.

Why Collaboration is Vital:

- **Early Warning System:** Sharing Indicators of Compromise (IoCs – malicious IP addresses, file hashes, domain names) and TTPs allows organizations to proactively search for and block threats *before* they cause significant damage. Information about an attack targeting one organization can serve as an early warning for others.
- **Collective Intelligence:** No single organization has complete visibility into the global threat landscape. Aggregating observations from many entities creates a much richer and more accurate picture of attacker campaigns, motivations, and evolving methods.
- **Resource Optimization:** Sharing threat intelligence prevents redundant effort. Instead of multiple organizations independently reverse-engineering the same malware sample or researching the same command-and-control infrastructure, shared analysis allows defenders to focus resources more effectively.
- **Improved Context:** Understanding *how* an attack unfolded elsewhere (the TTPs) provides crucial context for interpreting suspicious activity within one's own network. An isolated anomalous event might be dismissed, but if it matches a known TTP from a shared report, it warrants immediate investigation.
- **Benchmarking and Best Practices:** Collaboration allows organizations to share successful defensive strategies, mitigation techniques, incident response lessons learned, and effective security configurations, raising the bar for everyone.

Mechanisms for Collaboration:

- **Information Sharing and Analysis Centers (ISACs) and Organizations (ISAOs):** These are often sector-specific (e.g., Financial Services ISAC, Health ISAC, Energy ISAC) but can also be regional or cross-sector. They provide a trusted environment for member organizations to anonymously or openly share threat information, vulnerability data, and best practices relevant to their industry. They often provide curated threat feeds and analysis reports.

- **Government Agencies:** National cybersecurity agencies (like CISA in the US, NCSC in the UK, ENISA in the EU) play a vital role in collecting threat intelligence, issuing alerts and advisories, facilitating information sharing between public and private sectors, and coordinating responses to major incidents.
- **Vendor Threat Intelligence Networks:** Many cybersecurity vendors operate large-scale threat intelligence networks based on telemetry gathered (often anonymized) from their deployed products (firewalls, endpoint security, email gateways). This collective intelligence is used to update blocklists, detection rules, and AI models for all customers.
- **Open Source Intelligence (OSINT) Communities:** Security researchers, bloggers, and informal groups actively share findings about malware campaigns, vulnerabilities, and threat actor activity through platforms like Twitter, Mastodon, specialized forums, and collaborative analysis platforms (e.g., VirusTotal).
- **Formal and Informal Peer Groups:** Direct sharing between trusted peers in similar industries or regions remains a valuable channel, often facilitated by personal relationships and mutual trust.
- **Standardized Sharing Protocols:** Technologies like STIX (Structured Threat Information Expression) and TAXII (Trusted Automated Exchange of Intelligence Information) provide standardized formats and protocols for automated machine-to-machine sharing of cyber threat intelligence, making it easier to ingest and act upon shared data.

The Role of AI in Enhancing Collaboration:
AI can significantly amplify the benefits of collaboration:

- **Automated Intelligence Processing:** AI can rapidly process vast amounts of structured (e.g., STIX feeds) and unstructured (e.g., blog posts, news reports, security bulletins) threat intelligence from multiple sources, automatically extracting relevant IoCs, TTPs, and vulnerability information.
- **Correlation Across Sources:** AI excels at correlating information from diverse sharing platforms (ISACs, vendor feeds, OSINT) with an organization's internal telemetry (logs, network traffic, endpoint data). This quickly identifies which external threats are relevant and potentially active within the local environment.
- **Identifying Broader Campaigns:** By analyzing shared data from numerous organizations, AI can identify large-scale attack campaigns, track threat actor

infrastructure evolution, and spot emerging TTPs that might be missed when looking at isolated incidents.

- **Improving Signal-to-Noise Ratio:** Shared intelligence feeds can be voluminous. AI can help prioritize alerts based on relevance, severity, and corroborating evidence from other sources, allowing security teams to focus on the most critical threats.
- **Predictive Insights:** Analyzing historical shared data with AI can help predict future attack trends or likely targets, enabling more proactive defense postures.

7. CONCLUSION

AI-driven threat detection and response systems represent a transformative approach to cybersecurity, enabling organizations to better protect themselves against an ever-evolving threat landscape. By harnessing the power of AI, organizations can enhance their detection capabilities, improve response times, and ultimately reduce the impact of cyber threats. However, successful implementation requires careful consideration of challenges, continuous learning, and a commitment to staying ahead of emerging trends. As the digital landscape continues to evolve, the integration of AI into cybersecurity strategies will be essential for organizations seeking to safeguard their assets and maintain operational resilience.

The journey through the landscape of AI-driven threat detection and response reveals a fundamental transformation in how organizations must approach cybersecurity. It's no longer merely an enhancement but an increasingly essential evolution required to contend with a threat environment characterized by unprecedented speed, scale, and sophistication. Adversaries are themselves leveraging automation and advanced techniques, making traditional, purely human-driven security operations increasingly untenable.

AI represents a paradigm shift, moving cybersecurity from reactive, signature-based defense towards proactive, predictive, and adaptive strategies. By harnessing the power of machine learning and advanced algorithms, organizations gain the ability to:

- **Detect the Undetectable:** Identify subtle anomalies, zero-day threats, and complex attack patterns hidden within vast datasets that would overwhelm human analysts. AI's pattern recognition capabilities extend detection beyond known threats to encompass novel and evolving malicious behaviors.
- **Accelerate Response Dramatically:** Automate crucial steps in the incident response lifecycle – from initial alert triage and investigation enrichment to

containment actions and remediation orchestration. This drastically reduces attacker dwell time and minimizes the window for damage.

- **Optimize Security Resources:** Allow highly skilled human analysts to focus on strategic tasks, complex investigations, and threat hunting by automating repetitive, data-intensive processes, thereby alleviating the cybersecurity skills gap challenge.
- **Reduce Overall Impact:** Through faster detection and response, AI-driven systems directly contribute to minimizing the financial, operational, and reputational damage resulting from successful cyberattacks.

Collaboration and information sharing are foundational pillars of modern cybersecurity defense. They transform security from an isolated struggle into a collective effort, leveraging shared knowledge to stay ahead of adversaries. Initiatives like ISACs provide the platforms, while AI provides the tools to process, correlate, and act upon this shared intelligence at the speed and scale required to combat today's sophisticated cyber threats effectively. Fostering a culture of trust and utilizing enabling technologies for seamless sharing is essential for building resilient cyber defenses across industries and nations. However, the path to realizing these benefits is not without its hurdles. As explored, successful implementation demands strategic planning and careful consideration of significant challenges:

- **Data Quality and Integration:** Ensuring the AI has access to comprehensive, high-fidelity data from diverse sources is paramount, often requiring significant architectural effort.
- **Complexity and Expertise:** Deploying, configuring, tuning, and managing AI security systems requires specialized skills that may be scarce.
- **Trust and Transparency:** Overcoming the "black box" problem through Explainable AI (XAI) is crucial for analyst adoption, troubleshooting, and accountability.
- **Ethical and Regulatory Considerations:** Navigating data privacy regulations (like GDPR, CCPA) and ensuring fairness and bias mitigation are critical governance responsibilities.
- **Cost and Resource Allocation:** Implementing robust AI security solutions requires investment in technology, talent, and process re-engineering.

Furthermore, the cybersecurity domain is inherently dynamic. Continuous learning and adaptation are not optional, but mandatory. AI models require ongoing training and refinement with fresh data to remain effective against evolving threats. Security teams must continuously update their skills to leverage AI tools effectively. Equally important is a commitment to proactive adaptation, staying informed about emerging trends such as adversarial AI (attacks targeting AI systems themselves), the maturation of XAI techniques, evolving regulatory landscapes, and the increasing integration of AI across the entire security stack. Collaboration and information sharing, amplified by AI's analytical capabilities, become even more critical in this dynamic environment.

Ultimately, as organizations navigate an increasingly complex and perilous digital world, the integration of Artificial Intelligence into cybersecurity strategies transitions from a potential advantage to a fundamental requirement for survival and resilience. It is the key to safeguarding critical assets, ensuring business continuity, and maintaining trust in the digital age. This chapter has endeavored to provide a comprehensive and insightful exploration of AI-driven threat detection and response. By systematically examining:

- The nature of the current sophisticated threat landscape.
- The specific roles and capabilities of AI within cybersecurity defense.
- The practical implementation challenges and considerations.
- The importance of governance, ethics, and collaboration.
- The future trends shaping the next generation of AI in security.

It serves as a foundational resource. Whether you are a researcher investigating novel AI security algorithms, a practitioner evaluating or implementing these technologies, or an organizational leader shaping cybersecurity strategy, this chapter offers valuable knowledge. The inclusion of real-world applications and illustrative case studies aims to bridge theory and practice, providing tangible insights and actionable guidance for leveraging AI to build a more robust and adaptive cybersecurity posture.

In summary, this chapter aims to provide readers with a comprehensive understanding of AI-driven threat detection and response systems. By exploring the current threat landscape, the role of AI in cybersecurity, implementation challenges, and future trends, this chapter will serve as a valuable resource for researchers, practitioners, and organizations looking to enhance their cybersecurity posture through innovative technologies. The insights gained from real-world applications and case studies will further enrich the discussion, offering practical guidance for successful implementation.

REFERENCES

Alabdan, R. (2020). Phishing attacks survey: Types, vectors, and technical approaches. *Future Internet, 12*(10), 168. DOI: 10.3390/fi12100168

Anderson, R. (2020). *Security Engineering: A Guide to Building Dependable Distributed Systems*. Wiley. DOI: 10.1002/9781119644682

Böhme, R., & Moore, T. (2012). The Iterative Nature of Cybersecurity. *IEEE Security and Privacy, 10*(1), 71–75.

Bonfanti, M. E. (2022). *Artificial intelligence and the offence-defence balance in cyber security. Cyber Security: Socio-Technological Uncertainty and Political Fragmentation*. Routledge.

Chandana, P. and Gulzar, C.M., (2023). Securing Cyberspace: A Comprehensive Journey through AI's Impact on Cyber Security. Tuijin Jishu/Journal of Propulsion Technology, 44(2).

Ghasemshirazi, S., Shirvani, G., & Alipour, M. A. (2023). Zero Trust: Applications, Challenges, and Opportunities. arXiv preprint arXiv:2309.03582.

Iqbal, S., Rizvi, S. W. A., Haider, M. H., & Raza, S. (2023). Artificial Intelligence in Security and Defense: Explore the integration of AI in military strategies, security policies, and its implications for global power dynamics. *INTERNATIONAL JOURNAL OF HUMAN AND SOCIETY, 3*(4), 341–353.

Jabbarova, K. (2023). AI AND CYBERSECURITY-NEW THREATS AND OPPORTUNITIES. *The Journal of Research Administration, 5*(2), 5955–5966.

Jian, Y. L., & Luaus, C. (2023). Enhancing Power Grid Security: A Comprehensive Study on Cybersecurity Measures and Fault Diagnosis Strategies Amid Dynamic System Variations. *Revista Española de Documentación Cientifica, 17*(2).

Kaloudi, N., & Li, J. (2020). The ai-based cyber threat landscape: A survey. *ACM Computing Surveys, 53*(1), 1–34. DOI: 10.1145/3372823

Kumar, S., Gupta, U., Singh, A. K., & Singh, A. K. (2023). Artificial intelligence: Revolutionizing cyber security in the digital era. Journal of Computers. *Mechanical and Management, 2*(3), 31–42.

Markevych, M., & Dawson, M. (2023). A review of enhancing intrusion detection systems for cybersecurity using artificial intelligence (ai). In International conference KNOWLEDGE-BASED ORGANIZATION, Vol. 29, No. 3, pp. 30-37.

Mohsin, A., Janicke, H., Nepal, S., & Holmes, D. (2023). Digital Twins and the Future of their Use Enabling Shift Left and Shift Right Cybersecurity Operations. arXiv preprint arXiv:2309.13612. DOI: 10.1109/TPS-ISA58951.2023.00042

Padilla-Vega, R., Sanchez-Rivero, C., & Ojeda-Castro, A. (2023). Navigating the business landscape: Challenges and opportunities of implementing artificial intelligence in cybersecurity governance. *Issues in Information Systems*, *24*(4).

Rangaraju, S., Ness, S., & Dharmalingam, R. (2023). Incorporating AI-Driven Strategies in DevSecOps for Robust Cloud Security. *International Journal of Innovative Science and Research Technology*, *8*(23592365), 10–5281.

Steingartner, W., Galinec, D., & Kozina, A. (2021). Threat defense: Cyber deception approach and education for resilience in hybrid threats model. *Symmetry*, *13*(4), 597. DOI: 10.3390/sym13040597

Tanveer, M., Rajani, T., Rastogi, R., Shao, Y. H., & Ganaie, M. A. (2022). Comprehensive review on twin support vector machines. *Annals of Operations Research*, •••, 1–46.

Vegesna, V.V., (2023). Comprehensive Analysis of AI-Enhanced Defense Systems in Cyberspace. International Numeric Journal of Machine Learning and Robots, 7(7).

Vegesna, V.V., (2023). Enhancing Cyber Resilience by Integrating AI-Driven Threat Detection and Mitigation Strategies. Transactions on Latest Trends in Artificial Intelligence, 4(4).

Virupakshar, K. B., Asundi, M., Channal, K., Shettar, P., Patil, S., & Narayan, D. G. (2020). Distributed denial of service (DDoS) attacks detection system for OpenStack-based private cloud. *Procedia Computer Science*, *167*, 2297–2307. DOI: 10.1016/j.procs.2020.03.282

Zeadally, S., Adi, E., Baig, Z., & Khan, I. A. (2020). Harnessing artificial intelligence capabilities to improve cybersecurity. *IEEE Access : Practical Innovations, Open Solutions*, *8*, 23817–23837. DOI: 10.1109/ACCESS.2020.2968045

Chapter 9
Leveraging Explainable AI for Cybersecurity

Nasim Nezhadsistani
https://orcid.org/0009-0002-0693-8078
Communication Systems Group, Department of Informatics, University of Zürich, Switzerland

Burkhard Stiller
Communication Systems Group, Department of Informatics, University of Zürich, Switzerland

ABSTRACT

In recent years, cyber threats have grown exponentially. As organizations increasingly rely on digital infrastructures, robust cybersecurity solutions are increasingly necessary. The use of artificial intelligence (AI) has emerged as a promising tool for enhancing security, as it is capable of detecting threats in real-time, identifying anomalies, and automating response to incidents. While these AI systems are often referred to as "black boxes," they produce decisions that are difficult for cybersecurity analysts to interpret. Explainable AI (XAI) aims to address this issue by providing transparent and interpretable insights into how AI models arrive at their outputs. As a result of the combination of powerful AI-driven analytics combined with clear explanations, cybersecurity professionals can more confidently rely on machine learning models to detect threats. This chapter examines how Explainable AI can bolster cybersecurity, highlighting its core principles, defense applications, ethical concerns, and technical constraints.

DOI: 10.4018/979-8-3373-2200-1.ch009

1. INTRODUCTION

These days, in this digital age, where interlinked systems are the backbone of virtually every part of our everyday lives, it has become one of the most critical challenges of our times. With businesses, governments, and individuals all relying on large networks and cloud solutions to store, share, and process vital information, one security incident carries more weight than it ever has. But these threats are far from theoretical; they could have tangible impacts such as financial loss, downtime, legal ramifications and ruined reputations. As a result, defense strategies need to be more robust, dynamic, and intelligent if organizations are to continue to be competitive in a world where adversaries are becoming increasingly sophisticated (Goodfellow et al., 2018).

The traditional tools of cyber security, such as firewalls, antivirus based on signature patterns and detection systems based on rules have been the main tools supporting security solutions for many years. And as important as these measures continue to be, they are not enough. Cyber risks have evolved to more advanced and pervasive threats, exploiting sophisticated methodologies such as social engineering, zero-day vulnerabilities, and distributed denial-of-service (DDoS) attacks to circumvent traditional security controls. In this fast-changing world, there is a growing demand for higher-level, active and intelligent instruments. These needs had led to the development of Artificial Intelligence (AI) and Machine Learning (ML) technologies which provide new ways in detection, prevention and action when it comes to cyber threats. This means that these technologies are able to analyze vast quantities of data, looking for patterns and predicting risks much faster and with greater accuracy than a human analyst. AI-based solutions can enable businesses to automate routine tasks, reveal hidden vulnerabilities, and stay on their toes at all times by incorporating them into their security systems. Greater use of AI and ML, however, also presents its own set of challenges, mainly trust and transparency-related (Lundberg & Lee, 2017; Papernot et al., 2018).

The expression "black box" refers to complicated AI systems where their decision-making is not transparent and hard to understand. But even if such systems are capable of achieving high levels of accuracy and efficiency, the absence of an explanation is disturbing. Security analysts, regulators, and here most importantly consumers need to understand why a model made a certain prediction. Without this level of transparency, it becomes difficult to validate the effectiveness of AI solutions, to ensure compliance with legal standards, and to build stakeholder confidence (Doshi-Velez & Kim, 2017). This is where Explainable Artificial Intelligence (XAI) comes into play. By providing some level of understanding of AI model behavior and why it has produced a certain output, XAI addresses the fundamental need for transparency and confidence. Using XAI, cybersecurity experts can trace the sequence of actions that an algorithm takes to mark an offending file or identify abnormal network behavior. Apart from improving operational decisions, AI-based security also guarantees compliance with ethical standards, regulatory standards, and organizational security policies (Adadi & Berrada, 2018). XAI can bring multiple advantages to cybersecurity. It can help organizations to meet strict regulatory guidelines by giving well-documented reasons for AI decisions. It can also increase the speed of incident response times by allowing analysts to immediately process and respond to threats that have been flagged. This also can foster a greater degree of trust among all the players from the c-suite to IT staff to external auditors become in sync regarding the state of security (Nascita et al., 2024). As shown in Figure 1, XAI includes an explanation interface that facilitates user understanding and trust.

The aim of this chapter is to present a comprehensive study of XAI, including a study of the theory behind it and its application to applied issues in cybersecurity. Explainability is highlighted as a key concern in decision-making in cybersecurity because to be able to interpret and grasp AI-based decisions has the potential to enhance trust, utility, and accountability. It should be noted that in case of unexplainable or wrong output provided by AI models, extreme implications are involved, varying from unreported violations to misaligned responses. It is thus crucial that AI models should be explainable and transparent (Jagatheesaperumal et al., 2022).

In order to provide a solid foundation, seminal XAI methodologies such as LIME and SHAP are examined, as well as their potential applications to security challenges. By reviewing these approaches, readers will gain a deeper understanding of the underlying mechanisms that underlie explainability as well as how they can be used to uncover the reasoning behind complex AI decisions.

Figure 1. Traditional AI and XAI, based on (Srivastava et al., 2022)

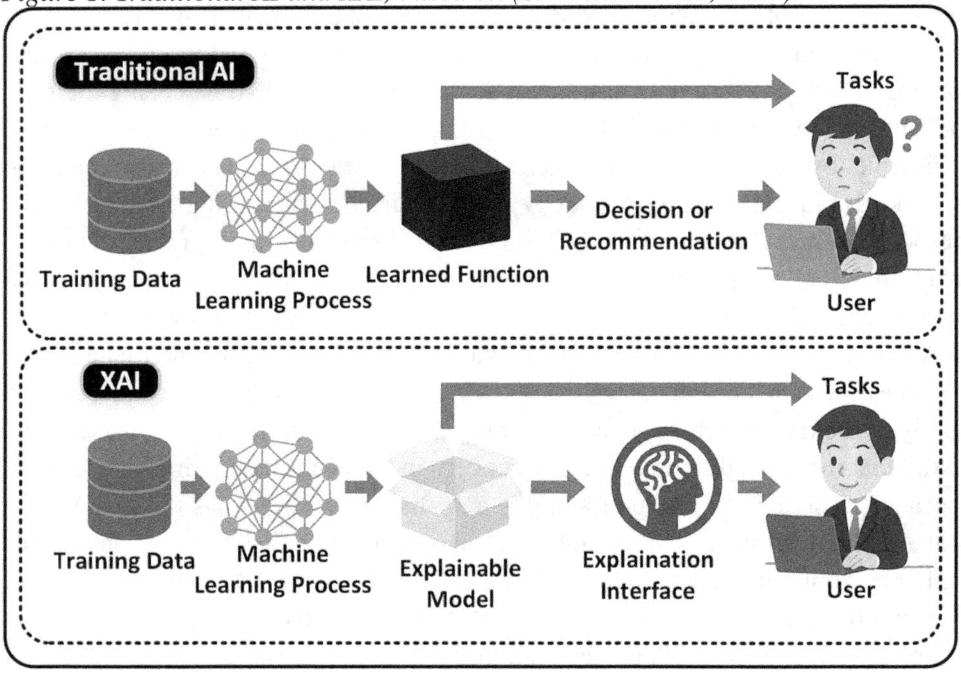

Moreover, the exploration will demonstrate how XAI can improve systems such as Network Intrusion Detection Systems (NIDS), malware classification accuracy, and insider threat detection. The examples provided here illustrate how explainability transforms AI solutions into trusted allies for those engaged in cybersecurity (Neupane et al., 2022; Sindiramutty et al., 2024).

Moreover, ethical, legal, and regulatory commitments under which XAI becomes the center of advanced cybersecurity planning is described. Alongside enabling the compliance of organizations with international data privacy regimes like GDPR and California Consumer Privacy Act (CCPA), open AI practice also induces accountability that clients, stakeholders, and regulators alike anticipate more intensely in today's climate. These requirements will help readers see why explainability is not merely a technical issue, but a key part of making sure there is consumer trust, compliance, and fairness (Faheem et al., 2022).

Following the technical challenges of XAI, the problems that need to be solved for its full potential to be harnessed are introduced. These are the resource-hungry nature of the majority of XAI methods, having efficient implementations on high-speed and low-resource platforms, and adversarial robustness of explainable models. To facilitate solutions to XAI to be readily integrated into dynamic and complex cybersecurity environments, these problems need to be solved.

Lastly, future directions are described, including the potential to combine XAI with hybrid defense systems, create specialized XAI libraries for use in cybersecurity operations, and create adaptive threat modeling methods that include explainability as a starting point. These forward-looking methods have the potential to not only improve existing defenses but also to create innovation in the overall strategy of cybersecurity.

2. BACKGROUND

Cyberattacks are also becoming more sophisticated and mass produced, and hence security analysts will have to rely on artificial intelligence-based solutions heavily (Capuano et al., 2022; Rai, 2020). The traditional signature-based systems that match known threat signatures against new data fails to detect zero-day exploits, or sophisticated evasion techniques. AI models can detect never-seen-before intrusions based on historical data, enabling predictive defence. However, there remain adoption challenges. These are the lack of interpretability abilities and understanding of what the model has learnt which results in lack of trust (Molnar, 2020). Unexplained false positives can exhaust security staff when operationalizing it in sensitive environments like defense and cybersecurity, and unexplained false negatives can fail catastrophically.

Explainable AI has emerged as a way to address the "black box" problem that many ML methods have (Wachter et al., 2017a). XAI technologies enable the decisions made by AI models to be interpreted and communicated in human-understandable ways, in order to build trust and enable higher-order monitoring. In the context of cybersecurity, this can help to clarify why a given alert was generated, allowing for better triaging and forensics.

Organizations globally operate in a changing regulatory environment that will increasingly require and expect transparent AI decision making (Simonyan et al., 2013). Regulations such as the EU's General Data Protection Regulation (GDPR) and the United States' CCPA include provisions regarding the explainability and fairness of automated decision-making. In addition to regulatory compliance, it is important to ensure that AI-powered cybersecurity measures are not inadvertently discriminative, violating of privacy norms, or eroding of civil liberties (Srivastava et al., 2022).

3. FOUNDATIONS OF EXPLAINABLE AI

XAI covers a broad array of methods with the aim of improving the transparency, interpretability, and trustworthiness of machine learning models. Note that researchers have suggested different taxonomies to categorize and study XAI methods in a systematic way, considering the heterogeneity of such methods (Arrieta et al., 2020; Carvalho et al., 2019). It should be noted, however, that these taxonomies are not rigid or exclusive. There are several techniques that possess attributes that fall under more than one category in practice. For example, a certain technique can be all post-hoc, model-agnostic, and locally centered at the same time. In addition, it should, therefore, be judged within its respective subcategory for each technique instead of trying to position it into one category. Therefore, it should be evaluated within the context of each method's specific subcategory rather than attempting to place it in one category. Figures and diagrams accompanying such taxonomies often serve as illustrations, and alternative visualizations may be employed in order to highlight different interpretive dimensions. To provide a structured overview, the taxonomy of XAI methods can be examined along three principal dimensions: (1) the timing of explanation (ante-hoc vs. post-hoc), (2) model dependence (model-specific vs. model-agnostic), and (3) the interpretive scope (local vs. global). In the following sections, these dimensions are described in more detail.

3.1. Ante-Hoc vs. Post-Hoc Explanations

XAI methods can be classified into ante-hoc and post-hoc approaches according to Figure 2, where post-hoc methods explain opaque models following training, whereas ante-hoc methods involve building interpretable models from the outset.

***Ante-hoc explanations*:** In the context of ant-hoc explanations, methods are either incorporated into the model architecture prior to training or designed to produce interpretability during training. It is through these methods that transparent models are produced, which are inherently interpretable. There are numerous types of decision trees, including Decision Trees and Sparse Linear Regressions, whose structure and parameters provide insight into the model's decision-making process.

Post-hoc explanations: In contrast, post-hoc explanations are applied externally after the model has been trained. This kind of technique aims to adjust a model's structure based on interpretability issues. Therefore, ante-hoc explanations are useful for use with models that are naturally interpretable. Furthermore, ante-hoc explanations might add to post-hoc explanations for greater clarity (Zhang et al., 2022).

Figure 2. XAI Explanation: Ante-hoc vs. Post-hoc, based on (Viswan et al., 2024).

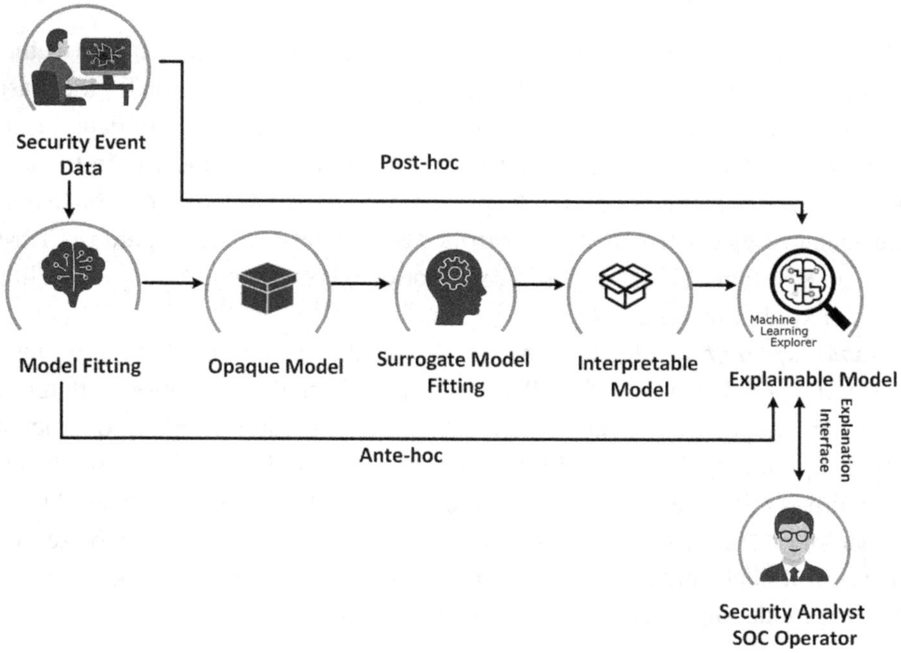

3.2. Model-Specific vs. Model-Agnostic Explanations

Classification is based on the degree to which a particular explanation technique is tailored to a particular type of model:

Model-specific methods: A model-specific, non-linear description of Deep Neural Networks (DNNs), a typical black box structure, necessitates expert methods due to their intricate, non-linear internal representation. These methods might inform us about the particular behavior of a particular model but cannot be applied to models of a different kind.

Model-agnostic methods: In these approaches, the explanation process is separated from the predictive model, allowing the same method to be applied across a variety of models. Therefore, model-agnostic methods are more flexible and reusable in practical applications due to the fact that they are model-independent.

3.3. Local vs. Global Explanations

This axis concerns the scope of interpretability provided by the explanation method:

Local explanations: A local explanation provides the explanation for the reason behind particular predictions for a particular point or a small group of data. In such techniques, model behavior is explained in a local neighborhood within the input space. It comes in handy where model predictions are controlled by certain features in particular cases instead of being controlled by general, applicable patterns. LIME (Local Interpretable Model-agnostic Explanations) is one such technique that illustrates this kind of method.

Global explanations: On the other hand, global explanations attempt to capture the overall model behavior for all the datasets. Global explanations attempt to expose general patterns, identify the most significant features, and find structural relationships among the model. Rather than studying predictions for particular cases, the aim is to create a general picture of the model's behavior in general (Belle & Papantonis, 2021). As shown in Figure 3, XAI models can be categorized into transparent models and post-hoc explainability methods, which can be further divided into model-agnostic and model-specific methods.

Figure 3. The Developed Taxonomic View on XAI Models, based on (Belle & Papantonis, 2021).

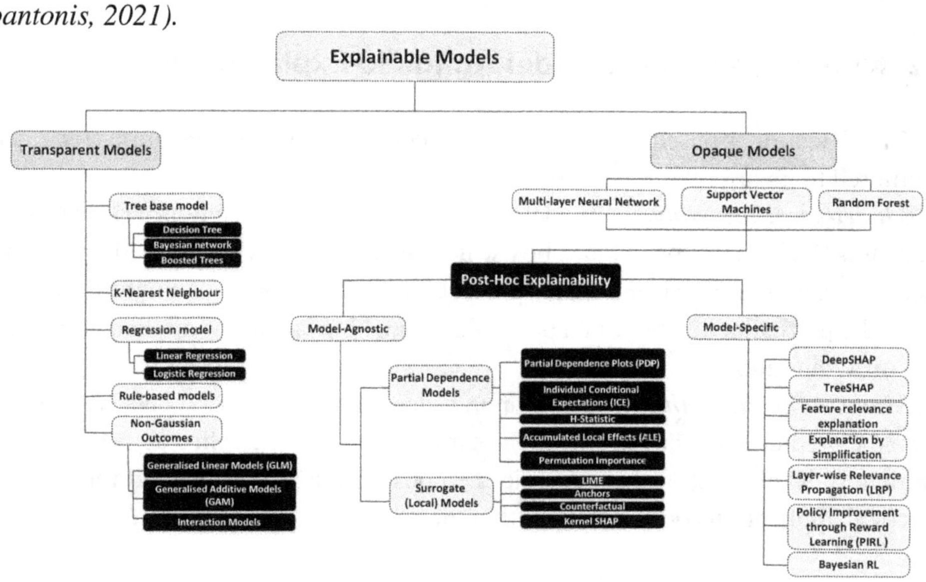

4. XAI MODELS

Over the past few years, XAI has witnessed rapid growth in the development of many algorithms based on various use cases and interpretability needs. In attempting to realize and believe in sophisticated machine learning models, such evolving techniques are essential. Here, six of the most common and powerful XAI strategies are considered with a focus on their interpretability, strengths, and weaknesses.

4.1. SHAP (SHapley Additive exPlanations)

One of the most employed methods in the XAI field is SHAP, which offers a strict, mathematically grounded approach to attributing model predictions to input variables. Through the use of Shapley values developed for cooperative game theory, SHAP gives the same contribution score for every feature as a function of its impact on prediction (Lundberg & Lee, 2017).

One unique feature of SHAP is that it can measure the effect of tiny changes in individual features on a particular prediction. SHAP With this two-way explainability, it is even more suitable not only for instance-level understanding but also for model-level assessment. SHAP can also allow for advanced interaction between features and detect possible biases, facilitating fairness assessment in predictive modeling. It should be noted that although SHAP is robust, it is not without its drawbacks, such as high computational requirements and some technical complexity that might be challenging for non-expert stakeholders.

Figure 4. Example of SHAP.

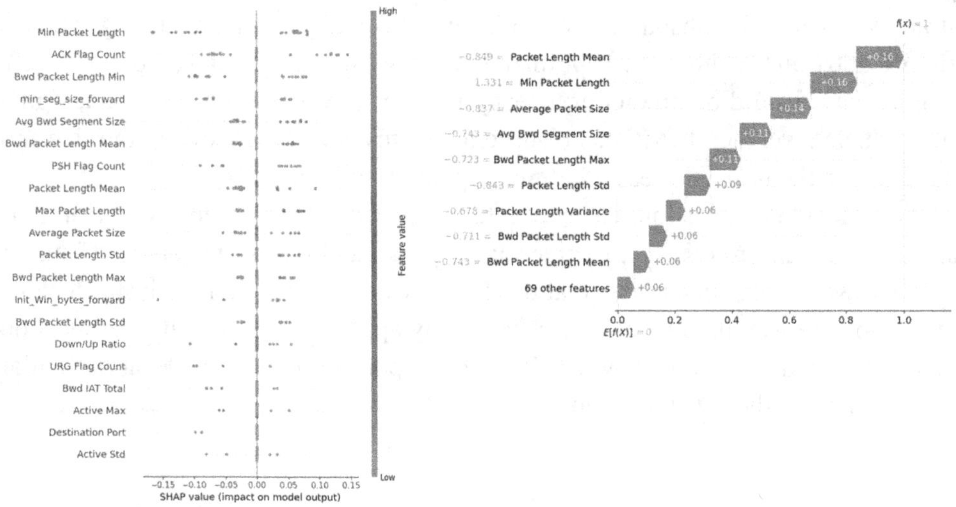

For example, imagine a communication network model that forecasts download speeds from input features like signal strength, network type (4G/5G), and device type. A SHAP summary plot can visualize the contribution of each feature to network performance by the spread and magnitude of Shapley values, allowing users to understand the most critical factors to network performance. An example of SHAP when analyzing global and local features is shown in Figure 4, which depicts the significance of global and local features by showing graphically the contribution of each feature to output for all model instances.

4.2. LIME (Local Interpretable Model-Agnostic Explanations)

Another widely used tool in XAI is LIME, which explains the behavior of any machine learning model locally near a particular prediction. The process entails creating a distribution of perturbed samples around the input point of interest and training a simple, interpretable surrogate model on the samples. Because the surrogate replicates the complexity of behavior of the complex model in a given area, it should be able to indicate some semblance of changes in input effects on the process of prediction. (Ribeiro et al., 2016).

The process starts by identifying the instance to interpret, and from it, slightly variant versions of this instance are generated. Depending on how similar the variant is to the original input, weights are computed according to the similarities between the variant and original input. These weighted examples are used to train a surrogate model so that it can give an interpretation of the behavior of the complex model.

Because of the model-agnostic property of LIME, it can be used for a broad spectrum of tasks and is therefore valuable in areas where explanations are needed on a per-instance basis. In spite of this, optimization of surrogate model and perturbation strategy can bring in substantial variability and the quality of understanding depends significantly on the choice and optimization of the surrogate model (Molnar, 2020). A good case would be predicting latency in a network based on user load, signal strength, and weather. LIME can be used to create a bar chart showing the size and direction of the impact of each feature on predicting latency.

To make model decisions easier to interpret, positive and negative contributions are generally color-coded (e.g., green for positive and red for negative). Figure 5 shows LIME's local linear explanation (LLE), where nearby sample instances in a prediction are weighted by closeness to locally approximate the complex decision boundary. Figure 6 shows how LIME picks important features making particular predictions and their weights and values.

Figure 5. Example of LIME LLE.

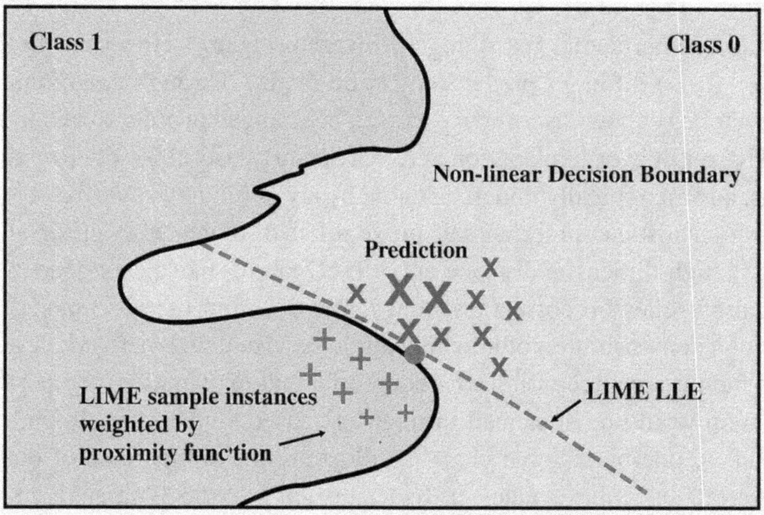

Figure 6. Example of LIME.

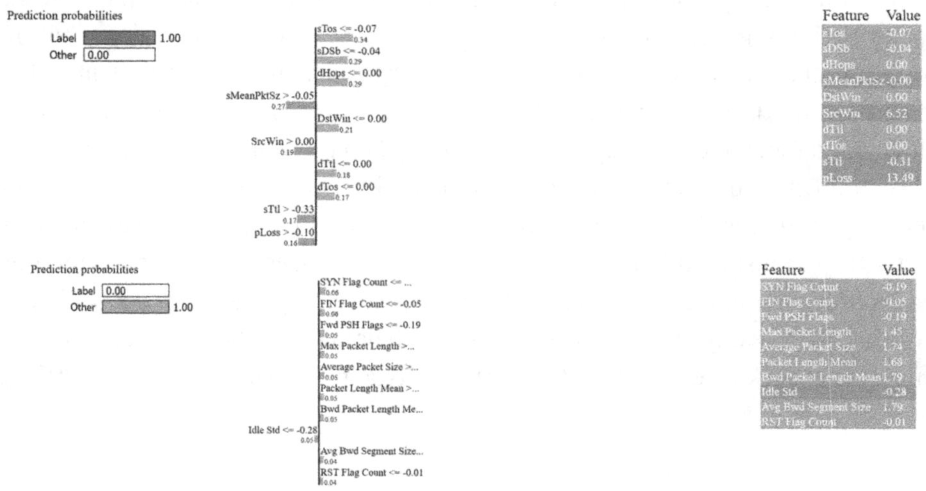

4.3. Counterfactual Explanations

In XAI, counterfactual reasoning involves the query: How can the input be changed so that a different prediction can be made? Through examining what-if cases, this strategy shows users how parts can be changed in order to obtain alternate results. These kinds of explanations are particularly useful to identify actionable directions, and are typically understandable by lay individuals (Verma et al., 2020). Despite this, realistic counterfactuals prove difficult to generate, especially where operating in high-dimensional space or with set features like age or gender. Validity in explanation relies on correctness and fairness within the base model. For the purposes of a demonstration of how this might be visualized, network performance has to be monitored. According to a counterfactual explanation, the performance of the system would be enhanced through increased signal strength and adjusted traffic load. A side-by-side bar chart, by illustrating a comparison of the original and counterfactual feature values, provides insight into the features that have been altered, and this makes us more aware of the model's decision-making.

4.4. Layer-wise Relevance Propagation (LRP)

LRP is a specially designed method for explaining deep neural networks. It's essentially back-propagating a model's output step by step in the layers of the network prior to attributing relevance scores to input features based on their contribution towards the end prediction. By tracing back layer by layer, one can comprehend what happens within during decision-making. An LRP analysis is usually followed by visualization tools like heatmaps, which help explain relevance scores. Because of its structural similarity with many different neural network architectures, LRP can be employed for post-hoc explanation since it is robust and versatile (Montavon et al., 2019). As illustrated in Figure 7, LRP mechanism assesses the contribution of each input feature to the model output by back-propagating relevance scores in the network. LRP rules are provided in Table 1, with their mathematical formulas and the particular network layer to which they are usually applied (Montavon et al., 2019).

Figure 7. The LRP Process, based on (Montavon et al., 2019).

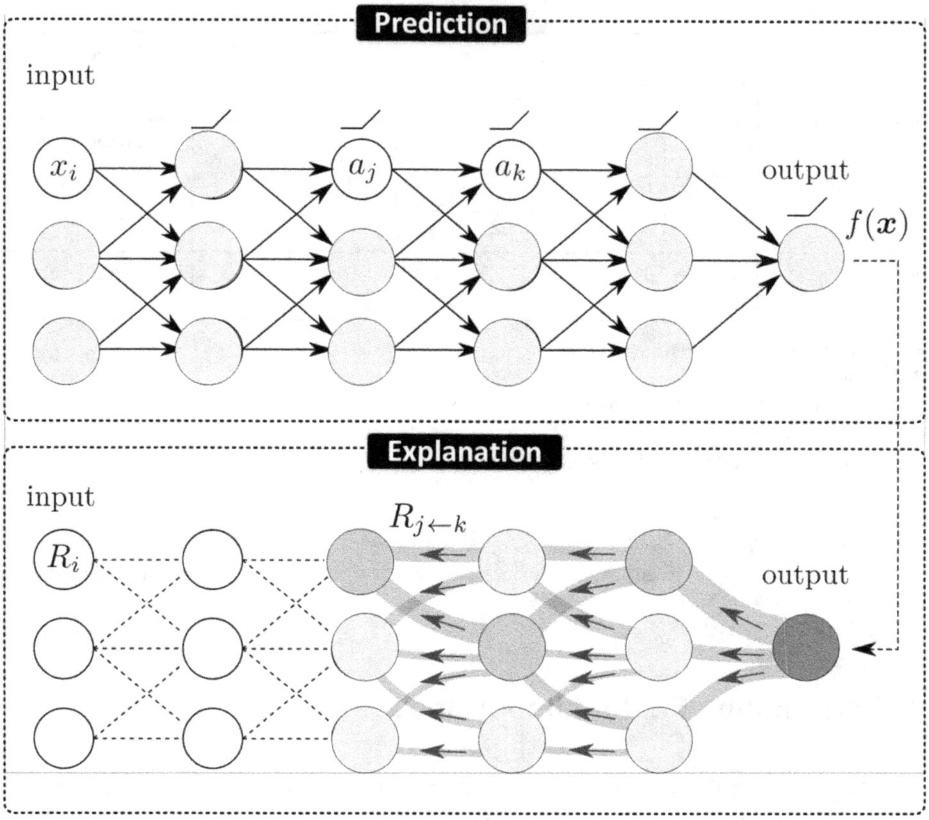

Table 1. Commonly Used LRP Rules, based on (Montavon et al., 2019).

LRP Rule Name	Equation	Used Layer
w^2-rule	$R_i = \sum_j \frac{w_{ij}^2}{\sum_i w_{ij}^2} R_j^1$	First layer ($\mathbb{R}^d$)
$z^{\mathcal{B}}$**-rule**	$R_i = \sum_j \frac{x_i^2 w_{ij} - l_i^3 w_{ij}^{+4} - h_i^5 w_{ij}^{-6}}{\sum_i x_i w_{ij} - l_i w_{ij}^{+} - h_i w_{ij}^{-}} R_j$	First layer (pixels)
LRP-0	$R_j = \sum_k \frac{a_j w_{jk}}{\sum_{0,j} a_j w_{jk}} R_k$	Upper layers
LRP- ϵ	$R_j = \sum_k \frac{a_j w_{jk}}{\epsilon^7 + \sum_{0,j} a_j w_{jk}} R_k$	Middle layers

continued on following page

Table 1. Continued

LRP Rule Name	Equation	Used Layer
LRP $-\gamma$[8]	$R_j = \frac{a_j\left(w_{jk} + \gamma w_{jk}^{+}\right)}{\epsilon + \sum_{0,j} a_j\left(w_{jk} + \gamma w_{jk}^{+}\right)} R_k$	Lower layers
LRP $-\gamma$[8]	$R_j = \sum_k \left(\alpha \frac{(a_j w_{jk})^{+}}{\sum_{0,j} (a_j w_{jk})^{+} - \beta \frac{(a_j w_{jk})^{-}}{\sum_{0,j} (a_j w_{jk})^{-}}} \right) R_k$	Lower layers
flat	$R_j = \sum_k \frac{1}{\sum_j 1} R_k$	Lower layers

1. Neuron j relevance score.
2. Input data i^{th} feature value.
3. Defines the lowest pixel value for input dimension.
4. $(.)^{+}$ indicates max $(0,\cdot)$.
5. Defines the highest pixel value for input dimension.
6. $(.)^{-}$ indicates min $(0,\cdot)$.
7. ε small and positive value.
8. γ controls the impact of positive contributions over negative.
9. α, β control the impact on positive contributions with α and negative contributions with β under the conservation constraint $\alpha = \beta + 1$.

4.5. Permutation Feature Importance (PI)

Permutation Feature Importance measures the importance of each input feature by seeing how model performance varies when the feature values are randomly permuted. Performance drops significantly, suggesting that the feature plays a significant role in making correct predictions, while a very small negligible change suggests that its contribution is insignificant (Fisher et al., 2019).

Figure 8. Permutation Feature Importance for Cybersecurity Application.

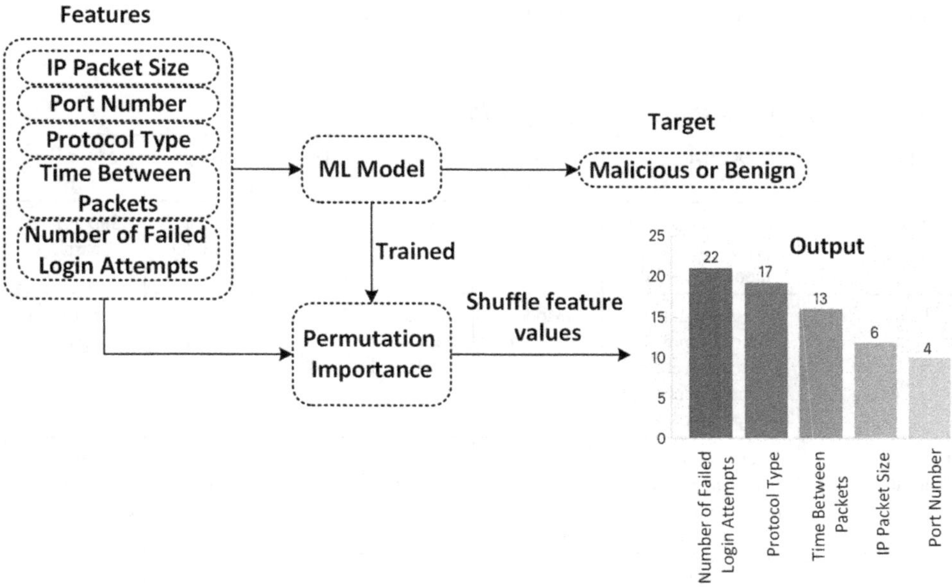

Unlike LIME, PI gives a global view of the importance of features in a dataset. It, however, consumes a lot of computational power, especially when used on a large dataset. Perturbing a feature once may be less representative of the actual importance of the feature if the feature is correlated with other features. As can be seen from Figure 8, permutation feature importance is utilized in a security context to identify if it would impact the capability of a machine learning model to label network traffic as malicious or not if input features were randomly permuted.

4.6. Bayesian Reinforcement Learning (Bayesian RL)

By bringing uncertainty into the decision-making process of the agent, Bayesian reinforcement learning combines probabilistic reasoning and reinforcement learning. By employing clear policies and posterior distributions, the method is more interpretable. With prior information and uncertainty estimates, Bayesian RL can improve the efficiency of learning and enable safer and more informative exploration of the solution space (Ghavamzadeh et al., 2015). Its explainability is because of the probabilistic nature of its choices, traceable to a mix of prior assumptions and seen consequences. The characteristics of Bayesian RL make it an appropriate fit for activities that demand flexibility along with interpretability. Table 2 presents a brief overview of XAI algorithms used across various learning paradigms, with descriptions of the model type, the level of explanation, the stage of application, and the top use cases for each algorithm.

Table 2. Overview of Popular XAI Algorithms.

Method	Description	Model Type	Scope	Type	Stage	Main Use Case
LIME	Construct a local approximation model to explain	Model Agnostic	Local	Surrogate	Post-Model	Supervised Learning
SHAP	Assign a contribution value to each feature in the model prediction	Model Agnostic	Local but also global	Surrogate	Post-Model	Supervised Learning
Counter-factual	Generate similar instances with different outputs to explain	Model Agnostic and Model Specific	Local but also global	Surrogate	Post-Model	Supervised Learning
LRP	A layer-by-layer backward propagation approach to explanation	Model Specific	Local	Visual	Post-Model	Deep Learning
PIRL	Explanations analyze feature interaction effects	Model Specific	Global	Surrogate	In-Model	RL
Bayesian RL	Use Bayesian inference, explains model decisions in uncertainty	Model Agnostic and Model Specific	Local	Visual	In/Post-Model	RL
Permutation Importance	Shuffle features and observe performance changes to explain	Model Agnostic	Global	Visual	Post-Model	Supervised Learning

5. EXPLAINABLE AI FOR CYBERSECURITY: USE CASES

Cyber defense today relies heavily on artificial intelligence. In recent years, deep learning models have been able to inspect gigabits of traffic per second, label hundreds of thousands of executable files every day, and monitor the behavior of entire workforces in real time. These systems are able to achieve accuracy far beyond that of conventional rule engines, but they also suffer from a critical defect: opacity.

Analysts are often left staring at a score of 0.92 malicious without understanding the evidence behind it. The uncertainty associated with incident response slows down incident response, adversely affects trust, and may even cause an organization to fall out of compliance with emerging regulations, such as the EU's NIS2 directive and the NIST AI Risk Management Framework. XAI addresses this issue by converting complex model internals into brief, human-readable explanations that explain why a particular decision was made. The purpose of this section is to examine four flagship use cases, namely network intrusion detection, malware analysis, insider threat detection, and phishing defense, and demonstrate how XAI improves performance, reduces analyst workload, and boosts user confidence through concrete examples.

5.1. Network Intrusion Detection Systems (NIDS)

A NIDS passively observes packets and flow records that traverse routers and switches. In high-speed environments, these flow vectors are fed into a short-term memory network (LSTM) that learns temporal patterns such as bursts of reconnaissance traffic followed by periods of silence, which often signal an impending attack. According to one enterprise study involving 2.6 billion packets, the LSTM increased zero day detection by nine percent, yet analysts ignored more than one quarter of its alerts due to the lack of clear reasoning. (Kalakoti et al.).

The XAI technology changes that dialogue. In the case of post hoc explainers, such as SHAP or Integrated Gradients, a ranked list of features that pushed the score over the danger line is returned for the ten percent of flows that appear most suspicious. As a result of a surge of SSH connections arriving at 03:17 UTC in the same study, SHAP attributed 31% of the risk to destination port 22 and 27% to irregular timing. Those two cues were sufficient for the on-call analyst to verify a brute force attempt and block the source address immediately. Across an entire month, the explanations reduced mean triage time by one third and reduced “alert fatigue,” the rate at which analysts discard notifications, by 41%. (Neupane et al., 2022).

Moving to specialized environments such as the Internet of Things complicates matters since smart home protocols, industrial field buses, and lightweight operating systems generate traffic that differs significantly from conventional TCP/IP. The SPIP ensemble, which combines SHAP and permutation importance, partial dependence plots, and individual conditional expectation curves, was able to reduce false positives by 41 percent in a simulated security operations center. (Keshk et al., 2023). As part of the next generation of research, there will be streaming explainers operating in real time and user-interfaces that will adapt the granularity of evidence to the analyst's role, such as high-level summaries for managers, or packet-level detail for forensic engineers (Manthena et al., 2025).

Table 3. Overview of Cyber-Attack Types, based on (Srivastava et al., 2022).

Category	Specific attack type	Core mechanism / objective	Real-world example
Malware	Ransomware	Encrypts data and demands payment for the decryption key	2021 REvil attack via Kaseya VSA: ≈1 M systems hit; US $70 M ransom demand; Coop (Sweden) closed 800 stores
	Spyware	Stealth software that records user activity, keystrokes, credentials or other private data	Pegasus used to monitor ~1 400 journalists & activists on WhatsApp in 2019
	Botnet	Network of hijacked devices used to launch automated attacks (e.g., DDoS)	2021 Meris botnet → 17 M RPS DDoS vs. Cloudflare finance client
	Fileless malware	Resides only in memory, abusing legitimate OS tools; leaves no files for AV scanners	Astaroth campaign (2019) on Windows, dumping credentials via native scripts
Phishing & social engineering	Spear phishing	Highly-targeted email/ social messages that install malware or steal funds	2015 Ubiquiti Networks lost US $46.7 M after spoofed finance emails
	Whaling	Spear phishing that impersonates or targets C-suite executives	2020 Australian hedge fund lost US $0.8 M after bogus Zoom link; firm collapsed
	Smishing & Vishing	Phishing via SMS (smishing) or voice/ VoIP calls (vishing) to harvest credentials	2020 Spectrum Health vishing scam sought patient IDs; USPS smishing campaign stole Google creds
	Pharming	Redirects users to spoofed sites to siphon log-ins/data	2019 Voluntarios por Venezuela" fake site captured thousands of volunteer records

continued on following page

Table 3. Continued

Category	Specific attack type	Core mechanism / objective	Real-world example
Man-in-the-middle (MITM)	ARP cache poisoning	Corrupts LAN ARP tables to intercept traffic	General technique; widely exploited with off-the-shelf tools
	DNS cache poisoning	Pollutes resolver caches, silently sending users to bogus domains	Common precursor to credential theft on banking sites
	HTTPS spoofing	Uses almost-identical HTTPS domains/certs to fool victims	Look-alike "secure" URLs harvest personal data
	Wi-Fi eavesdropping	Rogue/open hotspots sniff traffic for logins or card details	Attackers create hotspots with popular names in cafés/airports
	Session hijacking	Steals valid session cookies to take over active accounts	Often combined with packet sniffing on unsecured networks
Denial-of-Service	Denial-of-Service (DoS / DDoS)	Floods a service with bogus requests, exhausting resources and blocking legitimate users	Large-scale DDoS attacks regularly cripple online retailers & public services
Injection attacks	SQL Injection (SQLi)	Inserts malicious SQL into queries to dump or modify back-end data	Classic breach vector for user credentials and PII
Vulnerability exploitation	Zero-day exploit	Leverages a flaw before developers can patch it	Any newly disclosed CVE actively used in the wild before fix deployment
Data-exfiltration channel	DNS tunneling	Encodes outbound data/ commands in DNS queries over port 53 to evade firewalls	Malicious "DNS-over-HTTPS VPN" services abused for covert C2 traffic
Adversarial ML	Evasion attack	Perturbs inputs at inference-time to fool a learned model	White-box or black-box approaches; lowers detection accuracy
	Poisoning attack	Inserts crafted data during training to bias or degrade a model	Targeted (to chosen label) or random (to reduce overall accuracy)

There are a number of different types of cyber-attacks, all of which can be classified into Table 3, with descriptions of their specific mechanisms and examples of real-world attacks, including malware, phishing, MITMs, denial of service, injection exploits, and adversarial machine learnings.

5.2. Malware Classification and Analysis

In large organizations, antimalware pipelines ingest up to 800 000 binaries each day. A typical workflow involves the use of static features, such as Portable Executable headers and OPCode N-grams, in conjunction with dynamic traces captured in a sandbox. Approximately 0.6 percent of samples are then classified as high risk by convolutional neural networks (CNNs) or gradient-boosted forests, a subset that is too large to be reviewed manually.

SHAP-instrumented CNNs deployed within a public-cloud sandbox demonstrate how XAI streamlines the backlog. For each alert, the system draws a waterfall diagram that highlights the top five API calls or code regions. Reverse engineers can batch files that share the same dominant feature such as registry editing, process injection, or network exfiltration and write one analysis report instead of a number of them. As a result, the manual workload was reduced from six hours to approximately two hours per day in production. The organization published signatures for a new ransomware strain within 24 hours, well within the industry median of 72 hours (Card et al., 2024). As long as malware authors use packing and code obfuscation to conceal their behavior, robustness remains a challenge. A controlled benchmark injected polymorphic stubs into the training set and found that SHAP explanations degraded gracefully by 4%, while gradient-based attributions suffered a 15% loss in fidelity. (Saqib et al., 2024). This implies that perturbation-based explainers might be able to withstand evasion tactics more effectively than gradient methods. A research project in progress is attempting to test this hypothesis.

5.3. Insider Threat Detection

Insider threats differ from external attacks because the adversary has legitimate access to internal resources. AI is often used in behavioral analytics to detect anomalies in user logins, file access patterns, and communication logs. The use of an XAI-based system can provide clarification regarding the reasons behind certain flagged actions, such as unusual login times or atypical access to confidential data.

Internal attackers begin with legitimate credentials and, often, have privileged knowledge of internal workflows; external attackers are faced with firewalls and multifactor authentication. As a result, behavior-based detectors learn statistical baselines from login times, file system paths, VPN sessions, and e-mail metadata. An alert is generated when the score exceeds the anomaly threshold. In a study that protected five thousand employees, combining an autoencoder with SHAP explanations reduced false positive escalations by 19 percent because analysts could identify that the critical evidence was a 02:00 login to the HR directory followed by three attempts at escalation of privileges (Amiri-Zarandi et al., 2023).

Data movement within organizations that span multiple jurisdictions is restricted by privacy laws. A federated learning variant aggregates only noisy gradients and keeps raw telemetry on premises. Those global weights are then mapped back to local insights using a Shapley value "explanation head". Using a pilot deployment across three subsidiaries, fourteen rogue administrators were identified within forty-eight hours while adhering to strict data sovereignty requirements (Amiri-Zarandi et al., 2023). There are still many open questions, such as scaling to hundreds of thousands of users, ensuring that minority workflows are not unfairly flagged, and defending against insiders who adapt once they understand the explanatory policy. Causal inference layers that distinguish correlation from causation are being explored as well as epistemic uncertainty scores that advise analysts when the model is uncertain.

5.4. Phishing and Social Engineering Defense

Phishing remains the principal vector of entry for ransomware campaigns. Transformer classifiers, which are fine-tuned using e-mail corpora of approximately one gigabyte, achieve 98% accuracy on public benchmarks, but end users rarely understand why a message was blocked. In a controlled study of 10 000 users, the integration of LIME with a multi head attention LSTM highlighted token salience ("verify", "urgent"), entropy-based URL features, and sender reputation scores, resulting in a 50% reduction in false positives (Alotaibi et al., 2025).

SHAP or LIME attributions are channeled through a large-language model, EXPLICATE, which translates technical indicators into conversational warnings, such as "Suspicious Unicode in paypal.com redirect." In A/B tests conducted across four corporations, 94 percent of users were able to take action and the mean response time was 3.5 minutes, compared to 11 minutes for a baseline banner-only interface (Lim et al., 2025).

Future research is needed to address multilingual phishing, adversarial constructed prompts that manipulate explanation salience, and cognitive trade-offs between brevity and detail. In light of this, adaptive interfaces that modulate explanation granularity based on the recipient's security maturity (new hire versus SOC analyst) appear to be a promising approach. As shown in Table 4, there are a number of cybersecurity use cases where the application of XAI techniques has been successful, highlighting the data sources, models, explanation methods, operational benefits, and challenges of each application area.

Table 4. XAI for Cyber Security Use-case.

Use-Case	Primary Data Sources	Typical Models	XAI Techniques	Operational Gains	Key Challenges
NIDS	Packets, NetFlow, syslogs	LSTM, CNN, GNN	SHAP, IG, DeepLIFT, SPIP	−33% triage time; +9% zero-day detect.	Scale; adversarial traffic
Malware	PE headers, opcodes, sandbox traces	CNN, GBDT, Transformers	SHAP, IG, DeepLIFT	6 h → 2.3 h analyst load	Obfuscation; poisoned traces
Insider	IAM logs, file access, VPN sessions, e-mail	Auto-encoder, GMM, RNN	SHAP, Shapley	−19% false positives	Privacy; fairness
Phishing	E-mail text, URLs, headers	Transformer, LSTM	LIME, SHAP + LLM	94% user actionability	Multilingual; salience attacks

6. INTEGRATION OF XAI IN SECURITY OPERATION CENTERS

Security Operations Centers (SOs) have evolved into data-saturated, algorithm-driven control rooms that are capable of freezing client accounts, severing network ports, or notifying external regulators within seconds. XAI techniques have become an operational imperative as well as a legal requirement due to an increasing proportion of these actions now being triggered automatically by opaque machine learning models (Smuha). This section explores how XAI can be embedded at four tightly integrated layers within a Security Operations Center: log collection and forensics, real-time dashboards, human-in-the-loop collaboration, and governance.

6.1. Logging, Incident Reporting, and Forensics

The early investigations by Papernot et al. (2018) identified a "forensic blind spot": when a black-box detector blocks traffic or suspends a host without exposing its rationale, security teams face difficulties reconstructing the causal chain after the fact (Papernot et al., 2018). Contemporary SOs increasingly mitigate this risk by integrating model-agnostic explainers such as SHAP directly into log-shipping pipelines. Every event forwarded to the Security Information and Event Management (SIEM) platform is enriched with a vector of feature attributions for example, *JA3* hash = 0.31 or *dst_port 3389* = 0.27 so that the evidentiary trail remains intact.

In a controlled deployment at a large financial SO, an explainability-augmented intrusion-detection system (IDS) reduced the mean forensic triage time from 68 minutes to 39 minutes (a 42% improvement) while maintaining a 98% detection rate (MP, 2024). When the integrity of the model itself is under suspicion due to possible data poisoning or concept drift, AI forensics methods can trace a contested prediction back to the specific training artifacts that shaped it, providing admissible chain of custody documentation in court (Schneider & Breitinger, 2023).

6.2. Real-time Dashboards and Analytics Interfaces

The visual layer of the SO has evolved from static wallboards to explorers that provide analysts with multi-dimensional, interactive tools that enable them to pivot seamlessly between global heat maps and individual alert rationales. For example, HuntGPT combines SHAP visualizations with a LLM agent that paraphrases the explanation in plain English; Tier1 analysts validated alerts 30% faster and reported higher cognitive trust scores during field trials (Ali & Kostakos, 2023). According to survey data from 112 practitioners, confidence intervals and feature importance graphs are among the top five "missing capabilities" in commercial SIEM systems (Rastogi et al., 2025). According to Neupane et al. (2022), these findings are translated into the XIDS reference architecture, which specifies zoomable and role-aware explanations across hierarchies of nested alerts (Neupane et al., 2022).

6.3. Collaboration between SO Analysts and AI Models

Analyst feedback becomes doubly valuable when XAI artefacts accompany every alert: respondents label not only the verdict (true positive/false positive) but also the quality of the explanation. These second order signals can be captured by SOs and fed into nightly retraining jobs that optimize a multi objective loss by balancing predictive precision with "explanation usefulness." In a six-week pilot study, this setup was found to increase precision from 0.87 to 0.93 and explanation helpfulness scores from 3.1 to 4.2 on a five-point Likert scale (Rastogi et al., 2025). Furthermore, human factor experiments reveal a need for role-adaptive narratives: senior engineers prefer causal graphs and statistical confidence intervals, whereas junior analysts benefit more from simplified textual explanations (Rjoub et al., 2023). According to these insights, domain-specific explanation metrics are now being proposed that correlate directly with SO performance indicators such as mean time to response (MTTR). According to EU AI Act articles 13 and 48, most anomaly detection engines are considered "high risk" AI systems, and deployers are required to provide a sufficient level of transparency to enable users to interpret the output of a system and utilize it appropriately, while maintaining machine-generated logs for future examination. By storing the explanation vector alongside the raw event, both operational troubleshooting needs and statutory logging requirements are met. External auditors can replay historical alerts, regenerate the explanations under the exact model version, and verify whether human overrides are considered capabilities that several managed SO vendors have announced for their 2025 service offerings (Smuha). Scaling explanation techniques to billions of NetFlow records processed daily by large enterprise SOs requires hardware-accelerated Shapley approximations and sketching algorithms that compress high-cardinality features without distorting their attributions. A recent study has also exposed adversarial explanation attacks, in which threat actors craft inputs whose operational payload is malicious while their accompanying explanation appears innocent, reviving Papernot's original concerns about security-aware machine learning. Finally, case studies such as IsoEx suggest that combining lightweight unsupervised detectors with inherently interpretable models can alleviate analyst overload, but robust cross-role evaluation protocols for explanation quality are not yet available (Lavieille & Atlas, 2023). XAI research in SOs focused on bridging these gaps while maintaining real-time efficiency and regulatory compliance is a desirable agenda for the next wave of SO-oriented research.

6.4. Best Practices for Integrating XAI into an Enterprise SO

To ensure XAI brings real operational value to a modern SO, it must be implemented with a practical and resource-efficient approach. Interpretability is a key component of an effective response to high-impact alerts. Rather than generating explanations for every event, which would overwhelm analysts and infrastructure, explanations should be selectively applied to the most severe or high-confidence detections. It ensures that cognitive resources are directed to where they are most needed, without overwhelming the dashboard with low-value data.

One of the best practices is to implement hybrid detection pipelines. Using white-box models for initial filtering and triage, in addition to delegating more complex classification tasks to deep learning models, SOs can achieve a balance between accuracy and explainability. The outputs of the black box components can then be strategically explained by post-hoc explainers such as SHAP or LIME. It is, however, not advisable to blindly believe explanations. Whenever possible, models must be validated by experts to detect issues such as misaligned rationales or explanation spoofing, where the model appears benign through manipulated attribution results.

A growing body of adversarial research makes it imperative to red-team the explanation layer as well. Security teams should assume that explanation mechanisms can be targeted and simulate attacks designed to fool both the classifier and the generated rationales. Additionally, practical constraints on CPU, memory, and storage must be taken into account, especially in environments with high-throughput event ingestion or edge computing. In order to reduce latency and resource consumption, it is recommended to use lightweight or approximate explainers, batch explanation requests, or employ caching mechanisms.

Lastly, explanation data should be logged judiciously. By storing explanations in compressed formats or on secondary storage tiers, one can avoid SIEM overload, and by using summarization techniques one can further reduce the clutter. It is also crucial to monitor the impact of XAI tools on the overall performance of the system. It is possible for SO managers to make informed decisions about when and where explainability adds the most value by tracking metrics such as detection rate, false positives, and processing latency.

This approach embodies a defense-in-depth methodology that takes XAI beyond just being a transparency tool and treats it as an integral element of a scalable, secure, and analyst-friendly detection environment.

7. ETHICAL, LEGAL, AND REGULATORY CONSIDERATIONS

Transparency has evolved from an ethical aspiration to a legal obligation. The EU GDPR codifies a data subject right not to be subject to decisions solely based on automated processing (Art. 22) and requires controllers to provide "meaningful information about the logic involved." Legal scholarship, particularly Wachter et al. (2017b), emphasizes that even if the Regulation does not provide an unconditional right to explanation, opacity can already render many data driven systems unlawful (Wachter et al., 2017b).

Across the Atlantic, the CCPA and its 2020 amendment (CPRA) require firms to disclose the types of personal data they collect, their business purpose for collecting the data, and whether the data is shared or sold. While the statutes do not expressly mention "explainable AI," their disclosure and opt-out provisions impose practical pressure on model developers to create models whose outputs can be attributed to identifiable data sources (de la Torre, 2018).

At the technical-policy interface, the U.S. National Institute of Standards and Technology (NIST) AI Risk Management Framework 1.0 urges organizations to "map, measure, manage, and govern" AI risks, naming explainability as one of the core characteristics of trustworthy systems. As a result of the public endorsement of large cloud providers in 2024, the voluntary guidance has effectively become a standard for the industry (Tabassi, 2023).

The new Artificial Intelligence Act in Europe (Regulation (EU) 2024/1689) tightens the screws further: providers of high risk AI must maintain automatically generated logs that are sufficient to provide a traceability of the system's operation, provide documentation that "allows deployers to interpret the system's output," and provide end users with the opportunity to contest automated decisions (Act, 2024). A number of complementary *meta-governance* instruments are emerging. ISO/IEC 42001 (AI Management Systems) introduces an internationally recognized certification framework that entails firms setting measurable KPIs associated with transparency and assessing them on a regular basis (Benraouane, 2024). In corporate governance policies, high-level principles such as the OECD AI Principles (2019) and the EU's Ethics Guidelines for Trustworthy AI are routinely cited to ensure that KPIs are anchored in broader public values (Hleg, 2019; OECD, 2019).

When it comes to security contexts, opacity creates a double liability: false negatives undermine protection, while false positives can create a situation in which users are incorrectly locked out of critical services. Papernot et al. (2018) report that incident response teams are unable to reproduce detection outcomes when model internals are obscured, resulting in brittle playbooks and longer mean time to resolution (Papernot et al., 2018). GDPR and AI Act now mandate human oversight by establishing mechanisms by which individuals can obtain human review of contested actions. It is also important to note that explainability is fundamental to organizational accountability. Organizations create evidentiary trails for auditors, courts, and affected individuals when they tie every enforcement action to a human-readable rationale and store that rationale in tamper-evident logs. As a result of this entailment, NIST AI RMF treats these explanation artefacts as "risk controls," and ISO/IEC 42001 integrates them into its plan-do-check-act cycle in order to continuously improve the product (Benraouane, 2024). In the event that statistical correlates of malicious behavior overlap with protected characteristics, security models may themselves become vectors of discrimination. The most recent research on fair anomaly detection has shown that naive detectors disproportionately flag minority traffic; by adding group fairness constraints, equity can be significantly improved without sacrificing detection accuracy (Wu et al., 2024)

Responsible AI frameworks all have layered defenses. The EU Ethics Guidelines for Trustworthy AI suggest pre-deployment bias testing, in production monitoring, and post hoc explanation; the OECD Principles call for "transparency and responsible disclosure"; and the NIST RMF provides concrete measurement families for bias impact assessment, explanation completeness, and MLOps pipelines (Hleg, 2019; OECD, 2019). ISO/IEC 42001 requires organizations to declare fairness objectives (e.g., False Positive Rate parity), define metrics, and document corrective actions. As threat landscapes change, the standard requires continuous monitoring: fairness metrics are recalculated after every model update, and deviations trigger root cause analysis and remediation plans that can be audited at every stage. Together, transparency, accountability, and fairness constitute a governance stack. Legislation (GDPR, CCPA, AI Act) establishes minimum transparency and redress; voluntary but increasingly normative standards (NIST RMF, ISO 42001) operationalize these rights; and ethical principles (OECD, EU HLEG) shape the culture of the organization. With the aid of XAI techniques, security systems are provided with the technical foundation that allows them to satisfy every layer, making explanations no longer a luxury but a legal and ethical necessity.

8. TECHNICAL CHALLENGES AND LIMITATIONS

DNNs dominate state-of-the-art intrusion detection benchmarks due to their ability to handle the high dimensionality and non-stationarity of enterprise telemetry. In spite of this, their internal representations remain opaque, forcing security teams to trade some points of accuracy for the cognitive traction offered by simpler models. According to Molnar's handbook, this dilemma can be thought of as a Pareto frontier: every shift toward transparency (e.g., from an LSTM to a gradient-boosted tree or rule list) moves the model away from its global optimum (Molnar, 2020). Rudin goes further, arguing that black boxes are indefensible in high-stakes domains and that *ante-hoc* interpretability should be the default, not the exception (Rudin, 2019). Several studies on CICIDS 2017 conclude that CNN and LSTM detectors achieve 98% accuracy, but a random forest baseline whose decision paths can be inspected achieves 99.9% accuracy with 44% less inference time per flow. (Ali et al., 2025). This same study indicates that "opening the model" may reduce zero day recall because handcrafted features do not capture subtle polymorphic patterns. Hybrid pipelines (white box feature filters paired with black box deep encoders combined with white box surrogate explainers) are emerging as a compromise, but they still lack formal guarantees of integrity.

The discovery of adversarial example inputs designed to elicit incorrect predictions with imperceptible perturbations exposed a structural weakness of DNNs (Goodfellow et al., 2014). Adversaries can now target not only the classifier, but also the explanation surface of the classifier. A study demonstrated how to "scaffold" a biased model so that LIME and SHAP produce benignly looking rationales even when the underlying decision function remains malicious (Slack et al., 2020). These findings imply that XAI layers themselves must be red-teamed. For example, a data-exfiltration tool can inject benign header bytes that dominate the SHAP ranking, causing the SOC dashboard to highlight harmless features while the real exploit operates in the noise floor (Vadillo et al., 2025). Defenses such as adversarial training on explanations, or certifiably robust attribution are nascent and often computationally prohibitive. According to Pawlicki et al. (2024), XAI is both a shield and a new attack surface (Pawlicki et al., 2024).

In edge gateways, industrial IoT devices, and even tier-1 SoC pipelines that ingest millions of events per second, generating faithful explanations consumes memory, CPU/GPU cycles, and network bandwidth that are scarce commodities. According to Jagatheesaperumal et al. (2022), SHAP adds a 30–50% latency overhead to Raspberry Pi-class hardware unless coarse approximations are employed (Jagatheesaperumal et al., 2022). Jain et al. (2025) report that local explanations for every alert would increase SIEM storage by 1.2 TB per week and saturate analyst dashboards with low-value metadata, causing them to restrict explanations to the ten most severe events (Jain & Mitra, 2025).

As a result, while deep neural networks offer exceptional performance in intrusion detection, their lack of transparency leads to a persistent tradeoff between interpretability and accuracy. With the use of XAI, new complexities develop: it can reduce performance on novel threats, increase computational and storage overhead, and even introduce new vectors for adversaries to manipulate. These challenges reveal that current XAI methods are still far from being mature, ranging from the risk of explanation spoofing to the resource burden on edge devices and SIEM systems. To design robust, interpretable security systems, any future direction must take into account these structural, operational, and adversarial constraints.

9. FUTURE RESEARCH DIRECTIONS

9.1. Neuro-Symbolic Approaches

A growing body of neuro-symbolic research has demonstrated the capability of combining logic-based reasoning with deep-net pattern recognition to produce detectors that are both data-efficient and intrinsically interpretable. Surveys of the field describe a two-layer architecture in which a neural encoder produces latent features that are then constrained by a differentiable first-order logic module allowing the system to assert rules such as:

"if origin $\in$ {TOR, VPN} $\wedge$ payloadSize > x $\Rightarrow$ HIGH_RISK."

Early prototypes for malware triage already demonstrate a 3-to-5× reduction in analyst review time because violations of the symbolic rules surface as natural language justifications next to each alert. In future work, these methods must be generalized to streaming data and safety guarantees (e.g., no rule violations) need to be demonstrated under concept drift, a problem identified in the recent systematic review (Wang et al., 2022).

9.2. Domain-Specific XAI APIs

Generic toolkits such as SHAP or LIME do not support flows, ports, JA3 hashes, or MITRE ATT&CK tactics. Researchers therefore argue for domain-specific XAI APIs that encode typical SOC entities as first-class objects and ship with visual widgets (e.g., flow-timeline heat-maps, process-tree overlays). Based on an XAI extension, Nascita et al. (2021) improved analyst comprehension scores by 25% by automatically grouping packets into app-level sessions and coloring SHAP bars based on protocol (Nascita et al., 2021). Paredes et al. (2021) propose a design road-map listing functional requirements from packet-level counter-factuals to attack-path tracing that can serve as the blueprint for an open-source "XAI-for-Sec" SDK (Paredes et al., 2021).

9.3. Robustness Against Adversarial Attacks

Standard explanation techniques are surprisingly easy to *fool*. Slack et al. (2020) showed how minor, human-imperceptible perturbations can shift SHAP and LIME attributions while leaving the model decision unchanged a threat dubbed *fair-washing* or *explanation manipulation* (Slack et al., 2020). In recent surveys, more than thirty types of attacks have been documented, including gradient masking, partial dependency poisoning, and explanation inversion (Baniecki & Biecek, 2024). Additionally, the AUTOLYCUS framework takes advantage of explanation APIs to extract model decision boundaries with much fewer queries than classical methods of model extraction (Oksuz et al., 2024).

10. SUMMARY AND CONCLUSIONS

As cyberattacks grow more sophisticated, organizations will be compelled to utilize every resource at their disposal in an effort to protect digital assets. Technologies based on artificial intelligence will be responsible for real-time threat identification and mitigation. There are, however, serious concerns regarding trust, accountability, and compliance that emerge when unexplainable "black box" solutions are implemented. These concerns become even more acute as AI plays an increasingly critical role in incident detection and response.

XAI provides a solution that bridges the performance and interpretability gaps. This chapter outlined the core techniques (such as LIME, SHAP, or counterfactual explanations), highlighted use cases in intrusion detection, malware analysis, and insider threat identification, and discussed how XAI can be embedded within SOC workflows. While the implementation of XAI is not without technical challenges, such as computational complexity and vulnerability to adversarial manipulation, it has the potential to play a pivotal role in shaping the next generation of cybersecurity systems. As a result of cultivating transparent AI systems, organizations are able to enhance their defensive capabilities as well as user and stakeholder trust. Further, ethical and regulatory considerations highlight the importance of incorporating XAI into cyber defense strategies. It is anticipated that hybrid models, domain-specific XAI libraries, and robust adversarial defenses will enhance the capabilities of explainable AI in the future. Ultimately, the effectiveness of mitigating cyber threats in an ever-changing digital landscape will depend on the synergy between artificial intelligence and human expertise, reinforced by robust explainability.

REFERENCES

Act, A. I. (2024). Artificial Intelligence Act. *Regulamento da União Europeia (UE), 1689.*

Adadi, A., & Berrada, M. (2018). Peeking inside the black-box: A survey on explainable artificial intelligence (XAI). *IEEE Access : Practical Innovations, Open Solutions*, *6*, 52138–52160. DOI: 10.1109/ACCESS.2018.2870052

Ali, M. L., Thakur, K., Schmeelk, S., Debello, J., & Dragos, D. (2025). Deep Learning vs. Machine Learning for Intrusion Detection in Computer Networks: A Comparative Study. *Applied Sciences (Basel, Switzerland)*, *15*(4), 1903. DOI: 10.3390/app15041903

Ali, T., & Kostakos, P. (2023). Huntgpt: Integrating machine learning-based anomaly detection and explainable ai with large language models (llms). *arXiv preprint arXiv:2309.16021.*

Alotaibi, S. R., Alkahtani, H. K., Aljebreen, M., Alshuhail, A., Saeed, M. K., Ebad, S. A., Almukadi, W. S., & Alotaibi, M. (2025). Explainable artificial intelligence in web phishing classification on secure IoT with cloud-based cyber-physical systems. *Alexandria Engineering Journal*, *110*, 490–505. DOI: 10.1016/j.aej.2024.09.115

Amiri-Zarandi, M., Karimipour, H., & Dara, R. A. (2023). A federated and explainable approach for insider threat detection in IoT. *Internet of Things : Engineering Cyber Physical Human Systems*, *24*, 100965. DOI: 10.1016/j.iot.2023.100965

Arrieta, A. B., Díaz-Rodríguez, N., Del Ser, J., Bennetot, A., Tabik, S., Barbado, A., García, S., Gil-López, S., Molina, D., & Benjamins, R. (2020). Explainable Artificial Intelligence (XAI): Concepts, taxonomies, opportunities and challenges toward responsible AI. *Information Fusion*, *58*, 82–115. DOI: 10.1016/j.inffus.2019.12.012

Baniecki, H., & Biecek, P. (2024). Adversarial attacks and defenses in explainable artificial intelligence: A survey. *Information Fusion*, *107*, 102303. DOI: 10.1016/j.inffus.2024.102303

Belle, V., & Papantonis, I. (2021). Principles and practice of explainable machine learning. *Frontiers in Big Data*, *4*, 688969. DOI: 10.3389/fdata.2021.688969 PMID: 34278297

Benraouane, S. A. (2024). *AI Management System Certification According to the ISO/IEC 42001 Standard: How to Audit, Certify, and Build Responsible AI Systems*. CRC Press. DOI: 10.4324/9781003463979

Capuano, N., Fenza, G., Loia, V., & Stanzione, C. (2022). Explainable artificial intelligence in cybersecurity: A survey. *IEEE Access : Practical Innovations, Open Solutions, 10*, 93575–93600. DOI: 10.1109/ACCESS.2022.3204171

Card, Q., Simpson, D., Aryal, K., Gupta, M., & Islam, S. R. (2024). Explainable Deep Learning Models for Dynamic and Online Malware Classification. *2024 IEEE International Conference on Smart Computing (SMARTCOMP)*

Carvalho, D. V., Pereira, E. M., & Cardoso, J. S. (2019). Machine learning interpretability: A survey on methods and metrics. *Electronics (Basel), 8*(8), 832.

de la Torre, L. (2018). A guide to the california consumer privacy act of 2018. *Available atSSRN* 3275571. DOI: 10.2139/ssrn.3275571

Doshi-Velez, F., & Kim, B. (2017). Towards a rigorous science of interpretable machine learning. *arXiv preprint arXiv:1702.08608.*

Faheem, M. A., Kakolu, S., & Aslam, M. (2022). The Role of Explainable AI in Cybersecurity: Improving Analyst Trust in Automated Threat Assessment Systems. *Iconic Research and Engineering Journals, 6*(4), 173–182.

Fisher, A., Rudin, C., & Dominici, F. (2019). All models are wrong, but many are useful: Learning a variable's importance by studying an entire class of prediction models simultaneously. *Journal of Machine Learning Research, 20*(177), 1–81. PMID: 34335110

Ghavamzadeh, M., Mannor, S., Pineau, J., & Tamar, A. (2015). Bayesian reinforcement learning: A survey. *Foundations and Trends® in Machine Learning, 8*(5-6), 359-483.

Goodfellow, I., McDaniel, P., & Papernot, N. (2018). Making machine learning robust against adversarial inputs. *Communications of the ACM, 61*(7), 56–66. DOI: 10.1145/3134599

Goodfellow, I. J., Shlens, J., & Szegedy, C. (2014). Explaining and harnessing adversarial examples. *arXiv preprint arXiv:1412.6572.*

Hleg, A. (2019). Ethics guidelines for trustworthy AI. In.

Jagatheesaperumal, S. K., Pham, Q.-V., Ruby, R., Yang, Z., Xu, C., & Zhang, Z. (2022). Explainable AI over the Internet of Things (IoT): Overview, state-of-the-art and future directions. *IEEE Open Journal of the Communications Society, 3*, 2106–2136. DOI: 10.1109/OJCOMS.2022.3215676

Jain, V., & Mitra, A. (2025). Real-Time Threat Detection in Cybersecurity: Leveraging Machine Learning Algorithms for Enhanced Anomaly Detection. In Machine Intelligence Applications in Cyber-Risk Management (pp. 315-344). IGI Global Scientific Publishing.

Kalakoti, R., Vaarandi, R., Bahsi, H., & Nomm, S. Evaluating Explainable AI for Deep Learning-Based Network Intrusion Detection System Alert Classification.

Keshk, M., Koroniotis, N., Pham, N., Moustafa, N., Turnbull, B., & Zomaya, A. Y. (2023). An explainable deep learning-enabled intrusion detection framework in IoT networks. *Information Sciences*, *639*, 119000. DOI: 10.1016/j.ins.2023.119000

Lavieille, P., & Atlas, I. A. H. (2023). IsoEx: an explainable unsupervised approach to process event logs cyber investigation. *arXiv preprint arXiv:2306.09260.*

Lim, B., Huerta, R., Sotelo, A., Quintela, A., & Kumar, P. (2025). EXPLICATE: Enhancing Phishing Detection through Explainable AI and LLM-Powered Interpretability. *arXiv preprint arXiv:2503.20796.*

Lundberg, S. M., & Lee, S.-I. (2017). A unified approach to interpreting model predictions. *Advances in Neural Information Processing Systems*, **•••**, 30.

Manthena, H., Shajarian, S., Kimmell, J., Abdelsalam, M., Khorsandroo, S., & Gupta, M. (2025). Explainable Artificial Intelligence (XAI) for Malware Analysis: A Survey of Techniques, Applications, and Open Challenges. *IEEE Access : Practical Innovations, Open Solutions*, *13*, 61611–61640. DOI: 10.1109/ACCESS.2025.3555926

Molnar, C. (2020). *Interpretable machine learning*. Lulu. com.

Montavon, G., Binder, A., Lapuschkin, S., Samek, W., & Müller, K.-R. (2019). Layer-wise relevance propagation: an overview. *Explainable AI: interpreting, explaining and visualizing deep learning*, 193-209.

MP, P. J. (2024). An Explainable and Optimized Network Intrusion Detection Model using Deep Learning. *International Journal of Advanced Computer Science and Applications*, *15*(1).

Nascita, A., Aceto, G., Ciuonzo, D., Montieri, A., Persico, V., & Pescapé, A. (2024). A Survey on Explainable Artificial Intelligence for Internet Traffic Classification and Prediction, and Intrusion Detection. *IEEE Communications Surveys and Tutorials*, 1. DOI: 10.1109/COMST.2024.3504955

Nascita, A., Montieri, A., Aceto, G., Ciuonzo, D., Persico, V., & Pescapé, A. (2021). XAI meets mobile traffic classification: Understanding and improving multimodal deep learning architectures. *IEEE Transactions on Network and Service Management, 18*(4), 4225–4246. DOI: 10.1109/TNSM.2021.3098157

Neupane, S., Ables, J., Anderson, W., Mittal, S., Rahimi, S., Banicescu, I., & Seale, M. (2022). Explainable intrusion detection systems (x-ids): A survey of current methods, challenges, and opportunities. *IEEE Access : Practical Innovations, Open Solutions, 10*, 112392–112415. DOI: 10.1109/ACCESS.2022.3216617

OECD. (2019). OECD principles on artificial intelligence. In Paris, O. E. C. D. (Ed.).

Oksuz, A. C., Halimi, A., & Ayday, E. (2024). AUTOLYCUS: Exploiting Explainable Artificial Intelligence (XAI) for Model Extraction Attacks against Interpretable Models. *Proceedings on Privacy Enhancing Technologies*.

Papernot, N., McDaniel, P., Sinha, A., & Wellman, M. P. (2018). Sok: Security and privacy in machine learning. 2018 IEEE European symposium on security and privacy (EuroS&P).

Paredes, J. N., Teze, J. C. L., Simari, G. I., & Martinez, M. V. (2021). On the importance of domain-specific explanations in AI-based cybersecurity systems (technical report). arXiv preprint arXiv:2108.02006.

Pawlicki, M., Pawlicka, A., Kozik, R., & Choraś, M. (2024). The survey on the dual nature of xAI challenges in intrusion detection and their potential for AI innovation. *Artificial Intelligence Review, 57*(12), 1–32. DOI: 10.1007/s10462-024-10972-3

Rai, A. (2020). Explainable AI: From black box to glass box. *Journal of the Academy of Marketing Science, 48*(1), 137–141. DOI: 10.1007/s11747-019-00710-5

Rastogi, N., Dhanuka, D., Saxena, A., Mairal, P., & Nguyen, L. (2025). Survey Perspective: The Role of Explainable AI in Threat Intelligence. *arXiv preprint arXiv:2503.02065*.

Ribeiro, M. T., Singh, S., & Guestrin, C. (2016). " Why should i trust you?" Explaining the predictions of any classifier. *Proceedings of the 22nd ACM SIGKDD international conference on knowledge discovery and data mining* DOI: 10.18653/v1/N16-3020

Rjoub, G., Bentahar, J., Wahab, O. A., Mizouni, R., Song, A., Cohen, R., Otrok, H., & Mourad, A. (2023). A survey on explainable artificial intelligence for cybersecurity. *IEEE Transactions on Network and Service Management, 20*(4), 5115–5140. DOI: 10.1109/TNSM.2023.3282740

Rudin, C. (2019). Stop explaining black box machine learning models for high stakes decisions and use interpretable models instead. *Nature Machine Intelligence, 1*(5), 206–215. DOI: 10.1038/s42256-019-0048-x PMID: 35603010

Saqib, M., Mahdavifar, S., Fung, B. C., & Charland, P. (2024). A Comprehensive Analysis of Explainable AI for Malware Hunting. *ACM Computing Surveys, 56*(12), 1–40. DOI: 10.1145/3677374

Schneider, J., & Breitinger, F. (2023). Towards AI forensics: Did the artificial intelligence system do it? *Journal of Information Security and Applications, 76*, 103517. DOI: 10.1016/j.jisa.2023.103517

Simonyan, K., Vedaldi, A., & Zisserman, A. (2013). Deep inside convolutional networks: Visualising image classification models and saliency maps. *arXiv preprint arXiv:1312.6034.*

Sindiramutty, S. R., Tan, C. E., Lau, S. P., Thangaveloo, R., Gharib, A. H., Manchuri, A. R., Khan, N. A., Tee, W. J., & Muniandy, L. (2024). Explainable AI for cybersecurity. In *Advances in Explainable AI Applications for Smart Cities* (pp. 31–97). IGI Global Scientific Publishing. DOI: 10.4018/978-1-6684-6361-1.ch002

Slack, D., Hilgard, S., Jia, E., Singh, S., & Lakkaraju, H. (2020). Fooling lime and shap: Adversarial attacks on post hoc explanation methods. Proceedings of the AAAI/ACM Conference on AI, Ethics, and Society

Srivastava, G., Jhaveri, R. H., Bhattacharya, S., Pandya, S., Maddikunta, P. K. R., Yenduri, G., Hall, J. G., Alazab, M., & Gadekallu, T. R. (2022). XAI for cybersecurity: state of the art, challenges, open issues and future directions. *arXiv preprint arXiv:2206.03585.*

Tabassi, E. (2023). Artificial intelligence risk management framework (AI RMF 1.0).

Vadillo, J., Santana, R., & Lozano, J. A. (2025). Adversarial attacks in explainable machine learning: A survey of threats against models and humans. *Wiley Interdisciplinary Reviews. Data Mining and Knowledge Discovery, 15*(1), e1567. DOI: 10.1002/widm.1567

Verma, S., Dickerson, J., & Hines, K. (2020). Counterfactual explanations for machine learning: A review. *arXiv preprint arXiv:2010.10596, 2*(1), 1.

Viswan, V., Shaffi, N., Mahmud, M., Subramanian, K., & Hajamohideen, F. (2024). Explainable artificial intelligence in Alzheimer's disease classification: A systematic review. *Cognitive Computation, 16*(1), 1–44. DOI: 10.1007/s12559-023-10192-x

Wachter, S., Mittelstadt, B., & Floridi, L. (2017a). Transparent, explainable, and accountable AI for robotics. *Science Robotics*, *2*(6), eaan6080. DOI: 10.1126/scirobotics.aan6080 PMID: 33157874

Wachter, S., Mittelstadt, B., & Floridi, L. (2017b). Why a Right to Explanation of Automated Decision-Making Does Not Exist in the General Data Protection Regulation. *International Data Privacy Law*, *7*(2), 76–99. DOI: 10.1093/idpl/ipx005

Wang, W., Yang, Y., & Wu, F. (2022). Towards data-and knowledge-driven artificial intelligence: A survey on neuro-symbolic computing. *arXiv preprint arXiv:2210.15889.*

Wu, Z., Zheng, L., Yu, Y., Qiu, R., Birge, J., & He, J. (2024). Fair Anomaly Detection For Imbalanced Groups. *arXiv preprint arXiv:2409.10951.*

Zhang, Z., Al Hamadi, H., Damiani, E., Yeun, C. Y., & Taher, F. (2022). Explainable artificial intelligence applications in cyber security: State-of-the-art in research. *IEEE Access : Practical Innovations, Open Solutions*, *10*, 93104–93139. DOI: 10.1109/ACCESS.2022.3204051

Chapter 10
Federated Learning for Secure and Resilient AI Systems

Shaista Ashraf Farooqi
https://orcid.org/0009-0001-2066-5013
Asia e University, Pakistan

ABSTRACT

Federated Learning is a transformative approach to building secure and resilient AI systems by enabling decentralized model training without exposing raw data. As part of Challenges and Solutions for Cybersecurity and Adversarial Machine Learning, this chapter examines its role in enhancing cybersecurity and mitigating adversarial threats, emphasizing its privacy-preserving capabilities and robustness against attacks. Key security challenges, including adversarial model poisoning, communication risks, and data privacy concerns, are analyzed alongside solutions such as differential privacy, secure aggregation, and robust optimization techniques. The discussion extends to Federated Learning's applications in critical sectors such as healthcare, finance, and edge computing, where secure AI deployment is essential. Addressing these challenges and proposing viable solutions, the chapter provides a comprehensive perspective on Federated Learning's potential to enhance AI security and resilience in adversarial environments.

DOI: 10.4018/979-8-3373-2200-1.ch010

1. INTRODUCTION

The innovation of Artificial Intelligence (AI) has had sweeping impacts on the fields of health care, finance, transportation, and infrastructure management. With the growing integration of AI systems into everyday processes, the need for adaptive and secure learning frameworks escalates.

Federated Learning (FL) allows data pupils to collaboratively learn as multiple clients in a system without their raw data being exposed. This method maintains confidentiality and increases the strength of the system to possible attacks. The decentralized nature of FL means that data is kept on its local device and only the updates are sent, thus there is little opportunity for data trust leakage and regulatory compliance frameworks are more easily adhered to.

This chapter deals with how FL helps build secure AI systems within the context of Challenges and Solutions for Cybersecurity and Adversarial Machine Learning. It analyzes the architecture of FL, the security of its mechanisms, adversarial threats, and the applications of these mechanisms in some privacy-sensitive domains.

1.1 Overview of Cybersecurity Challenges in AI

Integration of AI technology into core functions such as health care, finance, and national security makes it an easy target for cyber-attacks. Unlike traditional programs, the software is an ever-growing entity and so is its range of vulnerabilities. This attack potential is driven by a code vulnerability as well as data-determined exploitation. These attacks leverage the same adaptiveness which supports the powering of intelligence in AI (Zhang et al., 2022) and violate the core security tenets encapsulated in the CIA triad.

AI systems face a significant risk in the form of adversarial attacks. Adversarial examples are inputs crafted by malicious users that attempt to manipulate the behavior of a model. Not only do these inputs often go unnoticed by humans, but they can also lead to erroneous conclusions in models pertaining to image classification, sensor data interpretation, and forecasting. In safety-critical areas, these failures could prove catastrophic. Chakraborty et al. (2021) discuss the data poisoning attack: an attacker compromising the training data with backdoors or damaging biases which in turn alters the trustworthiness, fairness and overall integrity of the system.

Moreover, both the static and dynamic structure of traditional machine learning models poses a serious risk to data security. Centralized storage of sensitive and classified information poses a serious threat, and once this data is aggregated its value increases exponentially for potential attackers. With the growing use of the Cloud and IoT devices, networked systems become more vulnerable, turning algorithms into ideal candidates for model inversion, membership inference and even model theft (Zhang et al., 2020).

The reliability and performance of AI systems are greatly affected by the threats of cybersecurity. Trust from the public also decreases, especially for mission-oriented and regulated AI, which increases demand for technologies that focus on security. The rise of federated learning technologies that can decentralize the problem of AI system security helps counter this.

1.2 Adversarial Machine Learning's Role

Adversarial machine learning (AML) is one of the most prominent disciplines situated at the interface of AI and cybersecurity. It analyzes how learning-based systems can be compromised and how to defend such attacks. AML deals with the problems of security of machine learning models and focuses their attention on what are known as "security issues," that is, how machine learning models fail to perform under attack situations with poisoned inputs or maliciously altered training data. As AI systems are assigned more critical tasks usually reserved for humans, it becomes increasingly necessary to understand all possible adversarial threats to ensure that dependable systems can be built (Bountakas et al., 2023).

A focus of AML is to understand that a large portion of deep learning neural networks are extremely brittle: They are susceptible to adversarial examples, modifications that aim to achieve misclassification of an intended target with bound reasoning. These forms of attack pose a risk in the digital and physical realms, affecting anything from image recognition to voice assistants and self-driving cars. Perhaps the most problematic aspect of adversarial examples is their transferability; an adversarial input generated for a one model will frequently trick others, even those trained on different datasets (Jegorova et al., 2022).

Along with inference-time attacks, AML considers training-time threats as well. Adding harmful data to a training set in order to alter how a model works constitutes a poisoning attack. Backdoor attacks conceal triggers that can later be used by foes to alter the outcomes of the model. Such changes are difficult to identify and are capable of seeping in throughout a model's lifecycle, which creates enduring threats (Goldblum et al., 2022).

Different facets of AI are assaulted by evasion, extraction, and inference attacks. Models are fooled into making decisions during a testing phase in evasion attacks. In extraction attacks, the functionality of the model is asked until it gets replicated. Inference attacks, such as membership inference, find out whether certain data points were used as part of the training set, which is a breach of privacy for the client.

The risks of AML are most significant in centralized AI systems because having a single point of control for the model or data pipeline could lead to catastrophic system-wide exposures. This kind of vulnerability has inspired researchers and practitioners to consider architectural solutions such as Federated Learning (FL), which partitions the training among numerous client devices. FL reduces some attack possibilities based on the lack of data aggregation, but this raises new questions of how to defend against these additional adversarial scenarios.

In light of this chapter, studying adversarial machine learning equips one with the necessary knowledge to analyze how Federated Learning could be developed, modified, and fortified fortify to withstand both established and new threats.

1.3 Definition and Significance of Federated Learning

Federated Learning (FL) refers to the way of training models where numerous clients such as mobile phones collaboratively build a model without needing to share their raw data. FL was proposed by Google in 2016 to enhance the privacy and security of data. This characteristic makes FL essential in the ethical advancement of AI.

The traditional approach of centralized learning gathers data in a single location, which poses the risk of sensitive information being leaked. Federated Learning (FL) functions differently. It trains models on data from numerous clients and keeps the data on the client side. Only partial model information is conveyed to the central system, such as model updates or local parameters. This technique enhances privacy and reduces the risk of exposure and breaches of sensitive data (Wen et al., 2023).

FL is experiencing rapid growth in industries that are privacy sensitive and heavily regulated. Data across these sectors is usually siloed due to legal, ethical, or technical barriers, posing challenges for centralized model training. FL addresses the problem by keeping the data on local devices or servers while allowing organizations to work together on model development.

Furthermore, as noted by Said et al. (2023), FL is in sync with contemporary frameworks like the GDPR, HIPAA, and new governance paradigms of AI, which stress data minimization and consent. Moreover, FL's architecture inherently restricts data centralization, allowing organizations to develop socially responsible machine learning technologies to safely innovate within the bounds of privacy regulations.

From a security perspective, Federated Learning also presents a paradigmatic change. FL offers advantages, such as reduced surfaces for centralized data leakage attacks, but it also presents new vulnerabilities, including poisoning attacks, model inversion, and free-rider problems. This dual characterization of weaknesses and strengths makes FL an intriguing subject in the study of secure and resilient AI systems (Li et al., 2020).

In adversarial machine learning and cybersecurity, Federated Learning (FL) is not a band-aid solution but an essential recalibration of training paradigms in the era of hyper-connectivity. Its distributed architecture is friendly to privacy, making FL an aid to robust AI in numerous domains. Diminishing control coupled with an increase in cyber threats makes it essential to protect against cyber threats while maintaining usable trust in systems.

2. BASICS OF FEDERATED LEARNING

Federated Learning (FL) is a method of implementing machine learning that enhances privacy since data does not need to be centralized. Mobile clients, such as smartphones or IoT devices, are able to collaboratively train a global model without sharing local data. They only need to send updates like gradients or weight updates to a central server.

The FedAvg (Federated Averaging) algorithm is used to aggregate these updates after several rounds of communication. Cross-device FL pertains to a heterogeneous collection of low-power devices, and cross-silo FL is for organizational units like hospitals or banks. Its decentralized nature minimizes security concerns, enables compliance with regulations, and control of local data. This also allows for the deployment of AI systems in sensitive and distributed setups.

2.1 Key Principles and Mechanisms

Federated Learning is different from centralized machine learning because it operates on a set of more foundational concepts. It has a principle of data locality which is responsible for keeping local data, such as sensitive information, on the client device to limit privacy risks. Each client performs model training on their local dataset instead of sending sensitive data to a centralized server. After model training, only model updates, usually in the form of gradients or weight changes, are sent to a central aggregator where further processing takes place (Zhang et al., 2021).

Another defining feature in Federated Learning is model aggregation where a new global model is created by merging the updates calculated by clients locally. FedAvg is the most commonly used method among others since it obtains a weighted average of client updates which is calculated based on the size of the client's local dataset. This approach is optimal in terms of fairness as well as computational expense, especially when client data is not homogeneous or non-independent and identically distributed (non-IID) (Zhao et al., 2018).

FL incorporates the basics of privacy preservation and efficiency of communication. Because of the high costs associated with communication and bandwidth limitations in edge environments, FL employs update compression, client sampling, and asynchronous communication. FL often supplements other privacy-preserving methods (such as differential privacy and secure multi-party computation) to safeguard confidential information, even from the central server (Mehta, 2024).

As such, heterogeneity robustness is an important feature for FL. In a federated environment, the clients can differ in the quality and quantity of the data, underlying computing resources, and network connectivity. Therefore, FL frameworks are designed to support a certain degree of non-attendance, dropout clients, and variation in local training sessions without losing functionality.

These guiding principles defend the position of federated learning as a responsive framework in need of sensitive, decentralized AI, especially in hostile and data-sensitive settings.

2.2 The Federated Learning Workflow

The Federated Learning (FL) approach combines local training and centralized control in a repetitive collaborative fashion. The methodology can be divided into five phases that pose privacy and other scalability challenges during model training on different clients (Farooqi et al., 2024).

Phase 1: Model Pre-Training and Client Module Design

At the start, a global machine learning algorithm will be constructed by the server. This largely consists of putting together a base ML model within the parameters that have either been pretrained or randomly generated. The server also selects a sample of clients, which can either be devices or data nodes, who will be active for the transitory phase of training. The sample clients can either be selected randomly, grouped by data availability, data quality, or some optimization procedures (e.g. conditional sampling, reinforcement learning) can be performed on the data to formulate a participating set of clients. Obtained clients receive the initial parameter set of the global model through a secure communication channel so that they can undertake local training.

Phase 2: Local Dataset Modelling on Client Devices

Different clients further refine the global model they received using their own datasets. The model makes certain guarantees that do not permit the uploading of any raw data from the device. Clients have the option of training for a number of epochs over their dataset using standard machine learning procedures like SGD, Adam, or DP-SGD with local modifications. A form of tracking known as local capture of distinctive features and patterns pertaining to each data source is integrated with the rest of computer science in the choreography of inter-client algorithmic interactions. This is necessary because client datasets may have non-IID distributions.

Phase 3: Secure Transmission of Learned Parameters

The trained parameters, which could include learned gradients or other model alterations, are sent back to the central server by the clients without sending raw data in a secure manner. In this situation, more than differential privacy can be utilized to protect the information being shared. Protection against dangerous privacy infringements that can arise from sophisticated methods such as homomorphic encryption or secure multiparty computation (SMPC) is possible. These methods prevent the reconstruction or inference of sensitive information based on the provided updates.

Phase 4: Aggregation and Global Model Updating at the Server

The central server gets and aggregates all the submitted encrypted or anonymized model updates from the participating clients. They then perform update aggregation using Federated Averaging (FedAvg) or similar approaches. This typically involves combining local models by means of a weighted average where most of the weights are derived from the size of the dataset or effort made by the particular client that is being aggregated. Model aggregation yields the resultant output which is a new global model that supersedes all previous ones, and this new global model incorporates the information of all users. It may also be useful to apply some kind of model fusion algorithm to remove redundant information without degrading performance. Additional aggregation techniques that could increase robustness of the model by increasing resilience against noisy malicious updates, so-called poison attacks, could also be added.

Phase 5: Allocating the Global Model and Continuing Iterative Rounds

After determining the global model, the server downloads the modifications to its parameters. Clients can now terminate communication while the server prepares to use the model for local training. The clients begin a new round of local training.

This iterative loop or regroup, train, aggregate, and redistribute, continues until the model reaches convergence or until a set target criteria performance has been reached.

This model provides an effective solution for constructing high-quality global models with sensitive, distributed, and heterogeneous data due to the privacy-preserving methodologies implemented in Federated Learning. The system's modular architecture allows for the incorporation of more advanced features such as additional client selection, asynchrony with updatable clients, and self-correcting faulted updates and enhances the usefulness of the FL system as a deployable AI infrastructure in cybersecurity, healthcare, or finance. Federated Learning process is illustrated in Figure 1, showing all five phases from system initialization to model iteration.

Figure 1. Five Phases of Federated Learning Process

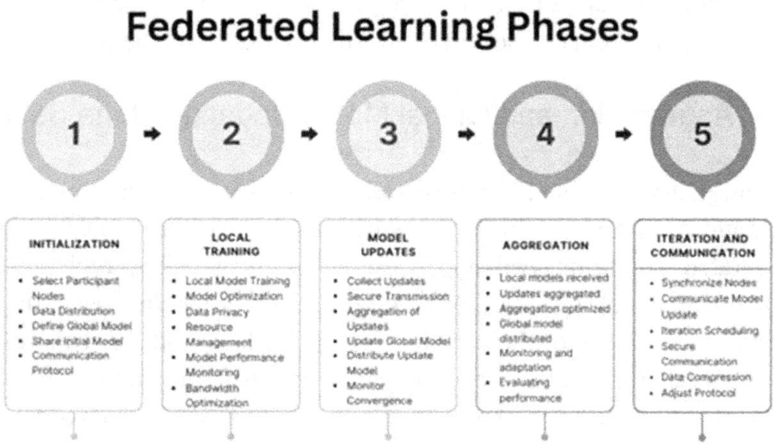

2.3 FL Architectures: Centralized, Decentralized, and Hierarchical

Federated Learning (FL) systems may take various forms based on the underlying architectural models. They differ in terms of their scalability, fault tolerance, efficiency in communication, and level of trust needed. The three principal types of architecture are configured around the most basic subdivisions of the system hierarchy concerning the distribution, collection, and management of model updates—centralized, decentralized, and hierarchical.

- **Centralized Architecture**

The centralized architecture takes all updates from the individual clients, creates a global model, and then sends it to an aggregate server that is both trusted and can store the model and perform the training. This is by far the simplest and the most common method. Nevertheless, in trustless domains, both the single point of failure and reliance on a trusted authority is a serious drawback (Drainakis et al., 2023).

- **Decentralized Architecture**

In comparison with other approaches, decentralized FL does not have a central coordinator. Instead, clients share and aggregate model updates, often using gossip protocols or ring-based topologies (Wink & Nochta 2021). In this more sophisticated model, client-to-client communication is more direct. This improves fault tolerance since an aggregator who may be targeted in an attack is no longer needed. However, this type of FL decentralization increases the problems of synchronization and convergence, as well as the system design's level of complexity.

- **Hierarchical Architecture**

An edge aggregator that sits between the central server and the clients is added. Clients send their updates to these local nodes, which are called edge aggregators. Local nodes do the primary aggregation on the shard and then send the combined result to the central server. Typically, this architecture is applicable for larger systems that are more distributed or those that are more geographically dispersed. Examples of such systems are smart cities and healthcare networks. The hierarchical model has been shown to reduce communication overhead, improve scalability, and allow some regional personalization of the model without losing the overall learning goal (Zhong et al. 2022).

Every federated learning (FL) architecture has distinctive operational and security capabilities. A federated learning model is selected depending on the system's scale, level of trust, communication limits, and privacy requirements of the specific application. Understanding these differences is critical for creating effective federated learning systems which are capable of solving complex problems in the real world. We discuss the advantages and disadvantages of three basic types of Federated Learning (FL) architectures that include centralized, decentralized and hierarchical in relation to their application in cybersecurity in Table 1.

Table 1. *Comparison of Federated Learning Architectures in Cybersecurity*

	FL Architecture	Advantage	Disadvantage	Use Case
1.	**Centralized**	Simple to implement Efficient model coordination Easier control and update management	Single point of failure Requires trust in central server Limited fault tolerance	Intrusion detection in enterprise networks Threat data aggregation from branch offices
2.	**Decentralized**	No single point of failure Greater fault tolerance Improved resilience in trustless environments	Complex communication and synchronization Slower convergence Higher bandwidth requirements	Peer-to-peer botnet mitigation Decentralized threat sharing among ISPs
3.	**Hierarchical**	Scalable for large, distributed systems Reduced communication cost Local customization with global insight	Requires layered infrastructure Intermediate nodes may become bottlenecks or vulnerabilities	Regional hospital malware detection Sector-wide smart grid security coordination

The table clearly indicates that the three approaches to FL—centralized, decentralized, and hierarchical—differ in terms of their effectiveness, resilience, and scalability. Based on these attributes, each design is tailored to specific cybersecurity requirements, ranging from enterprise-scale threat intelligence to sophisticated smart grid security for national infrastructure protection.

2.4 Communication Protocols and Aggregation Strategies

Communication and secure aggregation are among the most challenging problems in Federated Learning (FL). This is a greater challenge in bandwidth-constrained distributed systems with heterogeneous clients. Transmission costs must be reduced to scale FL. Client sampling, update compressing, and asynchronous communication are some ways to reduce these costs. Aggregation techniques such as Federated Averaging (FedAvg) along with outlier filtering, and secure multiparty computation not only protect the integrity of the model, but also ensure privacy. These approaches enable the design of practical FL systems that are capable of scaling and securing utility (Almanifi et al., 2023).

For FL (Federated Learning), communication protocols determine the delimitations of the steps where data is collected from clients and delivered to the server, which serves as the principal computer. Each exchange in a decentralized structure is managed at a peer-to-peer level. Extreme model updates tend to be very expensive in terms of bandwidth for large scale deployments. To improve this, some clients may be selected to participate in each training round through client sampling. Quantization or sparsification, which compresses model updates, reduces the quantity of data that is transmitted. Asynchronous communication allows clients to dispatch updates in sync, which increases fault tolerance and flexibility of the system (Aledhari et al., 2020).

On the server side, aggregation strategies determine the approaches for merging individual updates from clients to form a new global model. The most common technique is FedAvg which combines updates from the clients using a weighted average based on the size of their local datasets. While effective, FedAvg's main optimization concerns is with low honesty participants therefore it must contend with unreliable or malicious participants (Collins et al., 2022).

To increase robustness, secure aggregation allows the server to carry out global updates without having direct access to any of the clients' data. Techniques like homomorphic encryption, secret sharing, and SMPC upholds the privacy of the client's contributions which is vital in adversarial or semi-trustful settings (Zhou et al., 2024).

More sophisticated methods of aggregation also focus on dealing with the non-IID data distributions and untrustworthy clients. Krum, Median, Trimmed Mean, and Bulyan are designed to survive adversarial or faulty updates, focusing instead on contributions that are not outliers. These approaches are helpful in FL environments where there is a lack of trust or when the system's robustness is the main focus of design (Li et al., 2022; Wang et al., 2025).

3. SECURITY IMPLICATIONS OF FEDERATED LEARNING

Employing privacy methods like data aggregation in Federated Learning (FL) does not increase security in any manner. It is still open to attack. More specifically, the framework's architecture leaves if vulnerable to adversarial clients, poisoned updates, and leaking model details. The presence of untrusted settings further heightens the risk of such malicious attacks. During the model's communication, aggregation, or update phases, the models or information may be altered or exfiltrated (Zhang et al., 2022).

3.1 Principles of Data Protection Relating to Classification

As stated previously, Federated Learning is fundamentally centered around user privacy, and therefore, data is stored on client devices. Nevertheless, operating a model on a device poses certain dangers since updating model parameters carries the risk of privacy violations. The updates may consist of sensitive defining characteristics or data biased toward important features of the data centroid. In addressing these issues, FL systems utilize a wide array of methods aimed at enhancing privacy, especially confidentiality within the data lifecycle during the learning process (Jagarlamudi et al., 2024) (Jagarlamudi et al., 2024).

Differential Privacy (DP) is the first attempt in Federated Learning to secure the personal information of users when training a model. DP prevents the influence of a single datum from being visible and statistically identifiable by applying calibrated noise to shared outputs, like gradients or parameters. This implies that the amalgamated data can be protected even under malicious access since no sensitive details about the relevant people will be revealed. The degree of privacy can be adjusted with the so-called privacy budget (ε) which defines how much privacy versus accuracy a model will have (Farooqi et al., 2024).

Another crucial strategy is secure multi-party computation (SMPC). This allows clients to compute a clustered output, such as the summation of model weights, without revealing any of their private data. The possibility of protective conglomeration routines is made possible by SMPC, so that a curious server cannot obtain knowledge about one client's model update independently. Also, homomorphic encryption could be applied to the proposed updates to be encrypted and still allow the server to perform computations without decryption, thus adding more security (Zhou et al., 2024).

Alongside cryptography, Federated Learning (FL) frameworks utilize protective mechanisms such as gateways and secure transmission protocols (TLS/SSL) to limit participation to verified users. The multi-faceted approach to security helps ensure an environment where privacy is both assured and demonstrable (Jalali & Chen, 2023).

These considerations within Federated Learning enable compliance with contemporary legal standards for privacy while permitting collaboration across a vast number of organizations.

3.2 Resistance to Data Breaches and Insider Threats

Data security is enhanced through Federated Learning (FL) since sensitive information is kept on client devices, reducing risks of large-scale breaches. Centralized systems are more susceptible to attacks since aggregating all data creates a single point of failure. FL mitigates this risk by restricting direct exposure to sensitive data. As a result, attackers are forced to compromise individual clients in order to gain access to discrete datasets. This shift in design increases the vulnerability of FL's exposed face to external attacks.

Nonetheless, Federated Learning (FL) brings about new challenges with insider threats. Clients who are able to train data and are considered authorized can perform data poisoning, model inversion, or gradient leakage attacks. Such attacks may corrupt the global model or reveal information that is sensitive and confidential from other participants. Detecting and mitigating insider threats is very difficult due to the default trust placed on client updates within FL systems (Almutairi, & Barnawi, 2023).

To counter these risks, FL systems use defenses such as anomaly detection, reputation systems based on prior contributions, and robust aggregation strategies that vindicate the validity of the clients' submissions. Krum and Trimmed Mean techniques seek to minimize the impact that suspicious revisions have on outcomes, while identity management using blockchain along with zero-knowledge proofs shows great potential for verifying participants without exposing sensitive information.

The combination of architectural decentralization and intelligent security protocols allow Federated Learning to protect sensitive data and counteract cyber threats while safeguarding against potential external and internal risks that compromise trust and integrity within shared AI systems.

3.3 Counteraction to Adversarial Attacks in FL Model

The Federated Learning Models (FLMs) have become gradually more susceptible to attacks that aim to damage the training process or the global model. Although the Fl's default trust on client updates provides some security, it is not easy to attack due to its decentralized nature. Such defenses lack control while needing complete visibility.

i. Model Poisoning Attacks

In order mitigate self-optimizing conflicts regarding violating accuracy thresholds, models need to achieve a balance between autonomy and intervention. This, however, poses a serious risk of some clients launching model poisoning attacks that deteriorate model performance, intentionally or otherwise (Chen et al., 2023). Strategies such as robust aggregation with Krum, Median, or Trimmed Mean are useful to defend against these types of attackers by limiting harmful participants from tampering with the system's performance. Additionally, distrust score-based model assignments further guard against hostile clients by intentionally designating less influential role and seeking out pre-established meaningless suspicious channels.

ii. Backdoor Attacks

Backdoor attacks involve embedding imperceptible triggers hidden inside images that causes models to act in a desired manner but go rogue at some predetermined instances of the model's running time (Wan et al., 2024). Countermeasures include employing exposure techniques along the path of potential backdoor openings and employing anomaly detection strategies that may include client monitoring over time to highlight behavior patterns that appear atypical.

iii. Inference-Time Attacks

Inference-time attacks come into play during the deployment or testing stage of a model when input is altered deceitfully, but without any adjustments made to the underlying model, which leads to outputs that defy expectations (Queyrut et al., 2023). As for defenses, adversarial training at the client level and constraint-based security measures around model fluctuations at the lower bound of acceptable perturbation limits are some strategies.

iv. Data Leakage via Gradients Exploitation:

In Federated Learning, even though the raw data stays local, the gradients transmitted to the server may reveal sensitive information through either gradient leakage or model inversion attacks (Wang et al., 2022). To mitigate such risks, Differential Privacy disables individual contributions by adding noise, while Secure Aggregation facilitates summation of the encrypted updates, such that the server has no access to any client's data.

Likewise, the possibility of monitoring client behavior and trust scoring system assessing clients over time is currently being studied. When used in combination with other measures, they form an integrated defensive strategy that protects against threats in both the training and operational phases.

These protective measures embed advance persistent threats into the framework of the FL pipeline, ensuring that federated models can withstand manipulative attempts and remain reliable, accurate, and secure under adversarial conditions. The core adversarial and cybersecurity challenges commonly faced in AI systems which are proactive and prone to adversaries is described in table 2, with an illustration on supporting practical use cases around privacy-violating contexts Federated Learning can provide beauty fences through in the diverse scenarios from real life.

Table 2. Federated Learning Solutions to Key Cybersecurity and Adversarial AI Challenges

	Challenges	FL-Based Solutions	Use Cases
1.	Centralized Data Breaches	Keeps data decentralized, eliminating central points of failure	Collaborative disease prediction across hospitals.
2.	Privacy & Inference Attacks	Shares only model updates; adds differential privacy.	Mobile keyboard personalization without raw text logs.
3.	Regulatory Non-Compliance	Maintains data locality; aligns with GDPR, HIPAA.	Cross-border fraud detection in global banking.
4.	Insider Threats	Limits internal access to sensitive data.	Internal access control in healthcare data analytics.
5.	Data Silos	Enables secure collaboration without raw data exchange	Cyber threat intelligence sharing among ISPs.
6.	Model Poisoning & Backdoors	Uses robust aggregation and anomaly detection	Securing autonomous vehicle coordination systems.
7.	Lack of Trust in Collaboration	Employs blockchain and secure protocols to ensure trust.	Federated learning across competing financial firms.
8.	Latency & Scalability Constraints	Reduces bandwidth usage; supports edge and asynchronous training	Intrusion detection on IoT edge devices.

The table above summarizes how Federated Learning (FL) addresses core challenges in cybersecurity and privacy. FL manages issues like data leakage, insider risk, and compliance obligations by keeping data untangled, safeguarding model updates, and enabling protected cooperation. Moreover, it increases trust and deepens scalability, expanding its suitability for practical use in medicine, finance, and IoT.

4. APPLICATIONS OF FL IN CYBERSECURITY

Federated Learning (FL) is transforming the field of cybersecurity by permitting the detection and response to threats without the use of raw data. Threats are detected in real-time by training learning algorithms using data collected from critical infrastructures, healthcare systems, and IoT systems. With its decentralized architecture, FL facilitates cooperation among devices or separate organizations as long as data stays confidential. Anomic detection, intrusion prevention, and malware classification are reinforced through the secure construction of models. This part of the work emphasizes the use of FL in solving issues of cybersecurity while upholding privacy and regulatory compliance (Ghimire & Rawat, 2022).

4.1 Secure Healthcare Data Processing

Healthcare frameworks have to meet strict regulatory standards like HIPAA and GDPR when handling sensitive patient information. The traditional approach to machine learning usually involves data collection from multiple clinics or hospitals, which is challenging from a privacy and compliance standpoint. In contrast, Federated Learning enables backend integration of healthcare institutions with a secure model where raw data cannot be disclosed (Rani et al., 2023). In this case, hospitals and medical centers can perform local training of models on advanced clinical texts, images, and lab results and only send model updates to a central server or coordinating node in encrypted or anonymized form. This way, data privacy, confidentiality, and model utility is preserved.

Apart from blurry de-identification, Federated Learning shifts the paradigm of data management in medical systems. Tasks like disease diagnosis, medical imaging, and treatment can be done at both personalized and population levels. Integration of differential privacy, blockchain technologies, and secure aggregation enables better safeguarding of patient data from inference and other contextual attacks (Farooqi et al., 2025). Through enhanced data security, Federated Learning enables the efficient formulation of precise and legally-adhering AI algorithms in health organizations.

4.2 Privacy-Preserving Financial Fraud Detection

Due to the sensitive nature of customer data, financial institutions are at risk of suffering cyber threats. This risk highlights the necessity of incorporating fraud detection models to safeguard customer assets and trust. On the contrary, creating relevant models for fraud detection requires vast datasets from multiple banks, payment service providers, and even non-financial entities, which is a compliance and privacy nightmare. Federated Learning (FL) presents a remarkable solution to manage privacy compliance challenges during disbursed cooperative detection of fraud without requiring direct access to sensitive financial information (Kanamori et al., 2022).

With FL, every institution can train models for simulation on user behavioral and transaction data locally. The FL model allows users to share just the model updates with a main server or peer nodes instead of the raw data. This protects privacy and conflicts with PCI Data Security Standards (DSS) regulations or national banking privacy laws. Further, financial institutions are able to detect emerging fraud activities that are cross-platform or multi-regional in nature. As such fraud response becomes not only rapid but also more accurate.

The risks of data loss and model inversion attacks can be mitigated through the integration of advanced privacy-preserving techniques like secure multiparty computation, homomorphic encryption, and differential privacy into the Federated Learning (FL) architecture. This allows financial entities to effectively cooperate in enhancing fraud detection systems while observing utmost privacy and security with the data (Arora et al., 2024).

4.3 FL for IoT and Edge Security

The Internet of Things (IoT) includes billions of interconnected devices, many of which are situated at the network's edge and have limited processing power and bandwidth. These devices are particularly susceptible to a range of cyber threats, including botnet attacks, denial-of-service, and unauthorized access, highlighting the need for real-time threat detection and adaptive security measures. Federated Learning (FL) offers edge devices the capability to collaboratively train security models while keeping the data decentralized, rendering it a scalable, privacy-protecting solution (Bhavsar et al.,2024).

Any device or edge node can monitor local network traffic, look for sensor anomalies, or analyze behavior patterns within an FL-enabled IoT setting. They may also provide updates to a model that is aimed at intrusions or any malicious activity. This approach avoids adding latency, saves bandwidth, and minimizes the probability of prank data being intercepted or compromised during transmission. An FL framework is ideal in this situation due to its adaptability to local data distributions, support of asynchronous training, and the heterogeneous and dynamically changing nature of IoT ecosystems (Fenanir & Semchedine, 2023).

Also, the application of FL with light cryptographic methods and secure aggregation schemes grant access to learning even to constrained devices. As a result, the empowerment of edge defense and intelligence systems with Federated Learning increases the IoT system's resilience and autonomy. Consequently, the devices are better able to endure advanced cyber-attacks in real time (Imteaj et al., 2021).

4.4 Threat Intelligence Sharing Using FL

Threat intelligence sharing is one of the most important aspects of a cyber-defense strategy since it enables collaborative effort for the early detection, response, and mitigation of emerging cyber risks. This is particularly true when dealing with sensitive logs or proprietary information, as their legal, ethical, and practical approaches make sharing very difficult. Federated Learning offers an alternative solution that enables collaboration in a group context without exposing raw threat information (EL Jaouhari & Etiabi, 2023).

According to Koike et al., 2024, ISPs, business, and public sector institutions could apply Federated Learning (FL) to create and train a shared model at IOCs and network telemetry, in addition to malware signature specific to their region. In doing so, these stakeholders aid in the development of a centralized threat observation model without having to reveal sensitive information that is proprietary to their infrastructure. This bottom-up framework is characterized by strong data sovereignty and the full domain of potential targets to be used for faster and more accurate detection of cyber threat.

Threat intelligence sharing enhanced by Federated Learning (FL) could incorporate concepts such as differential privacy, removal of outliers, trustless verification, and blockchain-based participatory frameworks for ensuring trust, honesty, and accountability. As cyber threats become more intricate and nuanced, the collaborative learning frameworks provided through FL enables scaled responsive defenses while upholding confidentiality, thereby facilitating adaptive collective cyber resilience (Rahman et al., 2024).

Figure 2 shows the core applications of FL in cybersecurity alongside other sectors such as IoT, smart infrastructures, healthcare, finance, and compliance, showcasing the need to address diverse but sector-specific challenges. It also demonstrates the scope of Federated Learning in developing privacy-centric trust frameworks and multi-stakeholder AI systems across different industries.

Figure 2. Application Domains of Federated Learning in Cybersecurity

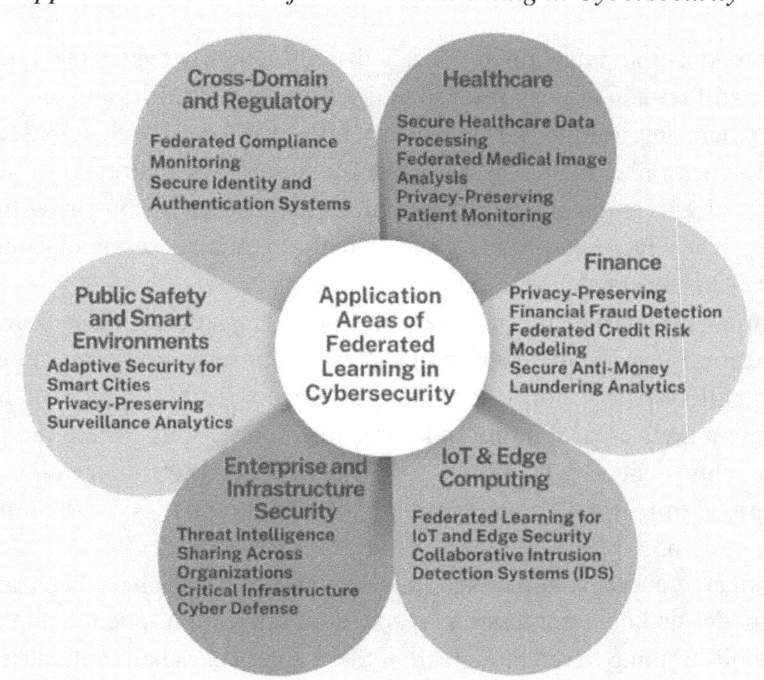

5. CHALLENGES AND GAPS OF FL APPLICATION IN CYBERSECURITY

The very optimistic benefits of FL in cybersecurity applications still have some obstacles which restrict smooth integration. Because of the technical difficulties associated with coordinating a distributed set of clients, providing secure communication, and maintaining consistent model performance in non-IID scenarios, there are problems on the engineering side. Additionally, Federated Learning systems are still vulnerable to many forms of adversarial attacks such as model poisoning and inference attacks, as well as selective and uncooperative participation from the clients. These problems, along with others, are compounded by limited processing resources on edge devices and the substantial communication costs involved in large-scale implementations (Alazab et al., 2021). Addressing these issues is crucial to harnessing the advantages of FL as a secure and scalable option for cybersecurity defenses.

5.1 Communication Overheads and Latency Issues

The broad communication overhead discrepancies between the clients and the server still remain at peak level in Federated Learning. FL, unlike centralized learning where the training occurs locally on a unified dataset, is based on the continual synchronization of model parameters across a multitude of separated units (or devices), requiring extensive tuning. This is especially true with greater bandwidth when increased models and numerous training sessions (rounds) are practiced (Almanifi et al., 2023).

Within an IoT architecture or even on a mobile platform, these demands on communication can impose substantial latency, consume additional power, and hinder overall system performance. Things get worse in heterogeneous networks with different device capabilities and unreliable connections, where the presence of delay clients—clients who either do not fulfill or complete their training within the predefined time or fail to meet training time constraints—slow the progress of the entire system.

To mitigate concerns, numerous optimization techniques have been suggested such as model update compression, sparse communication, client sampling, and asynchronous training. Even though all of these approaches help mitigate the communication overhead, they tend to incur some penalty in terms of convergence and accuracy. Accordingly, the routing of communication in relation to model performance remains a challenging problem when utilizing FL in cybersecurity contexts (Shah & Lau, 2021).

5.2 Risks of Model Poisoning and Gradient Leakage

The use of client devices that are both remote and potentially untrustworthy exposes Federated Learning to diverse new security concerns. The most prominent of these is model poisoning; we have malicious clients who will upload forged updates to destroy the global model or implant backdoors. These attacks tend to be inconspicuous and will be hard to identify in massive scale federated settings due to their lack of server visibility concerning individual data sources, which makes verification of local training integrity impossible (Yazdinejad et al., 2024).

An equally noteworthy issue is privacy susceptibility known as gradient leakage; a form of model updating attacks where protected data may be extracted. There is now abundant literature arguing that individuals with no physical access to sanitized data are able to reconstruct input data and even extract sensitive features from gradient analysis, which poses a serious threat to data confidentiality (Wang et al., 2022; Zafar et al, 2025).

Though differential privacy, blockchain technology, robust aggregation algorithms, and secure multi-party computation techniques provide some level of protection, they inflict trade-offs to model accuracy, efficacy, or scalability. The ongoing challenge is designing defenses that effectively balance all these trade-offs and simultaneously address poisoning and leakage threats. These strategies need to be implemented carefully to build trust in federated learning systems that are used in high-risk scenarios, such as those involving cybersecurity (Zhang et al., 2022).

5.3 Security and Integrity of Model Aggregation

Federated Learning (FL) architecture has two primary steps and the aggregation step, MD-EF-5, is critical to preserving the integrity and trust of the global model. This stage comprises a central server receiving model updates from various clients and merging these iterations by means of Federated Averaging. The refinement process in the current form is inherently dependent on a single coordinating server, which opens up attack vectors such as update-based attacks, aggregation control attacks, or complete server takeover (Qi et al., 2024).

A controlling adversary can tailor the global model to suit global frameworks, give biased injection frameworks or lessen the model's competency in identifying cybersecurity threats. Information transparency issues, especially trust, bring other severe risks in preliminary frameworks opening matters of auditability, controllability, and attribution of responsibility in cross organizational projects forming a net of organizations.

In order to strengthen aggregation security, FL systems increasingly utilize secure aggregation protocols that encrypt or mask client updates. Provable audit trails based on blockchain technology, zero-knowledge proofs, and other forms of aggregation modeling focused on decentralization are also being developed to enhance integrity and resilience. However, these approaches combine with performance and scalability issues, again highlighting secure aggregation as the primary challenge of FL within cybersecurity (So et al., 2023).

5.4 Comparative Perspective: Federated Learning Against Other Privacy Methods

In response to the increased concerns for privacy within AI systems, several privacy-enhancing and decentralized methods have been developed. Here, four core techniques are analyzed: Federated Learning, Federated Analytics, Edge AI, and Collaborative Learning, which, while differing in approach, combine scalability and cybersecurity with a focus on privacy.

i. Federated Learning (FL)

Federated Learning (FL) enables the training of a model in a distributed fashion by ensuring data remains on local devices. Each client trains its local model and only sends the resulting parameters to a central server where the parameters are aggregated. FL facilitates collaborative computation even when the data is non-IID across participants, and is highly scalable; however, it suffers from high communication costs and is vulnerable to poisoning attacks.

ii. Federated Analytics

Federated Analytics relates to the computation of aggregated sums, means, or frequencies from various distributed data sources without having to train complicated and expensive machine learning algorithms. It is more lightweight than FL, requires fewer rounds of communication, and is useful for things like privacy-preserving healthcare reporting. It does not permit full model learning; however, it is limited to gaining statistical insights.

iii. Edge AI

Edge AI encompasses model training and inference occurring entirely on the user end devices, including: connected sensors, mobile phones, and other embedded systems. As data does not leave the local environment, its privacy is guaranteed and low latency operations are enabled. Learning is also confined to single nodes, which creates problems when trying to generalize results across distributed environments. Resource constraints can also limit the complexity of models that can be used.

iv. Collaborative Learning

Collaborative Learning takes the approach of partitioning the model across the clients and the server. The clients perform the initial layers on their local data and send the intermediate representation to the server, which completes the remaining training. This approach afforded high privacy of the data features in the early stage as well as lower data transfer needs. The problem it poses is that it requires stable connections, and also brings operational complexity due to the logistics of splitting the model.

Table 3 summarizes prominent methods of preserving privacy by comparing their features, advantages, disadvantages, and uses in cybersecurity. It illustrates how techniques such as FL, FA, Edge AI, and Collaborative Learning implement various approaches to maintaining privacy and collaboration at different levels of scalability and security.

Table 3. Comparison of Federated Learning with Other Privacy-Preserving AI Techniques

Technique	Description	Advantages	Limitations	Cybersecurity Use Cases
Federated Learning (FL)	Decentralized model training without sharing raw data.	-Enables collaborative training -Supports non-IID data -Scalable to many clients	-Communication overhead -Vulnerable to model poisoning	Cross-organizational threat detection and anomaly detection
Federated Analytics (FA)	Computes aggregate statistics from distributed data sources.	-Lightweight -Requires fewer communication rounds	-Not suitable for complex model training	Privacy-preserving healthcare statistics or usage analytics
Edge AI	Models are trained and executed entirely on edge devices.	-Low latency -Data remains completely local	-Limited learning across nodes -Resource constraints	Real-time IoT device-level anomaly detection
Collaborative Learning	Model is split between client and server; partial computations are shared.	-High privacy for initial layers -Lower data transfer	-Requires continuous connection -Limited scalability	Secure image classification in medical imaging

5.5 Scalability and Regulatory Barriers

While Federated Learning (FL) has seen its potential in cybersecurity and other sensitive fields, the challenge of scaling FL systems to varying environments continues to be a problem. General applications involve the supervision of a heterogeneous network of devices, which can often exceed millions in number. This heterogeneity in system capabilities leads to inconsistent training results, range shrinking trains, and loss of model efficacy, particularly with low-bidis participation and sparse updates (Malik et al., 2024).

Apart from the technical level of scalability, policy constraints also have a noteworthy impact. The General Data Protection Regulation (GDPR) (Sharma, 2019) and HIPAA (Cohen & Mello, 2018) along with numerous national data protection laws offer stringent requirements for the counting, transferring, and processing of data, even when it is stored locally. More often than not, compliant implementation of Federated Learning tends to be laden with audits and transparency which in turn leads to operational silos (Li et al., 2021).

In addition, governance of data across borders can hinder the company's ability of carrying out FL with other international institutions. Differences in laws and policies on privacy, encryption, and security might provide barriers around standardizing FL frameworks. To fully harness the potential of FL towards cyber security, future studies need to focus on the integration of Controlled scalability alongside shifting regulatory frameworks.

6. SOLUTIONS AND FUTURE RESEARCH DIRECTIONS

Both scholars and practitioners continue to create novel solutions to the problems posed by Federated Learning (FL) in the context of cybersecurity. Some of the primary privacy, model robustness, and deployment issues associated with FL are being addressed. There are numerous wide-ranging proposals including secure aggregation, adaptive client participation, blockchain, and federated adversarial training. Alongside other considerations, future research seeks to enhance the interpretability and resource efficiency of FL as well as compliance with complex legal guidelines. This part discusses emerging solutions while also identifying gaps in the literature that seek to promote the understanding of FL as a secure, robust, and scalable solution for cybersecurity challenges.

6.1 Advances in Privacy-Preserving FL Techniques

Due to the importance of privacy in Federated Learning, constant work is being done towards improving data protection techniques and frameworks without hindering the efficiency of the model. Among numerous other developments, one of the most important is the use of differential privacy (DP) within FL pipelines. Differential Privacy (DP) ensures privacy by applying appropriately calibrated noise on model update data. Thus, even the most powerful inference attacks cannot ascertain the value of a particular secret, thus strong mathematical privacy guarantees are assured.

One of the most evolving aspects of Federated Learning works on improving secure aggregation protocols so that the global model can be calculated without revealing individual client updates. Client data is protected using secret sharing, secure multi-party computations (SMPC), and homomorphic encryption (HE). These methods maintain data privacy even when the server is only semi-trusted, or is a malicious actor. Recently, these methods have also been improved to be more efficient, which is ideal for mobile and IoT device implementation.

Other emerging methodologies target adaptive privacy, where privacy budgets can be allocated dynamically based on the sensitivity of a given data set, or the client's level of trust. This capability aids systems in striking the right balance between privacy and performance metrics for the model. Additionally, research focusing on privacy-preserving federated analytics broadens the scope of FL by shifting focus from model training and enabling the secure computation of statistical insights across decentralized datasets.

These developments, when combined, increase the level of privacy, usability, and scalability in Federated Learning, thereby accentuating its use as an approach for privacy-centric secure and trustworthy cybersecurity AI.

6.2 Integrating Blockchain Technology in Secure Federated Learning

Blockchain technology solves several problems associated with decentralized learning in Federated Learning (FL). In particular, it helps build trust and ensure transparency among the active clients. A blockchain stores in a distributed ledger all relevant activities including model updates, client participation, aggregations, and other relevant activities. These records are inherently secure and can be verified, allowing for craftsmanship and trust during the entire learning evolution. This increases the fidelity of FL systems in collaborative or cross-organizational cyber defense situations where there is no trust among participants (Ngoupayou Limbepe et al., 2025; Liu et al., 2024).

One of the examples of changing Federated Learning systems to include blockchain is the immutability, and traceability of contributions to the model. Contribution audits through the logs of updates and aggregation on the blockchain mitigate defacement claims by ensuring no alterations were made without proper authorization. Malignant or uncompliant clients are considered a risk, which these clients can prompt smart contracts through predefined rules to become automatic enforcers of client selection automation, contribution control, rewards, and penalties (Nguyen et al., 2021).

In addition, blockchains enable the creation of incentive structures in federated networks using token systems which reward virtuous behavior and resource contribution. It is especially important in trust-critical systems or confirmatory large scale/ open federated networks where users need to be motivated to contribute. Farooqi et al. (2025) detail how privacy-preserving techniques such as zero knowledge proofs allow sensitive information to remain confidential while still allowing for blockchain utilization.

The integration of blockchain with federated learning (FL) networks carries promise for developing audit-friendly and robust FL frameworks, especially for sensitive areas like cybersecurity (Qu et al., 2022). However, issues like scalability, energy use, and latency still require solutions.

6.3 Adaptive Security Based Reinforcement Learning (RL)

Reinforcement Learning (RL) has proven useful for augmenting the adaptability of Federated Learning (FL) systems, particularly within the rapidly evolving landscape of cybersecurity. Unlike static frameworks, RL permits model agility through learning from past experiences, altering their responses to different levels of threat, client activity, and overall network performance. The combination of FL and RL enables distributed counterpart agents such as edge nodes or intrusion detection systems to act autonomously and contextually act on preserved data (Pinto Neto et al., 2023).

In the context of cybersecurity, RL can shift the client selection process, allocate resources, or customize defenses strategies suited to evolving adversarial steps. As an example, RL policies can actively update from trusted clients, model anomaly detection, and selective application of differential privacy at different risk levels. This enhances the intelligence responsiveness of the FL process to security challenges, particularly with the presence of heterogeneous and unreliable participants (Wang et al., 2023).

In parallel, multi-agent reinforcement learning (MARL) enables collaborative defense in which several agents learn individually and subsequently coordinate their efforts to reinforce system resilience. This is of particular importance in the case of decentralized networks where collaboration needs to take place without sharing the actual data (Albrecht et al., 2024).

RL provides great potential together with FL, but also brings difficulties like increased computational requirements, designing reward signals, and maintaining convergence stability. The active investigations on lightweight and privacy preserving RL algorithms are increasing the possibility of integrating RL with FL. It is correct to say that reinforcement learning poses this challenge, since it seems that incorporating it will be the new focus for responsive and proactive FL based cybersecurity frameworks (Qi et al., 2021).

6.4 Standardization and Regulations Issues

With the integration of new technologies in sensitive domains such as cyber security, the need for clear standards and regulations becomes more crucial. While Federated Learning (FL) attempts to comply with laws like the GDPR and HIPAA, the legal issues that arise from its decentralized structure pose additional difficulties.

Issues such as cross-border data sharing, liability in cooperative frameworks, and the rationale behind the functioning of decentralized systems remain legally and morally problematic (Chalamala et al., 2022).

One major problem is the absence of uniform procedures for the integration of privacy-enhancing techniques, model auditing, and compliance verification on a federated level. Organizations might find it difficult to provide adequate legal compliance on their FL deployments in situations with multiple stakeholders from different regions with varying jurisdictions, risk profiles, as well as organizational cultures. Some efforts in framing compliant and secure documentations for federations have been made by standardization bodies like IEEE, ISO, and NIST, but their works are still at their infancy (Shahbazian, 2023).

Certification and governance frameworks are required to validate regulatory factors for FL systems in sensitive industries. Such frameworks must allocate jurisdiction concerning fault, liability, and breach of duty of care. Meeting increasing expectations around transparency and auditability is possible through blockchain and federated explainability technologies (Chen et al., 2025).

Closing the compliance and standardization gaps is imperative to foster trust and increase the adoption of Federated Learning (FL) in cybersecurity and other critical areas. These frameworks are essential for guiding the use of FL in these sensitive domains. The absence of such frameworks, however, poses challenges for organizations to freely deploy FL regardless of privacy concerns.

7. CONCLUSION

This chapter has shown how Flexible Learning (FL) is changing the paradigm of security in artificial intelligence (AI) by including privacy and collective efforts while enabling practitioners to have advanced secure, private, and robust AI systems. From a real-world perspective, these systems are not only achievable using Federated Learning (FL)— which disallows data exchanging but rather trains models on location information—instead of relying on a central repository of data, enhancing compliance with data protection regulations like HIPAA and GDPR.

We also highlighted how FL is already making a difference in various domains such as healthcare, finance, and IoT. Despite the rapid development of ideas and concepts around FL, many challenges remain unsolved. The issues that require immediate attention include high communication overhead, poor scalability, and relentless security vulnerabilities that continuously risk safety. We also presented supporting evidence for this chapter's claims by showcasing the most prominent flag bearers of these systems. To conclude this chapter, the main points highlighted include the core findings and prospective avenues for further work.

7.1 Key Takeaways

Federated Learning's (FL) potential has grown into an essential building block of AI security as a consequence of an ever interconnected and data heavy world. Traditional centralized learning approaches have had integrating modern needs for security as well privacy frameworks. Through Federated Learning (FL), multiple individuals can collaboratively train models while maintaining privacy, thus solving such healthcare challenges.

- **Decentralized Privacy and Data Sovereignty**

FL supports collaboration between numerous clients for training machine-learning models which use the raw sensitive data of clients for using sophisticated analytical methods. This architecture improves data protection across high-risk fields including IIoT, financial, healthcare professionals, and IoT systems. Clients have less chances of breaching datasets with sensitive details as clients are paramount in retaining dataset governance.

- **Adversarial Resilience and Emerging Threats**

Despite greatly limiting the central attack surface on a system, FL is still vulnerable to advanced centralized attacks like model poisoning, backdoor insertion, and gradient leakage. These risks create a necessity for constant evolutions in secure aggregation structures as well as advanced anomaly detection and differential privacy methods.

- **Cross-Environment Adaptability: Scalability**

FL is flexible and scalable at the same time, as it can manage learning across clients heterogeneously at varying levels of computation and network access. The two remaining challenges are achieving efficient communication and maintaining strong aggregation as the system grows.

- **Trust Building and Compliance with Standards**

By keeping data within definable boundaries and anonymous, FL facilitates compliance with applicable data protection laws like GDPR, HIPAA then CCPA. However, creating a reliable FL ecosystem of trust requires specially designed boundary and operational laws to make security policies, certification policies, and interoperability frameworks trusted beyond sector.

To put it differently, Federated Learning exists on the convergence of machine learning, privacy, and cyber security. It addresses problems related to the safe implementation of AI and facilitates robust multi-actor system collaboration and autonomous decision-making. With the increase in threats along with stringent regulations, Federated Learning can aid in the construction of secure, compliant, and trusted frameworks for AI systems.

Table 4 aims to summarize Federated Learning with a focus toward secure and resilient AI systems detailing the main architectural features and the provided solutions with regard to cybersecurity and privacy issues in distributed learning cyber systems.

Table 4. Key Takeaways on Federated Learning for Secure and Resilient AI Systems

Aspect	Key Insight	Impact on Cybersecurity
Decentralized Privacy	FL enables model training without raw data sharing, strengthening privacy across sectors like healthcare, finance, and IoT.	Reduces data breach risks and protects sensitive information.
Adversarial Resilience	FL lowers centralized risks but remains vulnerable to model poisoning, backdoors, and gradient leakage.	Highlights the need for continuous defense innovation.
Scalability Challenges	FL supports diverse clients but struggles with communication and aggregation as systems grow.	Affects real-world deployment in large, distributed networks.
Regulatory Compliance	By keeping data local, FL helps meet GDPR, HIPAA, and CCPA requirements, though standardization is needed.	Ensures legal compliance and builds trust in federated systems.

7.2 Future Direction and Research Areas

The growth of Federated Learning (FL) has a distinctly multifaceted potential across different domains, particularly in cybersecurity. FL's position is bound to escalate with increasing attention directed towards privacy and distributed intelligence.

- **Combining Blockchain with FL for Trust and Transparency**

The future development of FL is likely to benefit from integrating blockchain to construct decentralized, verifiable audit trails. Such measures ensure participant verification, model aggregation, and malicious poisoning safeguards on the learners. Trust-less participation agreements could also be managed via smart contracts without the need of a controlling party for bolstered trust among several untrusted clients.

- **Proactive and Resilient Defense Strategies**

Emerging more advanced paradigms such as Sybil (multiple fake clients) and slow drift poisoning (subtle slow corruption over time) attacks necessitate that FL systems keep pace with evolving adaptive defenses. Proposed systems should focus on shifting strategies for anomaly detection, reputation systems based on client behaviors, and aggregation strategies shielded from progressive adversarial actions across successive training epochs.

- **Communication Overhead and Edge Performance Improvement**

The communication overhead that comes with Federated Learning (FL) is still a profound challenge, especially considering IoT, mobile edge computing, and other resource-limited contexts. More work must be done to develop light update protocols, as well as asynchronous communication, client resource selection, and time estimation models that enhance accuracy but tailor resource expenditures. For broader adoption of Federated Learning (FL), restrictions on bandwidth use without degrading model performance need to be addressed.

- **Regulatory Compliance and Global Standardization**

The implementation of FL in various sectors dealing with sensitive data makes standard legal policies and operational procedures increasingly necessary. Further research is required on how FL implementations deal with regulatory compliance not only from a local perspective – like GDPR for Europe, HIPAA for the US – but also from an overarching viewpoint with autonomous certification frameworks. Movement toward a unified FL standard would facilitate ethical AI and more seamless international partnerships.

- **Personalized and Adaptive Federated Learning Frameworks**

In order for Federated Learning to function seamlessly in heterogeneous and dynamic conditions, context awareness and adaptability are critical focal points for future systems. Rather than treating each client the same, FL models should attempt to self-adjust and tailor to the distinctive features of each client's data. Furthermore, FL models should continue upholding privacy at all levels. Future works could aid this challenge through meta-learning by teaching models how to adapt efficiently, personalized aggregation methods that make use of local variances, and flexible hybrid structures that respond to changing network and user conditions while maintaining confidentiality over sensitive information.

FL forms a solid base for the design and construction of secure AI systems while still integrating the security of privacy mechanisms. The system is a candidate for further development of AI technologies. It receives praise for their federated techniques and in order to unlock its full capability, the additional works in the privacy mechanisms have to be mutually complementary to strong legal, ethical, and technical boundaries. These works need to focus on increasing federated defenses while reducing the ability to scale, adapting, and relying on the system. With the precision of detailed works done on the techniques of FL, it may stand as a pillar to defend systems in the age of AI.

REFERENCES

Alazab, M., Rm, S. P., Maddikunta, P. K. R., Gadekallu, T. R., & Pham, Q. V. (2021). Federated learning for cybersecurity: Concepts, challenges, and future directions. *IEEE Transactions on Industrial Informatics*, *18*(5), 3501–3509. DOI: 10.1109/TII.2021.3119038

Albrecht, S. V., Christianos, F., & Schäfer, L. (2024). *Multi-agent reinforcement learning: Foundations and modern approaches*. MIT Press.

Aledhari, M., Razzak, R., Parizi, R. M., & Saeed, F. (2020). Federated learning: A survey on enabling technologies, protocols, and applications. *IEEE Access : Practical Innovations, Open Solutions*, *8*, 140699–140725. DOI: 10.1109/ACCESS.2020.3013541 PMID: 32999795

Almanifi, O. R. A., Chow, C. O., Tham, M. L., Chuah, J. H., & Kanesan, J. (2023). Communication and computation efficiency in federated learning: A survey. *Internet of Things : Engineering Cyber Physical Human Systems*, *22*, 100742. DOI: 10.1016/j.iot.2023.100742

Almutairi, S., & Barnawi, A. (2023). Federated learning vulnerabilities, threats and defenses: A systematic review and future directions. *Internet of Things : Engineering Cyber Physical Human Systems*, *24*, 100947. DOI: 10.1016/j.iot.2023.100947

Arora, S., Beams, A., Chatzigiannis, P., Meiser, S., Patel, K., Raghuraman, S., & Zamani, M. (2024, December). Privacy-preserving financial anomaly detection via federated learning & multi-party computation. In *2024 Annual Computer Security Applications Conference Workshops (ACSAC Workshops)* (pp. 270-279). IEEE. DOI: 10.1109/ACSACW65225.2024.00038

Bhavsar, M. H., Bekele, Y. B., Roy, K., Kelly, J. C., & Limbrick, D. (2024). Fl-ids: Federated learning-based intrusion detection system using edge devices for transportation iot. *IEEE Access : Practical Innovations, Open Solutions*, *12*, 52215–52226. DOI: 10.1109/ACCESS.2024.3386631

Bountakas, P., Zarras, A., Lekidis, A., & Xenakis, C. (2023). Defense strategies for adversarial machine learning: A survey. *Computer Science Review*, *49*, 100573. DOI: 10.1016/j.cosrev.2023.100573

Chakraborty, A., Alam, M., Dey, V., Chattopadhyay, A., & Mukhopadhyay, D. (2021). A survey on adversarial attacks and defences. *CAAI Transactions on Intelligence Technology*, *6*(1), 25–45. DOI: 10.1049/cit2.12028

Chalamala, S. R., Kummari, N. K., Singh, A. K., Saibewar, A., & Chalavadi, K. M. (2022). Federated learning to comply with data protection regulations. *CSI Transactions on ICT, 10*(1), 47–60. DOI: 10.1007/s40012-022-00351-0

Chen, C., Liu, J., Tan, H., Li, X., Wang, K. I. K., Li, P., Sakurai, K., & Dou, D. (2025). Trustworthy federated learning: Privacy, security, and beyond. *Knowledge and Information Systems, 67*(3), 2321–2356. DOI: 10.1007/s10115-024-02285-2

Chen, J., Zhao, Y., Li, Q., Feng, X., & Xu, K. (2023). FedDef: Defense against gradient leakage in federated learning-based network intrusion detection systems. *IEEE Transactions on Information Forensics and Security, 18*, 4561–4576. DOI: 10.1109/TIFS.2023.3297369

Cohen, I. G., & Mello, M. M. (2018). HIPAA and protecting health information in the 21st century. *Journal of the American Medical Association, 320*(3), 231–232. DOI: 10.1001/jama.2018.5630 PMID: 29800120

Collins, L., Hassani, H., Mokhtari, A., & Shakkottai, S. (2022). Fedavg with fine tuning: Local updates lead to representation learning. *Advances in Neural Information Processing Systems, 35*, 10572–10586.

Drainakis, G., Pantazopoulos, P., Katsaros, K. V., Sourlas, V., Amditis, A., & Kaklamani, D. I. (2023). From centralized to Federated Learning: Exploring performance and end-to-end resource consumption. *Computer Networks, 225*, 109657. DOI: 10.1016/j.comnet.2023.109657

El Jaouhari, S., & Etiabi, Y. (2023, November). FedCTI: Federated Learning and Cyber Threat Intelligence on the Edge for secure IoT Networks. In *Proceedings of the 13th International Conference on the Internet of Things* (pp. 98-104). DOI: 10.1145/3627050.3627064

Farooqi, S. A., Abd Rahman, A., & Saad, A. (2024, January). Differential privacy based federated learning techniques in IoMT: A review. In *2024 18th International Conference on Ubiquitous Information Management and Communication (IMCOM)* (pp. 1-7). IEEE. DOI: 10.1109/IMCOM60618.2024.10418361

Farooqi, S. A., Abd Rahman, A., & Saad, A. (2025, January). A Theoretical Comparison of Federated Learning with Differential Privacy and Blockchain for Security and Privacy in IoMT. In *2025 19th International Conference on Ubiquitous Information Management and Communication (IMCOM)* (pp. 1-8). IEEE. DOI: 10.1109/IMCOM64595.2025.10857505

Fenanir, S., & Semchedine, F. (2023). Smart intrusion detection in IoT edge computing using federated learning. *Revue d'Intelligence Artificielle*, *37*(5), 1133–1145. DOI: 10.18280/ria.370505

Ghimire, B., & Rawat, D. B. (2022). Recent advances on federated learning for cybersecurity and cybersecurity for federated learning for internet of things. *IEEE Internet of Things Journal*, *9*(11), 8229–8249. DOI: 10.1109/JIOT.2022.3150363

Goldblum, M., Tsipras, D., Xie, C., Chen, X., Schwarzschild, A., Song, D., Madry, A., Li, B., & Goldstein, T. (2022). Dataset security for machine learning: Data poisoning, backdoor attacks, and defenses. *IEEE Transactions on Pattern Analysis and Machine Intelligence*, *45*(2), 1563–1580. DOI: 10.1109/TPAMI.2022.3162397 PMID: 35333711

Imteaj, A., Khan, I., Khazaei, J., & Amini, M. H. (2021). Fedresilience: A federated learning application to improve resilience of resource-constrained critical infrastructures. *Electronics (Basel)*, *10*(16), 1917. DOI: 10.3390/electronics10161917

Jagarlamudi, G. K., Yazdinejad, A., Parizi, R. M., & Pouriyeh, S. (2024). Exploring privacy measurement in federated learning. *The Journal of Supercomputing*, *80*(8), 10511–10551. DOI: 10.1007/s11227-023-05846-4

Jalali, N. A., & Chen, H. (2023). Federated learning security and privacy-preserving algorithm and experiments research under internet of things critical infrastructure. *Tsinghua Science and Technology*, *29*(2), 400–414. DOI: 10.26599/TST.2023.9010007

Jegorova, M., Kaul, C., Mayor, C., O'Neil, A. Q., Weir, A., Murray-Smith, R., & Tsaftaris, S. A. (2022). Survey: Leakage and privacy at inference time. *IEEE Transactions on Pattern Analysis and Machine Intelligence*, *45*(7), 9090–9108. DOI: 10.1109/TPAMI.2022.3229593 PMID: 37015684

Kanamori, S., Abe, T., Ito, T., Emura, K., Wang, L., Yamamoto, S., Phong, L. T., Abe, K., Kim, S., Nojima, R., Ozawa, S., & Moriai, S. (2022). Privacy-preserving federated learning for detecting fraudulent financial transactions in japanese banks. *Journal of Information Processing*, *30*(0), 789–795. DOI: 10.2197/ipsjjip.30.789

Koike, S., Tanaka, H., & Maeda, M. (2024). Federated learning-based ransomware detection via indicators of compromise.

Li, Q., Wen, Z., Wu, Z., Hu, S., Wang, N., Li, Y., Liu, X., & He, B. (2021). A survey on federated learning systems: Vision, hype and reality for data privacy and protection. *IEEE Transactions on Knowledge and Data Engineering*, *35*(4), 3347–3366. DOI: 10.1109/TKDE.2021.3124599

Li, T., Sahu, A. K., Talwalkar, A., & Smith, V. (2020). Federated learning: Challenges, methods, and future directions. *IEEE Signal Processing Magazine*, *37*(3), 50–60. DOI: 10.1109/MSP.2020.2975749

Li, Y., Sani, A. S., Yuan, D., & Bao, W. (2022). Enhancing federated learning robustness through clustering non-iid features. In *Proceedings of the Asian Conference on Computer Vision* (pp. 41-55).

Liu, Y., Jia, Z., Jiang, Z., Lin, X., Liu, J., Wu, Q., & Susilo, W. (2024). BFL-SA: Blockchain-based federated learning via enhanced secure aggregation. *Journal of Systems Architecture*, *152*, 103163. DOI: 10.1016/j.sysarc.2024.103163

Malik, P., Alirajpurwala, T., Kaushal, S., Patidar, T., Indore, I. I. I., & Padlak, S. (2024). Scalability and robustness of federated learning systems: Challenges and solutions. [IJSREM]. *International Journal of Scientific Research in Engineering and Management*, *8*(6), 1–5. DOI: 10.55041/IJSREM35575

Mehta, A. R. (2024). Privacy-Preserving AI: A Survey of Encrypted Techniques. *International IT Journal of Research, ISSN: 3007-6706, 2*(2), 84-94.

Ngoupayou Limbepe, Z., Gai, K., & Yu, J. (2025). Blockchain-Based Privacy-Enhancing Federated Learning in Smart Healthcare: A Survey. *Blockchains*, *3*(1), 1. DOI: 10.3390/blockchains3010001

Nguyen, D. C., Ding, M., Pham, Q. V., Pathirana, P. N., Le, L. B., Seneviratne, A., Li, J., Niyato, D., & Poor, H. V. (2021). Federated learning meets blockchain in edge computing: Opportunities and challenges. *IEEE Internet of Things Journal*, *8*(16), 12806–12825. DOI: 10.1109/JIOT.2021.3072611

Pinto Neto, E. C., Sadeghi, S., Zhang, X., & Dadkhah, S. (2023). Federated reinforcement learning in IoT: Applications, opportunities and open challenges. *Applied Sciences (Basel, Switzerland)*, *13*(11), 6497. DOI: 10.3390/app13116497

Qi, J., Zhou, Q., Lei, L., & Zheng, K. (2021). Federated reinforcement learning: Techniques, applications, and open challenges. *arXiv preprint arXiv:2108.11887.*

Qi, P., Chiaro, D., Guzzo, A., Ianni, M., Fortino, G., & Piccialli, F. (2024). Model aggregation techniques in federated learning: A comprehensive survey. *Future Generation Computer Systems*, *150*, 272–293. DOI: 10.1016/j.future.2023.09.008

Qu, Y., Uddin, M. P., Gan, C., Xiang, Y., Gao, L., & Yearwood, J. (2022). Blockchain-enabled federated learning: A survey. *ACM Computing Surveys*, *55*(4), 1–35. DOI: 10.1145/3524104

Queyrut, S., Schiavoni, V., & Felber, P. (2023, July). Mitigating adversarial attacks in federated learning with trusted execution environments. In *2023 IEEE 43rd International Conference on Distributed Computing Systems (ICDCS)* (pp. 626-637). IEEE. DOI: 10.1109/ICDCS57875.2023.00069

Rahman, S., Pal, S., Jadidi, Z., & Karmakar, C. (2024). Robust Cyber Threat Intelligence Sharing Using Federated Learning for Smart Grids. *IEEE Transactions on Computational Social Systems.*

Rani, S., Kataria, A., Kumar, S., & Tiwari, P. (2023). Federated learning for secure IoMT-applications in smart healthcare systems: A comprehensive review. *Knowledge-Based Systems, 274*, 110658. DOI: 10.1016/j.knosys.2023.110658

Said, A., Yahyaoui, A., & Abdellatif, T. (2023, November). HIPAA and GDPR compliance in IoT healthcare systems. In *International conference on model and data engineering* (pp. 198-209). Cham: Springer Nature Switzerland.

Shah, S. M., & Lau, V. K. (2021). Model compression for communication efficient federated learning. *IEEE Transactions on Neural Networks and Learning Systems, 34*(9), 5937–5951. DOI: 10.1109/TNNLS.2021.3131614 PMID: 34936557

Shahbazian, R. (2023). Enhancing IoT Security through Standardization: A Review. *Advances in the Standards & Applied Sciences, 1*(4).

Sharma, S. (2019). *Data privacy and GDPR handbook.* John Wiley & Sons. DOI: 10.1002/9781119594307

So, J., Ali, R. E., Güler, B., Jiao, J., & Avestimehr, A. S. (2023, June). Securing secure aggregation: Mitigating multi-round privacy leakage in federated learning. *Proceedings of the AAAI Conference on Artificial Intelligence, 37*(8), 9864–9873. DOI: 10.1609/aaai.v37i8.26177

Wan, Y., Qu, Y., Ni, W., Xiang, Y., Gao, L., & Hossain, E. (2024). Data and model poisoning backdoor attacks on wireless federated learning, and the defense mechanisms: A comprehensive survey. *IEEE Communications Surveys and Tutorials, 26*(3), 1861–1897. DOI: 10.1109/COMST.2024.3361451

Wang, H., Kaplan, Z., Niu, D., & Li, B. (2020, July). Optimizing federated learning on non-iid data with reinforcement learning. In *IEEE INFOCOM 2020-IEEE Conference on computer communications* (pp. 1698-1707). IEEE. DOI: 10.1109/INFOCOM41043.2020.9155494

Wang, J., Guo, S., Xie, X., & Qi, H. (2022, May). Protect privacy from gradient leakage attack in federated learning. In *IEEE INFOCOM 2022-IEEE Conference on Computer Communications* (pp. 580-589). IEEE. DOI: 10.1109/INFOCOM48880.2022.9796841

Wang, T., Zheng, Z., & Lin, F. (2025). Federated learning framework based on trimmed mean aggregation rules. *Expert Systems with Applications*, *270*, 126354. DOI: 10.1016/j.eswa.2024.126354

Wen, J., Zhang, Z., Lan, Y., Cui, Z., Cai, J., & Zhang, W. (2023). A survey on federated learning: Challenges and applications. *International Journal of Machine Learning and Cybernetics*, *14*(2), 513–535. DOI: 10.1007/s13042-022-01647-y PMID: 36407495

Wink, T., & Nochta, Z. (2021, June). An approach for peer-to-peer federated learning. In *2021 51st Annual IEEE/IFIP International Conference on Dependable Systems and Networks Workshops (DSN-W)* (pp. 150-157). IEEE. DOI: 10.1109/DSN-W52860.2021.00034

Yazdinejad, A., Dehghantanha, A., Karimipour, H., Srivastava, G., & Parizi, R. M. (2024). A robust privacy-preserving federated learning model against model poisoning attacks. *IEEE Transactions on Information Forensics and Security*, *19*, 6693–6708. DOI: 10.1109/TIFS.2024.3420126

Zafar, U., Teixeira, A., & Toor, S. (2025). Robust Federated Learning Against Poisoning Attacks: A GAN-Based Defense Framework. *arXiv preprint arXiv:2503.20884.*

Zhang, C., Xie, Y., Bai, H., Yu, B., Li, W., & Gao, Y. (2021). A survey on federated learning. *Knowledge-Based Systems*, *216*, 106775. DOI: 10.1016/j.knosys.2021.106775 PMID: 34909232

Zhang, J., Li, C., Ye, J., & Qu, G. (2020, September). Privacy threats and protection in machine learning. In *Proceedings of the 2020 on Great Lakes Symposium on VLSI* (pp. 531-536). DOI: 10.1145/3386263.3407599

Zhang, J., Zhu, H., Wang, F., Zhao, J., Xu, Q., & Li, H. (2022). Security and privacy threats to federated learning: Issues, methods, and challenges. *Security and Communication Networks*, *2022*(1), 2886795. DOI: 10.1155/2022/2886795

Zhang, Z., Ning, H., Shi, F., Farha, F., Xu, Y., Xu, J., Zhang, F., & Choo, K. K. R. (2022). Artificial intelligence in cyber security: Research advances, challenges, and opportunities. *Artificial Intelligence Review*, *55*(2), 1–25. DOI: 10.1007/s10462-021-09976-0

Zhao, Y., Li, M., Lai, L., Suda, N., Civin, D., & Chandra, V. (2018). Federated learning with non-iid data. *arXiv preprint arXiv:1806.00582*.

Zhong, Z., Bao, W., Wang, J., Zhu, X., & Zhang, X. (2022). Flee: A hierarchical federated learning framework for distributed deep neural network over cloud, edge, and end device. [TIST]. *ACM Transactions on Intelligent Systems and Technology*, *13*(5), 1–24. DOI: 10.1145/3514501

Zhou, I., Tofigh, F., Piccardi, M., Abolhasan, M., Franklin, D., & Lipman, J. (2024). Secure multi-party computation for machine learning: A survey. *IEEE Access : Practical Innovations, Open Solutions*, *12*, 53881–53899. DOI: 10.1109/ACCESS.2024.3388992

Chapter 11
Role of Federated Learning in Enhancing Security

Umme Ayeman Saqib Gani
https://orcid.org/0009-0000-2095-1100
Priyadarshini College of Engineering, India

ABSTRACT

Federated Learning (FL), which prioritises data privacy and reduces centralised risks, has emerged as a revolutionary technique for enhancing security in distributed machine learning systems. As opposed to traditional methods that rely on aggregating raw data, FL ensures that sensitive data remains localised while enabling cooperative model training across scattered devices. This study carefully looks at the critical role FL plays in addressing significant security issues like data breaches, hostile assaults, and regulatory compliance. At the centre of this discussion is an analysis of key techniques like secure aggregation, homomorphic encryption, and differential privacy, which collectively defend FL systems against malicious attacks while preserving model accuracy.The utility of FL is demonstrated by its application in sensitive domains such as healthcare, where patient data is protected during cooperative model training.

1. INTRODUCTION

Federated Learning (FL) has presented itself as a radical solution to enhance the security of distributed machine learning systems that maintains privacy of data as well as minimizes centralized dangers. Unlike the conventional techniques whose practice requires the need for aggregation of raw data, FL guarantees that the sensitive

DOI: 10.4018/979-8-3373-2200-1.ch011

data remain local and it enables cooperative model training regarding the distributed devices. This decentralised architecture lowers the probability of unauthorized access and data breach because this reduces the attack surface. However the following are distinctive security risks with FL quotient are Byzantine and model poisoning adversarial attacks which are aimed at distorting the global model or stopping convergence. These shortcomings except for FLs built in privacy keeping capabilities, which are compliant with regulatory frameworks like GDPR and HIPAA, making FL a potential good candidate as a privacy compliant AI solution to resolve issues in highly secured domains like cybersecurity, healthcare, and finance. (Alberto Blanco-Justicia, 2021) . The secure aggregation differential privacy and the cryptographic protocols, homomorphic encryption, among others, improve and secure FL respectively. These precautions, however, right these ensure that even the model updates, which are released during training, cannot leak personal information and improve new generation defense against malevolent against actors. As an example, differential privacy adds noise to updates to thwart inference attacks, while secure multi-party computation (SMPC) enables the aggregation of updates without disclosing individual contributions. Nevertheless, certain privacy-preserving techniques (such as SMC) may conflict with security features. like anomaly detection, making it still challenging to achieve security and privacy in FL. Future research areas will combine FL with state-of-the-art technologies like blockchain for decentralized trust and edge computing for real-time threat adaptation to develop scalable, secure, and privacy-conscious AI systems.

In distributed machine learning, federated learning (FL) has become a paradigm shift, especially in fields with strict data protection laws, like digital healthcare. Traditional centralized FL systems are effective, but they have significant drawbacks, including single points of failure, communication bottlenecks, and the potential for hostile servers to leak gradients. The efficacy and security of the system are compromised by these limitations, especially when handling sensitive data. To address these problems, decentralized FL frameworks have been proposed, such as the robust decentralised deep federated learning (RPDFL) system that protects privacy. The topology used by RPDFL is ring-based and advanced cryptographic techniques like threshold secret sharing to enhance security and ensure dependable and private model training even in dynamic settings where users may stop participating

(Youliang Tian, 2024). Applications like healthcare, where data sharing between companies is limited by privacy regulations like GDPR, benefit greatly from FL's security enhancements. FL lessens the risks of illegal access and data breaches by making it possible to train models cooperatively without exchanging raw data. By allowing the absence of the necessity of the central server, the decentralised FL designs also encourage scalability, as well as lower sensitivity to attacks. Methods like the use of Ring-Allreduce, Chinese Remainder Theorem (CRT) for effective private aggregation of model changes all increase security of the process. The presented RPDFL seems to preserve a marvel of the model accuracy and convergence while maintaining confidentiality which makes FL a cornerstone in secure distributed machine learning in places where privacy is to be protected.

The ability of Generative Adversarial Networks (GANs) to generate realistic data has catapulted them into the leading edge of the explosive growth of machine learning, especially in the production of synthetic data. However, data spread to several companies and each of them must adhere to privacy/confidentiality laws GAN training sometimes encounters problems when centralized. Federated learning (FL), a decentralized alternative allows for collaborative model training without the need to share data directly. Still, simply FL can be susceptible to privacy-brokenness like membership inference attack, enabling adversaries to model back private data from shared model variants (Ali Reza Ghavamipour, 2023). In order to solve these problems, this study recommends usage of PP-FedGAN, a hybrid architecture integrating homomorphic encryption (CKKS) and differential privacy (DP) in order to facilitate security in federated GAN training. With the help of this combination of techniques, PP- FedGAN can provide scalable accommodation to the industries like healthcare and finance where stringent data protection is necessary at the cost of strong privacy guarantees and model usefulness. In-depth tests of the framework in real-world datasets show its effectiveness and that it outperforms existing approaches on performance and security.

1.1 Importance of Security in Federated Learning

Sensitive to privacy industries like healthcare, banking or smart devices are attracted to federated learning (FL) because it enables cooperative but also protects local raw data, model training across scattered devices or organisations. Rather than the raw data one should share model updates but does not close security hole. Attackers not only exploit weaknesses in the FL pipeline, but they use it to change model behaviour, compromise training data, or reveal private information. Without robust safeguards, FL systems could inadvertently divulge private data, violate legal obligations, and undermine trust in distributed artificial intelligence.

These risks are demonstrated by real-world examples. In 2021, researchers showed that gradient inversion attacks could potentially rebuild high-resolution medical images using FL-trained models. This would be very risky for hospitals sharing patient diagnostic updates. Financial institutions that use FL for fraud detection may also inadvertently expose transaction patterns if model gradients are intercepted. It has been demonstrated that membership inference attacks, in which adversaries ascertain whether the training data of a particular individual, can succeed even in differentially private FL systems if privacy budgets are not appropriately adjusted.

These risks highlight the limitations of relying solely on encryption or basic noise insertion for data transmission .(Jinhua Li, 2024).

2. BACKGROUND AND RELATED WORK

In order to preserve privacy, the authors of (Xuanyu Cao, 2023) stress the importance of the goal of distributed learning in next-generation intelligent networks is to train models cooperatively among intelligent agents without the need for centralised raw data processing.. It does, however, draw attention to the problem of high communication overhead in resource-constrained wireless systems, which calls for the development of distributed learning algorithms that are effective at communicating. The authors of (Mingzhe Chen, Zhaohui Yang, 2021) offer a thorough analysis of FL algorithm training in authentic wireless network situations. They solve the combined optimisation problem of learning, wireless resource allocation, and user selection. The authors of (Zihan Chen, Jundong Li, 2023) propose a novel personalised FL algorithm, FEDACS, which emphasises collaboration among clients with similar data distributions to overcome the problems of non-IID data and data scarcity. An attention-based method of client selection is introduced by this algorithm. A GNN-based approach for DFL in D2D wireless networks is presented by the authors of (Chuiyang Meng, 2023) in order to enhance learning performance and decrease overall training delay. The proposed method incorporates a multi-head graph attention mechanism to capture various client and channel features, and a neighbour selection module that enables clients to choose participating neighbours in model aggregation. Recent literature has already documented DP deployment in FL environments. In particular, by introducing the idea of user-level differential privacy, the authors of (K. Wei, J. Li,2022) present a solution to privacy issues that arise in FL. The author of (Mamoun Alazab,2022) discusses three key elements that have greatly influenced the efficacy and broad application of machine learning (ML) techniques in the modern era. The first essential component is the availability of Big Data, which is gathered from various fields like mobile networking and image processing. The second component comes from newer learning models and recent advances in processing power. The third factor is the evolution of machine learning (ML) models and computing equipment from deep learning (DL) models, which have been used recently to indulge intelligence. One excellent illustration of the successful application of DL models is the board game Alpha-Go (1). The following are the primary causes of the majority of domains' inability to use machine learning in real time, despite its high success rate: 1) Users are more concerned about data privacy; 2) User data confidentiality is at risk because the server should gather the data for central learning; and 3) the enormous amount of data and processing power at the network edge is not being effectively used to improve learning.

There are still many privacy and confidentiality issues that need to be addressed, despite the fact that many companies provide highly qualified machine learning models to teach at lower computational costs.

Federated learning (FL) has been suggested as a promising machine learning concept to address the aforementioned issues. From a conceptual standpoint, Without exchanging data with the central server, FL enables multiple devices to learn a collaborative machine learning model (] J. Koneˇ cný, H. B. McMahan, 2016). In contrast to the central learning concept, which calls for all devices to send their data to the server for central storage and central learning, FL has the potential to address privacy concerns, reduce latency, and enhance scalability and reliability. With its edge computing capabilities, the learning server only needs to manage model aggregation and broadcasting, allowing these features. Learning and computing activities are distributed across a large number of networked devices. FL has also found many uses in the field of cybersecurity. Numerous attack types, including malware, intrusion detection, denial of service (DoS), zero-day attacks, and system flooding, are frequently encountered in cybersecurity. For instance, data collection and storage from edge and Internet-of-things (IoT) devices are necessary for the traditional intrusion detection system. Such centralised learning is ineffective due to a number of factors, such as the learning load on the centralised server, high communication and latency costs, and a reluctance to divulge private information (S. A. Rahman, 2020).

3. FUNDAMENTALS OF FEDERATED LEARNING

3.1. Overview of FL mechanisms

Federated Learning (FL) is a novel distributed machine learning framework that enables collaborative model training while effectively protecting locality and data privacy. Unlike conventional centralized learning models that require data aggregation, Multiple dispersed entities, such as edge devices, healthcare systems, and financial institutions, are made possible by FL, to collaboratively improve a global model while maintaining their private datasets on-premises. Participants in the paradigm compute model updates locally using their native data through an iterative process. For safe aggregation, they subsequently forward only the learned parameters—not the raw data—to a central coordinator. At the same time, this innovative strategy solves three serious issues faced by modern AI systems: First, it will hold data confidentiality at a high level in line with increasing privacy standards such as GDPR and HIPAA; (2) reduce communication costs associated with massive data transfers; and (3) encourage knowledge sharing across possibly varying data distributions. Among the crucial technical aspects that enhance the efficiency of FL systems are sophisticated aggregation algorithms (including Federated Averaging and its variations), robust privacy-protecting methods (e.g., secure multi-party computation and differential privacy), and sophisticated tools addressing statistical discrepancies between participating clients. Due to the above, the FL has emerged as a key approach for privacy sensitive applications, from intelligent user interfaces and customised medicine to industrial IoT systems and financial risk assessment.

Beyond privacy, FL makes a difference through solutions of problems in distributed computing and edge ecosystems. By decentralizing model training, FL enhances scalability, reduces latency and supports the real-time learning on limiting-resource devices. Yet, its usage will bring new areas of the research such as resilience to adversarial attacks, the attitude towards the diverse distributions of data, and communication-efficient optimisation. Its adjustability is illustrated with recent innovations like cross-silo FL for enterprise partnerships and federated transfer learning. There has been another boost in the use of TensorFlow Federated and Flower frameworks. By the integration with latest in technology such as blockchain for trust less aggregation and homomorphic encryption for extra security, FL is promising to usher in new developments in collaborative AI without compromising on the strict privacy promises. This paradigm change in thinking makes focused learning a major enabler for the next generation of distributed machine learning systems that seek to guard privacy.

3.2. Architecture of Federated Learning System

Similar to a team report, federated learning enables multiple individuals to remotely share their data in order to collaboratively train a single deep learning model, improving iteratively. The model, which is frequently a pre-trained foundation model, is downloaded by each participant from a cloud data centre. They condense and encrypt the modified configuration after feeding the model their personal data. The model updates are incorporated into the main model after they have been decrypted, averaged, and uploaded back to the cloud. The collaborative training process continues through iterations until the model is completely trained. as shown in **Figure: 1** below.

Figure 1. The Collaborative Training Process in Federated Learning

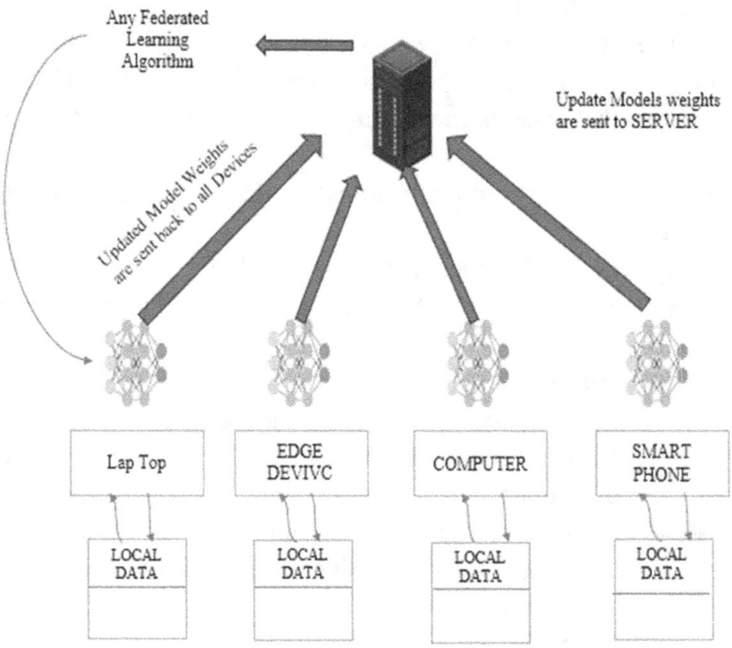

Federated learning (FL) is a decentralised machine learning method where a number of devices, or nodes, collaborate to create a model. while maintaining localised data. The architecture depicted in **Figure: 1** is designed to minimise data transit, leverage distributed computing resources, and handle privacy concerns. Below is a summary of a federated learning system's key components and architecture.

1. Essential Elements
    a) **Clients (Edge Devices or Nodes):** These comprise Internet of Things devices, local servers, and cell phones that participate in the federated learning process. Each client keeps its own private dataset and trains models locally. Sensors, smartphones, and hospital patient data are a few examples.
    b) **Central Server (Aggregator):** Federated Learning is supervised by a central server. The raw data kept on clients is not directly accessible to it. Its main responsibilities include promoting the global model and collecting client model updates.
    c) **Global Model:** This is the shared model that all clients are taught together. The server uses the collective input from all of the clients to update and maintain this model.

d) **Local Model:** Each client trains a local version of the global model using its own data; after training, the client only sends model updates, like weights or gradients, to the server.

e) **Communication Protocol:** It describes how clients and the server communicate, including how updates are sent and received, and it ensures that the server and its clients can communicate securely and effectively.

The following steps are commonly found in the architecture of a Federated Learning system:

Step 1: Setup: A global model with either random or pre-trained weights is initialised by the central server. All of the clients, who involve each, obtain a copy of the global model.

Step 2: Local Training: the global model will be downloaded from server to each client. The client trains their model from their own private dataset, locally. Stochastic gradient descent is one of the machines learning techniques which are popular when used for training.

Step 3: Model update: The client will instead use their own local data to calculate updates (weights or gradients) after local training. It is not raw data that's going to the server; it is updates.

Step 4: Aggregation: The server collects notification updates from all clients employed in this. The combination of these updates improves the global model. Federated averaging (FedAvg) is a weighted average of the local model updates that happen to be one of the common aggregation approaches. **Secure Aggregation:** This technique ensures privacy by overlapping updates such that the server cannot get to individual contributions.

Step 5: Global Model Update: The server makes an update of the global model from the aggregate update.

A copy of the revised global model updated to correspond to the next training session is then sent to each of the clients.

Step 6: Iteration: The steps from 2 to 5 are taken many times until the global model converge to ideal solution.

3.3.Key Algorithms of Federated Learning

3.3.1. Federated Averaging (FedAvg)

The Federated Averaging (FedAvg) algorithm that has been proposed by McMahan et al. (2017), represents the backbone of FL. This one allows the decentralised clients to be able to share training for a cooperative model while maintaining the data privacy through keeping the raw data local. FedAvg diverges from centralised datasets in the fact that the successive updates are used to generate a global model from each of the clients that computed its model updates locally. The given solution becomes most effective in cases when there is no access to data for logistical, legal or privacy reasons. FedAvg's main benefits include: **Privacy Protection:** Client's raw data stays on them; models are updated. **Communication Efficiency:** Less bandwidth is needed as compared to centrally based training. **Scalability:** Allows performing extensive distributed training on multiple devices.

Mathematical Formulation: Let $\mathscr{K}$ be the group of participants chosen for training in round **t,** and let be the global model at round . Using stochastic gradient descent (SGD) over its private dataset , each participant **k** updates its local model : = – (), where η is the rate of learning and () is the local loss function, which is defined as follows:: () = where the model prediction is denoted by and the loss function by . The server combines the models from each participant using a weighted average after local updates.: = where is the dataset size of participant k.

FedAvg is computationally efficient and works well when participant data distributions are approximately IID. However, its performance declines in non-IID environments or when participant datasets are highly unbalanced. In response, researchers have proposed variants like FedProx, which introduces a proximal term to stabilise convergence under heterogeneity.

3.3.2. Federated Stochastic Gradient Descent or (FedSGD)

A more straightforward option to FedAvg is FedSGD, in which users compute gradients locally and submit them straight to the server for aggregation.

Mathematical Formulation:

The gradient of the loss function is calculated by each participant k. ():=()

The server aggregates these gradients to update the global model: = –

Compared to FedAvg, FedSGD may have higher communication costs because players and the server communicate more frequently. It is theoretically sound, but for large-scale FL systems, its inefficiency makes it less practical.

3.3.3. Multi-Task Learning Approaches

In highly diverse environments, users can adapt the global model to fit their local data distributions by using personalised FL techniques. For example, Per-FedAvg (Personalised Federated Averaging) is a FedAvg extension that incorporates meta-learning ideas to enable personalisation. The technique alternates between global updates and local fine-tuning: = – (), followed by fine-tuning on the local dataset: = – (), where α and β are learning rates for global and local updates, respectively.

The limitations of a single global model are addressed in non-IID situations by customised approaches like Per-FedAvg, which enable participants to benefit from shared knowledge while maintaining local adaptability.

3.3.4. Asynchronous Federated Learning

By enabling participants to update the global model at different times, asynchronous FL makes scalability and idle time both better.

Mathematical Formulation:

The server supports the gradual update of the global model during asynchronous FL each time a participant completes its local update: = + , where is local update from participant ***k***, and is a factor of weighting (e.g., dataset size or staleness).

Such strategy is particularly useful in locations with unreliable or intermittent connectivity. However, to tackle problems such as stale updates and convergence problems, adaptive weighting or staleness-aware aggregation are necessary.

3.3.5. Hierarchical Federated Learning

Hierarchical FL prevents communication bottlenecks through presence of intermediary initiating node (e.g., edge server) that collects updates first before forwarding them to the main serving node.

Mathematical Formulation:

Let **S** denote the set of edge servers and the set of participants that are connected to edge server ***i***. The edge server compiles participant updates: = . Afterwards, all updates are aggregated by the central server.: = , Hierarchical FL suits large IoT or mobile network installations because it minimizes latency and increases scalability.

4. SECURITY CHALLENGES IN FEDERATED LEARNING (FL)

Federated learning (FL) is a decentralised machine learning method that allows for data locality to be maintained while several individuals can work together to train a shared model. This approach is especially beneficial in the security of data privacy due to the lack of need for transferring private data to the centralized server so, this approach can be used for IoT, healthcare and financial application. FL has a number of security issues that have to be taken care of for the system to be resilient. Among the most serious sources of concern are adversarial attacks like inference attacks where attackers try to deduce private information from shared gradients, and model poisoning where malicious individuals share poisons updates to modify global models. Furthermore, communication blockages and uneven data distribution for devices make it difficult to install secure FL systems (Li et al., 2002. Yang et al., 2019).

The researchers have recommended amongst others safe multi-party computation, differential privacy, and two reliable aggregation techniques such as Byzantine resilient algorithms to render these fears moot. In general, such strategies develop FL framework security and privacy without affecting their model accuracy and efficiency. Despite the above-mentioned advancements, people still struggle to create a proper balance between privacy, security and performance to create a real-world operational management of the FL (Kairouz et al. 2019). Such issues of concern must be addressed to ensure better trust and federated learning can be scaled usefully in practice.

4.1. Major Security Challenges in Federated Learning

4.1.1. Poisoning Attacks

Poisoning of data and poisoning of the model are two of the most studied risks in FL. Data poisoning is the activity of changing local data sets to corrupt the global model (Bagdasaryan et al., 2020). Model Poisoning, which often uses the well-designed gradients in order to create backdoors or to cause specific misclassification, corrupts directly the model update before distribution (Bhagoji et al., 2019). The performance of a model can be greatly diminished, even with the influence of just a fraction of malicious clients if aggregation rules are weak as recent research, Sun et al., 2021 has established.

4.1.2. Inference and Reconstruction Attacks

Although FL does not expose raw data, even model changes (gradients) can be compromising. Attackers can: Employ Membership Inference Attacks to identify whether a specific record was a member of the set of training data (Nasr et al., 2019). Model Inversion Attacks are employed to copy client inputs from shared updates (Zhu et al., 2019). The attacks grow even more serious where anonymity is reduced because of complex models and few participation numbers.

4.1.3. Byzantine Failures

Byzantine clients randomly or maliciously interrupt training by providing erroneous model updates (Blanchard et al., 2017). Byzantine attacks can be random (noise injection) or targeted (optimising harmful objectives). In extreme cases, a few Byzantine clients can steer global models towards adversarial goals (Baruch et al., 2019).

4.1.4. Communication Attacks

FL depends on the server and clients having secure communication. Potential risks include:

Man-in-the-Middle (MitM) attacks entail intercepting or altering model updates (Bonawitz et al., 2017). Replay Attacks: Learning processes may become confused if previously valid changes are sent again. Without encryption and secure session management, FL systems are vulnerable.

4.2. Attack Surfaces in Federated Learning

FL adds multiple dimensions to the conventional machine learning attack surface:

4.2.1 Local Devices:

Endpoints like smartphones and Internet of Things gadgets are susceptible.
Risk: Malware may alter local datasets or model training protocols.

4.2.2 Communication Channels:

During communication between a server and its clients, data such as model weights and gradients may be intercepted or changed. Replay attacks, gradient leakage, and communication jamming are among the dangers.

4.2.3 Aggregation Server:

Aggregation Server Even if an unprotected server isn't malicious, it can become a major point of failure. Risks include unauthorised aggregation, data modification, and leakage.

4.2.4 Global Model:

Following training, the global model itself may disclose information about the training data (property inference attacks). Risk: Violation of privacy even if raw data is not accessible.

4.2.5 Design of Protocols:

Protocols with inadequate encryption, authentication, or verification processes are vulnerable. Risk: Protocol attacks in which adversaries take advantage of bugs in update rules, or client selection.

5. METHODS FOR PRIVACY-PRESERVING IN FEDERATED LEARNING

There should be privacy preserving approaches for dealing with intrinsic privacy hazards of Federated Learning (FL). FL or Federated learning that leaves raw data at the devices themselves, by its nature, it protects privacy of user data. However, there are still vectors through which key information could play out during the model update exchange: Attacks based on property inference (Ganju et al.,2018), attacks based on membership inference (Shokriet al., 2017) and gradient inversion attacks (Zhu, et al., 2019). It has been seen that three primary privacy preserving strategies are adopted in order to reduce these risks as shown in **Table 1.**

Table 1. Privacy-Preserving Techniques in FL

Technique	Privacy Guarantee	Computational Overhead	Use Case
Secure Aggregation	Heuristic	Moderate	Cross-device FL
Homomorphic Encryption	Cryptographic	High	Cross-silo FL
Differential Privacy	Mathematical	Low-Medium	Regulatory compliance

5.1 Secure Aggregation (SecAgg)

A cryptographic protocol was designed called Secure Aggregation (SecAgg) that allows safe aggregations of local model updates from multiple players, without revealing individual contributions, to protect privacy in Federated Learning (FL). In FL, gradients or model updates are locally calculated, transmitted to a central server to be aggregated. Vulnerable information regarding the underlying data could be revealed by direct sharing of these changes. SecAgg solves this problem by letting users encrypt their updates so that each update is private and there is thus only so much the server can decrypt the output back into the entire output.

Masking and unmasking are usually the two main processes of the process. In masking, a secret key or random noise is added by each participant to his or her local update to make encrypted update random to other users. The server brings together each participant's masked changes as a single global update. Updates with masks: Client i sends: $= w_i + - \mathbf{mod}\ R$. The unmasking experience involves the collaborative process of stripping off noise or keys in such a way as to conceal individual contributions leaving the real aggregated result. This helps to protect the privacy of participants by making sure that server learns only the final aggregate.

Using such techniques as paired masking and additive secret sharing, one of the most commonly used SecAgg applications is one in which the players collaborate in sharing partial secrets in order to collectively generate the end aggregate. While SecAgg offers good privacy guarantees, there is a computational and communication price, particularly when the number of paper signers increases. Two other complications for SecAgg to be viable in real-world scenarios are managing dropouts; or participants who leave while the process takes place, and also the ability to resist malicious players (Bonawitz et al., 2017).

5.2 Homomorphic Encryption (HE) in Federated Learning(FL)

Calculations can be performed directly on encrypted data without first decrypting it thanks to a powerful cryptographic technique known as homomorphic encryption (HE), Because HE allows users to encrypt their local model updates prior to sending them to the central server. it offers a robust privacy-preserving technique in the context of Federated Learning (FL).The server can then combine these encrypted updates and perform any required computations, like averaging or summing, while the data is still encrypted. Since only the final aggregated output is decrypted, individual contributions are kept private at every stage.

Concealing information even as computations are carried out is the greatest advantage of HE. In the case where FL players use the gradients by encrypting them using an additive homomorphic encryption method, for instance, it yet without seeing the raw updates, the server is capable of computing the sum of encrypted gradients. This ensures that no private data relating to the training data below will ever be shared. But since the encryption and decryption are too complex, COST has large computational and communication overhead. Due to high resource needs, Fully Homomorphic Encryption (FHE), which works on certain calculations on encrypted data, is not easy to scale for large FL systems. PHE schemes are often used by researchers to get around issues because PHE schemes are less computationally expensive, yet only support a handful of operations (such as addition or multiplication).

In spite of these difficulties, HE has been able to be incorporated into FL frameworks for sectors that require high privacy assurances (banking, healthcare, etc.) Recent advances in hardware acceleration and HE protocol optimisation had made such approach more practical for the real-world deployment (Aono et al., 2017; Kairouz et al., 2019). By integrating HE with other FL systems may be used for strong privacy protection while maintaining model accuracy and scalability with privacy preserving strategy such as safe aggregation or differential privacy. Consider the following scenario: We would like to be able to add two numbers, "5" and "3" while keeping their encryption with a simple homomorphic encryption scheme built upon the RSA algorithm (partially homomorphic for addition). The following equations are utilised in this example: 1) Encryption: E(x), 2) Aggregation: E(x1) + E(x2) = E(x1 + x2), 3) Decryption: D(E(x1 + x2)) = x1 + x2

Procedure for encryption:

- **Public key:** Assume that the public key is (n, e), where n = 21 (the product of primes 3 and 7) and e = 5.
- **Encrypting** 5: (5^e) mod n = (5^5) mod 21 = 3125 mod 21 = 10
- **Encryption** 3: (3^e) mod n = (3^5) mod 21 = 243 mod 21 = 6

Including values that are encrypted: (10 + 6) mod 21 = 16.

Decryption:

- **Private key:** Assume that the private key is (n, d), where d = 11 (e's modular multiplicative inverse).
- **Decrypting the result:**(16^d) mod n = (16^11) mod 21 = 5 (the right sum of 5 + 3)
- In this case, after decryption, adding the plain text values (5 + 3) is equal to adding the encrypted values (10 + 6).

5.3. (DP) Differential Privacy for Federated Learning

Differential Privacy (DP), a powerful privacy preserving method, maintains the security of individual data points within a dataset through the deliberate application of noise on computations. DP is applied to FL to protect the shared updates of local models from shared participants. By injecting very carefully calibrated noise into the gradients or model param, DP enables the global model to discover significant patterns in the aggregated data without revealing anything specific about an individual's data from the aggregating ingress.

The principle that guides DP is the ability to render the final product hardly affected by whether or not individual participant data is used. This is achieved through the intervening mechanisms like Gaussian mechanism which injects random noise into the model updates themselves derived from Gaussian distribution. Privacy protection level is measured by The trade-off between privacy and utility is measured by the privacy budget (ε). Even though a smaller trained model with ε may do not perform as accurate as possible, it does offer better privacy guarantees. In case of FL, DP can be performed on different levels, with both the global one, that is noise added by the central server after aggregation, and the local one, i.e., noise added by each participant before sharing his/her updates.

Although DP provides excellent theoretical privacy guarantees, it is complicated to trade between privacy and the performance of a model. When there is a lack of data or when the data sets are very heterogeneous, too much noise may corrupt the quality of the global model. To counter this problem, researchers have explored adaptive DP methods, which vary the noise level in a dynamic manner, either with respect to the training process, or to the sensitivity of the data. Further, to maximize the benefits of privacy and reduce the negative effects of noise on the model, privacy can be combined with other methods, such as safe aggregation or homomorphic encryption (Kairouz et al., 2019; Abadi et al., 2016).

Illustrative model of how Federated Learning (FL) exploits Differential Privacy (DP) by applying numbers as how it affects model updates.

Let's assume that Federated Learning is used to train a naïve linear regression model. Each participant has their own local data for defining the gradient of the loss function for the model parameter. The aggregations of participant's gradients is used to update the global model.

Step 1: Local Gradients

Assume that each of the three participants (P1, P2, and P3) calculates a gradient for a single parameter w. The following are their local gradients:

- Gradient from $P1{:}g1{=}0.5$
- Gradient from $P2{:}g2{=}{-}0.3$
- Gradient from $P3{:}g3{=}0.8$

The true aggregated gradient is:

True Aggregated Gradient$=g1+g2+g3=0.5-0.3+0.8=1.0$

Step 2: Adding Noise for Differential Privacy

Before sharing their local gradient, each participant adds noise derived from a Gaussian distribution N(0,σ2) to ensure differential privacy. Assume that the noise scale σ=0.2, which correlates to a particular privacy budget ϵ, exists.

- Noise added by $P1{:}n1{\sim}N(0,0.22)=0.15$
- Noise added by $P2{:}n2{\sim}N(0,0.22)=-0.05$
- Noise added by $P3{:}n3{\sim}N(0,0.22)=0.20$

The noisy gradients shared by the participants are:

- Noisy gradient from $P1{:}g1'=0.5+0.15=0.65$
- Noisy gradient from $P2{:}g2'=-0.3-0.05=-0.35$
- Noisy gradient from $P3{:}g3'=0.8+0.20=1.0$

Step 3: Aggregating Noisy Gradients

The server aggregates the noisy gradients:

Noisy Aggregated Gradient$=g1'+g2'+g3'=0.65-0.35+1.0=1.3$

Step 4: Impact of Noise on Model Update

The noisy aggregated gradient is 1.3 because of the additional noise, whereas the true aggregated gradient was 1.0. Although the model update contains a tiny error as a result, the gradient's general direction stays the same. The noise averages out over a number of iterations, enabling the model to converge while guaranteeing that individual contributions are hidden.

Trade-offs in Privacy and Accuracy

Privacy Guarantee: of the gradient of any participant (e.g., g1=0.5). Impact on **Accuracy:** There is a slight deviation between the true gradient 1.0 and the noisy aggregated gradient 1.3. Nevertheless, the noise scale σ, which is selected according to the intended privacy budget ϵ, regulates the deviation. For instance: Higher accuracy and less noise are achieved with a smaller σ (e.g., σ=0.1), but privacy is compromised. Stronger privacy is offered by a larger σ (e.g., σ=0.5), but this may slow convergence and increase noise.

6. TRENDS, PROBLEMS, AND UNDEREXPLORED AREAS IN (FL) FEDERATED LEARNING

Even though Federated Learning (FL) has attracted a lot of interest because it allows for collaborative learning while protecting privacy, there are still a number of new developments., persistent problems, and uncharted territories that need further investigation. These include explainability, fairness, and energy efficiency, all of which are necessary to ensure that FL systems are not only safe and private but also transparent, egalitarian, and long-lasting.

6.1. Fairness in Federated Learning

Fairness is still a topic that has gotten relatively little attention in FL because of the decentralised distribution of data among members. Since data in FL is frequently identically distributed and non-independent (non-IID), diverse participants may contribute datasets with different distributions, sizes, and biases. This diversity can lead to under-representation of some people in models that disproportionately favour those with larger or more representative datasets. From for instance healthcare applications can purposefully or inadvertently overlook roles of hospitals with lack of data constraining biassed models with no outputs for under-represented population. More example of procedures that are critical to address fairness and ensure a fair representation during model aggregation include e.g. weighting scrambles based on diversity and data quality or fairness aware optimisation strategies. However, all these strategies are at initial stages and more research is needed to quantify justice against model convergence and accuracy.

6.2. Explainability and Transparency

Explainability is another important but lack of research topic in FL. As can be noted, dealing with several participants that train the FL models in a collaborative manner assumes that it is hard to understand how individual efforts influence the global model. This lack of transparency is an issue that calls accountability for high stakes industries such as finance/predict that industry/ healthcare and the criminal justice systems. For instance, it may be hard to identify the reason for biased or wrong prediction made by a federated model by virtue of the training distributed nature. The need arises to devise strategies for private interpretation of local updates and their effect to the global model to design explorable FL framework. Design of FL frameworks and techniques for private interpretation of local updates and influences on the global model is an imperative. Methods like SHAP (SHapley Additive exPlanations) and LIME (Local Interpretable Model-agnostic Explanations) could be modified for use in FL, but integration into privacy protecting schemes such as secure aggregation or differential privacy remains challenging.

6.3. Energy Efficiency and Sustainability

Energy efficiency is becoming increasingly important as FL grows to include vast networks of resource-constrained devices, like cell phones or Internet of Things sensors. Local model training consumes a significant amount of energy and processing power on edge devices, which can reduce battery life and increase operating costs. Additionally, frequent communication between participants and the central server, particularly in low bandwidth settings, exacerbates energy consumption. Despite efforts to improve FL algorithms for lower communication overhead (e.g., compression approaches, sparsification, or periodic averaging), comprehensive solutions for energy-efficient FL remain lacking. Future research should focus on energy-conscious participant selection strategies, flexible training plans, and lightweight model structures to lessen the financial and environmental impact of FL systems.

6.4. Other Underexplored Areas

Robustness to Non-IID Data: While most FL research assumes that the data is IID, real-world scenarios occasionally involve highly skewed or non-IID distributions. The problem of developing trustworthy algorithms capable of handling massive amounts of data remains unsolved. **Incentive Mechanisms:** FL participants may be highly or lowly motivated to participate, depending on their level of agreement with the project's goals or computational prowess. Developing incentive structures that encourage fair participation is one area that requires more study. **Cross-Domain Applications**: Despite extensive research in fields like healthcare and finance, FL's potential in more recent sectors like climate modelling, smart cities, and driverless cars has largely not yet been realised.

7. PRACTICAL CONSIDERATIONS AND ISSUES WITH FEDERATED LEARNING DEPLOYMENT

Federated Learning (FL) has many practical issues that need to be addressed before FL can be used in the real world to ensure scalability, efficiency, and resilience, even though decentralised computation and privacy are two of its main advantages. Implementation complexity, latency, device limitations, and data heterogeneity are significant variables that impact the feasibility and performance of FL systems.

7.1. Data Heterogeneity

One of the main issues with FL is the non-independent and identically distributed (non-IID) nature of the data across participants. In practice, local datasets often exhibit significant variations in terms of size, distribution, and quality. In a healthcare application, for example, different hospitals might have distinct patient demographics, diagnostic procedures, or data collection techniques. This diversity may result in departure or worst-case global models because the accumulated updates might not give just representation to the underling population. To solve this problem there are advanced techniques like

Personalised FL is yielding the individual learnt models for each participant drawing from one single global model. **Bias correction** means adjustment of sausage contributions in aggregation. **Data augmentation** is a process by which local datasets are augmented (increased) to provide better representation. Even with such strategies, in very diverse settings, convergence and fairness will still be problematic.

7.2 Device Limitations

FL typically employs such tools like smartphones, Internet of Things sensors or edge devices with low computing power, memory, and battery life. Training local machine-learning models on such systems, may greatly load the systems that may lead to: High computational overhead: This high level of processing requires resource demands of complex models to be a device performance limitation. Energy Consumption: Could drain batteries in the scenario of routine local trainings and the availability of servers on mobile devices.

Storage Limitations: Some of the devices may not have the space for big models or equations in between. In an attempt to solve these issues researchers have explored lightweight model architectures such as TinyML, quantisation and pruning which would minimise FL's resource needs. However, it is still important to discuss models complexity and capabilities of devices.

7.3. Latency and Communication Bottlenecks

FL participants may notice noticeable delays and bandwidth constraints due to their intensive communicating with the central server. To be visible to each participant, local model changes for every participant needs to be downloaded for every training cycle, as well as latest updated global model, large-scale deployments may well face a bottleneck. There are among the causes which led to the lapse:<|response|>Within the various causes, the following do: Network conditions: It may occur that the participants have unstable, slow connections particularly in rural or underdeveloped areas. Synchronisation Delays: Conflicts in scheduling may arise due to the large number of devices which submit their updates while time synchronizing them because some participants may be late or unresponsive. Scalability Issues: Because of the rose Communication overhead, the rose communication overhead, it becomes hard to scale the FL systems as the number of players increase. Fed-era-ted distillation, model compression, asynchronous updating etc. have been suggested as ways of achieving communication cost minimization. However, such systems typically integrate a trade-off between latency and accuracy or speed of convergence that calls for close tuning.

7. 4. Implementation Overhead

Actually getting Federated Learning (FL) off the ground isn't a walk in the park; there are some pretty big hurdles to jump over. For instance, the whole system can get incredibly complicated. You're not just building something simple; you need a good grasp of how distributed systems work, along with cryptography and, of course, machine learning. Then there's the issue of keeping things running smoothly. These FL systems can get even trickier when you're trying to handle troublemakers, network glitches, or when devices just drop off the radar. Security is another huge concern. To keep model updates private and untampered with, you often have to bring in some heavy-duty security techniques – things like homomorphic encryption, differential privacy, and secure aggregation. The catch? Using these can really ramp up how much processing power and communication bandwidth you need. And let's not forget about the rulebook. FL systems have to play by data protection laws like GDPR and HIPAA, and these can add even more restrictions on how data is managed and models are trained. All these challenges really underscore why we need more standardized frameworks and tools. We need things that can help us hit the mark on security, scale up effectively, and stay compliant, all while making it quicker to get these FL systems out there.

8. FUTURE DIRECTIONS IN FEDERATED LEARNING

To really get the most out of Federated Learning (FL) as it keeps developing, we'll need to tackle the problems we're already facing and also explore some areas that haven't gotten much attention yet. Future research really ought to focus on up-and-coming areas like explainability, how to build trust, deploying it at scale, and making sure it meets regulatory requirements. These aren't just about fixing current issues; they're also about paving the way for FL to be used much more widely across all sorts of industries.

1. **Explainability**: which is a really key part of trusting any machine learning system—is still an area that hasn't been studied enough in FL. This is mostly because the training is spread out, and we're using strategies to keep things private. To make FL more explainable:

We should create methods that use interpretable aggregation protocols. This would help us track how individual changes affect the global model, all while keeping who contributed what anonymous. Techniques we already know, like SHAP (SHapley Additive exPlanations) or LIME (Local Interpretable Model-agnostic Explanations), could potentially be adapted to work within FL frameworks. For **Post-hoc Justifications**: it's worth looking into methods for generating explanations for federated models *after* they've been deployed. This way, stakeholders can understand and trust the predictions. And when it comes to **Explainability Concerned with Privacy**: the goal is to develop explainability techniques that can work alongside privacy-preserving methods like safe aggregation or differential privacy, so we can have transparency without revealing personal information. Improving explainability won't just make systems more accountable; it will also encourage FL to be accepted more widely in high-stakes situations like criminal justice, healthcare, and finance.

2. **Trust-Building: Enhancing Confidence in FL Systems:** Trust is absolutely essential if FL is going to be widely adopted, especially in situations where different players might have competing interests. Future research in this area should concentrate on: **Robust Security Measures**: We can strengthen defenses against harmful attacks, like model poisoning and inference attacks, by integrating state-of-the-art cryptography techniques with systems that can detect anomalies. For **Fairness Audits**: We need to create tools that can evaluate and ensure fairness in FL systems. This is important for addressing concerns about bias and making sure there's equal representation in the global models. And for **Mechanisms of Incentive**: It's a good idea to develop incentive schemes that encourage everyone involved to contribute fairly and participate proactively, as this helps build trust and collaboration. Another way to promote trust is to create open governance frameworks that clearly lay out what roles participants have, what the policies are for data usage, and who is accountable for what.
3. **Regulation Compliance: Aligning with Legal and Ethical Standards:** It's crucial to make sure that FL systems comply with data protection laws (like GDPR and HIPAA) and ethical standards, especially since they're used in regulated industries. Future research here should look into: **Privacy-by-Frameworks for Design**: This means integrating privacy-preserving techniques, such as differential privacy and secure aggregation, right into the core architecture of FL systems so they can meet legal requirements. For **Auditability**: We need to establish

protocols to verify that FL systems are indeed complying with data protection regulations and that privacy guarantees are being maintained throughout the entire training stage. And regarding **Ethical Guidelines**: We should provide clear ethical guidelines for FL that address issues like openness, consent, and the potential misuse of models trained on personal data. Collaboration between researchers, lawmakers, and industry stakeholders will be incredibly important for developing regulatory frameworks that strike a good balance between innovation and accountability.

4. **Scalable Deployment: Overcoming Practical Barriers**: For FL to move from being a research prototype to something that's actually deployed, we need scalable solutions that can deal with the practical challenges of varying data (heterogeneity), limited resources on devices, and communication overhead. Key recommendations include: **Lightweight algorithms**: We should create compact, efficient models (like TinyML) for devices that have limited resources, which would help lower how much computation and energy they need. For **Asynchronous and Hierarchical FL**: It's worth examining asynchronous training protocols and hierarchical structures (like cross-silo FL) to handle large deployments where there's a wide variety of device capabilities and network conditions. We should also **Utilise edge computing** to reduce the strain on central servers and to preprocess data locally, which would make FL workflows faster and more efficient. And for **Energy-Saving Procedures**: We need to develop energy-efficient algorithms that improve FL's usability and sustainability by cutting down on battery consumption on mobile and Internet of Things devices. To make FL system implementation simpler and to lower the barrier to entry for developers and organisations, we also need standardised frameworks and tools for scalable deployment.

9.CONCLUSION

Federated Learning (FL) is a revolutionary machine learning method that gets around the usual drawbacks of needing to collect all data in one place. It allows for collaborative model training while keeping data private. Its decentralized structure makes it particularly useful in sensitive sectors like banking, healthcare, and the Internet of Things, where data security and following regulations are absolutely essential. Among the main challenges FL faces are things like inefficient communication, constraints on device resources, dealing with diverse data (heterogeneity), and adversarial attacks. To solve these issues, we need scalable deployment strategies, robust security measures, and ongoing advancements in methods for protecting privacy. Areas that haven't been studied enough, like explainability, fairness, and energy efficiency, also need to be prioritised to ensure that FL systems are transparent, fair to everyone, and sustainable in the long run.

Recommendations

In order to broaden the chapter's scope and make sure it aligns with the vision of the suggested book, the following recommendations are put forward: **Improve Problem Analysis**: It should offer an extensive examination of cases, much like what was done for issues such as latency, adversarial attacks, and non-IID data. **Extend Broader Implications**: It ought to include discussions on ethical dilemmas and the societal or economic impacts of foundational learning, as these are relevant to the broader implications of Federated Learning. **Create Multidisciplinary Connections**: To show how FL connects to distributed systems, game theory, cryptography, and economics, thereby reaching a wider audience, these connections should be included. **Include Real-World Applications**: It's important to provide full case studies and examples of Federated Learning in action to really demonstrate the value of FL. **Discuss New Trends**: The chapter should discuss the latest concepts like federated transfer learning, blockchain integration, and hybrid FL paradigms to show what's new. **Provide metrics for assessment**: To ensure consistency in deployment and research, common standards and metrics for assessing FL systems should be established and discussed. **Improve Graphic Visuals**: Diagrams, flowcharts, and tables can significantly help in making complex concepts more readable. **Analyse Regulatory Frameworks**: There should be a description of the legal and regulatory aspects, including standardisation efforts, liability, and accountability.

Final Remarks

Federated learning, a truly cutting-edge advancement in machine learning, makes it possible to build sophisticated algorithms through cooperation, all without compromising data privacy. As with any federated system, there isn't one central authority. To realize its true benefits, however, we'll need to overcome both social and technological hurdles. If implemented, the suggestions made in this chapter would help nurture a guide that not only educates readers but also stimulates innovative thinking for further inquiry. As FL evolves, achieving sustainability, upholding ethics, and ensuring social inclusion across various disciplines will be essential to foster the kind of transformational change it promises in many sectors.

REFERENCES

Abadi, M., Chu, A., & Goodfellow, I.. (2016). Deep Learning with Differential Privacy. *Proceedings of the 2016 ACM SIGSAC Conference on Computer and Communications Security (CCS)*. DOI: 10.1145/2976749.2978318

Alazab, M. (2022). *Swarna Priya RM, Parimala M, Praveen Kumar Reddy Maddikunta, Thippa Reddy Gadekallu, Senior Member, IEEE, and Quoc-Viet Pham*. Federated Learning for Cybersecurity.

Aono, Y., Hayashi, T., Trieu Phong, L., & Wang, L. (2017). Privacy-Preserving Deep Learning via Additively Homomorphic Encryption. *IEEE Transactions on Information Forensics and Security*.

Bagdasaryan, E., Veit, A., Hua, Y., Estrin, D., & Shmatikov, V. (2020). How to backdoor federated learning. *Proceedings of the 23rd International Conference on Artificial Intelligence and Statistics (AISTATS)*.

Baruch, G., Baruch, M., & Goldberg, Y. (2019). A little is enough: Circumventing defenses for distributed learning. *Advances in Neural Information Processing Systems (NeurIPS)*.

Bhagoji, A. N., Chakraborty, S., Mittal, P., & Calo, S. (2019). Analyzing federated learning through an adversarial lens. *International Conference on Machine Learning (ICML)*.

Blanchard, P., El Mhamdi, E. M., Guerraoui, R., & Stainer, J. (2017). Machine learning with adversaries: Byzantine tolerant gradient descent. *Advances in Neural Information Processing Systems (NeurIPS)*.

Blanco-Justicia, A., Domingo-Ferrer, J., Martínez, S., Sánchez, D., Flanagan, A., & Tan, K. E. (2021). Achieving security and privacy in federated learning systems: Survey, research challenges and future directions. *Engineering Applications of Artificial Intelligence*, *106*, 104468. DOI: 10.1016/j.engappai.2021.104468

Bonawitz, K.. (2017). Practical secure aggregation for privacy-preserving machine learning. *Proceedings of the 2017 ACM SIGSAC Conference on Computer and Communications Security*. DOI: 10.1145/3133956.3133982

Bonawitz, K., Ivanov, V., & Kreuter, B.. (2017). Practical secure aggregation for privacy-preserving machine learning. *Proceedings of the 2017 ACM SIGSAC Conference on Computer and Communications Security (CCS)*. DOI: 10.1145/3133956.3133982

Cao, X., Başar, T., Diggavi, S., Eldar, Y. C., Letaief, K. B., Poor, H. V., & Zhang, J. (2023). Communication-Efficient Distributed Learning: An Overview. *IEEE Journal on Selected Areas in Communications, 41*(4), 851–873. DOI: 10.1109/JSAC.2023.3242710

Chen, M., Yang, Z., Saad, W., Yin, C., Poor, H. V., & Cui, S. (2021). A Joint Learning and Communications Framework for Federated Learning Over Wireless Networks. *IEEE Transactions on Wireless Communications, 20*(1), 269–283. DOI: 10.1109/TWC.2020.3024629

Chen, Z., Li, J., & Shen, C. (2023). Personalized Federated Learning with Attention-based Client Selection. arXiv preprint arXiv:2312.15148 14 pages.

Fung, C., Yoon, C. J. M., & Beschastnikh, I. (2018). Mitigating Sybils in Federated Learning poisoning. *arXiv preprint arXiv:1808.04866.*

Geyer, R. C., Klein, T., & Nabi, M. (2017). Differentially private federated learning: A client level perspective. *arXiv preprint arXiv:1712.07557.*

Ghavamipour, A. R., Turkmen, F., Wang, R., & Liang, K. 2023.Federated Synthetic Data Generation with Stronger Security Guarantees.In *Proceedings of the 28th ACM Symposium on Access Control Models and Technologies (SACMAT '23)*, June 7–9, 2023, Trento, Italy. ACM, New York,NY, USA, 12 pages. DOI: 10.1145/3589608.3593835

Hitaj, B., Ateniese, G., & Perez-Cruz, F. (2017). Deep models under the GAN: Information leakage from collaborative deep learning. *Proceedings of the 2017 ACM SIGSAC Conference on Computer and Communications Security (CCS).* DOI: 10.1145/3133956.3134012

Kairouz, P., McMahan, H. B., & Avent, B.. (2019). Advances and Open Problems in Federated Learning. arXiv:1912.04977.

Kang, J., Xiong, Z., Niyato, D., Xie, S., & Zhang, J. (2019). Incentive mechanism for reliable federated learning: A joint optimization approach to combining reputation and contract theory. *IEEE Internet of Things Journal, 6*(6), 10700–10714. DOI: 10.1109/JIOT.2019.2940820

Konečný, J., McMahan, H. B., Yu, F. X., Richtárik, P., Suresh, A. T., & Bacon, D. (2016). Federated learning: Strategies for improving communication efficiency. arXiv preprint arXiv:1610.05492.

Li, J., He, J., Hu, L., & Wu, C. (2024, April). A Federated Learning Framework via Decentralized Data Valuation for Chronic Disease Healthcare. In *Proceedings of the 2024 6th International Conference on Intelligent Medicine and Image Processing* (pp. 60-65).

Li, Q., Wen, Z., He, B., & Li, J. (2020). A Survey on Federated Learning Systems: Vision, Hype and Reality for Data Privacy and Protection. *IEEE Transactions on Knowledge and Data Engineering.*

Li, T., Sahu, A. K., Talwalkar, A., & Smith, V. (2020). Federated learning: Challenges, methods, and future directions. *IEEE Signal Processing Magazine, 37*(3), 50–60. DOI: 10.1109/MSP.2020.2975749

Li, T., Sahu, A. K., Zaheer, M., Sanjabi, M., Talwalkar, A., & Smith, V. (2020). Federated optimization in heterogeneous networks. Proceedings of Machine learning and systems, 2, 429-450.

McMahan, B., Moore, E., & Ramage, D.. (2017). Communication-Efficient Learning of Deep Networks from Decentralized Data. arXiv:1602.05629.

McMahan, H. B., Moore, E., Ramage, D., Hampson, S., & Arcas, B. A. (2017). Communication-Efficient Learning of Deep Networks from Decentralized Data. *Proceedings of the 20th International Conference on Artificial Intelligence and Statistics (AISTATS).*

Meng, C., Tang, M., Setayesh, M., & Wong, V. W. (2023, December). GNN-based neighbor selection and resource allocation for decentralized federated learning. In GLOBECOM 2023-2023 IEEE Global Communications Conference (pp. 1223-1228). IEEE.

Nasr, M., Shokri, R., & Houmansadr, A. (2019). Comprehensive privacy analysis of deep learning: Passive and active white-box inference attacks against centralized and federated learning. *IEEE Symposium on Security and Privacy (SP).* DOI: 10.1109/SP.2019.00065

Nishio, T., & Yonetani, R. (2019). *Client selection for federated learning with heterogeneous resources in mobile edge.* IEEE ICC. DOI: 10.1109/ICC.2019.8761315

Phong, L. T., Aono, Y., Hayashi, T., Wang, L., & Moriai, S. (2018). Privacy-preserving deep learning via additively homomorphic encryption. *IEEE Transactions on Information Forensics and Security, 13*(5), 1333–1345. DOI: 10.1109/TIFS.2017.2787987

Rahman, S. A., Tout, H., Talhi, C., & Mourad, A. (2020, November/December). Internet of things intrusion detection: Centralized, on-device, or federated learning. *IEEE Network, 34*(6), 310–317. DOI: 10.1109/MNET.011.2000286

Smith, V., Chiang, C.-K., Sanjabi, M., & Talwalkar, A. (2017). Federated Multi-Task Learning. Advances in Neural Information Processing Systems (NeurIPS)

Sun, J., Kairouz, P., Suresh, A. T., McMahan, B., & Talwar, K. (2021). Can you really backdoor federated learning? *Advances in Neural Information Processing Systems (NeurIPS).*

Tian, Y., Wang, S., Xiong, J., Bi, R., Zhou, Z., & Md, Z. A. B. (2024). Robust and Privacy-Preserving Decentralized Deep Federated Learning Training: Focusing on Digital Healthcare Applications. IEEE/ACM TRANSACTIONS ON COMPUTATIONAL BIOLOGY AND BIOINFORMATICS, VOL. 21, NO. 4, JULY/AUGUST 2024.

Wei, K., Li, J., Ding, M., Ma, C., Su, H., Zhang, B., & Poor, H. (2022, September). User-Level Privacy-Preserving Federated Learning: Analysis and Performance Optimization. *IEEE Transactions on Mobile Computing*, *21*(09), 3388–3401. DOI: 10.1109/TMC.2021.3056991

Wu, X., Wu, Z., Li, H., & Chen, P. (2020). Backdoor defense in federated learning with poisoned data detection and model filtering. *IEEE Access : Practical Innovations, Open Solutions.*

Yang, Q., Liu, Y., Chen, T., & Tong, Y. (2019). Federated Machine Learning: Concept and Applications. *ACM Transactions on Intelligent Systems and Technology*, *10*(2), 1–19. DOI: 10.1145/3298981

Zhu, L., Liu, Z., & Han, S. (2019). Deep leakage from gradients. *Advances in Neural Information Processing Systems (NeurIPS).*

Ziller, A., Schneider, J. J., & Makarov, I. (2021). Explainability in Federated Learning. *Survey (London, England).* arXiv2103.09650

Chapter 12
Assessing the Suitability of IoT Security Datasets for IDS: A Comprehensive Review

Manasa Koppula
https://orcid.org/0000-0002-7585-2991
SR University, India

L. M. I. Leo Joseph
https://orcid.org/0000-0003-4269-7670
SR University, India

ABSTRACT

This chapter highlights the growing urgency for robust Intrusion Detection Systems (IDS) in the Internet of Things (IoT) security, focusing on sustainable cybersecurity strategies within the modern, highly interconnected digital ecosystem. As the rapid expansion of IoT devices presents vast attack surfaces, it is crucial to develop IDS that protect interconnected environments. This chapter performs a thorough analysis of IDS detection mechanisms and IoT security datasets, critically assessing the relevance and reliability. The evaluation emphasizes essential dataset attributes, including source authenticity, diversity, data volume, and real-world applicability. By systematically analyzing these criteria, the paper identifies datasets that offer comprehensive insights into IoT security's challenges, offering researchers a detailed resource for selecting datasets that align with the complexity of current IDS development. This review thus serves as a foundational guide for advancing IDS technology, aiming to foster more resilient and adaptive security solutions within the IoT landscape.

DOI: 10.4018/979-8-3373-2200-1.ch012

1.1 INTRODUCTION

IoT technology involves linking physical objects to the internet to enable data exchange with minimal human interaction. These objects are smart devices, sensors, & actuators that work together to sense, monitor, & monitor their surroundings. IoT applications span across different domains like home automation, smart cities, Industry 4.0, healthcare, transportation, & smart grids (Khanna & Kaur, 2020). The revolutionary connectivity of IoT devices has resulted in a generation of vast volumes of data that demand sophisticated transmission, storage, & processing capabilities. Processing such high volume of data involves a large amount of computing power, and it also induces significant delays in execution. In addition, transportation and storage of big data into cloud or fog environments are power & resource-scarce in nature. For servicing such challenges, the term "Green IoT" has emerged that suggests green algorithms & protocols in order to secure energy optimization & better info management for IoT networks (Alsharif et al., 2023).

IoT is growing strongly across many applications with the number of devices connected to Internet increasing continuously. By the year 2025, Cisco estimates, the total count of connected devices globally could reach 500 billion (Camhi, 2015). Nonetheless, the speedy evolution in the usage of IoT devices and the application of Green IoT models indicate the utmost necessity for overcoming data security issues and limiting unauthorized access or misuse, as required to secure sensitive data (Bartolucci et al., 2023). Security practices include numerous methods such as systemic security architecture & cryptographic solutions. Attacks on the network, as flood requests of IoT services or unauthorized access to certain resources, can have critical consequences (Yang, Shu, et al., 2022). To counter them, the deployment of IDS is critical for identifying malicious behavior and maintaining the availability and integrity of IoT networks. Yet, resource & power limitations of IoT devices typically limit feasibility in deploying sophisticated IDS solutions. An IDS scans network activity and health, triggering an alert to network administrator when intrusion is detected (Mbarek et al., 2015). Due to its capability to detect anomalies, unauthorized access, and possible cyber threats, the IDS becomes a must in the dynamic IoT era of diverse devices and gargantuan data flows. Its proactive approach has a central role in strengthening security infrastructure of IoT designs by offering a critical defensive mechanism that mitigates risks and ensures the resilience of the networked ecosystem.

Having an incorrect dataset for IoT security for IDS can indeed impact security solution performance. The ability to distinguish between likely threats and regular IoT device behaviour could be limited without trained models because of the wrong datasets. It could lead to false positives or negatives, which would decrease overall reliance upon IDSs. The model may not be able to handle the continuously changing security risk presented by real IoT deployments if the dataset is not sufficiently diverse. It may also decrease the generality and portability of the model to various diverse IoT deployments. Poor selection of datasets may lead to numerous problems ranging from inferior security performance, increased false alarms, and inferior capability to defend IoT ecosystems against new threats in cybersecurity. Sensitive selection of IoT security datasets is therefore vital when building effective and accurate anomaly-based IDS for IoT & IIoT networks (Essop et al., 2021).

Enhancing the detection performance, accuracy, and reliability of cybersecurity in IoT-based security systems is the aim of the learning-oriented methodology by Kandhro et al. (Kandhro et al., 2023). The use of non-IoT dataset-based sources like NSL-KDD (Mahbod et al., 2009) & UNSW-NB15 (Moustafa & Slay, n.d.), while they imply possible improvements, creates a concern about the effectiveness of the method for real-time IoT intrusion detection. To counteract IoT network security, Ahad et al. (Ahad et al., 2022) estimated IDS using a Random Forest classifier and performed better than earlier research. However, the results may not be as effective in actual IoT implementations since the NSL-KDD dataset employed is not representative of IoT device traffic patterns.

With notable detection accuracy, Yang, X. et al. (Yang, Peng, et al., 2022) presented lightweight IDS for IoT networks. However, dataset NSL-KDD, which doesn't represent real-world IoT-generated traffic, is used, which raises questions about how well their approach works in actual IoT environments. PSO-LightGBM, a reliable and scalable intrusion detection model for IoT, was introduced by Liu, J. et al. (Liu et al., 2021) and shown to be effective in identifying both legitimate and malicious data. Nonetheless, the assessment procedure employing the UNSW-NB15 dataset, which is unconnected to IoT gadgets, prompts apprehensions regarding the model's appropriateness for actual IoT contexts. Abbas, A. et al. (Abbas et al., 2022) present ensemble-based IDS model, surpassing existing models in accuracy for identifying malicious activities within IoT networks. Nevertheless, their reliance on the CICIDS 2017 (Sharafaldin et al., 2018) dataset, originating from a network of computers, raises questions about the model's generalizability to genuine IoT-generated traffic.

These investigations, taken as a whole, highlight how vital it is for IoT intrusion detection research to properly use datasets. Future research should prioritize datasets that accurately reflect the complexities of IoT-generated traffic, given the limitations associated with using non-IoT-specific datasets. This will ensure that IDSs are developed and evaluated in a way that is compatible with the difficulties encountered in real-world IoT environments.

To tackle increasing complexities & scope of IoT systems, the next section offers a fundamental exposition of IoT architecture, which is essential for comprehending the emergence of vulnerabilities.

1.2 IOT ARCHITECTURE AND SECURITY CHALLENGES

1.2.1 IoT Architecture

With the help of IoT, millions of different devices can be connected. Consequently, adaptive layered engineering is needed. Despite the increasing number of proposed concepts, a unified reference model for IoT has yet to be established (Eldrandaly et al., 2019). However, some initiatives, such as IoT-A (Silva et al., 2019), aim to align legacy practices with expert insights and market demands. Among the various proposed models, the foundational three-layer architecture stands out (Fu Bing, n.d.; Kaur & Sood, 2017; Wu et al., 2010). Three-layer architecture of IoT is depicted in Figure 1. This design consists of perception layer, also called sensing layer, serving as foundation; network layer, or transmission layer, positioned in middle; and application layer (business layer), forming the top tier. Recent research has introduced specialized models that enhance IoT design (Atzori et al., 2010; Babun et al., 2021; Navani et al., 2017; Virat et al., n.d.), but the three-layer approach remains a cornerstone of IoT systems. For large-scale IoT networks, scalable and self-configuring architectures have been proposed (Cirani et al., 2014). IoT can be classified into three domains: internet-based, sensor & actuator-based, & knowledge-based systems. Implementation of IoT technologies reflects modern societal trends, where devices and communities are interconnected through data systems enabled by wireless sensors (Tsai et al., 2014)

1.2.2 IoT Security Challenges

IoT/IIoT security faces significant challenges due to the diversity and limitations of its components. The IoT Security Challenges depicted in Figure 2. IoT systems consist of heterogeneous devices, including sensors and actuators, that range from advanced 32-bit processors to simpler 8-bit microcontrollers. This diversity demands software that is compatible across all device types while meeting requirements for functionality, storage, power efficiency, and scalability. Heterogeneity is a critical concern, as IoT architecture must support devices with diverse algorithms, protocols, and circuits. The difficulty is increased by making sure that software runs effectively with little memory and with little complexity (Hosseinzadeh et al., 2016).

Figure 1. Three-layer Architecture of IoT

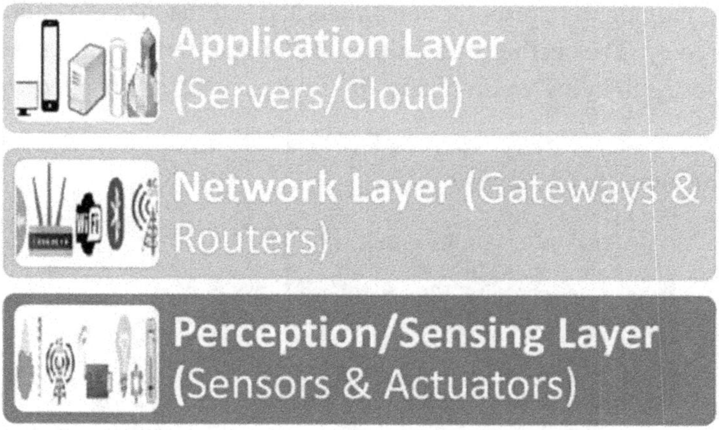

Data privacy is also a critical concern, particularly in applications where sensitive user data is involved, and compromises may leak personal data (Khanam et al., 2020). Energy efficiency is a basic IoT constraint, and protocols and algorithms need to reduce power consumption while ensuring performance (Butun et al., 2020). Communication issues are raised by technologies such as ZigBee and LPWAN, which need to be authenticated securely to avoid unauthorized access (Butun et al., 2020). Moreover, interoperability is essential to provide a smooth interaction between heterogeneous devices, but designing an exchangeable data format that is trustworthy is complex because of the heterogeneous nature of IoT devices (Butun et al., 2020).

Scalability is an urgent issue, as billions of IoT devices are being added to networks around the world every day, making conventional security schemes ineffective. Mobility is another challenge, with devices such as wearables joining and leaving networks frequently, making it difficult to apply static security algorithms (Kouicem et al., 2018).

Resource limitations, such as low battery, memory, and computational power, further hinder the deployment of energy-efficient encryption mechanisms (Kouicem et al., 2018). Effective data management is essential to holder vast quantities of information engendered by IoT devices while maintaining its integrity and privacy (Kouicem et al., 2018). Finally, updating security patches for remotely deployed devices is often impractical, leaving them vulnerable to potential threats (Khanam et al., 2020), and developing multi-protocol networking solutions that work across different communication standards remains a complex task (Khanam et al., 2020).

In a nutshell selecting the right IDS is crucial due to the many different issues with IoT security, ranging from resource constraints and heterogeneity to interoperability and data privacy. The section that follows explores a number of datasets created to aid IDS research in IoT environments in order to intensify this understanding.

Figure 2. IoT Security Challenges

1.3 AVAILABLE IOT DATASETS FOR IDS

The community has put forth several datasets for IoT cybersecurity in the early years. This segment explores a description of some of extensively utilized datasets for the development of IDS for IoT architecture. Table 1. offers a concise comparison of these datasets, outlining key attributes and characteristics.

1.3.1 N-BaIoT

Meidan et al. (Meidan et al., 2018) developed a dataset called N-BaIoT to assess a network-based anomaly detection system for spotting anomalous network traffic from compromised IoT devices. Test bed setup features nine IoT devices doorbells, baby monitors, thermostats, security cameras, & a webcam—along with sniffer host, access point, & a C&C server. Of over 7 million instances, dataset encompasses 115 features out of these features 23 are from five-time windows, including stream.

Normal traffic, captured post-installation, ensures no infected streams. While the dataset encompasses BASHLITE and Mirai botnets, it's limited to malicious attacks from these two, preventing the detection of other IoT attack types.

1.3.2 Bot-IoT

Developed by Koroniotis et al. (Koroniotis et al., 2019) at UNSW Canberra, the BotIoT dataset aims to identify botnets in IoT architecture by combining real and simulated network traffic. The lab setup includes network services & platforms with both authentic & malicious virtual machines (VM), a simulated smart home utilizing Node-RED for various devices, & forensics analytics utilizing Argus tool. This dataset, comprising more than 72 million records, includes PCAP files (69.3 GB) and flow traffic data (16.7 GB) with protocols like TCP, UDP, IGMP, ARP, ICMP, & RARP. It reports two types of features: real protocol parameters & engendered flow features. The malevolent traffic, simulated by cyberthreats from Kali Linux VMs, involves activities like probing, DoS/DDoS attacks, & information theft. However, it mostly depends on simulation tools for generating traffic. This a major drawback, because the applicability of Bot-IoT dataset is limited for real-time IoT networks.

Table 1. Comparison of Existing IoT based Attack datasets

Dataset	No. of Features	No. of Classes	No. of records	Pros	Cons
N-BaIoT (Meidan et al., 2018)	115	2	7,062,606	Suited for IIoT environment	Restricted to botnet-specific assaults; other IoT attack types are not included.
Bot-IoT (Koroniotis et al., 2019)	31	4	72,000,000	Traffic generation, modelling, and analysis are made easier by combining Node-red and Argus.	Restricted with simulation traffic
WUSTL-IIOT (Zolanvari et al., 2019)	41	4	1,194,464	Suited for IIoT environment	Not fit for IoT attacks
TON_IoT (Moustafa et al., n.d.)	133	9	64,342	Fit for IIoT/IoT environments	Engagement of virtual machines is substantially more
X-IIoTID (Al-Hawawreh et al., 2022)	67	19	820,834	Suited for IIoT environment	Not opt for IoT attacks

continued on following page

Table 1. Continued

Dataset	No. of Features	No. of Classes	No. of records	Pros	Cons
Edge-IIoT (Ferrag et al., 2022)	61	15	157,801	Realistic testbed, Appropriate for IIoT environment	Constricted generalizability
IDSIoT2024 (Koppula & Leo Joseph, 2025)	85	11	16,230,955	Realistic IoT Architecture, Involvement of virtual machines is very limited.	Attack vector is limited

1.3.3 WUSTL-IIOT

With careful modeling and emulation to mimic real-world industrial systems, Zolanvari et al.'s WUSTL-IIOT (Zolanvari et al., 2019) is a cybersecurity-focused dataset designed for IIoT applications. To accurately simulate real-world industrial applications, the built architecture includes a variety of IIoT components, including sensors, actuators, Human-Machine-Interface [HMI], Programmable-Logic-Controller [PLC], loggers, & warning devices. This dataset has 1,194,464 observations totaling 2.7 GB, collected over roughly 53 hours. Of those samples, 1,107,448 are benign & 87,016 are malicious samples including 41 carefully chosen features. The attacks include backdoor, reconnaissance, Denial of Service [DoS], & command injection. Nevertheless, dataset comprises information from an IIoT architectural context; it does not contain traffic, information, or threats from IoT-based devices, therefore it cannot be used to assess Intrusion IDS made especially for IoT scenarios.

1.3.4 TON-IOT

The TON-IoT (Moustafa et al., n.d.) dataset, which was produced by Moustafa et al. in the UNSW Canberra IoT lab, combines federated data from three key sources: network traffic, operating systems, & IoT services telemetry. Testbed is separated into 3 layers: Edge Layer, which houses networking & IoT devices; Fog Layer, which houses gateways & VMs; & the Cloud Layer, which offers services. TON-IoT dataset records attacks and regular traffic, with notable occurrences in the Windows 7 & Windows 10 datasets. There are 28,367 entries in Windows 7 dataset and 35,975 records in Windows 10 dataset, which includes both normal and attack observations. There is a representation for nine different attack types: DDoS/DoS, injection, XSS, ransomware, backdoor, scanning, password, & Man-In-the-Middle [MITM]. Dataset's use of virtual machines and Windows operating systems introduces a little diversion from a strict focus on IoT network traffic.

1.3.5 X-IIoTID

Al-Hawawreh et al. (Al-Hawawreh et al., 2022) from University of New South Wales in Canberra produced the X-IIoTID dataset. The lab's architecture extends three levels: edge, platform, and enterprise—installing a range of industrial & IoT devices, cloud services, protocols, & attack machines. With 421,417 normal samples, 399,417 malevolent samples, & 67 features obtained from device resources, device/alert logs, & network traffic, dataset employs protocols like Modbus, MQTT, CoAP, TCP, & SMTP. Malicious records are generated through frameworks like MALC, CKC, & ATT&CK. The testbed's attack process unfolds through stages like reconnaissance, lateral movement, weaponization, exploitation, command & control, tampering, exfiltration, crypto-ransomware, & DoS. While the current approach relies on centralized learning, exploring the inclusion of federated learning becomes imperative in diverse IoT/IIoT networks to address network, privacy, & storage concerns. The X-IIoTID is mostly suitable for only IIoT environment.

1.3.6 Edge-IIoTset

The Edge-IIoTset (Ferrag et al., 2022), introduced as a dataset, serves as a valued asset for designing, implementing, & evaluating contemporary IDS tailored to IIoT/IoT networks. The dataset originates from realistic testbed replicates real-world IIoT/IoT scenarios. Through simulations of various cyberattacks across categories include DoS/DDoS, MITM, Information gathering, Injection, & Malware attacks, the authors compiled a rich dataset capturing normal and anomalous traffic. The dataset is characterized by 61 features, including 43 numeric features and a mix of string and nominal features. While Edge-IIoTset provides a robust foundation, it's essential to note potential limitations for specific use cases and scenarios like regular upgradation of datasets.

1.3.7 IDSIoT2024

The IDSIoT2024 dataset (Koppula & Leo Joseph, 2025) is a real-world IoT security dataset designed to aid in the development of IDS using ML/DL techniques. It comprises 16,230,955 records collected over two months (June–August 2023) in a controlled IoT environment using the Wireshark tool. The dataset includes network traffic from seven smart devices, such as smartwatches, smartphones, surveillance cameras, smart vacuum robots, laptops, smart TVs, and smart lights. It covers five major attack categories with eleven subcategories, including DoS, Injection Attacks, Malware, MITM Attacks, Routing Attacks, & Vulnerability Analysis, all generated using Kali Linux tools. This dataset is acquirable in raw PCAP format & preprocessed CSV files (both imbalanced and balanced versions) to facilitate research. Researchers can use it for real-time anomaly detection, cyber threat intelligence, and security policy evaluation. Publicly hosted on the IEEE DataPort repository, IDSIoT2024 provides a valuable resource for advancing AI-driven cybersecurity solutions in IoT networks.

Notably, these do not include emulations of real-world IoT environments, and therefore their representation of real-world challenges encountered in real-world implementations may be limited. These datasets, varied in scope and purpose, form the empirical basis upon which IDS solutions are developed and tested. Knowledge of their strengths and weaknesses is essential to their suitability for custom IoT applications. The following section explains the classification of IDS based on their deployment architecture, which gives a structural overview of how these systems operate in networks.

1.4 INTRUSION DETECTION SYSTEMS IN IOT ARCHITECTURE

An IDS is an effective security for IoT systems that actively protects from security intrusions through scanning and identifying suspicious behavior across networks. This focused observation is facilitated by which identifies possible weaknesses and malicious activities before they manifest and fortifies the IoT ecosystems' defenses IDSs are essential in bolstering the security position of IoT systems as they continuously observe network traffic and provide real-time solutions to prevent dynamic cyber attacks. The Taxonomy of IDS is depicted in Figure 3. IDS Taxonomy is classified into three types placement strategies in IoT, data sources in IoT, and Detection Techniques.

1.4.1 Placement Strategies of IDS in IoT

IDS can be divided into groups according to how they are positioned to detect IoT attacks. In the context of the Internet of Things, IDS can be implemented using centralised, distributed, or hybrid approaches.

i. Distributed IDS

In distributed placement approaches, IoT devices actively monitor and evaluate the behavior of other devices, enabling a concerted and decentralized security framework. A Distributed Intrusion Detection System (DIDS) entails multiple IDS components deployed across a widespread IoT ecosystem. These components interconnect with each other or with a centralized server, facilitating evolved attack/threat detection, packet analysis, & incident response. Numerous IDS architectures implement distributed designs where subsets of the network monitor other nodes. DIDS offers important advantages over centralized systems, particularly in recognizing attack patterns across the entire IoT ecosystem. This capability enhances the prevention and detection of IoT-based threats by allowing early detection and restraint. For instance, a DIDS can detect the development of IoT botnets attempting to infiltrate corporate IoT infrastructures. By leveraging this information, incident analysts can initiate mitigation measures, such as isolating compromised devices to avert further spread and removing malicious components before they cause noteworthy harm (Jamalipour & Murali, 2022).

The prime benefit of a distributed IDS lies in its capability to decentralize monitoring. Each node is equipped with a full IDS implementation, allowing associations to share threat intelligence and detect distrustful activities. However, this strategy enforces a momentous load on IoT devices, as it need considerable computational and energy resources. To address these confines, "watchdog nodes" are often deployed. These nodes are in charge of monitoring specific tasks within the network and collaborating with IDS components employed on other devices, reducing resource straining on constrained IoT devices. Such a distributed approach enhances detection capabilities while maintaining scalability. Each node, identified by its individual ID, contributes to improved security. Nevertheless, the use of resources is still an essential issue, especially for limited IoT devices, which imposes the use of lightweight or optimized IDS solutions (Jamalipour & Murali, 2022).

Advances in lightweight IDS models focus on balancing computational efficiency and detection accuracy. Clustered federated learning frameworks, for instance, have been designed to enhance detection while minimizing computational overhead by grouping similar nodes and facilitating localized learning (Shan et al., 2024). Federated learning has proven to be a promising solution, with distributed environments capable of detecting intrusions without requiring centralized data aggregation. This technique preserves data privacy and security while maintaining detection performance (Mehta et al., 2024). Moreover, lightweight machine learning models for resource-constrained IoT devices are being researched to achieve scalable and effective intrusion detection within resource-constrained settings. Distributed IDS architectures are a viable solution to reporting the dynamic security threats of IoT ecosystems. Although they provide enhanced detection and early attack mitigation, further research needs to prioritize developing effective, lightweight models specific to resource-constrained IoT environments to ensure scalability and sustainability.

Figure 3. Taxonomy of IDS

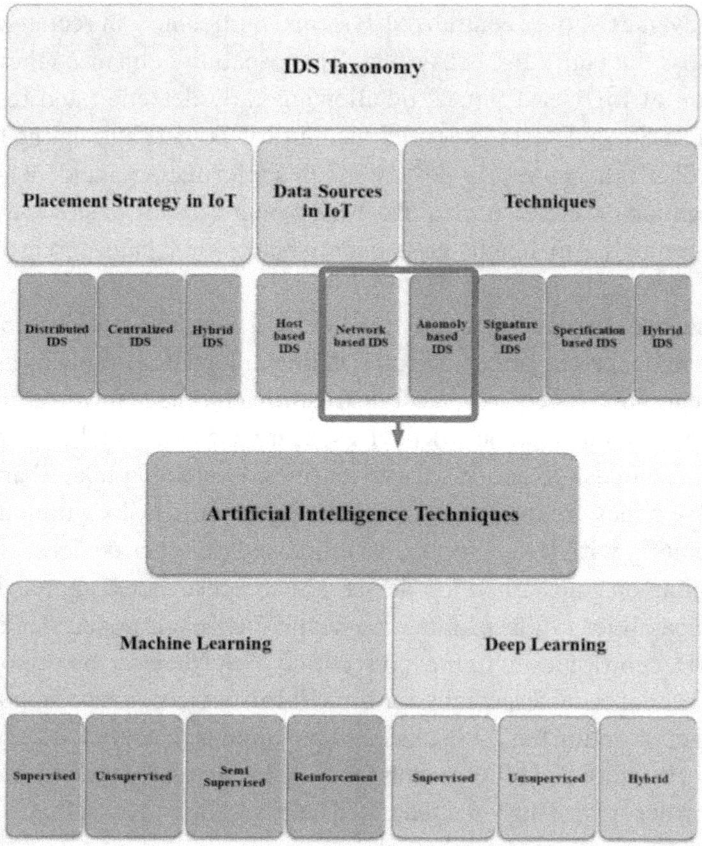

ii. Centralized IDS

In centralized IDS architectures, IDS is placed on a central node, e.g., a boundary switch or a special node. This central node may act as an aggregation point for all the data collected by IoT devices, allowing the IDS to examine packets passed between IoT devices & the rest of the network (Benkhelifa et al., 2018). Centralized IDS systems, via the analysis of network traffic drawn from sources like packet capture or NetFlow, can identify threats, including malicious activity initiated from external sources. Such systems, however, cannot effectively detect anomalies that directly affect individual IoT devices since they analyze network-wide traffic.

In centralized IDS installations, a single node with strong computational power, such as a root or head node of a cluster, is typically tasked with detection, data collection, and threat monitoring. This makes it possible to have extensive security scans because the central node will be capable of examining the traffic in depth. The middle node can also act as a firewall to ward off unwanted traffic and botnets. But such systems are tested by the monitoring of real-time network activity under simultaneous attacks and handling high data traffic in dynamic networks (Jamalipour & Murali, 2022).

iii. Hybrid IDS

Hybrid IDS deployment consolidates advantages of distributed & centralized approaches to produce maximum results. This approach is based on distributing computationally extensive tasks, e.g., information processing gathered from monitoring nodes & issuing security-related instructions, to central high-resource nodes. In parallel, low-resource nodes have lighter tasks such as monitoring surrounding nodes, passing traffic information, & responding to the central node's mitigation orders (Jamalipour & Murali, 2022). This approach is a balance between efficiency and resource utilization, facilitating quicker and more precise threat detection than that in centralized approaches and lower resource utilization than in a complete distribution of IDS. A hybrid IDS takes the benefits of both placement approaches, offering greater scalability and resiliency of security solutions to IoT settings.

The detection performance of IDS in detecting threats largely relies on where it is placed. To step in with a wider discussion of how different analytical approaches affect detection performance, the chapter now categorizes IDS based on their detection approach.

1.4.2 IDS Data Sources in IoT

Successful application of an intrusion detection strategy requires keen observation of deployment methods and the types of information sources examined. IDS generally fall into 2 broad categories depending on their focus of collecting data: Host-Based IDS (HIDS) & Network-Based IDS (NIDS). HIDS are developed to examine data collected directly from the host machines that they are deployed in. Meanwhile, NIDS focuses on checking & examining traffic over networks in order to detect potential threats (Zarpelão et al., 2017).

i. Host-based IDS

A Host-Based IDS is intended to monitor & analyze activities on specific computer systems to identify unauthorized access to system resources. It records suspicious behavior & alerts administrators or users to take suitable deeds. Essentially, a HIDS functions as a security agent, ensuring compliance with system security policies and identifying any internal or external breaches. The scrutinizing & event investigation mechanisms of HIDS rely solely on data collected from device. This info may include system records, user activity, services, & process-related information (Bace & Mell, n.d.). Arshad et al. (Arshad et al., 2019) introduced a host-based detection mechanism tailored for IoT nodes, utilizing signature detection techniques. The system detects events at the end nodes and forwards them to a centralized fog computing layer.

In another study, (Sudqi Khater et al., 2019), lightweight IDS leveraging Artificial Neural Networks (ANN) was anticipated to detect intrusions. The system achieved intrusion detection by analyzing system log data from devices. Similarly, (Pacheco et al., 2019) proposed ANN-based adaptive-IDS designed to detect malicious fog nodes and take necessary measures to ensure communication remains uninterrupted. This approach analyzes critical parameters, including memory usage, CPU activity, buffers, processes, and Ethernet traffic (Pacheco et al., 2019). Host-based approaches offer the advantage of being independent of network connectivity and are effective in detecting internal attacks. However, when deployed directly on IoT nodes, they can face significant memory and resource constraints. In contrast, HIDS implementations on fog devices are better equipped to detect attacks targeting the fog node itself but may struggle with addressing attacks that propagate across the network or multiple IoT devices.

ii. Network-based IDS

NIDS is accountable for monitoring & analyzing network traffic to classify mistrustful activities & protect network infrastructure. By inspecting incoming packets & associating them in contradiction of a database of familiar attack signatures, NIDS can notice anomalous patterns. Suspicious traffic is flagged based on its severity, prompting the system to either alert administrators or block network access from the attacker's IP address. However, efficiently analyzing network traffic under heavy loads remains a challenge (Liao et al., 2013). NIDS solutions are typically positioned on devices skilled of capturing and monitoring network traffic. They operate in promiscuous mode, enabling them to inspect all packets traversing the network. The system primarily focuses on analyzing data extracted from packet headers to identify potential threats. Additionally, distributed sensor nodes can be strategically placed at various points in the network to capture traffic efficiently, especially in complex IoT environments.

In IoT networks, NIDS approaches are often implemented in fog computing layers, enabling localized analysis and reducing latency. Prabavathy et al. (Prabavathy et al., 2018) suggested a detection strategy that decentralizes traditional cloud-based intrusion detection intelligence and redistributes it across fog nodes. This approach enhances the speed of attack detection by analyzing real-time streaming traffic within IoT applications. Similarly, (Kalnoor & Gowrishankar, 2021) introduced an Intelligent IDS (I-IDS). The system investigates packet data from distributed sensors, enabling precise detection of intrusions across IoT networks. The network-based detection approach offers significant advantages, such as noticing external bouts & being largely platform-independent (Mukherjee et al., 1994). Machine Learning (ML) & Deep Learning (DL) methods are mostly used to develop NIDS, with additional specifics provided in Section 1.5.

1.4.3 IDS Based on Detection Techniques in IoT

IDSs can be arranged into four main classes according to the detection methodologies: anomaly-based, signature-based, specification-based, & hybrid-based approaches.

i. Anomaly-based IDS

Anomaly-based IDS, often stated as behavior-based IDS, is an extensively adopted method in intrusion detection studies. This method assumes that any deviation from well-known normal behavior patterns indicates a potential intrusion. Activities that fail to line up with predefined behavioral norms are identified as attacks. A key advantage of anomaly detection deceits in its capability to classify novel attacks and differences from existing ones without necessitating prior knowledge of their signatures. ML and DL techniques are commonly used to model this strategy, with further particulars provided in Section 1.5.

ii. Signature-based IDS

Signature-based IDS focal point on monitoring incoming network traffic & identifying intrusions by scrutinizing observed traffic patterns against database of pre-stored attack signatures. However, this method faces challenges, such as trouble in sensing zero-day attacks & continuous effort required to update and maintain the signature database (Liao et al., 2013). In signature-based detection, monitored activities are matched against pre defined patterns of invasive behavior, commonly referred to as signatures (S. Northcutt et al., 2001). This approach is widely adopted in commercial antivirus systems.

To enhance detection capabilities, Wang et al. (Wang et al., 2018) introduced a method utilizing Rabin fingerprint algorithm, integrating it with IDS Snort signatures and network packet analysis to ensure both privacy and intrusion detection. Similarly, IDS Snort has been paired with two-state hidden Markov model to classify device statuses into distinct classes (Sandhu et al., 2017; Sohal et al., 2018). The authors (Mourad et al., 2021) suggested a real-time signature-based discovery method leveraging Aho–Corasick method to compare live system calls in contradiction of a pre-defined dataset. Additionally, frameworks combining both signature and anomaly-based detection have been introduced (Lawal et al., 2020, 2021). In a related effort, (Ghazi & Moulay Rachid, 2020) suggested a hybrid IDS that integrates cloud & fog computing. This design enables real-time monitoring, ensuring early detection and prevention of attacks before they propagate across the network.

Maintaining the Integrity of the Specifications. FIXIDS, an enhanced NIDS based on Internet Protocol Flow Information Export (IPFIX) that integrates HTTP intrusion detection signatures from Snort, is presented by Erlacher et al. (Erlacher & Dressler, 2022). Compared to Snort, FIXIDS performs better, managing four times as much network data at no time drops and maximizing security appliance performance through traffic offloading while preserving the same event detection rate. With the help of a filter engine acting as a secondary IDS, Abdiyeva-Aliyeva et al. (Abdiyeva-Aliyeva & Hematyar, 2022) describe a novel AI model for signature-based intrusion detection that updates attack lists on its own. Improved overall IDS accuracy and effective threat management are made possible by the model's IP-Factor and Non-IP-Factor blacklist, which also allows for automatic threat detection, database upgrades, and the creation of new attack features. Utilizing UNSW-NB15 dataset & a Ryu. The capacity of signature-based IDS SNORT to identify new attack signatures independently of humans and its inability to detect multi-stage attacks are the two issues addressed in this paper by (Farooq, n.d.). The paper discusses a multi-layer classification method utilizing neural networks and fuzzy logic in the second layer and a decision tree in the first. This approach enhances SNORT's ability to detect multi-stage attacks and enables automatic detection of new attack signatures. Ariffin et al. (S Ariffin et al., 2022) illustrate for assessing accuracy of IDS using a Software-Defined Network (SDN) IoTController with Snort IDS to detect DDoS attacks, the research conducts false positive & false negative tests. The findings validate SDN-IoT platform with Snort IDS accuracy in well reducing errors and confirming its promising potential in hardy intrusion detection in network security. Given regard to literature, SNORT has the capability of being among the best signature-based IDS. Snort can be applied in IoT appliances, but in order to effectively detect intrusions without interfering with the functioning of the appliance, one needs to scrutinize the capabilities of the device and the particular needs of the IoT environment carefully.

While signature-based IDS offers rapid threat detection and minimizes false alarms, its primary limitation remains the inability to identify previously unknown or zero-day attacks effectively.

iii. Specification-based IDS

Specification-based IDS works by defining suitable system behaviors and identifying any deviation from these predefined standards as potential security threats. While this approach shares similarities with anomaly-based IDS, the key distinction lies in the fact that specification-based IDS relies on behavior guidelines and standards explicitly defined by cybersecurity experts. This expert-driven approach results in extensively reduced false positive & negative rates (Glissa et al., 2016).

Ko et al. (Ko et al., n.d.) pioneered the concept of specification-based IDS. Their system, such as anomaly-based detection, identifies deviations from predefined normal behaviors. However, in this approach, the behavioral specifications are derived from the system's security policies and operational guidelines. Any activity that fails to adhere to these specifications is flagged as a security violation (Berthier & Sanders, 2011). Despite its advantages, the practical deployment of specification-based IDS faces challenges, particularly in accurately evaluating and maintaining the defined specifications. Nevertheless, this approach effectively integrates elements from both misuse-based and anomaly-based detection techniques, enabling it to defend against known attacks while offering resilience against emerging or previously unknown threats (Bostani & Sheikhan, 2017; Surendar & Umamakeswari, 2016).

iv. Hybrid IDS

Hybrid IDS combines the benefits of signature, specification, & anomaly-based sensing techniques to achieve exploiting strengths without limitations (Jamalipour & Murali, 2022). Hybrid IDS can balance detection accuracy, efficiency, and responsiveness by integrating these methods. A prominent example is the system described by Tabassum et al. (Tabassum et al., 2021), which balances the storage overhead of signature-based approaches with the computational complexity frequently found in anomaly-based methods. This blended strategy maximizes resource utilization while providing strong and reliable intrusion detection.

Each detection technique has its advantages and disadvantages, which are often influenced by the nature of the IoT context in which they are being applied. As explained in the following section, researchers are making more use of machine learning methods to improve the use of these approaches.

1.5 ARTIFICIAL INTELLIGENCE TECHNIQUES EMPLOYED FOR IDS

Artificial Intelligence (AI) is capable of emulating some aspects of human intellectual and reasoning habits. While AI does not have human intelligence, in the vast majority of circumstances it can execute activities with a level of proficiency and accuracy above human capabilities (Xin et al., 2018). Security experts are ever more adopting AI technologies in guarding systems against ever-increasing cyber attacks. AI contributes significantly to the IoT security journey by monitoring network traffic patterns in order to determine behaviors that may indicate likely attacks (Kuzlu et al., 2021). Rapid expansion of IoT technologies has driven increased focus on AI use for enhanced security provisions. Specifically, AI contributes to the development of NIDS and Anomaly-Based IDS, both of which play an integral part in safeguarding IoT ecosystems. Two front-running subtypes of AI, ML and DL, are highlighted in Figure 3. These have an important application in building intelligent systems capable of identifying and counteracting cyber attacks effectively.

1.5.1 Machine Learning-Based Detection Techniques

ML is a fluid branch of learning under the study of data science that is predominantly applied to teach algorithms to perform activities such as prediction and classification. In ML-based attack detection in IoT, ML algorithms are typically classified into four broad categories: supervised, unsupervised, semi-supervised, & reinforced learning.

i. Supervised Learning

Supervised learning, as the name implies, involves guidance throughout the learning process. In this approach, the algorithm is trained using labeled data, each input is allied with related output. This technique is primarily applied to solve classification and regression problems. Supervised learning methods comprise Decision Trees (DT), Neural Networks, Random Forests (RF), k-nearest Neighbor (K-NN), & Support Vector Machine (SVM), etc.

DTs are a subset of supervised learning methods primarily utilized for decision-making by addressing an initial set of questions. Among the most popular ML algorithms, DTs are effective in classification and grouping tasks (Charbuty & Abdulazeez, 2021). There are several DT based IDS (Dev & Eden, 2019; Maharaja et al., 2020; Nakano et al., 2017) were presented in recent years.

Decision Trees offer transparency and ease of use, making them highly interpretable and valuable tools for building predictive models. They classify samples based on conditional rules represented through tree branches and leaf nodes. While DTs excel at detecting known traffic patterns with high accuracy, they often face challenges when dealing with anomalous or novel traffic patterns. Additionally, as the number of trees in ensemble methods grows, they may require significant storage resources. Despite these limitations, DTs remain a robust and widely adopted approach in anomaly detection and classification tasks across various domains, including cybersecurity and IoT network IDSs.

RF is an ensemble-based ML technique designed to enhance the performance of DTs by decreasing overfitting & improving generalization. The findings of (Hosseini & Sardo, 2023; R. Kumar et al., 2022) collectively highlight RF's ability to deliver great accuracy & reliability in sensing network invasions, making it a preferred choice for modern intrusion detection frameworks.

SVMs are set of supervised learning algorithms extensively employed for regression, classification, & outlier detection tasks (Ahmad et al., 2021). They have proven highly effective in addressing challenges related to detection and prediction. The core principle behind SVM is discriminative classification, where the algorithm learns patterns from previously labeled data and applies this knowledge to classify new, unseen data. It achieves this by constructing a decision border, referred to as a hyperplane, which separates data points belonging to different classes (Bagaa et al., 2020; Carone et al., 2023; Z. Lu & Metghalchi, 2023).

KNN algorithm is widely recognized supervised ML practice employed for classification & regression (Mohammed et al., 2025). Alternatively, it retention training dataset & makes predictions based on closeness of new data points to existent ones in the feature space (Shenvi & Virani, 2023). This approach eliminates the need for an intensive training phase, as the algorithm focuses on evaluating the similarity between data points during the prediction stage. In k-NN based IDS (Pan et al., 2021), the algorithm's strength lies in its straightforward approach and adaptability to various datasets. Unlike many other ML techniques, kNN doesn't depend on assumptions about the fundamental data distribution, making it particularly versatile. However, it also requires efficient computation and storage, as it evaluates all training data points during each prediction. Despite these challenges, kNN remains a valuable tool in both research and practical applications, particularly in scenarios requiring dynamic and distributed decision-making systems (Saadeh et al., 2022; Sarker, 2021).

ii. Unsupervised Learning

Clustering techniques, primarily unsupervised, play a significant role in anomaly detection by identifying patterns and outliers within datasets. While unsupervised clustering remains the dominant approach, semi-supervised techniques have also been explored to bridge the gap between labeled and unlabeled data. Clustering methods group similar data points into clusters, this usual data typically exists in near cluster centroids or within dense, large clusters, while anomalies are often located in sparse or small clusters or at a significant distance from the nearest centroid.

One of the utmost popular unsupervised clustering methods is K-Means Clustering. At each iteration, the algorithm calculates the distance of data points from the centroids utilizing distance metrics like Euclidean distance & assigns them to the nearest cluster (Yuan & Yang, 2019). It proceeds until cluster assignments stabilize, ensuring low intra-cluster variance. Its simplicity and iterative nature have made K-Means a standard component in anomaly detection systems. Kernel-based Online Anomaly Detection (KOAD) expands clustering ability by using kernel functions to transform input information into a higher feature space, enabling the detection of complex patterns and relationships. KOAD is especially useful for real-time anomaly detection since it keeps updating its internal representation to learn from evolving data streams. In Ref. (Hu et al., 2021), a modified version of KOAD (E-KOAD) was incorporated into an IDS to particularly detect apprehensive points. Multi-Kernel K-Means is another important improvement over classic K-Means that involves using multiple kernel functions to accommodate non-linear data distributions & complex data structures.

In Ref. (Hu et al., 2021), this strategy was applied to IDS models and evaluated on datasets such as AWID & UNSW_NB15. The model performed better than conventional K-Means, with an accuracy rate of 93.80% versus 84.20%. Anticipated Distance Clustering (ADC) is yet another clustering algorithm, groups points by expected distance, a proximity metric designed for clustering purposes. In Ref. (Ferrag et al., 2020), ADC was used together with Density-Based Spatial Clustering of Applications with Noise (DBSCAN) for an IDS. DBSCAN is famous for detecting clusters of any shape and effectively identifying noise in datasets. The suggested method attained a commendable accuracy of 99.99%, underscoring the effectiveness of clustering as a preparatory phase for classification tasks.

Additionally, the research (Ravi & Shalinie, 2020) introduced a modified version of K-Means known as RRS-K-Means (Repeated-Random-Sampling-K-Means). This approach was integrated with DNN to notice irrupt in IoT environments. Overall, clustering techniques, whether traditional like K-Means or advanced like Multi-Kernel K-Means and ADC, endure to play a pivotal part in identifying anomalies in complex datasets. Their integration with other ML and DL methods further enhances their performance, making them indispensable in modern IDS.

iii. Semi-supervised Learning

This is a hybrid method that combines strengths of supervised & unsupervised techniques. It powers a blend of labeled & unlabeled data to train ML classifiers (Al-Garadi et al., 2020). While supervised learning remains more effective in achieving accurate attack detection, semi-supervised learning offers an alternative when labeled data is scarce. Despite its potential, semi-supervised learning has seen limited adoption in IoT security studies due to its relatively lower success rate in comparison to supervised methods. In the context of intrusion detection, the Semi-Supervised Fuzzy-C-Means (SFCM) method has been explored to enhance clustering performance by integrating prior knowledge into the clustering process.

Rathore et al. (Rathore & Park, 2018) introduced a hybrid model combining Extreme-Learning-Machine (ELM) & SFCM, known as ESFCM. In this method, the ELM classifier is initially trained on a labeled dataset. This distributed approach reduces computational overhead and ensures real-time detection capabilities. Experimental results using NSLKDD demonstrated an accuracy of 86.53%, highlighting the effectiveness of the ESFCM model in intrusion detection tasks. Overall, while semi-supervised learning remains underutilized in IoT security, its hybrid nature and ability to exploit both labeled and unlabeled data make it a promising approach for addressing challenges where labeled data is limited. The integration of clustering techniques, such as FCM, with classifiers like ELM demonstrates the potential for semi-supervised models to achieve reliable performance in complex intrusion detection scenarios.

iv. Reinforcement Learning

Reinforcement Learning (RL) is agent interacts with its surround & gains decision-making ability while knowing very little about its settings beforehand. This approach mimics human brain's processing and decision-making system, focusing on plotting environmental situations to actions to exploit a predefined numerical reward signal (Uprety & Rawat, 2021). RL solves optimization problems by dynamically adjusting parameters based on the environment, enabling it to adapt to complex and ever-changing scenarios. Given the dynamic and heterogeneous nature of IoT networks, which comprise numerous interconnected devices with varying functionalities, RL has gained significant attention for its effectiveness in multi-agent sceneries and was introduced in implementation of several IDS mechanisms (Caminero et al., 2019; Heartfield et al., 2021; H. Lu et al., 2018; Oh & Iyengar, 2019). RL offers promising results in addressing the dynamic and complex challenges posed by IoT environments. Through adaptive learning mechanisms, reward-based optimization, and integration with advanced techniques such as neural networks and Bayesian inference, RL-based approaches continue to enhance the effectiveness and robustness of IDSs in IoT networks.

IDS's capabilities have been revolutionised by use of ML, which makes threat detection more sophisticated & flexible. Significant progress has been made, especially in deep learning, as will be covered in the next section.

1.5.2 Deep Learning-Based Detection Techniques

DL is a specialized branch of ML focused on developing neural networks capable of analytical reasoning. These networks are designed to replicate the way humans process auditory, textual, and visual information. Deep learning techniques are broadly classified into supervised and unsupervised learning methods. Unlike traditional ML approaches, where feature extraction is performed manually, DL algorithms learn & extract related features from data. The following section provides overview of main categories of deep learning techniques.

i. Supervised Learning

Supervised learning trusts on labeled datasets for training ML models, allowing them to learn patterns and relationships between inputs & outputs. Among these, DNN, a subset of ANN is widely used due to its capacity to handle tangled patterns & high-dimensional info. Initially, the DNN learns patterns from the input data, and forecast output is contrasted with real output. The deviation, known as error, is minimized over activity called backpropagation. During backpropagation, model regulates weights & biases iteratively to reduce the error till it congregates to an optimal solution. When the error reaches its minimum feasible value, the DNN achieves higher accuracy and performs reliably. The ability of DNNs to represent increasingly complex functions comes from adding more hidden layers & neurons per layer. However, an excessive number of neurons in each layer does not necessarily improve performance and might introduce unnecessary computational overhead. For example, (Sahar et al., 2021) employed hidden ReLU layers with 768 & 512 neurons, correspondingly, while used 2 hidden layers with 32 & 16 neurons. In another study (Lalouani & Younis, 2021), 2 hidden layers with 64 neurons each employed the ReLU activation function, demonstrating its efficiency in terms of time and computational cost. Similarly, a layer with 16 & other with 12 neurons, using ReLU and dropout rate of 0.2, were utilized in (R. Kumar & Tripathi, 2021).

The ReLU activation function remains a prevalent excellent for hidden layers owing to its simplicity and effectiveness in avoiding issues such as vanishing gradients.

The authors have utilized Convolutional Neural Networks (CNNs) in the research work (Rodríguez et al., 2022; Ullah & Mahmoud, 2022). Their IDS is capable of detecting advanced patterns of attack by employing a CNN. Three such customized datasets constructed by authors have been rigorously tested by which they were showing robustness as well as learning capabilities for recognizing new types of attacks.

Long Short-Term Memory (LSTM) networks discuss the limitations of standard Recurrent-Neural-Networks (RNNs), primarily the vanishing gradient issue. LSTMs achieve this by having specialized memory blocks with three essential gates: input, output, & forget. These adjust flow of information, enabling model to decide which information to retain, update, or discard across time steps (Mittal et al., 2023). An extension of the standard LSTM is the Bidirectional LSTM (Bi-LSTM), which enhances the capability to capture sequential dependencies by processing input sequences in forward & backward orders. While traditional LSTMs consider only past dependencies, Bi-LSTMs simultaneously incorporate information from future time steps, allowing them to detect more nuanced relationships within sequential data (Shinde et al., 2023). This bidirectional processing is particularly valuable for tasks requiring contextual insights from both past and future inputs, leading to improved accuracy in prediction and classification tasks. However, this advantage originates at the cost of enlarged computational difficulty & lengthier training times associated to standard LSTMs.

Ferrag et al. (Ferrag et al., 2021) steered a detailed study on federated DL approaches to enhance IoT security. Their research examined vulnerabilities in federated systems and experimentally evaluated models based on CNNs, DNNs, and RNNs. The findings indicated that federated learning approaches outperformed their centralized counterparts, offering enhanced security and scalability. Similarly, (Syed et al., 2023) tailored a framework that employed distributed data processing & a feature selection phase, followed by application of Bi-LSTM & RNN architectures to detect threats effectively. The model was seriously tested on BoT-IoT dataset and showed it efficient enough to discover malicious traffic. LSTM networks remained a workhorse for intrusion detection mechanisms, mainly due to the ability to parse and predict patterns in sequential data (Ullah et al., 2021). Their capacity for learning long-range dependencies & temporal relationships makes them very appropriate in identifying anomalies as well as dangers in sophisticated IoT environments. With continued research, hybrid frameworks and federated solutions with LSTMs will be key in driving IoT security solutions.

ii. Unsupervised Learning

Unsupervised DL, also known as generative learning, is dedicated to hiding implicit patterns & structures in data in a manner that it does not require labeled data. Through this, models can learn semantic representations and produce new data records identical to the original data distribution. Unsupervised DL has the benefit of processing a lot of unstructured data, and thus it is of immense value when there is no labeled data in a particular scenario.

Generative Adversarial Networks (GANs), is unsupervised DL, rely on a competitive training process between two neural networks: generator & discriminator. GANs excel in tasks such as style transfer, image generation, & data augmentation, offering significant advantages in fields requiring synthetic data creation. Deep autoencoders are also widely used for representation learning, reducing data dimensionality without relying on manually constructed features. This allows them to learn more meaningful representations directly from the raw data. However, autoencoders require substantial processing time, and their performance may suffer if training data is not illustrative of testing data, making them sensitive to data quality and distribution (Al-Garadi et al., 2020).

Restricted Boltzmann Machines (RBMs) are another kind of generative-stochastic ANN that acts a crucial role in DL. They consist of two layers visible layer & hidden layer where nodes in different layers are fully connected, but connections within the same layer are absent (Al-Garadi et al., 2020). RBMs are highly effective in feature extraction tasks. These networks excel in unsupervised environments but come with high computational costs due to lengthy initialization and training procedures. Nevertheless, they have shown significant success in applications like malicious attack detection (Al-Garadi et al., 2020).

In recent research, (Basati & Faghih, 2023; Lahasan & Samma, 2022) light weight autoencoder (AE) based IDS were introduced. The AE design enabled efficient feature separation and improved classification performance, particularly in minority classes. Moreover, the lightweight architecture minimized computational overhead, making the system highly scalable and resource-efficient. Overall, autoencoders and their variants (Sohn, 2021), along with RBMs, DBNs, and GANs, represent essential tools in unsupervised deep learning. Their applications in feature extraction, anomaly detection, and generative tasks have significantly advanced fields such as intrusion detection, data preprocessing, and synthetic data generation. These techniques continue to evolve, addressing current challenges and broadening their scope across diverse domains.

Hybrid learning approaches are being investigated more and more to combine the advantages of several learning paradigms, which will be addressed in the next section. As seen, deep learning models offer strong tools for feature extraction and pattern recognition.

iii. Hybrid Learning

Hybrid learning combines multiple learning paradigms, often blending supervised and unsupervised DL techniques, to grease the assets of both methods for enhanced model performance. Hybrid models (Elsaeidy et al., 2021; Roopak et al., 2020; Telikani et al., 2022), like CNN+LSTM and GAN+CNN, are commonly employed to address the limitations of standalone architectures and improve overall accuracy, scalability, and adaptability to complex tasks.

Hybrid learning approaches like CNN+LSTM, SAE+CNN, and CNN+RBM demonstrate significant advancements in addressing the challenges associated with data imbalance, scalability, and computational efficiency in IDS models. These models offer a versatile and robust framework for detecting cyber threats in IoT environments, smart cities, and other critical infrastructure systems. By integrating optimisation methods, distributed processing environments, and heterogeneous data sets, hybrid learning methods remain at the cutting edge of intrusion detection theory and practical application.

By integrating the strengths of two or more learning paradigms, hybrid methods enhance the accuracy and responsiveness of IDS. The following section addresses their implementation in resource-limited and real-time IoT settings.

1.6 FUTURE DIRECTIONS IN IOT INTRUSION DETECTION SYSTEM

With the growth of the IoT ecosystem, it becomes ever more important to have strict security controls. New methods and technology hold promising opportunities to revolutionize IDS in Internet of Things environments. The future directions discussed in the following section include federated learning, adversarial robustness, and real-time deployment of IDS.

1.6.1 Federated Learning for Privacy-Preserving IDS

The need for aggregating data from multiple IoT devices in conventional centralised IDS systems poses concerns of scalability, communication overhead, and data privacy. Since it permits decentralised model training on devices without sharing raw data, federated learning (FL) is a very attractive strategy. Scalability is enhanced, network bandwidth consumption is reduced, and user privacy is maintained with this approach.

The performance of FL in IoT IDS tasks has been demonstrated in current research. For improving sensor accuracy & resilience in heterogeneous IoT networks, Nguyen and Beuran (Nguyen & Beuran, n.d.) proposed FedMSE, which is a semi-supervised FL model that incorporates the Shrink AE & Centroid one-class classifier. Just like this, Belenguer et al. (Belenguer et al., 2022) provided a comprehensive review of FL applications in IDS, highlighting how it can be utilized to address computational and privacy concerns in IoT environments.

1.6.2 Enhancing Adversarial Robustness in IDS

Adversarial attacks, under which malicious entities manipulate inputs to deceive detection algorithms, can target ML-based IDS. Integrity and reliability of IDS in IoT networks must be ensured to maintain dependability.

The vulnerability of IDS to adversarial examples was studied by Papadopoulos et al. (Papadopoulos et al., 2021), which demonstrated that attackers are likely to manipulate or evade detection methods. Future research should focus on developing robust IDS models that can resist such malicious tactics, possibly employing strategies such as ensemble methods, anomaly detection, and adversarial training.

1.6.3 Real-Time IDS Deployment in Resource-Constrained Environments

IDS systems must be light and also capable of real-time threat detection since IoT devices have limited resource requirements. One of the biggest challenges is providing low-latency responses without sacrificing detection accuracy.

Edge computing and computationally efficient machine learning models present possible solutions. Centralised systems usage is reduced by deploying IDS at the edge, enabling real-time detection and response to threats. Resource-constrained IoT devices are also supported due to model computation optimisation.

Real-time IDS deployment has dire challenges, particularly in resource-constrained environments, and edge computing and model optimisation are moving towards solving them. The practical and ethical aspects of exploiting IoT datasets must also be taken into consideration along with technical issues in deploying real-time IDS. Such important considerations as privacy, informed consent, and regulatory compliance in IoT contexts are discussed in the next section.

1.7 PRACTICAL AND ETHICAL ISSUES ON IOT DATASET USAGE

There are severe ethical and practical concerns in deploying IDS in real-world IoT systems. Providing data privacy is one of the greatest challenges, especially when datasets hold sensitive data generated by industrial or personal IoT devices. Such data, when inadvertently exposed publicly, can compromise user privacy and breach regulations like California Consumer Privacy Act (CCPA) in the US or General Data Protection Regulation (GDPR) in the EU (Pathmabandu et al., 2023).

In addition, IoT data collection and use pose ethical issues regarding informed consent, especially where the data is collected in consumer environments. Transparency, consent, and proper handling procedures are required for ethical data gathering to promote stakeholder trust (Sharjeel et al., n.d.).

One of the primary hindrances to deployment is the heterogeneity of IoT device capabilities. Heavy IDS approaches cannot be deployed in many IoT devices due to inadequate memory, processing capacity, & power. Lightweight IDS models & edge-based processing are crucial so as to bridge these limitations without sacrificing performance (Azam et al., n.d.).

The second key issue is regulatory compliance. To ensure confidence that IDS solutions are compliant with regulations in actual systems, they must be designed according to international standards and regulations. Guidelines of organizations such as the European Union Agency for Cybersecurity (ENISA) (Chiara, 2024) emphasize appropriate safety design and implementation of detection mechanisms in IoT networks.

Besides, new technologies like blockchain are being investigated to strengthen decentralised security and data integrity across IoT networks in a manner that supports privacy-preserving frameworks complying with regulatory requirements (Gugueoth et al., 2023). In general, resolving pragmatic and ethical concerns strengthens the reliability and acceptability of IDS in IoT settings towards ensuring technological advancement in accordance with legal requirements and social expectations.

1.8 CONCLUSION

In summary, this chapter answers the urgent need for efficient IDS in fast-changing environment of IoT security. With the increase in IoT devices, strong security mechanisms become essential, and IDS becomes a key element in protecting these connected environments. The thorough review carried out herein explores the detection mechanisms of IDS and assesses current IoT security datasets, keeping in mind vital criteria like authenticity, diversity, volume, and realism. The discourse covers the categories of IDS highlighting the significance of dataset selection in ensuring correct model training and the resulting impact on machine learning-based IDS performance. The paper presents a critical assessment of notable datasets, including N-BaIoT, Bot-IoT, WUSTL-IIOT, TON-IOT, X-IIoTID, Edge-IIoTset, and IDSIoT2024, highlighting their strengths, limitations, and applicability to IoT security scenarios. The comparative analysis aids researchers and practitioners in making informed decisions based on specific use cases. Furthermore, the paper underscores the necessity for future research to prioritize datasets accurately reflecting the intricacies of IoT-generated traffic, ensuring the development and evaluation of IDS aligned with real-world challenges. The journey through various datasets underscores the evolving strategies and technologies dedicated to strengthening IoT security through IDS. In a broader context, the review also mentions other widely used cybersecurity datasets that lack simulations of real-world IoT environments. This comprehensive overview serves as a valuable guide for navigating the intricate landscape of IoT security, offering insights for researchers & practitioners striving to intensify the resilience & potency of intrusion detection systems in IoT networks.

ACKNOWLEDGMENTS

The authors wish to acknowledge SR University for the support provided for research work.

REFERENCES

Abbas, A., Khan, M. A., Latif, S., Ajaz, M., Shah, A. A., & Ahmad, J. (2022). A New Ensemble-Based Intrusion Detection System for Internet of Things. *Arabian Journal for Science and Engineering*, *47*(2), 1805–1819. DOI: 10.1007/s13369-021-06086-5

Abdiyeva-Aliyeva, G., & Hematyar, M. (2022). Statistic Approached Dynamically Detecting Security Threats and Updating a Signature-Based Intrusion Detection System's Database in NGN. *Journal of Advances in Information Technology*, *13*(5), 524–529. DOI: 10.12720/jait.13.5.524-529

Ahad, U., Singh, Y., Anand, P., Sheikh, Z. A., & Singh, P. K. (2022). Intrusion Detection System Model for IoT Networks Using Ensemble Learning. *Journal of Interconnection Networks*, *22*(03), 2145008. Advance online publication. DOI: 10.1142/S0219265921450080

Ahmad, Z., Shahid Khan, A., Wai Shiang, C., Abdullah, J., & Ahmad, F. (2021). Network intrusion detection system: A systematic study of machine learning and deep learning approaches. *Transactions on Emerging Telecommunications Technologies*, *32*(1), e4150. Advance online publication. DOI: 10.1002/ett.4150

Al-Garadi, M. A., Mohamed, A., Al-Ali, A. K., Du, X., Ali, I., & Guizani, M. (2020). A Survey of Machine and Deep Learning Methods for Internet of Things (IoT) Security. *IEEE Communications Surveys and Tutorials*, *22*(3), 1646–1685. DOI: 10.1109/COMST.2020.2988293

Al-Hawawreh, M., Sitnikova, E., & Aboutorab, N. (2022). X-IIoTID: A Connectivity-Agnostic and Device-Agnostic Intrusion Data Set for Industrial Internet of Things. *IEEE Internet of Things Journal*, *9*(5), 3962–3977. DOI: 10.1109/JIOT.2021.3102056

Alsharif, M. H., Jahid, A., Kelechi, A. H., & Kannadasan, R. (2023). Green IoT: A Review and Future Research Directions. In *Symmetry* (Vol. 15, Issue 3). MDPI. DOI: 10.3390/sym15030757

Arbex, G. V., Machado, K. G., Nogueira, M., Batista, D. M., & Hirata, R. (2021). IoT DDoS Detection Based on Stream Learning. *2021 12th International Conference on Network of the Future (NoF)*, 1–8. DOI: 10.1109/NoF52522.2021.9609940

Ariffin, S. H., Le Chong, J., Latif, N. M. A. A., Abd Malik, N. N. N., Baharudin, M. A., Syed-Yusof, S. K., & Yusof, K. M. (2022). Intrusion detection system (IDS) accuracy testing for software defined network internet of things (SDN-IoT) testbed. *ELEKTRIKA-Journal of Electrical Engineering*, *21*(3), 23–27.

Arshad, J., Azad, M. A., Mahmoud Abdellatif, M., Ur Rehman, M. H., & Salah, K. (2019). COLIDE: A collaborative intrusion detection framework for Internet of Things. *IET Networks*, *8*(1), 3–14. DOI: 10.1049/iet-net.2018.5036

Atzori, L., Iera, A., & Morabito, G. (2010). The Internet of Things: A survey. *Computer Networks*, *54*(15), 2787–2805. DOI: 10.1016/j.comnet.2010.05.010

Azam, M., Mumtaz, G., & Mubeen, Z. (n.d.). *Securing IoT: Balancing Privacy and Attack Prediction.* https://doi.org/DOI: 10.56979/701/2024

Babun, L., Denney, K., Celik, Z. B., McDaniel, P., & Uluagac, A. S. (2021). A survey on IoT platforms: Communication, security, and privacy perspectives. *Computer Networks*, *192*, 108040. DOI: 10.1016/j.comnet.2021.108040

Bace, R., & Mell, P. (n.d.). *NIST Special Publication on Intrusion Detection Systems Intrusion Detection Systems.*

Bagaa, M., Taleb, T., Bernabe, J. B., & Skarmeta, A. (2020). A Machine Learning Security Framework for Iot Systems. *IEEE Access : Practical Innovations, Open Solutions*, *8*, 114066–114077. DOI: 10.1109/ACCESS.2020.2996214

Bartolucci, F., Donni, P. L., & Mira, A. (2023). Temporal analysis of hospital network data by hierarchical Bayesian p2 models with covariates. *Journal of the Royal Statistical Society. Series A, (Statistics in Society)*, *186*(3), 422–440. DOI: 10.1093/jrsssa/qnad036

Basati, A., & Faghih, M. M. (2023). APAE: An IoT intrusion detection system using asymmetric parallel auto-encoder. *Neural Computing & Applications*, *35*(7), 4813–4833. DOI: 10.1007/s00521-021-06011-9

Belenguer, A., Navaridas, J., & Pascual, J. A. (2022). *A review of Federated Learning in Intrusion Detection Systems for IoT.* http://arxiv.org/abs/2204.12443

Benkhelifa, E., Welsh, T., & Hamouda, W. (2018). A Critical Review of Practices and Challenges in Intrusion Detection Systems for IoT: Toward Universal and Resilient Systems. *IEEE Communications Surveys and Tutorials*, *20*(4), 3496–3509. DOI: 10.1109/COMST.2018.2844742

Berthier, R., & Sanders, W. H. (2011). Specification-Based Intrusion Detection for Advanced Metering Infrastructures. *2011 IEEE 17th Pacific Rim International Symposium on Dependable Computing*, 184–193. DOI: 10.1109/PRDC.2011.30

Bing, F. (2016, October). The research of IOT of agriculture based on three layers architecture. In 2016 2nd International Conference on Cloud Computing and Internet of Things (CCIOT) (pp. 162-165). IEEE.

Bostani, H., & Sheikhan, M. (2017). Hybrid of anomaly-based and specification-based IDS for Internet of Things using unsupervised OPF based on MapReduce approach. *Computer Communications*, *98*, 52–71. DOI: 10.1016/j.comcom.2016.12.001

Butun, I., Osterberg, P., & Song, H. (2020). Security of the Internet of Things: Vulnerabilities, Attacks, and Countermeasures. *IEEE Communications Surveys and Tutorials*, *22*(1), 616–644. DOI: 10.1109/COMST.2019.2953364

Camhi, J. (2015). *Former Cisco CEO John Chambers predicts 500 billion connected devices by 2025.*

Caminero, G., Lopez-Martin, M., & Carro, B. (2019). Adversarial environment reinforcement learning algorithm for intrusion detection. *Computer Networks*, *159*, 96–109. DOI: 10.1016/j.comnet.2019.05.013

Carone, S., Pappalettera, G., Casavola, C., De Carolis, S., & Soria, L. (2023). A Support Vector Machine-Based Approach for Bolt Loosening Monitoring in Industrial Customized Vehicles. *Sensors (Basel)*, *23*(11), 5345. DOI: 10.3390/s23115345 PMID: 37300075

Charbuty, B., & Abdulazeez, A. (2021). Classification Based on Decision Tree Algorithm for Machine Learning. *Journal of Applied Science and Technology Trends*, *2*(01), 20–28. DOI: 10.38094/jastt20165

Chiara, P. G. (2024). *The Internet of Things and EU Law* (Vol. 67). Springer Nature Switzerland., DOI: 10.1007/978-3-031-67663-5

Cirani, S., Davoli, L., Ferrari, G., Leone, R., Medagliani, P., Picone, M., & Veltri, L. (2014). A scalable and self-configuring architecture for service discovery in the internet of things. *IEEE Internet of Things Journal*, *1*(5), 508–521. DOI: 10.1109/JIOT.2014.2358296

Dev, V. A., & Eden, M. R. (2019). *Gradient Boosted Decision Trees for Lithology Classification.*, DOI: 10.1016/B978-0-12-818597-1.50019-9

El Ghazi, A., & Moulay Rachid, A. (2020). Machine learning and datamining methods for hybrid IoT intrusion detection. *2020 5th International Conference on Cloud Computing and Artificial Intelligence: Technologies and Applications (CloudTech)*, 1–6. DOI: 10.1109/CloudTech49835.2020.9365895

Eldrandaly, K. A., Abdel-Basset, M., & Shawky, L. A. (2019). Internet of Spatial Things: A New Reference Model With Insight Analysis. *IEEE Access : Practical Innovations, Open Solutions*, *7*, 19653–19669. DOI: 10.1109/ACCESS.2019.2897012

Elsaeidy, A. A., Jamalipour, A., & Munasinghe, K. S. (2021). A Hybrid Deep Learning Approach for Replay and DDoS Attack Detection in a Smart City. *IEEE Access : Practical Innovations, Open Solutions*, *9*, 154864–154875. DOI: 10.1109/ACCESS.2021.3128701

Erlacher, F., & Dressler, F. (2022). On High-Speed Flow-Based Intrusion Detection Using Snort-Compatible Signatures. *IEEE Transactions on Dependable and Secure Computing*, *19*(1), 495–506. DOI: 10.1109/TDSC.2020.2973992

Essop, I., Ribeiro, J. C., Papaioannou, M., Zachos, G., Mantas, G., & Rodriguez, J. (2021). Generating Datasets for Anomaly-Based Intrusion Detection Systems in IoT and Industrial IoT Networks. *Sensors (Basel)*, *21*(4), 1528. DOI: 10.3390/s21041528 PMID: 33672108

Farooq, M. (n.d.). Supervised Learning Techniques for Intrusion Detection System based on Multi-layer Classification Approach Machine Learning and Intrusion Detection System. In *IJACSA) International Journal of Advanced Computer Science and Applications* (Vol. 13, Issue 3). www.ijacsa.thesai.org

Ferrag, M. A., Friha, O., Hamouda, D., Maglaras, L., & Janicke, H. (2022). Edge-IIoTset: A New Comprehensive Realistic Cyber Security Dataset of IoT and IIoT Applications for Centralized and Federated Learning. *IEEE Access : Practical Innovations, Open Solutions*, *10*, 40281–40306. DOI: 10.1109/ACCESS.2022.3165809

Ferrag, M. A., Friha, O., Maglaras, L., Janicke, H., & Shu, L. (2021). Federated Deep Learning for Cyber Security in the Internet of Things: Concepts, Applications, and Experimental Analysis. *IEEE Access : Practical Innovations, Open Solutions*, *9*, 138509–138542. DOI: 10.1109/ACCESS.2021.3118642

Ferrag, M. A., Maglaras, L., Ahmim, A., Derdour, M., & Janicke, H. (2020). RDTIDS: Rules and Decision Tree-Based Intrusion Detection System for Internet-of-Things Networks. *Future Internet*, *12*(3), 44. DOI: 10.3390/fi12030044

Glissa, G., Rachedi, A., & Meddeb, A. (2016). A Secure Routing Protocol Based on RPL for Internet of Things. *2016 IEEE Global Communications Conference (GLOBECOM)*, 1–7. DOI: 10.1109/GLOCOM.2016.7841543

Gugueoth, V., Safavat, S., Shetty, S., & Rawat, D. (2023). A review of IoT security and privacy using decentralized blockchain techniques. *Computer Science Review*, *50*, 100585. DOI: 10.1016/j.cosrev.2023.100585

Heartfield, R., Loukas, G., Bezemskij, A., & Panaousis, E. (2021). Self-Configurable Cyber-Physical Intrusion Detection for Smart Homes Using Reinforcement Learning. *IEEE Transactions on Information Forensics and Security*, *16*, 1720–1735. DOI: 10.1109/TIFS.2020.3042049

Hosseini, S., & Sardo, S. R. (2023). Network intrusion detection based on deep learning method in internet of thing. *Journal of Reliable Intelligent Environments*, *9*(2), 147–159. DOI: 10.1007/s40860-021-00169-8

Hosseinzadeh, S., Hyrynsalmi, S., & Leppänen, V. (2016). Chapter 14 - Obfuscation and diversification for securing the internet of things (IoT). In *Internet of Things*. https://doi.org/DOI: 10.1016/B978-0-12-805395-9/00014-9

Hu, N., Tian, Z., Lu, H., Du, X., & Guizani, M. (2021). A multiple-kernel clustering based intrusion detection scheme for 5G and IoT networks. *International Journal of Machine Learning and Cybernetics*, *12*(11), 3129–3144. DOI: 10.1007/s13042-020-01253-w

Jamalipour, A., & Murali, S. (2022). A Taxonomy of Machine-Learning-Based Intrusion Detection Systems for the Internet of Things: A Survey. *IEEE Internet of Things Journal*, *9*(12), 9444–9466. DOI: 10.1109/JIOT.2021.3126811

Kalnoor, G., & Gowrishankar, S. (2021). RETRACTED ARTICLE: IoT-based smart environment using intelligent intrusion detection system. *Soft Computing*, *25*(17), 11573–11588. DOI: 10.1007/s00500-021-06028-1

Kandhro, I. A., Alanazi, S. M., Ali, F., Kehar, A., Fatima, K., Uddin, M., & Karuppayah, S. (2023). Detection of Real-Time Malicious Intrusions and Attacks in IoT Empowered Cybersecurity Infrastructures. *IEEE Access : Practical Innovations, Open Solutions*, *11*, 9136–9148. DOI: 10.1109/ACCESS.2023.3238664

Kaur, N., & Sood, S. K. (2017). An Energy-Efficient Architecture for the Internet of Things (IoT). *IEEE Systems Journal*, *11*(2), 796–805. DOI: 10.1109/JSYST.2015.2469676

Khanam, S., Ahmedy, I., Idna Idris, M. Y., Jaward, M. H., & Bin Md Sabri, A. Q. (2020). A Survey of Security Challenges, Attacks Taxonomy and Advanced Countermeasures in the Internet of Things. *IEEE Access : Practical Innovations, Open Solutions*, *8*, 219709–219743. DOI: 10.1109/ACCESS.2020.3037359

Khanna, A., & Kaur, S. (2020). Internet of Things (IoT), Applications and Challenges: A Comprehensive Review. In *Wireless Personal Communications* (Vol. 114, Issue 2, pp. 1687–1762). Springer. DOI: 10.1007/s11277-020-07446-4

Ko, C., Ruschitzka, M., & Levitt, K. (n.d.). Execution monitoring of security-critical programs in distributed systems: a specification-based approach. *Proceedings. 1997 IEEE Symposium on Security and Privacy (Cat. No.97CB36097)*, 175–187. DOI: 10.1109/SECPRI.1997.601332

Koppula, M., & Leo Joseph, L. M. I. (2025). A Real-World Dataset "IDSIoT2024" for Machine Learning/Deep Learning Based Cyber Attack Detection System for IoT Architecture. *2025 3rd International Conference on Intelligent Data Communication Technologies and Internet of Things (IDCIoT)*, 1757–1764. DOI: 10.1109/IDCIOT64235.2025.10914935

Koroniotis, N., Moustafa, N., Sitnikova, E., & Turnbull, B. (2019). Towards the development of realistic botnet dataset in the Internet of Things for network forensic analytics: Bot-IoT dataset. *Future Generation Computer Systems*, *100*, 779–796. DOI: 10.1016/j.future.2019.05.041

Kouicem, D. E., Bouabdallah, A., & Lakhlef, H. (2018). Internet of things security: A top-down survey. In *Computer Networks* (Vol. 141, pp. 199–221). Elsevier B.V., DOI: 10.1016/j.comnet.2018.03.012

Kumar, P. (2021). Design of Anomaly-Based Intrusion Detection System Using Fog Computing for IoT Network. *Automatic Control and Computer Sciences*, *55*(2), 137–147. DOI: 10.3103/S0146411621020085

Kumar, P., Gupta, G. P., & Tripathi, R. (2021). An ensemble learning and fog-cloud architecture-driven cyber-attack detection framework for IoMT networks. *Computer Communications*, *166*, 110–124. DOI: 10.1016/j.comcom.2020.12.003

Kumar, R., Kumar, P., Tripathi, R., Gupta, G. P., Garg, S., & Hassan, M. M. (2022). A distributed intrusion detection system to detect DDoS attacks in blockchain-enabled IoT network. *Journal of Parallel and Distributed Computing*, *164*, 55–68. DOI: 10.1016/j.jpdc.2022.01.030

Kumar, R., & Tripathi, R. (2021). DBTP2SF: A deep blockchain-based trustworthy privacy-preserving secured framework in industrial internet of things systems. *Transactions on Emerging Telecommunications Technologies, 32*(4), e4222. Advance online publication. DOI: 10.1002/ett.4222

Kuzlu, M., Fair, C., & Guler, O. (2021). Role of Artificial Intelligence in the Internet of Things (IoT) cybersecurity. *Discover Internet of Things, 1*(1), 7. DOI: 10.1007/s43926-020-00001-4

Lahasan, B., & Samma, H. (2022). Optimized Deep Autoencoder Model for Internet of Things Intruder Detection. *IEEE Access : Practical Innovations, Open Solutions, 10*, 8434–8448. DOI: 10.1109/ACCESS.2022.3144208

Lalouani, W., & Younis, M. (2021). Robust Distributed Intrusion Detection System for Edge of Things. *2021 IEEE Global Communications Conference (GLOBECOM)*, 01–06. DOI: 10.1109/GLOBECOM46510.2021.9685361

Lawal, M. A., Shaikh, R. A., & Hassan, S. R. (2020). An Anomaly Mitigation Framework for IoT Using Fog Computing. *Electronics (Basel), 9*(10), 1565. DOI: 10.3390/electronics9101565

Lawal, M. A., Shaikh, R. A., & Hassan, S. R. (2021). A DDoS Attack Mitigation Framework for IoT Networks using Fog Computing. *Procedia Computer Science, 182*, 13–20. DOI: 10.1016/j.procs.2021.02.003

Liao, H.-J., Richard Lin, C.-H., Lin, Y.-C., & Tung, K.-Y. (2013). Intrusion detection system: A comprehensive review. *Journal of Network and Computer Applications, 36*(1), 16–24. DOI: 10.1016/j.jnca.2012.09.004

Liu, J., Yang, D., Lian, M., & Li, M. (2021). Research on Intrusion Detection Based on Particle Swarm Optimization in IoT. *IEEE Access : Practical Innovations, Open Solutions, 9*, 38254–38268. DOI: 10.1109/ACCESS.2021.3063671

Lu, H., Li, Y., Mu, S., Wang, D., Kim, H., & Serikawa, S. (2018). Motor Anomaly Detection for Unmanned Aerial Vehicles Using Reinforcement Learning. *IEEE Internet of Things Journal, 5*(4), 2315–2322. DOI: 10.1109/JIOT.2017.2737479

Lu, Z., & Metghalchi, H. (2023). Prediction of Laminar Burning Speed of Propane/Hydrogen/Air Mixtures Using Power-Law Correlation and Two Machine Learning Models. *ASME Open Journal of Engineering, 2*, 021038. Advance online publication. DOI: 10.1115/1.4062745

Maharaja, R., Iyer, P., & Ye, Z. (2020). A hybrid fog-cloud approach for securing the Internet of Things. *Cluster Computing, 23*(2), 451–459. DOI: 10.1007/s10586-019-02935-z

Mahbod, T., Ebrahim, B., Wei, L., & Ali, A. G. (2009). A Detailed Analysis of the KDD CUP 99 Data Set, 2009 : [Ottawa, Canada, 8-10 July 2009]. *IEEE Symposium on Computational Intelligence for Security and Defense Applications (CISDA)*.

Mbarek, B., Meddeb, A., Ben Jaballah, W., & Mosbah, M. (2015). A secure authentication mechanism for resource constrained devices. *2015 IEEE/ACS 12th International Conference of Computer Systems and Applications (AICCSA)*, 1–7. DOI: 10.1109/AICCSA.2015.7507270

Mehta, S., Khurana, M., Dogra, A., & Hariharan, S. (2024). Advancing IoT Security through Federated Learning: A Comprehensive Approach. *2024 3rd International Conference on Applied Artificial Intelligence and Computing (ICAAIC)*, 561–566. DOI: 10.1109/ICAAIC60222.2024.10575903

Meidan, Y., Bohadana, M., Mathov, Y., Mirsky, Y., Shabtai, A., Breitenbacher, D., & Elovici, Y. (2018). N-BaIoT-Network-based detection of IoT botnet attacks using deep autoencoders. *IEEE Pervasive Computing*, *17*(3), 12–22. DOI: 10.1109/MPRV.2018.03367731

Mittal, M., Kumar, K., & Behal, S. (2023). Deep learning approaches for detecting DDoS attacks: A systematic review. *Soft Computing*, *27*(18), 13039–13075. DOI: 10.1007/s00500-021-06608-1 PMID: 35103047

Mohammed, B. H., Sallehudin, H., Satar, N. S. M., Murhg, H. D., Mohamed, S. A., Alaba, F. A., Rocha, A., & Bianchi, I. (2025). Anomaly Detection of Distributed Denial of Service (DDoS) in IoT Network Using. *Machine Learning*, *577*, 41–64. DOI: 10.1007/978-3-031-78412-5_3

Mourad, A., Tout, H., Wahab, O. A., Otrok, H., & Dbouk, T. (2021). *Ad Hoc* Vehicular Fog Enabling Cooperative Low-Latency Intrusion Detection. *IEEE Internet of Things Journal*, *8*(2), 829–843. DOI: 10.1109/JIOT.2020.3008488

Moustafa, N., Keshk, M., Debie, E., & Janicke, H. (n.d.). *Federated TON IoT Windows Datasets for Evaluating AI-based Security Applications*. https://doi.org/DOI: 10.1109/TrustCom50675.2020.00114/20/$31.00

Moustafa, N., & Slay, J. (n.d.). *UNSW-NB15: A Comprehensive Data set for Network Intrusion Detection systems (UNSW-NB15 Network Data Set)*. https://cve.mitre.org/

Mukherjee, B., Heberlein, L. T., & Levitt, K. N. (1994). Network intrusion detection. *IEEE Network*, *8*(3), 26–41. DOI: 10.1109/65.283931

Nakano, M., Takahashi, A., & Takahashi, S. (2017). Fuzzy logic-based portfolio selection with particle filtering and anomaly detection. *Knowledge-Based Systems*, *131*, 113–124. DOI: 10.1016/j.knosys.2017.06.006

Navani, D., Jain, S., & Nehra, M. S. (2017). The internet of things (IoT): A study of architectural elements. *Proceedings - 13th International Conference on Signal-Image Technology and Internet-Based Systems, SITIS 2017, 2018-January*, 473–478. DOI: 10.1109/SITIS.2017.83

Nguyen, V. T., & Beuran, R. (n.d.). *FedMSE: Semi-supervised federated learning approach for IoT network intrusion detection.* https://ssrn.com/abstract=4990105 DOI: 10.1016/j.cose.2025.104337

Northcutt, S., Cooper, M., Fearnow, M., & Frederick, K. (2001). *Intrusion Signatures and Analysis*. New Riders.

Oh, M., & Iyengar, G. (2019). Sequential Anomaly Detection using Inverse Reinforcement Learning. *Proceedings of the 25th ACM SIGKDD International Conference on Knowledge Discovery & Data Mining*, 1480–1490. DOI: 10.1145/3292500.3330932

Otoum, Y., Liu, D., & Nayak, A. (2022). DL-IDS: A deep learning–based intrusion detection framework for securing IoT. *Transactions on Emerging Telecommunications Technologies*, *33*(3), e3803. Advance online publication. DOI: 10.1002/ett.3803

Pacheco, J., Benitez, V., & Félix, L. (2019). Anomaly Behavior Analysis for IoT Network Nodes. *Proceedings of the 3rd International Conference on Future Networks and Distributed Systems*, 1–6. DOI: 10.1145/3341325.3342008

Pan, J.-S., Fan, F., Chu, S.-C., Zhao, H.-Q., & Liu, G.-Y. (2021). A Lightweight Intelligent Intrusion Detection Model for Wireless Sensor Networks. *Security and Communication Networks*, *2021*, 1–15. DOI: 10.1155/2021/5540895

Papadopoulos, P., Thornewill von Essen, O., Pitropakis, N., Chrysoulas, C., Mylonas, A., & Buchanan, W. J. (2021). Launching Adversarial Attacks against Network Intrusion Detection Systems for IoT. *Journal of Cybersecurity and Privacy*, *1*(2), 252–273. DOI: 10.3390/jcp1020014

Pathmabandu, C., Grundy, J., Chhetri, M. B., & Baig, Z. (2023). Privacy for IoT: Informed consent management in Smart Buildings. *Future Generation Computer Systems*, *145*, 367–383. DOI: 10.1016/j.future.2023.03.045

Prabavathy, S., Sundarakantham, K., & Shalinie, S. M. (2018). Design of cognitive fog computing for intrusion detection in Internet of Things. *Journal of Communications and Networks (Seoul)*, *20*(3), 291–298. DOI: 10.1109/JCN.2018.000041

Rathore, S., & Park, J. H. (2018). Semi-supervised learning based distributed attack detection framework for IoT. *Applied Soft Computing*, *72*, 79–89. DOI: 10.1016/j.asoc.2018.05.049

Ravi, N., & Shalinie, S. M. (2020). Semisupervised-Learning-Based Security to Detect and Mitigate Intrusions in IoT Network. *IEEE Internet of Things Journal, 7*(11), 11041–11052. DOI: 10.1109/JIOT.2020.2993410

Rodríguez, E., Valls, P., Otero, B., Costa, J. J., Verdú, J., Pajuelo, M. A., & Canal, R. (2022). Transfer-Learning-Based Intrusion Detection Framework in IoT Networks. *Sensors (Basel), 22*(15), 5621. DOI: 10.3390/s22155621 PMID: 35957178

Roopak, M., Tian, G. Y., & Chambers, J. (2020). An Intrusion Detection System Against DDoS Attacks in IoT Networks. *2020 10th Annual Computing and Communication Workshop and Conference (CCWC)*, 0562–0567. DOI: 10.1109/CCWC47524.2020.9031206

Saadeh, H., Saadeh, M., Almobaideen, W., & Al-Tawil, M. (2022). Evaluating the Optimal Number of Clusters to Identify Similar Gene Expression Patterns During Erythropoiesis. *2022 International Conference on Computer, Information and Telecommunication Systems (CITS)*, 1–5. DOI: 10.1109/CITS55221.2022.9832988

Sahar, N., Mishra, R., & Kalam, S. (2021). *Deep Learning Approach-Based Network Intrusion Detection System for Fog-Assisted IoT.*, DOI: 10.1007/978-981-15-8377-3_4

Sandhu, R., Sohal, A. S., & Sood, S. K. (2017). Identification of malicious edge devices in fog computing environments. *Information Security Journal: A Global Perspective, 26*(5), 213–228. DOI: 10.1080/19393555.2017.1334843

Sarker, I. H. (2021). Machine Learning: Algorithms, Real-World Applications and Research Directions. *SN Computer Science, 2*(3), 160. DOI: 10.1007/s42979-021-00592-x PMID: 33778771

Shan, Y., Yao, Y., Zhou, X., Zhao, T., Hu, B., & Wang, L. (2024). CFL-IDS: An Effective Clustered Federated Learning Framework for Industrial Internet of Things Intrusion Detection. *IEEE Internet of Things Journal, 11*(6), 10007–10019. DOI: 10.1109/JIOT.2023.3324302

Sharafaldin, I., Lashkari, A. H., & Ghorbani, A. A. (2018). Toward generating a new intrusion detection dataset and intrusion traffic characterization. *ICISSP 2018 - Proceedings of the 4th International Conference on Information Systems Security and Privacy, 2018-January*, 108–116. DOI: 10.5220/0006639801080116

Sharjeel, M., Ahmed Sumra, I., Sattar, A., & Arshad, M. (n.d.). *A Comprehensive Analysis on Privacy and Security for IoT Solutions.* https://doi.org/DOI: 10.56979/801/2024

Shenvi, N., & Virani, H. (2023). Comparative Analysis of Machine learning techniques for Forecasting Ionospheric Total Electron Content Data. *2023 4th International Conference for Emerging Technology (INCET)*, 1–6. DOI: 10.1109/INCET57972.2023.10169972

Shinde, S. A., Pawar, R. R., Jagtap, A. A., Tambewagh, P. A., Rajput, P. U., Mali, M. K., Kale, S. D., & Mulik, S. V. (2023). Deceptive opinion spam detection using bidirectional long short-term memory with capsule neural network. *Multimedia Tools and Applications*, *83*(15), 45111–45140. DOI: 10.1007/s11042-023-17348-9

Shitharth, S., Kshirsagar, P. R., Balachandran, P. K., Alyoubi, K. H., & Khadidos, A. O. (2022). An Innovative Perceptual Pigeon Galvanized Optimization (PPGO) Based Likelihood Naïve Bayes (LNB) Classification Approach for Network Intrusion Detection System. *IEEE Access : Practical Innovations, Open Solutions*, *10*, 46424–46441. DOI: 10.1109/ACCESS.2022.3171660

Siddharthan, H., Deepa, T., & Chandhar, P. (2022). SENMQTT-SET: An Intelligent Intrusion Detection in IoT-MQTT Networks Using Ensemble Multi Cascade Features. *IEEE Access : Practical Innovations, Open Solutions*, *10*, 33095–33110. DOI: 10.1109/ACCESS.2022.3161566

Silva, J. D. C., Rodrigues, J. J. P. C., Saleem, K., Kozlov, S. A., & Rabelo, R. A. L. (2019). M4DN.IoT-A Networks and Devices Management Platform for Internet of Things. *IEEE Access : Practical Innovations, Open Solutions*, *7*, 53305–53313. DOI: 10.1109/ACCESS.2019.2909436

Sohal, A. S., Sandhu, R., Sood, S. K., & Chang, V. (2018). A cybersecurity framework to identify malicious edge device in fog computing and cloud-of-things environments. *Computers & Security*, *74*, 340–354. DOI: 10.1016/j.cose.2017.08.016

Sohn, I. (2021). Deep belief network based intrusion detection techniques: A survey. *Expert Systems with Applications*, *167*, 114170. DOI: 10.1016/j.eswa.2020.114170

Sudqi Khater, B., Abdul Wahab, A. W., Idris, M. Y. I. B., Abdulla Hussain, M., & Ahmed Ibrahim, A. (2019). A Lightweight Perceptron-Based Intrusion Detection System for Fog Computing. *Applied Sciences (Basel, Switzerland)*, *9*(1), 178. DOI: 10.3390/app9010178

Surendar, M., & Umamakeswari, A. (2016). InDReS: An Intrusion Detection and response system for Internet of Things with 6LoWPAN. *2016 International Conference on Wireless Communications, Signal Processing and Networking (WiSPNET)*, 1903–1908. DOI: 10.1109/WiSPNET.2016.7566473

Syed, N. F., Ge, M., & Baig, Z. (2023). Fog-cloud based intrusion detection system using Recurrent Neural Networks and feature selection for IoT networks. *Computer Networks*, *225*, 109662. DOI: 10.1016/j.comnet.2023.109662

Tabassum, A., Erbad, A., Mohamed, A., & Guizani, M. (2021). Privacy-Preserving Distributed IDS Using Incremental Learning for IoT Health Systems. *IEEE Access : Practical Innovations, Open Solutions*, *9*, 14271–14283. DOI: 10.1109/ACCESS.2021.3051530

Telikani, A., Shen, J., Yang, J., & Wang, P. (2022). Industrial IoT Intrusion Detection via Evolutionary Cost-Sensitive Learning and Fog Computing. *IEEE Internet of Things Journal*, *9*(22), 23260–23271. DOI: 10.1109/JIOT.2022.3188224

Tsai, C. W., Lai, C. F., & Vasilakos, A. V. (2014). Future Internet of Things: Open issues and challenges. *Wireless Networks*, *20*(8), 2201–2217. DOI: 10.1007/s11276-014-0731-0

Ullah, I., & Mahmoud, Q. H. (2022). Design and Development of RNN Anomaly Detection Model for IoT Networks. *IEEE Access : Practical Innovations, Open Solutions*, *10*, 62722–62750. DOI: 10.1109/ACCESS.2022.3176317

Ullah, I., Raza, B., Ali, S., Abbasi, I. A., Baseer, S., & Irshad, A. (2021). Software Defined Network Enabled Fog-to-Things Hybrid Deep Learning Driven Cyber Threat Detection System. *Security and Communication Networks*, *2021*, 1–15. DOI: 10.1155/2021/6136670

Uprety, A., & Rawat, D. B. (2021). Reinforcement Learning for IoT Security: A Comprehensive Survey. *IEEE Internet of Things Journal*, *8*(11), 8693–8706. DOI: 10.1109/JIOT.2020.3040957

Virat, M. S., Bindu, S. M., Aishwarya, B., Dhanush, B. N., & Kounte, M. R. (2018, May). Security and privacy challenges in internet of things. In 2018 2nd International Conference on Trends in Electronics and Informatics (ICOEI) (pp. 454-460). IEEE.

Wang, Y., Meng, W., Li, W., Li, J., Liu, W.-X., & Xiang, Y. (2018). A fog-based privacy-preserving approach for distributed signature-based intrusion detection. *Journal of Parallel and Distributed Computing*, *122*, 26–35. DOI: 10.1016/j.jpdc.2018.07.013

Wu, M., Lu, T. J., Ling, F. Y., Sun, J., & Du, H. Y. (2010). Research on the architecture of Internet of Things. *3rd International Conference on Advanced Computer Theory and Engineering (ICACTE).*

Xin, Y., Kong, L., Liu, Z., Chen, Y., Li, Y., Zhu, H., Gao, M., Hou, H., & Wang, C. (2018). Machine Learning and Deep Learning Methods for Cybersecurity. *IEEE Access : Practical Innovations, Open Solutions*, *6*, 35365–35381. DOI: 10.1109/ACCESS.2018.2836950

Yang, X., Peng, G., Zhang, D., & Lv, Y. (2022). An Enhanced Intrusion Detection System for IoT Networks Based on Deep Learning and Knowledge Graph. *Security and Communication Networks*, *2022*, 1–21. DOI: 10.1155/2022/3317048

Yang, X., Shu, L., Liu, Y., Hancke, G. P., Ferrag, M. A., & Huang, K. (2022). Physical Security and Safety of IoT Equipment: A Survey of Recent Advances and Opportunities. *IEEE Transactions on Industrial Informatics*, *18*(7), 4319–4330. DOI: 10.1109/TII.2022.3141408

Yuan, C., & Yang, H. (2019). Research on K-Value Selection Method of K-Means Clustering Algorithm. *J*, *2*(2), 226–235. DOI: 10.3390/j2020016

Zarpelão, B. B., Miani, R. S., Kawakani, C. T., & de Alvarenga, S. C. (2017). A survey of intrusion detection in Internet of Things. *Journal of Network and Computer Applications*, *84*, 25–37. DOI: 10.1016/j.jnca.2017.02.009

Zolanvari, M., Teixeira, M. A., Gupta, L., Khan, K. M., & Jain, R. (2019). Machine Learning-Based Network Vulnerability Analysis of Industrial Internet of Things. *IEEE Internet of Things Journal*, *6*(4), 6822–6834. DOI: 10.1109/JIOT.2019.2912022

Chapter 13

Security Vulnerabilities and Countermeasures for Wireless Sensor Networks in Cyber-Physical Systems

T. C. Swetha Priya
https://orcid.org/0000-0002-0644-4329
Stanley College of Engineering and Technology for Women, India

R. Sridevi
Jawaharlal Nehru Technological University, Hyderabad, India

ABSTRACT

Wireless Sensor Networks (WSNs) are fundamental to Cyber-Physical Systems (CPS), enabling the real-time collection and transmission of data for diverse critical uses including industrial automation, healthcare, smart cities, and environmental monitoring. Owing to their intrinsic weaknesses, such as restricted computational resources, unprotected communication pathways, and decentralized structures, the WSN is particularly susceptible to various security risks. These vulnerabilities present considerable dangers to the confidentiality, integrity, and availability of data exchanged within CPS, possibly resulting in serious outcomes like system break-downs, data manipulation, and unauthorized access. This chapter offers an in-depth examination of the security issues faced by WSNs in CPS settings. It examines the key vulnerabilities of WSNs across different network layers, including physical layer attacks (like eavesdropping and jamming), network layer attacks (such as routing and DOS attacks), and data integrity attacks at the application layer. The threats

DOI: 10.4018/979-8-3373-2200-1.ch013

from insiders and assaults on the energy efficiency of WSNs are also addressed. To address these threats, this chapter offers a range of countermeasures aimed at enhancing the security of WSNs in CPS. This includes cryptographic methods, secure routing protocols, intrusion detection systems, trust management frameworks, and energy-efficient security approaches. The chapter additionally emphasizes various case studies from actual CPS applications like smart grids and healthcare systems to showcase the real-world security implementations. Ultimately, new trends such as machine learning-driven intrusion detection and block chain for ensuring data integrity are explored as possible future pathways for enhancing the security of WSNs in progressively intricate CPS settings. This study seeks to establish a basic comprehension of the security challenges faced by WSN and the necessary countermeasures to safeguard CPS against emerging cyber threats.

1. INTRODUCTION

Cyber-Physical Systems (CPS) represents a novel framework that combines physical and computational processes to facilitate smooth interaction between the digital and physical realms. This leads to improved system automation and oversight, boosting the productivity and effectiveness of utilizing real-time environments. Employing different technologies and methods enables diverse interactions among humans, machines, and the environment, enhancing both operational and user efficiency.

The central component of CPS is Wireless Sensor Networks, known as WSNs. A network of sensors located in various geographical areas that utilize wireless communication to collect and send data is referred to as a WSN. These sensors can monitor various physical traits, including temperature, movement, humidity, and respiratory conditions. Given that WSNs form the foundation for CPS to operate and make decisions quickly, real-time integration is greatly reliant on the data gathered from them.

It is evident that WSNs are significant in CPS applications. WSNs offer intelligent infrastructure management in smart cities by tracking energy consumption, traffic trends, and the city's cleanliness. When cities are constructed and utilized for particular purposes, it fosters development that is guided by intention.

Data integrity protection, privacy assurance, and availability maintenance are some of the critical aspects considered during such deployment, across a variety of applications (Halim, T et al., 2012). As reliance on these networks continues to grow, security should take precedence to shield sensitive information and guarantee the uninterrupted performance of these systems.

2. WIRELESS SENSOR NETWORKS IN CYBER-PHYSICAL SYSTEMS

2.1. WSN Features

i) **Large scale**

Sensor nodes cover huge amount of information and receive a greater amount of information. This is because of a large amount of sensor nodes. However, a huge amount of sensor nodes makes maintenance difficult. In addition, the particular application area of the sensor nodes can make it challenging to replace them especially in environments with high temperatures and pressures or high radiation levels. (Sharma et al., 2021)

ii) Limited battery capacity

The working state of sensor nodes and their stability has a direct relationship with the battery power. Generally, the batteries are not reusable. So there is a need to replace them in a timely manner in order to prevent power loss and network failure. But such replacement is difficult in critical environments. To ensure reliable data transmission across nodes it is important to maintain battery life of nodes and network.

iii) Weak communication capabilities

Generally, sensors are poorly equipped in multi-hop network technology in terms of communication and have to be routed properly when communicating with each other and other nodes. Multi-hop network transmission technology passes the information to the aggregated node and that node can forward information sent by other sensor nodes. Even if a single sensor node fails, the gathered data can be transmitted through other nodes.

iv) Prone to faults

The sensor nodes are prone to few faults such as power failure or damage. Therefore, the entire network must have a strong coordination capability among nodes in order to resist from data loss.

2.2 Wireless Sensor Networks(WSN) Architecture

2.2.1. Key Components of WSNs

Sensors serve as the fundamental components of WSNs, intended to identify and quantify physical phenomena like temperature, humidity, light, motion, and pressure. The sensors transform physical constraints into electric signals that can be digitized consequently to involve processing. A wide range of data gathering is possible in wide range of areas by installing sensors for various applications such as healthcare, environment monitoring and smart urban environments.

Actuators are the devices that help in the execution of various actions as response to the information gathered by sensors. As an example, consider farming where this actuator manages all the irrigation systems based on the moisture level information present in the soil given by sensors. The cooperation between sensors and the actuators must be good enough to facilitate the changes in the readings and improve the efficiency of applications.

Communication nodes play a major role in the transmission of data across the network. These nodes direct data from the sensors to remaining nodes and then finally to gateways. These nodes support multi-hop communication to cover wide network ranges and also to ensure network's reliability in critical environments.

The connection between WSN and other networks such as internet or cloud services is possible with **Gateways**. Gateways collect information from several sensors and communication nodes. Then this information is refined and processed to send it further to advanced systems for analysis. They play major role in incorporation of WSNs into Cyber physical Systems to facilitate smooth data transmission and communication with additional elements.

2.2.2. Layered Architecture of WSNs

Figure 1. WSN Architecture

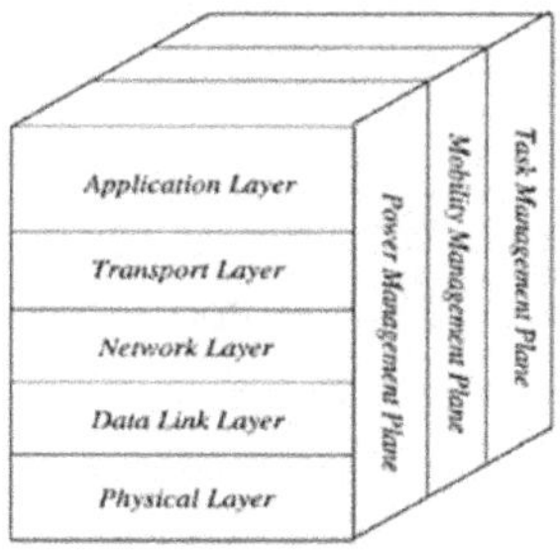

In general, the WSN architecture is organized in layered manner resembling the OSI model as shown in Figure 1. This layered approach simplifies the administration of network tasks and also improves modularity (Jondhale et al.,2022; Ojeda et al, 2023). The layered approach consists of 5 Layers that are explained as follows:

1. **Application Layer:** This layer is responsible for managing data traffic and provides software to various applications that convert unreadable data into proper form that is useful for analysis. There are several applications in which sensors are used such as industrial automation, Smart agriculture, Military, Healthcare etc. This layer also acts as interface between applications and the devices.
2. **Transport Layer:** This layer is provides reliability and congestion control and data transmission. It may provide data transmission either upstream or downstream. It also employs mechanisms like positive and negative acknowledgements for detection of lost segments and data recovery. TCP is not suitable for WSN because it consumes more energy. The transport protocols are classified into packet driven and event driven. Some of the popular protocols in this layer that supports sensors are Sensor Transmission Control Protocol (STCP),price-oriented reliable transport protocol(PORT) and Pump slow fetch Quick(PSFQ) protocol. This layer guarantees that information reaches accurately to intended node.
3. **Network Layer:** The primary function of this layer is routing data among nodes. The challenges faced by this layer are limited memory and power saving. The sensors do not maintain global identification information and are self organized. This layer provides reliable paths for data transmission between nodes. To provide energy efficiency, approaches like data fusion and data aggregation are employed along with data centric routing. Some hierarchy routing protocols such as LEACH, SPAN, ASCENT etc., are used to reduce power consumption.
4. **Data Link Layer:** This layer multiplexes data streams, detects data frames, provides medium access control, error control and provides reliability for point-to-point or point-to-multipoint connections. This layer resists against multipath fading and co-channel interference. The MAC protocol used in this layer provides reliability, high throughput and energy efficiency.
5. **Physical Layer:** This layer provides transmission of bits over physical channel by providing an interface. It also helps in selection of frequency bands, carrier frequency, modulation and detection of signals. IEEE 802.15.4 was one of the standard used for low rate small area to maximize Network lifetime, reduce complexity and cost.

2.2.3. Cross-Layer Management Planes

There are three cross planes in WSN architecture. They are power management plane, mobility management plane and task management plane. These planes help in controlling network operation as well as making the sensors function appropriately in order to enhance the network performance. These planes are explained as follows:

1. **Power Management Layer:** This plane helps in controlling the consumption of energy of sensor nodes which is important for restricted battery devices such as sensor nodes, IoT sensors etc,. Efficient power management approaches can then be used to enhance lifetime of a network.
2. **Mobility Management plane:** This plane helps in the detection of movement of sensor nodes. These nodes can keep track of their neighboring nodes and balances power levels.
3. **Task Management Plane**: This plane helps in scheduling the tasks for sensing a particular area in a WSN. It also determines which nodes are active and which nodes are dead. This helps in improving the network lifetime.

2.3 Applications of WSNs in Cyber-Physical Systems (CPS)

In cyber physical systems, the WSNs play a major role across several fields. Real-time monitoring, automated control and data gathering can be done easily with WSN providing efficient decision making.

Few applications of WSNs in Cyber Physical Systems(CPS) are discussed below:

i. Industrial Automation

In many manufacturing industries, the Sensor networks are deployed to monitor the equipment, environment and production works. These sensors gather data and transmit it to cloud servers or central storage for analysis. Then algorithms are applied on this data to determine certain patterns and find abnormal data patterns and take action accordingly before the situation gets worse. The actuators are generally used to respond automatically and act immediately according to the changing data. For example, machinery actuation in industries is done automatically according to the changes in real-time data (Popescu et al., 2020).

ii. Smart Farming

Traditional farming techniques are being replaced by introducing WSNs in agriculture sector (Suhaimi et al., 2021). The different type of sensors are deployed in the farming fields to monitor moisture levels in the soil, temperature and nutrient levels to give farmers a deep insight about the crop health conditions. This will help farmers in making sound decisions on irrigation, fertilization, and pest control hence increasing yield and resource efficiency. Integration of WSNs with cloud computing provides data storage and data management, thus enabling farmers to receive real-time information from anywhere. Besides, the actuators can automate an irrigation system for ensuring proper water supply directed by the information obtained from sensors.

iii. Healthcare

In the healthcare industry, the WSNs are used for monitoring and managing patients remotely (Sadeghi et al., 2022; Dey et al.,2018). The wearable sensors can continuously monitor the heart Beat rate, blood pressure, and temperature data which has to be transmitted in real-time to health service providers. This offers an opportunity for timely interventions and personalized care for patients with chronic illnesses. The exchange of data through WSNs into cloud servers will help in collecting and analyzing the data about the patients leading to much better health conditions. So, one could integrate actuators into different medical equipment to ensure automated drug delivery or alert healthcare professionals in emergencies.

iv. Smart Transportation

WSNs are of significant importance for intelligent transportation systems. By using sensors all over roads, it can monitor real-time traffic condition providing data on the flow of vehicles, congestion, and environmental parameters. This information can be analyzed through cloud systems to optimize traffic management strategies-like on traffic signals or driving directions to drivers. Not only this, but WSNs can also synchronize with actuators installed in vehicles allowing adaptive cruise control and parking assistance which elevates safety and efficiency on roads. Very few of them are dedicated to environmental monitoring.

v. Environmental monitoring

Environmental monitoring includes monitoring air and water quality as well as weather conditions. WSN deployment can include a variety of locations with their sensors measuring air and water pollutants, temperature, and humidity levels.

2.4 Challenges in WSN Security

In the course of the applications from environment monitoring to industrial automation, the increasing deployment of Wireless Sensor Networks (WSNs) presents some security challenges due to the inherent constraints of the networks and the environment in which they function. Hence, it is important to get to know the challenges for the implementation of an effective security method to maintain the integrity and functionality of WSNs.

i. Resource Constraints

The main challenge to be encountered when securing WSNs lies in the limited resources on the sensor nodes. Normally they are battery-powered that operate on restricted energy consumption. As a result, security protocols need to be devised with energy efficiency and the overhead caused by encryption, authentication, and integrity checks on data should be kept as low as possible. The energy consumed in communication tends to drain the battery quickly on sensor nodes leading to network failure. Besides energy restrictions, sensor nodes often possess low processing capacity. This limitation makes the execution of computationally heavy cryptographic algorithms very effective in a typical computing environment by practically making it impossible for WSNs. Security solutions must thus be lightweight and be able to run on devices with limited processing power. This balance is required between the security provided and the consumption of resources used by the security mechanism.

ii. Hostile Environment

WSNs may have their environment being potentially hostile, which further makes it difficult to carry out the security. The sensors are easily compromised and may also be subject to environmental changes or malicious attacks. Because the sensors are deployed ad hoc, the sensors cannot be associated with a specific location; thus, security measures cannot be easily adopted when they rely on a relatively stable network topology. The dynamic character of WSNs makes it quite difficult to assure secure communications. Failure of nodes and addition of new nodes may result in rapid changes in network topology. So, security schemes must require adaptive protocols to respond to these topology changes. Furthermore, the nodes may be easily compromised leading to requirement for good intrusion detection schemes in resource-constrained environments. In resource-constrained environments, IDSs play a crucial role in identifying the compromised nodes.

iii. Long Range Communication requirements

To transmit the gathered data to the base station and cloud servers, long range communication is required. The communication over long distances exposes data to few security risks such as interception of data, traffic analysis and eavesdropping. Maintaining the confidentiality and data integrity during data transmission over insecure channels is one of the major issues. Efficient encryption techniques and secure routing protocols are required to protect data from unauthorized users and ensure transmission of data through reliable nodes.

3. SECURITY VULNERABILITIES IN WSNS FOR CPS

When the Wireless Sensor Networks are setup in CPS applications, malicious nodes may interfere with the normal physical operations damaging the information gathered by the sensor nodes and even resulting in failure of whole system (Keerthika et al., 2021). So, identifying the potential security vulnerabilities in such networks is primary issue in making the CPS reliable.

3.1. Physical Layer Vulnerabilities

The physical layer in WSNs is responsible for radio-frequency (RF) communication and direct hardware access. Since sensor nodes are deployed in unsecured and remote environments, they are prone to various physical and signal-based attacks.

a. Eavesdropping

Because WSNs rely on wireless communication, the signals they transmit can be intercepted by anyone within range of the sensor nodes. Attackers who manage to position themselves close enough can passively listen to the communication channel. Unauthorized access to sensor data can compromise user privacy and intellectual property. This passive eavesdropping may allow them to gather sensitive information, including cryptographic keys, personal data from health sensors, or industrial process data. This attack causes lack of confidentiality. Figure 2 demonstrates the Eavesdropping attack.

Figure 2. Eavesdropping Attack

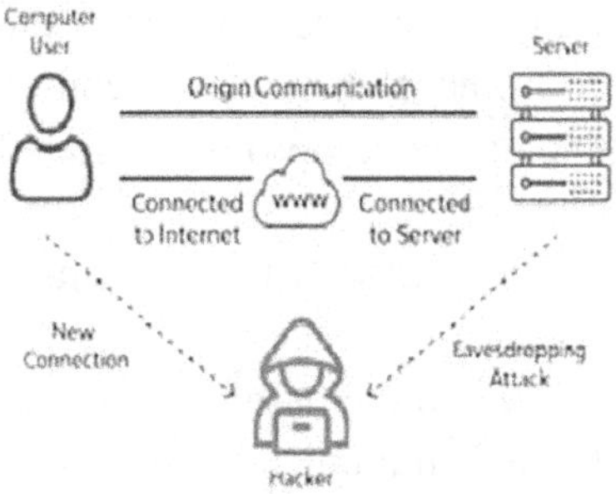

b. Signal Jamming

Signal jamming involves the deliberate emission of radio frequency (RF) noise or other disruptive signals to interfere with legitimate communications. The attacker continuously emits high-power noise, blocking any legitimate communication. The attacker sends interference signals only at specific times, such as when they detect a packet transmission, to remain undetected for longer periods. Jamming is typically easy to initiate but can be resource-intensive for the attacker, as they need a transmitter with enough power to overwhelm the signals of the WSN.

c. Spoofing Attacks

Spoofing at the physical layer can involve an attacker mimicking legitimate nodes by transmitting signals that appear to come from authorized sources. By doing this, the attacker can manipulate the network's topology, redirect traffic, or feed false data into the system. Spoofing attack is demonstrated as shown in figure 3.

Figure 3. Spoofing Attack

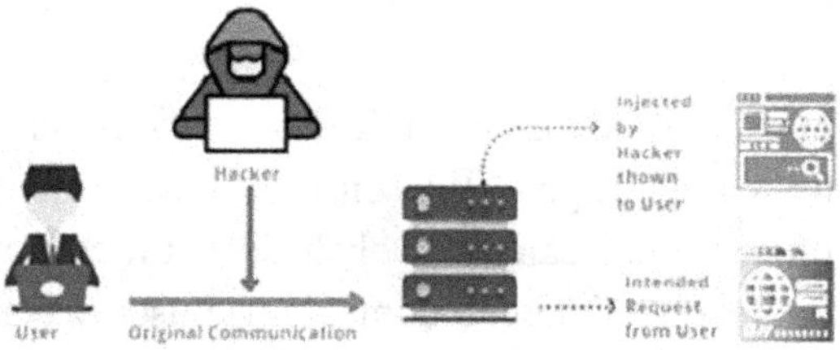

3.2 Network Layer Vulnerabilities

The network layer is responsible for routing and data forwarding between nodes. Various attacks target this layer to disrupt communication and manipulate routing protocols.

a. Routing Attacks

Routing protocols in WSNs often assume cooperative behaviour from all nodes. Because of the resource constraints in sensor nodes, many routing protocols may lack strong cryptographic protections. This makes them vulnerable to attacks such as:

i. Wormhole Attack

Two colluding attackers create a "tunnel" between distant parts of the network. They capture packets in one location and quickly replay them at another, effectively making nodes believe that they are neighbors. This can severely disrupt routing and create routing loops or false routes.

ii. Sybil Attack

A single malicious node presents multiple identities to the network. This undermines redundancy mechanisms and can skew voting-based protocols or disrupt load balancing.

iii. Sinkhole Attack

The adversary advertises a very attractive (e.g., low-cost) route to a base station, luring much of the network's traffic through the compromised node. Once traffic is concentrated, the attacker can selectively forward or drop packets.

iv. Blackhole Attack

An attacker simply drops all packets that come its way, acting like a "black hole" in the network. This attack can be used to create a DoS for certain parts of the network.

b. Denial-of-Service (DoS) Attacks

DoS attacks often involve flooding the network with spurious requests or exploiting weaknesses in routing protocols. For example, Sending large volumes of routing requests or data packets to overload network resources and Broadcasting powerful "HELLO" messages that trick many nodes into thinking the attacker is within range. Figure 4 demonstrates the working of DOS attack.

Figure 4. Denial-of-Service (DoS)

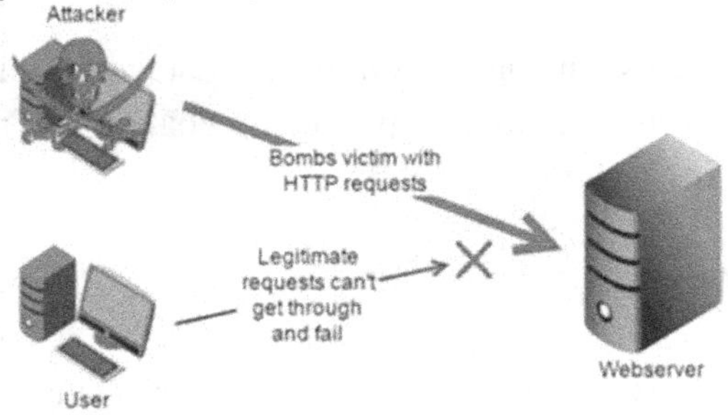

c. Network Sniffing and Traffic Analysis

Even if the data is encrypted, attackers can perform traffic analysis to learn about network topology and patterns of communication. By analyzing who communicates with whom, an adversary may identify key nodes like cluster heads or base stations, which then become prime targets for more direct attacks.

3.3 Data Link and Application Layer Vulnerabilities

The data link layer manages data integrity and access control, while the application layer handles sensor data processing and user interactions. At the data link layer, frames can be altered, duplicated, or dropped if an attacker gains access to communication channels or compromised nodes.

At the application layer, software vulnerabilities in sensor firmware or gateway applications can be exploited to corrupt sensor readings or trigger incorrect operations.

a. Tampering and Resource Manipulation

Physical tampering with sensor nodes is a significant risk because sensors are often deployed in remote or unsupervised environments. Once an attacker gains physical access to a sensor node, they can perform the following:

Extract Cryptographic Keys: If keys are stored in memory without proper protection.

Modify Firmware: Inject malicious code that changes how the sensor collects or reports data.

Sabotage Hardware:

This attack causes damage to the node and nodes reports erroneous readings or stops proper functionality of nodes.

b. Privacy Concerns

WSNs gather personal or sensitive information in many application layer scenarios such as healthcare monitoring, smart home, etc,. The attacker can compromise privacy by modifying the sensitive information if the application layer does not encrypt data properly.

3.4 Insider and Collusion Attacks

In this type of attacks, the compromised nodes cooperate with each other to interfere with network functionality.

a. Insider Threats

This type of attack originates from nodes that were initially incorporated inside the network legitimately but later turn into compromised nodes over time. This causes a significant risk as insider nodes possess legitimate cryptographic credentials, reliable pathways, and direct access to information. Attackers control a node physically to retrieve keys or modify its programming. Harmful updates or firmware faults enable attackers to take control.

b. Collusion Attacks

This type of attack takes place when a large number of compromised nodes work together to cause an attack. As a group, the compromised nodes can initiate stronger sinkhole or black hole attacks. This attack leads to significant data modifications causing an impact on the dependability of system.

3.5 Energy-Consumption and Battery Drain Vulnerabilities

Compromised nodes causes more energy consumption leading to network failure since the sensor nodes depend on limited battery power.

a. Resource Constraints in WSNs

Limited battery power and limited processing power constraints of a sensor node may be considered by attackers to exploit resources prematurely

b. Battery Drain Attacks

An attacker may repeatedly request for data or force the nodes to continuously transmit, receive, or perform computational tasks.

4. THREAT MODEL FRAMEWORK FOR WSN IN CYBER-PHYSICAL SYSTEMS

Even though the WSNs are used for monitoring and controlling the physical environments in Cyber Physical systems, these types of networks encounter several threats that weakens reliability and performance. To counter such attacks, several threat models are employed to examine possible attack surfaces and weaknesses.

4.1 Common Threat Models in WSN for Cyber Physical Systems

a. **Compromised Node Attacks** – In this type of attacks, the compromised sensor nodes physically access the sensitive information or reprogram the other nodes to act maliciously
b. **Eavesdropping & Data Interception** – The attackers intercept the data being transmitted and analyze the packets that are transmitted over the network.
c. **Denial-of-Service (DoS)** – The attackers flood the network with excessive data or disrupt the communication channels, making the system unresponsive.
d. **Routing Attacks** – Compromised nodes create false routing tables or manipulate the routing information to mislead the packets to wrong destinations leading to packet dropping or network failure.
e. **Sybil Attacks** – A single malicious node can create multiple fake identities to confuse the network and disrupts the decision-making processes.

4.2. Security goals and Requirements for WSNs in CPS

WSNs are most commonly employed in harsh or remote environments making them vulnerable to several threats. A security breach can cause severe consequences disrupting critical services causing physical damage or loss to confidential information. A few security goals for WSNs are Confidentiality, Integrity, Authentication and Availability.

4.3 Common Attack Models

a. **Man-in-the-Middle (MITM) Attack:** An attacker may intercept the data communication between two nodes by eavesdropping or false data injection.
b. **Replay Attacks:** An attacker captures data traffic and replays data for malicious purposes.
c. **Impersonation Attacks:** A malicious node acts as a legitimate node to gain unauthorized access or disrupt normal operations.

5. COUNTERMEASURES FOR SECURING WIRELESS SENSOR NETWORKS IN CPS

5.1 Cryptographic Techniques for WSN Security

Lightweight encryption protocols are used to provide secure data communication between nodes. Such cryptographic algorithms are designed for devices with limited computational resources such as sensors, RFID tags, and embedded systems (Priya et al., 2024). The main features of these protocols are:

- **Low Computational Complexity:** Designed for fast execution and minimal use of CPU cycles.
- **Small Memory Footprint:** Require less RAM and storage, making them suitable for constrained devices.
- **Energy Efficiency:** Reduce battery drain, crucial for battery-operated or hard-to-access devices.
- **Adequate Security:** Provide confidentiality, integrity, and authentication without sacrificing essential protection.

The Common Lightweight Encryption Algorithms are shown in Table 1.

Table 1. Lightweight Encryption Algorithms

Algorithm	Type	Key Features	Standardization/Status
ASCON	Block cipher	AEAD, NIST standard, low resource use	NIST Lightweight Crypto Standard
PRESENT	Block cipher	64-bit block, 80/128-bit key, ISO/IEC	ISO/IEC 29192, widely used
CLEFIA	Block cipher	128-bit block, 128/192/256-bit key	ISO/IEC 29192, Sony-developed

continued on following page

Table 1. Continued

Algorithm	Type	Key Features	Standardization/Status
Grain v1	Stream cipher	Low power, suitable for RFID	eSTREAM portfolio
Trivium	Stream cipher	Simple, low hardware cost	eSTREAM portfolio
MICKEY v2	Stream cipher	Lightweight, for constrained hardware	eSTREAM portfolio

The comparison of Traditional and Lightweight Encryption is given in Table 2.

Table 2. Traditional Vs Lightweight Encryption

Feature	Lightweight Encryption	Traditional Encryption
Resource Usage	Minimal	Moderate to High
Security Level	Sufficient for IoT	High
Suitable for Constrained	Yes	Sometimes
Standardization	ISO/IEC, NIST	NIST, ISO/IEC

Lightweight encryption protocols are essential in securing the data transmitted over connected devices providing robust protection.

5.2 Authentication Protocols for WSN Security

To guarantee secure communication between sensor nodes, protect data confidentiality, and prevent unauthorized access or attacks, robust authentication protocols are needed. Several authentication protocols are proposed to focus on lightweight, efficient, and secure mechanisms that are suitable for resource-constrained sensor nodes. Some of the authentication protocols are as follows:

i. Trust-Based Authentication Protocols

Protocols based on trusted computing architectures aim to prevent node capture and malicious attacks by establishing trust relationships between nodes before granting access.

ii. Lightweight Mutual Authentication Protocols

Protocols like WSN-SLAP provide secure and lightweight mutual authentication tailored to WSN environments. These protocols address security weaknesses in earlier schemes and reduce computational overhead, making them suitable for sensor nodes with limited resources.

iii. Secure Mobile Sensor Network (SMSN) Authentication Protocol

The SMSN protocol suite is designed for mobile sensor nodes and user nodes in dynamic WSN environments. It supports multiple concurrent secure connections and uses a ticket-based re-authentication mechanism to reduce communication and computational complexity. The suite includes key agreement, key retrieval, and key management protocols, enabling mutual authentication between sensor nodes, sink nodes, and users.

iv. User Authentication Protocols with Authentication and Key Agreement (UAP-AKA)

UAP-AKA technique is used to create session keys that can be shared between users and sensor nodes to ensure secure data communication. These protocols typically involve a trusted gateway that validates users and sensor nodes, enabling mutual authentication and session key security with low computational and communication overhead. They use lightweight operations such as secure hash algorithms and XOR operations to provide support for resource-constrained devices.

v. Enhanced Secure Authentication Protocols

These protocols primarily focus on authentication and secure data transmission among sensor nodes to improve security measures and providing efficiency.

Table 3. Secure Authentication protocols

Protocol/ Approach	Mutual Authentication	Lightweight	Supports Mobility	Key Management	Suitable for IoT Integration
Trusted -Based	Yes	Moderate	No	Yes	Limited
WSN-SLAP	Yes	Yes	No	Yes	Moderate
SMSN Authentication	Yes	Yes	Yes	Yes	Yes

continued on following page

Table 3. Continued

Protocol/ Approach	Mutual Authentication	Lightweight	Supports Mobility	Key Management	Suitable for IoT Integration
UAWSNA-IoT (AKA-based)	Yes	Yes	Yes	Yes	Yes
SAPWSN	Yes	Yes	No	Yes	Moderate

Table 3 shows the authentication protocols that support mobility and concurrent connections, to be suitable for the emerging IoT scenarios.

5.3 Secure Routing Protocols

These protocols ensure data confidentiality and reliability irrespective of malicious nodes and resource constraints (Singh et al., 2018) addressing the lightweight sensor node challenges.

The key challenges faced by Secure Routing protocols are as follows:

In-network aggregation: The communication overhead of data over the network can be reduced by aggregating the data while maintaining security.

Routing attacks: These protocols suffer from Sybil attacks, packet dropping, modification of data and Denial of Service attacks

5.4 Prominent Secure Routing Protocol Approaches

1. Trust-Based Secure Routing

Trust based secure routing protocols measures and assigns the trust values to the nodes based on their performance in terms of count of packet drops, packet forwards and decides whether the node is malicious or not (Sreevidya et al., 2024). They also assign a threshold value based on which the nodes may be revoked from data transmission over a communication network by increasing the resistance against attacks such as routing interference.

2. LEACH-Based Secure Routing Protocols

Low-Energy Adaptive Clustering Hierarchy is one of the most commonly used routing protocol that is based on the concept of Clustering. Clustering is used for energy efficiency. It includes rotation of Cluster heads randomly to distribute the load on nodes uniformly in order to improve energy efficiency. It also employs secure data aggregation protocols to minimize data transmission overhead on all nodes and uses various encryption techniques and MAC to provide data confidentiality and Integrity.

3. Information-Aware Secure Routing

Information aware secure routing protocols takes the malicious nodes also into consideration and dynamically changes the routing table information and selects secure paths that are efficient in data transmission. Such protocols help in providing network efficiency and security by using trust level of nodes and recognising threats.

Table 4. Information-aware Secure Routing protocols

Feature	Description
Trust Mechanisms	Use trust evaluation to exclude malicious nodes from routing paths.
Clustering & Energy Efficiency	LEACH-based protocols rotate cluster heads and integrate secure data aggregation for energy savings.
Cryptographic Authentication	Use of secret keys, session keys, encryption, and MACs to verify node identity and data integrity.
Attack Resilience	Defend against routing attacks such as packet dropping, Sybil, and DoS attacks.
Adaptability	Information-aware routing adapts to network conditions and threats.

Table 4 represents the information aware secure routing protocols that combines cryptographic algorithms, trust based routing and energy efficient clustering based routing protocols for providing robust security and combat various threats in sensor networks. These protocols are integrated to provide a balance between security and energy efficiency.

5.5 Data Integrity and Authenticity Protection

To ensure data integrity and authenticity, it is crucial to maintain consistency, accuracy and reliability of data. To safeguard data from unauthorized modifications and data origin authenticity, different techniques are employed. The major techniques to safeguard data integrity are explained as follows:

i. Data Validation and Verification

Validation of input data at several stages is required to confirm whether the data adheres to specific rules and formats. Verification of data is required for comparison of data against some reliable sources such as checksum values to identify unauthorized data modifications during transmission and data storage.

ii. Access Control and Authentication

It allows data access to only the authorized users based on Role based Access control mechanisms, passwords, and multi-factor authentication. This helps in assuring that the data is secure only with authenticated users.

iii. Encryption of data

The data must be secured when it is stored as well as during transit so this can be achieved with the help of various cryptographic techniques such as AES and other protocols such as SSL/TLS, HTTPs, SFTP, etc,. Encryption is used to secure data privacy and prevents unauthorized modification of data during data transmission.

iv. Hash Functions

Hash functions are used to generate a fixed size unique fingerprint that can be used to identify unauthorized data modifications. A small change in information results in a drastic change in hash value resulting in identification of data corruption easily.

v. Digital Signatures

Asymmetric cryptography based digital signatures are used in guaranteeing the data integrity and validation of data. They validate the sender's identity by signing the data and adding it to data and use a verification algorithm to verify the sender's identity.

vi. Audit Trails and Logs

Audit logs maintain a detailed record of the data accesses, modifications, and user activities. Reviewing the logs helps in detection of suspicious activities, unauthorized logins and also supports forensic analysis in case of severities.

vii. Regular Backups and Recovery Plans

Backup of data provides safeguarding against data loss. Ensuring proper restore points and recovery plan can guarantee data recovery in situations of node crashes.

viii. Versioning of Data and Timestamps

Using version numbers to data and time stamping can help in identifying the data modifications and recovering data back to original versions in case if unauthorized data changes are identified.

ix. Error Handling Mechanisms

Implement techniques to detect, log and correct data inconsistencies or errors promptly, minimizing the impact of data manipulation.

Table 5. Data Protection Methods

Method	Purpose	Key Benefit
Data Validation & Verification	Ensure accuracy and consistency at entry and storage	Prevents erroneous or malicious data input
Access Control & Authentication	Restrict data access to authorized users	Prevents unauthorized data modification
Data Encryption	Protect data confidentiality and integrity	Secures data in transit and at rest
Hash Functions & Checksums	Detect unauthorized data changes	Enables integrity verification
Digital Signatures	Verify data origin and integrity	Confirms authenticity and non-repudiation
Audit Trails & Logs	Record data access and changes	Supports monitoring and forensic analysis
Regular Backups & Recovery	Safeguard against data loss	Enables data restoration after incidents
Data Versioning & Timestamps	Track data changes over time	Facilitates accountability and rollback
Error Handling	Identify and correct data errors	Maintains data consistency

Table 5 shows data protection methods to ensure that the data remains accurate, consistent, and trustworthy while verifying the authenticity of its source thereby maintaining the overall security and reliability of information.

5.6 Intrusion Detection Systems (IDS) for WSNs

To improve data security, Intrusion Detection Systems play a major role. IDS serves as a second layer in providing defense to enhance preventive security measures such as encryption and authentication against insider threats and complex attacks that prevention strategies alone cannot mitigate (Hosseini et al., 2024).

5.6.1. IDS Architecture in WSNs

An IDS consists of 3 key modules:

- **Information Collection Module:** Gathers data and events from sensor nodes.
- **Detection Engine Module:** Analyzes collected data to identify abnormal or malicious node behaviour.
- **Response Module:** Response module alerts the administrators for reconfiguring the network when intrusion behaviour of node is detected.

5.6.2. Classification of IDS in WSNs

The classification of Intrusion Detection Systems based on their architecture and response to intrusions is shown in table 6.

Table 6. Classification of Intrusion Detection Systems

Classification	Description
Centralized IDS	A central node (or base station) collects and analyzes data from the entire network. Suitable for simple networks but may create bottlenecks and single points of failure.
Distributed IDS	Each node or cluster head participates in detection and response, improving scalability and resilience but increasing resource consumption.

5.6.3. Detection Techniques

IDS in WSNs employ various detection techniques, each with its own strengths and limitations. The Intrusion detection techniques and their performance analysis is shown in Table 7 and 8.

Table 7. Intrusion Detection Techniques

Technique	Detects Known Attacks	Detects Unknown Attacks	Resource Usage	False Alarm Rate	Suitable for WSNs
Signature-Based	Yes	No	Low	Low	Moderate
Anomaly-Based	No	Yes	Moderate/High	Higher	Yes
Specification-Based	Yes	Limited	Moderate	Moderate	Yes
Hybrid	Yes	Yes	High	Lower	Increasingly

Table 8. Performance of Intrusion Detection Techniques

Technique	Description & Example	Pros	Cons
Signature-Based	Detects attacks by matching known patterns (signatures) of malicious activity.	Fast, low false positives	Cannot detect unknown attacks
Anomaly-Based (Shirvani et al., 2024; Mohammadi et al, 2020)	Identifies deviations from normal behavior using statistical or machine learning models.	Can detect novel attacks	Higher false positives, resource-intensive
Specification-Based	Monitors adherence to predefined protocol or behavior rules.	Effective for protocol-specific attacks	Requires accurate specifications
Hybrid Approaches	Combine two or more techniques for better accuracy and coverage.	Balance detection and efficiency	Increased complexity

5.7 Comparison of Countermeasures for securing WSNs

Table 9 compares the purpose, advantages and disadvantages of Cryptographic Techniques, Authentication Protocols, Secure Routing Protocols, Data Integrity & Authenticity and Intrusion Detection Systems (IDS).

Table 9. Countermeasures for Securing Wireless Sensor Networks in CPS

Category	Technique/ Protocol	Purpose	Advantages	Limitations
Cryptographic Techniques	Symmetric (e.g., AES), Asymmetric (e.g., ECC)	Confidentiality, Authentication, Integrity	Lightweight, Strong security	Key distribution, high cost
Authentication Protocols	SPINS, TinySec, μTESLA	Verifies sender identity	Efficient, Support for resource-constrained devices	Delay in key disclosure, Scalability issues
Secure Routing Protocols	INSENS, SPINS, ARAN	Prevent routing attacks (e.g., sinkhole)	Enhances network resilience, mitigates malicious paths	Higher latency, increased overhead
Data Integrity & Authenticity	Message Authentication Codes (MAC), Hashing	Ensures that the data is not altered or forged	Efficient verification, small overhead	Shared key management needed, not resistant to physical capture
Intrusion Detection Systems (IDS)	Anomaly-based, Signature-based, Hybrid	Detects unauthorized activity or node behavior	Detects unknown attacks (anomaly), precise (signature)	False positives (anomaly), signature updates needed

6. CASE STUDIES AND PRACTICAL APPLICATIONS

6.1 Security in Smart Grids

6.1.1. Role of WSNs in smart grids and specific Cyber Security challenges they face

WSNs are an essential component of the networked future world, also referred to as the Internet of Things, that will be extensively utilized for control, connectivity, security, and overall awareness of things big or small, near or far, wired or wireless (Rejeb et al., 2023). WSNs are a network of small, low-power devices referred to as sensors used to collect data from the surroundings. They are applied in many areas such as healthcare, environmental monitoring, and military surveillance. Nonetheless, employing wireless communication in WSNs creates a big security challenge because hostile nodes might attempt to undermine the confidentiality, availability, and integrity of data. Therefore, security is a major concern in the design and implementation of WSNs. A comprehensive security framework should be established to ensure the protection of the network against attacks. The WSNs provide special challenges for security protocol designers due to the following unique characteristics:

1. All wireless channels use the same frequency band and have the same radio interface.
2. Most protocols for WSNs do not consider necessary security techniques in their design stage, as in the case of the Internet.
3. Due to their complexity and the limited capabilities of sensor nodes, it is extremely hard to support strong security algorithms on a sensor node platform.
4. More resources at sensor nodes are needed for stronger security protocols.
5. WSNs are usually deployed in hostile areas (unguarded areas) with no fixed infrastructure.
6. Dynamic topology changes and low communication bandwidth.
7. Random deployment and large-scale use of WSNs require security mechanisms that must be adapted to cope with dynamic deployment environments and ensure sensor effectiveness.

6.1.2. Real-world solutions to secure WSNs within smart grid environments

In Smart Grid environments, Wireless Sensor Networks (WSNs) must be secured to ensure grid stability is maintained, cyberattacks are avoided, and reliable energy management is ensured. Deploying WSNs for data collection, load balancing, and power flow automation, smart grids integrate renewable resources, two-way energy flow, and real-time monitoring. These networks are susceptible to virus attacks, eavesdropping, data tampering, DoS attacks, and other cyber-attacks that can pose threats to national security and system integrity. To recognize threats automatically in real-time, some of the effective real-world solutions such as AI-driven anomaly detection, end-to-end encryption and Intrusion detection systems. The network strength can further be improved by employing strong authentication, self-recovery techniques and segmentation of network to block unauthorized access to network by maintaining constant communication. To identify abnormal network patterns and anomalies prior to causing disruption, Machine learning algorithms can be used(Leong et al, 2020). By adopting such security mechanisms, Smart Grids can attain reliability and efficiency against cyber threats guaranteeing efficient power distribution and secure integration of renewable energy.

6.2 Healthcare Systems

A major issue in remote patient monitoring systems (RPMS) is to safeguard the patient's personal health information sent through WSNs. RPMS uses WSN to track the blood pressure levels, sugar levels and oxygen saturation levels continously. These technologies help in improving emergency response, identifies diseases prior to causing situations worsen. They also enable patients to continuosly monitor the regular activities while undergoing treatment. There are some issues regarding privacy and security of patient data during transmission over sensor nodes via WSN. In order to maintain Confidentiality, integrity, and availability, the patient data must be protected by using secure authentication and encryption techniques.

6.3 Industrial Automation

Wireless sensor networks (WSNs) have become crucial especially in Supervisory Control and Data Acquisition (SCADA) and automation in industries. These networks must be structured using various topologies such as mesh, star, and cluster-tree, and comprise of several sensor nodes that come up with microcontrollers, storage, sensors, ADCs, transceivers, and power supplies. Because wireless communication increases power utilization and energy efficiency continues to be a major issue. To improve energy efficiency, data aggregation techniques can be used. WSNs encounter extra challenges in industrial environments because of co-channel interferences, multi-path propagation and the interference from signals of large machines. These elements might be vulnerable to data integrity. Despite these challenges, WSNs are commonly deployed in industrial CPS applications as they provide efficient automation, real-time monitoring and effective control systems.

Their application ensures smooth communication in industrial environments and ranges from cellular and satellite systems to short-range personal area networks. To create robust, interference-resistance and energy-constrained networks that fulfils industrial reliability standards, the complexity of WSN applications in these situations demands competence in various fields.

For reliable industrial automation in manufacturing, secure communication between actuators and sensors is an important task. Actuators convert electrical inputs into mechanical signals, and sensors convert mechanical signals to electrical outputs. Some of the advanced materials such as Liquid crystal elastomers (LCEs), ferroelectric polymers, and dielectric elastomers offers flexibility but has to be well-insulated to prevent signal interference. Low-voltage actuation of robots and prosthetics is enhanced by ionic electroactive polymers (iEAPs); however, cybersecurity threats and electromagnetic interference (EMI) need to be minimized by encryption and shielding. Ionic liquids (ILs) guarantee precise data transmission with increased stability in electrochemical sensors. In addition, the integration of these materials with self-healing and 3D printing technology enhances the durability of industrial applications. System integrity relies upon the use of secure communication protocols like interference-resilient networking and real-time encryption of data. By combining material innovation with robust communication strategies, modern manufacturing environments can achieve reliable, secure, and efficient sensor-actuator integration for industrial automation and smart factory operations (Huanan et al., 2021).

7. EMERGING TRENDS AND FUTURE DIRECTIONS

7.1. Role of Quantum cryptography and post-quantum encryption in securing future WSNs.

Even though wireless sensor networks (WSNs) are crucial to critical infrastructure, smart cities, and healthcare, they are being increasingly vulnerable to cybersecurity threats, particularly with the imminent emergence of quantum computers. Traditional public-key encryption methods like elliptic curve cryptography and RSA are based on mathematical problems that can be solved efficiently using quantum algorithms, especially Shor's algorithm. Security in WSN, which relies on encryption to protect data and ensure secure transmission, is highly threatened by this (Oztoprak et al., 2024).

Post-quantum cryptography (PQC) was designed to resist from quantum attacks to address such challenges. They ensure security even in 3was advanced quantum computers as they rely on intricate mathematical structures like error-correcting codes and high-dimensional lattices. Quantum Key Distribution is another security approach provided by Quantum cryptography to provide security. It allows the two parties to share the encryption keys securely preventing from eavesdropping attack. It provides more security in critical applications that include high risk. Further, development must be done to enhance technologies to secure data in resource-constrained WSN nodes.

7.2 Machine Learning for Intrusion Detection

Deep Learning techniques have improved the detection rates while traditional ML methods struggle to scale in extensive networks. Deep belief networks (DBN) aimed at enhancing intrusion classification and trust-based models for identifying malicious users. These methods represent few advancements in intrusion detection systems. The PRO-DLBIDCPS framework combines block chain technology with an attention-based bi-directional gated recurrent neural network (ABi-GRNN) for classifying intrusions and utilizes an adaptive harmony search algorithm (AHSA) for selecting features. This AI-driven approach ensures robust threat identification in CPS environments, boosts security, and optimizes resource utilization. Many simulations confirm its effectiveness, demonstrating the capabilities of AI and ML in safeguarding CPS against evolving cyber threats (Ahmad et al., 2022).

While the Machine learning-based Intrusion Detection Systems present strong detection capabilities they are also susceptible to adversarial attacks in which the attackers exploit weaknesses in the model through fake inputs or poisoned data. Integrating Adversarial Machine Learning-resilient systems is therefore essential in current Cyber Physical System environments.

7.3 Adversarial Machine Learning in CPS Security

Adversarial Machine Learning (Sheikh et al., 2023) is an area of Machine Learning that focuses on the study of defending against adversarial attacks that deceives the machine learning models by providing a misleading input. It includes the creation and detection of adversarial datasets that are given as inputs to deceive classifier models. Such adversarial machine learning attacks have been extensively explored in some areas such as image classification and spam detection. There are 2 types of attacks in adversarial Machine Learning. In a white-box attack, the attacker has complete access to the target model including the model's architecture and its parameters. In a black box attack, the attacker has no access to the model and can only observe the outputs of the targeted model. Most common attacks in adversarial machine learning include data poisoning attacks, evasion attacks, Byzantine attacks and model extraction attacks. There are a huge number of adversarial attacks against machine learning systems. Most of these systems work on the concepts of deep learning and traditional ML models such as Support Vector Machines (SVMs) and linear regression (Ibitoye et al., 2019).

The major aim of the adversarial machine learning is to deteriorate the classifier performance. Adversarial attacks can be categorized as shown categories:

i. Poisoning Attacks

In this attack, the attacker controls the training data or its labels to cause the model to underperform during deployment. This is an adversarial contamination of training data. As the Machine Learning systems can be re-trained using data collected during operation, an attacker may poison the data by inserting malicious samples during operation that may subsequently disrupt or influence re-training.

ii. Evasion Attacks

In this attack, attacker tries to deceive the trained classifiers. Such attacks comes under practical attacks as they are performed at the deployment stage. The attackers tries to evade detection by concealing the content of malware or spam emails. Therefore, samples are modified to bypass detection as they are classified as legitimate without directly impacting the training data. Some examples are spoofing attacks against biometric verification systems.

iii. Model Extraction Attacks

This is also known as Model stealing where an attacker enters into a black box machine learning system to rebuild the model or extract the data that was trained on. This is significant when either the training data or the model data itself is sensitive and confidential. For example, such type of attacks can be used by adversaries to steal stock market prediction model for their own financial beneficiary.

iv. Byzantine Attacks

Byzantine attacks in adversarial machine learning refers to malicious attacks on distributed machine learning systems especially federated learning where the exploited participants (clients) send misleading or corrupted data to poison the training process or compromise the global model. These attacks exploit the decentralized nature of distributed systems to disrupt training leading to decrease in the model performance or even malicious backdoors.

It is difficult to identify and prevent adversarial machine learning because adversarial inputs are subtle and stealthy making the model fail even though they appear normal to humans. Defensive strategies result in a continuous race with attackers because they are less generalized and degrade model accuracy. Defence is made more difficult by the lack of uniform evaluation benchmarks, high processing costs, and restricted interpretability. Furthermore, domain-specific vulnerabilities and contexts with limited resources make protection a challenging issue. These challenges make it more difficult to safely implement Machine Learning in crucial applications like banking, healthcare and self-governing systems.

Defending against Adversarial machine learning attacks requires a versatile approach by combining robust model training, data sanitization, and hybrid detection strategies. One of the core technique is robust model training i.e., adversarial training where the models can be trained on both clean and adversarial examples to enhance resilience. This method increases training time but the robustness is improved by reducing the precision values on standard inputs. Defensive distillation is another approach to smoothen the model's decision boundaries by training secondary model based on predictions from basic model. This approach is good enough in terms of performance but cannot resist adaptive attacks. The adversarial inputs are filtered out by data sanitization filters by pre-processing data using auto encoders where as anomaly-aware updates allows the models to identify unusual patterns that indicates adversarial behaviour over time. Hybrid approaches that combines AI-based detection and rule-based systems can be used to strengthen the defense. Such integrated approaches make use of heuristic rules to identify anomalies while using ML. Such techniques improve robustness across several threat models in adversarial ML.

7.4 Integration of Block Chain for Data Integrity

In applications such as Smart cities, Healthcare, Industrial automation and environment monitoring, Smart Wireless Sensor Networks are widely used (Swetha Priya et al., 2020). Such networks use sensor nodes to send gathered information for processing and decision making. Nevertheless, challenges such as data integrity, confidentiality, reliability and security are common. To overcome such challenges, Blockchain technology presents a suitable solution. With the help of Blockchain technology, compromised nodes cannot modify the sensor data because of the decentralized nature and secure ledger system providing data immutability. This technology is most significant in situations where precision of data is essential.

7.5 Secure Multi-Network Integration

A challenging task when multiple WSNs are integrated to form a single CPS is in maintaining security at different stages of data transmission. WSNs are mainly deployed in mission critical environments such as military, healthcare etc., as they are prone to severe security issues. A few challenges in such integrated environments are change in network topologies, power requirements and security measures. Secure communication between layers from sensor nodes to base stations and cloud-based e-Health systems requires authentication, intrusion detection, and robust encryption. In CPS-integrated WSNs, sophisticated methods including energy-efficient cryptographic protocols, gateway-based access management, and self-organizing and self-healing networks can improve security and guarantee dependable and continuous data flow.

8. CONCLUSION

In Cyber physical systems, the WSNs play a major role in real-time monitoring, control and data collection in some of the applications such as smart cities, industrial automation, healthcare, and environmental monitoring. The WSN comprises of sensors, actuators, communication nodes and gateways that form a backbone for CPS to facilitate reliable transmission of data and interaction with cloud and other control systems. Due to the Wireless and decentralized WSN behaviour, security emerges as a major issue rendering CPS susceptible to threats like eavesdropping, routing assaults, data alteration, insider threats, and energy exhaustion attacks. These attacks jeopardize data integrity, privacy, and availability, which are crucial for CPS reliability and safety. A multi-tier approach is necessary to incorporate the cryptographic techniques, secure routing protocols, IDSs, Trust management systems and protection at physical layer to address such challenges. The latest technologies like quantum-resistant cryptography, machine learning-driven intrusion detection, blockchain and secure interoperability across various networks shows the potential to enhance WSN security in future CPS deployments. Some of the case studies on smart grid, healthcare, and industrial automation demonstrate the actual security challenges and solutions, emphasizing the need for tailored security frameworks that protect confidential data and ensure smooth operation of CPS. In conclusion, safeguarding WSNs in CPS is essential to secure the communication and services they support. An efficient security plan that reconciles resource constraints with advanced countermeasures can guarantee utilization of CPS technologies securely. In future, there is need for continuous research and development in security frameworks and protocols to counter evolving threats and maintain trust in Cyber Physical Systems.

REFERENCES

Ahmad, R., Wazirali, R., & Abu-Ain, T. (2022). Machine learning for wireless sensor networks security: An overview of challenges and issues. *Sensors (Basel), 22*(13), 4730. DOI: 10.3390/s22134730 PMID: 35808227

Dey, N., Ashour, A. S., Shi, F., Fong, S. J., & Tavares, J. M. R. (2018). Medical cyber-physical systems: A survey. *Journal of Medical Systems, 42*(4), 1–13. DOI: 10.1007/s10916-018-0921-x PMID: 29525900

Halim, T., & Islam, M. R. (2012). A study on the security issues in WSN. *International Journal of Computer Applications, 53*(1), 26–32. DOI: 10.5120/8386-1992

Hosseini Shirvani, M., & Akbarifar, A. (2024). A survey study on intrusion detection system in wireless sensor network: Challenges and considerations. [JECEI]. *Journal of Electrical and Computer Engineering Innovations, 12*(2), 449–474.

Huanan, Z., Suping, X., & Jiannan, W. (2021). Security and application of wireless sensor network. *Procedia Computer Science, 183*, 486–492. DOI: 10.1016/j.procs.2021.02.088

Ibitoye, O., Abou-Khamis, R., Shehaby, M. E., Matrawy, A., & Shafiq, M. O. (2019). The Threat of Adversarial Attacks on Machine Learning in Network Security—A Survey. arXiv preprint arXiv:1911.02621.

Jondhale, S. R., Maheswar, R., & Lloret, J. (2021). *Received signal strength based target localization and tracking using wireless sensor networks*. Springer Nature.

Keerthika, M., & Shanmugapriya, D. (2021). Wireless sensor networks: Active and passive attacks-vulnerabilities and countermeasures. *Global Transitions Proceedings, 2*(2), 362–367. DOI: 10.1016/j.gltp.2021.08.045

Leong, A. S., Ramaswamy, A., Quevedo, D. E., Karl, H., & Shi, L. (2020). Deep reinforcement learning for wireless sensor scheduling in cyber–physical systems. *Automatica, 113*, 108759.

Mohammadi Rouzbahani, H., Karimipour, H., Rahimnejad, A., Dehghantanha, A., & Srivastava, G. (2020). Anomaly detection in cyber-physical systems using machine learning. Handbook of big data privacy, 219-235.

Ojeda, F., Mendez, D., Fajardo, A., & Ellinger, F. (2023). On wireless sensor network models: A cross-layer systematic review. *Journal of Sensor and Actuator Networks, 12*(4), 50. DOI: 10.3390/jsan12040050

Oztoprak, A., Hassanpour, R., Ozkan, A., & Oztoprak, K. (2024). Security challenges, mitigation strategies, and future trends in wireless sensor networks: A review. *ACM Computing Surveys*, *57*(4), 1–29. DOI: 10.1145/3706583

Perrig, A., Stankovic, J., & Wagner, D. (2004). Security in wireless sensor networks. *Communications of the ACM*, *47*(6), 53–57. DOI: 10.1145/990680.990707

Popescu, G. H., Zvarikova, K., Machova, V., & Mihai, E. A. (2020). Industrial big data, automated production systems, and Internet of Things sensing networks in cyber-physical system-based manufacturing. *Journal of Self-Governance and Management Economics*, *8*(3), 30–36.

Priya, T. S., Sridevi, R., & Rao, K. S. (2024). Lightweight encryption techniques: Types, challenges and security issues. In *Computational Methods in Science and Technology* (pp. 266–273). CRC Press. DOI: 10.1201/9781003501244-41

Sadeghi, S., Soltanmohammadlou, N., & Nasirzadeh, F. (2022). Applications of wireless sensor networks to improve occupational safety and health in underground mines. *Journal of Safety Research*, *83*, 8–25. DOI: 10.1016/j.jsr.2022.07.016 PMID: 36481040

Salehi, S. A., Razzaque, M. A., Naraei, P., & Farrokhtala, A. (2013, July). Security in wireless sensor networks: Issues and challanges. In *2013 IEEE International Conference on Space Science and Communication (IconSpace)* (pp. 356-360). IEEE. DOI: 10.1109/IconSpace.2013.6599495

Sayın, A. Anomaly detection scenarios in cyber-physical systems.

Sharma, S., & Kaur, A. (2021, July). Survey on wireless sensor network, its applications and issues. [). IOP Publishing.]. *Journal of Physics: Conference Series*, *1969*(1), 012042. DOI: 10.1088/1742-6596/1969/1/012042

Sheikh, Z. A., Singh, Y., Singh, P. K., & Gonçalves, P. J. S. (2023). Defending the defender: Adversarial learning based defending strategy for learning based security methods in cyber-physical systems (cps). *Sensors (Basel)*, *23*(12), 5459. DOI: 10.3390/s23125459 PMID: 37420626

Singh, R., Kathuria, K., & Sagar, A. K. (2018, December). Secure routing protocols for wireless sensor networks. In 2018 4th international conference on computing communication and automation (ICCCA) (pp. 1-5). IEEE. DOI: 10.1109/CCAA.2018.8777557

Sreevidya, B., & Supriya, M. (2024). Trust based routing–A novel approach for data security in WSN based data critical applications. *Journal of Wireless Mobile Networks, Ubiquitous Computing and Dependable Applications, 15*(1), 27–41. DOI: 10.58346/JOWUA.2024.I1.003

Suhaimi, A. F., Yaakob, N., Saad, S. A., Sidek, K. A., Elshaikh, M. E., Dafhalla, A. K., Lynn, O. B., & Almashor, M. (2021, July). IoT based smart agriculture monitoring, automation and intrusion detection system. [). IOP Publishing.]. *Journal of Physics: Conference Series, 1962*(1), 012016. DOI: 10.1088/1742-6596/1962/1/012016

Swetha Priya, T. C., & Kanaka Durga, A. (2020). Clustering-based blockchain technique for securing wireless sensor networks. In *Data Engineering and Communication Technology: Proceedings of 3rd ICDECT-2K19* (pp. 461–471). Springer Nature Singapore. DOI: 10.1007/978-981-15-1097-7_39

Swetha Priya, T. C., & Sridevi, R. (2023, March). Protecting the Privacy of IoMT-Based Health Records Using Blockchain Technology. In International Conference on Network Security and Blockchain Technology (pp. 409-423). Singapore: Springer Nature Singapore.

Teymourzadeh, M., Vahed, R., Alibeygi, S., & Dastanpour, N. (2020). Security in wireless sensor networks: Issues and challenges. arXiv preprint arXiv:2007.05111.

Chapter 14
Addressing Data Privacy Concerns in Digital Emerging Technologies:
Strategies and Best Practices

Hanan Aldowah
https://orcid.org/0000-0003-1020-2389
Universiti Sains Malaysia, Malaysia

Shafiq Ul Rehman
Kingdom University, Bahrain

Sohail Ahmed Shahani
Universiti Teknologi Petronas, Malaysia

ABSTRACT

In this digital age, data is one of the most valuable assets for organizations. Recent advances in the Internet of Things (IoT), cloud computing, and data analytics have enabled efficient data collection. IoT, a crucial set of smart technologies, is anticipated to drive the next information technology revolution and the development of big data analytics. However, widespread data collection and the lack of security in IoT devices raise significant privacy concerns. This study reviews current literature and discusses concepts and approaches for data privacy in IoT from various perspectives. It identifies several challenges and provides comprehensive solutions to address data privacy issues. The proposed solutions encompass technical, academic, and industry viewpoints. Additionally, the integration of machine learning (ML) and deep learning (DL) technologies into IoT systems introduces further privacy and security challenges. ML and DL models often require access to large datasets containing sensitive information, necessitating advanced privacy-preserving techniques such as

DOI: 10.4018/979-8-3373-2200-1.ch014

differential privacy and federated learning. These methods aim to protect individual data while enabling robust model training. Furthermore, the study explores the impact of adversarial attacks on ML and DL models within IoT environments and discusses strategies to enhance model robustness and security. Despite these efforts, major issues remain in designing and deploying IoT solutions. This study concludes with recommendations and future research directions to enhance IoT privacy and security, particularly in the context of emerging ML and DL technologies.

1. INTRODUCTION

Modern technologies such as IoT along with ML and DL advance at a high pace to introduce an emerging wave of information management systems. These technologies help institutions enhance operational efficiency alongside developing data handling systems that increase individual well-being (Subramanian, 2023). These recent updates to technology systems present critical privacy and cybersecurity risks for users. Research demonstrates that broad data collection by these technologies reveals security flaws because of inadequate cryptographic defenders. The susceptibility of IoT devices produces two main issues: security breaches of information systems and weakened protection of sensitive data (Chaudhary, Kumar, & Saxena, 2024). Researchers such as Tawalbeh et al. (2020) conducted an examination of IoT and emerging technology studies to explore data privacy solutions and different perspectives and problem solutions. IoT integration in daily use creates new privacy concerns since almost all present-day items function as internet-connected devices. Unsecure cybersecurity standards between connecting devices result in three primary privacy threats that occur during ongoing operations. Ramos and Skármeta (2020) report that the complications increase when IoT devices operate based on their independent intelligence and make their own decisions.

The protection of user privacy in IoT research requires innovative analysis management techniques together with data collection protection methods and analysis management. The realization of IoT systems' complete internet capabilities depends on the provision of simple security measures that users can easily control. User privacy protocols integrated with multiple privacy expectations and data management systems lead to improved benefits from IoT for users. Implementing safety standards which resolve privacy conflicts but reduce potential risks will advance the adoption of IoT technology (Ren, Li, Dai, Yang, & Lin, 2018). Traditional solutions derived from wireless sensor networks (WSNs) and the Internet need adaptation to meet the unique dimensions of IoT challenges, which often depend on centralized architectures unsuitable for the vast and diverse nature of IoT applications. This paper advocates for varied and distributed approaches to better address these complexities (Zhou,

Jia, Peng, Zhang, & Liu, 2018). Furthermore, a singular strategy is inadequate for the varied privacy challenges of IoT. New legal and technical measures must be developed to safeguard individual privacy rights and foster a dialogue among governments, NGOs, public interest groups, and the private sector to establish effective privacy and data protection frameworks (Karale, 2021). This paper surveys different solutions from academic, technical, and industrial perspectives, extending previous work that focused on security and trust aspects in IoT. By integrating these diverse approaches, the study aims to provide insights and propose solutions that address the key privacy issues identified in IoT environments. The goal is to guide future research toward implementing specific mechanisms and approaches that mitigate these challenges, with particular attention to industrial and technical solutions.

The paper structure is organized as follows: IoT and cloud, IoT privacy and big data, research scope and methodology are described in section 2. the main challenges and issues that are associated with IoT technologies and their considerations are stated in section 3. Machine Learning and Deep Learning Privacy and Security Issues in Emerging Technologies in section 4. Some of the solutions provided by academic researchers, technician, and industry experts are presented in section 5 while the findings of the review are discussed in Section 5. Conclusion, recommendations, and future work are summarized in Section 6.

1.1 IoT Privacy and Big Data

The Internet of Things (IoT) is a complex network of interconnected devices, objects, and sensors that enables continuous data collection across various environments. Unlike conventional big data, multiple heterogeneous data components from IoT sources create complex problems for analysis and management due to high noise levels.

The main sources of IoT big data originate from smart cities along with transportation sectors and industries and healthcare services and agricultural domains (Stergiou et al., 2018). The availability of large data collections supports improved urban methods of strategic planning and service recommendations. System security along with privacy concerns become crucial when datasets contain individual information. Numerous entry points emerge for unauthorized access and cyberattacks because the massive quantity and various types of IoT data (Awan et al., 2023; Yang et al., 2019). The integration of health data collection with regular daily inputs creates serious privacy issues for wearable technology along with home sensors. The privacy-protection necessities become clear through products such as Apple iWatch and Google Fit (Sollins, 2019). Solving these problems requires an integration between modern privacy-security tools such as cryptographic systems with federated learning protocols to secure data operations and movements. An existing framework should protect data while determining data ownership and user permission systems. Standards for privacy need data protection systems and clear definitions about how users gain access to their information and own it. Artificial immune systems show great promise as emerging security features (Stergiou et al., 2023). According to Stergiou et al. (2023) hybrid immune system artificial methods create progressively improved defense solutions for security measures. A blend of IoT technology and cloud computing and big data systems results in privacy concerns therefore automatic access solutions need dynamic capabilities for responding to current situations (Yang et al., 2019).

In conclusion, the necessary protections for privacy must strengthen because IoT technology continues to establish increasing connections between big data systems. Users require security-based protection frameworks that will be developed through joint efforts between data management specialists and IT experts during IoT research.

2. RESEARCH SCOPE AND METHODOLOGY

This study aims to critically review IoT privacy issues, challenges, and the solutions proposed by previous research, with a special emphasis on contributions from the industrial sector to the successful application of IoT. Unlike other reviews, this study pays particular attention to technical and industrial solutions that address IoT privacy problems. These solutions, presented in the form of new methods, approaches, algorithms, mechanisms, and frameworks, are believed to guide future research in employing such strategies to resolve specific privacy concerns within IoT contexts. The initial step in this review involved conducting a comprehensive search across several databases to gather relevant studies on IoT privacy and its myriad topics and issues. Key databases included Web of Science, Scopus, Science Direct, IEEE Xplore, and Google Scholar. Research terms used in the search encompassed "Internet of Things issues," "IoT issues," "IoT challenges," "privacy in IoT," "IoT privacy challenges," "IoT privacy issues," and "IoT privacy solutions." Inclusion and exclusion criteria were meticulously applied to evaluate the literature, focusing on works that contribute to solving and enhancing IoT privacy. This review spans a wide array of privacy topics within IoT, providing a thorough overview of existing solutions up to the present day. The aim is to offer a comprehensive picture of available IoT privacy solutions and to shed light on how the utilization of specific proposed mechanisms, algorithms, and platforms can enhance the deployment of IoT technologies with greater confidence. Articles considered for this review were selected based on their publication in internationally recognized journals and conference proceedings indexed in ISI and Scopus. The focus was on empirical studies that offer practical solutions in terms of algorithms, frameworks, and mechanisms that are applicable to real-world scenarios.

3. PRIVACY ISSUES AND CHALLENGES

We currently operate in a fast-growing network of Internet-connected devices which transforms how we transfer data throughout personal spaces and infrastructure systems. The internet-based transmission of data through IoT networks generates negative impacts on both network functions and data measurement procedures. People use IoT to enhance daily function while risking privacy so we must create urgent solutions and new privacy approaches now. The protection of privacy requires an active mindset for building full-scale protections across the IoT ecosystem. Careful attention must be paid to establishing broad privacy regulations that will secure the operational levels of the IoT system.

Emerging Privacy Challenges: As the IoT becomes increasingly integrated into our daily lives, it connects a vast network of devices from smart TVs and wearable technologies to home appliances and city infrastructure. Advanced devices now gather big datasets that help them monitor activities along with health information and geographic positions of users. IoT devices acquire extensive repositories of data which enables them to track exact user events such as positional data and health metrics. Huge amounts of valuable data are quickly accumulating leading to several privacy vulnerabilities which are increasing the chances of the misuse of personal data along with unauthorized probing done on system. Autonomous IoT chips that tie together different applications from hospitals to smart homes require a full reassessment of privacy and security. The special characteristics of IoT result in privacy concerns with regards to exposed private data along with occurrence of data breaches as well require strong data security measures for privacy of user data across all sectors. Hasan, Chamoli, and Alam (2020) reinforced this finding together with Tawalbeh et al. (2020), and Chaurasia and Kumar (2023). The strategies need to handle multiple privacy issues that result from the IoT integration in homes and industry while maintaining modern privacy security measures. The necessity demands a focused method for developing and implementing extensive privacy safeguards that should protect the Internet of Things ecosystem in every operational stage.

Layered Security Concerns: To achieve IoT security one must handle weaknesses across the entire IoT stack which consists of perception layers along with network layers and application layers. Deep et al. (2022) highlighted that most security issues emerge from the misuse of protection layers together with network layers and application layers. Therefore, IoT system needs developed security protocols that must defend all of its layers while keeping the entire framework private.

Standardization of Privacy Protocols: Current IoT devices with inconsistent platforms create barriers for privacy protection efforts. The development of uniform privacy guidelines serves as a necessity to construct uniform data protection frameworks across different IoT systems. Standard enforcement demands secure deletion processes and systems need to reveal information about their operations (Tawalbeh et al., 2020).

Architectural and Design Challenges: The complete protection of IoT system privacy requires detailed investigations into architectural and design needs. A successful IoT security implementation relies on using preventive measures involving well-designed IoT systems that extend from devices to cloud computing levels (Khan et al., 2022).

Privacy by Design: Privacy by Design creates its essential nature by integrating privacy concerns into products and services of IoT during their initial design phase. Businesses that integrate user privacy concerns at the beginning of IoT development protocols enable security elements to be embedded in systems before complete deployment occurs. Multiple data sources in IoT data analysis lead to detailed individual profiles that can trigger severe privacy breaches (Karale, 2021).

Technical and Regulatory Responses: Addressing IoT privacy issues needs both perfect state-of-the-art technical measures together with extensive regulatory systems. Technologies such as anonymization, pseudonymity, and strong encryption are essential for protecting data within IoT networks, ensuring that user interactions remain confidential and secure from unauthorized access (Bhattacharjya, Zhong, Wang, & Li, 2019; Karale, 2021).

Regulatory and Standards Development: IoT requires adaptable regulatory systems which should maintain synchronization with innovations within the industry. The protection of individual privacy and standard compliance for IoT developers and manufacturers requires new laws and standards. Karale (2021) highlighted the need for standardized IoT regulations because IoT technology problems exceed the limits of single countries.

Pseudonymity and Unlinkability: Pseudonymity and unlinkability serve essential functions to manage IoT privacy and security issues that come from the extensive interconnected device networks. Pseudonymity performs the function of anonymity by connecting each IoT action to a unique pseudonym instead of providing personal identifying information. This allows actions to be authenticated and linked to a pseudonym holder without revealing their real identity, thereby maintaining privacy while ensuring accountability (Haider, Höberl, & Rinner, 2016; Sucasas, Mantas, Bastos, Damião, & Rodriguez, 2019). Establishing successful pseudonymity together with unlinkability requires standardized solutions which must span across all IoT domains. Developing end-to-end effective pseudonymity and unlinkability solutions demands standardized protected communication across the broad spectrum of IoT sectors and domains. Most present-day IoT architectures and systems fail to provide single integrated privacy solutions which thoroughly protect against privacy breaches from device level to cloud-level domains (Akil, Islami, Fischer-Hübner, Martucci, & Zuccato, 2020). The application of unlinkability creates challenges because it requires identifying and defining untraceable patterns while understanding attacker potentials (Sucasas et al., 2019). Despite these mechanisms, the pervasive connectivity of IoT presents significant exposure and vulnerability risks, highlighting the need for enhanced privacy measures embedded within both software and hardware, like antivirus and firewalls, to secure user data and ensure system integrity (Attarian & Hashemi, 2021; Vasilomanolakis et al., 2015).

Ethical and Safety Considerations: Solving IoT privacy issues demands both moral choices about safety alongside technological implementation. The long-term trust that public users place in IoT technology requires maintaining both strict privacy standards and safety standards There is still a clear need to expand discussions about ethical design practices and IoT deployment within private and public areas to resolve these larger privacy issues (Atlam & Wills, 2020). User consent along with data ownership and technical safeguards operate as fundamental elements which protect privacy throughout IoT systems. The unawareness of users about IoT device data-collection processes results in difficulties regarding transparency and accountability (Coiduras-Sanagustín et al., 2024). A notable example is the case of smart home devices, such as Amazon Alexa, inadvertently recording and transmitting private conversations without user consent, leading to significant public backlash and regulatory scrutiny (Chung et al., 2017; Ha et al., 2021). Privileged patient data released from healthcare infrastructure medical devices with IoT capabilities has become a major security and privacy problem (Alsubaei, Abuhussein, & Shandilya, 2023). Companies face legal troubles with clients who lose trust because they did not obtain clear consent and their ownership of data remained unclear. Social trust in IoT deployment requires ethical solutions (Alaba & Rocha, 2024).

Global Privacy Concerns and User Awareness: The way users understand privacy threats from Internet-of-Things devices proves essential for addressing worldwide privacy issues. Users often overlook the fact that devices like smart TVs and game consoles gather user data which gets transmitted to external entities. Users face substantial privacy violations because IoT providers need to build privacy features at the beginning and also need to teach users regarding their data rights and device protection measures (Akil et al., 2020). The process of tracking presence at home together with health activities demands strict privacy rules for users to trust the system because IoT technologies enhance daily situations (Mugariri et al., 2022). The global nature of IoT exacerbates these privacy concerns, necessitating international cooperation to develop and enforce robust privacy laws that can keep pace with technological advancements. The protection of effective privacy requires users to understand their IoT device privacy threats and acquire tools to properly manage their personal data. The establishment of user rights for device data collection needs exact understanding between IoT devices and data protection procedures (Karale, 2021). Unified privacy measures within a single system protect user privacy in secure IoT environments across all cultural territories.

AI-Driven Threats and Deepfake Attacks: Rapid technological development requires extensive new security strategies to deal with changes in privacy operations. The use of artificial intelligence by computers enables criminal creation of sophisticated automated threats that pose the leading security issue in cyberattacks. This includes the creation of deepfake content, advanced phishing schemes, and misinformation campaigns that are increasingly difficult to detect (Gilbert & Gilbert, 2024; Gupta et al., 2023). Additionally, insider threats have become more complex, with nation-states employing covert tactics to infiltrate organizations (Jones, 2024; Joubert & Eloff, 2024). Businesses need to deploy latest security protocols with modern detection systems to fight against advancing infrastructure intrusions. Geopolitical tensions further exacerbate the situation, leading to heightened cyber espionage and frequent attacks on critical infrastructure (World Economic Forum, 2025; Reuters, 2024).

Regulatory Fragmentation: The divided approach to regulating the IoT remains an everlasting difficulty in securing IoT privacy. The fast-paced evolution of IoT technologies creates challenges for law to formally keep up leading to unharmonized privacy standards and weak regulatory enforcement. Such inconsistent regulations block organizations from meeting data sovereignty requirements and cross-border compliance standards and standardized privacy requirements. The deployment of uniform protections in Global IoT ecosystems becomes challenging because different existing laws from separate legal jurisdictions remain non-uniform.

In conclusion, combining efforts between technologists and policymakers with users will address the widespread privacy challenges within IoT devices. These strategies must address the technical, ethical, and regulatory dimensions to mitigate privacy risks and enhance user trust in IoT technologies.

4. KEY CHALLENGES AND STRATEGIC SOLUTIONS IN IOT PRIVACY AND CLOUD COMPUTING

Cloud computing and IoT offer transformative solutions for managing applications, services, and resources within IoT ecosystems. This integration facilitates the evolution of traditional systems into advanced frameworks that automatically handle complexities and adapt to changes, enhancing operational efficiencies and capabilities. For instance, cloud computing provides expansive, on-demand services and a pool of shared resources that address the vast data requirements of IoT systems, thereby meeting the intricate architecture needs of modern IoT solutions protection (Stergiou, Psannis, Kim, & Gupta, 2018). However, alongside these advancements, several critical challenges arise that need to be addressed to fully optimize the integration of IoT and cloud computing. The following challenges outline the main issues that require careful consideration to ensure secure, scalable, and efficient integration:

Standardization Challenges: The integration of IoT with cloud computing introduces significant standardization challenges, as the rapid development of IoT solutions has resulted in a diverse array of devices from various manufacturers. This diversity complicates the integration of IoT ecosystems, which often include components from different vendors with unique architectural frameworks. Such diversity makes it difficult to create cohesive systems, as various stages of the system lifecycle from design and implementation to end-user exploitation often employ inconsistent concepts and methodologies across different solution classes (Szczepaniuk & Szczepaniuk, 2022). Standardized protocols together with APIs and interfaces require development given the technical complexity. Through data integration and service delivery standards solve interoperability problems. Through data integration and service delivery standards solve interoperability problems. The connection between standardized protocols and interfaces and APIs between devices and cloud services results in better functionality as well as improved user experience for IoT devices (Singh et al., 2017). Standards development initiatives focus on simplifying technical and logical architectures beside seeking standardization of programming languages and development frameworks and application paradigms throughout all phases. Standards to secure reliable data transfers need to be developed for the various communication protocols found in the IoT environment. Cybersecurity standardization is equally critical. thropological systems require continuous preservation of both data confidentiality and integrity and availability because such systems process critical sensitive information on a regular basis. The suggested IoT standardization framework by Szczepaniuk & Szczepaniuk (2022) delivers structure which helps improve IoT system compatibility and scalability and their interoperability and security capabilities. Through this standardized framework developers can create systemic approaches to IoT standardization by having access to a complete roadmap that resolves technological difficulties that emerge from IoT progress (Botterman, (Botterman, Cave, & Doria, 2020).

Integration Complexity: Real-time decision systems including data processing depend heavily on the effective linking of IoT devices to cloud platforms. Performing all tasks in a unified system and connecting cloud systems to intelligent devices leads to simplicity in service delivery throughout different fields. Cloud computing delivers improved IoT capabilities by providing its on-demand scalable services for Sensing as a Service (SaaS) Database as a Service (DBaaS) Video Surveillance as a Service (VSaaS). The complex implementations of architecture depend on communication protocols REST, COAP, MQTT that work with networking technologies 6LoWPAN and IPv6 over Bluetooth Low Energy (Malik & Om, 2018). Through their partnership cloud, fog, and edge computing brings forth fast-responsive adaptable infrastructure that works in real-time for application demands. The implementation of different paradigms brings both positive and negative aspects to latency reduction and bandwidth optimization and security enhancement approaches. Interesting frameworks create an essential base which promotes smart cities telemedicine along with advanced distance learning (Kuchuk & Malokhvii, 2024). Long-term surveillance of security issues alongside privacy matters remains crucial for IoT-based big data cloud systems operating in digital twin settings. Stergiou, Bompoli, and Psannis (2023) explained that current data security protocols require enhanced protection protocols for protected information. Achieving secure and efficient integration between IoT and cloud depends upon continuous innovation as an essential practice. All important aspects of cybersecurity together with energy efficiency and standardization mechanisms should not be ignored because they assist IoT applications in adapting to altering requirements.

Scalability Issues: For optimal performance IoT devices and their produced data demand systems which adapt their capabilities to remain effective. Cloud computing establishes critical processing infrastructure for big data collections that improves the effective connectivity of IoT applications. Modern cloud architectures and improved data management platforms enable systems to adjust their performance automatically according to rising IoT requirements (Bertino, 2016). The rapid deployment of IoT through 5G, Wi-Fi, BT, NFC, RFID and IPv6 technology creates major scalability problems and reliability problems and performance problems. Fog computing enables better quality of service through cloud services by providing improved protocols and frameworks that handle unstructured "Big Data" while ensuring system scalability (Luntovskyy & Globa, 2019). Scalable solutions that incorporate edge computing become essential for the mobile Internet of Things (MIoT) system to function properly. The technique allows device localization using worldwide cloud resources to resolve issues related to managing large-scale distributed mobile devices. Fog computing lesson studies demonstrate a need for fresh classification systems to enable smooth IoT system interoperability (Bellavista, Corradi, & Zanni, 2017).

Data privacy protection needs urgent attention in IoT operational networks that continue to grow larger in number.

The Cloud of Things (CoT) architecture combining IoT and cloud computing must be extensively risk audited with current security practices in place to face increasing levels of privacy and security challenges (Abba Ari et al., 2024). Generally, large-scale implementation of IoT-cloud synergy requires more innovative solutions which not only deals with big data, performance reliability and user security and privacy but also takes account of systems security. The current systems demand answers from Fog and edge computation structures to meet their novel technological specifications.

Security and Privacy Concerns: Security concerns pose an increasing threat because cloud computing combines with IoT systems to process large amounts of sensitive information. Recommendations warn for unified architectural implementations to use multi-layer security including end-to-end encryption with blockchain-based access management solutions. Aqeel et al. (2022) emphasized adopting multi-dimensional frameworks which support heterogeneous IoT devices through ethical and regulatory standards for operational use by (2022).

The research done by Tawalbeh et al. (2020) demonstrated that encryption must operate alongside policies which meet global privacy regulations. Lee and Ahmed (2021) uses privacy-preserving analytics through encrypted data-processing ML models. preserving utility without compromising privacy. Karale (2021) extended this knowledge by examining ethical and legal and user rights perspectives to create integrated solutions for secure data procedures. The defence against IoT systems includes whole cryptographic solutions and design arrangement as well as moral and legitimate necessities for securing client information, to manufacture frame trust.

Energy Efficiency and Data Management: Cloud platforms can also be considered as one of the important features of IoT to promote efficiency in energy use and support operations on data. Modern data services enable these platforms reduce power usage by efficient communication protocols and caching that in addition to conserve data usage. With the bundling of these technologies, IoT operations become more eco-friendly and energy-efficient and data reusable. Cloud-based software together with middleware helps organizations track data over extended periods to improve their entire system performance. According to Bahrami, Khan, and Singhal (2016) and Singhal (2016), Dual-function security systems protect data confidentiality while preserving power conservation for specific mobile cloud IoT devices. Humayun et al. (2020) discussed privacy protection and energy optimization within 5G-content industrial IoT systems, presenting how 5G integration does both in a better way. Barua et al. (2024) provided a framework for IoT-based energy management favouring privacy, alongside performance, privacy aware compliance. These developments highlight the growing alignment between energy efficiency, data management, and privacy in cloud-based IoT systems. Cloud technology development now enables improved sustainability alongside better security and deployment effectiveness for IoT systems.

In summary, the merge of IoT and cloud computing provides companies a more recent technology infrastructure that enhances the data processing power of an organization but still incorporates flexible systems along with stronger operative abilities. This increased synchronization of such systems gives rise to better privacy and security problems that need to be addressed with good technology solutions along with the right rules. The full kind of IoT and cloud computing impinges upon additional accrual of the ambition for standards, alongside passive security and data administration protocols to secure use information, security.

5. MACHINE LEARNING AND DEEP LEARNING PRIVACY AND SECURITY ISSUES IN EMERGING TECHNOLOGIES

Machine learning (ML) and deep learning (DL) technologies have become integral to developing advanced predictive analytics and automating decision-making processes across various industries, including healthcare, finance, and autonomous systems (Paracha et al., 2024). However, the implementation of these technologies generates substantial privacy problems along with security risks.

Personal data protection stands as the main essential issue. Most Machine Learning and Deep Learning deployments that require large volumes of data process sensitive information including Personably Identifiable Information (PII). The protection of personal data emerges as the primary concern because model training operations become more challenging. Differential Privacy solutions and federated learning approaches now provide hopeful ways. There is the incorporation of differential privacy to the AI models where it secure both the people in the dataset as well as the app privacy (Xu, Baracaldo, & Joshi, 2021).

Federated learning enables models to learn across decentralized devices or servers possessing local data itmes without even swapping information on them, while maintaining privacy and obtain a robust training model (Awan et al., 2023; Nguyen et al., 2024). Model accuracy can suffer when multiple implementation methods are employed in addition to original training methods. The Predictive leverage of ML models is still highly susceptible to failure whenever attackers deceive input facts in order to deceive predictions. Said security systems based on ML models and that of Autonomous vehicle it persists crucial vulnerabilities (Salem, Azzam, Emam, & Abohany, 2024). The ongoing research aims to develop resilient models despite the main research hurdle being the unstable model performance (Wang et al., 2024). Attackers can break privacy by the invasion methods extracting information from function model and datasets training. Defending against these requires new security measures, such as encrypting model parameters, which may lead to computational inefficiencies inefficiencies (Abba Ari et al., 2024; Wang et al., 2024).

Both biases and unfairness present substantial obstacles for combined models of ML and DL. Biase maintained from training data affects practical applications using these models which causes unfair outcomes especially during law enforcement and recruitment systems. To work within ethical and legal frameworks organizations need algorithms which detect and fix biases in their systems. Organizations that apply ML and DL to process data struggle with GDPR compliance in Europe and CCPA compliance in California because of existing regulatory standards. Ensuring that model decisions are interpretable and auditable conflicts with the often ambiguous nature of deep learning models, complicating efforts to meet these regulatory standards (Nguyen et al., 2024).

Overall, addressing the privacy and security challenges in ML and DL requires a comprehensive approach that includes developing cryptographic techniques, robust modeling methods, and adherence to regulatory and ethical standards. This multidisciplinary effort is crucial for safeguarding sensitive information, maintaining user trust, and ensuring compliance with legal requirements (Dhinakaran, Sankar, Selvaraj, & Raja, 2024; Wang et al., 2024).

6. EXISTING AND COMMON PRIVACY SOLUTIONS IN EMERGING TECHNOLOGIES

For these technical privacy-enhancing methods to make sense, one needs to have some background in IoT privacy issues first. The way IoT systems operate to collect process and share user data without explicit user consent creates these oppositions. The privacy problem in IoT extends further than technical elements because it involves ethical and legal and social specifics too. Technical innovation must unite with efforts toward enhanced transparency and user trust alongside systems designed to improve accountability, and user trust.

The evolution of privacy technology functions as the key solution to overcome current problems in data collection and analytical systems. The use of multiple privacy techniques ensures privacy is maintained in ML and DL sensitive information from the loss of model performance. With **differential privacy methods** ML systems output results that is completely private from individual data even in the case of massive amounts of data (Subramanian, 2023). The process of model training in the **federated learning** makes it possible to run distributed system without bringing the raw data to the device but update location sensible data (Cummings et al., 2023). Research work has made them more efficient with solutions that reduce communication overheads and varying model types (Chaudhary et al., 2024). **Homomorphic encryption** enables calculations on data that stays encrypted from start to finish of processing (Salem et al., 2024), while newer developments decrease its processing requirements (Gong et al., 2024). These privacy-preserving approaches are fundamental to ethically and securely deploy ML and DL in sectors such as finance, healthcare, and autonomous systems (Cummings et al., 2023).

The IoT faces its most substantial challenge through privacy-related issues which remain an essential concern in this domain. IoT systems operating without limitations because of their anytime anywhere with anything nature cause major privacy issues because they permit the transfer and management of highly sensitive information between IoT networks (Karale, 2021). Accordingly, IoT developers need to actively solve privacy problems which affect the technology. Security risk management demands improved protective measures because an excessive number of connected devices exist. New solutions need development since forthcoming IoT ecosystem challenges require new protective methods and mechanisms and innovative architectural frameworks (Akil et al., 2020).

The primary role of IoT privacy solutions is to design safe information protection systems that hide user identity data so that the unknown parties cannot trace out or misuse user's activities. Protecting privacy stands as a vital priority for IoT operations since the produced data materials sensitive personal information related to individual lives. Conversation papers comprise of scholastic and modern innovation and production/proficient horizons focused on specialists recommended alternatives characterized by imaginative architectures and advancements and system strategies to shield the IoT biological system security and duty strings. Academic studies achieved that achevments in unertaking of privacy requirements through developing solutions that are put in place for access controls protection and data privacy as well as user identity protection ((Kouicem et al., 2018). Sicari et al. (2015) highlighted end-to-end security deployment requirements which need to offer authentication together with confidential features, access control functions, user-device trust operations while following existing privacy regulations (Vishal Sharma et al., 2020). In terms of authentication and access control, patients for instance, gain entry through authentication methods employed by Elliptic Curve Cryptography (ECC) session keys which represent a lightweight encryption technique. The keys work in conjunction with an attribute authority for mutual authentication between users and sensor nodes to fulfill security requirements of the IoT (Sharma et al., 2024). Moreover, combining ECC with blockchain enhances both security and privacy in IoT environments ((Guo et al., 2024).

In the field of data privacy, a widely used mechanism is data tagging, which associates additional tags with data. The management of secure private data flows takes place through trusted computing entities who prevent the identification of data controllers (McIntyre, 2023). While the main approach named Zero Knowledge Proof (ZKP) enables communication between two parties referred to as prover and verifier. The prover can show evidence of holding particular data through ZKP without showing actual details of the data (Chatzigiannakis et al., 2011). This is widely used by the developers to make privacy security protocols (PrimaFelicitas, 2024). Under **K-anonymity** each record becomes indistinguishable from its **k−1** counterpart records in the dataset to prevent sensitive information detection (Sweeney, 2002). This method serves multiple applications in cloud computing along with big data systems to safeguard streaming data from unauthorized users. The application of **K-anonymity** through clustering methods serves IoT research for location data protection of sensor nodes in wireless sensor networks (di Vimercati et al., 2023; Ling et al., 2023; Mahanan et al., 2020). Improved privacy solutions emerge through the acquisition and processing of distributed sensor node data. The protection of IoT devices against security threats demands manufacturers to deliver succinct security alerts about vulnerabilities to users at the time of purchasing IoT devices. Organizations need to offer full training programs which teach users how to construct powerful passwords and maintain security updates that stops unauthorized applications and spam mail hazards. User consciousness about IoT security advances simultaneously with this strategy (Estrada, Tawalbeh, & Vinaja, 2020).

Henze et al. (2016) presented a useful strategy for resolving critical application areas' severe privacy problems including assisted living and public mobility assistance. The study developed UPECSI as an approach that links different technologies with organizational procedures to allow users to enforce privacy rules on cloud-based IoT services. Through this method end-users secure their private data prior to cloud transmission with benefits for cloud service developers who can integrate privacy elements smoothly (Henze et al., 2016). The system offers users a user-friendly interface that delivers adjustable and clear privacy setting controls (G. Yang, 2022). Hernandez-Ramos together with Bernabe and Skarmeta (2016) developed the ARMY architectural design through the ARM framework for continuous IoT security and privacy management. Various European IoT initiatives implemented this architecture to stimulate the growth of privacy and security-based IoT services according to Tawalbeh et al. (2020). Peng et al. (2013) established a key-changed mutual authentication protocol that ensures security for WSN and RFID systems. The security system with its real-time key refresh mechanism includes key backup features and random number generation and one-way hash functions to defend against attack forms that include replay attacks and replications attempts and denial-of-service intrusions and spoofing threats and tag tracking vulnerabilities (Sharmila et al., 2023). The PPDM techniques examined by Ukil, Bandyopadhyay, and Pal (2014) yielded findings towards establishing a privacy management system to evaluate security risks of sharing confidential information (Dhinakaran et al., 2024).

To improve IoT privacy, the research group led by Su et al. (2014) established ePASS as an ABS system that integrated attribute trees to build policy conditions for user authorization without compromising user anonymity in IoT environments. They introduced an attribute-based signature (ABS) scheme named ePASS, that utilizes the concept of the attribute tree defined AND/OR policy conditions and permits only allowed users to signify messages along with the preservation of anonymity

(Gong et al., 2023). Furthermore, Sicari, Cappiello, et al. (2014) proposed a UML-based conceptual design of IoT questions, including luxury questions and premium complexities factoring (Bazza et al., 2023). For evaluating data quality, security, and privacy in IoT, Sicari et al. (2014) developed a layered architecture that integrates data from various sources to meet customer needs and improve privacy and data quality (Laghari et al., 2024). Furthermore, Harbor (2016) proposed a three-step framework to guide governments, institutions, and companies in implementing IoT security and privacy. A comprehensive IoT security approach requires impact assessments together with core security function management including identification and access management and encryption abilities and analytics capabilities and network security implementation (Yang, 2022).

The industrial sector depends heavily on the IoT because IoT delivers valuable automation possibilities. The fundamental goal of IoT implementation centres on improving production levels as well as efficiency and reliability and control of finished products (Parra-Sánchez, 2024). Privacy in IoT maintains essential importance from design until implementation stages of development (Yang, 2022). Various industry workshops together with professional conferences have demonstrated that companies must implement strong security and privacy measures for their IoT products in order to establish customer confidence. Three main privacy challenges exist around collecting massive customer information alongside the unexpected application of collected data and maintaining data safety. Enterprises need to implement best practices including privacy by design together with data minimization and transparency to provide users with both notification and selection options regarding unexpected data use (Tawalbeh et al., 2020).

Privacy by design presents a usable approach that matches our present circumstances through which users control their data access. Through dynamic tools users have the ability to provide access to specific services for their data (Sharmila et al., 2023). To prevent unwanted processing of individual data mechanisms must be implemented and users need to receive information regarding data processing including its purposes and processor identity along with methods to exercise their privacy rights. Optimized design of products and procedures necessitates the examination of privacy goals when creating new products as well as during their complete execution process (IEEE, 2023). The application of this methodology begins at system development onset to protect privacy rights through multiple principles which establish both data protection compliance and privacy risk reduction. Cavoukian, Taylor, and Abrams (2010) identified seven foundational principles of privacy by design: (1) privacy should be proactive and preventative, not reactive and remedial; (2) privacy should be the default setting; (3) privacy should be embedded into the design of a product or interaction, not an add-on; (4) privacy should not impede the full functionality of a product; (5) security should protect privacy throughout the entire system and data lifecycle; (6) privacy procedures should be visible and transparent to support accountability and trust; and (7) privacy design should respect users' interests and empower them to manage their data through consent, accuracy, access, and compliance (UCSC, 2023). Data protection requirements such as purpose limitation as well as data minimization and data deletion present significant challenges in the IoT environment since automatic communication between things and people remains essential (EpiSensor, 2023).

On the other hand, data minimization establishes requirements for companies to reduce the amount of data they collect and maintain and permanently remove data when it becomes unnecessary. Various policy initiatives integrate portability as a key element which protects privacy. Businesses should collect data only for specific purposes and dispose of it safely to reduce the risks of data breaches and misuse (Forbes Technology Council, 2024).

To minimize these risks, companies have to examine their data operations to define proper restrictions for both data acquisition and storage (ISACA, 2021). Every entity must deliver privacy notices which explain their practices regarding personal information collection along with processing and retention and data sharing. Clear and transparent privacy notices help users understand how their data is handled and their rights (IAPP, 2025). Providing notice along with choice requirements play a critical role in IoT operations because their framework generates substantial data collections. Despite the challenges, it is critical to offer users clear options and information about data practices to mitigate potential privacy and security risks (TrustCloud, 2025). Research supports these practices, highlighting the importance of data minimization in machine learning models to comply with GDPR and enhance privacy (Staab, Jovanović, Balunović, & Vechev, 2024).

The combination of complex and modern cyber threats, including AI-powered attacks, deepfakes, and smart phishing, along with anomalous inputs, is overwhelming traditional IoT security systems. Addressing these evolving risks requires AI-augmented cybersecurity, which enhances detection and response by analyzing large data volumes, identifying anomalies, and enabling real-time, automated incident handling (Nadella & Gonaygunta, 2024; Sindiramutty, 2023). They also prepare the ground for the move to both autonomous threat hunting capabilities and predictive risk analytics systems. The changing legal environment keeps the pace for businesses to change data privacy and compliance requirement (Hodgins, 2024). The monotony of intelligent security systems has been augmented by the norm of compliance, and organizations are now more effective in resisting threats and protecting sensitive data which exists presently in online systems.

In summary, a complete framework for IoT privacy demands devices and services designed with privacy in mind as well as models aligned with user interests and minimum data collection and defensive AI systems. These techniques form a multi-faceted strategy, to safeguard data whilst building trust with your users. Solutions to these bottlenecks, such as scalability dilemmas and integration points with current systems as well as inadequate user engagement are difficult. The efficacy of privacy systems is hampered by ethical issues when information is moved across borders along with varied rules. A systematic review and adjusted risk management strategies and unified standards need to be developed to ensure proper benefits assessment of IoT privacy solutions. Several strategies are needed to enhance IoT privacy individually, integrating technological advances as well as regulatory standards with ethical concepts and user engagement to ensure continued security in both technical and non-technical domains.

7. FINDINGS AND DISCUSSION

The review emphasized the importance of both easy-to-use interfaces in addition to strict privacy protection for IoT systems. Privacy protection encounters essential obstacles that match the challenges encountered by IoT system security and trust. Remote system communication through IoT device connections to the global web resulted in emerging privacy issues stemming from data privacy and anonymity alongside unclear privacy policies and privacy rights and social acceptance and pseudonymity and unlinkability and accountability issues (Tawalbeh et al., 2020). To protect sensitive information and enable legitimate users to gather and share data while preventing third-party access, further research is needed to design effective privacy measures for IoT platforms. Appropriate encryption algorithms must be implemented to ensure authenticity, integrity, anonymity, and data privacy, while ensuring efficient data processing (Yang, 2022).

Privacy in IoT technologies is fundamental and poses many challenges. Intuitive solutions are needed that seamlessly integrate with the physical world. Collaboration among scholars, academicians, and technicians is crucial to develop solutions that address these issues and reduce associated risks (Mohammad et al., 2024). This review identified common IoT privacy concerns, including data privacy, risks in data collection and usage, user privacy rights, and unclear policies. It was also found that more mechanisms should be developed to educate users about processing and providing information about the processor, the purpose of the processing, and how to practice data subject rights, especially since most IoT applications are expected to work in the background, unnoticed by users. To mitigate increased threats, governments, companies, and academic institutions should change their approach to IoT privacy and other IoT issues. They should understand the advantages and disadvantages of new technologies, the nature of new challenges, and potential risks. Additionally, companies should concentrate on discovering cutting-edge methods to address IoT privacy concerns while identifying current gaps and recognizing absent elements (Dhinakaran et al., 2024). To provide a clearer understanding of how data privacy can be addressed in IoT systems, the following flow diagrams illustrate the general process and the roles of different stakeholders in protecting privacy within digital emerging technologies.

Figure 1. General Process for Addressing IoT Privacy Issues

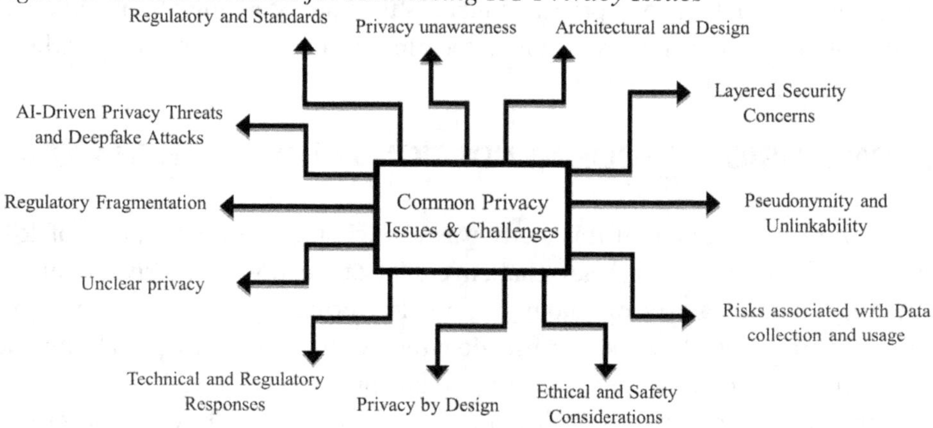

Data privacy challenges initiate the process with the assessment of risks stemming from data collection as well as unclear privacy policies. Developing solutions requires innovative algorithms along with frameworks. Privacy measures are implemented within IoT systems. Continuous education for users and stakeholders is essential. Finally, privacy practices must be regularly monitored and updated to address emerging threats. Furthermore, to complement the general process illustrated above, the following diagram (Figure 2) highlights the roles and responsibilities of different stakeholders in ensuring effective IoT privacy management.

Figure 2. Roles of Different Stakeholders in IoT Privacy Management

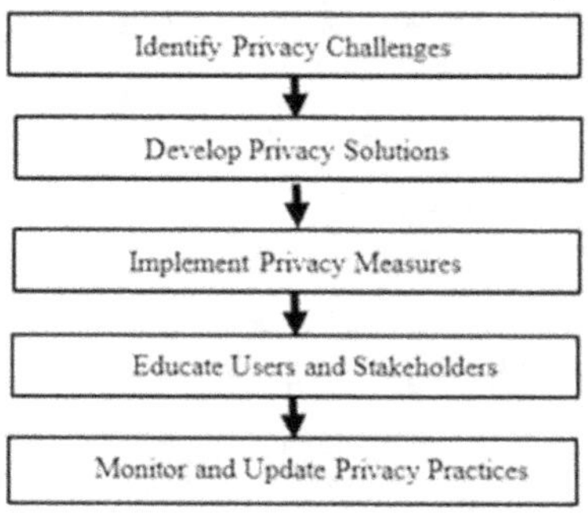

Various stakeholders play critical roles in ensuring IoT privacy. Developers and system designers are responsible for building privacy-compliant applications. Data protection managers oversee the enforcement of privacy policies. Governments and academic institutions conduct research and provide education. End-users are encouraged to actively manage their privacy settings and understand their rights.

These flow diagrams provide a structured view of the essential steps and stakeholder involvement required to address data privacy concerns effectively in emerging IoT technologies. Visualizing the process enhances the understanding of how practical implementation can be achieved, complementing the discussion provided earlier.

8. CONCLUSION, RECOMMENDATIONS AND FURTHER WORK

The primary objective of this study was to review the critical aspects of IoT, with a particular focus on privacy challenges. It examined various privacy-related issues, including data privacy, anonymity, unclear privacy policies, privacy rights and expectations, social acceptance, pseudonymity, unlinkability, accountability, and other common concerns related to user rights and privacy policies. This review also summarized existing solutions from academic, technical, and industry perspectives. These solutions include new methods, approaches, architectures, and mechanisms aimed at enhancing user privacy in IoT platforms. However, many open issues and potential gaps remain in existing solutions that need to be addressed. In conclusion, IoT platforms embrace a complex set of privacy policy considerations across various stakeholders. As the world moves towards Industry 4.0, IoT developers, academicians, technicians, industries, and governments need to consider robust solutions when designing and deploying IoT technologies.

REFERENCES

Abba Ari, A. A., Ngangmo, O. K., Titouna, C., Thiare, O., Mohamadou, A., & Gueroui, A. M. (2024). Enabling privacy and security in Cloud of Things: Architecture, applications, security & privacy challenges. *Applied Computing and Informatics, 20*(1/2), 119–141. DOI: 10.1016/j.aci.2019.11.005

Akil, M., Islami, L., Fischer-Hübner, S., Martucci, L. A., & Zuccato, A. (2020). Privacy-preserving identifiers for IoT: A systematic literature review. *IEEE Access : Practical Innovations, Open Solutions, 8*, 168470–168485. DOI: 10.1109/ACCESS.2020.3023659

Aqeel, M., Ali, F., Iqbal, M. W., Rana, T. A., Arif, M., & Auwul, M. R. (2022). A review of security and privacy concerns in the internet of things (IoT). *Journal of Sensors, 2022*(1), 5724168. DOI: 10.1155/2022/5724168

Atlam, H. F., & Wills, G. B. (2020). IoT security, privacy, safety and ethics. *Digital twin technologies and smart cities*, 123-149.

Attarian, R., & Hashemi, S. (2021). An anonymity communication protocol for security and privacy of clients in IoT-based mobile health transactions. *Computer Networks, 190*, 107976. DOI: 10.1016/j.comnet.2021.107976

Awan, K. A., Din, I. U., Almogren, A., & Rodrigues, J. J. (2023). Privacy-preserving big data security for IoT with federated learning and cryptography. *IEEE Access : Practical Innovations, Open Solutions, 11*, 120918–120934. DOI: 10.1109/ACCESS.2023.3328310

Bahrami, M., Khan, A., & Singhal, M. (2016). *An energy efficient data privacy scheme for IoT devices in mobile cloud computing*. Paper presented at the 2016 IEEE International Conference on Mobile Services (MS). DOI: 10.1109/MobServ.2016.37

Barua, E., Chowhan, S. S., Jain, S. K., & Vekariya, V. (2024). A novel framework for privacy and data protection in internet of things-based energy management systems. *International Journal of System Assurance Engineering and Management*, •••, 1–10. DOI: 10.1007/s13198-024-02620-4

Bellavista, P., Corradi, A., & Zanni, A. (2017). Integrating mobile internet of things and cloud computing towards scalability: Lessons learned from existing fog computing architectures and solutions. *International Journal of Cloud Computing, 6*(4), 393–406. DOI: 10.1504/IJCC.2017.090198

Bertino, E. (2016). *Data privacy for IoT systems: Concepts, approaches, and research directions.* Paper presented at the 2016 IEEE International Conference on Big Data (Big Data). DOI: 10.1109/BigData.2016.7841030

Bhattacharjya, A., Zhong, X., Wang, J., & Li, X. (2019). Security challenges and concerns of Internet of Things (IoT). *Cyber-Physical Systems: architecture, security and application*, 153-185.

Botterman, M., Cave, J., & Doria, A. (2020). Standardization issues. *ICT Policy, Research, and Innovation: Perspectives and Prospects for EU-US Collaboration*, 309-330.

Cavoukian, A., Taylor, S., & Abrams, M. E. (2010). Privacy by Design: Essential for organizational accountability and strong business practices. *Identity in the Information Society, 3*(2), 405–413. DOI: 10.1007/s12394-010-0053-z

Chatzigiannakis, I., Pyrgelis, A., Spirakis, P. G., & Stamatiou, Y. C. (2011). *Elliptic curve based zero knowledge proofs and their applicability on resource constrained devices.* Paper presented at the Mobile Adhoc and Sensor Systems (MASS), 2011 IEEE 8th International Conference on. DOI: 10.1109/MASS.2011.77

Chaudhary, R. K., Kumar, R., & Saxena, N. (2024). A systematic review on federated learning system: A new paradigm to machine learning. *Knowledge and Information Systems*, •••, 1–104.

Chaurasia, N., & Kumar, P. (2023). A comprehensive study on issues and challenges related to privacy and security in IoT. *e-Prime-Advances in Electrical Engineering. Electronics and Energy, 4*, 100158.

Chung, H., Iorga, M., Voas, J., & Lee, S. (2017). Alexa, can I trust you? *Computer, 50*(9), 100–104. DOI: 10.1109/MC.2017.3571053 PMID: 29213147

Cummings, R., Desfontaines, D., Evans, D., Geambasu, R., Huang, Y., Jagielski, M., . . . Ohrimenko, O. (2023). Advancing differential privacy: Where we are now and future directions for real-world deployment. *arXiv preprint arXiv:2304.06929.*

Deep, S., Zheng, X., Jolfaei, A., Yu, D., Ostovari, P., & Kashif Bashir, A. (2022). A survey of security and privacy issues in the Internet of Things from the layered context. *Transactions on Emerging Telecommunications Technologies, 33*(6), e3935. DOI: 10.1002/ett.3935

Dhinakaran, D., Sankar, S., Selvaraj, D., & Raja, S. E. (2024). Privacy-preserving data in IoT-based cloud systems: A comprehensive survey with AI integration. *arXiv preprint arXiv:2401.00794.*

di Vimercati, S. D. C., Foresti, S., Livraga, G., & Samarati, P. (2023). k-Anonymity: From Theory to Applications. *Transactions on Data Privacy*, *16*(1), 25–49.

EpiSensor. (2023). *IoT Data Privacy: Ensuring Compliance with GDPR and Other Regulations*. Retrieved from EpiSensor.

Estrada, D., Tawalbeh, L. A. A., & Vinaja, R. (2020). How secure having IoT devices in our homes?.

Gong, B., Guo, C., Guo, C., Sun, Y., Waqas, M., & Chen, S. (2023). SLIM: A secure and lightweight multi-authority attribute-based signcryption scheme for IoT. *IEEE Transactions on Information Forensics and Security*, *19*, 1299–1312.

Gong, Y., Chang, X., Mišić, J., Mišić, V. B., Wang, J., & Zhu, H. (2024). Practical solutions in fully homomorphic encryption: A survey analyzing existing acceleration methods. *Cybersecurity*, *7*(1), 5. DOI: 10.1186/s42400-023-00187-4

Guo, C., Gong, B., Waqas, M., Alasmary, H., Tu, S., & Chen, S. (2024). An efficient pairing-free ciphertext-policy attribute-based encryption scheme for Internet of Things. *Sensors (Basel)*, *24*(21), 6843. DOI: 10.3390/s24216843 PMID: 39517740

Haider, I., Höberl, M., & Rinner, B. (2016). *Trusted Sensors for Participatory Sensing and IoT Applications based on Physically Unclonable Functions.* Paper presented at the Proceedings of the 2nd ACM International Workshop on IoT Privacy, Trust, and Security. DOI: 10.1145/2899007.2899010

Henze, M., Hermerschmidt, L., Kerpen, D., Häußling, R., Rumpe, B., & Wehrle, K. (2016). A comprehensive approach to privacy in the cloud-based Internet of Things. *Future Generation Computer Systems*, *56*, 701–718. DOI: 10.1016/j.future.2015.09.016

Humayun, M., Jhanjhi, N., Alruwaili, M., Amalathas, S. S., Balasubramanian, V., & Selvaraj, B. (2020). Privacy protection and energy optimization for 5G-aided industrial Internet of Things. *IEEE Access : Practical Innovations, Open Solutions*, *8*, 183665–183677. DOI: 10.1109/ACCESS.2020.3028764

IAPP. (2025). *US State Privacy Legislation Tracker*. Retrieved from IAPP.

IEEE. (2023). *What Is Privacy-by-Design and Why It's Important?* Retrieved from IEEE.

ISACA. (2021). *Data Minimization—A Practical Approach*. Retrieved from ISACA.

Karale, A. (2021). The challenges of IoT addressing security, ethics, privacy, and laws. *Internet of Things : Engineering Cyber Physical Human Systems*, *15*, 100420. DOI: 10.1016/j.iot.2021.100420

Khan, Y., Su'ud, M. B. M., Alam, M. M., Ahmad, S. F., Salim, N. A., & Khan, N. (2022). Architectural threats to security and privacy: A challenge for internet of things (IoT) applications. *Electronics (Basel)*, *12*(1), 88. DOI: 10.3390/electronics12010088

Kouicem, D. E., Bouabdallah, A., & Lakhlef, H. (2018). Internet of Things Security: A top-down survey. *Computer Networks*, *141*, 199–221. DOI: 10.1016/j.comnet.2018.03.012

Kuchuk, H., & Malokhvii, E. (2024). Integration of IoT with cloud, fog, and edge computing: A review. *Advanced Information Systems*, *8*(2), 65–78. DOI: 10.20998/2522-9052.2024.2.08

Laghari, A. A., Li, H., Khan, A. A., Shoulin, Y., Karim, S., & Khani, M. A. K. (2024). Internet of Things (IoT) applications security trends and challenges. *Discover Internet of Things*, *4*(1), 36. DOI: 10.1007/s43926-024-00090-5

Lee, C., & Ahmed, G. (2021). Improving IoT privacy, data protection and security concerns. [IJTIM]. *International Journal of Technology Innovation and Management*, *1*(1), 18–33. DOI: 10.54489/ijtim.v1i1.12

Ling, C., Zhang, W., & He, H. (2023). K-anonymity privacy-preserving algorithm for IoT applications in virtualization and edge computing. *Cluster Computing*, *26*(2), 1495–1510. DOI: 10.1007/s10586-022-03755-4

Luntovskyy, A., & Globa, L. (2019). *Performance, reliability and scalability for IoT.* Paper presented at the 2019 International Conference on Information and Digital Technologies (IDT). DOI: 10.1109/DT.2019.8813679

Mahanan, W., Chaovalitwongse, W. A., & Natwichai, J. (2020). Data anonymization: A novel optimal k-anonymity algorithm for identical generalization hierarchy data in IoT. *Service Oriented Computing and Applications*, *14*(2), 89–100. DOI: 10.1007/s11761-020-00287-w

Malik, A., & Om, H. (2018). Cloud computing and internet of things integration: Architecture, applications, issues, and challenges. *Sustainable cloud and energy services: Principles and practice*, 1-24.

Mohammad, N., Khatoon, R., Nilima, S. I., Akter, J., Kamruzzaman, M., & Sozib, H. M. (2024). Ensuring Security and Privacy in the Internet of Things: Challenges and Solutions. *Journal of Computer and Communications*, *12*(8), 257–277. DOI: 10.4236/jcc.2024.128016

Mugariri, P., Abdullah, H., Garcia-Torres, M., Parameshchari, B., & Abdul Sattar, K. N. (2022). Promoting information privacy protection awareness for internet of things (IoT). *Mobile Information Systems*, *2022*(1), 4247651. DOI: 10.1155/2022/4247651

Nguyen, G., Sáinz-Pardo Díaz, J., Calatrava, A., Berberi, L., Lytvyn, O., Kozlov, V., Tran, V., Moltó, G., & López García, Á. (2024). Landscape of machine learning evolution: Privacy-preserving federated learning frameworks and tools. *Artificial Intelligence Review*, *58*(2), 51. DOI: 10.1007/s10462-024-11036-2

Paracha, A., Arshad, J., Farah, M. B., & Ismail, K. (2024). Machine learning security and privacy: A review of threats and countermeasures. *EURASIP Journal on Information Security*, *2024*(1), 10. DOI: 10.1186/s13635-024-00158-3

Parra-Sánchez, D. T. (2024). Exploring the Internet of Things adoption in the Fourth Industrial Revolution: a comprehensive scientometric analysis. *Journal of Innovative Digital Transformation*.

Peng, L., Ru-chuan, W., Xiao-yu, S., & Long, C. (2013). *Privacy Protection Based on Key-changed Mutual Authentication Protocol in Internet of Things.* Paper presented at the China Conference Wireless Sensor Networks.

Ramos, J. H., & Skármeta, A. (2020). *Security and privacy in the internet of things: Challenges and solutions* (Vol. 27). IOS Press.

Salem, A. H., Azzam, S. M., Emam, O., & Abohany, A. A. (2024). Advancing cybersecurity: A comprehensive review of AI-driven detection techniques. *Journal of Big Data*, *11*(1), 105. DOI: 10.1186/s40537-024-00957-y

Sharma, V., Kumar, A., & Sharma, K. (2024). Digital twin: Securing IoT networks using integrated ECC with blockchain for healthcare ecosystem. *Knowledge and Information Systems*, •••, 1–32.

Sharma, V., You, I., Andersson, K., Palmieri, F., Rehmani, M. H., & Lim, J. (2020). Security, privacy and trust for smart mobile-Internet of Things (M-IoT): A survey. *IEEE Access : Practical Innovations, Open Solutions*, *8*, 167123–167163. DOI: 10.1109/ACCESS.2020.3022661

Sharmila, K., Kumar, P., Bhushan, S., Kumar, M., & Alazab, M. (2023). Secure key management and mutual authentication protocol for wireless sensor network by linking edge devices using hybrid approach. *Wireless Personal Communications*, *130*(4), 2935–2957. DOI: 10.1007/s11277-023-10410-7

Sicari, S., Cappiello, C., De Pellegrini, F., Miorandi, D., & Coen-Porisini, A. (2014). A security-and quality-aware system architecture for Internet of Things. *Information Systems Frontiers*, •••, 1–13.

Sicari, S., Rizzardi, A., Coen-Porisini, A., & Cappiello, C. (2014). *A NFP model for internet of things applications.* Paper presented at the 2014 IEEE 10th International Conference on Wireless and Mobile Computing, Networking and Communications (WiMob). DOI: 10.1109/WiMOB.2014.6962181

Sicari, S., Rizzardi, A., Grieco, L. A., & Coen-Porisini, A. (2015). Security, privacy and trust in Internet of Things: The road ahead. *Computer Networks*, *76*, 146–164. DOI: 10.1016/j.comnet.2014.11.008

Singh, V. P., Dwarakanath, V. T., Haribabu, P., & Babu, N. S. C. (2017). *IoT standardization efforts—An analysis.* Paper presented at the 2017 International Conference On Smart Technologies For Smart Nation (SmartTechCon). DOI: 10.1109/SmartTechCon.2017.8358536

Sollins, K. R. (2019). IoT big data security and privacy versus innovation. *IEEE Internet of Things Journal*, *6*(2), 1628–1635. DOI: 10.1109/JIOT.2019.2898113

Staab, R., Jovanović, N., Balunović, M., & Vechev, M. (2024). *From principle to practice: Vertical data minimization for machine learning.* Paper presented at the 2024 IEEE Symposium on Security and Privacy (SP). DOI: 10.1109/SP54263.2024.00089

Stergiou, C., Psannis, K. E., Kim, B.-G., & Gupta, B. (2018). Secure integration of IoT and cloud computing. *Future Generation Computer Systems*, *78*, 964–975. DOI: 10.1016/j.future.2016.11.031

Stergiou, C. L., Bompoli, E., & Psannis, K. E. (2023). Security and privacy issues in IoT-based big data cloud systems in a digital twin scenario. *Applied Sciences (Basel, Switzerland)*, *13*(2), 758. DOI: 10.3390/app13020758

Su, J., Cao, D., Zhao, B., Wang, X., & You, I. (2014). ePASS: An expressive attribute-based signature scheme with privacy and an unforgeability guarantee for the Internet of Things. *Future Generation Computer Systems*, *33*, 11–18. DOI: 10.1016/j.future.2013.10.016

Subramanian, R. (2023). Have the cake and eat it too: Differential Privacy enables privacy and precise analytics. *Journal of Big Data*, *10*(1), 117. DOI: 10.1186/s40537-023-00712-9

Sucasas, V., Mantas, G., Bastos, J., Damião, F., & Rodriguez, J. (2019). A signature scheme with unlinkable-yet-accountable pseudonymity for privacy-preserving crowdsensing. *IEEE Transactions on Mobile Computing*, *19*(4), 752–768. DOI: 10.1109/TMC.2019.2901463

Szczepaniuk, H., & Szczepaniuk, E. K. (2022). Standardization of IoT ecosystems: Open challenges, current solutions, and future directions [CRC Press.]. *Internet of Things : Engineering Cyber Physical Human Systems*, •••, 23–42.

Tawalbeh, L., Muheidat, F., Tawalbeh, M., & Quwaider, M. (2020). IoT Privacy and security: Challenges and solutions. *Applied Sciences (Basel, Switzerland)*, *10*(12), 4102. DOI: 10.3390/app10124102

TrustCloud. (2025). *Data Privacy in the Age of IoT: Securing Connected Devices*. Retrieved from TrustCloud.

UCSC. (2023). *Privacy by Design: The 7 Foundational Principles*. Retrieved from UCSC.

Ukil, A., Bandyopadhyay, S., & Pal, A. (2014). *Iot-privacy: To be private or not to be private*. Paper presented at the Computer Communications Workshops (INFOCOM WKSHPS), 2014 IEEE Conference on. DOI: 10.1109/INFCOMW.2014.6849186

Vasilomanolakis, E., Daubert, J., Luthra, M., Gazis, V., Wiesmaier, A., & Kikiras, P. (2015). *On the security and privacy of Internet of Things architectures and systems*. Paper presented at the 2015 International Workshop on Secure Internet of Things (SIoT). DOI: 10.1109/SIOT.2015.9

Wang, T., Bi, Z., Zhang, Y., Liu, M., Hsieh, W., Feng, P., . . . Liu, J. (2024). Deep Learning Model Security: Threats and Defenses. *arXiv preprint arXiv:2412.08969*.

Xu, R., Baracaldo, N., & Joshi, J. (2021). Privacy-preserving machine learning: Methods, challenges and directions. *arXiv preprint arXiv:2108.04417*.

Yang, G. (2022). An overview of current solutions for privacy in the Internet of Things. *Frontiers in Artificial Intelligence*, *5*, 812732. DOI: 10.3389/frai.2022.812732 PMID: 35310954

Yang, Y., Zheng, X., Guo, W., Liu, X., & Chang, V. (2019). Privacy-preserving smart IoT-based healthcare big data storage and self-adaptive access control system. *Information Sciences*, *479*, 567–592. DOI: 10.1016/j.ins.2018.02.005

Zhou, W., Jia, Y., Peng, A., Zhang, Y., & Liu, P. (2018). The effect of IoT new features on security and privacy: New threats, existing solutions, and challenges yet to be solved. *IEEE Internet of Things Journal*, *6*(2), 1606–1616. DOI: 10.1109/JIOT.2018.2847733

Compilation of References

Abadi, M., Chu, A., & Goodfellow, I.. (2016). Deep Learning with Differential Privacy. *Proceedings of the 2016 ACM SIGSAC Conference on Computer and Communications Security (CCS)*. DOI: 10.1145/2976749.2978318

Abba Ari, A. A., Ngangmo, O. K., Titouna, C., Thiare, O., Mohamadou, A., & Gueroui, A. M. (2024). Enabling privacy and security in Cloud of Things: Architecture, applications, security & privacy challenges. *Applied Computing and Informatics*, *20*(1/2), 119–141. DOI: 10.1016/j.aci.2019.11.005

Abbas, A., Khan, M. A., Latif, S., Ajaz, M., Shah, A. A., & Ahmad, J. (2022). A New Ensemble-Based Intrusion Detection System for Internet of Things. *Arabian Journal for Science and Engineering*, *47*(2), 1805–1819. DOI: 10.1007/s13369-021-06086-5

Abdirashid Abukar Ahmed, N. N. (2024, September 04). A Comparative Analysis of Adversarial Attack Methods on Machine Learning Models. *Indian Scientific Journal Of Research In Engineering And Management*, *8*(08), 1–16. DOI: 10.55041/IJSREM37340

Abdiyeva-Aliyeva, G., & Hematyar, M. (2022). Statistic Approached Dynamically Detecting Security Threats and Updating a Signature-Based Intrusion Detection System's Database in NGN. *Journal of Advances in Information Technology*, *13*(5), 524–529. DOI: 10.12720/jait.13.5.524-529

Abdul Awal Mintoo, A. R. (2024). Adversarial Machine Learning In Network Security: A Systematic Review Of Threat Vectors And Defense Mechanisms. *01*(01), 80 - 98. DOI: 10.70937/itej.v1i01.9

Abinaya, K., Palaniappan, D., & Vedaraj, M. (2023). A Novel Hyper-Spectral Model to Optimize the Prediction Rate for Heart Disease in Modern Healthcare Networks. *Engineering Proceedings*, *59081*, 59081. Advance online publication. DOI: 10.3390/engproc2023059081

Acemoğlu, D., Autor, D., Hazell, J., & Restrepo, P. (2022). Artificial Intelligence and Jobs: Evidence from Online Vacancies. In Journal of Labor Economics (Vol. 40). University of Chicago Press. DOI: 10.1086/718327

Act, A. I. (2024). Artificial Intelligence Act. *Regulamento da União Europeia (UE), 1689.*

Adadi, A., & Berrada, M. (2018). Peeking inside the black-box: A survey on explainable artificial intelligence (XAI). *IEEE Access : Practical Innovations, Open Solutions*, *6*, 52138–52160. DOI: 10.1109/ACCESS.2018.2870052

Adeola N. Raji, A. O. (2024). Integrating Artificial Intelligence, machine learning, and data analytics in cybersecurity: A holistic approach to advanced threat detection and response. *World Journal Of Advanced Research and Reviews.* DOI: 10.30574/wjarr.2024.24.2.3197

Afees Olanrewaju Akinade, P. A. (2023). 10 30). Evaluating AI and ML in Cybersecurity: A USA and global perspective. *GSC Advanced Research and Reviews*, *17*(1), 138–148. DOI: 10.30574/gscarr.2023.17.1.0409

Ahad, U., Singh, Y., Anand, P., Sheikh, Z. A., & Singh, P. K. (2022). Intrusion Detection System Model for IoT Networks Using Ensemble Learning. *Journal of Interconnection Networks*, *22*(03), 2145008. Advance online publication. DOI: 10.1142/S0219265921450080

Ahmad, R., Wazirali, R., & Abu-Ain, T. (2022). Machine learning for wireless sensor networks security: An overview of challenges and issues. *Sensors (Basel)*, *22*(13), 4730. DOI: 10.3390/s22134730 PMID: 35808227

Ahmad, Z., Shahid Khan, A., Wai Shiang, C., Abdullah, J., & Ahmad, F. (2021). Network intrusion detection system: A systematic study of machine learning and deep learning approaches. *Transactions on Emerging Telecommunications Technologies*, *32*(1), e4150. Advance online publication. DOI: 10.1002/ett.4150

Ahmed, M., Nazeeruddin, M., & Hashem, I. A. T. (2016). Machine learning algorithms for intrusion detection: A survey. *International Journal of Security and Networks*, *11*(3), 173–182.

Akhtar, N., Mian, A., Kardan, N., & Shah, M. (2021). Advances in adversarial attacks and defenses in computer vision: A survey. *IEEE Access : Practical Innovations, Open Solutions*, *9*, 155161–155196. DOI: 10.1109/ACCESS.2021.3127960

Akhtar, Z. B., & Rawol, A. T. (2024). Enhancing cybersecurity through AI-powered security mechanisms. *IT Journal Research and Development*, *9*(1), 50–67. DOI: 10.25299/itjrd.2024.16852

Akil, M., Islami, L., Fischer-Hübner, S., Martucci, L. A., & Zuccato, A. (2020). Privacy-preserving identifiers for IoT: A systematic literature review. *IEEE Access : Practical Innovations, Open Solutions, 8*, 168470–168485. DOI: 10.1109/ACCESS.2020.3023659

Alabdan, R. (2020). Phishing attacks survey: Types, vectors, and technical approaches. *Future Internet, 12*(10), 168. DOI: 10.3390/fi12100168

Alam, T. (2018). A Reliable Communication Framework and Its Use in Internet of Things (IoT). *International Journal of Scientific Research in Computer Science, Engineering and Information Technology, Vol 3(5).*

Alazab, M. (2022). *Swarna Priya RM, Parimala M, Praveen Kumar Reddy Maddikunta, Thippa Reddy Gadekallu, Senior Member, IEEE, and Quoc-Viet Pham.* Federated Learning for Cybersecurity.

Alazab, M., Rm, S. P., Maddikunta, P. K. R., Gadekallu, T. R., & Pham, Q. V. (2021). Federated learning for cybersecurity: Concepts, challenges, and future directions. *IEEE Transactions on Industrial Informatics, 18*(5), 3501–3509. DOI: 10.1109/TII.2021.3119038

Albrecht, S. V., Christianos, F., & Schäfer, L. (2024). *Multi-agent reinforcement learning: Foundations and modern approaches*. MIT Press.

Aledhari, M., Razzak, R., Parizi, R. M., & Saeed, F. (2020). Federated learning: A survey on enabling technologies, protocols, and applications. *IEEE Access : Practical Innovations, Open Solutions, 8*, 140699–140725. DOI: 10.1109/ACCESS.2020.3013541 PMID: 32999795

Al-Garadi, M. A., Mohamed, A., Al-Ali, A. K., Du, X., Ali, I., & Guizani, M. (2020). A Survey of Machine and Deep Learning Methods for Internet of Things (IoT) Security. *IEEE Communications Surveys and Tutorials, 22*(3), 1646–1685. DOI: 10.1109/COMST.2020.2988293

Al-Hawawreh, M., Sitnikova, E., & Aboutorab, N. (2022). X-IIoTID: A Connectivity-Agnostic and Device-Agnostic Intrusion Data Set for Industrial Internet of Things. *IEEE Internet of Things Journal, 9*(5), 3962–3977. DOI: 10.1109/JIOT.2021.3102056

Ali, T., & Kostakos, P. (2023). Huntgpt: Integrating machine learning-based anomaly detection and explainable ai with large language models (llms). *arXiv preprint arXiv:2309.16021.*

Ali, M. L., Thakur, K., Schmeelk, S., Debello, J., & Dragos, D. (2025). Deep Learning vs. Machine Learning for Intrusion Detection in Computer Networks: A Comparative Study. *Applied Sciences (Basel, Switzerland)*, *15*(4), 1903. DOI: 10.3390/app15041903

Al-Maliki, S., Qayyum, A., Ali, H., Abdallah, M., Qadir, J., Hoang, D. T., Niyato, D., & Al-Fuqaha, A. (2024). Adversarial machine learning for social good: Reframing the adversary as an ally. *IEEE Transactions on Artificial Intelligence*, *5*(9), 4322–4343. DOI: 10.1109/TAI.2024.3383407

Almanifi, O. R. A., Chow, C. O., Tham, M. L., Chuah, J. H., & Kanesan, J. (2023). Communication and computation efficiency in federated learning: A survey. *Internet of Things : Engineering Cyber Physical Human Systems*, *22*, 100742. DOI: 10.1016/j.iot.2023.100742

Almutairi, S., & Barnawi, A. (2023). Federated learning vulnerabilities, threats and defenses: A systematic review and future directions. *Internet of Things : Engineering Cyber Physical Human Systems*, *24*, 100947. DOI: 10.1016/j.iot.2023.100947

Alotaibi, S. R., Alkahtani, H. K., Aljebreen, M., Alshuhail, A., Saeed, M. K., Ebad, S. A., Almukadi, W. S., & Alotaibi, M. (2025). Explainable artificial intelligence in web phishing classification on secure IoT with cloud-based cyber-physical systems. *Alexandria Engineering Journal*, *110*, 490–505. DOI: 10.1016/j.aej.2024.09.115

Alrawi, O., Lever, C., Antonakakis, M., & Monrose, F. (2019). SoK: Security evaluation of home-based IoT deployments. In *2019 IEEE Symposium on Security and Privacy (SP)* (pp. 1362–1380). IEEE. DOI: 10.1109/SP.2019.00013

Alsharif, M. H., Jahid, A., Kelechi, A. H., & Kannadasan, R. (2023). Green IoT: A Review and Future Research Directions. In *Symmetry* (Vol. 15, Issue 3). MDPI. DOI: 10.3390/sym15030757

Altun, İ. Z., & Özkök, A. E. (2024, April). Securing artificial intelligence: Exploring attack scenarios and defense strategies. In *2024 12th International Symposium on Digital Forensics and Security (ISDFS)* (pp. 1-6). IEEE.

Amiri-Zarandi, M., Karimipour, H., & Dara, R. A. (2023). A federated and explainable approach for insider threat detection in IoT. *Internet of Things : Engineering Cyber Physical Human Systems*, *24*, 100965. DOI: 10.1016/j.iot.2023.100965

Amirkhanova, G., Amirkhanov, B., Tyulepberdinova, G., & Ishmurzin, T. "Application of Machine Learning Algorithms in Digital Twin Monitoring Systems: An Overview of Approaches, Methods, and Prospects." In *2024 International Conference on Intelligent Computing and Next Generation Networks (ICNGN)*, pp. 01-05. IEEE, 2024. DOI: 10.1109/ICNGN63705.2024.10871832

Anderson, R. (2020). *Security Engineering: A Guide to Building Dependable Distributed Systems*. Wiley. DOI: 10.1002/9781119644682

Andrei Costin, J. Z. (2014). A Large-Scale Analysis of the Security of Embedded Firmwares.

Aono, Y., Hayashi, T., Trieu Phong, L., & Wang, L. (2017). Privacy-Preserving Deep Learning via Additively Homomorphic Encryption. *IEEE Transactions on Information Forensics and Security*.

Apruzzese, G., Anderson, H. S., Dambra, S., Freeman, D. E., Pierazzi, F., & Roundy, K. (2023). *Real Attackers Don't Compute Gradients*. Bridging the Gap Between Adversarial ML Research and Practice., DOI: 10.1109/SaTML54575.2023.00031

Aqeel, M., Ali, F., Iqbal, M. W., Rana, T. A., Arif, M., & Auwul, M. R. (2022). A review of security and privacy concerns in the internet of things (IoT). *Journal of Sensors*, *2022*(1), 5724168. DOI: 10.1155/2022/5724168

Arbex, G. V., Machado, K. G., Nogueira, M., Batista, D. M., & Hirata, R. (2021). IoT DDoS Detection Based on Stream Learning. *2021 12th International Conference on Network of the Future (NoF)*, 1–8. DOI: 10.1109/NoF52522.2021.9609940

Arianna Armijos, E. C. (2023). The absence of effective defenses, such as signature-based antivirus systems, makes these attacks particularly dangerous. 1-6. DOI: 10.1109/C358072.2023.10436218

Ariffin, S. H., Le Chong, J., Latif, N. M. A. A., Abd Malik, N. N. N., Baharudin, M. A., Syed-Yusof, S. K., & Yusof, K. M. (2022). Intrusion detection system (IDS) accuracy testing for software defined network internet of things (SDN-IoT) testbed. *ELEKTRIKA-Journal of Electrical Engineering*, *21*(3), 23–27.

Arjovsky, M., Chintala, S., & Bottou, L. (2017). Wasserstein generative adversarial networks. In *International conference on machine learning* (pp. 214-223). PMLR.

Arjun, E. R. R., Kulkarni, P., Govindarajulu, Y., Shah, H., & Parmar, M. (2024, October). Evasion Attacks on Object Detection Models using Attack Transferability. In *2024 IEEE Secure Development Conference (SecDev)* (pp. 28-34). IEEE.

Arora, S., Beams, A., Chatzigiannis, P., Meiser, S., Patel, K., Raghuraman, S., & Zamani, M. (2024, December). Privacy-preserving financial anomaly detection via federated learning & multi-party computation. In *2024 Annual Computer Security Applications Conference Workshops (ACSAC Workshops)* (pp. 270-279). IEEE. DOI: 10.1109/ACSACW65225.2024.00038

Arrieta, A. B., Díaz-Rodríguez, N., Del Ser, J., Bennetot, A., Tabik, S., Barbado, A., García, S., Gil-López, S., Molina, D., & Benjamins, R. (2020). Explainable Artificial Intelligence (XAI): Concepts, taxonomies, opportunities and challenges toward responsible AI. *Information Fusion*, *58*, 82–115. DOI: 10.1016/j.inffus.2019.12.012

Arshad, J., Azad, M. A., Mahmoud Abdellatif, M., Ur Rehman, M. H., & Salah, K. (2019). COLIDE: A collaborative intrusion detection framework for Internet of Things. *IET Networks*, *8*(1), 3–14. DOI: 10.1049/iet-net.2018.5036

Arun K. Kanuparthi, R. K. (2014). Hardware and embedded security in the context of internet of things. *Computer and Communications Security*, 61 - 64. DOI: 10.1145/2517968.2517976

Athalye, A., Carlini, N., & Wagner, D. (2018). Obfuscated gradients give a false sense of security: Circumventing defenses to adversarial examples. In *International conference on machine learning* (pp. 274-283). PMLR.

Atlam, H. F., & Wills, G. B. (2020). IoT security, privacy, safety and ethics. *Digital twin technologies and smart cities*, 123-149.

Attarian, R., & Hashemi, S. (2021). An anonymity communication protocol for security and privacy of clients in IoT-based mobile health transactions. *Computer Networks*, *190*, 107976. DOI: 10.1016/j.comnet.2021.107976

Atzori, L., Iera, A., & Morabito, G. (2010). The internet of things: A survey. *Computer Networks*, *54*(15), 2787–2805. DOI: 10.1016/j.comnet.2010.05.010

Awan, K. A., Din, I. U., Almogren, A., & Rodrigues, J. J. (2023). Privacy-preserving big data security for IoT with federated learning and cryptography. *IEEE Access : Practical Innovations, Open Solutions*, *11*, 120918–120934. DOI: 10.1109/ACCESS.2023.3328310

Azam, M., Mumtaz, G., & Mubeen, Z. (n.d.). *Securing IoT: Balancing Privacy and Attack Prediction*. https://doi.org/DOI: 10.56979/701/2024

Babun, L., Denney, K., Celik, Z. B., McDaniel, P., & Uluagac, A. S. (2021). A survey on IoT platforms: Communication, security, and privacy perspectives. *Computer Networks*, *192*, 108040. DOI: 10.1016/j.comnet.2021.108040

Bace, R., & Mell, P. (n.d.). *NIST Special Publication on Intrusion Detection Systems Intrusion Detection Systems.*

Badjie, B., Cecílio, J., & Casimiro, A. (2024). Adversarial attacks and countermeasures on image classification-based deep learning models in autonomous driving systems: A systematic review. *ACM Computing Surveys*, *57*(1), 1–52. DOI: 10.1145/3691625

Bagaa, M., Taleb, T., Bernabe, J. B., & Skarmeta, A. (2020). A Machine Learning Security Framework for Iot Systems. *IEEE Access : Practical Innovations, Open Solutions*, *8*, 114066–114077. DOI: 10.1109/ACCESS.2020.2996214

Bagdasaryan, E., Veit, A., Hua, Y., Estrin, D., & Shmatikov, V. (2020). How to backdoor federated learning. *Proceedings of the 23rd International Conference on Artificial Intelligence and Statistics (AISTATS).*

Bahrami, M., Khan, A., & Singhal, M. (2016). *An energy efficient data privacy scheme for IoT devices in mobile cloud computing.* Paper presented at the 2016 IEEE International Conference on Mobile Services (MS). DOI: 10.1109/MobServ.2016.37

Balamurugan, M. (2024). Guardians at Risk: The Challenge of Adversarial Attacks on Authentication Systems and Artificial Intelligence. *International Journal of Scientific Research.*

Baniecki, H., & Biecek, P. (2024). Adversarial attacks and defenses in explainable artificial intelligence: A survey. *Information Fusion*, *107*, 102303. DOI: 10.1016/j.inffus.2024.102303

Barik, K., & Misra, S. (2024). Adversarial attack defense analysis: An empirical approach in cybersecurity perspective. *Software Impacts*, *21*, 100681. DOI: 10.1016/j.simpa.2024.100681

Barreno, M., Nelson, B., Joseph, A. D., & Tygar, J. D. (2010). The security of machine learning. *Machine Learning*, *81*(2), 121–148. DOI: 10.1007/s10994-010-5188-5

Barreno, M., Nelson, B., Sears, R., Joseph, A. D., & Tygar, J. D. (2006, March). Can machine learning be secure? In *Proceedings of the 2006 ACM Symposium on Information, computer and communications security* (pp. 16-25). DOI: 10.1145/1128817.1128824

Bartolucci, F., Donni, P. L., & Mira, A. (2023). Temporal analysis of hospital network data by hierarchical Bayesian p2 models with covariates. *Journal of the Royal Statistical Society. Series A, (Statistics in Society)*, *186*(3), 422–440. DOI: 10.1093/jrsssa/qnad036

Barua, E., Chowhan, S. S., Jain, S. K., & Vekariya, V. (2024). A novel framework for privacy and data protection in internet of things-based energy management systems. *International Journal of System Assurance Engineering and Management*, •••, 1–10. DOI: 10.1007/s13198-024-02620-4

Baruch, G., Baruch, M., & Goldberg, Y. (2019). A little is enough: Circumventing defenses for distributed learning. *Advances in Neural Information Processing Systems (NeurIPS).*

Basati, A., & Faghih, M. M. (2023). APAE: An IoT intrusion detection system using asymmetric parallel auto-encoder. *Neural Computing & Applications*, *35*(7), 4813–4833. DOI: 10.1007/s00521-021-06011-9

Bastounis, A., Hansen, A. C., & Vlačić, V. (2021). The mathematics of adversarial attacks in AI—Why deep learning is unstable despite the existence of stable neural networks. *arXiv preprint arXiv:2109.06098.*

Belenguer, A., Navaridas, J., & Pascual, J. A. (2022). *A review of Federated Learning in Intrusion Detection Systems for IoT*. http://arxiv.org/abs/2204.12443

Bellavista, P., Corradi, A., & Zanni, A. (2017). Integrating mobile internet of things and cloud computing towards scalability: Lessons learned from existing fog computing architectures and solutions. *International Journal of Cloud Computing*, *6*(4), 393–406. DOI: 10.1504/IJCC.2017.090198

Belle, V., & Papantonis, I. (2021). Principles and practice of explainable machine learning. *Frontiers in Big Data*, *4*, 688969. DOI: 10.3389/fdata.2021.688969 PMID: 34278297

Benkhelifa, E., Welsh, T., & Hamouda, W. (2018). A Critical Review of Practices and Challenges in Intrusion Detection Systems for IoT: Toward Universal and Resilient Systems. *IEEE Communications Surveys and Tutorials*, *20*(4), 3496–3509. DOI: 10.1109/COMST.2018.2844742

Bennouna, A., Lucas, R., & Parys, B. V. (2023). Certified Robust Neural Networks: Generalization and Corruption Resistance. In arXiv (Cornell University). Cornell University. https://doi.org//arxiv.2303.02251DOI: 10.48550

Benraouane, S. A. (2024). *AI Management System Certification According to the ISO/IEC 42001 Standard: How to Audit, Certify, and Build Responsible AI Systems*. CRC Press. DOI: 10.4324/9781003463979

Berthier, R., & Sanders, W. H. (2011). Specification-Based Intrusion Detection for Advanced Metering Infrastructures. *2011 IEEE 17th Pacific Rim International Symposium on Dependable Computing*, 184–193. DOI: 10.1109/PRDC.2011.30

Bertino, E. (2016). *Data privacy for IoT systems: Concepts, approaches, and research directions.* Paper presented at the 2016 IEEE International Conference on Big Data (Big Data). DOI: 10.1109/BigData.2016.7841030

Bhagoji, A. N., Chakraborty, S., Mittal, P., & Calo, S. (2019). Analyzing federated learning through an adversarial lens. *International Conference on Machine Learning (ICML).*

Bhattacharjya, A., Zhong, X., Wang, J., & Li, X. (2019). Security challenges and concerns of Internet of Things (IoT). *Cyber-Physical Systems: architecture, security and application*, 153-185.

Bhatt, D., Patel, C., Talsania, H., Patel, J., Vaghela, R., Pandya, S., Modi, K., & Ghayvat, H. (2021). CNN variants for computer vision: History, architecture, application, challenges and future scope. *Electronics (Basel), 10*(20), 2470. DOI: 10.3390/electronics10202470

Bhavsar, M. H., Bekele, Y. B., Roy, K., Kelly, J. C., & Limbrick, D. (2024). Fl-ids: Federated learning-based intrusion detection system using edge devices for transportation iot. *IEEE Access : Practical Innovations, Open Solutions, 12*, 52215–52226. DOI: 10.1109/ACCESS.2024.3386631

Biasin, E., Kamenjašević, E., & Ludvigsen, K. R. (2024). Cybersecurity of AI medical devices: risks, legislation, and challenges. In *Edward Elgar Publishing eBooks* (p. 57). Edward Elgar Publishing., DOI: 10.4337/9781802205657.00010

Biggio, B., Corona, I., Maiorca, D., Nelson, B., Šrndić, N., Laskov, P., . . . Roli, F. (2013). Evasion attacks against machine learning at test time. In *Machine learning and knowledge discovery in databases: European conference, ECML pKDD 2013, prague, czech Republic, September 23-27, 2013, proceedings, part III* 13 (pp. 387-402). Springer Berlin Heidelberg. DOI: 10.1007/978-3-642-40994-3_25

Biggio, B., Nelson, B., & Laskov, P. (2012). Poisoning attacks against support vector machines. arXiv preprint arXiv:1206.6389.

Bing, F. (2016, October). The research of IOT of agriculture based on three layers architecture. In 2016 2nd International Conference on Cloud Computing and Internet of Things (CCIOT) (pp. 162-165). IEEE.

Blanchard, P., El Mhamdi, E. M., Guerraoui, R., & Stainer, J. (2017). Machine learning with adversaries: Byzantine tolerant gradient descent. *Advances in Neural Information Processing Systems (NeurIPS).*

Blanco-Justicia, A., Domingo-Ferrer, J., Martínez, S., Sánchez, D., Flanagan, A., & Tan, K. E. (2021). Achieving security and privacy in federated learning systems: Survey, research challenges and future directions. *Engineering Applications of Artificial Intelligence, 106*, 104468. DOI: 10.1016/j.engappai.2021.104468

Blum, A., & Mitchell, T. (1998). Combining labeled and unlabeled data with co-training. In *Proceedings of the eleventh annual conference on computational learning theory* (pp. 92-100). DOI: 10.1145/279943.279962

Böhme, R., & Moore, T. (2012). The Iterative Nature of Cybersecurity. *IEEE Security and Privacy, 10*(1), 71–75.

Bonawitz, K.. (2017). Practical secure aggregation for privacy-preserving machine learning. *Proceedings of the 2017 ACM SIGSAC Conference on Computer and Communications Security*. DOI: 10.1145/3133956.3133982

Bonawitz, K., Eichner, H., Grieskamp, W., Huba, D., Ingerman, A., Ivanov, V., & Van Overveldt, T. (2019). Towards federated learning at scale: System design. *Proceedings of Machine Learning and Systems, 1*, 374–388.

Bonfanti, M. E. (2022). *Artificial intelligence and the offence-defence balance in cyber security. Cyber Security: Socio-Technological Uncertainty and Political Fragmentation*. Routledge.

Bostani, H., & Sheikhan, M. (2017). Hybrid of anomaly-based and specification-based IDS for Internet of Things using unsupervised OPF based on MapReduce approach. *Computer Communications, 98*, 52–71. DOI: 10.1016/j.comcom.2016.12.001

Botterman, M., Cave, J., & Doria, A. (2020). Standardization issues. *ICT Policy, Research, and Innovation: Perspectives and Prospects for EU-US Collaboration*, 309-330.

Bountakas, P., Zarras, A., Lekidis, A., & Xenakis, C. (2023). Defense strategies for adversarial machine learning: A survey. *Computer Science Review, 49*, 100573. DOI: 10.1016/j.cosrev.2023.100573

Bousmalis, K., Silberman, N., Dohan, D., Erhan, D., & Krishnan, D. (2017). Unsupervised pixel-level domain adaptation with generative adversarial networks. In *Proceedings of the IEEE conference on computer vision and pattern recognition* (pp. 3722-3731). DOI: 10.1109/CVPR.2017.18

Breiman, L. (2001). Random forests. *Machine Learning, 45*(1), 5–32. DOI: 10.1023/A:1010933404324

Buczak, A. L., & Guven, E. (2016). A survey of data mining and machine learning methods for cyber security intrusion detection. *IEEE Communications Surveys and Tutorials*, *18*(2), 1153–1176. DOI: 10.1109/COMST.2015.2494502

Butun, I., Osterberg, P., & Song, H. (2020). Security of the Internet of Things: Vulnerabilities, Attacks, and Countermeasures. *IEEE Communications Surveys and Tutorials*, *22*(1), 616–644. DOI: 10.1109/COMST.2019.2953364

Calinescu, R., Imrie, C., Mangal, R., Rodrigues, G. N., Păsăreanu, C., Santana, M. A., & Vázquez, G. (2024). Controller synthesis for autonomous systems with deep-learning perception components. *IEEE Transactions on Software Engineering*, *50*(6), 1374–1395. DOI: 10.1109/TSE.2024.3385378

Camhi, J. (2015). *Former Cisco CEO John Chambers predicts 500 billion connected devices by 2025.*

Caminero, G., Lopez-Martin, M., & Carro, B. (2019). Adversarial environment reinforcement learning algorithm for intrusion detection. *Computer Networks*, *159*, 96–109. DOI: 10.1016/j.comnet.2019.05.013

Cao, X., Başar, T., Diggavi, S., Eldar, Y. C., Letaief, K. B., Poor, H. V., & Zhang, J. (2023). Communication-Efficient Distributed Learning: An Overview. *IEEE Journal on Selected Areas in Communications*, *41*(4), 851–873. DOI: 10.1109/JSAC.2023.3242710

Cao, Y., Xiao, C., Cyr, B., Fang, J., Yang, J., Tramèr, F., & Kolter, J. Z. (2019). Adversarial sensor attack on LiDAR-based perception in autonomous driving. *Proceedings of the 2019 ACM SIGSAC Conference on Computer and Communications Security (CCS)*. DOI: 10.1145/3319535.3339815

Capuano, N., Fenza, G., Loia, V., & Stanzione, C. (2022). Explainable artificial intelligence in cybersecurity: A survey. *IEEE Access : Practical Innovations, Open Solutions*, *10*, 93575–93600. DOI: 10.1109/ACCESS.2022.3204171

Card, Q., Simpson, D., Aryal, K., Gupta, M., & Islam, S. R. (2024). Explainable Deep Learning Models for Dynamic and Online Malware Classification. *2024 IEEE International Conference on Smart Computing (SMARTCOMP)*

Carlini, N., & Wagner, D. (2017). Towards evaluating the robustness of neural networks. In *2017 IEEE symposium on security and privacy (SP)* (pp. 39-57). IEEE. DOI: 10.1109/SP.2017.49

Carlini, N., & Wagner, D. (2017). *Towards evaluating the robustness of neural networks. In 2017 IEEE symposium on security and privacy*. IEEE.

Carone, S., Pappalettera, G., Casavola, C., De Carolis, S., & Soria, L. (2023). A Support Vector Machine-Based Approach for Bolt Loosening Monitoring in Industrial Customized Vehicles. *Sensors (Basel), 23*(11), 5345. DOI: 10.3390/s23115345 PMID: 37300075

Carrara, F., Amato, G., Brombin, L., Falchi, F., & Gennaro, C. (2021). Combining gans and autoencoders for efficient anomaly detection. In *2020 25th International Conference on Pattern Recognition (ICPR)* (pp. 3939-3946). IEEE. DOI: 10.1109/ICPR48806.2021.9412253

Carvalho, D. V., Pereira, E. M., & Cardoso, J. S. (2019). Machine learning interpretability: A survey on methods and metrics. *Electronics (Basel), 8*(8), 832.

Casper, S., Ezell, C., Siegmann, C., Kolt, N., Curtis, T. L., Bucknall, B., Haupt, A., Wei, K., Scheurer, J., Hobbhahn, M., Sharkey, L., Krishna, S., Hagen, M. V., Alberti, S., Chan, A., Sun, Q., Gerovitch, M., Bau, D., Tegmark, M., & Hadfield-Menell, D. (2024). Black-Box Access is Insufficient for Rigorous AI Audits. In *2022 ACM Conference on Fairness, Accountability, and Transparency* (p. 2254). DOI: 10.1145/3630106.3659037

Cavoukian, A., Taylor, S., & Abrams, M. E. (2010). Privacy by Design: Essential for organizational accountability and strong business practices. *Identity in the Information Society, 3*(2), 405–413. DOI: 10.1007/s12394-010-0053-z

Chakraborty, A., Alam, M., Dey, V., Chattopadhyay, A., & Mukhopadhyay, D. (2021). A survey on adversarial attacks and defences. *CAAI Transactions on Intelligence Technology, 6*(1), 25–45. DOI: 10.1049/cit2.12028

Chalamala, S. R., Kummari, N. K., Singh, A. K., Saibewar, A., & Chalavadi, K. M. (2022). Federated learning to comply with data protection regulations. *CSI Transactions on ICT, 10*(1), 47–60. DOI: 10.1007/s40012-022-00351-0

Chandana, P. and Gulzar, C.M., (2023). Securing Cyberspace: A Comprehensive Journey through AI's Impact on Cyber Security. Tuijin Jishu/Journal of Propulsion Technology, 44(2).

Chander, B., John, C., Warrier, L., & Gopalakrishnan, K. (2025). Toward trustworthy artificial intelligence (TAI) in the context of explainability and robustness. *ACM Computing Surveys, 57*(6), 1–49. DOI: 10.1145/3675392

Chandola, V., Banerjee, A., & Kumar, V. (2009). Anomaly detection: A survey. *ACM Computing Surveys, 41*(3), 1–58. DOI: 10.1145/1541880.1541882

Charbuty, B., & Abdulazeez, A. (2021). Classification Based on Decision Tree Algorithm for Machine Learning. *Journal of Applied Science and Technology Trends*, *2*(01), 20–28. DOI: 10.38094/jastt20165

Chatzigiannakis, I., Pyrgelis, A., Spirakis, P. G., & Stamatiou, Y. C. (2011). *Elliptic curve based zero knowledge proofs and their applicability on resource constrained devices.* Paper presented at the Mobile Adhoc and Sensor Systems (MASS), 2011 IEEE 8th International Conference on. DOI: 10.1109/MASS.2011.77

Chaudhary, R. K., Kumar, R., & Saxena, N. (2024). A systematic review on federated learning system: A new paradigm to machine learning. *Knowledge and Information Systems*, •••, 1–104.

Chaurasia, N., & Kumar, P. (2023). A comprehensive study on issues and challenges related to privacy and security in IoT. *e-Prime-Advances in Electrical Engineering. Electronics and Energy*, *4*, 100158.

Chen, B., Carvalho, W., Baracaldo, N., Ludwig, H., Edwards, B., Lee, T., . . . Srivastava, B. (2018). Detecting backdoor attacks on deep neural networks by activation clustering. *arXiv preprint* arXiv:1811.03728.

Chen, Z., Li, J., & Shen, C. (2023). Personalized Federated Learning with Attention-based Client Selection. arXiv preprint arXiv:2312.15148 14 pages.

Chen, C., Liu, J., Tan, H., Li, X., Wang, K. I. K., Li, P., Sakurai, K., & Dou, D. (2025). Trustworthy federated learning: Privacy, security, and beyond. *Knowledge and Information Systems*, *67*(3), 2321–2356. DOI: 10.1007/s10115-024-02285-2

Chen, J., Jia, C., Zheng, H., Chen, R., & Fu, C. (2022). Is Multi-Modal Necessarily Better? Robustness Evaluation of Multi-modal Fake News Detection. In arXiv (Cornell University). Cornell University. https://doi.org/DOI: 10.48550/arXiv.2206

Chen, J., Wang, H., & Li, H. (2022). Defects detection in weld joints based on visual attention and deep learning. In *NDT & E International* (Vol. 133, p. 102764). Elsevier BV., DOI: 10.1016/j.ndteint.2022.102764

Chen, J., Zhao, Y., Li, Q., Feng, X., & Xu, K. (2023). FedDef: Defense against gradient leakage in federated learning-based network intrusion detection systems. *IEEE Transactions on Information Forensics and Security*, *18*, 4561–4576. DOI: 10.1109/TIFS.2023.3297369

Chen, M., Yang, Z., Saad, W., Yin, C., Poor, H. V., & Cui, S. (2021). A Joint Learning and Communications Framework for Federated Learning Over Wireless Networks. *IEEE Transactions on Wireless Communications*, *20*(1), 269–283. DOI: 10.1109/TWC.2020.3024629

Chen, S., Cornelius, C., Martin, C., & Song, D. (2020). ShapeShifter: Adversarial traffic sign attacks against vision-based autonomous vehicles. *USENIX Security Symposium.*

Chiara, P. G. (2024). *The Internet of Things and EU Law* (Vol. 67). Springer Nature Switzerland., DOI: 10.1007/978-3-031-67663-5

Chi, L., & Msahli, M. (2025). LaserGuard: Efficiently Detecting Laser-based Physical Adversarial Attacks in Autonomous Driving. *IEEE Access : Practical Innovations, Open Solutions, 13*, 35219–35229. DOI: 10.1109/ACCESS.2025.3540653

Chi, L., Msahli, M., Zhang, Q., Qiu, H., Zhang, T., Memmi, G., & Qiu, M. (2024). Adversarial attacks on autonomous driving systems in the physical world: A survey. *IEEE Transactions on Intelligent Vehicles*, 1–22. DOI: 10.1109/TIV.2024.3484152

Choraś, M., & Woźniak, M. (2022). The double-edged sword of AI: Ethical Adversarial Attacks to counter artificial intelligence for crime. *AI and Ethics*, *2*(4), 631–634. DOI: 10.1007/s43681-021-00113-9

Chung, H., Iorga, M., Voas, J., & Lee, S. (2017). Alexa, can I trust you? *Computer*, *50*(9), 100–104. DOI: 10.1109/MC.2017.3571053 PMID: 29213147

Chutia, T., & Baruah, N. (2024). A review on emotion detection by using deep learning techniques [Review of A review on emotion detection by using deep learning techniques]. Artificial Intelligence Review, 57(8). Springer Science+Business Media. DOI: 10.1007/s10462-024-10831-1

Cinà, A. E., Grosse, K., Demontis, A., Vascon, S., Zellinger, W., Moser, B. A., Oprea, A., Biggio, B., Pelillo, M., & Roli, F. (2023). Wild patterns reloaded: A survey of machine learning security against training data poisoning. *ACM Computing Surveys*, *55*(13s), 1–39. DOI: 10.1145/3585385

Cirani, S., Davoli, L., Ferrari, G., Leone, R., Medagliani, P., Picone, M., & Veltri, L. (2014). A scalable and self-configuring architecture for service discovery in the internet of things. *IEEE Internet of Things Journal*, *1*(5), 508–521. DOI: 10.1109/JIOT.2014.2358296

Cohen, I. G., & Mello, M. M. (2018). HIPAA and protecting health information in the 21st century. *Journal of the American Medical Association*, *320*(3), 231–232. DOI: 10.1001/jama.2018.5630 PMID: 29800120

Colaco, V. O., & Nadjm-Tehrani, S. (2024, October). Fast Evasion Detection & Alert Management in Tree-Ensemble-Based Intrusion Detection Systems. In 2024 IEEE 36th International Conference on Tools with Artificial Intelligence (ICTAI) (pp. 404-412). IEEE.

Collins, L., Hassani, H., Mokhtari, A., & Shakkottai, S. (2022). Fedavg with fine tuning: Local updates lead to representation learning. *Advances in Neural Information Processing Systems*, *35*, 10572–10586.

Costa, J. C., Roxo, T., Proença, H., & Inácio, P. R. (2024). How deep learning sees the world: A survey on adversarial attacks & defenses. *IEEE Access : Practical Innovations, Open Solutions*, *12*, 61113–61136. DOI: 10.1109/ACCESS.2024.3395118

Cummings, R., Desfontaines, D., Evans, D., Geambasu, R., Huang, Y., Jagielski, M., . . . Ohrimenko, O. (2023). Advancing differential privacy: Where we are now and future directions for real-world deployment. *arXiv preprint arXiv:2304.06929.*

Dalvi, N., & Domingos, P., Mausam, Sanghai, S., & Verma, D. (2004, August). Adversarial classification. In *Proceedings of the tenth ACM SIGKDD international conference on Knowledge discovery and data mining* (pp. 99-108).

Damodharan, P., & Ravichandran, C. S. (2019). Applicability Evaluation of Web Mining in Healthcare E-Commerce towards Business Success and a derived Cournot Model. In Journal of Medical Systems (Vol. 43, Issue 8). Springer Science+Business Media. DOI: 10.1007/s10916-019-1395-1

Das, S., Tariq, A., Santos, T., Kantareddy, S. S., & Banerjee, I. (2023). Recurrent neural networks (RNNs): architectures, training tricks, and introduction to influential research. *Machine learning for Brain disorders*, 117-138.

David Noever, S. E. (2021). Deep Learning for Identifying Malicious Firmware. DOI: 10.5121/csit.2021.111506

de la Torre, L. (2018). A guide to the california consumer privacy act of 2018. *Available atSSRN* 3275571. DOI: 10.2139/ssrn.3275571

Deep, S., Zheng, X., Jolfaei, A., Yu, D., Ostovari, P., & Kashif Bashir, A. (2022). A survey of security and privacy issues in the Internet of Things from the layered context. *Transactions on Emerging Telecommunications Technologies*, *33*(6), e3935. DOI: 10.1002/ett.3935

Delobelle, P., Temple, P., Perrouin, G., Frénay, B., Heymans, P., & Berendt, B. (2021). Ethical adversaries: Towards mitigating unfairness with adversarial machine learning. *SIGKDD Explorations*, *23*(1), 32–41. DOI: 10.1145/3468507.3468513

Dev, V. A., & Eden, M. R. (2019). *Gradient Boosted Decision Trees for Lithology Classification.*, DOI: 10.1016/B978-0-12-818597-1.50019-9

Dey, N., Ashour, A. S., Shi, F., Fong, S. J., & Tavares, J. M. R. (2018). Medical cyber-physical systems: A survey. *Journal of Medical Systems*, *42*(4), 1–13. DOI: 10.1007/s10916-018-0921-x PMID: 29525900

Dhinakaran, D., Sankar, S., Selvaraj, D., & Raja, S. E. (2024). Privacy-preserving data in IoT-based cloud systems: A comprehensive survey with AI integration. *arXiv preprint arXiv:2401.00794*.

di Vimercati, S. D. C., Foresti, S., Livraga, G., & Samarati, P. (2023). k-Anonymity: From Theory to Applications. *Transactions on Data Privacy*, *16*(1), 25–49.

Didem Genç, M. Ö. (2023). A Taxonomic Survey of Model Extraction Attacks. DOI: 10.1109/CSR57506.2023.10224959

Dietterich, T. G. (2000). Ensemble methods in machine learning. In *Multiple classifier systems* (pp. 1–15). Springer. DOI: 10.1007/3-540-45014-9_1

Diksha Dhiman, A. B. (2024). Artificial Intelligence and Machine Learning-Enabled Cybersecurity Tools and Techniques. In *Advance techniques and applications of cybersecurity and forensics* (pp. 35–56). Informa., DOI: 10.1201/9781003386926-3

Doshi-Velez, F., & Kim, B. (2017). Towards a rigorous science of interpretable machine learning. *arXiv preprint arXiv:1702.08608*.

Drainakis, G., Pantazopoulos, P., Katsaros, K. V., Sourlas, V., Amditis, A., & Kaklamani, D. I. (2023). From centralized to Federated Learning: Exploring performance and end-to-end resource consumption. *Computer Networks*, *225*, 109657. DOI: 10.1016/j.comnet.2023.109657

Dwork, C. (2008). Differential Privacy: A Survey of Results. In Agrawal, M., Du, D., Duan, Z., & Li, A. (Eds.), Lecture Notes in Computer Science: Vol. 4978. *Theory and Applications of Models of Computation. TAMC 2008*. Springer. DOI: 10.1007/978-3-540-79228-4_1

Ebrahimi, J., Rao, A., Lowd, D., & Dou, D. (2018). HotFlip: White-box adversarial examples for text classification. *Proceedings of the 56th Annual Meeting of the Association for Computational Linguistics (ACL)*. DOI: 10.18653/v1/P18-2006

El Ghazi, A., & Moulay Rachid, A. (2020). Machine learning and datamining methods for hybrid IoT intrusion detection. *2020 5th International Conference on Cloud Computing and Artificial Intelligence: Technologies and Applications (CloudTech)*, 1–6. DOI: 10.1109/CloudTech49835.2020.9365895

El Jaouhari, S., & Etiabi, Y. (2023, November). FedCTI: Federated Learning and Cyber Threat Intelligence on the Edge for secure IoT Networks. In *Proceedings of the 13th International Conference on the Internet of Things* (pp. 98-104). DOI: 10.1145/3627050.3627064

Eldrandaly, K. A., Abdel-Basset, M., & Shawky, L. A. (2019). Internet of Spatial Things: A New Reference Model With Insight Analysis. *IEEE Access : Practical Innovations, Open Solutions, 7*, 19653–19669. DOI: 10.1109/ACCESS.2019.2897012

Elsaeidy, A. A., Jamalipour, A., & Munasinghe, K. S. (2021). A Hybrid Deep Learning Approach for Replay and DDoS Attack Detection in a Smart City. *IEEE Access : Practical Innovations, Open Solutions, 9*, 154864–154875. DOI: 10.1109/ACCESS.2021.3128701

Elsayed, G., Krishnan, B., Tavel, A., Papernot, N., & Goldstein, T. (2018). Adversarial reprogramming of neural networks. *arXiv preprint arXiv:1806.00057.*

Enuma Edmund, A. E., & Aliyu Enemosah, . (2024). AI and machine learning in cybersecurity: Leveraging AI to predict, detect, and respond to threats more efficiently. *International Journal of Science and Research Archive, 11*(2), 2625–2645. DOI: 10.30574/ijsra.2024.11.1.0083

EpiSensor. (2023). *IoT Data Privacy: Ensuring Compliance with GDPR and Other Regulations*. Retrieved from EpiSensor.

Erlacher, F., & Dressler, F. (2022). On High-Speed Flow-Based Intrusion Detection Using Snort-Compatible Signatures. *IEEE Transactions on Dependable and Secure Computing, 19*(1), 495–506. DOI: 10.1109/TDSC.2020.2973992

Essop, I., Ribeiro, J. C., Papaioannou, M., Zachos, G., Mantas, G., & Rodriguez, J. (2021). Generating Datasets for Anomaly-Based Intrusion Detection Systems in IoT and Industrial IoT Networks. *Sensors (Basel), 21*(4), 1528. DOI: 10.3390/s21041528 PMID: 33672108

Esteva, A., Kuprel, B., Novoa, R. A., Ko, J., Swetter, S. M., Blau, H. M., & Thrun, S. (2017). Dermatologist-level classification of skin cancer with deep neural networks. *Nature, 542*(7639), 115–118. DOI: 10.1038/nature21056 PMID: 28117445

Estrada, D., Tawalbeh, L. A. A., & Vinaja, R. (2020). How secure having IoT devices in our homes?.

Eykholt, K., Evtimov, I., Fernandes, E., Li, B., Rahmati, A., Xiao, C., & Song, D. (2018). Robust physical-world attacks on deep learning visual classification. *Proceedings of the IEEE Conference on Computer Vision and Pattern Recognition (CVPR)*. DOI: 10.1109/CVPR.2018.00175

Fahad Mira, I. A. (2019). Review of Analysis on IoT Components, Devices and Layers Security. DOI: 10.1109/ICISCT47635.2019.9012037

Faheem, M. A., Kakolu, S., & Aslam, M. (2022). The Role of Explainable AI in Cybersecurity: Improving Analyst Trust in Automated Threat Assessment Systems. *Iconic Research and Engineering Journals*, *6*(4), 173–182.

Farooq, M. (n.d.). Supervised Learning Techniques for Intrusion Detection System based on Multi-layer Classification Approach Machine Learning and Intrusion Detection System. In *IJACSA) International Journal of Advanced Computer Science and Applications* (Vol. 13, Issue 3). www.ijacsa.thesai.org

Farooqi, S. A., Abd Rahman, A., & Saad, A. (2024, January). Differential privacy based federated learning techniques in IoMT: A review. In *2024 18th International Conference on Ubiquitous Information Management and Communication (IMCOM)* (pp. 1-7). IEEE. DOI: 10.1109/IMCOM60618.2024.10418361

Farooqi, S. A., Abd Rahman, A., & Saad, A. (2025, January). A Theoretical Comparison of Federated Learning with Differential Privacy and Blockchain for Security and Privacy in IoMT. In *2025 19th International Conference on Ubiquitous Information Management and Communication (IMCOM)* (pp. 1-8). IEEE. DOI: 10.1109/IMCOM64595.2025.10857505

Feinman, R., Curtin, R., Shintre, S., & Gardner, A. B. (2017). Detecting adversarial samples from artifacts. *arXiv preprint arXiv:1711.00105.*

Fenanir, S., & Semchedine, F. (2023). Smart intrusion detection in IoT edge computing using federated learning. *Revue d'Intelligence Artificielle*, *37*(5), 1133–1145. DOI: 10.18280/ria.370505

Fernández-Caramés, T. M., & Fraga-Lamas, P. (2018). A review on the use of blockchain for the Internet of Things. *IEEE Access : Practical Innovations, Open Solutions*, *6*, 32979–33001. DOI: 10.1109/ACCESS.2018.2842685

Ferrag, M. A., Friha, O., Hamouda, D., Maglaras, L., & Janicke, H. (2022). Edge-IIoTset: A New Comprehensive Realistic Cyber Security Dataset of IoT and IIoT Applications for Centralized and Federated Learning. *IEEE Access : Practical Innovations, Open Solutions*, *10*, 40281–40306. DOI: 10.1109/ACCESS.2022.3165809

Ferrag, M. A., Friha, O., Maglaras, L., Janicke, H., & Shu, L. (2021). Federated Deep Learning for Cyber Security in the Internet of Things: Concepts, Applications, and Experimental Analysis. *IEEE Access : Practical Innovations, Open Solutions*, *9*, 138509–138542. DOI: 10.1109/ACCESS.2021.3118642

Ferrag, M. A., Maglaras, L., Ahmim, A., Derdour, M., & Janicke, H. (2020). RDTIDS: Rules and Decision Tree-Based Intrusion Detection System for Internet-of-Things Networks. *Future Internet, 12*(3), 44. DOI: 10.3390/fi12030044

Ferrag, M. A., Maglaras, L., Janicke, H., & Jiang, J. (2020). Deep learning for cyber security intrusion detection: Approaches, datasets, and comparative study. *Journal of Information Security and Applications, 50*, 102419. DOI: 10.1016/j.jisa.2019.102419

Finlayson, S. G., Bowers, J. D., Ito, J., Zittrain, J. L., Beam, A. L., & Kohane, I. S. (2019). Adversarial attacks on medical machine learning. *Science, 363*(6433), 1287–1289. DOI: 10.1126/science.aaw4399 PMID: 30898923

Fisher, A., Rudin, C., & Dominici, F. (2019). All models are wrong, but many are useful: Learning a variable's importance by studying an entire class of prediction models simultaneously. *Journal of Machine Learning Research, 20*(177), 1–81. PMID: 34335110

Fredrikson, M., Jha, S., & Ristenpart, T. (2015). Model inversion attacks that exploit confidence information and basic countermeasures. In *Proceedings of the 22nd ACM SIGSAC conference on computer and communications security* (pp. 1322-1333). DOI: 10.1145/2810103.2813677

Fung, C., Yoon, C. J. M., & Beschastnikh, I. (2018). Mitigating Sybils in Federated Learning poisoning. *arXiv preprint arXiv:1808.04866.*

Gal, Y., & Ghahramani, Z. (2016). Dropout as a bayesian approximation: Representing model uncertainty in deep learning. In *International conference on machine learning* (pp. 1050-1059). PMLR.

Gama, J., Žliobaitė, I., Pechenizkiy, M., & Bifet, A. (2014). A survey on concept drift adaptation. *ACM Computing Surveys, 46*(4), 1–37. DOI: 10.1145/2523813

Ganin, Y., Ustinova, E., Ajakan, H., Germain, P., Larochelle, H., Laviolette, F., & Lempitsky, V. (2016). Domain-adversarial training of neural networks. *Journal of Machine Learning Research, 17*(59), 1–35.

Geyer, R. C., Klein, T., & Nabi, M. (2017). Differentially private federated learning: A client level perspective. *arXiv preprint arXiv:1712.07557.*

Ghasemshirazi, S., Shirvani, G., & Alipour, M. A. (2023). Zero Trust: Applications, Challenges, and Opportunities. arXiv preprint arXiv:2309.03582.

Ghavamipour, A. R., Turkmen, F., Wang, R., & Liang, K. 2023.Federated Synthetic Data Generation with Stronger Security Guarantees.In *Proceedings of the 28th ACM Symposium on Access Control Models and Technologies (SACMAT '23)*, June 7–9, 2023, Trento, Italy. ACM, New York,NY, USA, 12 pages. DOI: 10.1145/3589608.3593835

Ghavamzadeh, M., Mannor, S., Pineau, J., & Tamar, A. (2015). Bayesian reinforcement learning: A survey. *Foundations and Trends® in Machine Learning, 8*(5-6), 359-483.

Ghimire, B., & Rawat, D. B. (2022). Recent advances on federated learning for cybersecurity and cybersecurity for federated learning for internet of things. *IEEE Internet of Things Journal, 9*(11), 8229–8249. DOI: 10.1109/JIOT.2022.3150363

Glissa, G., Rachedi, A., & Meddeb, A. (2016). A Secure Routing Protocol Based on RPL for Internet of Things. *2016 IEEE Global Communications Conference (GLOBECOM)*, 1–7. DOI: 10.1109/GLOCOM.2016.7841543

Goldblum, M., Tsipras, D., Xie, C., Chen, X., Schwarzschild, A., Song, D., Madry, A., Li, B., & Goldstein, T. (2022). Dataset security for machine learning: Data poisoning, backdoor attacks, and defenses. *IEEE Transactions on Pattern Analysis and Machine Intelligence, 45*(2), 1563–1580. DOI: 10.1109/TPAMI.2022.3162397 PMID: 35333711

Gong, B., Guo, C., Guo, C., Sun, Y., Waqas, M., & Chen, S. (2023). SLIM: A secure and lightweight multi-authority attribute-based signcryption scheme for IoT. *IEEE Transactions on Information Forensics and Security, 19*, 1299–1312.

Gong, Y., Chang, X., Mišić, J., Mišić, V. B., Wang, J., & Zhu, H. (2024). Practical solutions in fully homomorphic encryption: A survey analyzing existing acceleration methods. *Cybersecurity, 7*(1), 5. DOI: 10.1186/s42400-023-00187-4

Goodfellow, I. J., Shlens, J., & Szegedy, C. (2014). Explaining and harnessing adversarial examples. *arXiv preprint arXiv*:1412.6572.

Goodfellow, I. J., Pouget-Abadie, J., Mirza, M., Xu, B., Warde-Farley, D., Ozair, S., & Bengio, Y. (2014). Generative adversarial nets. *Advances in Neural Information Processing Systems*, •••, 27.

Goodfellow, I. J., Shlens, J., & Szegedy, C. (2015). Explaining and harnessing adversarial examples. *International Conference on Learning Representations (ICLR).*

Goodfellow, I., McDaniel, P., & Papernot, N. (2018). Making machine learning robust against adversarial inputs. *Communications of the ACM, 61*(7), 56–66. DOI: 10.1145/3134599

Grosse, K., Papernot, N., Manoharan, P., Backes, M., & McDaniel, P. (2017). Adversarial examples for malware detection. *European Symposium on Research in Computer Security (ESORICS).*

Gu, T., Dolan-Gavitt, B., & Garg, S. (2017). *BadNets: Identifying vulnerabilities in deep learning-based autonomous control systems.* arXiv preprint arXiv:1708.06733.

Gu, T., Dolan-Gavitt, B., & Garg, S. (2017). Badnets: Identifying vulnerabilities in the machine learning model supply chain. *arXiv preprint arXiv:1708.06733.*

Guesmi, A., Hanif, M. A., Ouni, B., & Shafique, M. (2023). Physical adversarial attacks for camera-based smart systems: Current trends, categorization, applications, research challenges, and future outlook. *IEEE Access : Practical Innovations, Open Solutions, 11*, 109617–109668. DOI: 10.1109/ACCESS.2023.3321118

Gugueoth, V., Safavat, S., Shetty, S., & Rawat, D. (2023). A review of IoT security and privacy using decentralized blockchain techniques. *Computer Science Review, 50*, 100585. DOI: 10.1016/j.cosrev.2023.100585

Gujar, S. S. (2024, November). Enhancing Adversarial Robustness in AI Systems: A Novel Defense Mechanism Using Stable Diffusion. In *2024 2nd DMIHER International Conference on Artificial Intelligence in Healthcare, Education and Industry (IDICAIEI)* (pp. 1-6). IEEE. DOI: 10.1109/IDICAIEI61867.2024.10842888

Guo, C., Gong, B., Waqas, M., Alasmary, H., Tu, S., & Chen, S. (2024). An efficient pairing-free ciphertext-policy attribute-based encryption scheme for Internet of Things. *Sensors (Basel), 24*(21), 6843. DOI: 10.3390/s24216843 PMID: 39517740

Gupta, M., Jain, J., Agarwal, G., Modake, R., & Tanikonda, A. (2025). Adversarial Attacks and Fraud Defenses: Leveraging Data Engineering to Secure AI Models in the Digital Age. *Authorea Preprints, 20.*

Haider, I., Höberl, M., & Rinner, B. (2016). *Trusted Sensors for Participatory Sensing and IoT Applications based on Physically Unclonable Functions.* Paper presented at the Proceedings of the 2nd ACM International Workshop on IoT Privacy, Trust, and Security. DOI: 10.1145/2899007.2899010

Halim, T., & Islam, M. R. (2012). A study on the security issues in WSN. *International Journal of Computer Applications, 53*(1), 26–32. DOI: 10.5120/8386-1992

Hannun, A. Y., Rajpurkar, P., Haghpanahi, M., Tison, G. H., Bourn, C., Turakhia, M. P., & Ng, A. Y. (2019). Cardiologist-level arrhythmia detection and classification in ambulatory electrocardiograms using a deep neural network. *Nature Medicine, 25*(1), 65–69. DOI: 10.1038/s41591-018-0268-3 PMID: 30617320

Han, S., Lin, C., Shen, C., Wang, Q., & Guan, X. (2023). Interpreting adversarial examples in deep learning: A review. *ACM Computing Surveys*, *55*(14s), 1–38. DOI: 10.1145/3594869

Heartfield, R., Loukas, G., Bezemskij, A., & Panaousis, E. (2021). Self-Configurable Cyber-Physical Intrusion Detection for Smart Homes Using Reinforcement Learning. *IEEE Transactions on Information Forensics and Security*, *16*, 1720–1735. DOI: 10.1109/TIFS.2020.3042049

He, L., Wei, B., Hao, K., Gao, L., & Peng, C. (2025). Bio-inspired deep neural local acuity and focus learning for visual image recognition. *Neural Networks*, *181*, 106712. DOI: 10.1016/j.neunet.2024.106712 PMID: 39388996

Henna, S., & Amjath, M. (2024, December). Front-running Attack Detection in Blockchain using Conditional Packing Generative AI. In *2024 IEEE International Conference on Big Data (BigData)* (pp. 5585-5591). IEEE.

Henry, E. (2024). Adversarial Machine Learning Developing Robust Defense Mechanisms Against Evolving Threat Models in AI Systems.

Henze, M., Hermerschmidt, L., Kerpen, D., Häußling, R., Rumpe, B., & Wehrle, K. (2016). A comprehensive approach to privacy in the cloud-based Internet of Things. *Future Generation Computer Systems*, *56*, 701–718. DOI: 10.1016/j.future.2015.09.016

Hernández-Castro, C. J., Liu, Z., Serban, A., Tsingenopoulos, I., & Joosen, W. (2022). Adversarial machine learning. In *Security and Artificial Intelligence: A Crossdisciplinary Approach* (pp. 287–312). Springer International Publishing. DOI: 10.1007/978-3-030-98795-4_12

He, X., Yang, H., Hu, Z., & Lv, C. (2022). Robust lane change decision making for autonomous vehicles: An observation adversarial reinforcement learning approach. *IEEE Transactions on Intelligent Vehicles*, *8*(1), 184–193. DOI: 10.1109/TIV.2022.3165178

Hinton, G. E., & Salakhutdinov, R. R. (2006). Reducing the dimensionality of data with neural networks. *Science*, *313*(5786), 504–507. DOI: 10.1126/science.1127647 PMID: 16873662

Hitaj, B., Ateniese, G., & Perez-Cruz, F. (2017). Deep models under the GAN: Information leakage from collaborative deep learning. *Proceedings of the 2017 ACM SIGSAC Conference on Computer and Communications Security (CCS)*. DOI: 10.1145/3133956.3134012

Hleg, A. (2019). Ethics guidelines for trustworthy AI. In.

Hoang, V. T., Ergu, Y. A., Nguyen, V. L., & Chang, R. G. (2024). Security risks and countermeasures of adversarial attacks on AI-driven applications in 6G networks: A survey. *Journal of Network and Computer Applications*, *232*, 104031. DOI: 10.1016/j.jnca.2024.104031

Hossain, M. T., Afrin, R., & Biswas, M. A. A. (2024). A Review on Attacks against Artificial Intelligence (AI) and Their Defence Image Recognition and Generation Machine Learning, Artificial Intelligence. *Control Systems and Optimization Letters*, *2*(1), 52–59. DOI: 10.59247/csol.v2i1.73

Hosseini Shirvani, M., & Akbarifar, A. (2024). A survey study on intrusion detection system in wireless sensor network: Challenges and considerations. [JECEI]. *Journal of Electrical and Computer Engineering Innovations*, *12*(2), 449–474.

Hosseini, S., & Sardo, S. R. (2023). Network intrusion detection based on deep learning method in internet of thing. *Journal of Reliable Intelligent Environments*, *9*(2), 147–159. DOI: 10.1007/s40860-021-00169-8

Hosseinzadeh, S., Hyrynsalmi, S., & Leppänen, V. (2016). Chapter 14 - Obfuscation and diversification for securing the internet of things (IoT). In *Internet of Things*. https://doi.org/DOI: 10.1016/B978-0-12-805395-9/00014-9

Hsiao-Ying Lin, B. B. (2021). Adversarial Machine Learning: Attacks From Laboratories to the Real World. *Computer*, *54*(5), 56–60. DOI: 10.1109/MC.2021.3057686

Huanan, Z., Suping, X., & Jiannan, W. (2021). Security and application of wireless sensor network. *Procedia Computer Science*, *183*, 486–492. DOI: 10.1016/j.procs.2021.02.088

Humayun, M., Jhanjhi, N., Alruwaili, M., Amalathas, S. S., Balasubramanian, V., & Selvaraj, B. (2020). Privacy protection and energy optimization for 5G-aided industrial Internet of Things. *IEEE Access : Practical Innovations, Open Solutions*, *8*, 183665–183677. DOI: 10.1109/ACCESS.2020.3028764

Hu, N., Tian, Z., Lu, H., Du, X., & Guizani, M. (2021). A multiple-kernel clustering based intrusion detection scheme for 5G and IoT networks. *International Journal of Machine Learning and Cybernetics*, *12*(11), 3129–3144. DOI: 10.1007/s13042-020-01253-w

Hussain, S., & Elson, A. (2024). Adversarial Machine Learning: Identifying and Mitigating AI-Powered Cyber Attacks.

IAPP. (2025). *US State Privacy Legislation Tracker*. Retrieved from IAPP.

Ibitoye, O., Abou-Khamis, R., Shehaby, M. E., Matrawy, A., & Shafiq, M. O. (2019). The Threat of Adversarial Attacks on Machine Learning in Network Security—A Survey. arXiv preprint arXiv:1911.02621.

IEEE. (2023). *What Is Privacy-by-Design and Why It's Important?* Retrieved from IEEE.

Ijiga, O. M., Idoko, I. P., Ebiega, G. I., Olajide, F. I., Olatunde, T. I., & Ukaegbu, C. (2024). Harnessing adversarial machine learning for advanced threat detection: AI-driven strategies in cybersecurity risk assessment and fraud prevention. *J. Sci. Technol, 11*, 001-024.

Ilyas, A., Santurkar, S., Tsipras, D., Engstrom, L., Tran, B., & Madry, A. (2019). Adversarial examples are not bugs, they are features. *Advances in Neural Information Processing Systems*, •••, 32.

Imteaj, A., Khan, I., Khazaei, J., & Amini, M. H. (2021). Fedresilience: A federated learning application to improve resilience of resource-constrained critical infrastructures. *Electronics (Basel)*, *10*(16), 1917. DOI: 10.3390/electronics10161917

Iqbal, S., Rizvi, S. W. A., Haider, M. H., & Raza, S. (2023). Artificial Intelligence in Security and Defense: Explore the integration of AI in military strategies, security policies, and its implications for global power dynamics. *INTERNATIONAL JOURNAL OF HUMAN AND SOCIETY*, *3*(4), 341–353.

ISACA. (2021). *Data Minimization—A Practical Approach.* Retrieved from ISACA.

Islam, S., Elmekki, H., Elsebai, A., Bentahar, J., Drawel, N., Rjoub, G., & Pedrycz, W. (2024). A comprehensive survey on applications of transformers for deep learning tasks. *Expert Systems with Applications*, *241*, 122666. DOI: 10.1016/j.eswa.2023.122666

Jabbarova, K. (2023). AI AND CYBERSECURITY-NEW THREATS AND OPPORTUNITIES. *The Journal of Research Administration*, *5*(2), 5955–5966.

Jagarlamudi, G. K., Yazdinejad, A., Parizi, R. M., & Pouriyeh, S. (2024). Exploring privacy measurement in federated learning. *The Journal of Supercomputing*, *80*(8), 10511–10551. DOI: 10.1007/s11227-023-05846-4

Jagatheesaperumal, S. K., Pham, Q.-V., Ruby, R., Yang, Z., Xu, C., & Zhang, Z. (2022). Explainable AI over the Internet of Things (IoT): Overview, state-of-the-art and future directions. *IEEE Open Journal of the Communications Society*, *3*, 2106–2136. DOI: 10.1109/OJCOMS.2022.3215676

Jain, V., & Mitra, A. (2025). Real-Time Threat Detection in Cybersecurity: Leveraging Machine Learning Algorithms for Enhanced Anomaly Detection. In Machine Intelligence Applications in Cyber-Risk Management (pp. 315-344). IGI Global Scientific Publishing.

Jalali, N. A., & Chen, H. (2023). Federated learning security and privacy-preserving algorithm and experiments research under internet of things critical infrastructure. *Tsinghua Science and Technology*, *29*(2), 400–414. DOI: 10.26599/TST.2023.9010007

Jamalipour, A., & Murali, S. (2022). A Taxonomy of Machine-Learning-Based Intrusion Detection Systems for the Internet of Things: A Survey. *IEEE Internet of Things Journal*, *9*(12), 9444–9466. DOI: 10.1109/JIOT.2021.3126811

Javed, H., El-Sappagh, S., & Abuhmed, T. (2025). Robustness in deep learning models for medical diagnostics: Security and adversarial challenges towards robust AI applications. *Artificial Intelligence Review*, *58*(1), 1–107.

Jegorova, M., Kaul, C., Mayor, C., O'Neil, A. Q., Weir, A., Murray-Smith, R., & Tsaftaris, S. A. (2022). Survey: Leakage and privacy at inference time. *IEEE Transactions on Pattern Analysis and Machine Intelligence*, *45*(7), 9090–9108. DOI: 10.1109/TPAMI.2022.3229593 PMID: 37015684

Jian, Y. L., & Luaus, C. (2023). Enhancing Power Grid Security: A Comprehensive Study on Cybersecurity Measures and Fault Diagnosis Strategies Amid Dynamic System Variations. *Revista Española de Documentación Cientifica*, *17*(2).

Jondhale, S. R., Maheswar, R., & Lloret, J. (2021). *Received signal strength based target localization and tracking using wireless sensor networks*. Springer Nature.

Joshi, H. C., & Kumar, S. (2024). Artificial Intelligence Failures in Autonomous Vehicles: Causes, Implications, and Prevention. *Computer*, *57*(11), 18–30. DOI: 10.1109/MC.2024.3449435

Kairouz, P., McMahan, H. B., & Avent, B.. (2019). Advances and Open Problems in Federated Learning. arXiv:1912.04977.

Kalakoti, R., Vaarandi, R., Bahsi, H., & Nomm, S. Evaluating Explainable AI for Deep Learning-Based Network Intrusion Detection System Alert Classification.

Kalnoor, G., & Gowrishankar, S. (2021). RETRACTED ARTICLE: IoT-based smart environment using intelligent intrusion detection system. *Soft Computing*, *25*(17), 11573–11588. DOI: 10.1007/s00500-021-06028-1

Kaloudi, N., & Li, J. (2020). The ai-based cyber threat landscape: A survey. *ACM Computing Surveys*, *53*(1), 1–34. DOI: 10.1145/3372823

Kanamori, S., Abe, T., Ito, T., Emura, K., Wang, L., Yamamoto, S., Phong, L. T., Abe, K., Kim, S., Nojima, R., Ozawa, S., & Moriai, S. (2022). Privacy-preserving federated learning for detecting fraudulent financial transactions in japanese banks. *Journal of Information Processing*, *30*(0), 789–795. DOI: 10.2197/ipsjjip.30.789

Kandhro, I. A., Alanazi, S. M., Ali, F., Kehar, A., Fatima, K., Uddin, M., & Karuppayah, S. (2023). Detection of Real-Time Malicious Intrusions and Attacks in IoT Empowered Cybersecurity Infrastructures. *IEEE Access : Practical Innovations, Open Solutions*, *11*, 9136–9148. DOI: 10.1109/ACCESS.2023.3238664

Kanervisto, A. (2022). Advances in Deep Learning for Playing Video Games.

Kang, J., Xiong, Z., Niyato, D., Xie, S., & Zhang, J. (2019). Incentive mechanism for reliable federated learning: A joint optimization approach to combining reputation and contract theory. *IEEE Internet of Things Journal*, *6*(6), 10700–10714. DOI: 10.1109/JIOT.2019.2940820

Kannan, Y. (2024). AI AND MACHINE LEARNING FOR NETWORK SECURITY: APPLICATIONS AND CASE STUDIES. [IJAIML]. *International Journal of Artificial Intelligence and Machine Learning*, *3*(02), 1–13.

Karale, A. (2021). The challenges of IoT addressing security, ethics, privacy, and laws. *Internet of Things : Engineering Cyber Physical Human Systems*, *15*, 100420. DOI: 10.1016/j.iot.2021.100420

Karras, T., Aila, T., Laine, S., & Lehtinen, J. (2017). Progressive growing of GANs for improved quality, stability, and variation. *arXiv preprint* arXiv:1710.10196.

Karras, T., Laine, S., & Aila, T. (2019). A style-based generator architecture for generative adversarial networks. In *Proceedings of the IEEE/CVF conference on computer vision and pattern recognition* (pp. 4401-4410). DOI: 10.1109/CVPR.2019.00453

Kashyap, S., Sharma, A., Gautam, S., Sharma, R., & Chauhan, S. (2024, May). Adversarial Attacks and Defenses in Deep Learning. In *2024 International Conference on Emerging Innovations and Advanced Computing (INNOCOMP)* (pp. 318-323). IEEE.

Kaur, N., & Sood, S. K. (2017). An Energy-Efficient Architecture for the Internet of Things (IoT). *IEEE Systems Journal*, *11*(2), 796–805. DOI: 10.1109/JSYST.2015.2469676

Kaviani, S., Han, K. J., & Sohn, I. (2022). Adversarial attacks and defenses on AI in medical imaging informatics: A survey. *Expert Systems with Applications*, *198*, 116815. DOI: 10.1016/j.eswa.2022.116815

Kavitha, D., & Thejas, S. (2024). Ai enabled threat detection: Leveraging artificial intelligence for advanced security and cyber threat mitigation. *IEEE Access : Practical Innovations, Open Solutions*.

Kearns, M., & Li, M. (1988). Learning in the presence of malicious errors. In *Proceedings of the twentieth annual ACM symposium on Theory of computing* (pp. 267-280). DOI: 10.1145/62212.62238

Keerthika, M., & Shanmugapriya, D. (2021). Wireless sensor networks: Active and passive attacks-vulnerabilities and countermeasures. *Global Transitions Proceedings*, *2*(2), 362–367. DOI: 10.1016/j.gltp.2021.08.045

Keramati, M. (2017). 09 15). An Attack Graph Based Method for Predictive Risk Evaluation of Zero-Day Attacks. *International Journal of Information and Communication Technology Research*, *9*(3), 7–16. https://ijict.itrc.ac.ir/article-1-30-en.html

Keshk, M., Koroniotis, N., Pham, N., Moustafa, N., Turnbull, B., & Zomaya, A. Y. (2023). An explainable deep learning-enabled intrusion detection framework in IoT networks. *Information Sciences*, *639*, 119000. DOI: 10.1016/j.ins.2023.119000

Khairnar, S., Gite, S., Mahajan, K., Pradhan, B., Alamri, A., & Thepade, S. D. (2024). Advanced Techniques for Biometric Authentication: Leveraging Deep Learning and Explainable AI. *IEEE Access : Practical Innovations, Open Solutions*, *12*, 153580–153595. DOI: 10.1109/ACCESS.2024.3474690

Khakurel, U., Abdelmoumin, G., Bajracharya, A., & Rawat, D. B. (2022). Exploring bias and fairness in artificial intelligence and machine learning algorithms. In *Artificial Intelligence and Machine Learning for Multi-Domain Operations Applications IV* (Vol. 12113, pp. 629–638). SPIE. DOI: 10.1117/12.2621282

Khaleel, T. A. (2024, May). Developing robust machine learning models to defend against adversarial attacks in the field of cybersecurity. In *2024 International Congress on Human-Computer Interaction, Optimization and Robotic Applications (HORA)* (pp. 1-7). IEEE. DOI: 10.1109/HORA61326.2024.10550799

Khaleel, Y. L., Habeeb, M. A., Albahri, A. S., Al-Quraishi, T., Albahri, O. S., & Alamoodi, A. H. (2024). Network and cybersecurity applications of defense in adversarial attacks: A state-of-the-art using machine learning and deep learning methods. *Journal of Intelligent Systems*, *33*(1), 20240153. DOI: 10.1515/jisys-2024-0153

Khalil, U., Malik, O. A., Uddin, M., & Chen, C. (2022). A Comparative Analysis on Blockchain versus Centralized Authentication Architectures for IoT-Enabled Smart Devices in Smart Cities: A Comprehensive Review, Recent Advances, and Future Research Directions [Review of A Comparative Analysis on Blockchain versus Centralized Authentication Architectures for IoT-Enabled Smart Devices in Smart Cities: A Comprehensive Review, Recent Advances, and Future Research Directions]. Sensors, 22(14), 5168. Multidisciplinary Digital Publishing Institute. DOI: 10.3390/s22145168

Khanam, S., Ahmedy, I., Idna Idris, M. Y., Jaward, M. H., & Bin Md Sabri, A. Q. (2020). A Survey of Security Challenges, Attacks Taxonomy and Advanced Countermeasures in the Internet of Things. *IEEE Access : Practical Innovations, Open Solutions*, *8*, 219709–219743. DOI: 10.1109/ACCESS.2020.3037359

Khan, M. M., Shah, N., Shaikh, N., Thabet, A., & Belkhair, S. (2024). Towards secure and trusted AI in healthcare: A systematic review of emerging innovations and ethical challenges. *International Journal of Medical Informatics*, •••, 105780. PMID: 39753062

Khanna, A., & Kaur, S. (2020). Internet of Things (IoT), Applications and Challenges: A Comprehensive Review. In *Wireless Personal Communications* (Vol. 114, Issue 2, pp. 1687–1762). Springer. DOI: 10.1007/s11277-020-07446-4

Khan, O. U., Abdullah, S. M., Olajide, A. O., Sani, A. I., Faisal, S. M. W., Ogunola, A. A., & Lee, M. D. (2024). The Future of Cybersecurity: Leveraging Artificial Intelligence to Combat Evolving Threats and Enhance Digital Defense Strategies. *Journal of Computational Analysis and Applications*, *33*(8).

Khan, Y., Su'ud, M. B. M., Alam, M. M., Ahmad, S. F., Salim, N. A., & Khan, N. (2022). Architectural threats to security and privacy: A challenge for internet of things (IoT) applications. *Electronics (Basel)*, *12*(1), 88. DOI: 10.3390/electronics12010088

Kiranbabu, M. N. V., Viji, A. J., Chandanan, A. K., Birchha, V., Pandey, T. K., & Sar, S. K. (2025). The Challenge of Adversarial Attacks on AI-Driven Cybersecurity Systems. *Journal of Cybersecurity & Information Management*, *15*(1).

Knowing Your Hardware. (2022). In *System firmware* (pp. 45 - 143). Apress eBooks. DOI: 10.1007/978-1-4842-7939-7_2

Ko, C., Ruschitzka, M., & Levitt, K. (n.d.). Execution monitoring of security-critical programs in distributed systems: a specification-based approach. *Proceedings. 1997 IEEE Symposium on Security and Privacy (Cat. No.97CB36097)*, 175–187. DOI: 10.1109/SECPRI.1997.601332

Kohonen, T., & Honkela, T. (2007). Kohonen network. *Scholarpedia Journal, 2*(1), 1568. DOI: 10.4249/scholarpedia.1568

Koike, S., Tanaka, H., & Maeda, M. (2024). Federated learning-based ransomware detection via indicators of compromise.

Konečný, J., McMahan, H. B., Yu, F. X., Richtárik, P., Suresh, A. T., & Bacon, D. (2016). Federated learning: Strategies for improving communication efficiency. arXiv preprint arXiv:1610.05492.

Koppula, M., & Leo Joseph, L. M. I. (2025). A Real-World Dataset "IDSIoT2024" for Machine Learning/Deep Learning Based Cyber Attack Detection System for IoT Architecture. *2025 3rd International Conference on Intelligent Data Communication Technologies and Internet of Things (IDCIoT)*, 1757–1764. DOI: 10.1109/IDCIOT64235.2025.10914935

Koroniotis, N., Moustafa, N., Sitnikova, E., & Turnbull, B. (2019). Towards the development of realistic botnet dataset in the Internet of Things for network forensic analytics: Bot-IoT dataset. *Future Generation Computer Systems, 100*, 779–796. DOI: 10.1016/j.future.2019.05.041

Kothinti, R. R. (2024). Deep learning in healthcare: Transforming disease diagnosis, personalized treatment, and clinical decision-making through AI-driven innovations.

Kouicem, D. E., Bouabdallah, A., & Lakhlef, H. (2018). Internet of things security: A top-down survey. In *Computer Networks* (Vol. 141, pp. 199–221). Elsevier B.V., DOI: 10.1016/j.comnet.2018.03.012

Krijnen, T., & Tamke, M. (2015). Assessing implicit knowledge in BIM models with machine learning. In *Modelling Behaviour: Design Modelling Symposium 2015* (pp. 397-406). Springer International Publishing. DOI: 10.1007/978-3-319-24208-8_33

Kuchuk, H., & Malokhvii, E. (2024). Integration of IoT with cloud, fog, and edge computing: A review. *Advanced Information Systems, 8*(2), 65–78. DOI: 10.20998/2522-9052.2024.2.08

Kumar, B. G., & Shanthini, E. (2024, December). From Attacks to Insights: XAI and Defense in Network Security. In *2024 International Conference on Sustainable Communication Networks and Application (ICSCNA)* (pp. 395-401). IEEE.

Kumar, P. (2021). Design of Anomaly-Based Intrusion Detection System Using Fog Computing for IoT Network. *Automatic Control and Computer Sciences, 55*(2), 137–147. DOI: 10.3103/S0146411621020085

Kumar, P., Gupta, G. P., & Tripathi, R. (2021). An ensemble learning and fog-cloud architecture-driven cyber-attack detection framework for IoMT networks. *Computer Communications*, *166*, 110–124. DOI: 10.1016/j.comcom.2020.12.003

Kumar, R., Jain, V., Leong, H. W., & Teyarachakul, S. (2023). Convergence of IoT, Blockchain, and Computational Intelligence in Smart Cities. In *CRC Press eBooks*. Informa., DOI: 10.1201/9781003353034

Kumar, R., Kumar, P., Tripathi, R., Gupta, G. P., Garg, S., & Hassan, M. M. (2022). A distributed intrusion detection system to detect DDoS attacks in blockchain-enabled IoT network. *Journal of Parallel and Distributed Computing*, *164*, 55–68. DOI: 10.1016/j.jpdc.2022.01.030

Kumar, R., & Tripathi, R. (2021). DBTP2SF: A deep blockchain-based trustworthy privacy-preserving secured framework in industrial internet of things systems. *Transactions on Emerging Telecommunications Technologies*, *32*(4), e4222. Advance online publication. DOI: 10.1002/ett.4222

Kumar, S., Gupta, U., Singh, A. K., & Singh, A. K. (2023). Artificial intelligence: Revolutionizing cyber security in the digital era. Journal of Computers. *Mechanical and Management*, *2*(3), 31–42.

Kurakin, A., Goodfellow, I., & Bengio, S. (2016). Adversarial machine learning at scale. *arXiv preprint* arXiv:1611.01236.

Kurakin, A., Goodfellow, I. J., & Bengio, S. (2018). Adversarial examples in the physical world. In *Artificial intelligence safety and security* (pp. 99–112). Chapman and Hall/CRC. DOI: 10.1201/9781351251389-8

Kuzlu, M., Fair, C., & Guler, O. (2021). Role of Artificial Intelligence in the Internet of Things (IoT) cybersecurity. *Discover Internet of Things*, *1*(1), 7. DOI: 10.1007/s43926-020-00001-4

Laghari, A. A., Li, H., Khan, A. A., Shoulin, Y., Karim, S., & Khani, M. A. K. (2024). Internet of Things (IoT) applications security trends and challenges. *Discover Internet of Things*, *4*(1), 36. DOI: 10.1007/s43926-024-00090-5

Lahasan, B., & Samma, H. (2022). Optimized Deep Autoencoder Model for Internet of Things Intruder Detection. *IEEE Access : Practical Innovations, Open Solutions*, *10*, 8434–8448. DOI: 10.1109/ACCESS.2022.3144208

Lahoti, P., Beutel, A., Chen, J., Lee, K., Prost, F., Thain, N., & Chi, E. (2020). Fairness without demographics through adversarially reweighted learning. *Advances in Neural Information Processing Systems*, *33*, 728–740.

Lalouani, W., & Younis, M. (2021). Robust Distributed Intrusion Detection System for Edge of Things. *2021 IEEE Global Communications Conference (GLOBECOM)*, 01–06. DOI: 10.1109/GLOBECOM46510.2021.9685361

Lau, J., Zimmerman, B., & Schaub, F. (2018). Alexa, are you listening? Privacy perceptions, concerns and privacy-seeking behaviours with smart speakers. *Proceedings of the ACM on Human-Computer Interaction, 2*(CSCW), Article 102.

Lavieille, P., & Atlas, I. A. H. (2023). IsoEx: an explainable unsupervised approach to process event logs cyber investigation. *arXiv preprint arXiv:2306.09260.*

Lawal, M. A., Shaikh, R. A., & Hassan, S. R. (2020). An Anomaly Mitigation Framework for IoT Using Fog Computing. *Electronics (Basel), 9*(10), 1565. DOI: 10.3390/electronics9101565

Lawal, M. A., Shaikh, R. A., & Hassan, S. R. (2021). A DDoS Attack Mitigation Framework for IoT Networks using Fog Computing. *Procedia Computer Science, 182*, 13–20. DOI: 10.1016/j.procs.2021.02.003

Lecun, Y., Bengio, Y., & Hinton, G. (2015). Deep learning. *Nature, 521*(7553), 436–444. DOI: 10.1038/nature14539 PMID: 26017442

Lee, C., & Ahmed, G. (2021). Improving IoT privacy, data protection and security concerns. [IJTIM]. *International Journal of Technology Innovation and Management, 1*(1), 18–33. DOI: 10.54489/ijtim.v1i1.12

Leong, A. S., Ramaswamy, A., Quevedo, D. E., Karl, H., & Shi, L. (2020). Deep reinforcement learning for wireless sensor scheduling in cyber–physical systems. *Automatica, 113*, 108759.

Li, T., Sahu, A. K., Zaheer, M., Sanjabi, M., Talwalkar, A., & Smith, V. (2020). Federated optimization in heterogeneous networks. Proceedings of Machine learning and systems, 2, 429-450.

Li, Y., Zhao, Y., Liu, G., & Liao, X. (2024, May). THE APPLICATION OF DEEP LEARNING IN THE FINANCIAL SECTOR: A COMPREHENSIVE REVIEW. In *The 21st International scientific and practical conference "Innovative solutions in public communications and international relations"(May 28–31, 2024) Sofia, Bulgaria. International Science Group. 2024. 382 p.* (p. 316).

Liang, H., He, E., Zhao, Y., Jia, Z., & Li, H. (2022). Adversarial Attack and Defence: A Survey. *Electronics (Basel), 11*(8), 1283. DOI: 10.3390/electronics11081283

Liao, H.-J., Lin, C.-H. R., Lin, Y.-C., & Tung, K.-Y. (2013). Intrusion detection system: A comprehensive review. *Journal of Network and Computer Applications*, *36*(1), 16–24. DOI: 10.1016/j.jnca.2012.09.004

Li, B., Qi, P., Liu, B., Di, S., Liu, J., Pei, J., Yi, J., & Zhou, B. (2023). Trustworthy AI: From principles to practices. *ACM Computing Surveys*, *55*(9), 1–46. DOI: 10.1145/3555803

Li, J., He, J., Hu, L., & Wu, C. (2024, April). A Federated Learning Framework via Decentralized Data Valuation for Chronic Disease Healthcare. In *Proceedings of the 2024 6th International Conference on Intelligent Medicine and Image Processing* (pp. 60-65).

Lim, B., Huerta, R., Sotelo, A., Quintela, A., & Kumar, P. (2025). EXPLICATE: Enhancing Phishing Detection through Explainable AI and LLM-Powered Interpretability. *arXiv preprint arXiv:2503.20796.*

Ling, C., Zhang, W., & He, H. (2023). K-anonymity privacy-preserving algorithm for IoT applications in virtualization and edge computing. *Cluster Computing*, *26*(2), 1495–1510. DOI: 10.1007/s10586-022-03755-4

Li, Q., Wen, Z., He, B., & Li, J. (2020). A Survey on Federated Learning Systems: Vision, Hype and Reality for Data Privacy and Protection. *IEEE Transactions on Knowledge and Data Engineering.*

Li, Q., Wen, Z., Wu, Z., Hu, S., Wang, N., Li, Y., Liu, X., & He, B. (2021). A survey on federated learning systems: Vision, hype and reality for data privacy and protection. *IEEE Transactions on Knowledge and Data Engineering*, *35*(4), 3347–3366. DOI: 10.1109/TKDE.2021.3124599

Li, T., Sahu, A. K., Talwalkar, A., & Smith, V. (2020). Federated learning: Challenges, methods, and future directions. *IEEE Signal Processing Magazine*, *37*(3), 50–60. DOI: 10.1109/MSP.2020.2975749

Liu, F. T., Ting, K. M., & Zhou, Z. H. (2008). Isolation forest. In *2008 eighth IEEE international conference on data mining* (pp. 413-422). IEEE. DOI: 10.1109/ICDM.2008.17

Liu, J., Feng, W., & Zhu, H. (2021). Backdoor vulnerabilities in AI-driven decentralized finance systems. *Proceedings of the ACM Conference on Computer and Communications Security (CCS).*

Liu, J., Yang, D., Lian, M., & Li, M. (2021). Research on Intrusion Detection Based on Particle Swarm Optimization in IoT. *IEEE Access : Practical Innovations, Open Solutions*, *9*, 38254–38268. DOI: 10.1109/ACCESS.2021.3063671

Liu, Y., Jia, Z., Jiang, Z., Lin, X., Liu, J., Wu, Q., & Susilo, W. (2024). BFL-SA: Blockchain-based federated learning via enhanced secure aggregation. *Journal of Systems Architecture*, *152*, 103163. DOI: 10.1016/j.sysarc.2024.103163

Liu, Y., & Lyu, T. (2025). Real-time monitoring of lower limb movement resistance based on deep learning. *Alexandria Engineering Journal*, *111*, 136–147. DOI: 10.1016/j.aej.2024.09.031

Liu, Y., Ma, S., Aafer, Y., Lee, W. C., Zhai, J., Wang, W., & Zhang, X. (2018). Trojaning attack on neural networks. *25th Network and Distributed System Security Symposium (NDSS)*. DOI: 10.14722/ndss.2018.23291

Li, Y., Sani, A. S., Yuan, D., & Bao, W. (2022). Enhancing federated learning robustness through clustering non-iid features. In *Proceedings of the Asian Conference on Computer Vision* (pp. 41-55).

Li, Y., Xie, B., Guo, S., Yang, Y., & Xiao, B. (2024). A survey of robustness and safety of 2d and 3d deep learning models against adversarial attacks. *ACM Computing Surveys*, *56*(6), 1–37. DOI: 10.1145/3636551

Lowd, D., & Meek, C. (2005). Good Word Attacks on Statistical Spam Filters. In *CEAS* (Vol. 2005).

Lu, H., Li, Y., Mu, S., Wang, D., Kim, H., & Serikawa, S. (2018). Motor Anomaly Detection for Unmanned Aerial Vehicles Using Reinforcement Learning. *IEEE Internet of Things Journal*, *5*(4), 2315–2322. DOI: 10.1109/JIOT.2017.2737479

Lundberg, S. M., & Lee, S.-I. (2017). A unified approach to interpreting model predictions. *Advances in Neural Information Processing Systems*, •••, 30.

Lunghi, D., Simitsis, A., & Bontempi, G. (2024, July). Assessing adversarial attacks in real-world fraud detection. In *2024 IEEE International Conference on Web Services (ICWS)* (pp. 27-34). IEEE.

Luntovskyy, A., & Globa, L. (2019). *Performance, reliability and scalability for IoT.* Paper presented at the 2019 International Conference on Information and Digital Technologies (IDT). DOI: 10.1109/DT.2019.8813679

Lu, Z., & Metghalchi, H. (2023). Prediction of Laminar Burning Speed of Propane/Hydrogen/Air Mixtures Using Power-Law Correlation and Two Machine Learning Models. *ASME Open Journal of Engineering*, *2*, 021038. Advance online publication. DOI: 10.1115/1.4062745

Madry, A., Makelov, A., Schmidt, L., Tsipras, D., & Vladu, A. (2017). Towards deep learning models resistant to adversarial attacks. *arXiv preprint* arXiv:1706.06083.

Mahanan, W., Chaovalitwongse, W. A., & Natwichai, J. (2020). Data anonymization: A novel optimal k-anonymity algorithm for identical generalization hierarchy data in IoT. *Service Oriented Computing and Applications*, *14*(2), 89–100. DOI: 10.1007/s11761-020-00287-w

Maharaja, R., Iyer, P., & Ye, Z. (2020). A hybrid fog-cloud approach for securing the Internet of Things. *Cluster Computing*, *23*(2), 451–459. DOI: 10.1007/s10586-019-02935-z

Mahbod, T., Ebrahim, B., Wei, L., & Ali, A. G. (2009). A Detailed Analysis of the KDD CUP 99 Data Set, 2009 : [Ottawa, Canada, 8-10 July 2009]. *IEEE Symposium on Computational Intelligence for Security and Defense Applications (CISDA).*

Mahjabeen, F., & Islam, M. A. (2024). The Role of AI and Machine Learning in Strengthening Cybersecurity Defenses. [BESTEC]. *Bulletin of Engineering Science and Technology*, *1*(02), 109–124.

Malatji, M., & Tolah, A. (2024). Artificial intelligence (AI) cybersecurity dimensions: A comprehensive framework for understanding adversarial and offensive AI. *AI and Ethics*, •••, 1–28.

Malik, A., & Om, H. (2018). Cloud computing and internet of things integration: Architecture, applications, issues, and challenges. *Sustainable cloud and energy services: Principles and practice*, 1-24.

Malik, P., Alirajpurwala, T., Kaushal, S., Patidar, T., Indore, I. I. I., & Padlak, S. (2024). Scalability and robustness of federated learning systems: Challenges and solutions. [IJSREM]. *International Journal of Scientific Research in Engineering and Management*, *8*(6), 1–5. DOI: 10.55041/IJSREM35575

Manogna, R. L., & Anand, A. (2024). A bibliometric analysis on the application of deep learning in finance: Status, development and future directions. *Kybernetes*, *53*(12), 5951–5971. DOI: 10.1108/K-04-2023-0637

Manthena, H., Shajarian, S., Kimmell, J., Abdelsalam, M., Khorsandroo, S., & Gupta, M. (2025). Explainable Artificial Intelligence (XAI) for Malware Analysis: A Survey of Techniques, Applications, and Open Challenges. *IEEE Access : Practical Innovations, Open Solutions*, *13*, 61611–61640. DOI: 10.1109/ACCESS.2025.3555926

Markevych, M., & Dawson, M. (2023). A review of enhancing intrusion detection systems for cybersecurity using artificial intelligence (ai). In International conference KNOWLEDGE-BASED ORGANIZATION, Vol. 29, No. 3, pp. 30-37.

Ma, X., Niu, Y., Gu, L., Wang, Y., Zhao, Y., Bailey, J., & Lu, F. (2021). Understanding adversarial attacks on deep learning based medical image analysis systems. *Pattern Recognition, 110*, 107332. DOI: 10.1016/j.patcog.2020.107332

Mbarek, B., Meddeb, A., Ben Jaballah, W., & Mosbah, M. (2015). A secure authentication mechanism for resource constrained devices. *2015 IEEE/ACS 12th International Conference of Computer Systems and Applications (AICCSA)*, 1–7. DOI: 10.1109/AICCSA.2015.7507270

McMahan, B., Moore, E., & Ramage, D.. (2017). Communication-Efficient Learning of Deep Networks from Decentralized Data. arXiv:1602.05629.

McMahan, H. B., Moore, E., Ramage, D., Hampson, S., & Arcas, B. A. (2017). Communication-Efficient Learning of Deep Networks from Decentralized Data. *Proceedings of the 20th International Conference on Artificial Intelligence and Statistics (AISTATS).*

Mehrabi, N., Morstatter, F., Saxena, N., Lerman, K., & Galstyan, A. (2019). A survey on bias and fairness in machine learning. *arXiv preprint arXiv:1908.09635.*

Mehta, A. R. (2024). Privacy-Preserving AI: A Survey of Encrypted Techniques. *International IT Journal of Research, ISSN: 3007-6706, 2*(2), 84-94.

Mehta, S., Khurana, M., Dogra, A., & Hariharan, S. (2024). Advancing IoT Security through Federated Learning: A Comprehensive Approach. *2024 3rd International Conference on Applied Artificial Intelligence and Computing (ICAAIC)*, 561–566. DOI: 10.1109/ICAAIC60222.2024.10575903

Meidan, Y., Bohadana, M., Mathov, Y., Mirsky, Y., Shabtai, A., Breitenbacher, D., & Elovici, Y. (2018). N-BaIoT-Network-based detection of IoT botnet attacks using deep autoencoders. *IEEE Pervasive Computing, 17*(3), 12–22. DOI: 10.1109/MPRV.2018.03367731

Melnik, A., Miasayedzenkau, M., Makaravets, D., Pirshtuk, D., Akbulut, E., Holzmann, D., Renusch, T., Reichert, G., & Ritter, H. (2024). Face generation and editing with stylegan: A survey. *IEEE Transactions on Pattern Analysis and Machine Intelligence, 46*(5), 3557–3576. DOI: 10.1109/TPAMI.2024.3350004 PMID: 38224501

Meng, C., Tang, M., Setayesh, M., & Wong, V. W. (2023, December). GNN-based neighbor selection and resource allocation for decentralized federated learning. In GLOBECOM 2023-2023 IEEE Global Communications Conference (pp. 1223-1228). IEEE.

Metri, P., Balla, S., Pawar, S., Sharma, A., & Sakunde, P. (2024, December). Image Forgery Detection Using Hybrid Model. In *2024 IEEE International Conference on Intelligent Signal Processing and Effective Communication Technologies (INSPECT)* (pp. 1-6). IEEE.

Mienye, I. D., & Swart, T. G. (2024). A hybrid deep learning approach with generative adversarial network for credit card fraud detection. *Technologies*, *12*(10), 186. DOI: 10.3390/technologies12100186

Mirza, M., & Osindero, S. (2014). Conditional generative adversarial nets. *arXiv preprint* arXiv:1411.1784.

Mittal, M., Kumar, K., & Behal, S. (2023). Deep learning approaches for detecting DDoS attacks: A systematic review. *Soft Computing*, *27*(18), 13039–13075. DOI: 10.1007/s00500-021-06608-1 PMID: 35103047

Mittelstadt, B. D., Allo, P., Taddeo, M., Wachter, S., & Floridi, L. (2016). Principles alone are not enough for ethical AI. *Nature Machine Intelligence*, *1*(11), 501–507. DOI: 10.1038/s42256-019-0114-4

Mohammadi Rouzbahani, H., Karimipour, H., Rahimnejad, A., Dehghantanha, A., & Srivastava, G. (2020). Anomaly detection in cyber-physical systems using machine learning. Handbook of big data privacy, 219-235.

Mohammad, N., Khatoon, R., Nilima, S. I., Akter, J., Kamruzzaman, M., & Sozib, H. M. (2024). Ensuring Security and Privacy in the Internet of Things: Challenges and Solutions. *Journal of Computer and Communications*, *12*(8), 257–277. DOI: 10.4236/jcc.2024.128016

Mohammed, B. H., Sallehudin, H., Satar, N. S. M., Murhg, H. D., Mohamed, S. A., Alaba, F. A., Rocha, A., & Bianchi, I. (2025). Anomaly Detection of Distributed Denial of Service (DDoS) in IoT Network Using. *Machine Learning*, *577*, 41–64. DOI: 10.1007/978-3-031-78412-5_3

Mohsin, A., Janicke, H., Nepal, S., & Holmes, D. (2023). Digital Twins and the Future of their Use Enabling Shift Left and Shift Right Cybersecurity Operations. arXiv preprint arXiv:2309.13612. DOI: 10.1109/TPS-ISA58951.2023.00042

Molnar, C. (2020). *Interpretable machine learning*. Lulu. com.

Montavon, G., Binder, A., Lapuschkin, S., Samek, W., & Müller, K.-R. (2019). Layer-wise relevance propagation: an overview. *Explainable AI: interpreting, explaining and visualizing deep learning*, 193-209.

Mourad, A., Tout, H., Wahab, O. A., Otrok, H., & Dbouk, T. (2021). *Ad Hoc* Vehicular Fog Enabling Cooperative Low-Latency Intrusion Detection. *IEEE Internet of Things Journal*, *8*(2), 829–843. DOI: 10.1109/JIOT.2020.3008488

Moustafa, N., & Slay, J. (n.d.). *UNSW-NB15: A Comprehensive Data set for Network Intrusion Detection systems (UNSW-NB15 Network Data Set)*. https://cve.mitre.org/

Moustafa, N., Keshk, M., Debie, E., & Janicke, H. (n.d.). *Federated TON IoT Windows Datasets for Evaluating AI-based Security Applications*. https://doi.org/DOI: 10.1109/TrustCom50675.2020.00114/20/$31.00

MP, P. J. (2024). An Explainable and Optimized Network Intrusion Detection Model using Deep Learning. *International Journal of Advanced Computer Science and Applications*, *15*(1).

Mridha, K., Kumbhani, S., Pandey, A. P., & Damodharan, P. "Automatically Detect the coronavirus (COVID-19) disease using Chest X-ray and CT images," 2021 IEEE 6th International Conference on Computing, Communication and Automation (ICCCA), Arad, Romania, 2021, pp. 150-156, DOI: 10.1109/ICCCA52192.2021.9666304

Mugariri, P., Abdullah, H., Garcia-Torres, M., Parameshchari, B., & Abdul Sattar, K. N. (2022). Promoting information privacy protection awareness for internet of things (IoT). *Mobile Information Systems*, *2022*(1), 4247651. DOI: 10.1155/2022/4247651

Mukherjee, B., Heberlein, L. T., & Levitt, K. N. (1994). Network intrusion detection. *IEEE Network*, *8*(3), 26–41. DOI: 10.1109/65.283931

Mutaz Wahed, M. S.-B. (2024). Comprehensive Assessment of Cybersecurity Measures: Evaluating Incident Response, AI Integration, and Emerging Threats. 1-8. DOI: 10.1109/NETAPPS63333.2024.10823603

Nabavirazavi, S., Taheri, R., & Iyengar, S. S. (2024). Enhancing federated learning robustness through randomization and mixture. *Future Generation Computer Systems*, *158*, 28–43. DOI: 10.1016/j.future.2024.04.009

Najim, A. H., Al-sharhanee, K. A. M., Al-Joboury, I. M., Kanellopoulos, D., Sharma, V. K., Hassan, M. Y., Issa, W., Abbas, F. H., & Abbas, A. H. (2025). An IoT healthcare system with deep learning functionality for patient monitoring. *International Journal of Communication Systems*, *38*(4), e6020. DOI: 10.1002/dac.6020

Nakano, M., Takahashi, A., & Takahashi, S. (2017). Fuzzy logic-based portfolio selection with particle filtering and anomaly detection. *Knowledge-Based Systems*, *131*, 113–124. DOI: 10.1016/j.knosys.2017.06.006

Nargesi, A. A., Adejumo, P., Dhingra, L. S., Rosand, B., Hengartner, A., Coppi, A., Benigeri, S., Sen, S., Ahmad, T., Nadkarni, G. N., Lin, Z., Ahmad, F. S., Krumholz, H. M., & Khera, R. (2025). Automated identification of heart failure with reduced ejection fraction using deep learning-based natural language processing. *Heart Failure, 13*(1), 75–87. DOI: 10.1016/j.jchf.2024.08.012 PMID: 39453355

Nascita, A., Aceto, G., Ciuonzo, D., Montieri, A., Persico, V., & Pescapé, A. (2024). A Survey on Explainable Artificial Intelligence for Internet Traffic Classification and Prediction, and Intrusion Detection. *IEEE Communications Surveys and Tutorials*, 1. DOI: 10.1109/COMST.2024.3504955

Nascita, A., Montieri, A., Aceto, G., Ciuonzo, D., Persico, V., & Pescapé, A. (2021). XAI meets mobile traffic classification: Understanding and improving multimodal deep learning architectures. *IEEE Transactions on Network and Service Management, 18*(4), 4225–4246. DOI: 10.1109/TNSM.2021.3098157

Nasr, M., Shokri, R., & Houmansadr, A. (2019). Comprehensive privacy analysis of deep learning: Passive and active white-box inference attacks against centralized and federated learning. *IEEE Symposium on Security and Privacy (SP)*. DOI: 10.1109/SP.2019.00065

Navani, D., Jain, S., & Nehra, M. S. (2017). The internet of things (IoT): A study of architectural elements. *Proceedings - 13th International Conference on Signal-Image Technology and Internet-Based Systems, SITIS 2017, 2018-January*, 473–478. DOI: 10.1109/SITIS.2017.83

Neupane, S., Ables, J., Anderson, W., Mittal, S., Rahimi, S., Banicescu, I., & Seale, M. (2022). Explainable intrusion detection systems (x-ids): A survey of current methods, challenges, and opportunities. *IEEE Access : Practical Innovations, Open Solutions, 10*, 112392–112415. DOI: 10.1109/ACCESS.2022.3216617

Ngo, A. T., Luqman, A., Jonathan, C. C. M., & Chattopadhyay, A. (2024). A Systematic Approach Toward Robust Perception in (Semi-) Autonomous Vehicles. *Computer, 57*(11), 41–48. DOI: 10.1109/MC.2024.3448220

Ngoupayou Limbepe, Z., Gai, K., & Yu, J. (2025). Blockchain-Based Privacy-Enhancing Federated Learning in Smart Healthcare: A Survey. *Blockchains, 3*(1), 1. DOI: 10.3390/blockchains3010001

Nguyen, D. C., Ding, M., Pham, Q. V., Pathirana, P. N., Le, L. B., Seneviratne, A., Li, J., Niyato, D., & Poor, H. V. (2021). Federated learning meets blockchain in edge computing: Opportunities and challenges. *IEEE Internet of Things Journal, 8*(16), 12806–12825. DOI: 10.1109/JIOT.2021.3072611

Nguyen, G., Sáinz-Pardo Díaz, J., Calatrava, A., Berberi, L., Lytvyn, O., Kozlov, V., Tran, V., Moltó, G., & López García, Á. (2024). Landscape of machine learning evolution: Privacy-preserving federated learning frameworks and tools. *Artificial Intelligence Review, 58*(2), 51. DOI: 10.1007/s10462-024-11036-2

Nguyen, V. T., & Beuran, R. (n.d.). *FedMSE: Semi-supervised federated learning approach for IoT network intrusion detection.* https://ssrn.com/abstract=4990105 DOI: 10.1016/j.cose.2025.104337

Nishio, T., & Yonetani, R. (2019). *Client selection for federated learning with heterogeneous resources in mobile edge.* IEEE ICC. DOI: 10.1109/ICC.2019.8761315

Northcutt, S., Cooper, M., Fearnow, M., & Frederick, K. (2001). *Intrusion Signatures and Analysis.* New Riders.

OECD. (2019). OECD principles on artificial intelligence. In Paris, O. E. C. D. (Ed.).

Oh, M., & Iyengar, G. (2019). Sequential Anomaly Detection using Inverse Reinforcement Learning. *Proceedings of the 25th ACM SIGKDD International Conference on Knowledge Discovery & Data Mining*, 1480–1490. DOI: 10.1145/3292500.3330932

Ojeda, F., Mendez, D., Fajardo, A., & Ellinger, F. (2023). On wireless sensor network models: A cross-layer systematic review. *Journal of Sensor and Actuator Networks, 12*(4), 50. DOI: 10.3390/jsan12040050

Ojo, B., & Aghaunor, C. T. (2024). AI-driven cybersecurity solutions for real-time threat detection in critical infrastructure. *International Journal of Science and Research Archive, 12*(02), 1716–1726. DOI: 10.30574/ijsra.2024.12.2.1401

Okoli, U. I., Obi, O. C., Adewusi, A. O., & Abrahams, T. O. (2024). Machine learning in cybersecurity: A review of threat detection and defense mechanisms. *World Journal of Advanced Research and Reviews, 21*(1), 2286–2295. DOI: 10.30574/wjarr.2024.21.1.0315

Oksuz, A. C., Halimi, A., & Ayday, E. (2024). AUTOLYCUS: Exploiting Explainable Artificial Intelligence (XAI) for Model Extraction Attacks against Interpretable Models. *Proceedings on Privacy Enhancing Technologies.*

Oloyede, J. (2024). AI-Driven Cybersecurity Solutions: Enhancing Defense Mechanisms in the Digital Era. *Available atSSRN* 4976103. DOI: 10.2139/ssrn.4976103

Olutimehin, A. T., Ajayi, A. J., Metibemu, O. C., Balogun, A. Y., Oladoyinbo, T. O., & Olaniyi, O. O. (2025). Adversarial threats to AI-driven systems: Exploring the attack surface of machine learning models and countermeasures. *Available atSSRN* 5137026.

Oniani, D., Hilsman, J., & Peng, Y. COL, Poropatich, R. K., Pamplin, C. J. C., Legault, L. G. L., & Wang, Y. (2023). From Military to Healthcare: Adopting and Expanding Ethical Principles for Generative Artificial Intelligence. In arXiv (Cornell University). Cornell University. https://doi.org/DOI: 10.48550/arXiv.2308

Otoum, Y., Liu, D., & Nayak, A. (2022). DL-IDS: A deep learning–based intrusion detection framework for securing IoT. *Transactions on Emerging Telecommunications Technologies*, *33*(3), e3803. Advance online publication. DOI: 10.1002/ett.3803

Oye, E., & Owen, A. (2024). Adversarial Attacks and Defenses in Machine Learning.

Ozay, M., Vural, F. T. Y., Tappert, C., & Moghadam, P. (2016). Machine learning attack and defense strategies in power grid state estimation. *IEEE Transactions on Neural Networks and Learning Systems*.

Oztoprak, A., Hassanpour, R., Ozkan, A., & Oztoprak, K. (2024). Security challenges, mitigation strategies, and future trends in wireless sensor networks: A review. *ACM Computing Surveys*, *57*(4), 1–29. DOI: 10.1145/3706583

Pacheco, J., Benitez, V., & Félix, L. (2019). Anomaly Behavior Analysis for IoT Network Nodes. *Proceedings of the 3rd International Conference on Future Networks and Distributed Systems*, 1–6. DOI: 10.1145/3341325.3342008

Padilla-Vega, R., Sanchez-Rivero, C., & Ojeda-Castro, A. (2023). Navigating the business landscape: Challenges and opportunities of implementing artificial intelligence in cybersecurity governance. *Issues in Information Systems*, *24*(4).

Pan, J.-S., Fan, F., Chu, S.-C., Zhao, H.-Q., & Liu, G.-Y. (2021). A Lightweight Intelligent Intrusion Detection Model for Wireless Sensor Networks. *Security and Communication Networks*, *2021*, 1–15. DOI: 10.1155/2021/5540895

Papadopoulos, P., Thornewill von Essen, O., Pitropakis, N., Chrysoulas, C., Mylonas, A., & Buchanan, W. J. (2021). Launching Adversarial Attacks against Network Intrusion Detection Systems for IoT. *Journal of Cybersecurity and Privacy*, *1*(2), 252–273. DOI: 10.3390/jcp1020014

Papernot, N., McDaniel, P., & Goodfellow, I. (2016). Transferability in machine learning: from phenomena to black-box attacks using adversarial samples. *arXiv preprint* arXiv:1605.07277.

Papernot, N., McDaniel, P., Jha, S., Fredrikson, M., Celik, Z. B., & Swami, A. (2016). *The limitations of deep learning in adversarial settings.* 2016 IEEE European Symposium on Security and Privacy (EuroS&P). DOI: 10.1109/EuroSP.2016.36

Papernot, N., McDaniel, P., Sinha, A., & Wellman, M. P. (2018). Sok: Security and privacy in machine learning. 2018 IEEE European symposium on security and privacy (EuroS&P).

Papernot, N., McDaniel, P., Wu, X., Jha, S., & Swami, A. (2016). Distillation as a defence to adversarial perturbations against deep neural networks. In *2016 IEEE symposium on security and privacy (SP)* (pp. 582-597). IEEE.

Papernot, N., McDaniel, P., Wu, X., Jha, S., & Swami, A. (2016). Distillation as a defense to adversarial perturbations against deep neural networks. In *2016 IEEE symposium on security and privacy (SP)* (pp. 582-597). IEEE. DOI: 10.1109/SP.2016.41

Papernot, N., McDaniel, P., Goodfellow, I., Jha, S., Celik, Z. B., & Swami, A. (2017). Practical black-box attacks against machine learning. In *Proceedings of the 2017 ACM on Asia conference on computer and communications security* (pp. 506-519).

Papernot, N., McDaniel, P., Sinha, A., & Wellman, M. (2018). SoK: Security and privacy in machine learning. In *IEEE European Symposium on Security and Privacy* (pp. 399-414). IEEE. DOI: 10.1109/EuroSP.2018.00035

Paracha, A., Arshad, J., Farah, M. B., & Ismail, K. (2024). Machine learning security and privacy: A review of threats and countermeasures. *EURASIP Journal on Information Security, 2024*(1), 10. DOI: 10.1186/s13635-024-00158-3

Paredes, J. N., Teze, J. C. L., Simari, G. I., & Martinez, M. V. (2021). On the importance of domain-specific explanations in AI-based cybersecurity systems (technical report). arXiv preprint arXiv:2108.02006.

Parihar, A., Prajapati, J. B., Prajapati, B. G., Trambadiya, B., Thakkar, A., & Engineer, P. (2024). Role of IOT in healthcare: Applications, security & privacy concerns.

Parra-Sánchez, D. T. (2024). Exploring the Internet of Things adoption in the Fourth Industrial Revolution: a comprehensive scientometric analysis. *Journal of Innovative Digital Transformation.*

Patel, C. D., Aggarwal, M., & Chaubey, N. K. (2025). Enhancing Cyber-Physical Systems Security Through Advanced Defense Mechanisms. In *Advancing Cyber Security Through Quantum Cryptography* (pp. 307–342). IGI Global.

Pathmabandu, C., Grundy, J., Chhetri, M. B., & Baig, Z. (2023). Privacy for IoT: Informed consent management in Smart Buildings. *Future Generation Computer Systems, 145*, 367–383. DOI: 10.1016/j.future.2023.03.045

Patrick Jungwirth, T. B.-H. (2017). Rootkits and the OS friendly microprocessor architecture. *10185*, 1018503. DOI: 10.1117/12.2258235

Pawlicki, M., Pawlicka, A., Kozik, R., & Choraś, M. (2024). The survey on the dual nature of xAI challenges in intrusion detection and their potential for AI innovation. *Artificial Intelligence Review*, *57*(12), 1–32. DOI: 10.1007/s10462-024-10972-3

Pendey, B. (2023). Artificial Intelligence And Cyber Security. *Journal transnational universal studies, 1*(2), 93 - 99. DOI: 10.58631/jtus.v1i2.15

Peng, L., Ru-chuan, W., Xiao-yu, S., & Long, C. (2013). *Privacy Protection Based on Key-changed Mutual Authentication Protocol in Internet of Things*. Paper presented at the China Conference Wireless Sensor Networks.

Perrig, A., Stankovic, J., & Wagner, D. (2004). Security in wireless sensor networks. *Communications of the ACM*, *47*(6), 53–57. DOI: 10.1145/990680.990707

Petihakis, G., Farao, A., Bountakas, P., Sabazioti, A., Polley, J., & Xenakis, C. (2024, July). AIAS: AI-ASsisted cybersecurity platform to defend against adversarial AI attacks. In *Proceedings of the 19th International Conference on Availability, Reliability and Security* (pp. 1-7). DOI: 10.1145/3664476.3669920

Phong, L. T., Aono, Y., Hayashi, T., Wang, L., & Moriai, S. (2018). Privacy-preserving deep learning via additively homomorphic encryption. *IEEE Transactions on Information Forensics and Security*, *13*(5), 1333–1345. DOI: 10.1109/TIFS.2017.2787987

Pinto Neto, E. C., Sadeghi, S., Zhang, X., & Dadkhah, S. (2023). Federated reinforcement learning in IoT: Applications, opportunities and open challenges. *Applied Sciences (Basel, Switzerland)*, *13*(11), 6497. DOI: 10.3390/app13116497

Polemi, N., Praça, I., Kioskli, K., & Bécue, A. (2024). Challenges and efforts in managing AI trustworthiness risks: A state of knowledge. *Frontiers in Big Data*, *7*, 1381163. DOI: 10.3389/fdata.2024.1381163 PMID: 38798307

Popescu, G. H., Zvarikova, K., Machova, V., & Mihai, E. A. (2020). Industrial big data, automated production systems, and Internet of Things sensing networks in cyber-physical system-based manufacturing. *Journal of Self-Governance and Management Economics*, *8*(3), 30–36.

Prabavathy, S., Sundarakantham, K., & Shalinie, S. M. (2018). Design of cognitive fog computing for intrusion detection in Internet of Things. *Journal of Communications and Networks (Seoul)*, *20*(3), 291–298. DOI: 10.1109/JCN.2018.000041

Prasad, T. S. L., Manikandan, K. B., & Vinoj, J. (2024, December). Shielding NLP Systems: An In-depth Survey on Advanced AI Techniques for Adversarial Attack Detection in Cyber Security. In *2024 3rd International Conference on Automation, Computing and Renewable Systems (ICACRS)* (pp. 1059-1067). IEEE.

Priya, T. S., Sridevi, R., & Rao, K. S. (2024). Lightweight encryption techniques: Types, challenges and security issues. In *Computational Methods in Science and Technology* (pp. 266–273). CRC Press. DOI: 10.1201/9781003501244-41

Qi, J., Zhou, Q., Lei, L., & Zheng, K. (2021). Federated reinforcement learning: Techniques, applications, and open challenges. *arXiv preprint arXiv:2108.11887.*

Qian, Z., Huang, K., Wang, Q. F., & Zhang, X. Y. (2022). A survey of robust adversarial training in pattern recognition: Fundamental, theory, and methodologies. *Pattern Recognition*, *131*, 108889. DOI: 10.1016/j.patcog.2022.108889

Qi, P., Chiaro, D., Guzzo, A., Ianni, M., Fortino, G., & Piccialli, F. (2024). Model aggregation techniques in federated learning: A comprehensive survey. *Future Generation Computer Systems*, *150*, 272–293. DOI: 10.1016/j.future.2023.09.008

Queyrut, S., Schiavoni, V., & Felber, P. (2023, July). Mitigating adversarial attacks in federated learning with trusted execution environments. In *2023 IEEE 43rd International Conference on Distributed Computing Systems (ICDCS)* (pp. 626-637). IEEE. DOI: 10.1109/ICDCS57875.2023.00069

Qu, Y., Uddin, M. P., Gan, C., Xiang, Y., Gao, L., & Yearwood, J. (2022). Blockchain-enabled federated learning: A survey. *ACM Computing Surveys*, *55*(4), 1–35. DOI: 10.1145/3524104

Radford, A., Metz, L., & Chintala, S. (2015). Unsupervised representation learning with deep convolutional generative adversarial networks. *arXiv preprint* arXiv:1511.06434.

Rahman, A., Debnath, T., Kundu, D., Khan, M. S. I., Aishi, A. A., Sazzad, S., Sayduzzaman, M., & Band, S. S. (2024). Machine learning and deep learning-based approach in smart healthcare: Recent advances, applications, challenges and opportunities. *AIMS Public Health*, *11*(1), 58–109. DOI: 10.3934/publichealth.2024004 PMID: 38617415

Rahman, S. A., Tout, H., Talhi, C., & Mourad, A. (2020, November/December). Internet of things intrusion detection: Centralized, on-device, or federated learning. *IEEE Network*, *34*(6), 310–317. DOI: 10.1109/MNET.011.2000286

Rahman, S., Pal, S., Jadidi, Z., & Karmakar, C. (2024). Robust Cyber Threat Intelligence Sharing Using Federated Learning for Smart Grids. *IEEE Transactions on Computational Social Systems*.

Rai, A. (2020). Explainable AI: From black box to glass box. *Journal of the Academy of Marketing Science*, *48*(1), 137–141. DOI: 10.1007/s11747-019-00710-5

Raja, A., Njilla, L., & Yuan, J. (2022). Adversarial attacks and defenses toward ai-assisted uav infrastructure inspection. *IEEE Internet of Things Journal, 9*(23), 23379–23389. DOI: 10.1109/JIOT.2022.3206276

Ramesh, A., Patel, R., & Singh, P. (2020). Hidden adversarial triggers in reinforcement learning-based robotic control. *Proceedings of the International Conference on Intelligent Robots and Systems (IROS).*

Ramos, J. H., & Skármeta, A. (2020). *Security and privacy in the internet of things: Challenges and solutions* (Vol. 27). IOS Press.

Rangaraju, S., Ness, S., & Dharmalingam, R. (2023). Incorporating AI-Driven Strategies in DevSecOps for Robust Cloud Security. *International Journal of Innovative Science and Research Technology, 8*(23592365), 10–5281.

Rani, S., Kataria, A., Kumar, S., & Tiwari, P. (2023). Federated learning for secure IoMT-applications in smart healthcare systems: A comprehensive review. *Knowledge-Based Systems, 274*, 110658. DOI: 10.1016/j.knosys.2023.110658

Rastogi, N., Dhanuka, D., Saxena, A., Mairal, P., & Nguyen, L. (2025). Survey Perspective: The Role of Explainable AI in Threat Intelligence. *arXiv preprint arXiv:2503.02065.*

Rathore, S., & Park, J. H. (2018). Semi-supervised learning based distributed attack detection framework for IoT. *Applied Soft Computing, 72*, 79–89. DOI: 10.1016/j.asoc.2018.05.049

Rath, S., Das, T., & Sengupta, S. (2024). Improvise, adapt, overcome: Dynamic resiliency against unknown attack vectors in microgrid cybersecurity games. *IEEE Transactions on Smart Grid, 15*(4), 4245–4258. DOI: 10.1109/TSG.2024.3372643

Ratinder Kaur, M. S. (2014). *Automatic Evaluation and Signature Generation Technique for Thwarting Zero-Day Attacks.* Springer., DOI: 10.1007/978-3-642-54525-2_27

Ravi, N., & Shalinie, S. M. (2020). Semisupervised-Learning-Based Security to Detect and Mitigate Intrusions in IoT Network. *IEEE Internet of Things Journal, 7*(11), 11041–11052. DOI: 10.1109/JIOT.2020.2993410

Raza, S. A., Syed, D., Rizwan, S., & Ahmed, M. (2025). Quantum Computing and Its Implications for Financial Markets. In *The Global Evolution, Changing Landscape and Future of Financial Markets: From Traditional to Digital* (pp. 119-131). Emerald Publishing Limited. DOI: 10.1108/978-1-83549-330-420251010

Rebentrost, P., Mohseni, M., & Lloyd, S. (2014). Quantum support vector machine for big data classification. *Physical Review Letters, 113*(13), 130503. DOI: 10.1103/PhysRevLett.113.130503 PMID: 25302877

Ren, H., Huang, T., & Yan, H. (2021). Adversarial examples: Attacks and defenses in the physical world. *International Journal of Machine Learning and Cybernetics, 12*(11), 3325–3336. DOI: 10.1007/s13042-020-01242-z

Ren, S., Dai, H., Wu, X., Zhang, L., & Yu, P. S. (2020). TextBugger: Generating adversarial text against real-world applications. *26th Network and Distributed System Security Symposium (NDSS).*

Ribeiro, M. T., Singh, S., & Guestrin, C. (2016). " Why should i trust you?" Explaining the predictions of any classifier. *Proceedings of the 22nd ACM SIGKDD international conference on knowledge discovery and data mining* DOI: 10.18653/v1/N16-3020

Ribouh, S., & Hadid, A. (2024, April). Is Semantic Communication for Autonomous Driving Secured against Adversarial Attacks? In 2024 IEEE 6th International Conference on AI Circuits and Systems (AICAS) (pp. 139-143). IEEE.

Rigaki, M., & Garcia, S. (2023). A survey of privacy attacks in machine learning. *ACM Computing Surveys, 56*(4), 1–34. DOI: 10.1145/3624010

Rjoub, G., Bentahar, J., Wahab, O. A., Mizouni, R., Song, A., Cohen, R., Otrok, H., & Mourad, A. (2023). A survey on explainable artificial intelligence for cybersecurity. *IEEE Transactions on Network and Service Management, 20*(4), 5115–5140. DOI: 10.1109/TNSM.2023.3282740

Rodríguez, E., Valls, P., Otero, B., Costa, J. J., Verdú, J., Pajuelo, M. A., & Canal, R. (2022). Transfer-Learning-Based Intrusion Detection Framework in IoT Networks. *Sensors (Basel), 22*(15), 5621. DOI: 10.3390/s22155621 PMID: 35957178

Roopak, M., Tian, G. Y., & Chambers, J. (2020). An Intrusion Detection System Against DDoS Attacks in IoT Networks. *2020 10th Annual Computing and Communication Workshop and Conference (CCWC)*, 0562–0567. DOI: 10.1109/CCWC47524.2020.9031206

Rossolini, G.. (2023). On the real-world adversarial robustness of real-time semantic segmentation models for autonomous driving. *IEEE Transactions on Neural Networks and Learning Systems*. PMID: 37782588

Ruan, W., Yi, X., & Huang, X. (2021). Adversarial Robustness of Deep Learning: Theory, Algorithms, and Applications. In arXiv (Cornell University). Cornell University. https://doi.org/DOI: 10.48550/arXiv.2108

Rudin, C. (2019). Stop explaining black box machine learning models for high stakes decisions and use interpretable models instead. *Nature Machine Intelligence*, *1*(5), 206–215. DOI: 10.1038/s42256-019-0048-x PMID: 35603010

Saadeh, H., Saadeh, M., Almobaideen, W., & Al-Tawil, M. (2022). Evaluating the Optimal Number of Clusters to Identify Similar Gene Expression Patterns During Erythropoiesis. *2022 International Conference on Computer, Information and Telecommunication Systems (CITS)*, 1–5. DOI: 10.1109/CITS55221.2022.9832988

Sabini, M., & Rusak, G. (2018). Painting outside the box: Image outpainting with GANs. *arXiv preprint* arXiv:1808.08483.

Sadeghi, S., Soltanmohammadlou, N., & Nasirzadeh, F. (2022). Applications of wireless sensor networks to improve occupational safety and health in underground mines. *Journal of Safety Research*, *83*, 8–25. DOI: 10.1016/j.jsr.2022.07.016 PMID: 36481040

Sahana, N. S., Palaniappan, N. D., Bobade, N. S. D., & Rafi, N. S. M. (2022). Deep Learning ensemble model for the prediction of traffic accidents using social media data. *Journal of Pharmaceutical Negative Results*, •••, 485–495. DOI: 10.47750/pnr.2022.13.S09.055

Sahar, N., Mishra, R., & Kalam, S. (2021). *Deep Learning Approach-Based Network Intrusion Detection System for Fog-Assisted IoT.*, DOI: 10.1007/978-981-15-8377-3_4

Said, A., Yahyaoui, A., & Abdellatif, T. (2023, November). HIPAA and GDPR compliance in IoT healthcare systems. In *International conference on model and data engineering* (pp. 198-209). Cham: Springer Nature Switzerland.

Sajeed Mohammad, F. F. (2024). FortBoot. *Fortifying Rooted-in-Device-Specific Security Through Secure Booting.*, *1-4*, 1–4. Advance online publication. DOI: 10.1109/VLSI-SoC62099.2024.10767821

Salehi, S. A., Razzaque, M. A., Naraei, P., & Farrokhtala, A. (2013, July). Security in wireless sensor networks: Issues and challanges. In *2013 IEEE International Conference on Space Science and Communication (IconSpace)* (pp. 356-360). IEEE. DOI: 10.1109/IconSpace.2013.6599495

Salem, A. H., Azzam, S. M., Emam, O., & Abohany, A. A. (2024). Advancing cybersecurity: A comprehensive review of AI-driven detection techniques. *Journal of Big Data*, *11*(1), 105. DOI: 10.1186/s40537-024-00957-y

Salimans, T., Goodfellow, I., Zaremba, W., Cheung, V., Radford, A., & Chen, X. (2016). Improved techniques for training GANs. *Advances in Neural Information Processing Systems*, •••, 29.

Samek, W., Wiegand, T., & Müller, K. (2019). Explainable artificial intelligence: Understanding, visualizing, and interpreting deep learning models. *IEEE Signal Processing Magazine*, *36*(4), 20–28.

Samuel, A. L. (1959). Some studies in machine learning using the game of checkers. *IBM Journal of Research and Development*, *3*(3), 210–229. DOI: 10.1147/rd.33.0210

Sandhu, R., Sohal, A. S., & Sood, S. K. (2017). Identification of malicious edge devices in fog computing environments. *Information Security Journal: A Global Perspective, 26*(5), 213–228. DOI: 10.1080/19393555.2017.1334843

Sangaiah, A. K., Wang, X., Obaidat, M. S., & Patrick, C. K. (2024). Huang, and Kannan Govindan. "Guest Editorial Data-Driven Innovation and Adversarial Learning Models for Industry 5.0 Toward Consumer Digital Ecosystems.". *IEEE Transactions on Consumer Electronics*, *70*(2), 4878–4881. DOI: 10.1109/TCE.2024.3383608

Sankaram, M., Roopesh, M., Rasetti, S., & Nishat, N. (2024). A Comprehensive review of artificial intelligence applications in enhancing cybersecurity threat detection and response mechanisms. *Management*, *3*(5).

Saqib, M., Mahdavifar, S., Fung, B. C., & Charland, P. (2024). A Comprehensive Analysis of Explainable AI for Malware Hunting. *ACM Computing Surveys*, *56*(12), 1–40. DOI: 10.1145/3677374

Sarker, I. H. (2021). Machine Learning: Algorithms, Real-World Applications and Research Directions. *SN Computer Science*, *2*(3), 160. DOI: 10.1007/s42979-021-00592-x PMID: 33778771

Sayın, A. Anomaly detection scenarios in cyber-physical systems.

Schmidhuber, J. (1991). A possibility for implementing curiosity and boredom in model-building neural controllers. In *Proc. of the international conference on simulation of adaptive behavior: From animals to animats* (pp. 222-227). DOI: 10.7551/mitpress/3115.003.0030

Schneider, J., & Breitinger, F. (2023). Towards AI forensics: Did the artificial intelligence system do it? *Journal of Information Security and Applications*, *76*, 103517. DOI: 10.1016/j.jisa.2023.103517

Shahbazian, R. (2023). Enhancing IoT Security through Standardization: A Review. *Advances in the Standards & Applied Sciences, 1*(4).

Shah, S. M., & Lau, V. K. (2021). Model compression for communication efficient federated learning. *IEEE Transactions on Neural Networks and Learning Systems*, *34*(9), 5937–5951. DOI: 10.1109/TNNLS.2021.3131614 PMID: 34936557

Shamoo, Y. (2025). Adversarial Attacks and Defense Mechanisms in the Age of Quantum Computing. In *Leveraging Large Language Models for Quantum-Aware Cybersecurity* (pp. 301–344). IGI Global Scientific Publishing. DOI: 10.4018/979-8-3373-1102-9.ch010

Shandilya, S. K., Datta, A., Kartik, Y., & Nagar, A. (2024). Advancing security and resilience. In *Digital Resilience: Navigating Disruption and Safeguarding Data Privacy* (pp. 459–529). Springer Nature Switzerland. DOI: 10.1007/978-3-031-53290-0_8

Shan, Y., Yao, Y., Zhou, X., Zhao, T., Hu, B., & Wang, L. (2024). CFL-IDS: An Effective Clustered Federated Learning Framework for Industrial Internet of Things Intrusion Detection. *IEEE Internet of Things Journal, 11*(6), 10007–10019. DOI: 10.1109/JIOT.2023.3324302

Sharafaldin, I., Lashkari, A. H., & Ghorbani, A. A. (2018). Toward generating a new intrusion detection dataset and intrusion traffic characterization. *ICISSP 2018 - Proceedings of the 4th International Conference on Information Systems Security and Privacy, 2018-January*, 108–116. DOI: 10.5220/0006639801080116

Sharif, M., Bhagavatula, S., Bauer, L., & Reiter, M. K. (2016). Accessorize to a crime: Real and stealthy attacks on state-of-the-art face recognition. *Proceedings of the 2016 ACM SIGSAC Conference on Computer and Communications Security*. DOI: 10.1145/2976749.2978392

Sharjeel, M., Ahmed Sumra, I., Sattar, A., & Arshad, M. (n.d.). *A Comprehensive Analysis on Privacy and Security for IoT Solutions*. https://doi.org/DOI: 10.56979/801/2024

Sharma, S. (2019). *Data privacy and GDPR handbook*. John Wiley & Sons. DOI: 10.1002/9781119594307

Sharma, S., & Kaur, A. (2021, July). Survey on wireless sensor network, its applications and issues. [). IOP Publishing.]. *Journal of Physics: Conference Series, 1969*(1), 012042. DOI: 10.1088/1742-6596/1969/1/012042

Sharma, V., Kumar, A., & Sharma, K. (2024). Digital twin: Securing IoT networks using integrated ECC with blockchain for healthcare ecosystem. *Knowledge and Information Systems*, •••, 1–32.

Sharma, V., You, I., Andersson, K., Palmieri, F., Rehmani, M. H., & Lim, J. (2020). Security, privacy and trust for smart mobile-Internet of Things (M-IoT): A survey. *IEEE Access : Practical Innovations, Open Solutions*, *8*, 167123–167163. DOI: 10.1109/ACCESS.2020.3022661

Sharmila, K., Kumar, P., Bhushan, S., Kumar, M., & Alazab, M. (2023). Secure key management and mutual authentication protocol for wireless sensor network by linking edge devices using hybrid approach. *Wireless Personal Communications, 130*(4), 2935–2957. DOI: 10.1007/s11277-023-10410-7

Sheikh, Z. A., Singh, Y., Singh, P. K., & Gonçalves, P. J. S. (2023). Defending the defender: Adversarial learning based defending strategy for learning based security methods in cyber-physical systems (cps). *Sensors (Basel), 23*(12), 5459. DOI: 10.3390/s23125459 PMID: 37420626

Shenvi, N., & Virani, H. (2023). Comparative Analysis of Machine learning techniques for Forecasting Ionospheric Total Electron Content Data. *2023 4th International Conference for Emerging Technology (INCET)*, 1–6. DOI: 10.1109/INCET57972.2023.10169972

Shinde, S. A., Pawar, R. R., Jagtap, A. A., Tambewagh, P. A., Rajput, P. U., Mali, M. K., Kale, S. D., & Mulik, S. V. (2023). Deceptive opinion spam detection using bidirectional long short-term memory with capsule neural network. *Multimedia Tools and Applications, 83*(15), 45111–45140. DOI: 10.1007/s11042-023-17348-9

Shitharth, S., Kshirsagar, P. R., Balachandran, P. K., Alyoubi, K. H., & Khadidos, A. O. (2022). An Innovative Perceptual Pigeon Galvanized Optimization (PPGO) Based Likelihood Naïve Bayes (LNB) Classification Approach for Network Intrusion Detection System. *IEEE Access : Practical Innovations, Open Solutions, 10*, 46424–46441. DOI: 10.1109/ACCESS.2022.3171660

Shokri, R., Stronati, M., Song, C., & Shmatikov, V. (2017). Membership inference attacks against machine learning models. In *2017 IEEE symposium on security and privacy (SP)* (pp. 3-18). IEEE. DOI: 10.1109/SP.2017.41

Shoniwa, M., Veerabudren, K., & Sharma, M. (2024, October). AI-based Malware Threat Prediction through CNN-SVM Ensemble. In *2024 International Conference on Next Generation Computing Applications (NextComp)* (pp. 1-6). IEEE.

Shrivastava, A., Kumar, V., & Maurya, J. P. (2024, December). Cutting-Edge Image Recognition Leveraging Deep Learning and Machine Learning for Enhanced Accuracy. In *2024 International Conference on Artificial Intelligence and Quantum Computation-Based Sensor Application (ICAIQSA)* (pp. 1-6). IEEE.

Shukla, A. (2022). Leveraging AI and ML for Advance Cyber Security. DOI: 10.47363/JAICC/2022(1)142

Sicari, S., Rizzardi, A., Coen-Porisini, A., & Cappiello, C. (2014). *A NFP model for internet of things applications.* Paper presented at the 2014 IEEE 10th International Conference on Wireless and Mobile Computing, Networking and Communications (WiMob). DOI: 10.1109/WiMOB.2014.6962181

Sicari, S., Cappiello, C., De Pellegrini, F., Miorandi, D., & Coen-Porisini, A. (2014). A security-and quality-aware system architecture for Internet of Things. *Information Systems Frontiers*, •••, 1–13.

Sicari, S., Rizzardi, A., Grieco, L. A., & Coen-Porisini, A. (2015). Security, privacy and trust in Internet of Things: The road ahead. *Computer Networks*, *76*, 146–164. DOI: 10.1016/j.comnet.2014.11.008

Siddharthan, H., Deepa, T., & Chandhar, P. (2022). SENMQTT-SET: An Intelligent Intrusion Detection in IoT-MQTT Networks Using Ensemble Multi Cascade Features. *IEEE Access : Practical Innovations, Open Solutions*, *10*, 33095–33110. DOI: 10.1109/ACCESS.2022.3161566

Silva, J. D. C., Rodrigues, J. J. P. C., Saleem, K., Kozlov, S. A., & Rabelo, R. A. L. (2019). M4DN.IoT-A Networks and Devices Management Platform for Internet of Things. *IEEE Access : Practical Innovations, Open Solutions*, *7*, 53305–53313. DOI: 10.1109/ACCESS.2019.2909436

Simonyan, K., Vedaldi, A., & Zisserman, A. (2013). Deep inside convolutional networks: Visualising image classification models and saliency maps. *arXiv preprint arXiv:1312.6034*.

Sindiramutty, S. R., Tan, C. E., Lau, S. P., Thangaveloo, R., Gharib, A. H., Manchuri, A. R., Khan, N. A., Tee, W. J., & Muniandy, L. (2024). Explainable AI for cybersecurity. In *Advances in Explainable AI Applications for Smart Cities* (pp. 31–97). IGI Global Scientific Publishing. DOI: 10.4018/978-1-6684-6361-1.ch002

Singh, R., Kathuria, K., & Sagar, A. K. (2018, December). Secure routing protocols for wireless sensor networks. In 2018 4th international conference on computing communication and automation (ICCCA) (pp. 1-5). IEEE. DOI: 10.1109/CCAA.2018.8777557

Singh, V. P., Dwarakanath, V. T., Haribabu, P., & Babu, N. S. C. (2017). *IoT standardization efforts—An analysis.* Paper presented at the 2017 International Conference On Smart Technologies For Smart Nation (SmartTechCon). DOI: 10.1109/SmartTechCon.2017.8358536

Sivajothi, E., Diana, S. M. C., Rekha, M., Lincy, R. B., Damodharan, P., & J, J. R. (2024). A future prediction for cyber-attacks in the network domain with the visualisation of patterns in cyber-security tickets with machine learning. In International Journal of Electronic Security and Digital Forensics (Vol. 16, Issue 5, p. 648). Inderscience Publishers. DOI: 10.1504/IJESDF.2024.140758

Slack, D., Hilgard, S., Jia, E., Singh, S., & Lakkaraju, H. (2020). Fooling lime and shap: Adversarial attacks on post hoc explanation methods. Proceedings of the AAAI/ACM Conference on AI, Ethics, and Society

Smith, V., Chiang, C.-K., Sanjabi, M., & Talwalkar, A. (2017). Federated Multi-Task Learning. Advances in Neural Information Processing Systems (NeurIPS)

Sohal, A. S., Sandhu, R., Sood, S. K., & Chang, V. (2018). A cybersecurity framework to identify malicious edge device in fog computing and cloud-of-things environments. *Computers & Security*, *74*, 340–354. DOI: 10.1016/j.cose.2017.08.016

Sohn, I. (2021). Deep belief network based intrusion detection techniques: A survey. *Expert Systems with Applications*, *167*, 114170. DOI: 10.1016/j.eswa.2020.114170

So, J., Ali, R. E., Güler, B., Jiao, J., & Avestimehr, A. S. (2023, June). Securing secure aggregation: Mitigating multi-round privacy leakage in federated learning. *Proceedings of the AAAI Conference on Artificial Intelligence*, *37*(8), 9864–9873. DOI: 10.1609/aaai.v37i8.26177

Sollins, K. R. (2019). IoT big data security and privacy versus innovation. *IEEE Internet of Things Journal*, *6*(2), 1628–1635. DOI: 10.1109/JIOT.2019.2898113

Sommer, R., & Paxson, V. (2010). *Outside the closed world: On using machine learning for network intrusion detection. In 2010 IEEE symposium on security and privacy*. IEEE.

Sreevidya, B., & Supriya, M. (2024). Trust based routing–A novel approach for data security in WSN based data critical applications. *Journal of Wireless Mobile Networks, Ubiquitous Computing and Dependable Applications*, *15*(1), 27–41. DOI: 10.58346/JOWUA.2024.I1.003

Srivastava, G., Jhaveri, R. H., Bhattacharya, S., Pandya, S., Maddikunta, P. K. R., Yenduri, G., Hall, J. G., Alazab, M., & Gadekallu, T. R. (2022). XAI for cybersecurity: state of the art, challenges, open issues and future directions. *arXiv preprint arXiv:2206.03585.*

Staab, R., Jovanović, N., Balunović, M., & Vechev, M. (2024). *From principle to practice: Vertical data minimization for machine learning*. Paper presented at the 2024 IEEE Symposium on Security and Privacy (SP). DOI: 10.1109/SP54263.2024.00089

Stefano Righi, N. K. (2007). Retrieved from https://patents.google.com/patent/US8352721B1/en

Steingartner, W., Galinec, D., & Kozina, A. (2021). Threat defense: Cyber deception approach and education for resilience in hybrid threats model. *Symmetry*, *13*(4), 597. DOI: 10.3390/sym13040597

Stergiou, C. L., Bompoli, E., & Psannis, K. E. (2023). Security and privacy issues in IoT-based big data cloud systems in a digital twin scenario. *Applied Sciences (Basel, Switzerland)*, *13*(2), 758. DOI: 10.3390/app13020758

Stergiou, C., Psannis, K. E., Kim, B.-G., & Gupta, B. (2018). Secure integration of IoT and cloud computing. *Future Generation Computer Systems*, *78*, 964–975. DOI: 10.1016/j.future.2016.11.031

Subramanian, R. (2023). Have the cake and eat it too: Differential Privacy enables privacy and precise analytics. *Journal of Big Data*, *10*(1), 117. DOI: 10.1186/s40537-023-00712-9

Sucasas, V., Mantas, G., Bastos, J., Damião, F., & Rodriguez, J. (2019). A signature scheme with unlinkable-yet-accountable pseudonymity for privacy-preserving crowdsensing. *IEEE Transactions on Mobile Computing*, *19*(4), 752–768. DOI: 10.1109/TMC.2019.2901463

Sudqi Khater, B., Abdul Wahab, A. W., Idris, M. Y. I. B., Abdulla Hussain, M., & Ahmed Ibrahim, A. (2019). A Lightweight Perceptron-Based Intrusion Detection System for Fog Computing. *Applied Sciences (Basel, Switzerland)*, *9*(1), 178. DOI: 10.3390/app9010178

Suhaimi, A. F., Yaakob, N., Saad, S. A., Sidek, K. A., Elshaikh, M. E., Dafhalla, A. K., Lynn, O. B., & Almashor, M. (2021, July). IoT based smart agriculture monitoring, automation and intrusion detection system. [). IOP Publishing.]. *Journal of Physics: Conference Series*, *1962*(1), 012016. DOI: 10.1088/1742-6596/1962/1/012016

Suhas Shivanna, S. B. (2014). Retrieved from https://www.freepatentsonline.com/y2017/0315798.html

Su, J., Cao, D., Zhao, B., Wang, X., & You, I. (2014). ePASS: An expressive attribute-based signature scheme with privacy and an unforgeability guarantee for the Internet of Things. *Future Generation Computer Systems*, *33*, 11–18. DOI: 10.1016/j.future.2013.10.016

Sun, J., Kairouz, P., Suresh, A. T., McMahan, B., & Talwar, K. (2021). Can you really backdoor federated learning? *Advances in Neural Information Processing Systems (NeurIPS)*.

Su, P., Yan, Y., Li, H., Wu, H., Liu, C., & Huang, W. (2025). Images and deep learning in human and urban infrastructure interactions pertinent to sustainable urban studies: Review and perspective. *International Journal of Applied Earth Observation and Geoinformation*, *136*, 104352. DOI: 10.1016/j.jag.2024.104352

Surendar, M., & Umamakeswari, A. (2016). InDReS: An Intrusion Detection and response system for Internet of Things with 6LoWPAN. *2016 International Conference on Wireless Communications, Signal Processing and Networking (WiSPNET)*, 1903–1908. DOI: 10.1109/WiSPNET.2016.7566473

Swapno, S. M. M. R., Nobel, S. N., Meena, P., Meena, V. P., Azar, A. T., Haider, Z., & Tounsi, M. (2024). A reinforcement learning approach for reducing traffic congestion using deep Q learning. *Scientific Reports*, *14*(1), 30452. DOI: 10.1038/s41598-024-75638-0 PMID: 39668197

Swetha Priya, T. C., & Sridevi, R. (2023, March). Protecting the Privacy of IoMT-Based Health Records Using Blockchain Technology. In International Conference on Network Security and Blockchain Technology (pp. 409-423). Singapore: Springer Nature Singapore.

Swetha Priya, T. C., & Kanaka Durga, A. (2020). Clustering-based blockchain technique for securing wireless sensor networks. In *Data Engineering and Communication Technology: Proceedings of 3rd ICDECT-2K19* (pp. 461–471). Springer Nature Singapore. DOI: 10.1007/978-981-15-1097-7_39

Syed, A. S., Sierra-Sosa, D., Kumar, A., & Elmaghraby, A. (2021). IoT in Smart Cities: A Survey of Technologies, Practices and Challenges. *Smart Cities*, *4*(2), 429–475. DOI: 10.3390/smartcities4020024

Syed, N. F., Ge, M., & Baig, Z. (2023). Fog-cloud based intrusion detection system using Recurrent Neural Networks and feature selection for IoT networks. *Computer Networks*, *225*, 109662. DOI: 10.1016/j.comnet.2023.109662

Szczepaniuk, H., & Szczepaniuk, E. K. (2022). Standardization of IoT ecosystems: Open challenges, current solutions, and future directions [CRC Press.]. *Internet of Things : Engineering Cyber Physical Human Systems*, •••, 23–42.

Szegedy, C., Zaremba, W., Sutskever, I., Bruna, J., Erhan, D., Goodfellow, I., & Fergus, R. (2013). Intriguing properties of neural networks. *arXiv preprint arXiv*:1312.6199.

Tabassi, E. (2023). Artificial intelligence risk management framework (AI RMF 1.0).

Tabassum, A., Erbad, A., Mohamed, A., & Guizani, M. (2021). Privacy-Preserving Distributed IDS Using Incremental Learning for IoT Health Systems. *IEEE Access : Practical Innovations, Open Solutions*, *9*, 14271–14283. DOI: 10.1109/ACCESS.2021.3051530

Tanveer, M., Rajani, T., Rastogi, R., Shao, Y. H., & Ganaie, M. A. (2022). Comprehensive review on twin support vector machines. *Annals of Operations Research*, •••, 1–46.

Tarade, R., & Das, S. (2025). Cybersecurity in the Age of Al-Enhancing Defences for Today's Threats. *Critical Phishing Defense Strategies and Digital Asset Protection*, 309.

Tawalbeh, L., Muheidat, F., Tawalbeh, M., & Quwaider, M. (2020). IoT Privacy and security: Challenges and solutions. *Applied Sciences (Basel, Switzerland)*, *10*(12), 4102. DOI: 10.3390/app10124102

Telikani, A., Shen, J., Yang, J., & Wang, P. (2022). Industrial IoT Intrusion Detection via Evolutionary Cost-Sensitive Learning and Fog Computing. *IEEE Internet of Things Journal*, *9*(22), 23260–23271. DOI: 10.1109/JIOT.2022.3188224

Tesauro, G. (1992). Practical Issues in Temporal Difference Learning. *Machine Learning*, *8*(3-4), 257–277. DOI: 10.1007/BF00992697

Teymourzadeh, M., Vahed, R., Alibeygi, S., & Dastanpour, N. (2020). Security in wireless sensor networks: Issues and challenges. arXiv preprint arXiv:2007.05111.

Thanh-Tung, H., Tran, T., & Venkatesh, S. (2019). Improving generalization and stability of generative adversarial networks. *arXiv preprint* arXiv:1902.03984.

Tian, Y., Wang, S., Xiong, J., Bi, R., Zhou, Z., & Md, Z. A. B. (2024). Robust and Privacy-Preserving Decentralized Deep Federated Learning Training: Focusing on Digital Healthcare Applications. IEEE/ACM TRANSACTIONS ON COMPUTATIONAL BIOLOGY AND BIOINFORMATICS, VOL. 21, NO. 4, JULY/AUGUST 2024.

Tiwari, V., Rajasekar, D., & Wang, J. (2024, October). A Survey: Emerging Cybersecurity Threats in Driverless Cars. In 2024 IEEE 15th Annual Ubiquitous Computing, Electronics & Mobile Communication Conference (UEMCON) (pp. 183-189). IEEE.

Toutouh, J., Hemberg, E., & O'Reilly, U. M. (2019). Spatial evolutionary generative adversarial networks. In *Proceedings of the genetic and evolutionary computation conference* (pp. 472-480). DOI: 10.1145/3321707.3321860

Tramèr, F., Kurakin, A., Papernot, N., Goodfellow, I., Boneh, D., & McDaniel, P. (2017). Ensemble adversarial training: Attacks and defenses. *arXiv preprint* arXiv:1705.07204.

Tramèr, F., Zhang, F., Juels, A., Reiter, M. K., & Kocher, P. (2016). *Stealing machine learning models via prediction apis.*

Tripathi, H., & Pandey, D. C. K. (2024). *Enhancing Security Against Adversarial Attacks Using Robust Machine Learning. International Journal of Advanced Engineering and Nano Technology.* IJAENT.

TrustCloud. (2025). *Data Privacy in the Age of IoT: Securing Connected Devices.* Retrieved from TrustCloud.

Tsai, C. W., Lai, C. F., & Vasilakos, A. V. (2014). Future Internet of Things: Open issues and challenges. *Wireless Networks*, *20*(8), 2201–2217. DOI: 10.1007/s11276-014-0731-0

UCSC. (2023). *Privacy by Design: The 7 Foundational Principles.* Retrieved from UCSC.

Ukil, A., Bandyopadhyay, S., & Pal, A. (2014). *Iot-privacy: To be private or not to be private.* Paper presented at the Computer Communications Workshops (INFOCOM WKSHPS), 2014 IEEE Conference on. DOI: 10.1109/INFCOMW.2014.6849186

Ullah, I., & Mahmoud, Q. H. (2022). Design and Development of RNN Anomaly Detection Model for IoT Networks. *IEEE Access : Practical Innovations, Open Solutions*, *10*, 62722–62750. DOI: 10.1109/ACCESS.2022.3176317

Ullah, I., Raza, B., Ali, S., Abbasi, I. A., Baseer, S., & Irshad, A. (2021). Software Defined Network Enabled Fog-to-Things Hybrid Deep Learning Driven Cyber Threat Detection System. *Security and Communication Networks*, *2021*, 1–15. DOI: 10.1155/2021/6136670

Uprety, A., & Rawat, D. B. (2021). Reinforcement Learning for IoT Security: A Comprehensive Survey. *IEEE Internet of Things Journal*, *8*(11), 8693–8706. DOI: 10.1109/JIOT.2020.3040957

Vadillo, J., Santana, R., & Lozano, J. A. (2025). Adversarial attacks in explainable machine learning: A survey of threats against models and humans. *Wiley Interdisciplinary Reviews. Data Mining and Knowledge Discovery*, *15*(1), e1567. DOI: 10.1002/widm.1567

Vasilomanolakis, E., Daubert, J., Luthra, M., Gazis, V., Wiesmaier, A., & Kikiras, P. (2015). *On the security and privacy of Internet of Things architectures and systems.* Paper presented at the 2015 International Workshop on Secure Internet of Things (SIoT). DOI: 10.1109/SIOT.2015.9

Vegesna, V.V., (2023). Comprehensive Analysis of AI-Enhanced Defense Systems in Cyberspace. International Numeric Journal of Machine Learning and Robots, 7(7).

Vegesna, V.V., (2023). Enhancing Cyber Resilience by Integrating AI-Driven Threat Detection and Mitigation Strategies. Transactions on Latest Trends in Artificial Intelligence, 4(4).

Venkata Subbaiah Desanamukula, M. P. (2023). A Comprehensive Analysis of Machine Learning and Deep Learning Approaches towards IoT Security. *2023 4th international conference on Electronics and Sustainable Communication Systems (ICESC), Coimbatore, India, 2023* (pp. 1165 - 1168). IEEE. DOI: 10.1109/ICESC57686.2023.10193209

Venugopal, H., & Christo, M. S. (2024, August). Strengthening Healthcare Cybersecurity by Optimizing Adversarial Attack Defences in Deep Learning Models using GPU and Parallel Processing Technologies. In *2024 7th International Conference on Circuit Power and Computing Technologies (ICCPCT)* (Vol. 1, pp. 1266-1272). IEEE. DOI: 10.1109/ICCPCT61902.2024.10672871

veria Hoseini, S., Suutala, J., Partala, J., & Halunen, K. (2024). Threat modeling AI/ML with the Attack Tree. IEEE Access.

Verma, S., Dickerson, J., & Hines, K. (2020). Counterfactual explanations for machine learning: A review. *arXiv preprint arXiv:2010.10596, 2*(1), 1.

Virat, M. S., Bindu, S. M., Aishwarya, B., Dhanush, B. N., & Kounte, M. R. (2018, May). Security and privacy challenges in internet of things. In 2018 2nd International Conference on Trends in Electronics and Informatics (ICOEI) (pp. 454-460). IEEE.

Virupakshar, K. B., Asundi, M., Channal, K., Shettar, P., Patil, S., & Narayan, D. G. (2020). Distributed denial of service (DDoS) attacks detection system for OpenStack-based private cloud. *Procedia Computer Science*, *167*, 2297–2307. DOI: 10.1016/j.procs.2020.03.282

Viswan, V., Shaffi, N., Mahmud, M., Subramanian, K., & Hajamohideen, F. (2024). Explainable artificial intelligence in Alzheimer's disease classification: A systematic review. *Cognitive Computation*, *16*(1), 1–44. DOI: 10.1007/s12559-023-10192-x

Voigt, P., & Von dem Bussche, A. (2017). *The EU General Data Protection Regulation (GDPR): A Practical Guide*. Springer. DOI: 10.1007/978-3-319-57959-7

Vorobeychik, Y. (2023). The Many Faces of Adversarial Machine Learning. *Proceedings of the ...AAAI Conference on Artificial Intelligence, 37*(13), 15402 - 15409. DOI: 10.1609/aaai.v37i13.26796

Wachter, S., Mittelstadt, B., & Floridi, L. (2017a). Transparent, explainable, and accountable AI for robotics. *Science Robotics, 2*(6), eaan6080. DOI: 10.1126/scirobotics.aan6080 PMID: 33157874

Wachter, S., Mittelstadt, B., & Floridi, L. (2017b). Why a Right to Explanation of Automated Decision-Making Does Not Exist in the General Data Protection Regulation. *International Data Privacy Law, 7*(2), 76–99. DOI: 10.1093/idpl/ipx005

Wallace, E., Feng, S., Kandpal, N., Gardner, M., & Singh, S. (2020). *Universal adversarial triggers for attacking and analyzing NLP models.* Empirical Methods in Natural Language Processing (EMNLP).

Wang, H., Kaplan, Z., Niu, D., & Li, B. (2020, July). Optimizing federated learning on non-iid data with reinforcement learning. In *IEEE INFOCOM 2020-IEEE Conference on computer communications* (pp. 1698-1707). IEEE. DOI: 10.1109/INFOCOM41043.2020.9155494

Wang, J., Guo, S., Xie, X., & Qi, H. (2022, May). Protect privacy from gradient leakage attack in federated learning. In *IEEE INFOCOM 2022-IEEE Conference on Computer Communications* (pp. 580-589). IEEE. DOI: 10.1109/INFOCOM48880.2022.9796841

Wang, T., Bi, Z., Zhang, Y., Liu, M., Hsieh, W., Feng, P., . . . Liu, J. (2024). Deep Learning Model Security: Threats and Defenses. *arXiv preprint arXiv:2412.08969.*

Wang, W., Yang, Y., & Wu, F. (2022). Towards data-and knowledge-driven artificial intelligence: A survey on neuro-symbolic computing. *arXiv preprint arXiv:2210.15889.*

Wang, J., Wang, S., & Zhang, Y. (2025). Deep learning on medical image analysis. *CAAI Transactions on Intelligence Technology, 10*(1), 1–35. DOI: 10.1049/cit2.12356

Wang, T., Zheng, Z., & Lin, F. (2025). Federated learning framework based on trimmed mean aggregation rules. *Expert Systems with Applications, 270*, 126354. DOI: 10.1016/j.eswa.2024.126354

Wang, Y., Meng, W., Li, W., Li, J., Liu, W.-X., & Xiang, Y. (2018). A fog-based privacy-preserving approach for distributed signature-based intrusion detection. *Journal of Parallel and Distributed Computing, 122*, 26–35. DOI: 10.1016/j.jpdc.2018.07.013

Wang, Y., Zhang, Y., & Wang, X. (2022). Adversarial machine learning in blockchain security. *IEEE Transactions on Information Forensics and Security.*

Wan, Y., Qu, Y., Ni, W., Xiang, Y., Gao, L., & Hossain, E. (2024). Data and model poisoning backdoor attacks on wireless federated learning, and the defense mechanisms: A comprehensive survey. *IEEE Communications Surveys and Tutorials, 26*(3), 1861–1897. DOI: 10.1109/COMST.2024.3361451

Weber, R. H. (2010). Internet of Things—New security and privacy challenges. *Computer Law & Security Review, 26*(1), 23–30. DOI: 10.1016/j.clsr.2009.11.008

Wei, H., Tang, H., Jia, X., Wang, Z., Yu, H., Li, Z., Satoh, S., Van Gool, L., & Wang, Z. (2024). Physical adversarial attack meets computer vision: A decade survey. *IEEE Transactions on Pattern Analysis and Machine Intelligence, 46*(12), 9797–9817. DOI: 10.1109/TPAMI.2024.3430860 PMID: 39024087

Wei, K., Li, J., Ding, M., Ma, C., Su, H., Zhang, B., & Poor, H. (2022, September). User-Level Privacy-Preserving Federated Learning: Analysis and Performance Optimization. *IEEE Transactions on Mobile Computing, 21*(09), 3388–3401. DOI: 10.1109/TMC.2021.3056991

Wen, J., Zhang, Z., Lan, Y., Cui, Z., Cai, J., & Zhang, W. (2023). A survey on federated learning: Challenges and applications. *International Journal of Machine Learning and Cybernetics, 14*(2), 513–535. DOI: 10.1007/s13042-022-01647-y PMID: 36407495

Wiatrak, M., Albrecht, S. V., & Nystrom, A. (2019). Stabilizing generative adversarial networks: A survey. *arXiv preprint* arXiv:1910.00927.

Wilson, A. C., Roelofs, R., Stern, M., Srebro, N., & Recht, B. (2017). The marginal value of adaptive gradient methods in machine learning. *Advances in Neural Information Processing Systems*, •••, 30.

Wink, T., & Nochta, Z. (2021, June). An approach for peer-to-peer federated learning. In *2021 51st Annual IEEE/IFIP International Conference on Dependable Systems and Networks Workshops (DSN-W)* (pp. 150-157). IEEE. DOI: 10.1109/DSN-W52860.2021.00034

Wong, E., & Kolter, J. Z. (2018). Provable defences against adversarial examples via the convex outer adversarial polytope. In *International conference on machine learning* (pp. 5286-5295). PMLR.

Wu, Z., Zheng, L., Yu, Y., Qiu, R., Birge, J., & He, J. (2024). Fair Anomaly Detection For Imbalanced Groups. *arXiv preprint arXiv:2409.10951.*

Wu, M., Lu, T. J., Ling, F. Y., Sun, J., & Du, H. Y. (2010). Research on the architecture of Internet of Things. *3rd International Conference on Advanced Computer Theory and Engineering (ICACTE).*

Wu, X., Wu, Z., Li, H., & Chen, P. (2020). Backdoor defense in federated learning with poisoned data detection and model filtering. *IEEE Access : Practical Innovations, Open Solutions.*

Xie, J., Wang, Y., & He, X. (2021). Adversarial machine learning in smart grid: Attacks and countermeasures. *IEEE Transactions on Smart Grid.*

Xin, Y., Kong, L., Liu, Z., Chen, Y., Li, Y., Zhu, H., Gao, M., Hou, H., & Wang, C. (2018). Machine Learning and Deep Learning Methods for Cybersecurity. *IEEE Access : Practical Innovations, Open Solutions*, *6*, 35365–35381. DOI: 10.1109/ACCESS.2018.2836950

Xu, R., Baracaldo, N., & Joshi, J. (2021). Privacy-preserving machine learning: Methods, challenges and directions. *arXiv preprint arXiv:2108.04417.*

Xu, H., Yan, Z., Ji, B., Huang, P., Cheng, J., & Wu, X. (2021). Defect detection in welding radiographic images based on semantic segmentation methods. In *Measurement* (Vol. 188, p. 110569). Elsevier BV., DOI: 10.1016/j.measurement.2021.110569

Xu, J., Wang, Y., Chen, H., & Shen, Z. (2025). Adversarial Machine Learning in Cybersecurity: Attacks and Defenses. *International Journal of Management Science Research*, *8*(2), 26–33.

Xu, Y., T. L. (2018). A Search-based Firmware Code Analysis Method for IoT Devices. *Communications and Networking Symposium*, 1-2. DOI: 10.1109/CNS.2018.8433163

Yang, C.-H., Maina, B. M., Cheng, S.-M., & Lee, H.-M. (2024). An Adversarial Attack on Artificial Intelligence Malware Detection in Consumer Internet of Things. *IEEE Consumer Electronics Magazine.*

Yang, G. (2022). An overview of current solutions for privacy in the Internet of Things. *Frontiers in Artificial Intelligence*, *5*, 812732. DOI: 10.3389/frai.2022.812732 PMID: 35310954

Yang, L., Zhang, Z., Song, Y., Hong, S., Xu, R., Zhao, Y., Zhang, W., Cui, B., & Yang, M. H. (2023). Diffusion models: A comprehensive survey of methods and applications. *ACM Computing Surveys*, *56*(4), 1–39. DOI: 10.1145/3626235

Yang, Q., Liu, Y., Chen, T., & Tong, Y. (2019). Federated machine learning: Concept and applications. [TIST]. *ACM Transactions on Intelligent Systems and Technology*, *10*(2), 1–19. DOI: 10.1145/3298981

Yang, X., Peng, G., Zhang, D., & Lv, Y. (2022). An Enhanced Intrusion Detection System for IoT Networks Based on Deep Learning and Knowledge Graph. *Security and Communication Networks*, *2022*, 1–21. DOI: 10.1155/2022/3317048

Yang, X., Shu, L., Liu, Y., Hancke, G. P., Ferrag, M. A., & Huang, K. (2022). Physical Security and Safety of IoT Equipment: A Survey of Recent Advances and Opportunities. *IEEE Transactions on Industrial Informatics*, *18*(7), 4319–4330. DOI: 10.1109/TII.2022.3141408

Yang, Y., Zheng, X., Guo, W., Liu, X., & Chang, V. (2019). Privacy-preserving smart IoT-based healthcare big data storage and self-adaptive access control system. *Information Sciences*, *479*, 567–592. DOI: 10.1016/j.ins.2018.02.005

Yazdinejad, A., Dehghantanha, A., Karimipour, H., Srivastava, G., & Parizi, R. M. (2024). A robust privacy-preserving federated learning model against model poisoning attacks. *IEEE Transactions on Information Forensics and Security*, *19*, 6693–6708. DOI: 10.1109/TIFS.2024.3420126

Yogi, M. K. (2023). 09 01). A Comprehensive Study of Zero-Day Attacks. *Journal of Information Technology and Digital World*, *5*(3), 253–273. DOI: 10.36548/jitdw.2023.3.003

Yuan, C., & Yang, H. (2019). Research on K-Value Selection Method of K-Means Clustering Algorithm. *J*, *2*(2), 226–235. DOI: 10.3390/j2020016

Zafar, U., Teixeira, A., & Toor, S. (2025). Robust Federated Learning Against Poisoning Attacks: A GAN-Based Defense Framework. *arXiv preprint arXiv:2503.20884*.

Zarpelão, B. B., Miani, R. S., Kawakani, C. T., & de Alvarenga, S. C. (2017). A survey of intrusion detection in Internet of Things. *Journal of Network and Computer Applications*, *84*, 25–37. DOI: 10.1016/j.jnca.2017.02.009

Zeadally, S., Adi, E., Baig, Z., & Khan, I. A. (2020). Harnessing artificial intelligence capabilities to improve cybersecurity. *IEEE Access : Practical Innovations, Open Solutions*, *8*, 23817–23837. DOI: 10.1109/ACCESS.2020.2968045

Zhang, T., Wang, J., & Meng, M. Q. H. (2021). Generative adversarial network-based heuristics for sampling-based path planning. *IEEE/CAA Journal of Automatica Sinica*, 9(1), 64-74.

Zhang, Z. (2024). Reinforcement Learning-Based Approaches for Enhancing Security and Resilience in Smart Control: A Survey on Attack and Defense Methods. *arXiv preprint arXiv:2402.15617*.

Zhang, C., Hu, M., Li, W., & Wang, L. (2024). Adversarial attacks and defenses on text-to-image diffusion models: A survey. *Information Fusion*, •••, 102701.

Zhang, C., Xie, Y., Bai, H., Yu, B., Li, W., & Gao, Y. (2021). A survey on federated learning. *Knowledge-Based Systems, 216*, 106775. DOI: 10.1016/j.knosys.2021.106775 PMID: 34909232

Zhang, H., Yu, Y., Jiao, J., Xing, E., El Ghaoui, L., & Jordan, M. (2019). Theoretically principled trade-off between robustness and accuracy. In *International conference on machine learning* (pp. 7472-7482). PMLR.

Zhang, J., Li, C., Ye, J., & Qu, G. (2020, September). Privacy threats and protection in machine learning. In *Proceedings of the 2020 on Great Lakes Symposium on VLSI* (pp. 531-536). DOI: 10.1145/3386263.3407599

Zhang, J., Zhu, H., Wang, F., Zhao, J., Xu, Q., & Li, H. (2022). Security and privacy threats to federated learning: Issues, methods, and challenges. *Security and Communication Networks, 2022*(1), 2886795. DOI: 10.1155/2022/2886795

Zhang, X., Xu, L., & Ma, H. (2021). Adversarial perturbations in robotic perception systems. *IEEE Robotics and Automation Letters*.

Zhang, Z., Al Hamadi, H., Damiani, E., Yeun, C. Y., & Taher, F. (2022). Explainable artificial intelligence applications in cyber security: State-of-the-art in research. *IEEE Access : Practical Innovations, Open Solutions, 10*, 93104–93139. DOI: 10.1109/ACCESS.2022.3204051

Zhang, Z., Ning, H., Shi, F., Farha, F., Xu, Y., Xu, J., Zhang, F., & Choo, K. K. R. (2022). Artificial intelligence in cyber security: Research advances, challenges, and opportunities. *Artificial Intelligence Review, 55*(2), 1–25. DOI: 10.1007/s10462-021-09976-0

Zhao, Y., Li, M., Lai, L., Suda, N., Civin, D., & Chandra, V. (2018). Federated learning with non-iid data. *arXiv preprint arXiv:1806.00582*.

Zhao, P., Shan, J. W., Zhang, Y. J., & Zhou, Z. H. (2024). Exploratory machine learning with unknown unknowns. *Artificial Intelligence, 327*, 104059. DOI: 10.1016/j.artint.2023.104059

Zheng, H., Paiva, A. R., & Gurciullo, C. S. (2020). Advancing from predictive maintenance to intelligent maintenance with AI and IIoT. *arXiv preprint arXiv:2009.00351*.

Zhong, Z., Bao, W., Wang, J., Zhu, X., & Zhang, X. (2022). Flee: A hierarchical federated learning framework for distributed deep neural network over cloud, edge, and end device. [TIST]. *ACM Transactions on Intelligent Systems and Technology, 13*(5), 1–24. DOI: 10.1145/3514501

Zhou, I., Tofigh, F., Piccardi, M., Abolhasan, M., Franklin, D., & Lipman, J. (2024). Secure multi-party computation for machine learning: A survey. *IEEE Access : Practical Innovations, Open Solutions, 12*, 53881–53899. DOI: 10.1109/ACCESS.2024.3388992

Zhou, S., Liu, C., Ye, D., Zhu, T., Zhou, W., & Yu, P. S. (2022). Adversarial attacks and defenses in deep learning: From a perspective of cybersecurity. *ACM Computing Surveys, 55*(8), 1–39. DOI: 10.1145/3547330

Zhou, W., Jia, Y., Peng, A., Zhang, Y., & Liu, P. (2018). The effect of IoT new features on security and privacy: New threats, existing solutions, and challenges yet to be solved. *IEEE Internet of Things Journal, 6*(2), 1606–1616. DOI: 10.1109/JIOT.2018.2847733

Zhu, L., Liu, Z., & Han, S. (2019). Deep leakage from gradients. *Advances in Neural Information Processing Systems (NeurIPS).*

Ziller, A., Schneider, J. J., & Makarov, I. (2021). Explainability in Federated Learning. *Survey (London, England).* arXiv2103.09650

Zolanvari, M., Teixeira, M. A., Gupta, L., Khan, K. M., & Jain, R. (2019). Machine Learning-Based Network Vulnerability Analysis of Industrial Internet of Things. *IEEE Internet of Things Journal, 6*(4), 6822–6834. DOI: 10.1109/JIOT.2019.2912022

Zou, J., Zhang, S., & Qiu, M. (2024, July). Different Attack and Defense Types for AI Cybersecurity. In *International Conference on Knowledge Science, Engineering and Management* (pp. 179-192). Singapore: Springer Nature Singapore. DOI: 10.1007/978-981-97-5498-4_14

Zügner, D., Akbarnejad, A., & Günnemann, S. (2018). Adversarial attacks on neural networks for graph data. *Proceedings of the 24th ACM SIGKDD International Conference on Knowledge Discovery & Data Mining*. DOI: 10.1145/3219819.3220078

About the Contributors

Shafiq Ul Rehman is an experienced educator and professional consultant with a background in curriculum development and educational technology. With over 10 years in the field, Dr. Shafiq has worked with various educational institutions to implement sustainable practices and innovative teaching strategies. Dr. Shafiq received his Ph.D. degree from Universiti Sains Malaysia (USM), Malaysia, in 2017. He was a Postdoctoral Research Fellow at Singapore University of Technology and Design (SUTD), Singapore, from 2017 to 2020. He is currently Acting Dean, College of Information Technology and Chairman Department of Computer Science, Kingdom University, Bahrain. He is also an Assistant Professor with research interests in cybersecurity, artificial intelligence, and the latest emerging IT technologies. He lectures in various Computer Science and IT courses, including developing curriculum and courseware in tandem with current technology trends. He has authored and coauthored more than 50 peer reviewed publications, published in journals, conference proceedings, and book chapters. He supervises Ph.D., postgraduate, and undergraduate students. He also gives talks and training on cybersecurity, artificial intelligence, and the latest emerging IT technologies at various organizations, conferences, seminars, and workshops.

Hanan Aldowah is currently a senior lecturer at Universiti Sains Malaysia (USM), where she has earned both a Ph.D. and a Master's degree in Instructional Technology and Multimedia. Aldowah possesses a comprehensive educational background. This is further enriched by a Bachelor's in computer science, offering a versatile skill set honed through practical experience and academic achievements.. Her extensive expertise spans diverse domains, including Business Analytics, Data Mining, Machine Learning, Artificial Intelligence, Internet of Things, Engineering Pedagogical Research, Cognitive Maps, VR & Augmented Reality, and Instructional Technology. Aldowah holds a keen interest in online learning, E-learning, educational technology, and the application of emerging technologies such as AI, IoT, ML, and sentiment analysis to enhance various sectors, including management, education, computer education, engineering education. Driven by a commitment to contribute to experiential education research and develop robust evaluation strategies. Aldowah's impactful research operates at the intersection of Computer Science and educational technology.

Bulent Gursel Emiroğlu is working at Kırıkkale University, Engineering and Natural Sciences Faculty, Computer Engineering Department as an Associate Professor. During his 25 years academic career, He contributed to the fields of Artificial Intelligence, Machine Learning, Deep Learning, Cyber Security, Software Engineering, Medical Informatics, Financial Technologies, Human Computer Interaction, Educational Technology and Instructional Systems. He is giving Software Engineering, Web / Internet Technologies, Computer Networks, Wireless Networks, Object Oriented Programming, Programming Languages courses at both Undergraduate and Graduate Levels.

Rituraj Jain is currently working in the Department of Information Technology, Marwadi University, Rajkot, GUjarat, India. He has published many papers in International Journals and Conferences. He has published 4 books. He is an Oracle Database SQL Certified Expert. He is also associated with professional bodies like the Indian Society of Technical Education (ISTE), Computer Science Teachers Association (CSTA), Academy & Industry Research Collaboration Center (AIRCC), International Association of Computer Science and Information Technology (IACSIT), International Association of Engineers (IAENG). His research interests include Cloud Computing, Machine Learning, Deep Learning, Fuzzy Logic, IoT, Genetic Algorithms, Big Data and Software Engineering.

L.M.I. Leo Joseph is working as an Associate Dean (School of Engineering) at SR University, Warangal, Telangana. He received his PhD in VLSI from Sathyabama Institute of Science and Technology, Chennai. His area of research is on deep learning neural networks.He has published several patents and Journals in Image processing, Artificial Neural Networks. He had hosted several International and National level FDP on online education. He is the winner of a global entrepreneurship competition by the Jack M. Wilson Center for Entrepreneurship, USA. He has rich experience in digital circuit design using VHDL, TinkerCAD. MATLAB, SCILAB are additions to his expertise. He has 23 years of teaching experience along with, different academic and administrative positions

G.Kirubasri is working as an Assistant Professor in the Department of Computer Science and Engineering at Sona College of Technology. I completed PhD in Information and Communication Engineering, Anna University at 2019.

She has received her M.E-CSE from Anna University, Trichy, with a Gold Medal at 2010 and B.E-CSE from Bharathidasan University, Trichy at 2001. She has published about 20 research articles and participated in various National and International conferences. She is a Red Hat Certified System Administrator. Her research interest includes Wireless Senor Networks, Network Security, Internet of Things and Machine Learning, Deep Learning

Manasa Koppula received her MTech in Embedded Systems from Megha Institute of Engineering in 2014 and Technology for Women, Hyderabad and BTech in Electronics and Communication Engineering from Balaji Institute of Engineering and Sciences, Warangal in 2012. She is currently pursuing her PhD at SR University. Her current research interests include Internet of Things and Cyber Security.

Nasim Nezhadsistani received the BS. and MSc degrees in electrical engineering in 2014 and 2017, respectively, and is currently pursuing the PhD degree in electrical engineering at the Isfahan University of Technology, Isfahan, Iran. Since 2022, she has been a Research Assistant with the Communication Systems Group CSG at the University of Zürich UZH. Her research interests include blockchain technologies, distributed systems, machine learning, network security, and privacy-preserving mechanisms in peer-to-peer systems.

Damodharan Palaniappan works as an Associate Professor & Head in the Department of Information Technology, Marwadi University, Rajkot, Gujarat. He completed his Ph.D. at Anna University, Chennai, M.E. in Computer Science and Engineering at C.I.E.T, Coimbatore and B.E. in Computer Science and Engineering at CSI College of Engineering, Ketty, Nilgiri. He has 19 years' experience of teaching and research. Currently, he guides 6 Ph.D. research scholars. He has authored 8 book chapters, and he has published research papers in reputed journals. His interested areas of research are Data Mining, Image Processing, Software, Machine Learning and Deep Learning.

Sohail Ahmed Shahani serves as a Universiti Teknologi PETRONAS (UTP) in Malaysia. His doctoral research, culminating in a PhD in Chemical Engineering with a focus on pharmaceuticals and life sciences, has equipped him with strong skills in computational simulations and modeling. His current work applies these techniques to challenges within the food and pharmaceutical industries. His specific areas of expertise include the development of drug delivery formulations, assessment of biodegradability and cytotoxicity, and the analysis of solubility and stability. Dr. Shahani's research makes significant contributions to the field of biochemical engineering.

Elizaveta Sokolova Specialist in the Department of Scientometry, R&D and Ratings, lecturer at the Department of Business Informatics, consultant to the Student Scientific Society of the Ural State University of Economics, Yekaterinburg, Russia. Research interests include bibliometrics, scientometrics, general issues of management of technical activities, and information technology.

R Sridevi is a Professor of CSE with 23 years of teaching experience. Presently working as Professor, Director, Directorate of Entrepreneurship, Innovation and Start-ups, JNTUH & Coordinator for Centre of Excellence in Cyber Security, JNTUH. She has lead various roles as Head of the CSE Department for nearly 3 years, Additional Controller of Examinations(EDEP), Additional Controller of Examinations(Result Processing). Worked as Chairman, Board of Studies for Department of CSE, JNTUHUCEH, Hyderabad. She has organized several Workshops, FDPs, curricular and extra-curricular events and 3 international conferences. Established three Research Labs: IoT Lab, Digital Forensics Lab & Big Data Analytics Lab and one smart classroom under TEQIP in the department. She guided 7 Ph. Ds & published several research papers in various national and international conferences and reputed journals with high indexing factor.

Burkhard Stiller received his Dipl.-Inform. (MSc) degree in Computer Science and PhD degree from the University of Karlsruhe, Germany, in 1990 and 1994, respectively. Since 2004 he chairs the Communication Systems Group CSG, Department of Informatics IfI, University of Zürich UZH, Switzerland as a Full Professor. His main research interests are published in more than 400 papers, addressing decentralized systems with fully decentralized control, network and service management, IoT, and telecommunication economics.

T C Swetha Priya is pursuing her Ph.D under the Department of CSE at Jawaharlal Nehru Technological University, Hyderabad. She is currently working as Assistant professor in Stanley College of Engineering and Technology for Women under the Department of Information Technology. She has 8 years of Teaching experience and 3 years Research Experience. She has published over 16 papers in various International journals, National and International Conferences. She has attended several FDP's, Workshops and Seminars at National and International level.

Muhammad Usman Tariq has more than 16+ year's experience in industry and academia. He has authored more than 200+ research articles, 110+ case studies, 130+ book chapters and several books other than 4 patents. He is founder and CEO of The Case HQ, a unique repository for courses, narrative and video case studies. He has been working as a consultant and trainer for industries representing six sigma, quality, health and safety, environmental systems, project management, and information security standards. His work has encompassed sectors in aviation, manufacturing, food, hospitality, education, finance, research, software and transportation. He has diverse and significant experience working with accreditation agencies of ABET, ACBSP, AACSB, WASC, CAA, EFQM and NCEAC. Additionally, Dr. Tariq has operational experience in incubators, research labs, government research projects, private sector startups, program creation and management at various industrial and academic levels. He is Certified Higher Education Teacher from Harvard University, USA, Certified Online Educator from HMBSU, Certified Six Sigma Master Black Belt and has been awarded PFHEA, SFSEDA, SMIEEE, and CMBE.

Shafiq Ul Rehman received his Ph.D. degree from Universiti Sains Malaysia (USM), Malaysia, in 2017. He was a Postdoctoral Research Fellow at Singapore University of Technology and Design (SUTD), Singapore, from 2017 to 2020. He has more than 10 years of teaching and research experience. He is currently the Acting Dean, College of Information Technology and Chairman Department of Computer Science, College of Information Technology, Kingdom University, Bahrain. He is also an Assistant Professor specializing in cybersecurity, artificial intelligence, Internet of Things / Industry 4.0, and cloud/edge computing. He has authored and coauthored more than 50 papers in peer- reviewed journals, conference proceedings, and book chapters. He is involved in various research projects related to cybersecurity, IoT in healthcare, Industry 4.0, and emerging technologies using open-source platforms. He has experience building AI tools for healthcare, security systems for communication protocols, IoT devices, and cloud/edge computing architecture.

Index

A

B

C

D

E

F

H

I

T

V

www.ingramcontent.com/pod-product-compliance
Lightning Source LLC
LaVergne TN
LVHW080352011026
849161LV00009B/2284